In the Author's Hand

Islamic History and Civilization

STUDIES AND TEXTS

VOLUME 171

The titles published in this series are listed at *brill.com/ihc*

In the Author's Hand

Holograph and Authorial Manuscripts in the Islamic Handwritten Tradition

Edited by

Frédéric Bauden
Élise Franssen

BRILL

LEIDEN | BOSTON

The Library of Congress Cataloging-in-Publication Data is available online at http://catalog.loc.gov
LC record available at http://lccn.loc.gov/2019048156

Typeface for the Latin, Greek, and Cyrillic scripts: "Brill". See and download: brill.com/brill-typeface.

ISSN 0929-2403
ISBN 978-90-04-41316-0 (hardback)
ISBN 978-90-04-41317-7 (e-book)

This book is printed on acid-free paper and produced in a sustainable manner.

Contents

Preface VII
List of Authors' Handwritings Appearing on the Cover Image X
List of Figures XI
List of Diagrams and Tables XVI
List of Abbreviations XVIII
Notes on Contributors XIX

1 Introduction 1

2 Comment reconnaître un autographe parmi les papyrus littéraires grecs ? L'exemple du *P. Oxy*. 74.4970 38
Marie-Hélène Marganne

3 Arabic Holographs: Characteristics and Terminology 55
Adam Gacek

4 *"Bi-khaṭṭ mu'allifihi"* … Vraiment?! L'apport de l'analyse judiciaire d'écritures à l'étude des manuscrits arabes 78
Élise Franssen

5 Maqriziana XV: The Characteristics of al-Maqrīzī's Handwriting 136
Frédéric Bauden

6 The Art of Copying: Mamlūk Manuscript Culture in Theory and Practice 232
Elias Muhanna

7 The Holograph Notebooks of Akmal al-Dīn Muḥammad b. Mufliḥ (d. 1011/1603) 260
Kristina Richardson

8 Al-ʿAynī's Working Method for His Chronicles: Analysis of His Holograph Manuscripts 277
Nobutaka Nakamachi

9 Textual Criticism of the Manuscripts of Ibn Khaldūn's *Autobiography* 300
Retsu Hashizume

10 Les *safīnas* yéménites 323
Julien Dufour et Anne Regourd

List of Quoted Manuscripts 437
Index of Names 444
Index of Places 449
Index of Technical Terms 450

Preface

This volume is the material achievement of an international conference entitled *Autograph/Holograph and Authorial Manuscripts in Arabic Script* that took place at Liège University on 10–11 October 2013. At the conference, seventeen participants gathered to share best practices and to think collectively about the issues raised by these specific manuscripts, that is, the autograph, holograph, and authorial manuscripts. Next to the necessary theoretical frame, we focused on the practical approach to the manuscripts.

Indeed, research specifically dealing with holograph, autograph, or authorial manuscripts in Arabic script is often unplanned and erratic. Nevertheless, these manuscripts raise numerous important questions of interest to a variety of disciplines, such as paleography, codicology, textual criticism, linguistics, and intellectual history (working methods and methodology). These disciplines pose questions such as:

- How can we identify handwriting with a degree of scientific confidence, beyond intuition?
- What are the discriminating criteria? Is there a method to be used/developed?
- Can these books be analyzed like other manuscripts?
- What kinds of information do their specific characteristics offer?
- How important is this category of manuscripts in an editorial process?
- When more than one authorial manuscript of the same text is available, how should we choose the one to use in an editorial process?
- What importance should we give to the status of a manuscript—fair copy, draft, copybook, notebook, etc.—and how should we classify these versions?
- How could holographs improve our knowledge of Arabic?
- What information can we deduce from different authorial versions of the same text?
- What about originality, plagiarism, or even authority?

Among these issues, paleography is particularly significant. In the field of Islamic manuscripts studies, handwriting identification is still a question of experience: experienced scholars can recognize one handwriting at first glance, but no one teaches how to do this. Paleography courses deal with the deciphering and dating of handwritings, not with the specific characteristics that are personal to the scribes, with the only exceptions being some renowned calligraphers or some handwritings in old Qurʾāns. There is no study of informal handwritings or scholars' hands, and even fewer courses about them. Since both of us are working on a celebrated scholar—respectively al-Maqrīzī (d. 845/1442) and al-Ṣafadī (d. 764/1363)—or on a particular manuscript tradition whose origin is related to a given person—the Egyptian recension of the *Thousand and One Nights*—, accurate and efficient handwriting identification is crucial for our research work.

We organized this conference because we wanted to think collectively, to give space and time to questions, to share knowledge and experience, discussions, and debate, but also to cross the usual boundaries marking the various fields. Hence, the conference convened not only renowned researchers in Arabic manuscripts (literary, historical, philosophical, or encyclopedic manuscripts), but also specialists of ancient and Byzantine Greek documents, manuscripts, and papyri, and a judicial expert in handwriting identification. The latter delivered a very detailed and pragmatic speech about the methods applied in the legal community. The papers were distributed in five panels, dealing with terminology and methodology; codicology; working methods; paleography; and textual criticism, respectively. The conference discussions were extremely rich and these proceedings are their faithful reflection.

We would like to warmly thank all the participants to the conference and the members of the scientific and organizing committees: Cécile Bonmariage (Catholic University of Louvain-la-Neuve, Belgium), Yehoshua Frenkel (University of Haifa, Israel), Adam Gacek (formerly McGill University, Montreal, Canada), Retsu Hashizume (Chiba Institute of Science, Japan), Stephen Hirtenstein (Muhyiddin Ibn ʿArabi Society, UK), Caroline Macé (Catholic University of Leuven, Belgium), Marie-Hélène Marganne (Liège University, Belgium), Elias Muhanna (Brown University, USA), Nobutaka Nakamachi (Konan University, Kobe, Japan), Anne Regourd (CNRS, France), Kristina Richardson (Queens College, New York), Valentina Sagaria Rossi (Accademia Nazionale dei Lincei, Italy), Tilman Seidensticker (Friedrich-Schiller-Universität, Jena, Germany), Aida Shalar Gasimova (Baku State University, Azerbaijan), Suha Taji-Farouki (University of Exeter, UK), Anne-Marie Verjans (freelance researcher, Belgium), and Jan Just Witkam (formerly Leiden University, Netherlands). We also express our deepest gratitude to Professor Robert Wisnovsky (McGill University, Montreal, Canada) for sharing with us reproductions of manuscripts quoted by Adam Gacek in his article. Another special thank goes to the two anonymous reviewers whose remarks and critical comments were helpful.

Last but not least, the organization of the conference would not have been possible without the assistance and support of the personnel of Liège University Library, particularly the curator of the Department of Old Prints and Manuscripts, Cécile Oger, whose support was critical for the launch of the small exhibition of manuscripts especially organized on the occasion of the conference. It is also our pleasure to acknowledge the financial and material support of the Faculty of Humanities and the Patrimoine of Liège University, as well as the Fund for Scientific Research (F.R.S.-FNRS, Fédération Wallonie-Bruxelles), without whom this conference could not have been organized.

Frédéric Bauden and Élise Franssen

List of Authors' Handwritings Appearing on the Cover Image

Ibn Iyās (d. 930/1524)
Ibn Fahd (d. 885/1480)
al-Biqāʿī (d. 885/1480)
Ibn Khaldūn (d. 808/1406)
al-Dhahabī (d. 748/1348)
Ibn Duqmāq (d. 809/1406)
al-Sakhāwī (d. 902/1497)
al-Maqrīzī (d. 845/1442)
Ibn Ḥajar (d. 852/1449)
al-Damīrī (d. 808/1405)
al-Ṣafadī (d. 764/1363)
Ibn Shākir al-Kutubī (d. 764/1363)

Reading of the inscriptions: Ibn Iyās: *Muḥammad b. Aḥmad b. Iyās*; Ibn Fahd: *Muḥammad al-madʿū ʿUmar b. Muḥammad b. Muḥammad b. Abī l-Khayr Muḥammad b. Fahd al-Hāshimī l-Makkī*; al-Biqāʿī: *Ibrāhīm al-Biqāʿī*; Ibn Khaldūn: *wa-kataba muʾallifuhā ʿAbd al-Raḥmān b. Khaldūn*; al-Dhahabī: *kātibuhu Muḥammad b. Aḥmad b. ʿUthmān b. al-Dhahabī*; Ibn Duqmāq: *Ibrāhīm b. Muḥammad b. Aydamur Duqmāq*; al-Sakhāwī: *Muḥammad b. ʿAbd al-Raḥmān al-Sakhāwī*; al-Maqrīzī: *Aḥmad b. ʿAlī b. ʿAbd al-Qādir b. Muḥammad al-Maqrīzī l-Shāfiʿī*; Ibn Ḥajar: *li-kātibihi Aḥmad b. ʿAlī b. Ḥajar*; al-Damīrī: *Muḥammad b. Yūnus al-Damīrī l-Shāfiʿī*; al-Ṣafadī: *wa-kataba Khalīl b. Aybak b. ʿAbdallāh al-Ṣafadī*; Ibn Shākir al-Kutubī: *ʿalā yad jāmiʿihi Muḥammad b. Shākir b. Aḥmad al-Kutubī.*

Sources: al-Biqāʿī: MS Ayasofya 3139 (Süleymaniye Kütüphanesi, Istanbul); al-Damīrī: MS Ayasofya 4110 (Süleymaniye Kütüphanesi, Istanbul); al-Dhahabī: MS Ayasofya 3007 (Süleymaniye Kütüphanesi, Istanbul); Ibn Duqmāq: MS A2832 (TSMK, Istanbul); Ibn Fahd: MS Feyzullah 1413 (Milli Kütüphanesi, Istanbul); Ibn Ḥajar: MS Ayasofya 3139 (Süleymaniye Kütüphanesi, Istanbul); Ibn Iyās: MS Fatih 4197 (Süleymaniye Kütüphanesi, Istanbul); Ibn Khaldūn: MS 1936 (Atıf Efendi Kütüphanesi, Istanbul); Ibn Shākir al-Kutubī: MS A2922 (TSMK, Istanbul); al-Maqrīzī: MS Or. 560 (Universiteitsbibliotheek, Leiden); al-Sakhāwī: MS Ayasofya 3139 (Süleymaniye Kütüphanesi, Istanbul); al-Ṣafadī: MS Ayasofya 2968 (Süleymaniye Kütüphanesi, Istanbul)

Figures

1.1 MS Garrett 3570 Y (Princeton, University Library), f. 33, al-Ṣafadī's *Tadhkira* 5
1.2 Adler's Arabic Alphabet 11
1.3 Ibn Khaldūn, *al-Muqaddima*, MS Atıf Efendi 1936 (Istanbul, Süleymaniye Kütüphanesi), fol. VII[a] 17
1.4 al-Mawṣilī, *Ghāyat al-wasāʾil ilā maʿrifat al-awāʾil* (Istanbul, Süleymaniye Kütüphanesi, MS Reisülküttab 862) 19
2.1 "The Bankes Homer", P. Lit. Lond. 28, Brit. Libr. inv. 114 (London, British Library) 42
2.2 P. Rein. 2.82, inv. Sorb. 2070 (Paris, Sorbonne Université, Institut de Papyrologie) 46
2.3 P. Oxy. 74.4970, The Egypt Exploration Society and the University of Oxford Imaging Papyri Project (Oxford, Oxford University Sackler Library, Oxyrhynchus Papyrus) 49
3.1 MS Arabic 3945, fol. 137[b] (Dublin, Chester Beatty Library) 57
3.2 MS Garrett 3520Y, fol. 37[b] (Princeton, University Library) 58
3.3 MS Arabic 3456, fol. 225[b] (Dublin, Chester Beatty Library) 59
3.4 MS Arabic 4731, fol. 2[a] (Dublin, Chester Beatty Library) 61
3.5 MS W 591, fol. 78[a] (Baltimore, Walters Art Museum) 62
3.6 MS Ayasofya 2662, fol. 69[a] (Istanbul, Süleymaniye Kütüphanesi) 63
3.7 MS Damad Ibrahim Paşa 822, fol. 354[b] (Istanbul, Süleymaniye Kütüphanesi) 64
3.8 MS 1153, fol. 1[a] (Tehran, Kitābkhāna-yi Millī-i Jumhūrī-i Islāmī-i Īrān) 65
3.9 MS Yeni Cami 763, fol. 198[b] (Istanbul, Süleymaniye Kütüphanesi) 66
3.10 MS Or. 7969, fol. 3[a] (London, British Library) 66
3.11 MS Fazıl Ahmed Paşa 1618, fol. 43[a] (Istanbul, Köprülü Yazma Eser Kütüphanesi) 67
3.12 MS 792, fol. 214[a] (Istanbul, Rağıb Paşa Kütüphanesi) 67
3.13 MS Carullah 1442, fol. 1[a] (Istanbul, Süleymaniye Kutüphanesi) 68
3.14 MS Carullah 1442, fol. 51[b] (Istanbul, Süleymaniye Kutüphanesi) 68
3.15 MS Ayasofya 4732, fol. Ab (Istanbul, Süleymaniye Kutüphanesi) 70
3.16 MS Or. Oct. 3806, fol. 1[a] (Berlin, Staatsbibliothek) 71
3.17 MS Arab. Add. 83, fol. 154[a] (Copenhagen, Kongelige Bibliotek) 72
3.18 MS Fazıl Ahmed Paşa 867, fol. 1[a] (Istanbul, Köprülü Yazma Eser Kütüphanesi) 73
3.19 MS Fazıl Ahmed Paşa 831, fol. 142[a] (Istanbul, Köprülü Yazma Eser Kütüphanesi) 74
3.20 MS 781, fol. 229[a] (Istanbul, Rağıb Paşa Kütüphanesi) 74

3.21 MS Esad Efendi 3733, fol. 47a (Istanbul, Süleymaniye Kütüphanesi) 75
3.22 MS 12388, fol. 190a (Qum, Marʿashī Kitābkhānah) 76
4.1 Schéma et lexique de description des graphies 85
4.2 Comparaison de formules introductives des *Nuits* 98
4.3 Scribe 1 (Saint-Petersburg, Institute of Oriental Manuscripts, MS B-1114, vol. 2, f. 302) 101
4.4 Scribe 1 (Liège, Liège Université, Bibliothèque d'Architecture, Lettres, Philosophie, Histoire et Arts, MS 2241, f. 404) 102
4.5 Scribe 1 (London, British Library, MS Or. 2917, f. 57) 103
4.6 ʿAlī l-Anṣārī (Paris, BnF, MS Ar. 3602, f. 34) 104
4.7 ʿAlī l-Anṣārī (Munich, Bayerische Staatsbibliothek, MS Cod. ar. 624, f. 328) 105
5.1 Handwriting identified as being al-Awḥadī's (Istanbul, TSMK, MS Emanet Hazinezi 1405, fol. 83b) 143
5.2 al-Maqrīzī's handwriting at the age of 28 (Istanbul, Süleymaniye Kütüphanesi, MS Murat Molla 575, fol. 3b) 143
5.3 Timeline of al-Maqrīzī's holograph and authorial manuscripts 147
5.4 Al-Maqrīzī's consultation note in Ibn Faḍl Allāh al-ʿUmarī's *Masālik al-abṣār*, vol. 3 (Istanbul, Süleymaniye Kütüphanesi, MS Ayasofya 3416, fol. 1a) 148
5.5 Abū Dāwūd, *al-Sunan* (Istanbul, Köprülü Yazma Eser Kütüphanesi, MS Fazıl Ahmed Paşa 294, fol. 327a), Ibn Ḥajar's colophon 155
5.6 Abū Dāwūd, *al-Sunan* (Istanbul, Köprülü Yazma Eser Kütüphanesi, MS Fazıl Ahmed Paşa 294, fol. 1b), beginning of the text in Ibn Ḥajar's restrained handwriting 155
5.7 Abū Dāwūd, *al-Marāsīl* (Istanbul, Köprülü Yazma Eser Kütüphanesi, MS Fazıl Ahmed Paşa 294, fol. 356a), Ibn Ḥajar's unrestrained handwriting 156
5.8 Spacing between words and the overlapping of words (above: IM [Istanbul, Murat Molla Kütüphanesi, MS 575], fol. 20, l. 9, 47 letters; below: IY [Istanbul, Süleymaniye Kütüphanesi, MS Şehit Ali Paşa 1847], fol. 28 a, l. 19, 57 letters) 167
5.9 The word *ithnān* in Lg (Liège, Liège Université, Bibliothèque d'Architecture, Lettres, Philosophie, Histoire et Arts, MS 2232), fol. 166a, l. 17 (left: *thnān*) and IF3 (Istanbul, Süleymaniye Kütüphanesi, MS Fatih 4340), fol. 117a, l. 2 (right: *thnatay*) 168
5.10 The word *allafa* in Lg (Liège, Liège Université, Bibliothèque d'Architecture, Lettres, Philosophie, Histoire et Arts, MS 2232), fol. 8b, l. 20 (left: *allafahā*) and IY (Istanbul, Süleymaniye Kütüphanesi, MS Şehit Ali Paşa 1847), fol. 4a, marginal addition, last l. (*fa-allaftu*) 168
5.11 Examples of the use of *matres lectionis* and of diacritical dots to specify the phonological value of a letter: Lg (Liège, Liège Université, Bibliothèque d'Architecture, Lettres, Philosophie, Histoire et Arts, MS 2232), fol. 64a, l. 12 (left:

laḥiqū); An (Ann Arbor, University of Michigan, Special Collections Library, MS Isl. 605), p. 8, l. 18 (center: *al-ʿaskar*); IF3 (Istanbul, Süleymaniye Kütüphanesi, MS Fatih 4340), fol. 125ᵃ, l. 5 (right: *ʿarīb*) 170
5.12 Occurrences of abusive ligatures, contractions, and *sīn/shīn muʿallaqa* in Lg* (Liège, Liège Université, Bibliothèque d'Architecture, Lettres, Philosophie, Histoire et Arts, MS 2232) 178
5.13 An almost similar line in three different manuscripts 185
5.14 A sliding window patch (left) and patches of connected components (right) (Boiarov et al., Arabic Manuscript 3, figs. 3–4) 195
5.15 The word *madrasa* penned by al-Awḥadī (Istanbul, TSMK, MS Emanet Hazinesi 1405, fol. 96ᵇ, l. 10 (left); fol. 98ᵇ, l. 1 (right)) 196
5.16 The word *madrasa* penned by al-Maqrīzī (right) (Istanbul, TSMK, MS Emanet Hazinesi 1405, respectively fol. 97ᵃ, l. 12 (left); fol. 96ᵇ, l. 9 (right)) 196
5.17 A: IT2 (Istanbul, TSMK, MS Emanet Hazinesi 1405), fol. 83ᵃ (with the exception of two words added in the margin by al-Maqrīzī, the leaf, contains nineteen lines in al-Awḥadī's hand) 198
5.18 B: IT1 (Istanbul, TSMK, MS Emanet Hazinesi 1405), fol. 54ᵇ (entirely in al-Maqrīzī's hand) 198
5.19 C: Du (Dushanbe, Kitobhona-i milli-i Todjikiston, MS 1790), fol. 77ᵇ (entirely in al-Maqrīzī's hand) 198
5.20 D: MS 702, fol. 2ᵇ (Afyon Karahisar, Gedik Ahmet Paşa Kütüphane: *al-Dhakhāʾir wa-l-tuḥaf*, entirely in Ibn Duqmāq's hand) 199
5.21 E: MS cod. ar. 437, fol. 3ᵃ (Munich, Bayerische Staatsbibliothek: Ibn Duqmāq, *Naẓm al-jumān fī ṭabaqāt aṣḥāb imāminā al-Nuʿmān*, unknown copyist) 199
5.22 F: MS Fazıl Ahmed Paşa 242, fol. 39ᵇ (Istanbul, Köprülü Yazma Eser Kütüphanesi: Ibn Manda, *al-Tārīkh al-mustakhraj min kutub al-nās*, unknown copyist, seventh/thirteenth c.) 199
5.23 G: IM (Istanbul, Murat Molla Kütüphanesi, MS 575), fol. 21ᵃ (entirely in al-Maqrīzī's hand) 199
5.24 H: L4 (Leiden, Universiteit Leiden, Universiteitsbibliotheek, MS Or. 14533), fol. 348ᵃ (seven lines in al-Maqrīzī's hand (top), ten lines in Ibn Ḥajar's hand (bottom)) 200
5.25 I: Lg (Liège, Liège Université, Bibliothèque d'Architecture, Lettres, Philosophie, Histoire et Arts, MS 2232), fol. 48ᵇ (entirely in al-Maqrīzī's hand) 200
5.26 MS Al (Alexandria, Bibliotheca Alexandrina, MS 2125 dāl Tārīkh), fol. 4ᵇ 210
5.27 MS An (Ann Arbor, University of Michigan, Special Collections Library, MS Isl. 605), p. 8 211
5.28 MS Du (Dushanbe, Kitobhona-i milli-i Todjikiston, MS 1790), fol. 37ᵇ 212
5.29 MS G1 (Gotha, Forschungs- und Landesbibliothek, MS Ar. 1652), fol. 10ᵇ 213
5.30 MS IA (Istanbul, Süleymaniye Kütüphanesi, MS Aya Sofya 3362), fol. 74ᵇ 214

5.31 MS IM (Istanbul, Murat Molla Kütüphanesi, MS 575), fol. 15b 215
5.32 MS IY (Istanbul, Süleymaniye Kütüphanesi, MS Şehit Ali Paşa 1847), fol. 12b 216
5.33 MS IT2 (Istanbul, TSMK, MS Emanet Hazinesi 1405), fol. 16b 217
5.34 MS IY (Istanbul, Süleymaniye Kütüphanesi, MS Yeni Cami 887), fol. 28a 218
5.35 MS L5 (Leiden, Universiteit Leiden, Universiteitsbibliotheek, MS Or. 560), fol. 9b 219
5.36 MS Lg (Liège, Liège Université, Bibliothèque d'Architecture, Lettres, Philosophie, Histoire et Arts, MS 2232), fol. 131a 220
5.37 MS Lg* (Liège, Liège Université, Bibliothèque d'Architecture, Lettres, Philosophie, Histoire et Arts, MS 2232), fol. 188a 221
6.1 Volume 25 of al-Nuwayrī's *Nihāyat al-arab fī funūn al-adab*. (Leiden, University Library, MS Or. 2i) 247
6.2 Leiden, University Library, MSS Or. 2i (top) and Or. 2l (bottom), al-Nuwayrī's *Nihāyat al-arab fī funūn al-adab*, vols 24–25 and 26–27 249
6.3 Colophon of al-Nuwayrī's *Nihāyat al-arab fī funūn al-adab* (Leiden, University Library, MS Or. 2f) (chap. 5). 250
6.4 Leiden, University Library, MS Or. 2d 251
6.5 The Yūnīniyya recension of al-Bukhārī's *Kitāb al-Jāmiʿ al-Ṣaḥīḥ*, copied by al-Nuwayrī in 725/1325. MS Fazıl Ahmed Paşa 362 (Istanbul, Köprülü Yazma Eser Kütüphanesi), fols. 17b–18a (title page) 253
6.6 MS Fazıl Ahmed Paşa 362 (Istanbul, Köprülü Yazma Eser Kütüphanesi), fols. 19b–20a 254
6.7 Final pages of the Yūnīniyya manuscript. MS Fazıl Ahmed Paşa 362 (Istanbul, Köprülü Yazma Eser Kütüphanesi), fols. 314b–315a 255
7.1 The Banū Mufliḥ Family Tree 272
7.2 MS We. 408 (Berlin, Staatsbibliothek), fol. 99a 273
7.3 MS 1004 (Beirut, American University Library), fols. 9b–10a 274
7.4 MS Pococke 26 (Oxford, Oxford University Library), fols. 62b–63a 275
8.1 MS A2911/A18 (Istanbul, TSMK), fols. 16b–17a 279
8.2 MS Arabe 1544 (Paris, BnF), fols. 102b–103a 280
8.3 MS Süleymaniye 830 (Istanbul, Süleymaniye Kütüphanesi), fols. 216b–217a 295
9.1 MS Ahmet III 2924/13–14 (Istanbul, TSMK), fol. 374a 315
9.2 MS Ayasofya 3200 (Istanbul, Süleymaniye Kütüphanesi), fol. 63a 316
9.3 MS Ar. 1528 (Paris, BnF), fol. 36a 317
9.4 MS Ayasofya 3200 (Istanbul, Süleymaniye Kütüphanesi), fol. 1a 317
9.5 MS Ayasofya 3200 (Istanbul, Süleymaniye Kütüphanesi), fol. 1a 317
9.6 MS Ayasofya 3200 (Istanbul, Süleymaniye Kütüphanesi), fol. 1b 318
9.7 MS Ayasofya 3200 (Istanbul, Süleymaniye Kütüphanesi), fol. 11b 318
9.8 MS Ayasofya 3200 (Istanbul, Süleymaniye Kütüphanesi), fols. 11b–12a 319
9.9 MS Ta'rīkh 109 mīm (Cairo, Dār al-Kutub al-Miṣriyya), fol. 1b 320

9.10 MS Ta'rīkh 109 mīm (Cairo, Dār al-Kutub al-Miṣriyya), fol. 2[a] 320
9.11 MS Ar. 1528 (Paris, BnF), fol. 3[b] 320
9.12 MS Ṭal'at Ta'rīkh 2106 (Cairo, Dār al-Kutub al-Miṣriyya), fol. 160[b] 320
9.13 MS Ṭal'at Ta'rīkh 2106 (Cairo, Dār al-Kutub al-Miṣriyya), fol. 161[a] 321
9.14 MS Esad Efendi 2268 (Istanbul, Süleymaniye Kütüphanesi), fol. 2[a] 321
9.15 MS Esad Efendi 2268 (Istanbul, Süleymaniye Kütüphanesi), fol. 13[a] 321
9.16 MS Ayasofya 3200 (Istanbul, Süleymaniye Kütüphanesi), fol. 14[a] 322
9.17 MS Esad Efendi 2268 (Istanbul, Süleymaniye Kütüphanesi), fol. 15[b] 322
10.1 *Safīna* 2 (Sanaa, Dār al-makhṭūṭāt, MS Adab 2336), *Dīwān* d' al-Ahdal, fol. 1–p. 23 325
10.2 *Safīna* 2 (Sanaa, Dār al-Makhṭūṭāt, MS Adab 2336), *Dīwān* d' al-Ahdal, fol. 83–p. 191 337
10.3 *Safīna* 2 (Sanaa, Dār al-Makhṭūṭāt, MS Adab 2336), *Dīwān* d' al-Ahdal, fol. 84–p. 193 (fol. supérieur) et p. 191 (fol. inférieur) 338
10.4 MS Sharaf al-dīn (Sanaa, collection privée). 112[a]. Reliure. 112[b]. Reliure, marque de propriété. 112c. Reliure, contreplat (partiel) et dos (vue interne), cahiers et couture. 112d. Cahiers et couture, gaze, contreplat (partiel). 112e. Tranchefile et dos (vue interne) 340
10.5 MS Sharaf al-dīn (Sanaa, collection privée) 341

Diagrams and Tables

Diagrams

9.1 Lineage of *al-Taʿrīf* manuscripts based on Ibn Tāwīt's conclusion 302
9.2 Lineage of *al-Taʿrīf* manuscripts according to the archetypes 304
9.3 Lineage of *al-Taʿrīf* manuscripts according to Hashizume 306

Tables

4.1 Reconstitution de trois ensembles complets fondée sur l'analyse des graphies 117
4.2 Tableau d'analyse des graphies 118
4.3 Tableau d'analyse de lettres spécifiques 130
5.1 Paces of al-Maqrīzī's manuscripts 161
5.2 List of the sizes of al-Maqrīzī's manuscripts 163
5.3 Comparative table of occurrences of *lām-alif* (unconnected and connected) 175
5.4 Number of occurrences of abusive ligatures and contractions 178
5.5 Some examples of contraction (*idghām*) and curtailment (*ikhtilās*) 179
5.6 Comparative table of the word *ḥattā* 180
5.7 Comparative table of occurrences of *sīn/shīn muḥaqqaqa* and *muʿallaqa* 184
5.8 Comparative table of occurrences of *yāʾ mabsūṭa* and *rājiʿa* and of the two shapes of *fī* 184
5.9 Comparative table of occurrences of *kāf mabsūṭa* (left) and *mashkūla* (right) 186
5.10 Examples of *lām-alif* and of *dāl* with a hanging stroke 189
5.11 Examples of pressure causing the widening of the nib 189
5.12 Examples of problems of coordination 191
5.13 Examples of tremor 192
5.14 Comparative table of letters *alif-sīn* 202
5.15 Comparative table of letters *ṣād-qāf* 204
5.16 Comparative table of letters *kāf-nūn* 206
5.17 Comparative table of letters *hāʾ-yāʾ* and of some ligatures in specific combinations 208
6.1 Manuscripts of the *Nihāyat al-arab* attributed to al-Nuwayrī 240
6.2 A Timeline of al-Nuwayrī's Compilation of the *Nihāyat al-arab* 246
8.1 Holograph manuscripts of *ʿIqd al-jumān* 278

8.2 Handwritings in MS Ar. 1544 (BnF) 280
8.3 Descriptions of the year 801/1398–9 282
8.4 Descriptions of the year 816/1413–4 289
8.5 Number of topics in al-ʿAynī's chronicles 292
8.6 Famine and high price in Egypt in 816/1413 293
8.7 Death of Sultan Barqūq in 801/1399 294
8.8 Appointment of Fatḥ Allāh b. Nafīs in 801/1399 297
10.1 Description du contenu de la *Safīna* 4 358
10.2 Description du contenu de la *Safīna* 5 376
10.3 Description du contenu de la *Safīna* 6 396

Abbreviations

BK	Beyazıt Kütüphanesi
BnF	Bibliothèque nationale de France, Paris
CEDOPAL	CEntre de DOcumentation de PApyrologie Littéraire, Liège Université
COMSt	Comparative Oriental Manuscripts Studies
DaM	Dār al-Makhṭūṭāt, Sanaa
DH	Digital Humanities
DKM	Dār al-Kutub al-Miṣriyya, Cairo
EI^2	*The Encyclopaedia of Islam*. New Edition, ed. C.E. Bosworth et al. (Leiden: Brill, 1960–2007), 11 vols.
GAL	Brockelmann, C., *Geschichte der arabischen Litteratur*, Leiden, 1937–42, 2 vols. and 3 vols. of supplement.
GAS	Sezgin, F., *Geschichte des arabischen Schriftums*, Leiden and Frankfurt 1967–84, 17 vols.
GRAPHEM	Grapheme based Retrieval and Analysis for PaleograpHic Expertise of Middle Age manuscripts
MS	Manuscript
MSS	Manuscripts
MZbAT	Mu'assasat Zayd b. ʿAlī l-Thaqāfiyya, Sanaa
OCR	Optical Character Recognition
PUL	Princeton University Library
SHOE	Standard Handwriting Objective Examination
SK	Süleymaniye Kütüphanesi
Spr.	Sprenger (a collection of Berlin Staatsbibliothek)
TEI	Text Encoding Initiative
TSMK	Topkapı Sarayı Müzesi Kütüphanesi, Istanbul
UbL	Universiteitsbibliotheek, Leiden
We	Wetzstein (a collection of Berlin Staatsbibliothek)
XML	eXtensible Markup Language
YMDI	Yemeni Manuscripts Digitization Initiative

Notes on Contributors

Frédéric Bauden
Ph.D. (1996), is Professor of Arabic Language and Islamic Studies at Liège University. His research focuses on Mamlūk historiography, diplomatics, and codicology. He is the editor of the *Bibliotheca Maqriziana* (Leiden) and the author of the forthcoming *Al-Maqrīzī's Collection of Opuscules: An Introduction* (Leiden).

Julien Dufour
(PhD 2007, HDR 2016) is Associate Professor at the University of Strasbourg. He has published a monograph (*Huit siècles de poésie chantée au Yémen. Langue, mètres et formes du* ḥumaynī, Presses Universitaires de Strasbourg, 2011) and articles on Yemeni poetry, Yemeni Arabic dialects and Modern South Arabian languages.

Élise Franssen
Ph.D. (2012), is Marie Skłodowska Curie Fellow at the Università Ca' Foscari, Venice (2018–21). A specialist of codicology, she is currently working on the holograph copy of al-Ṣafadī's *Tadhkira* and on her book on the manuscripts of the Egyptian recension of the *Thousand and One Nights*.

Adam Gacek
former Head of the Islamic Studies Library and Faculty Lecturer in Arabic manuscript studies at the Institute of Islamic Studies, McGill University (Montreal), is the author of many catalogues, articles and book chapters on Arabic and Persian manuscripts and printed rare books.

Retsu Hashizume
Ph.D. (2009), The University of Tokyo, Graduate School of Humanities and Sociology, is instructor in History at Chiba Institute of Science. He has published various monographs (in Japanese), among which *The Internal Structure of the Buwayhid Dynasty* (Keio U.P., 2016).

Marie-Hélène Marganne
Ph.D. (1983), Liège University, is Director of the Centre de Documentation de Papyrologie Littéraire (CEDOPAL) and Professor of papyrology. She is the author of numerous publications on medical papyri and ancient books and libraries, including the third electronic edition of the *Catalogue des papyrus littéraires grecs et latins*.

Elias Muhanna

Ph.D. (2012), Harvard University, is Associate Professor of Comparative Literature at Brown University. His books include *The Ultimate Ambition in the Arts of Erudition* (Penguin, 2016), *The Digital Humanities and Islamic & Middle East Studies* (De Gruyter, 2016), and *The World in a Book: al-Nuwayri and the Islamic Encyclopedic Tradition* (Princeton University Press, 2018).

Nobutaka Nakamachi

Ph.D. (2007), The University of Tokyo, is a Professor at Konan University. He has written many articles on Mamlūk history, including "Life in the Margins: Shihāb al-Dīn Aḥmad al-ʿAynī, a Non-Elite Intellectual in the Mamlūk Period," *Orient* 48 (2013).

Anne Regourd

Ph.D (1987), University of Copenhagen, Department of Cross-Cultural Studies, and CNRS. Her publications deal with codicology, catalography, paper studies, papyrology, and epigraphy. She worked extensively on Yemeni manuscripts, and more recently on Ethiopian manuscripts.

Kristina Richardson

Ph.D. (2008), University of Michigan-Ann Arbor, is Associate Professor of History at Queens College and the CUNY Graduate Center. She is the author of *Difference and Disability in the Medieval Islamic World* (Edinburgh University Press, 2012).

CHAPTER 1

Introduction

In recent years, a growing interest in "Oriental manuscripts" in all their aspects, including the extrinsic ones, has been observed.[1] The COMSt project is certainly emblematic of this interest, and the manual, published as a result of the activities of the group, is its best achievement.[2] The inter- and trans-disciplinary "Centre for the Study of Manuscript Cultures" created in Hamburg University reflects a similar interest. In addition, new notions like "social codicology" or "collectology," coined by Olly Akkerman,[3] have appeared and open new perspectives of research. Konrad Hirschler's current project and talks about Ibn ʿAbd al-Hādī's *Fihrist* of the manuscripts of the ʿUmariyya Madrasa of Damascus are part of this new trend, to cite only these few examples.

Nevertheless, specific questions raised by the exceptional manuscripts that are holographs have yet to be investigated. Some of the aspects to be scrutinized include their intrinsic value in terms of philology, textual criticism and ecdotics, codicology or paleography, their importance for our understanding of the working methods of past scholars, for our apprehension of book culture and the publication process, for our grasp of the transmission of knowledge, or more simply, the necessity that we compare these specific manuscripts in order to acknowledge other holograph manuscripts or autograph notes by the same author.

The question of terminology should be addressed before we begin. We must first clarify and precisely define "autograph," "holograph," and "authorial manuscript." Chapter 3 in this volume shows eloquent examples of possible case studies, and within the scope of this introduction, we offer a theoretical clarification of the situation. But first and foremost stands the question of authorship: could there be a holograph without any author?

---

1 Frédéric Bauden wrote the sections "Holographs as Collectibles" and "Ecdotics (Textual Criticism)" while Élise Franssen is the author of the remainder.

2 Bausi et al., *Comparative*.

3 She refers to "codicological ethnography" as well, see the title of her PhD: Akkerman, *The Bohra dark archive* (and its review by Bhalloo). The title of the workshop she organized in October 2018 at the Netherlands Institute in Morocco and at the Centre Jacques Berque in Rabat was entitled "Social Codicology: The Multiple Lives of Texts in Muslim Societies"; one of the panels was called "collectology."

 | DOI:10.1163/9789004413177_002

1 Authorship

The notion of authorship in pre-modern Islam is not as simple as it is at the present time: the isolated scholar composing his texts alone is not the only reality attested. As eloquently exposed by Lale Behzadi and Jaakko Hämeen-Anttila, we can observe different degrees of authorship.[4] The intellectual paternity of texts is not the only way to consider authors in pre-modern Islam. If we turn to the expressions used in the sources and in the colophons, we find many different terms: next to the *kātib*, we have the *muṣannif*, the *muʾallif*, the *jāmiʿ*, the *murattib*, etc. Each one refers to different aspects of authority, from the material activity of writing (*kātib*), to the intellectual process of creating a text (*muṣannif*), to the arrangement and compilation process (*muʾallif, jāmiʿ, murattib*). It is important to note that the activity of a compiler, who chooses to gather together different texts is understood to be creative work, to a certain degree, since it gives birth to a new work, with new meanings coming into reality from the union of the different pre-existing texts.[5] In this sense, the person who compiles a notebook or a commonplace book (*tadhkira*), a collection of tales or an anthology of poems, can be considered an author as well (see chapter 4, pp. 78–135, and chapter 10, pp. 323–431).

Finally, we should include a note on orality, since it adds a new layer of authority: we have examples of texts which, after publication (in the first sense, i.e., after having been rendered public) were modified in order to suit their audience (e.g., recited poems that were then written and distributed, or texts for which an *ijāza* was issued that were later modified by their author).[6] The context and transmission process thus play a significant role in the very nature of the text. In the same sense, an amorphous collection of tales with a common structure but also notable differences—like the *Thousand and One Nights*—does not always present the same texts, in the same order. Various textual traditions or recensions exist, and sometimes more than one manuscript contains the same text. The identification of a particular hand traceable in different manuscripts of a same textual recension is thus similar to the identification of holograph manuscripts.

4 Behzadi and Hämeen-Anttila, Preface 7 and n. 2; Behzadi, Introduction 13–7.
5 On the Arabic terminology applied to the different functions of an author and for examples, see Ghersetti, A pre-modern anthologist 24–6.
6 Bauer, Ibn Nubātah al-Miṣrī 28. Or simply because authors' knowledge and work was going forward. See the example of Maimonides as well, Sirat, *Writing as handwork* 479.

2 Terminology

Etymologically speaking, the word "holograph" comes from late Latin "hŏlŏgrăphus, a, um" (from the Greek ὁλόγραφος) and means "entirely written by the author's hand."[7] The legal terminology kept the term: a holograph will is fully handwritten by its author, and hence considered more faithful to one's last wishes, while a typed will hand signed by the testator bears an autograph of the latter, the autograph being the signature. In French, the term "*holographe*," also spelled more faithfully to its Greek etymology "*olographe*," is attested as early as 1235, in its form "*orograff*," whereas "*autographe*" is first attested only in 1553 in the form "*aftographe*."[8] In English, both the terms "holograph" and "autograph" derive from the French and appear in the seventeenth or eighteenth century.[9] Following Gacek,[10] we recommend the use of this precise terminology: a *holograph* is a manuscript entirely written by its author. An *autograph* is a short inscription by a person bearing his/her name (in the frame of manuscript studies, typically a signed colophon, an ownership mark, or a consultation note).

An *authorial manuscript* is defined here as a manuscript copied by a scribe and then revised by the author of the text, who left *autograph* interventions, such as corrections, emendations, cancellations or comments, in the margins or in any blank space of the manuscript (interlinear space, title page, margin, etc.). This is typically the case of MS Or. 560 (Leiden, Universiteitsbibliotheek), al-Maqrīzī's *Collection of opuscules* that is currently being edited separately in the *Bibliotheca Maqriziana* series.[11] At the time he published these works, al-Maqrīzī was already in his old age. He asked a scribe to make a fair copy of his opuscules and he then collated the manuscript. He was right to do this, because

7 See Gaffiot, *Dictionnaire* 751: "hŏlŏgrăphus, a, um (ὁλόγραφος), olographe, écrit en entier de la main de l'auteur: Sid. Ep. 9. 11; Ibid. 19, 22, 14." The dictionary by Lewis and Short says: "entirely autograph (late Lat.): epistula, entirely written by one's own hand, autograph, Hier. adv. Ruf. 3, 5: membrana, Sid. Ep. 9, 11 med.: testamentum, Isid. Orig. 5, 24."

8 Both references come from the Lexical portal of the Centre National des Ressources Textuelles et Lexicales: http://www.cnrtl.fr.

9 Hoad, *Concise* 28, 219; Onions et al., *The Oxford* 63, 445; Barnhart, *The Barnhart* 66, 487.

10 Gacek, *Vademecum* 14: "Both 'autograph' and 'holograph' are used as nouns and adjectives, and often interchangeably, although strictly speaking a 'holograph' is a manuscript *wholly* written by the author. An 'autograph', on the other hand, can mean a person's own signature or a short statement signed by him."

11 Thus far, three opuscules have been published (see https://brill.com/view/serial/BIMA).

he had to correct many passages in his own hand. He also added a comment at the end of each treatise, sometimes complaining about the poor quality of the scribe's work.[12]

With regard to texts copied by a famous author, scholar or calligrapher, Adam Gacek tackled the well-known case of Khalīl b. Aybak al-Ṣafadī (d. 764/1363) whose handwriting was handsome; thus, he served as a scribe, calligrapher, and illuminator on various occasions.[13] But if the text is not an original work handwritten by the author, the manuscript cannot be called a holograph—otherwise, any manuscript would be the holograph of its scribe. We have no particular word to refer to such manuscripts, we are reduced to using an expression as precise as possible, like "MS X by So-and-so, in the hand of So-and-so, with the autograph comments of So-and-so."

Some authors indeed played the role of copyists, perhaps to earn a living—chancery secretaries were especially gifted in this activity, since beautiful handwriting was necessary for such work,[14]—or for scholarship. We can assume that the features of the final manuscript differed according to its final destination: a manuscript penned to be sold was usually more nicely copied, with a steady handwriting, careful *mise en page*, regular margins, on even and good quality paper, and with the use of text dividers and rubrication when necessary. By contrast, if the manuscript was intended for the personal use of the writer/scholar, the result might be much more messy and hardly legible, the support might be reused paper, the lines of the writing may go in different directions, with hardly any margin delimited. Nevertheless, some medieval scholars who worked in the chancery were accustomed to writing well, such that they could not help doing it and even their drafts or personal notebooks resembled fair copies. Once again, this is the case with al-Ṣafadī who, even in his commonplace book (*tadhkira*), took the trouble to use red ink and to center the titles or subtitles of the book extract he was writing (see fig. 1.1). The same is valid for his drafts: MS Ayasofya 1970, the tenth volume of *Aʿyān al-ʿaṣr*, al-Ṣafadī's biographical dictionary of his contemporaries, shows obvious marks of a work in progress—parts of pages are left blank, others present many marginal glosses and additions, slips of paper are added in the binding—, but it is still very well structured, with a centered inscription in larger script at

12 See Bauden, *Al-Maqrīzī's collection* as well as chapter 5 in this volume, pp. 136–231.

13 See Gacek, The Copenhagen manuscript as well as chapters 3 (pp. 55–77) and 6 (pp. 232–69, regarding al-Nuwayrī) in this volume.

14 In this regard, see Bauden, Mamluk diplomatics 50. See also chapter 5 in this volume (pp. 136–231).

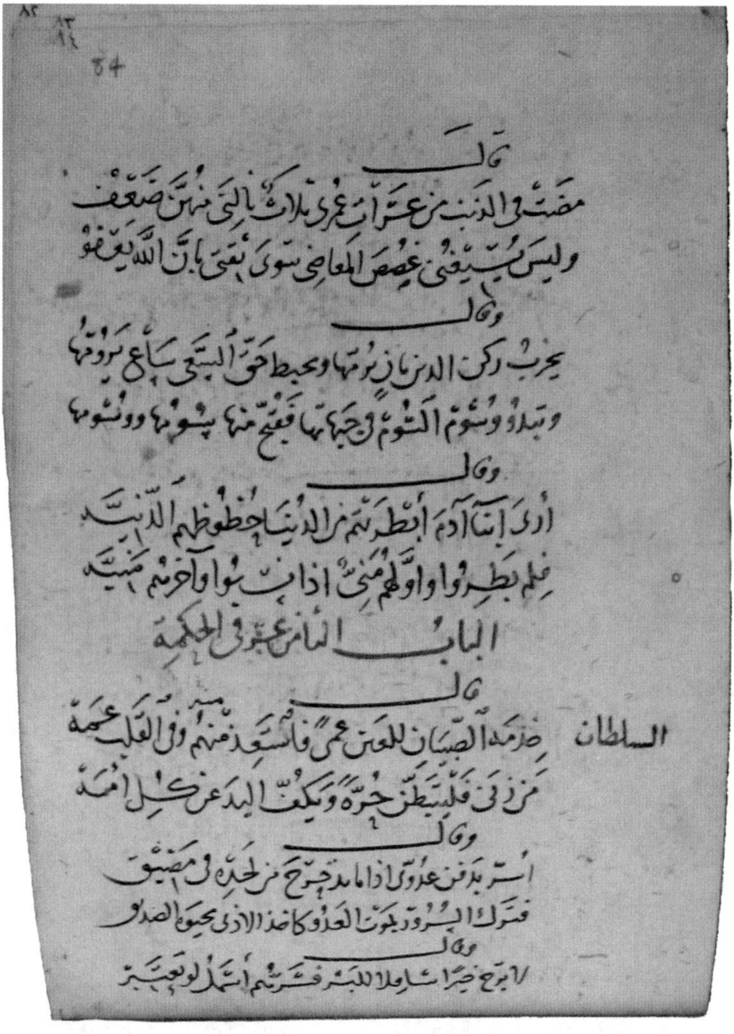

FIGURE 1.1 MS PUL Garrett 3570 Y, f. 33, al-Ṣafadī's *Tadhkira*, Holograph MS

every change of letter, the beginning of the names of each person cited is in red ink, it has even margins, and a beautiful and careful though quick handwriting.

Finally, we should mention some specific manuscripts in which a scholar copied a text by another author and commented upon it, adding his personal notes. These are in-between cases, and we designate them on a case-by-case basis that we explain individually. The *tadhkiras* do not enter into this category since they gather excerpts from more than one text, by more than one author; however, the copy of al-Ḥarīrī's *al-Maqāmāt* penned and illuminated by al-Ṣafadī, now in the Danish Royal Library,[15] is a good example, since the manuscript presents an impressive number of glosses, in red, next to the actual text by al-Ḥarīrī. In such a case, we must talk of a manuscript in al-Ṣafadī's hand, one that includes his personal textual commentary.

In other fields of research, such as classical,[16] medieval, or Renaissance manuscript studies, the word "holograph" is not used, rather "autograph" is preferred, though "autograph" is not the only expression in use and we can observe a certain inconsistency in terminology. A brief overview of the situation will stimulate reflection and, we hope, justify our choices.

When the paleographer Paul Lehmann established the first list of medieval "autograph" manuscripts in 1920, the only criterion he used to define a medieval manuscript as an "autograph" was its handwriting, that is, it had to be that of the author of the text.[17] Most later scholars, like Denis Muzerelle[18] or Eef Overgaauw,[19] use the same straightforward definition—though other specialists consider texts that are dictated by their author to a scribe to be "autograph manuscripts." Olivier Delsaux and Tania van Hemelryck hold this view and even go a step further, adding to the family of the "autograph manuscripts" the manuscripts that were corrected by the author, calling them "*manufactures autographes*," but also "manuscripts whose production was authorized ("*manuscrit original*") or supervised ("*manuscrit auctorial*") by the author of the text,"[20] even if these manuscripts do not show *any* trace of the author's handwriting. In 2014, the two scholars wrote a "Research Guide" on the question, but to date, there has not been any consensus on the terminology in their field of medieval and modern manuscript studies.[21] Since the vocabulary has not been

---

15 MS Cod. Arab. Add. 83, see Perho, *Catalogue* iii, 1416–21.

16 Few Greek and Latin documents (rolls or codex) are preserved in their author's hand. Chapter 2 (pp. 38–54) updates our knowledge of "autograph" Greek literary papyri, and the way to identify them.

17 Lehmann, Autographe and Lehmann, Autographe (updated version 1941).

18 "Autographe: qui est écrit de la propre main de l'auteur ou du personnage en question," Muzerelle, *Vocabulaire*.

19 "Un autographe est, selon notre définition, un manuscrit qui contient un texte écrit de la propre main de l'auteur," Overgaauw, Comment 3.

20 "… nous avons également retenu les manuscrits dont la production a été autorisée (*manuscrit original*) ou supervisée (*manuscrit auctorial*) par l'auteur du texte," Delsaux and van Hemelryck, *Les Manuscrits* 7.

21 This was confirmed by the eminent specialist of medieval manuscripts in Old French, Prof. Michèle Goyens, during her talk at the École nationale des Chartes, Paris, on 12 February 2018. The video of the talk is available: http://www.chartes.psl.eu/fr/actualite/les-defis-de-l-edition-d-un-manuscrit-autographe.

firmly settled, scholars working on these peculiar manuscripts must forge ad hoc expressions and explain their approach in each of their contributions.

In this field of study—i.e., medieval and modern manuscript studies—, the percentage of manuscripts (as outlined above, e.g., *manufactures autographes, manuscrit original, manuscrit auctorial*) that are more than "simple" copies of a given text (i.e., that are holograph, autograph or authorial manuscripts) is relatively low,[22] hence, such a fluid terminology is not really problematic. Our field—the field of manuscripts in Arabic script—is different because (among other factors) the late adoption of the movable-type printing press means that the total number of manuscripts in Arabic script is far higher. Consequently, holographs and manuscripts showing traces of their author's activity are more numerous as well, and thus, a widely accepted and precise terminology is required. Furthermore, if classical, medieval, and modern manuscripts in Occidental languages only rarely state, explicitly, that their scribe is also the author of the text,[23] Arabic sources and manuscripts themselves show a wide gamut of expressions referring to this fact. These can allude to the handwriting (*bi-khaṭṭ Fulān* "in So-and-so's hand"/*bi-khaṭṭihi* "in his hand") or to the stage of the redaction of the text: a manuscript can be an *aṣl*, i.e., an author's personal copy that he modified, emended, or corrected; a *musawwada* (draft); or a *mubayyaḍa* (fair copy). The mere fact that the author's intervention in the manuscript is stated (or not) provides us with information about the perception of authorship on both sides of the Mediterranean.

3 Repertory of Holographs

As just shown, contrary to what exists for medieval Europe,[24] we do not have a comprehensive study devoted to the specific category of autograph notes, holograph or authorial manuscripts and the problems they pose for the Arabic manuscript tradition. One of the first Orientalists who demonstrated the relevance of a careful identification of holographs was Reinhart Dozy, who published, as early as 1847–51, a study of al-Maqrīzī's holographs preserved in Lei-

22 Delsaux and van Hemelryck's repertoire cites a bit more than 400 manuscripts, of which only one-quarter is what we call holographs, see the list in Delsaux and van Hemelryck, *Les Manuscrits* 57–127 (and 129–53 for the arrangement by type of manuscript).

23 Overgaauw, Comment 5. Note that the fact that the word "autograph" only appears in the sixteenth century shows that, in contrast to medieval scholars in the Islamic world, the question was not seen as important by medieval scholars in Europe.

24 Delsaux and van Hemelryck, Les Manuscrits.

den.[25] Dozy concluded his study emphasizing the necessity of producing facsimiles of autograph notes or holograph manuscripts in order to allow proper identification of the authorship of other manuscripts. With a few exceptions, this call has not been answered. One may quote Bernhard Moritz's paleographic album,[26] but it is limited in the sense that it does not display any manuscript created later than the year 1000 AH. Georges Vajda's paleographic album is more comprehensive and arranged both geographically and chonologically,[27] but is restricted to the manuscripts of the BnF; in addition, the scribes are not all identified, and the manuscripts are not all penned by the authors to which they are attributed. Arthur J. Arberry was very interested in handwriting studies and published a compilation of excerpts of India Office manuscripts to contribute to the field of paleographical studies.[28] His catalogue of the Chester Beatty Library, renowned for the huge number of holographs it preserves,[29] is also extremely useful because it often provides illustrations; but again, in these two cases, the scope is limited to one library. Ṣalāḥ al-Dīn al-Munajjid's *al-Kitāb al-ʿarabī l-makhṭūṭ* is worth consulting as well because it shows plates of manuscripts preserved in the Islamic world,[30] and folios containing paratextual elements, such as certificates of audition (*samāʿāt*) and licenses of transmission (*ijāzāt*).[31] Finally, we can cite Khayr al-Dīn al-Ziriklī's biographical dictionary,[32] where the reproduction of a sample of the handwriting compensates for the lack of photographs. Interestingly, in this case, handwriting is placed on the same level as a portrait: indeed, both are entirely personal and representative of a specific individual.[33]

The lack of a general study of the holograph manuscripts produced in the Islamic world is probably because holographs are only mentioned casually in catalogues, articles, and studies,[34] and the researcher does not have access to

25 Dozy, Découverte. See also chapter 5 in this volume, pp. 136–231.
26 Moritz, *Arabic palaeography*.
27 Vajda, *Album*.
28 Arberry, *Specimens*.
29 Arberry, *The Chester Beatty Library*.
30 Al-Munajjid, *al-Kitāb*.
31 On *ijāzāt*, see *EI*² iii, 1020–2; on *samāʿāt*, see *EI*² viii, 1019–20. On both terms and concepts, see Görke and Hirschler, *Manuscript notes*.
32 Al-Ziriklī, *al-Aʿlām*. Three other (old) publications can be mentioned in this category: Cheikho, *Spécimens*; Smith Lewis and Dunlop Gibson, *Forty-one facsimiles*; Tisserant, *Specimina*.
33 The material embodiment of the immaterial spirit of the individual as Roger Chartier expressed it (see the quotations at the beginning of chapter 4 and 5 in this volume, pp. 78 and 136).
34 One may cite Ritter, Autographs, or studies of a particular author's manuscript(s), such as: Bauden, Maqriziana I-1; Bauden, Maqriziana I-2; Bauden, Maqriziana II; Bonebakker,

an exhaustive and unique repertoire which he/she could browse through to identify the particular handwriting of a given person. Such a repertoire would be most useful as a searchable online database that displays dated samples of handwritings in the form of autograph notes and representative leaves of manuscripts.[35]

The *FiMMOD, Fichier des Manuscrits Moyen-Orientaux Datés* ("Repertoire of dated Middle-Eastern manuscripts")[36] is another useful tool. For each manuscript, a record is created that contains basic information (language, library, shelf number, place and date of copy, name of the copyist, author, title, *waqf*, seals and dated paratextual elements, basic codicological description), a full-page picture of a folio, if possible in the original scale, and the detail of the colophon. These records are extremely useful for a paleographical approach to the holograph manuscripts, such as the one presented in chapter 5 in this volume (pp. 136–231).[37]

4 Paleography

In order to identify and study holograph manuscripts and autograph notes, it is necessary to develop sound paleographic skills. As it is often the case, research in manuscript and philological studies is more advanced for the classical world than for the Islamic world. The Italian school is brightly represented, with Dorandi's seminal work *Le stylet et la tablette*[38] certainly being the major one; it goes beyond paleographical questions and delves into methodological considerations. But Petrucci's,[39] Ammirati's, Capasso's, and Cavallo's research is no less significant;[40] Cavallo and Wilson are particularly relevant for Byzantine studies, especially Byzantine paleography.[41] With Byzantium, we are closer to the Islamic world. In addition, we know that "Greek scholars of the fourteenth

An autograph; Bora, A Mamluk historian's holograph; Makdisi, Ibn Taimiya's autograph manuscript; Reisman, A holograph; Richardson, Reconstructing; Sublet, Le Manuscrit; Witkam, Les Autographes; Zaydān, *al-Makhṭūṭāt*, etc.

35 Like Dutschke, Digital, for instance. For a similar claim, see Chapter 3, p. 76.

36 About FiMMOD, see https://maxvanberchem.org/fr/activites-scientifiques/projets/epigraphie-calligraphie-codicologie-litterature/13-epigraphie-calligraphie-codicologie-litterature/92-fimmod-2003.

37 Unfortunately, the project was terminated some years ago and only a few hundred cards were published.

38 Dorandi, *Le stylet*.

39 Petrucci, *La scrittura*; Petrucci, Au-delà; Petrucci, *Prima lezione*.

40 Ammirati et al., *Sul libro*.

41 Cavallo and Maehler, *Greek bookhands*; Wilson, *Mediaeval Greek bookhands*.

to sixteenth centuries were often active as scribes,"[42] a situation comparable to what we know for the Mamlūk period. Studies in Byzantine book culture are well advanced and very inspiring for us.[43]

For right-to-left scripts, Hebrew paleography studies are worth considering. Malachi Beit-Arié is recognized as the world expert in Hebrew manuscripts and has obviously addressed questions of paleography as well.[44] Judith Olszowy-Schlanger directed a seminar at the EPHE (École Pratique des Hautes Études, Paris) on the methods used to identify hands in Hebrew manuscripts and documents.[45] This method is comparable in spirit with the one suggested in chapter 4 in this volume (see pp. 78–135), but is obviously not directly applicable to Arabic scripts because of the intrinsic cursive nature of Arabic writing, which is the opposite of the dissected Hebrew script. Nevertheless, working independently and unaware of the work of the other, Élise Franssen and Judith Olszowy-Schlanger took the method developed by the same legal expert in handwriting (Marie-Jeanne Sedeyn)[46] as a source of inspiration for the establishment of their methodology, and thus attest to an objective approach to the problem. This question of the identification of handwriting is crucial for the advance of Hebrew manuscript and documentary studies since most of the time it is the only way to reconstruct manuscripts from their *membra disjecta* that are scattered in bindings or notarial files around the world.[47]

For Latin scripts, the bibliography of studies in handwriting identification in the field of forensics is given in chapter 4 in this volume. For more historical studies, in addition to the works of Olivier Delsaux and Tania van Hemelryck, the proceedings of conferences organized by the International Committee for Latin Paleography are of foremost importance, especially those published in 2013, since the question of the holograph/autograph manuscripts is the general theme of the publication.[48]

As regards the paleography of Arabic script, the first occurrence of the word "paleography" itself, in the context of Arabic studies, is found in 1782, in the pen

42 Bausi et al., *Comparative* 52; Cavallo, Sodalizi.

43 Cavallo, *Le biblioteche*; Cavallo, *Libri*; Hunger, *Schreiben*; Reynolds and Wilson, *Scribes*; Steel and Macé, Georges Pachymère; Waring, Byzantine book culture; Wilson, *Scholars*.

44 For instance, see Engel and Beit-Arié, *Specimens*.

45 Olszowy-Schlanger, Manuscrits, contains "Programme de l'année 2011–2012: Identifier la main du scribe: petit guide paléographique appliqué aux écritures hébraïques documentaires." In addition, Olszowy-Schlanger, *Un petit guide*, is more complete.

46 The method is called SHOE (Standard Handwriting Objective Examination).

47 See the project "Books within Books" at http://www.hebrewmanuscript.com.

48 Golob, *Medieval*.

FIGURE 1.2 Adler's Arabic Alphabet

of Jacob Georg Christian Adler, in his *Museum Cuficum Borgianum Velitris*[49] where he gathers the reading, translation, and explanations of inscriptions, seals, medals, and coins, as well as their engravings. In addition, the German clergyman provided a table of an alphabet showing the forms of the letters in manuscripts and coins, as well as some peculiar cases (see fig. 1.2); thus, he demonstrated the real methods of paleography. Several of his successors have already been mentioned—Moritz, Vajda, Arberry, al-Munajjid—, and to this list we could add the recent *Paleography between East and West*, which gathers contributions related to both Latin and Arabic paleography.[50]

In paleographical studies of Arabic scripts, the clear prevalence of studies of calligraphic hands, and the few studies about simple, informal, bookhands is

49 Adler, *Museum*, 32 cited by Déroche, La Paléographie. A short biography of Adler is found in Behn, *Concise biographical companion* i, 12–3.

50 See pp. 7–8, nn. 23–27 for the references to the previously cited references, and d'Ottone, *Paleography*.

striking.[51] This may be explained by a general preference for studies of exceptional artifacts—very old or very beautiful—even if to our eyes, very common and ordinary manuscripts reveal more information about the culture in which they were created.[52] An eloquent example of this phenomen is Nourane Ben Azzouna's excellent recent book,[53] in which she analyzes in detail the great Iraqi calligrapher's Yāqūt al-Mustaʿṣimī's hand:[54] the latter was called "*qiblat al-kuttāb*" (the point of reference of calligraphers), because he was seen as the third and last great calligrapher after Ibn Muqla[55] and Ibn al-Bawwāb[56] (one of his masters). Ben Azzouna meticulously describes the letterforms, diacritics, and orthoepics and underlines the variety of forms within the general unity of this mastered handwriting.[57]

Next to the very beautiful manuscripts, there are studies of the very old manuscripts, and François Déroche's research in this field is seminal, especially his classification of *Ḥijāzī* and Abbasid scripts, published in the first tome of the *Catalogue des manuscrits arabes*.[58] The French scholar gives a series of characteristics worth analyzing to describe a handwriting or, of interest for him, a style of handwritings. These include the verticality or obliquity of the letters, the weight of the handwriting, and several letters: the *alif*, the *ʿayn*, the *mīm*, the final *nūn*, the *hāʾ*, the *lām-alif* and the shape of the ligatures (in U or V) placed under the baseline.[59] Indeed, Déroche's main objects of study are the oldest Qurʾāns known at that time and, as a traditional paleographer, his aim was to be able to date the manuscripts based on their handwriting. Marcus Fraser follows the same methodology, with the same goal.[60]

But it would be erroneous to say that there are no paleographical studies of Arabic bookhands of later periods. In this regard, the Maghribī world is extremely well represented, and offers the majority share of all studies in Arabic scripts, starting from the nineteenth century. Indeed the first of the long

51 The following studies perfectly illustrate this fact: Atanasiu, *Le Phénomène calligraphique*; Atanasiu, Les Réalités subjectives; Blair, *Islamic calligraphy*; George, *The rise*; Ifrak, Le *Mabsūṭ*; Micheau, La Calligraphie; Polosin, Ibn Muqlah; etc.

52 See Franssen, A *Maġribī* copy, and above all, Franssen, What was there.

53 Ben Azzouna, *Aux origines du classicisme*.

54 On Yāqūt al-Mustaʿṣimī, see *EI*^{2} xi, 263–4; Ben Azzouna, *Aux origines du classicisme* 39–48 (biography) and sqq.

55 *EI*^{2} iii, 886–7.

56 *EI*^{2} iii, 736–7.

57 Ben Azzouna, *Aux origines du classicisme* 74–84.

58 Déroche, *Catalogue*.

59 Ibid. 17–8.

60 Fraser, The earliest.

series is Houdas' study dating back to 1886.[61] Many other scholars, including François Déroche,[62] Nico van den Boogert[63] and others,[64] considered the question, but it is only very recently that Umberto Bongianino theorized a subclassification within the broad category of *maghribī*.[65] Indeed, even if it shows a great unity at first sight, this style of handwriting could not possibly remain identical over the course of the ten centuries of its history! Nevertheless, we can explain the fact that the *maghribī* script has been more studied than any other bookhand by its easily recognizable attributes, notably because of the typical shapes of its *fāʾ*, with a dot behind the loop, and *qāf*, with only one dot above. In addition, it is rather well defined, geographically speaking, since this typical handwriting is only used by writers who learned to write in the western part of the Islamic world (from al-Andalus to halfway through Libya, including Muslim African regions, to the latitude of Senegal). This typical handwriting was taught in a different way to children, as attested by Ibn Khaldūn (d. 808/1405) himself.[66] But as is clearly shown in chapter 9 in this volume (pp. 300–22) where Ibn Khaldūn's manuscripts are scrutinized, a writer from the Maghrib could change style in the course of his lifetime. Calligraphers easily changed their styles as well, as underlined by Carine Juvin, who cites a certain Ibn Musdī l-Andalusī l-Gharnāṭī who, according to his biography by the Meccan historian al-Fāsī, used both the Occidental and the Oriental styles, "*maghribī* and *mashriqī*," she says.[67]

The term "*mashriqī*" is not often used.[68] Nevertheless, it seems to us the best way to qualify bookhands used in the region corresponding to the Mashriq. These are still too often described as "*naskh*" or "*naskhī*,"—words that do not mean much, since they are used to describe very different handwritings.[69] In addition, *naskh* is originally a calligraphic style, hence it is not an accurate description for informal bookhands. As for "*naskhī*," it is a neologism forged

61 Houdas, Essai.

62 Déroche, O. Houdas; Déroche, Tradition; Déroche, Les Écritures.

63 Van den Boogert, Some notes.

64 Franssen, *Une copie en* maġribī 123–7; Franssen, A *Maġribī* copy 69–70; d'Ottone, *al-Ḫaṭṭ al-maġribī*; Maghraoui, Uṣūl.

65 Bongianino, *The origin*; see also Bongianino, Quelques remarques; Bongianino, Le Manuscrit X 56 Sup.

66 Quoted in Déroche, Les Écritures 67.

67 Juvin, Calligraphy 155–6.

68 Next to Juvin, to the best of our knowledge, we are the only ones to use the word: Bauden, *Catalogue passim*; Franssen, What was there 321. Nevertheless, the word was already used by Ibn Khaldūn, see Chap. 9, 309 n. 28.

69 Jan Just Witkam has already underlined this, see Witkam, Seven specimens 18, as well as Déroche, Les études de paléographie 366–7.

by Nabia Abbott in the twentieth century.[70] Using calligraphic terminology to describe bookhands is quite understandable, given that it is the only existing original Arabic terminology.[71] This is the approach Gacek has brilliantly undertaken for numerous years,[72] but this terminology cannot be used without nuance: talking of *nastaʿlīq* when referring to a non-calligraphic bookhand is not correct, though referring to it as a "nastaʿlīq-ish script" is fine. In this sense, Abbott's "*naskhī*" is also acceptable, but since it is constructed as a *nisba*-adjective, it looks like a genuine Arabic word and is thus a bit misleading.

As a calligrapher, Yāqūt al-Mustaʿṣimī easily changed style as well, but it is worth remarking that even within the same style, he could write the same letter in different ways.[73] This shows that when analyzing a handwriting, one should not go too deep into details and that an analysis of lettershapes is not enough. Thus, the most important question is, which characteristics remain? What is really typical of one's particular hand? According to Nikolaj Serikoff,[74] text density, ratio between the height of the *alif* and the width of the final *bāʾ*, and the angle of the *alif* and of the *kāf* are the decisive criteria that even allow for a chronological or geographical attribution. We cannot follow him to this degree, but we do agree that a body of evidence is necessary in order to accurately describe a given handwriting. But how precisely can we describe a handwriting? This is one of the questions addressed in chapter 5 of this volume with regard to al-Maqrīzī's handwriting (pp. 136–231). Chapter 4 (pp. 78–135) also illustrates the test of another much more complete method and answers the question as well.

5 Holographs as Collectibles

If rationally proving that a particular manuscript is effectively in the hand of a certain author is arduous, practically speaking, there have always been connoisseurs able to recognize prestigious hands. Noticing that the number of preserved holographs of European authors particularly surged from the mid-eighteenth century, Roger Chartier linked the increasing interest in this category of manuscripts with the need to guarantee the authenticity of an

70 See Abbott, *The rise* 34, 37.

71 Because we all agree that epithets like "*ḥasan*" or "*ṭayyib*," often found in biographies to refer to one's handwriting, do not mean much. Examples are extremely numerous, among others in Juvin, Calligraphy.

72 Gacek, Arabic scripts; Gacek, al-Nuwayrī's classification; Gacek, The diploma; Gacek, Some technical terms; Gacek, The head-serif.

73 Ben Azzouna, *Aux origines du classicisme* 74–99.

74 Serikoff, Image and letter 58 and *passim*.

author's works.[75] He characterized the greed for this category of manuscripts as a fetishism of the author's hand, a phenomenon that exists for Islamic manuscripts as well.[76] Numerous references found in the literature demonstrate the importance Muslim scholars gave to holograph works that survived their authors. One such case is reported by Yāqūt al-Rūmī (d. 626/1229), with regard to Abū l-Faraj al-Iṣbahānī's *Kitāb al-Aġānī* (Book of songs), a multi-volume work composed in the fourth/tenth century. It became known that the draft of this book had passed into the hands of a bookseller and was to be offered for sale. The person in question, who was eager to own such a precious witness of Abū l-Faraj's work, asked a friend to contact the owner to negotiate a price. After an inquiry, the inquirer informed his friend that the book had already been sold at auction for the amount of 4,000 dirhams. He specified that the manuscript was mainly written on the back of (loose?) leaves (*ẓuhūr*)[77] and was in a handwriting used for note-taking (*bi-khaṭṭ al-taʿlīq*). He also provided the name of the potential buyer but, when contacted, the latter answered that he knew nothing about this manuscript. Despite a deep search, no trace of this manuscript could be found.[78] This anecdote—whether true or fabricated—shows how highly a manuscript in the author's handwriting was valued by some scholars and collectors.

Holographs could indeed become collectibles. If twenty-four volumes in al-Maqrīzī's hand are still preserved in various libraries around the world, it is due to the fact that al-Maqrīzī was famous during his lifetime and some of his works—particularly his *opus magnum* on the topography of Cairo (*al-Mawāʿiẓ wa-l-iʿtibār*)—became what would now be described as a bestseller. Even his notebooks, the most significant witness of his writing activity and *modus operandi*, given that they are composed of résumés and various notes, were deemed valuable enough to survive and be kept in the libraries of some famous scholars. These notebooks are generally anonymous in the sense that his name does not appear in the manuscript; this means that some scholars were able to identify his handwriting, even several centuries after his death (see chapter 5 in this volume, esp. p. 164, n. 98). Al-Maqrīzī's case may seem exceptional, but hundreds, if not thousands, of holographs are preserved in libraries, particularly from the seventh/thirteenth century onwards.[79] Some scholars,

75 Chartier, *From the author's hand* 10.

76 Ibid. 8.

77 Sic! This reading does not make much sense. The word *ẓuhūr* must perhaps be read as *ṭurūs* (palimpsests).

78 Yāqūt al-Ḥamawī, *Muʿjam al-udabāʾ* 1719.

79 For the Mamlūk period, see Sublet, Le Manuscrit autographe.

like the judge Ibn Jamāʿa (d. 790/1388) who never gave up trying to purchase the holograph of a text, deployed huge resources to collect holographs. In the meantime, he would acquire a copy which, in case he eventually purchased the author's holograph, he never parted with. His library was so renowned for its quality and the number of holographs it contained that most of it was bought by a Mamlūk amir who wanted it for his madrasa, for the benefit of students and scholars.[80]

Those who were eager to purchase holographs were ready to disburse huge amounts for them. Scholars and collectors, two categories of potential buyers, were not necessarily driven by the same desire. The scholar wished to acquire a holograph because it was the tangible witness of its author's work, as imperfect as it might have been—for instance, loose sheets could be misplaced—, the work in the author's hand that does not contain scribal errors usually found in copies. What is written and how it is written stirred the scholar's interest. By contrast, the collector was attracted to the holograph for other reasons: he wanted to build a library that contributed to his social status, to possess a much desired manuscript that no one owns, to be known and appreciated for owning a holograph that other scholars would dream of having in their libraries. Scholars and collectors competed to purchase the rarest items, though the latter usually had greater financial means. "God sends nuts to those who have no teeth" said an unlucky scholar who failed to buy a precious copy that was acquired by a nobleman whose interest in the book was purely material.[81]

Once the precious object of desire was in the possession of a scholar or a bibliophile, its owner often left a trace attesting to his acquisition. Ibn Khaldūn's personal copy of his *al-Muqaddima*, with an autograph note (later framed) indicating that it represented his draft (*musawwada*), is a perfect example of this phenomenon: the first leaf—not a title page in the full sense of the word—is covered with ownership marks added at various periods in the history of this singular manuscript (see fig. 1.3). Some owners also loaned their books to scholars who were eager to access what was sometimes a unique copy.[82] As readers, scholars did not refrain from leaving notes testifying that they had accessed the copy on a certain date and in a given place. Ownership statements and consul-

80 Ibn Ḥajar, *Inbāʾ al-ghumr* i, 355. The amir was Maḥmūd al-Ustādār and the collection came to be known as al-Maḥmūdiyya, which was the name of his madrasa. A note on the title page of each volume was added, stressing the conditions of the *waqf*. Kyle Wynter-Stoner is currently studying this library in the framework of his PhD dissertation at the University of Chicago.

81 Al-Maqqarī, *Nafḥ al-ṭīb* i, 463. See also Touati, *L'Armoire à sagesse* 31–4.

82 On book lending, see F. Sayyid, Naṣṣān qadīmān.

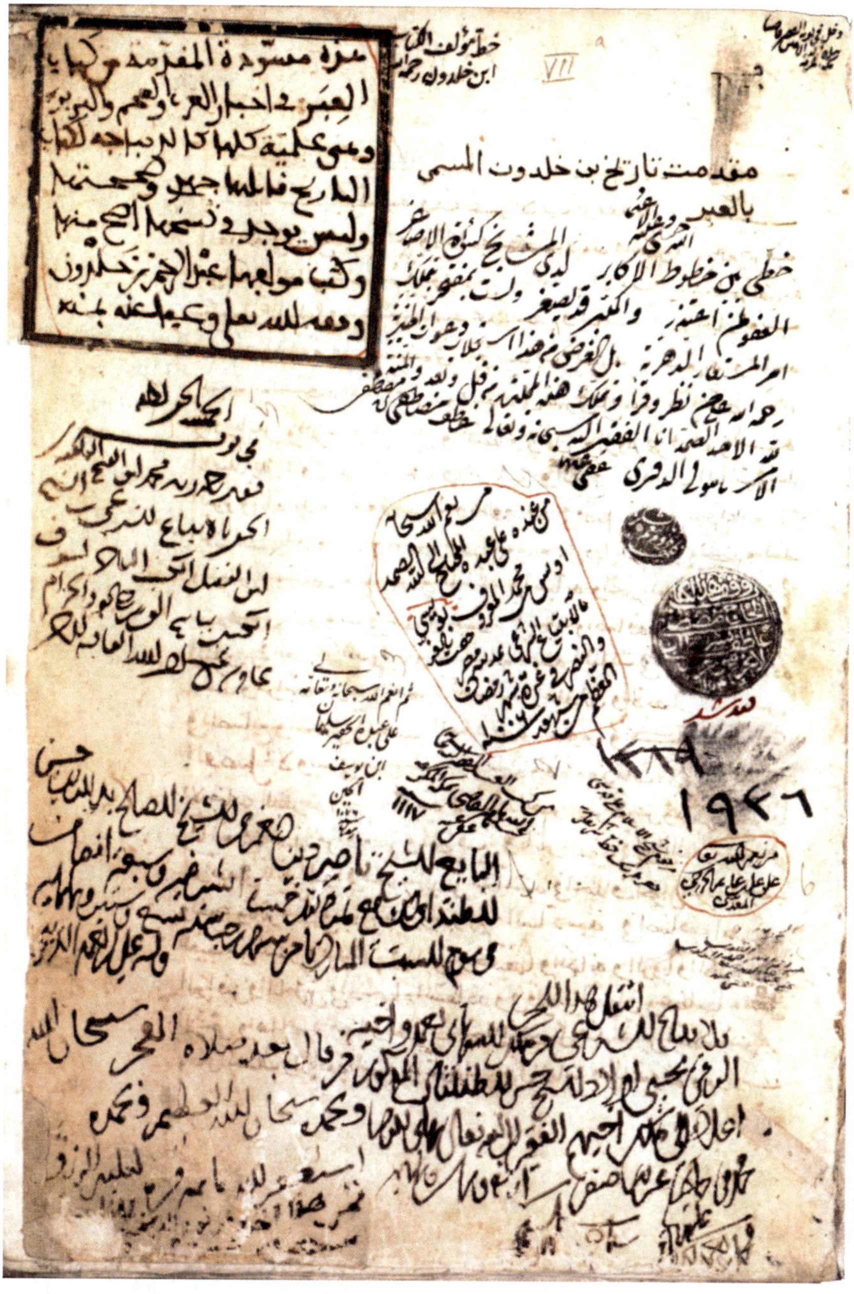

FIGURE 1.3 Ibn Khaldūn, *al-Muqaddima*, MS Atıf Efendi 1936, fol. VII[a]
SÜLEYMANIYE KÜTÜPHANESI, ISTANBUL

tation notes have received little attention so far.[83] Clearly, they do provide us with critical data on the history of libraries, particularly those of scholars', and on the fortune and diffusion of specific works in certain milieus, aspects that touch on issues related to the sociology of culture.[84] Perhaps as importantly, they represent additional—and sometimes unique—examples of a scholar's handwriting. These autograph notes added a special value to a manuscript, because of the fame of the person who penned them.[85] Unsurprisingly, like holographs (see chapter 3 in this volume, particularly p. 63), they sometimes stimulated greed. False attributions were thus not rare in this respect. It is difficult to assess this phenomenon because of the lack of studies, but the example found in fig. 1.4 is eloquent: one of the ownership marks states that the book was owned by a certain Aḥmad b. ʿAlī (*min kutub Aḥmad b. ʿAlī sanat 811*). A later possessor identified this owner with the famous historian al-Maqrīzī,[86] whose name was indeed Aḥmad b. ʿAlī. While the name and the date seem likely, the handwriting does not tally with al-Maqrīzī's hand and the content of the mark does not correspond to his practice of always using his family name (see fig. 5.4 in chapter 5, p. 148). Nevertheless, once attributed to this renowned historian, this specific mark could represent a valid reason for its purchase and increase its value in the eyes of a potential buyer.

6 Ecdotics (Textual Criticism)

Holographs are precious as collectibles, for their monetary value, but also for their philological value, since they clearly have a special status in the transmission history of a text. Indeed, when considering the critical edition of a text, scholars still consider the most reliable—and at times most accurate—witness to be the holograph.[87] Usually presented as the most desirable state of

83 See Gacek, Ownership statements; Touati, *L'Armoire à sagesse* 97–100; Liebrenz, The library; Liebrenz, *Die Rifāʿīya*; as well as the recent special issue (vol. 9, 2018) of the *Journal of Islamic Manuscripts* directed by B. Liebrenz and entitled *The history of books and collections through manuscript notes*.

84 See Akkerman's works, cited above, 1 n. 3.

85 Ownership marks and consultation statements are sometimes circled when they were penned by a famous scholar. See figs. 1.3–1.4.

86 The note is in Ottoman Turkish: *Maqrīzīniñ khaṭṭīdir* ("al-Maqrīzī's hand").

87 Literature about textual criticism applied to Arabic is abundant. For an assessment of this literature, see the excellent review presented by al-Qāḍī in her How 'sacred' is the text, particularly 13–22. Regarding issues linked to textual criticism, see also Witkam's reflections in his Establishing the stemma.

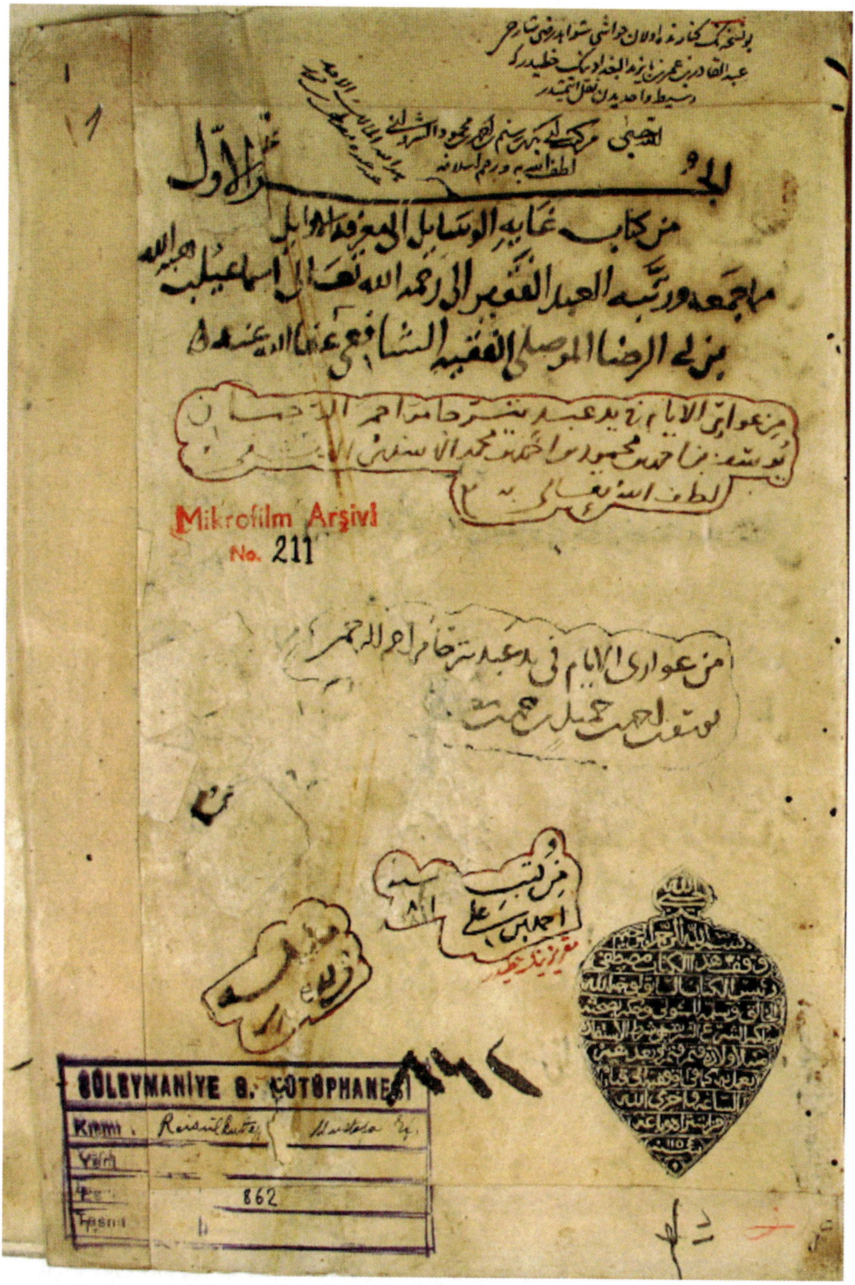

FIGURE 1.4 al-Mawṣilī, *Ghāyat al-wasāʾil ilā maʿrifat al-awāʾil* (MS Reisülküttab 862)
SÜLEYMANIYE KÜTÜPHANESI, ISTANBUL

a text, the holograph still raises concerns. Should the author's obvious handwriting errors be faithfully reproduced or corrected and duly indicated in the apparatus? What about the orthography: should it be standardized according to the rules applied since printing started on a large scale in the Arab world (thirteenth/nineteenth century) or left unchanged? Should grammatical errors be corrected or left in the text? Beside these legitimate questions, the editor also faces other problems. The holograph copy that has been preserved may represent only one stage in the elaboration of the text: it could be an early or intermediary draft, a fair copy used as a working copy which the author continued to modify through various means (inserts, cancellations, marginal or interlinear additions, etc). Even if the holograph corresponds to the fair copy that was ultimately 'published', which can be regarded as the most desirable witness of a text, it is legitimate to ask if it exempts the editor from considering other copies (for example, apographs, i.e., copied on the holograph or the authorial manuscript, or later copies). As with any other manuscript, holographs could be exposed to various vicissitudes. Perhaps more than other copies, holographs, depending on the stage of the text they corresponded to, were more amenable to alterations: inserts and loose leaves could be lost or marginal additions could be trimmed during the binding process, etc. In fact, the existence of a holograph does not make it less necessary to investigate other witnesses. An author could modify his text even after its publication, a process that might explain the presence of variants.[88]

The collation of the holograph with later copies may also reveal differences, sometimes notable ones. All too often, the editor is eager to offer the reader the most 'complete' text. When Ayman Fuʾād Sayyid tackled the critical edition of al-Maqrīzī's *al-Mawāʿiẓ wa-l-iʿtibār*, he relied as much as possible on the two volumes of the draft (*musawwada*), which only cover about one half of the final work, and he collated them with later copies.[89] In so doing, he neglected to take into consideration that al-Maqrīzī worked on this text over a period of some thirty years, and the two volumes of the draft represented one version—the first—of the work. During the collation process, he noticed that the draft sometimes contained more detailed descriptions and also, sometimes, mentioned monuments whose entries were reduced or left out of the final version. As an editor, he faced a dilemma: which version should be kept in the critically edited text? Anxious to print the most exhaustive version of al-Maqrīzī's text, he opted to mix the two versions, sticking to the draft each time it offered more

88 On this specific issue, see Sobieroj, *Variance*.
89 Al-Maqrīzī, *al-Mawāʿiẓ wa-l-iʿtibār* (1st ed.).

data, thus succombing to the temptation to prioritize comprehensiveness over the author's intent.[90]

Holograph and authorial manuscripts also bear crucial information about their author's working method. Indeed, the steps of the composition may have been preserved (drafts, fair copies, notebooks, commonplace books) and various aspects of the author's methodology are visible in these written traces: inserts, signs showing that a certain passage needs to be moved to another place in the work, words crossed out or cancelled, glosses referring to other works, etc. All these witnesses correspond to what has been termed the "avant-textes," i.e., what precedes the published version. Hence, holograph and authorial manuscripts constitute major evidence that *must* not only be taken into account for the elaboration of a critical edition, but also for the study of the author's methodology. Despite the quantity of material available, as outlined above, so far, this promising field of research has not drawn much attention from scholars working on Arabic manuscripts.[91] Beside the obvious interest in the way an author conceived and composed his work, the study of his methodology can also offer solutions to a scholar interested in editing the 'final' version of a text but willing, at the same time, to publish the most 'complete' text. As stressed above, each version of a text represents one step in the author's creative process and the mixing of several of these versions, in an attempt to publish the most comprehensive version, should be avoided as it does not represent the author's intent. Genetic criticism is the way forward for anyone wishing to consider as much of the "avant-textes" as possible together with the 'final' version of a text.[92] Rather than focusing on one particular state of the text, this approach consists of encompassing all the traces left by an author (notes, sketches, drafts, fair copies, correspondence, library) with the ultimate goal of presenting a genetic edition.[93] The study of the process which led to the production of the 'final' version is considered as significant as this 'final' version. As specialists of this field state: "... a genetic edition is more than a

---

90 See Bauden's review in *Mamlūk Studies Review* VIII/1 (2004), 169–76. These issues were not addressed in the second revised edition he published in 2013: Al-Maqrīzī, *al-Mawāʿiẓ wa-l-iʿtibār* (2nd rev. ed.). Theoretical works about author's variants are abundant for European literature, see for instance Ciociola, 'Storia.'

91 In addition to the work being done on al-Maqrīzī's working method by Frédéric Bauden in the framework of his Maqriziana studies, see chapter 7 in this volume (pp. 260–76, as well as Élise Franssen's current analysis of al-Ṣafadī's commonplace book (*al-Tadhkira*), and Reisman, A holograph.

92 On Genetic criticism, see Deppman et al., *Genetic criticism*.

93 Or an edition including the author's variants as it used to be called, see Ciociola, 'Storia' and many others.

'critical gathering' of primary documents. In a genetic edition it is possible to present the documents and texts that lead to the printed version of a particular work and also the variation among these printed texts."[94] To produce a genetic edition, scholars now have at their disposal electronic scholarly editing mainly made possible by the existence of the XML encoding language (eXtensible Markup Language) essentially in the frame of the TEI (Text Encoding Initiative). The genetic edition allows editors to combine a digital archive of all the written witnesses left by an author with an edition that fully embraces the two most favored approaches to digital editing: text- and document-oriented approaches. Nowadays, this process constitutes the best way to combine the necessity to take into consideration the form of the edited text and the requirement to reconstruct the dynamics of the composition process.[95] Undoubtedly, it should be considered for some Muslim authors like al-Maqrīzī, whose 'avant-textes' and texts in holograph form have been preserved in sufficient number.[96]

7 Digital Humanities

As just underlined, the Digital Humanities (DH) offer new possibilities for various aspects of our research. In philology, we see the great advantages of digital editions. In terms of the tools of research, they make possible the computational analysis of texts, for instance, thanks to efficient tagging methods, some of which are semi-automatic. The tagging system OpenITI mARkdown, developed by Maxim Romanov, is an excellent and user-friendly tool that renders texts machine readable and thus allows large corpus analyses.[97] The KITAB project (for "Knowledge, Information Technology, and the Arabic

94 See http://www.textualscholarship.org/gencrit/index.html.

95 Unsurprisingly, projects in this field mainly address modern and contemporary authors. See, for instance, the Samuel Beckett Digital Manuscript Project (https://www.beckettarchive.org).

96 The *Bibliotheca Maqriziana* project (https://brill.com/view/serial/BIMA) aims to publish critical editions with annotated translations and thorough studies of al-Maqrīzī's oeuvre on the basis of the exceptional corpus of holograph and authorial manuscripts that have reached us. Each editor takes great pain to track any of the author's modifications and emendations that are noticeable in the manuscripts and report these in the apparatus. The facsimile published at the end of each volume allows readers to visually become cognizant of these traces of the working process. Nevertheless, such a project would greatly benefit from genetic criticism for the creation of a digital archive including the manuscripts al-Maqrīzī consulted.

97 See https://alraqmiyyat.github.io/mARkdown/.

Book"), whose PI is Sarah Savant,[98] developed a software that can detect text reuse and thus unveil the sources used by an author for a particular chapter. The same approach allows the detection of different styles of language and gives the same kind of information, i.e., the source(s) used by an author.[99] In philology, and more precisely in ecdotics, in terms of displaying possibilities, we are no longer limited by the size of a book page and many different views of the same text edition can be seen; we do not have to choose between critical and diplomatic editions, since we can now display the edited text next to the image of the folio, or next to the collation notes tab, or the biographical information tab, or a map relevant to the text under study, or a representation of the network of sources or scholars represented by the text, etc.[100] Thus, we have in hand a global contextualization of the manuscripts and of the edited text.

In the field of paleography, for the identification of hands, various approaches have been undertaken. For instance, the "paleographic metrology" that aims at applying quantitative-statistical methods to paleography,[101] or the "spatial gray level dependence,"[102] a method of "texture analysis" that applies "a segmentation-free approach" that allows researchers to determine a time-span for the copying of manuscripts, should be improved and refined in order to achieve more precise results. The table of contents of the *Proceedings of 2017 IEEE International Workshop on Arabic Script Analysis and Recognition*[103] leads us to hope for substantial solutions: more than forty percent of the communications deal with Arabic handwritten text recognition, using different techniques: "deep convolutional networks," "neural network based recognition," "trajectory recovery technique," "sequential minimal optimization," and "dynamic bayesian networks." Yet, we did not find a single name of a colleague trained to work with Arabic manuscripts, not even with the mention "with the collaboration of" … We could not read all these very specialized articles, but hope to hear about their results, and hope the majority of them will be more accurate than the one referred to in this volume with regard to al-Maqrīzī's holographs:[104] as shown in chapter 5 (pp. 136–231), the results are not exactly convincing for a specialist of Arabic manuscripts, though they were for the authors of the study.

98 For the complete list of KITAB team's members, see http://kitab-project.org/team/.
99 The software is called "passim", see http://kitab-project.org/text-reuse-methods/.
100 These possibilities are offered by EVT (Edition Visualization Technology), a free open-source software developed at the University of Pisa, see http://evt.labcd.unipi.it.
101 See Rehbein et al. *Kodikologie*; Fischer et al. *Kodikologie*.
102 Abd Al-Aziz et al., Recognition.
103 Available online: http://toc.proceedings.com/36341webtoc.pdf.
104 Boiarov et al., Arabic manuscript.

The *Gazette du Livre médiéval* special double issue published in 2011 under the direction of Denis Muzerelle and Maria Gurrado[105] contains inspiring studies as well, and more traditional but still effective methods are exposed in Peter Rück's book.[106] Among these new approaches, the GRAPHEM project[107] is interesting because it uses a variety of methods to develop a global vision of the handwritings. Using the *Catalogue des manuscrits datés portant des indications de dates ou de copiste*[108] as a sample, the project developed a co-occurrence matrix based on the computer analysis of the letters contours pixels, and on wavelets[109] of the manuscript pictures that allow the automatic extraction of the main characteristics chosen a priori (for instance, the verticals) of the writing. In addition, it conducts an analysis of the inclination of the script, and a description of the ductus, in order to reconstruct the scriptor's hand movement. This description uses the automatic identification of the strokes, of their number and direction, and analyzes the thickness of the strokes and their color intensity. This exhaustive approach sounds excellent, but to the best of our knowledge, no tangible result has been published to date. This is too frequently the conclusion we come to: the same can be said of the ENTRAP software[110] that gave (excellent) test results, but nothing more. One article published in 2012 in the *International Journal of Computer Applications*, promised the "automatic reading of historical Arabic MSS."[111] All these innovative methods are extremely promising and we look forward to reading successful results in the near future.

105 Muzerelle and Gurrado, *Analyse* (http://www.persee.fr/issue/galim_0753-5015_2011_num_56_1).

106 Rück, *Methoden*.

107 This interdisciplinary project was financed by the French Agence Nationale de la Recherche between 2008 and 2011 and involved five different CNRS laboratories, in Computer sciences (LIRIS based in Lyon, LIPADE based in Paris, and LIFO, based in Orléans), the IRHT (Institut de Recherche en Histoire des Textes), and the École nationale des Chartes. See Gurrado, Ricerche and the bibliography cited there.

108 Realized under the patronage of the "Comité international de Paléographie latine," the CMD-France is online and searchable, see http://cmdf.irht.cnrs.fr.

109 This technique derives from the theories developed in the nineteenth century by Joseph Fourier, a French mathematician, and today are mainly used in image compressing: it reduces the amount of information for each image and stores the residuals (that are easier to store) elsewhere in order to recontruct the original image. The new image is thus lighter. On Fourier and the wavelets technique and function, see Koppe, Joseph Fourier. On Fourier, see Arago, Éloge.

110 Rezvan and Kondybaev, The ENTRAP software.

111 Farag, Handwritten text recognition system.

Dominique Stutzmann's effort, in the field of medieval and Renaissance Latin manuscripts, is highly interesting as well, since paleographical analysis is not her only final objective.[112] Indeed, she argues that the level of compliance to the norms (that is, the respect given to handwriting models) represents the extent to which the handwriting of a certain society has been normalized. Her research in script identification and machine reading of medieval manuscripts is extremely successful as well: she developed an OCR for manuscripts that is able to take into account the abbreviations as well.[113] The technique used, convolutional neural networks, "which mimick[s] the way we learn"[114] is the one used by the OpenITI team to develop their Optical Character Recognition software for the Arabic script.[115] They argue that the same methodology could be applied to manuscripts, since they are currently training the machine to read manuscripts.

8 An Insight into the Contents[116]

Before addressing issues linked to the Islamic world, an opening to the classical world was deemed useful because of the great experience gathered by scholars working on this period. In chapter 2 (pp. 38–54), Marie-Hélène Marganne presents the current state of research in Greek literary autograph papyri. In classical Greece, the copying of manuscripts was seen as a servile activity: authors used to dictate their texts to their scribes, as attested by the literary sources and by the iconography; while in Rome, authors sometimes wrote their texts themselves. This is another factor, in addition to the passage of time that has destroyed documents, and explains why the number of Greek holographs/autographs is so low. Of the 7,000 Greek literary papyri preserved, the

---

112 Her research project, first entitled ORIFLAMMS (Ontology Research, Image Features, Letterform Analysis on Multilingual Medieval Scripts), is now called ECMEN ("Écriture médiévale & numérique"). See Stutzmann, Système graphique.

113 Kestemont and Stutzmann, Script identification.

114 As expressed by Romanov et al., Important new developments 2.

115 On OpenITI (Open Islamicate Texts Initiative), see the website https://alraqmiyyat.github.io/OpenITI/. On the OCR software, see Romanov et al., Important new developments.

Note that two other important achievements in textual analysis were possible thanks to machine readable texts; these are Jedli, developed by Peter Verkinderen and José Haro Peralta, see Haro Peralta and Verkinderen, *Jedli*; and Qawl, developed by Sébastien Moureau, see https://uclouvain.be/qawl/.

116 A Conference review was published a couple of months after the conference in COMSt Newletters, see Franssen, Autograph/holograph.

author presents an up-to-date list of autographs, adding five to the list that was established by Tiziano Dorandi, and thus reaching the number of twenty-nine. Since the author's name is seldom given, in order to identify these papyrus as autographs, the scholar must build on a body of evidence: the form and quality of the medium, the page layout, the hand, the state of the text, the literary genre, and the context of the redaction of the text, all while keeping in mind the characteristics of the scribal work *a contrario*. Then, Marganne gives a detailed analysis of each manuscript listed, of their extrinsic and intrinsic features. Finally, she analyzes the medical papyri in depth, more precisely of P. Oxy. 74.4970.[117]

Another methodological contribution can be found in chapter 3 (pp. 55–77). It opens with a short terminological clarification and quickly passes to richly illustrated explanations about the different types of holographs in the Islamic manuscript tradition. If drafts are easy to identify as holographs thanks to their specific features—a special type of book, the messy layout, informal hand, numerous *marginalia*, blanks, etc.—, and, sometimes, indications in their colophon, fair copies are more difficult to authenticate because they are more polished. Furthermore, for some of them, it is impossible to ensure that they are actually in their author's hand, since no other sample of their author's handwriting is preserved. Gacek also tackles the case of working copies, sometimes heavily glossed by other authors. Then, he exposes the Arabic terminology related to the question, before passing to the method used to avoid being trapped by fraudulent statements. Indeed, as already tackled, owners sometimes sought to increase the value of their manuscripts by stating that the latter are in the hand of the original author. One needs to confront all the information available about the author, his biography, his time, his habits, his handwriting, his signature, and the invocation added after his name.

Chapter 4 (pp. 78–135) is methodological and practical at the same time, since it concerns the actual testing of a forensic method for the identification of the handwritings of Arabic manuscripts, more precisely of a sub-group of the Egyptian recension of *The Thousand and One Nights*. The Egyptian recension appeared at the end of the twelfth/eighteenth century to the beginning of the

117 It is worth mentioning that during the conference, Caroline Macé, a reputed Byzantinist, presented her work on Georges Pachymeres, more precisely of MS Gr. 1810 (BnF, Paris), in which he acts both as a scribe and an author, since he added a scholarly comment to the text he copied. The material she presented during the conference was already published, and for this reason her work is not included in this volume. See Steel and Macé, Georges Pachymère.

thirteenth/nineteenth century with two main protagonists at work: a scribe and a compiler. Élise Franssen's aim was to ascertain, based on the very detailed method called SHOE ("Standard Handwriting Objective Examination"), which manuscripts were in their respective hand. After an exhaustive account of the method, with remarks and considerations about its adaptation to the Arabic alphabet, the case studies are carefully examined. This analysis proved convincing, in fact, an examination of only part of the criteria exposed is sufficient to reach meaningful conclusions. In this case, we can apprehend the genesis of the group of manuscripts and propose a change in the distribution of the volumes in three of the groups of manuscripts.

The second part of the volume, in which the contributions deal with a specific author, opens with chapter 5 (pp. 136–231). In this article, Frédéric Bauden answers the question of the very essence of al-Maqrīzī's handwriting, especially over the passage of time, by examining twenty-four holographs and one authorial manuscript, written over a period of some fifty years. Al-Maqrīzī makes an excellent case study, because numerous holographs of his, of different types (notebooks, drafts, fair copies …), have been preserved, as have other types of autograph notes (ownership marks, consultation statements, marginal comments in manuscripts he consulted). Therefore, after a recap of al-Maqrīzī's biography, especially of his probable training in calligraphy, Bauden uses various paratexts by al-Maqrīzī as samples of the scholar's handwriting, and considers all the aspects of the manuscripts studied, noticing for instance, a change of *misṭara* at a precise point in the author's lifetime and precisely distinguishing drafts and fair copies. In conclusion, for the very first time, we gain a clear view of this great historian's handwriting and its peculiarities.

Al-Nuwayrī is the next author examined, in chapter 6 (pp. pp. 232–59). The analysis of al-Nuwayrī's holographs allows for an immersion into an encyclopedist's working method, and shows his strategies to cope with the great quantity of information available then. Al-Nuwayrī is an excellent candidate for such research in more than one respect. As a matter of fact, we have at our disposal information about his activity as an author and scribe of his own works from different sources: biographical sources (al-Udfuwī, al-Ṣafadī, and al-Maqrīzī recount interesting facts about his copying ability), theoretical sources (his own *Nihāyat al-arab* has a whole chapter about it), and material sources, since thirty holograph volumes of his are preserved. A question of terminology is also brought to our attention: the word *nāsikh* not only means copyist, but also compiler, anthologist, or editor. Finally, Elias Muhanna exposes the possible discovery of a copy of al-Bukhārī's *al-Jamīʿ al-ṣaḥīḥ* in al-Nuwayrī's hand. Al-Nuwayrī made this copy when he was in need of funds, to retire and devote his time to writing. The issue of handwriting identification is particularly relevant in this case, since al-Nuwayrī was a highly skilled calligrapher and mastered different styles.

Chapter 7 (pp. 260–76) deals with particular holographs and their difficult identification: three miscellanies consist of three volumes of Akmal al-Dīn b. Mufliḥ's *Tadhkira* or commonplace book. Since personal information about the author's family is included in each of the three volumes, these can be used as an archive of a family history, a matter of particular importance in this case since Akmal al-Dīn b. Mufliḥ was accused of manipulating his genealogy in order to seize *waqf*s. Kristina Richardson begins with an account of Ibn Mufliḥ's biography, based on biographical sources and on paratextual elements found in various manuscripts. She continues with a list of examples of Mamlūk and early Ottoman-period notebooks, then goes on to describe the three manuscripts she has identified as volumes of Akmal al-Dīn b. Mufliḥ's *Tadhkira*. These manuscripts allow her to draw a genealogy of the *qāḍī* which figures in the end of the article.

Chapter 8 (pp. 277–99) tackles al-ʿAynī and the intricate relationships between three of his holographs on one hand, and with the works of his rival al-Maqrīzī on the other hand. The accurate and precise observations help to solve the puzzle. Contrary to previous assumptions, the texts of the three manuscripts appear to be three different works, dealing with roughly the same events. The analysis of the paratexts and *marginalia* of one of them allows Nobutaka Nakamachi to ascertain the mutual influence that existed between al-ʿAynī and al-Maqrīzī. Finally, the importance of al-ʿAynī's younger brother as a historian of some concern is revealed.

Chapter 9 (pp. 300–22) focuses on Ibn Khaldūn's *al-Taʿrīf*. Retsu Hashizume begins with a reconsideration of the lineage the editor of the text established, and convincingly proves that this needs to be corrected. This fine analysis of the textual tradition—mainly based on the marginal annotations and cancellations that were neglected by the editor of the text—leads him to identify a holograph draft that must have existed. He also explains his discovery of three other manuscripts of the text. Finally, he raises the issue of the handwriting, since the draft he has identified is not in *maghribī*, as one would expect from a native of the Maghrib, but in *mashriqī* script. Biographical sources about Ibn Khaldūn indicate that he mastered both styles, but the author prudently concludes that this requires further investigation.

The final contribution, chapter 10 (pp. 323–435), is the combined effort of two specialists of Yemeni manuscripts and literature, Julien Dufour and Anne Regourd. It deals with particular manuscripts: Yemeni personal poetic anthologies in the form of *safīna* (vertical format, with horizontal binding) that are progressively called, by metonymy, *safīna*s themselves. Dufour and Regourd begin with a historical account of the *safīna* as a book form and as a literary genre in the Persian and Turkish worlds, then address the particular case of Yemen. The contents of Yemeni *safīna*s are then more precisely exposed, with interesting considerations about *ḥumaynī* poetry. The descriptions of six *safīnas* follow.

Thus, the second, fourth and last chapters of this volume deal with peculiar holographs: holographs whose author is unknown. Holograph manuscripts are representative of their authors, and if the latter is unknown, they give information about his time and culture. Indeed, this volume aims at examining the topic from all sides, theoretical and practical, particular and general, codicological, paleographical, and philological: these exceptional manuscripts deserve our focus and from their careful analysis, we can learn a great deal about the Islamic world in general.

Bibliography

Primary Sources

Ibn Ḥajar, *Inbāʾ al-ghumr bi-abnāʾ al-ʿumr*, ed. Ḥ. Ḥabashī, Cairo 1969–72 (repr. 1994–8), 4 vols.

al-Maqqarī, *Nafḥ al-ṭīb min ghuṣn al-Andalus al-raṭīb*, ed. I. ʿAbbās, Beirut 1988, 8 vols.

al-Maqrīzī, *al-Mawāʿiẓ wa-l-iʿtibār bi-dhikr al-khiṭaṭ wa-l-āthār*, ed. A. Fuʾād Sayyid, London 2002–4 (1st ed.), London 2013 (2nd rev. ed.), 6 vols.

Yāqūt al-Ḥamawī, *Muʿjam al-udabāʾ: Irshād al-arīb ilā maʿrifat al-adīb*, Beirut 1993, 7 vols.

Secondary Sources

Abd Al-Aziz, A.M., M., Gheith, and A. Fuʾād Sayyid, Recognition for old Arabic manuscripts using spatial gray level dependence (SGLD), *Egyptian Informatics Journal* 12 (2011), 37–43.

Abbott, N., *The rise of the North Arabic script and its Kurʾanic development, with a full description of the Kurʾan manuscripts in the Oriental Institute*, Chicago 1939.

Adler, J.G.C., *Museum cuficum borgianum Velitris*, Rome 1782.

Akimushkin, O.F., Textological studies and the "critical text" problem, *Manuscripta orientalia* 1/2 (1995), 22–8.

Akkerman, O., *The Bohra dark archive and the language of secrecy: a codicological ethnography of the Royal Alawi Bohra Library in Baroda*, PhD, Frei Universität Berlin, 2014.

Al-Qāḍī, W., How 'sacred' is the text of an Arabic medieval manuscript? The complex choices of the editor-scholar, in J. Pfeiffer and M. Kropp, *Theoretical approaches to the transmission and edition of Oriental manuscripts: Proceedings of a symposium held in Istanbul, March 28–30, 2001*, Würzburg 2007, 13–53.

Ammirati, S., M. Capasso, and G. Cavallo, *Sul libro latino antico: ricerche bibliologiche e paleografiche*, Pisa and Rome 2015.

Arago, F., Éloge historique de Joseph Fourier, lu à la séance publique du 18 novembre 1833, *Mémoires de l'Académie des sciences de l'Institut de France*, Paris 1836, LXIX–CXXXVIII.

Arberry, A.J., *Specimens of Arabic and Persian palæography*, London 1939.

Arberry, A.J., *The Chester Beatty Library: A handlist of the Arabic manuscripts*, Dublin 1955.

Atanasiu, V., *Le Phénomène calligraphique à l'époque du sultanat mamluk. Moyen-Orient, XIIIe–XVIe siècle* (PhD École pratique des Hautes Études, Paris 1 Sorbonne), 2003.

Atanasiu, V., Les Réalités subjectives d'un paléographe arabe du Xe siècle, *Gazette du Livre médiéval*, 43 (2003), 14–21.

Barnhart, R.K., *The Barnhart dictionary of etymology*, New York 1988.

Bauden, F., *Al-Maqrīzī's collection of opuscules: An introduction*, Leiden and Boston (forthcoming).

Bauden, F., *Catalogue of the Arabic, Persian and Turkish manuscripts in Belgium*. Vol. I: *Handlist*. Part I: *Université de Liège*, Leiden and Boston 2017.

Bauden, F., Maqriziana I: Discovery of an autograph manuscript of al-Maqrīzī: Towards a better understanding of his working method, Description: Section 1, *Mamlūk Studies Review* VII (2003), 21–68.

Bauden, F., Maqriziana I: Discovery of an autograph manuscript of al-Maqrīzī: Towards a better understanding of his working method, Description: Section 2, *Mamlūk Studies Review* X (2006), 81–139.

Bauden, F., Maqriziana II: Discovery of an autograph manuscript of al-Maqrīzī: Towards a better understanding of his working method, Analysis, *Mamlūk Studies Review* XII (2008), 51–118.

Bauden, F., Mamluk diplomatics: The present state of research, in F. Bauden, and M. Dekkiche (eds.), *Mamluk Cairo, a crossroads for embassies. Studies on diplomacy and diplomatics*, Leiden and Boston 2019, 1–104.

Bauden, F., Review of Ayman Fu'ād Sayyid's edition of al-Maqrīzī, *al-Mawāʿiẓ wa-l-iʿtibār fī dhikr al-khiṭaṭ wa-l-āthār*, vols. 1–2, London 2002–3, *Mamlūk Studies Review* VIII/1 (2004), 169–76.

Bauden, F., and M. Dekkiche (eds.), *Mamluk Cairo, a crossroads for embassies. Studies on diplomacy and diplomatics*, Leiden and Boston 2019.

Bauer, T., Ibn Nubātah al-Miṣrī (686–768/1287–1366): Life and works. Part II: The *Dīwān* of Ibn Nubātah, *Mamlūk Studies Review* XII-2 (2008), 25–69.

Bausi, A., P.G. Borbone, F. Briquel-Chatonnet, P. Buzi, J. Gippert, C. Macé, M. Maniaci,

Z. Melissakis, L.E. Parodi, and W. Witakowski (eds.), *Comparative Oriental manuscript studies: An introduction*, Hamburg 2015.

Behn, W.H., *Concise biographical companion to Index Islamicus: An international who's who in Islamic studies from its beginnings down to the twentieth century*, Leiden and Boston 2004, 3 vols.

Behzadi, L., and J. Hämeen-Anttila (eds.), *Concepts of authorship in pre-modern Arabic texts*, Bamberg 2015.

Behzadi, L., Introduction: The concepts of polyphony and the author's voice, in L. Behzadi and J. Hämeen-Anttila (eds.), *Concepts of authorship in pre-modern Arabic texts*, Bamberg 2015, 9–22.

Ben Azzouna, N., *Aux origines du classicisme: Calligraphes et bibliophiles au temps des dynasties mongoles (les Ilkhanides et les Djalayirides, 656–814 / 1258–1411)*, Leiden and Boston 2018.

Bhalloo, Z., Review of Olly Akkerman, "The Bohra Dark Archive and the Language of Secrecy: A Codicological Ethnography of the Royal Alawi Bohra Library in Baroda", Doctorat, Université libre de Berlin 2014, 360 p., *Chroniques des manuscrits du Yémen* 25 (2018), 5–9.

Blair, S.S., *Islamic calligraphy*, Edinburgh 2006.

Boiarov, A., A. Senovy, A. Knysh, and D. Shalymov, Arabic manuscript author verification using deep convolutional networks, *2017 IEEE International Workshop on Arabic Script Analysis and Recognition (ASAR). Proceedings of a meeting held 3–5 April 2017, Nancy, France*, [New York] 2017, 1–5.

Bonebakker, S.A., An autograph by at-Tibrizi in the National Library of Tunis, *Bibliotheca Orientalis* (1965), 245–47.

Bongianino, U., Le Manuscrit x 56 sup. (*Kitāb Sībawayh*) de la Bibliothèque Ambrosienne et les écritures de l'Occident arabe avant la diffusion du *maġribī* arrondi, *Les Rencontres du CJB* 6 (2015), 5–25.

Bongianino, U., Quelques remarques sur l'origine des écritures coraniques arrondies en al-Andalus (v^e^/xie–vi^e^/xiie siècles), *al-Qanṭara* XXXVIII-2 (2017), 153–87.

Bongianino, U., *The origin and development of Maghribī scripts: Epigraphic and calligraphic traditions of the western Islamic lands*, PhD, EPHE, 2017.

Bora, F., A Mamluk historian's holograph. Messages from a *musawwada* of *Taʾrīkh*, *Journal of Islamic Manuscripts* 3–2 (2012), 119–53.

Cavallo, G., *Le biblioteche nel mondo antico e medievale*, Bari 2004 (7th ed.).

Cavallo, G., *Libri, editori e pubblico nel mondo antico. Guida storica e critica*, Bari 2004 (4th ed.).

Cavallo, G., Sodalizi eruditi e pratiche di scrittura a Bisanzio, in J. Hamesse (ed.), *Bilan et perspectives des études médiévales (1993–1998). Euroconférence (Barcelone, 8–12 juin 1999)*, Turnhout 2004, 649–69.

Cavallo, G., and H. Maehler, *Greek bookhands of the early Byzantine period, A.D. 300–800*, London 1987.

Chartier, R., *From the author's hand to the printer's mind: Who is an author in early modern Europe?*, San Diego 2013.

Cheikho, L., *Spécimens de cent écritures arabes pour la lecture des manuscrits anciens et modernes*, Beirut 1885.

Ciociola, C., 'Storia della tradizione' e varianti d'autore (Barbi, Pasquali, Contini), in C. Ciociola, and C. Vela (eds.), *La tradizione dei testi, Atti del Convegno, Cortona, 21–23 settembre 2017*, Rome 2018, 3–22.

Delsaux, O., and T. Van Hemelryck, *Les Manuscrits autographes français à la fin du Moyen Âge: guide de recherches*, Turnhout 2014.

Deppman, J., D. Ferrer, and M. Groden, *Genetic criticism: Texts and avant-textes*, Philadelphia 2004.

Déroche, F., *Catalogue des manuscrits arabes. Deuxième partie: manuscrits musulmans. Tome I, 1: Les manuscrits du Coran. Aux origines de la calligraphie coranique*, Paris 1983.

Déroche, F., La Paléographie des écritures livresques dans le domaine arabe, *Gazette du Livre médiéval* 28 (1996), 1–8.

Déroche, F., Les Écritures maghrébines, in M.-G. Guesdon and A. Vernay-Nouri (eds.), *L'Art du livre arabe*, Paris 2001, 65–9.

Déroche, F., Les Études de paléographie des écritures livresques arabes: quelques observations, *al-Qanṭara* XIX (1998), 365–81.

Déroche, F., O. Houdas et les écritures maghrébines, in A.-C. Binebine, *Le Manuscrit arabe et la codicologie. Actes du colloque qui s'est tenu du 27 au 29 février 1992, à l'Université Mohammed V de Rabat*, Rabat 1994, 75–81.

Déroche, F., Tradition et innovation dans la pratique de l'écriture au Maghreb pendant les IVe/Xe et Ve/XIe siècles, in S. Lancel (ed.), *Numismatique, langue, écriture et arts du livre, spécificités des arts figurés. Actes du VIIe colloque international sur l'histoire et l'archéologie de l'Afrique du Nord*, Paris 1999, 233–47.

Dorandi, T., *Le Stylet et la tablette: dans le secret des auteurs antiques*, Paris 2000.

d'Ottone, A., *Al-Ḫaṭṭ al-maġribī* et le fragment bilingue latin-arabe Vat. Lat. 12900: quelques observations, in M. Jaouhari, *Les Écritures des manuscrits de l'Occident musulman. Journée d'études, Rabat, 29 Novembre 2012*, Rabat 2013, 7–18.

d'Ottone Rambach, A. (ed.), *Paleography between East and West. Proceedings of the seminars on Arabic palaeography held at Sapienza, University of Rome*, Rome and Pisa 2018.

Dozy, R.P.A., Découverte de trois volumes du *Mokaffá* d'Al-Makrízí, in R.P.A. Dozy, *Notices sur quelques manuscrits arabes*, Leiden 1847–51, 8–16.

Dutschke, C., Digital scriptorium as a construction site for ascertained manuscripts, in N. Golob (ed.), *Medieval autograph manuscripts. Proceedings of the XVIIth Colloquium of the Comité International de Paléographie Latine, held in Ljubljana, 7–10 September 2010*, Turnhout 2013, 281–89.

Engel, E., and M. Beit-Arié, *Specimens of mediaeval Hebrew scripts*, Jerusalem 1987–2017, 3 vols.

Farag, M.S., Handwritten text recognition system for automatic reading of historical Arabic manuscripts, *International Journal of Computer Applications* 60/13 (2012), 31–7.

Fischer, F., C. Fritze, G. Vogeler, B. Assmann, P. Sahle, and M. Rehbein, *Kodikologie und Paläographie im Digitalen Zeitalter 2 / Codicology and Palaeography in the Digital Age 2*, Norderstedt 2010.

Franssen, É., A *Maġribī* copy of the *Kitāb al-Faraj baʿd aš-Šidda*, by the ʿIrāqī qāḍī at-Tanūḫī. Study of a manuscript of Liège University (Belgium), *Journal of Islamic Manuscripts* 1–1 (2010), 61–78.

Franssen, É., Autograph/holograph and authorial manuscripts in Arabic Script [Conference review], *COMSt Newsletter* 7 (2014), 10–1.

Franssen, É., *Une copie en* maġribī *du* Kitāb al-Faraj baʿd aš-Šidda *d'at-Tanūḫī. Analyse d'un manuscrit de l'Université de Liège*, MA thesis, University of Liège 2008.

Franssen, É., What was there in a Mamluk amīr's library? Evidence from a fifteenth-century manuscript, in Y. Ben Bassat (ed.), *Developing perspectives in Mamluk history. Essays in honor of Amalia Levanoni*, Leiden 2017, 311–32.

Fraser, M., The earliest Qur'anic scripts, in M. Graves (ed.), *Islamic art, architecture and material culture: New perspectives (Proceedings from a workshop held at the Centre for the Advanced Study of the Arab World, University of Edinburgh)*, Oxford 2012, 121–32.

Gacek, A., *Arabic manuscripts: A vademecum for readers*, Leiden 2009.

Gacek, A., Arabic scripts and their characteristics as seen through the eyes of Mamluk authors, *Manuscripts of the Middle East* 4 (1989), 126–30.

Gacek, A., The Copenhagen manuscript of the *Maqāmāt al-Ḥārīriyya*, Copied, illuminated and glossed by the Mamluk litterateur Ṣalāḥ al-Dīn aṣ-Ṣafadī, in R.M. Kerr and T. Milo (eds.), *Writings and writing from another world and another era. Investigations in Islamic text and script in honour of Dr. Januarius Justus Witkam, Professor of codicology and palaeography of the Islamic world at Leiden University*, Cambridge 2010, 143–66.

Gacek, A., The diploma of the Egyptian calligrapher Ḥasan al-Rushdī, *Manuscripts of the Middle East* 4 (1989), 44–60.

Gacek, A., The head-serif (*Tarwīs*) and the typology of Arabic scripts: Preliminary observations, *Manuscripta Orientalia* 9–3 (2003), 27–33.

Gacek, A., al-Nuwayrī's classification of Arabic scripts, *Manuscripts of the Middle East* 2 (1987), 126–30.

Gacek, A., Ownership statements and seals in Arabic manuscripts, *Manuscripts of the Middle East* 2 (1987), 88–95.

Gacek, A., Some technical terms relative to the execution of Arabic manuscripts, *Middle East Librarians Association Notes (MELA Notes)* 50–51 (1990), 13–8.

Gaffiot, F., *Dictionnaire latin-français*, Paris 1934.

George, A., *The rise of Islamic calligraphy*, London, San Francisco, and Beirut 2010.

Ghersetti, A., A pre-modern anthologist at work: The case of Muḥammad b. Ibrāhīm al-Waṭwāṭ (d. 718/1318), in L. Behzadi and J. Hämeen-Anttila (eds.), *Concepts of authorship in pre-modern Arabic texts*, Bamberg 2015, 23–45.

Golob, N., *Medieval autograph manuscripts. Proceedings of the XVIIth Colloquium of the Comité International de Paléographie Latine, held in Ljubljana, 7–10 September 2010*, Turnhout 2013.

Görke, A, and K. Hirschler (eds.), *Manuscript notes as documentary sources*, Würzburg 2011.

Gurrado, M., Ricerche di paleografia digitale: il progetto "GRAPHEM", in N. Golob (ed.), *Medieval autograph manuscripts. Proceedings of the XVIIth Colloquium of the Comité International de Paléographie Latine, held in Ljubljana, 7–10 September 2010*, Turnhout 2013.

Haro Peralta, J., and P. Verkinderen, *Jedli: A textual analysis toolbox for digitized Arabic texts*, Hamburg 2016.

Hoad, T.F., *Concise Oxford dictionary of English etymology*, Oxford 1996.

Houdas, O., Essai sur l'écriture maghrébine, *Nouveaux mélanges orientaux. Mémoires, textes et traductions publiés par les Professeurs de l'École spéciale des langues orientales vivantes, à l'occasion du 7e Congrès international des Orientalistes réuni à Vienne (septembre 1886)*, IIe Série, Vol. XIX, Paris 1886, 85–112.

Hunger, H., *Schreiben und Lesen in Byzanz: die byzantinische Buchkultur*, Munich 1989.

Ifrak, K., Le *Mabsūṭ* d'al-Qandūsī, autopsie d'un style, in M. Jaouhari (ed.), *Les Écritures des manuscrits de l'Occident musulman. Journée d'études tenue à Rabat le 29 Novembre 2012*, Rabat 2013, 31–6.

Juvin, C., Calligraphy and writing activities in Mecca during the medieval period (twelfth–fifteenth centuries), *Proceedings of the Seminar for Arabian Studies*. Volume 43. *Papers from the forty-sixth meeting of the Seminar for Arabian Studies held at the British Museum, London, 13 to 15 July 2012*, Oxford 2013, 153–66.

Kestemont, M., and D. Stutzmann, Script identification in medieval Latin manuscripts using convolutional neural networks, *Digital Humanities 2017: Book of Astracts*, 283–85.

Koppe, M., Joseph Fourier transforme toujours la science, *CNRS. Le Journal*, 21 mars 2018 (online: https://lejournal.cnrs.fr/articles/joseph-fourier-transforme-toujours-la-science).

Lehmann, P., Autographe und Originale namhafter lateinischer Schrifsteller des Mittelalters, *Zeitschrift des Deutschen Vereins für Buchwesen und Schrifttum* 3 (1920), 6–16.

Lehmann, P., Autographe und Originale nahmafter lateinischer Schriftsteller, *Erforschung des Mittelalters. Aussgewählte Abhandlungen und Aufsätze 1*, Leipzig 1941, 359–81.

Lewis, C.T., and C. Short, *Harpers' Latin dictionary: A new Latin dictionary founded on the translation of Freund's Latin-German lexicon edited by E.A. Andrews*, Oxford 1800.

Liebrenz, B., *Die Rifāʿīya aus Damaskus. Eine Privatbibliothek im osmanischen Syrien und ihr kulturelles Umfeld*, Leiden 2016.

Liebrenz, B. (ed.), *The history of books and collections through manuscript notes*, special issue of the *Journal of Islamic Manuscripts*, Brill 2018.

Liebrenz, B., The library of Aḥmad al-Rabbāṭ. Books and their audience in 12th to 13th/18th to 19th century Syria, in R. Elger and U. Pietruschka (eds.), *Marginal perspectives on early modern Ottoman culture: Missionaries, travellers, booksellers*, Halle (Saale), 2013, 17–59.

Maghraoui, M., Uṣūl wa-taṭawwur al-khuṭūṭ al-maghribiyya ilā l-ʿaṣr al-wasīṭ, in M. Jaouhari (ed.), *Les Écritures des manuscrits de l'Occident musulman. Journée d'études, Rabat, 29 Novembre 2012*, Rabat 2013, 37–58.

Makdisi, G., Ibn Taimiya's autograph manuscript on *Istihsân*: Materials of the study of Islamic legal thought, in *Arabic and Islamic studies in honor of Hamilton A.R. Gibb*, Leiden 1969, 446–79.

Micheau, F., La Calligraphie du *Kitāb al-diryāq* de la Bibliothèque nationale de France: entre sens et esthétique, in C. Müller and M. Roiland-Rouabah (eds.), *Les Non-Dits du nom. Onomastique et documents en terres d'Islam. Mélanges offerts à Jacqueline Sublet*, Beirut 2013, 29–52.

Moritz, B., *Arabic palaeography: A collection of Arabic texts from the first century of the hidjra till the year 1000*, Cairo 1905.

al-Munajjid, Ṣ. al-D., *al-Kitāb al-ʿarabī l-makhṭūṭ ilā l-qarn al-ʿāshir al-hijrī* (= *Le Manuscrit arabe jusqu'au Xᵉ s. de l'H.*), Cairo 1960.

Muzerelle, D., *Vocabulaire codicologique: répertoire méthodique des termes français relatifs aux manuscrits, avec leurs équivalents en anglais, italien, espagnol, édition hypertextuelle*, Paris 1985 (online http://codicologia.irht.cnrs.fr).

Muzerelle, D., and M. Gurrado, *Analyse d'images et paléographie systématique. L'écriture entre histoire et science, Gazette du Livre médiéval* 56–7.

Olszowy-Schlanger, J., Manuscrits hébreux et judéo-arabes médiévaux, *Annuaire de l'École pratique des hautes études* (EPHE), *Section des sciences historiques et philologiques* 144 (2013), 10–2.

Olszowy-Schlanger, J., Un petit guide de description des écritures hébraïques: identifier la main du scribe, *Instrumenta BwB*, 1 (2013) (online: http://www.hebrewmanuscript.com/instrumenta.htm).

Onions, C.T., with the assistance of R.W. Burchfield, and G.W.S. Friedrichsen, *The Oxford dictionary of English etymology*, New York and Oxford 1966.

Overgaauw, E., Comment reconnaître un autographe du Moyen Âge?, in N. Golob (ed.), *Medieval autograph manuscripts. Proceedings of the XVIIth Colloquium of the Comité*

International de Paléographie Latine, held in Ljubljana, 7–10 September 2010, Turnhout 2013, 3–16.

Perho, I., *Catalogue of Arabic manuscripts. Codices arabici and codices arabici additamenta* (3 vols.), Copenhagen 2008.

Petrucci, A., Au-delà de la paléographie: histoire de l'écriture, histoire de l'écrit, histoire de l'écrire, *Bulletin de la Classe des lettres et des sciences morales et politiques de l'Académie royale de Belgique* 6/7 (1996), 123–35.

Petrucci, A., *La scrittura. Ideologia e rappresentazione*, Turin 1986.

Petrucci, A., *Prima lezione di paleografia*, Rome and Bari, 2002 (6th ed. 2011).

Polosin, V., Ibn Muqlah and the Qur'anic manuscripts in oblong format, *Mélanges de l'Université Saint-Joseph* 59 (2006), 309–17.

Rehbein, M., P. Sahle, T. Schaßan, B. Assmann, F. Fischer, and C. Fritze, *Kodikologie und Paläographie im digitalen Zeitalter / Codicology and palaeography in the digital age*, Norderstedt 2009.

Reisman, D., A holograph MS of Ibn Qāḍī Shuhbāh's 'Dhayl', *Mamlūk Studies Review* II (1998), 19–49.

Reynolds, L.D., and N.G. Wilson, *Scribes and scholars: A guide to the transmission of Greek and Latin literature*, Oxford 1991 (3rd ed.).

Rezvan, E.A., and N.S. Kondybaev, The ENTRAP software: Test results, *Manuscripta Orientalia* 5–2 (1999), 58–64.

Richardson, K., Reconstructing the autograph corpus of Shams al-Dīn Muḥammad Ibn Ṭūlūn, *JAOS* 135(2) (2015), 319–27.

Ritter, H., Autographs in Turkish libraries, *Oriens* 6–1 (1953), 63–90.

Romanov, M., M.T. Miller, S.B. Savant, and B. Kiessling, Important new developments in arabographic optical character recognition (OCR), *al-ʿUṣūr al-Wusṭā* 25 (2017), 1–13.

Rück, P., *Methoden der Schriftbeschreibung: historische Hilfwissenschaften*, Stuttgart 1999.

Sayyid, F., Naṣṣān qadīmān fī iʿārat al-kutub, in *Majallat Maʿhad al-Makhṭūṭāt al-ʿArabiyya/Revue de l'Institut des manuscrits arabes* 4 (1958), 125–36.

Serikoff, N., Image and letter: "Pace" in Arabic script (a thumb-nail index as a tool for a catalogue of Arabic manuscripts: Principles and criteria for its construction), *Manuscripta Orientalia* 7–4 (2001), 55–66.

Sirat, C., *Writing as handwork: A history of handwriting in Mediterranean and Western culture*, Turnhout 2006.

Smith Lewis, A., and M. Dunlop Gibson, *Forty-one facsimiles of dated Christian Arabic manuscripts, with text and English translation. With introductory observations on Arabic calligraphy by the Rev. D.S. Margoliouth*, Cambridge 1907.

Sobieroj, F., *Variance in Arabic manuscripts: Arabic didactic poems from the eleventh to the seventeenth centuries: Analysis of textual variance and its control in the manuscripts*, Berlin and Boston 2016.

Steel, C., and C. Macé, Georges Pachymère philologue: le commentaire de Proclus sur le *Parménide* dans le manuscrit Parisinus gr. 1810, in M. Cacouros and M.-H. Congourdeau (eds.), *Philosophie et sciences à Byzance de 1204 à 1453. Les textes, les doctrines et leur transmission: actes de la Table Ronde organisée au XXe Congrès International d'Etudes Byzantines (Paris, 2001)*, Leuven 2006, 77–99.

Stutzmann, D., Système graphique et normes sociales: pour une analyse électronique des écritures médiévales, in N. Golob (ed.), *Medieval autograph manuscripts. Proceedings of the XVIIth Colloquium of the Comité International de Paléographie Latine, held in Ljubljana, 7–10 September 2010*, Turnhout 2013, 429–34.

Sublet, J., Le Manuscrit autographe: un statut particulier? Des exemples à l'époque mamelouke, in A. Görke and K. Hirschler (eds.), *Manuscript notes as documentary sources*, Würzburg 2011, 173–81.

Tisserant, E., *Specimina codicum orientalium*, Bonn 1914.

Touati, H., *L'Armoire à sagesse: bibliothèques et collections en Islam*, Paris 2003.

Vajda, G., *Album de paléographie arabe*, Paris 1958.

van den Boogert, N., Some notes on Maghribi script, *Manuscripts of the Middle East* 4 (1989), 30–43.

Waring, J., Byzantine book culture, in L. James (ed.), *A Companion to Byzantium*, Malden, Oxford, and Chichester 2010, 275–88.

Wilson, N.G., *Mediaeval Greek bookhands: Examples selected from Greek manuscripts in Oxford libraries*, Cambridge (MA) 1973.

Wilson, N.G., *Scholars of Byzantium*, London and Baltimore 1983.

Witkam, J.J., Establishing the stemma: Fact or fiction?, *Manuscripts of the Middle East* 3 (1988), 88–101.

Witkam, J.J., Les Autographes d'al-Maqrizi, in A.C. Binebine (ed.), *Le Manuscrit arabe et la codicologie*, Rabat 1994, 89–98.

Witkam, J.J., *Seven specimens of Arabic manuscripts preserved in the Library of the University of Leiden presented to the 9th Congress of Arabic and Islamic Studies, Amsterdam, 1–6 September 1978*, Leiden 1978.

Zaydān, Y., *al-Makhṭūṭāt al-muwaqqaʿa: aʿmāl al-muʾtamar al-duwalī l-thānī li-Markaz al-Makhṭūṭāt (Abrīl 2005)*, Alexandria 2008.

al-Ziriklī, Kh. al-D., *al-Aʿlām: Qāmūs tarājim li-ashhar al-rijāl wa-l-nisāʾ min al-ʿArab wa-l-mustaʿribīna wa-l-mustashriqīna*, Beirut 2002, 8 vols.

CHAPTER 2

Comment reconnaître un autographe parmi les papyrus littéraires grecs ? L'exemple du *P. Oxy.* 74.4970

Marie-Hélène Marganne

À la différence des manuscrits médiévaux qui ont transmis, à la suite de copies successives, les œuvres des auteurs grecs et latins antiques, les papyrus littéraires grecs et, dans une moindre mesure, latins, permettent d'observer sur le vif des témoignages de première main de l'élaboration d'un texte littéraire à toutes ses étapes, des premières notes prises par un auteur à la rédaction en cours ou terminée, et de sa copie personnelle ou de travail à sa copie calligraphique.

La plupart des papyrus grecs et latins ont été découverts en Égypte, où le climat sec a assuré leur conservation. Ceux-ci datent, *grosso modo*, des IVe/IIIe siècles avant notre ère aux VIIe/VIIIe siècles de notre ère, c'est-à-dire de la période qui s'étend de l'installation en Égypte de nombreux Grecs, suite à l'annexion de ce pays par Alexandre le Grand, en 332 avant notre ère, jusqu'à la conquête arabe, en 641 de notre ère. Parmi ces pièces, on distingue deux grandes catégories : les papyrus littéraires (restes de livres, de manuels, de brouillons, d'exercices scolaires, etc.), et les papyrus documentaires (documents officiels, rapports légaux, contrats, testaments, lettres privées, signalements, certificats de décès, inventaires, listes, etc.). Eu égard au thème étudié ici, ce sont les papyrus littéraires, dont plus de 7.000 sont actuellement répertoriés[1], – du moins pour les textes profanes –, qui retiendront notre atten-

1 Dans le texte et les notes, l'abréviation MP[3] ou Mertens-Pack[3] désigne la 3e édition, mise à jour en permanence par nos soins, du *Catalogue des papyrus littéraires grecs et latins*, accessible sur le site web du CEDOPAL, à l'adresse http://cipl93.philo.ulg.ac.be/Cedopal/MP3/dbsearch.aspx. Ses deux premières éditions avaient été réalisées par Roger A. Pack : voir Pack, *The Greek and Latin literary texts*. Pour les abréviations papyrologiques, on se référera à la *Checklist of editions of Greek, Latin, Demotic and Coptic papyri, ostraca and tablets*, régulièrement mise à jour, à l'adresse http://papyri.info/docs/checklist. Dans les notices MP[3], les dates avant notre ère sont indiquées par [a] en exposant (abréviation d'*ante Christum natum*) ; in. indique le début (*ineunte*) et ex., la fin (*exeunte*) d'un siècle ; précisant les notions de recto et de verso, les flèches → et ↓ indiquent le sens des fibres du papyrus.

 | DOI:10.1163/9789004413177_003

tion. Ceux-ci se présentent sous la forme de rouleaux ou de coupons de papyrus, de *codices* de papyrus ou de parchemin, et aussi de tablettes de bois et d'ostraca.

Des autographes sont-ils attestés dans les papyrus littéraires grecs et latins? Quoique leur identification soit malaisée, plusieurs ont pu être identifiés parmi les papyrus littéraires grecs. Leur petit nombre pourrait s'expliquer par le fait que l'écriture autographe des œuvres littéraires, – fût-ce des traités techniques –, n'était pas très répandue dans l'antiquité gréco-romaine. Comme le confirme à plusieurs reprises le médecin Galien (129-*c.* 216)[2] dans ses traités, les auteurs grecs dictaient la plupart du temps leurs œuvres à des scribes, qui pouvaient être tachygraphes (sténographes)[3]. De fait, à la différence de l'Égypte pharaonique, où le statut du scribe était élevé[4], le monde hellénique considérait la copie manuelle d'un texte comme une activité servile. Il s'ensuit que les orateurs, les philosophes, les poètes, les médecins grecs, etc., ont été généralement représentés, soit un rouleau fermé à la main, soit en train de lire, et pratiquement jamais en train d'écrire. Par exemple, dans les illustrations du fameux manuscrit grec connu sous le nom de "Dioscoride de Vienne" (*Vindobonensis Medicus Graecus* 1), élaboré, vers 512, à Constantinople, la plupart des écrivains médecins sont représentés, non pas en train d'écrire, mais bien tenant un rouleau (ainsi, au fol. 2^{v}, Machaon, Pamphile, Xénocrate, Sextius Niger, Héraclide et Mantias groupés autour du centaure Chiron; au fol. 3^{v}, Cratévas, Apollonios, Andréas [de Caryste?], Dioscoride, Nicandre et Rufus entourant Galien, ainsi que Dioscoride au fol. 4^{v}) ou un codex fermés (Galien, au fol. 3^{v}) à la main. La seule exception à cette règle est, au fol. 5^{v}, la seconde repré-

2 Boudon-Millot, *Galien. Sur ses propres livres.*

3 Voir not. Galien, *Sur ses propres livres* 1.12, dans l'édition, traduite et commentée de Boudon-Millot, 139, 187-8 n. 1: ἐδεήθη μού τις φίλος ἐπαχθῶς ἔχων πρὸς αὐτὸν ὑπαγορεῦσαι τὰ ῥηθέντα τῷ πεμφθησομένῳ παρ'αὐτοῦ πρός με διὰ σημείων εἰς τάχος ἠσκημένῳ γράφειν, "un de mes amis qui ne pouvait supporter [Martialios], me demanda de dicter mes paroles à la personne qu'il m'enverrait et qui était entraînée à prendre des notes en sténographie (…)"; voir aussi Galien, *De propriorum animi cuiuslibet affectuum dignotione et curatione*, 9.9, dans l'édition de de Boer, *Galeni De propriorum animi* 32.15-18 (de Boer 1937, p. 32, 15-8 = V 48 Kühn) (en ligne http://cmg.bbaw.de/epubl/online/cmg_05_04_01_01.html): βλέπω γάρ σε μήτ'εἰς τὰ καλὰ τῶν ἔργων δαπανῆσαι τολμῶντα, μήτ'εἰς βιβλίων ὠνὴν καὶ κατασκευὴν καὶ τῶν γραφόντων ἄσκησιν ἤτοι γ'εἰς τάχος διὰ σημείων ἢ εἰς κάλλος ⟨καὶ⟩ ἀκρίβειαν, ὥσπερ γε οὐδὲ τῶν ἀναγινωσκόντων ὀρθῶς, "Je vois que tu n'oses pas dépenser pour de nobles actions, ni pour l'achat et la fabrication de livres, ni pour exercer les scribes à écrire soit rapidement au moyen de signes, soit avec élégance et précision, ni encore pour exercer les lecteurs à lire correctement" (traduction française, légèrement modifiée, de Barras et al., *Galien. L'âme et ses passions* 35); voir aussi les commentaires de Dorandi, *Le stylet* 65; Del Corso, Ercolano 160.

4 Piacentini, Scribes.

sentation de Dioscoride qui, semble-t-il, écrit sur une page de codex reposant sur ses genoux, tandis que l'illustrateur (Cratévas ?) peint une planche fixée sur un chevalet[5]. Cependant, comme l'indiquent le décor et les vêtements du peintre, ce tableau n'appartient plus à l'antiquité, mais à la période byzantine. Le contexte culturel est différent. À la suite de l'émergence du christianisme, religion du livre, copier, – surtout les livres saints –, n'est plus considéré comme une activité servile[6]. La situation semble plus complexe dans le monde romain. Si Pline l'Ancien (23/24-79) paraît évoquer d'anciens documents (*longinqua monimenta*) autographes (*manus*) de personnages et d'auteurs célèbres, dans le passage suivant :

> J'ai vu moi-même, au bout de deux cents ans ou presque, chez Pomponius Secundus, poète et citoyen très illustre, des autographes de Tiberius et Caius Gracchus. Quant à ceux de Cicéron, du divin Auguste et de Virgile, nous en voyons souvent[7],

il n'en va pas de même de Quintilien (*c.* 35-100), qui se réfère bel et bien aux écrits littéraires autographes (*manus*) de Cicéron et de Virgile, lorsqu'il précise, à propos d'une particularité orthographique,

> leurs manuscrits attestent que [Cicéron] lui-même et Virgile aussi ont usé de cette graphie[8].

Au début, l'attitude des Latins envers l'écriture et les écrits semble bien différente de celle des Grecs. Comme l'a remarqué le regretté Paolo Radicciotti[9], l'examen de la production graphique latine la plus ancienne montre qu'à Rome, pour longtemps, il n'y a pas eu de séparation nette entre l'écriture des livres et celle des textes liés à la vie quotidienne (documents) :

> Les Romains, encore à l'époque de Caton le Censeur (234-149), acceptent l'idée qu'un livre soit directement écrit par l'auteur et puis conservé dans

5 Mazal, *Wiener Dioskurides* 17-25.

6 Cavallo, Pratiche.

7 Pline, *Histoire naturelle* 13.83 : *Tiberi Gaique Gracchorum manus apud Pomponium Secundum uatem ciuemque clarissimum uidi annos fere post ducentos ; iam uero Ciceronis ac Diui Augusti Vergilique saepenumero uidemus*. Nous sommes responsable de la traduction française.

8 Quintilien, *Institution* 1.7.20 : *quo modo et ipsum et Vergilium quoque scripsisse manus eorum docent*. Toutefois, Dorandi, *Le stylet* 65-6, considère les témoignages de Pline l'Ancien et de Quintilien comme douteux.

9 Radiciotti, Della genuità et Radiciotti, Ercolano.

> les archives de la maison, comme le serait un document holographe. La présence de l'interponction (c'est-à-dire les points qui séparent les mots), soit dans les documents, soit dans les écrits de la vie quotidienne, soit dans les livres latins les plus antiques, serait encore unc conséquence de ce manque de séparation nette entre ce qui est un livre et ce qui ne l'est pas. C'est d'autant plus important qu'à l'origine de ce phénomène, il y a l'absence, dans la tradition graphique latine la plus antique, d'un groupe de scribes professionnels en mesure de produire des livres. C'est seulement avec le processus de lente hellénisation que se distinguent des pratiques de vie intellectuelle plus "modernes", à travers l'acceptation du modèle du livre-*volumen*, la conception de l'acte matériel d'écrire comme activité privée de signification diacritique et donc comme *opus* servile, et, enfin, la naissance des bibliothèques latines[10].

Comment identifier des autographes dans les papyrus littéraires grecs? L'opération est délicate car, en papyrologie littéraire, il est souvent malaisé de distinguer entre un manuscrit autographe et une copie privée, d'une part[11], entre un manuscrit autographe et un exercice scolaire, qu'il soit effectué par l'élève ou préparé par le maître, d'autre part. En revanche, ces types d'écrits diffèrent nettement des copies professionnelles reconnaissables par un certain nombre de caractéristiques dont font partie l'usage de papyrus neuf, plutôt que recyclé ("opisthographe" au sens antique, à savoir réutilisé au verso dans le cas d'un rouleau de papyrus), la présence de marques stichométriques, celle de variantes notées par une seconde main et d'autres signes prouvant la (re)lecture, l'usage intensif de signes de lecture, l'attention soigneuse à l'iota adscrit, l'orthographe évitant l'iotacisme, la coupure syllabique en fin de ligne, la régularité du format, et, éventuellement, la présence d'une étiquette pour un rouleau, ou d'une page de titre pour un codex[12].

Les recherches d'Armando Petrucci[13] et surtout de Tiziano Dorandi[14] ont montré que, pour identifier un autographe, très rarement signalé par le nom de son auteur dans les papyrus, il fallait se fonder sur un faisceau d'indices tirés de l'examen du support et de la forme de la pièce écrite, de sa mise en page, de

10 Radiciotti, Della genuità 371.

11 Fressura, Tipologie (spéc. 106, n. 125); Manetti, Autografi (spéc. 48-9).

12 Parsons, Copyists (spéc. 263).

13 Petrucci, Minuta; alors qu'elle est intitulée "Autografi", la contribution de Petrucci, Autografi ne sera pas utilisée ici, car elle est relative à l'épistolographie.

14 Dorandi, Den Autoren; Dorandi, *Le stylet* 51-75 (chapitre 3: *Sua manu scripsit*) et Dorandi, *Nell'officina* 47-64 (3. Tra autografia e dettato).

FIGURE 2.1 Exemple de copie professionnelle : fin du rouleau de papyrus contenant le chant XXIV de l'*Iliade* d'Homère, avec écriture calligraphique, titre final, esprits, accents et noms des personnages notés dans la marge ("The Bankes Homer", P. Lit. Lond. 28, Brit. Libr. inv. 114, Éléphantine ?, IIe siècle de notre ère)

sa main, de l'état du texte, du genre littéraire auquel il appartient, ainsi que du contexte dans lequel il a été mis par écrit. En procédant de la sorte, à la suite d'une première liste établie par Maryline Parca[15], T. Dorandi a identifié une vingtaine d'autographes, sans compter tous les textes littéraires de la composition et de la main de Dioscore d'Aphrodité, le notaire et poète de Thébaïde du VIe siècle[16], dont on connaît à coup sûr l'écriture par ses archives notariales[17]. En voici la liste[18] :

15 Parca, *Ptocheia* 3-4, n. 7.
16 Mac Coull, *Dioscorus* 2-3 ; Fournet, *Hellénisme*.
17 Del Corso, Le scritture (spéc. 103-8 : textes littéraires et paralittéraires, et 111-3 : autographes des œuvres en vers).
18 Dorandi, *Le stylet* 58-60, écarte de la liste 1) *T. Berol.* inv. 14283 (MP³ 1436), provenance inconnue, I, tablette de cire contenant une élégie qui pourrait être de Posidippe de Pella (IIIa), et qui serait plutôt une copie personnelle ; 2) plusieurs *P. Herc.* où l'on avait cru déceler des corrections et des additions autographes de Philodème de Gadara ; 3) *P. Berol.*

1 *P. Cairo Masp.* 1.67097 (MP^3 348), Aphrodité, 567, écrit → sur le ↓ (→ doc.: comptes), Dioscore d'Aphrodité, brouillon de trois poèmes de circonstance, dont deux adressés au duc Athanasios et un à l'empereur Justin II, avec des modifications marginales ou interlinéaires;

2 *P. Cairo Masp.* 2.67131 (MP^3 348.09), Aphrodité, 565/566-573, écrit → sur le ↓ (→ doc.), Dioscore d'Aphrodité, restes de deux poèmes de circonstance adressés au praeses Biktôr et à Théodoros;

3 *P. Cairo Masp.* 2.67184 (MP^3 384.04), Aphrodité, *c.* 551, écrit → et ↓, palimpseste (*script. sup.*; *script. inf.*: doc.), Dioscore d'Aphrodité, poème de circonstance adressé à Dôrothéos le Silentiaire;

4 *P. Hibeh* 2.182 (MP^3 2084), Hibeh, milieu III^a, → (↓ écriture peu lisible), Vie et dits de Socrate, avec des corrections et additions marginales et interlinéaires par la même main à tendance cursive;

5 *P. Köln* 3.128 (MP^3 1763.4), provenance inconnue, I^a/I, ↓, ainsi qu'un doc. écrit →, mais tête-bêche (autre face → doc.), épigramme avec notes interlinéaires pour amender le texte ou la métrique, écriture à tendance cursive;

6 *PSI* 15.1482 (MP^3 1861.1), provenance inconnue, I, opisthographe, brouillon d'un hymne à Eirènè en hexamètres écrit sur le recto et le verso d'un feuillet de papyrus, d'abord 15 vers sur le recto, puis réécriture des 10 premiers vers au verso, avec une suite et une fin différentes du recto, et des variantes entre les lignes, main experte à tendance cursive;

7 *P. Yale* 2.105 (MP^3 2495), Thèbes, I, rouleau, déclamation contre un général accusé d'avoir abandonné ses hommes, vivants ou morts, après un combat naval (exercice rhétorique ou copie privée?), tendance cursive, présence d'abréviations;

8 *P. Lit. Lond.* 62 (MP^3 1853.1), Fayoum?, I, d'un rouleau composite contenant aussi des documents et, sur l'autre face, des parties de trois plaidoiries légales (*P. Lit. Lond.* 138 = MP^3 2515), épigramme encomiastique en l'honneur d'Auguste à Actium (d'une école de rhétorique?), écriture informelle;

9 *P. Gissen Kuhlmann* 4.4 (MP^3 1853.2 = *P. Giss.* 3), Hermopolis (origine: Apollinopolis), 117, composition en mètres variés et prose rythmée retrouvée

inv. 10559/10558 (MP^3 1851), Hermopolis, IV, coupon de papyrus contenant deux épitaphes pour des professeurs de Beyrouth, qui auraient plutôt été écrites par un copiste professionnel sous la dictée de l'auteur; 4) *P. Cairo Zen.* 59532 (MP^3 1761), Philadelphie, III^a, deux épitaphes anonymes pour Tauron, le chien de chasse de Zénon de Caunos, intendant du diécète (ministre des finances) Apollonios.

dans les archives du stratège Apollonios et destinée à célébrer l'accession au trône de l'empereur Hadrien, main à tendance cursive;

10 *P. Berol.* inv. 11632 (MP^3 2207), provenance inconnue, II, pièce en prose sur le siège de Rhodes, en 304^a, par Démétrius Poliorcète, avec nombreuses corrections interlinéaires, main à tendance cursive;

11 *P. Oxy.* 54.3723 (MP^3 1757.31), Oxyrhynque, II, rouleau de petit format, ↓ (→ doc.), élégie sur le goût des dieux pour les éphèbes, petite écriture informelle à tendance cursive;

12 *P. Berol.* inv. 6870v + 14097v (MP^3 1706.1), provenance inconnue, 2e moitié II, au verso des restes d'un *Pridianum cohortis I Augustae Praetoriae Lusitanorum Equitatae*, en latin, daté du 31.08.156, textes poétiques avec notation musicale, parfois effacée et corrigée, ou tragédie classique ou hellénistique avec notation musicale?, main informelle;

13 *P. Oxy.* 53.3702 (MP^3 2451.01), Oxyrhynque, II/III, ↓ (→ doc.), résumé mythologique en prose: les chefs contre Troie, les Prétendants de Pénélope, les Danaïdes, liste des Argonautes (manuel?), main informelle;

14 *P. Ross. Georg.* 1.11 (MP^3 1861), Fayoum?, III, ↓ (→ doc.), hymne en hexamètres à Dionysos, avec ratures et corrections de la même main informelle à tendance cursive;

15 *P. Oxy.* 37.2816 (MP^3 1873.1), Oxyrhynque, II/III, ↓ (→ brouillon [de lettre?] postérieur à 200), hexamètres d'une invocation aux Muses de Piérie, et d'une cosmogonie, main informelle à tendance cursive;

16 *P. Köln* 6.245 (MP^3 1965.41), Haute-Égypte?, III, → (↓ blanc), restes d'un poème en trimètres iambiques (tragédie?) sur Ulysse mendiant (πτωχός) à Troie, avec des corrections qui relèvent du vocabulaire, de la grammaire et de la métrique, comme dans un brouillon;

17 *P. Oxy.* 7.1015 (MP^3 1847), Oxyrhynque, 2e moitié III, coupon de papyrus, éloge anonyme en hexamètres d'un certain Théon, avec un titre marginal et un titre final, ainsi que des corrections interlinéaires et marginales, des accents et des signes diacritiques, main à tendance cursive;

18 *P. Oxy.* 50.3537 (MP^3 1857.32), Oxyrhynque, IIIex./IVin., → (↓ MP^3 1849.1), éthopée intitulée "Ce qu'aurait dit Hésiode lorsqu'il fut inspiré par les Muses,", avec additions entre les lignes et ratures, main semi-littéraire à tendance cursive;

19 *P. Oxy.* 50.3539 (MP^3 1942.9), Oxyrhynque, III/IV, vers d'un poème mélique (avec notations rythmiques?), main documentaire;

20 *PSI* 1.17 (MP^3 1608), Hermopolis, IV/V, opisthographe, restes de 6 rédactions avec variantes et corrections d'une épitaphe pour un Euprépios inconnu, copiées sur le recto et le verso d'un coupon de papyrus, sans respect de la côlométrie, avec des corrections, main à tendance cursive;

21 *PSI* 14.1399 (MP^3 2518), provenance inconnue, VIex./VIIin., ↓ (→ blanc), brouillon d'un discours en prose en l'honneur d'un certain Appion (peut-être le *praefectus praetorio per Orientem* du VIin.) à l'époque d'Anastasios Ier, avec des ratures, des renvois, des additions interlinéaires de la même main;

22 *P. Wash. Univ.* 2.70 (MP^3 1982.22), provenance inconnue, VI/VII, ↓ (→ *P. Wash. Univ.* 2.104, doc.), coupon de papyrus, hexamètres, phrases en prose et trimètres avec variantes, notes d'un poète;

23 *PSI* 13.1303 (MP^3 420), Oxyrhynque, III, ↓ (→ doc.), pastiche d'une scène des *Phéniciennes* d'Euripide, texte revu ou composition originale d'un poète amateur?, nombreuses fautes d'orthographe;

24 *P. Lit. Lond.* 165 (MP^3 2339), "Anonyme de Londres", Hermopolite, I, rouleau de papyrus (3,36 m × 0,23 m; 39 colonnes) écrit → (↓ deux passages médicaux relatifs au recto écrits par la même main, une recette[19] et la copie plus tardive d'une lettre de Marc Antoine[20] par deux autres mains), doxographie médicale[21]. C'est D. Manetti[22] qui, la première, a évoqué la possibilité d'un autographe en 1985 après avoir soumis le papyrus à un examen très approfondi lors d'un séjour de recherches à la British Library, où il est conservé. Ainsi a-t-elle pu relever notamment les caractéristiques suivantes: si l'écriture, personnelle ou cursive, dénote une main experte et désinvolte, le scripteur a souvent utilisé des abréviations et s'est livré à de très nombreuses corrections et additions, non seulement interlinéaires et marginales, mais aussi au dos du papyrus, ainsi qu'à de fréquents changements de construction grammaticale. Tout cela joint au fait que le texte s'interrompt brusquement, donne l'impression que le scripteur était en plein travail de rédaction au moment où il écrivait, et qu'il avait parfois des remords.

Dans le catalogue informatisé des papyrus littéraires grecs et latins du CEDOPAL[23], 54 papyrus sont répertoriés comme autographes, dont 28 de Dioscore d'Aphrodité, à la main aisément reconnaissable. Les 26 restants comprennent 5 papyrus non répertoriés par T. Dorandi, dont voici la liste:

---

19 Andorlini, La ricetta.

20 Ricciardetto, La lettre.

21 Voir la nouvelle édition de l'Anonyme de Londres, traduit pour la première fois en français, par Ricciardetto, *L'Anonyme*.

22 Manetti, Note; Manetti, Doxograpjhical Deformation; Manetti, Autografi; Manetti, *Anonymous*; Dorandi, Per l'autografia; Del Corso, Ercolano 158-9.

23 http://cipl93.philo.ulg.ac.be/Cedopal/MP3/dbsearch.aspx.

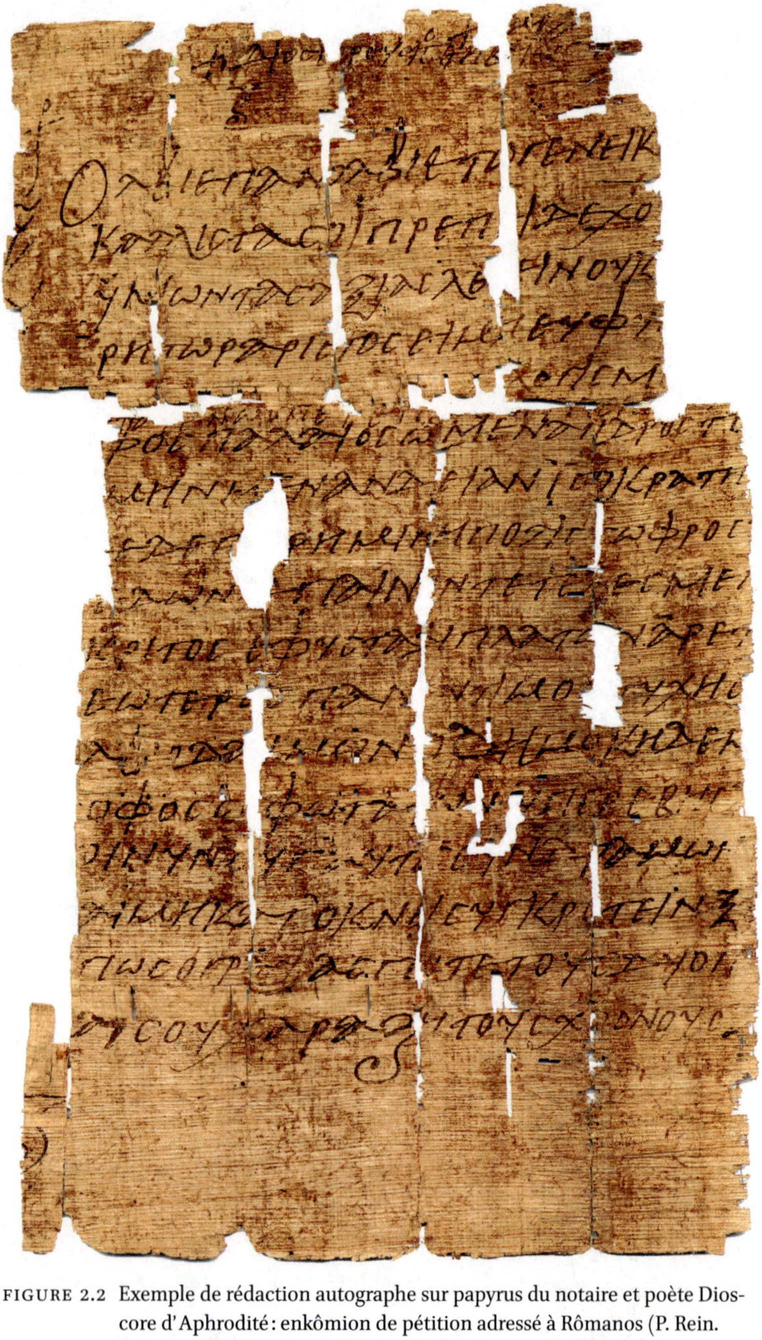

FIGURE 2.2 Exemple de rédaction autographe sur papyrus du notaire et poète Dioscore d'Aphrodité : enkômion de pétition adressé à Rômanos (P. Rein. 2.82, inv. Sorb. 2070, Aphrodité, vers 551)

25 *P. Oslo* inv. 1413 A-B (MP^3 1706), Oxyrhynque?, *c.* 80-120, deux textes tragiques (d'une anthologie?), avec notation musicale, présence de corrections et de ratures, main à tendance cursive;

26 *PSI* inv. 1357v (MP^3 1949.01), provenance inconnue, 2e moitié II/IIIin., ↓ (→ doc. 2e moitié II), notes de commentaire à un texte poétique, avec des abréviations, main informelle à tendance cursive;

27 *P. Strasb.* inv. G 90 + *P. Ryl.* 1.29a + 29b (MP^3 2379), provenance inconnue, II, recto et verso utilisés, recettes utilisées en ophtalmologie et en stomatologie et étiologie de plusieurs affections des yeux;

28 *P. Cair. Masp.* 2.67141 (MP^3 2406), Aphrodité, VIex., prescriptions médicales peut-être de la main de Dioscore, dans une page de comptes;

29 *P. Mich.* 17.758 (MP^3 2407.01), provenance inconnue, IV, codex de papyrus, recettes médicales ajoutées dans la marge inférieure, par le propriétaire du codex.

Si l'on applique à tous ces papyrus considérés comme autographes la grille d'analyse de la fiche Mertens-Pack^3 du CEDOPAL (auteur, œuvre, date, provenance, forme, matériau, mise en page, main) et si on les compare, on observe les caractéristiques suivantes. Le seul auteur sûrement identifié est Dioscore d'Aphrodité. Tous les autres papyrus sont anonymes (*adespota*), ce qui n'est pas étonnant, d'une part en raison de la perte énorme des œuvres littéraires grecques au cours des siècles et, d'autre part, en raison du caractère personnel ou privé de certaines pièces littéraires qui n'étaient sans doute pas destinées à être publiées. Le genre le mieux représenté est la poésie, avec 18 pièces, particulièrement la poésie de circonstance (n° 1, 2, 3, 8, 17, 20), éventuellement accompagnée de notations musicales (n° 12, 19, 25). La prose réunit 11 papyrus, dont 5 relèvent de la rhétorique (n° 4, 7, 9, 18, 21), spécialement de circonstance, elle aussi (n° 9, 21), et 4, de médecine (n° 24 et 27-29). En ce qui concerne la datation, on trouve un seul papyrus d'époque hellénistique (n° 4), 18 d'époque romaine (n° 5 à 17 et 23 à 27) et 10 appartenant à la période byzantine (n° 1, 2, 3, 18, 19, 20, 21, 22, 28 et 29). Si la provenance de 9 papyrus est inconnue, Aphrodité est la localité la mieux représentée, avec tous les papyrus appartenant à l'archive de Dioscore. Les autres lieux de provenance sont Oxyrhynque (7, ou peut-être 8 papyrus), Hermopolis et l'Hermopolite (3 papyrus), peut-être le Fayoum (2 papyrus), Hibeh (1 papyrus), Thèbes (1 papyrus) et peut-être la Haute-Égypte (1 papyrus). Pour la forme et le matériau, tous les textes ont été écrits sur du papyrus, presque toujours de réemploi (↓), et se présentant le plus souvent sous la forme d'un coupon. Cinq exceptions notables sont les rouleaux des n° 7, 8, 11 et de l'Anonyme de Londres (n° 24), encore que la qualité du papyrus utilisé pour ceux-ci soit plutôt médiocre, et le codex pharmaceutique de Michigan (n° 29). Toutes les écritures de ces papyrus sont informelles et leur mise en page est non livresque[24]. Dans la grande majorité des cas, on relève la présence de ratures, de corrections et de variantes trahissant des hésitations et des repentirs de la part des auteurs des textes. L'emploi d'abréviations n'est pas rare. Souvent aussi, l'auteur intervient dans le texte à la première personne, soit du singulier ("je"), soit du pluriel ("nous"). On note également des changements de construction grammaticale dans une même phrase. Enfin, l'écrit présente parfois un caractère inachevé.

On a pu constater que quatre papyrus considérés comme autographes sont médicaux[25]. L'Anonyme de Londres (n° 24) contient l'œuvre d'un intellectuel qui médite sur le texte qu'il est en train d'écrire de sa propre main. Le *P. Strasb.* inv. G 90 + *P. Ryl.* 1.29a + 29b (MP^3 2379 = n° 27) est un manuel médical du IIe siècle, qui contient, notées au recto et au verso (opisthographe), apparemment par la même main, – celle du médecin –, mais à des époques différentes, des recettes variées utilisées en ophtalmologie et en stomatologie, des recommandations pour l'administration de collyres et l'étiologie de plusieurs maladies des yeux[26]. Les deux cas suivants sont un peu différents, car ceux qui ont écrit les textes n'en sont peut-être pas les auteurs, mais seulement les copistes. Dans le premier, ce pourrait être Dioscore, le notaire et poète d'Aphrodité, qui a copié deux recettes contre la migraine au bas d'une page en partie blanche (*P. Cair. Masp.* 2.67141 = MP^3 2406, f° IIr = n° 28)[27] d'un codex documentaire de la fin du VIe siècle. Dans le deuxième, c'est le propriétaire probable du codex pharmaceutique de Michigan (*P. Mich.* 17.758 = MP^3 2407.01 = n° 29), qui a ajouté de sa main des recettes dans la marge inférieure[28]. On peut leur comparer la recette d'*artèriakè*, remède pour la trachée et les bronches (*P. Oxy.* 54.3724, fr. 1r, col. 3, 1-6 = MP^3 2410.11), qui a été notée, – par le propriétaire de l'écrit? –, au-dessus d'une colonne d'un rouleau ou d'un feuillet de papyrus opisthographe contenant une collection d'épigrammes et d'*incipit* d'épigrammes (*P. Oxy.* 54.3724 = MP^3 1596.21, Oxyrhynque, fin du Ier siècle de notre ère). On pourrait imaginer que le remède en question était destiné à éclaircir la voix lors de la récitation des poèmes.

24 Fressura, Tipologie 106, n. 125.
25 Marganne, *Le livre* 90-1.
26 Marganne, *L'ophtalmologie* 133-46.
27 Fournet, Un papyrus 320 et n. 22; Fournet, *Hellénisme* 2.671 et n. 9.
28 Youtie, *P. Michigan XVII*, ainsi que les commentaires de Hanson, Introduction; Andorlini, *I papiri* 20-7.

FIGURE 2.3 Exemple de rédaction autographe du début d'un discours ou d'un manuel médical écrite au verso d'un coupon de papyrus de réemploi, d'abord utilisé au recto pour un registre foncier (P. Oxy. 74.4970, Oxyrhynque, IIe siècle de notre ère)
COURTESY OF THE EGYPT EXPLORATION SOCIETY AND THE UNIVERSITY OF OXFORD IMAGING PAPYRI PROJECT

Un papyrus littéraire grec médical récemment édité[29] et daté paléographiquement du IIe siècle (*P. Oxy.* 74.4970 = MP^3 2354.11) semble présenter plusieurs caractéristiques d'un autographe. Provenant d'Oxyrhynque, il se présente comme un coupon de papyrus mesurant 17 cm de large sur 6,4 cm de haut et contient, au recto (→), un document (registre foncier). Le verso (↓), qui nous intéresse ici, semble intact, sauf à droite. La marge supérieure mesure 1,7 cm, et la marge inférieure, 1,1 cm. Il porte 6 lignes en rapport avec la médecine, dont voici le texte et la traduction :

τῶν νέων τοῖ[ς κ]ατὰ λόγον εἰς τὴν ἰατρικὴ̣ν [ε]ἰ̣σα̣[γ]ομέν[οις]
θεωρήματα, π[ρο]σ̣ῆκόν ἐστιν, ὡς ἔγωγαι διαλαμβάνω̣,
ἐν πρώτοις ἀπὸ̣ τοῦ Ἱπποκρατίου ὅρκου τὴν ἀρχὴν τῆς
μαθήσεως ποιε[ῖ]σ̣θαι, ὥσπερ νόμου δικαιοτάτου κα[ὶ]
σφρόδρα βιωφελο[ῦ]ς̣ καθεστῶτος. Τοῖς γὰρ διὰ τοῦτο μ[υ]-
σταγωγηθεῖσ⟨ι⟩ ἄ[π]τ̣αιστον ἅμα τὸν ἐν τῷ̣ ἰατρεύειν̣[

1 ϊατρικην 2 lire ἔγωγε 3 lire Ἱπποκρατείου 6 ϊατρευειν

29 Le papyrus a été édité par Leith, *The Oxyrhyncus Papyri* 51-5 et pl. I. Une image digitale du papyrus est également disponible sur le site "POxy – Oxyrhynchus Online!" (http://www.papyrology.ox.ac.uk/POxy/).

1 À ceux des jeunes qui débutent en médecine normalement,
2 il convient, comme je l'explique moi-même, en tant que principes,
3 de commencer leur instruction d'abord par le *Serment* hippocratique,
4 comme loi établie la plus juste et
5 puissamment utile à la vie. De fait, pour ceux qui, pour cette raison,
6 sont initiés, ... sans faux pas... en même temps que le (ou la)... dans l'art de guérir ...

Ce texte qui fait état de la nécessité, pour les débutants en médecine, de "commencer leur instruction d'abord par le *Serment* hippocratique comme loi établie la plus juste et puissamment utile à la vie"[30], a été noté, par une main informelle, au verso d'un coupon de papyrus déjà utilisé pour un texte documentaire. Loin d'être livresque, la mise en page vise à tirer parti du maximum d'espace sur le support d'écriture. Les lignes d'écritures sont donc longues. Parmi les imperfections orthographiques et grammaticales, on relève deux diérèses inorganiques sur l'iota (l. 1: ϊατρικην; l. 6: ϊατρευειν), un cas d'étacisme (l. 2: ἔγωγαι au lieu d'ἔγωγε), un cas d'iotacisme (l. 3: Ἱπποκρατίου au lieu d'Ἱπποκρατείου), la correction de ce qui est probablement une "coquille" (l. 5: au départ, la dernière lettre de Τοῖς était un gamma, qui, ensuite, a été transformé en sigma lunaire), une lettre manquante (l. 6: l'iota final dans σταγωγηθεῖσ⟨ι⟩) et une incohérence dans la construction grammaticale de la première phrase. L'auteur intervient dans le texte (l. 2: ὡς ἔγωγαι διαλαμβάνω̣), qui s'interrompt abruptement à la fin de la ligne 6. La dernière phrase est incomplète. Toutes ces caractéristiques suggèrent que le texte est un autographe et qu'il correspond probablement au brouillon d'une introduction à un manuel[31]

30 Sur la réception du *Serment* hippocratique, particulièrement dans la documentation papyrologique, voir la synthèse de Leith, Hippocratic oath (avec bibliographie).

31 Comparer Hipp., *Du médecin* 2, dans l'édition, avec traduction française, de Littré, *Oeuvres complètes d'Hippocrate* 206-7: τὰ δὲ ἐς τὴν ἰατρικὴν τέχνην παραγγέλματα, δι'ὧν ἔστιν εἶναι τεχνικόν, ἀπ'ἀρχῆς συνοπτέον, ἀφ'ὧν καὶ μανθάνειν ὤνθρωπος ἄρξαιτο, "Relativement aux préceptes touchant l'art médical, à l'aide desquels on peut devenir artiste, il faut d'abord considérer ceux par lesquels on commencera son instruction". Selon Jouanna, *Hippocrate* 550, ce traité est entré tardivement dans la *Collection hippocratique*, à l'époque hellénistique ou romaine, mais sa déontologie correspond à celle des écrits hippocratiques plus anciens. Comparer aussi *PSI* 12.1275 verso (MP^3 2345.1), Oxyrhynque, II, ↓ (→ *PSI* 12.1275 recto = MP^3 1011, Homère, *Iliade* 23.887-97, avec titre et n° du chant + collema médical en rapport avec le verso), qui conserve également une sorte de brouillon ou de copie personnelle d'une introduction à un manuel conseillant plutôt de commencer l'étude de la médecine par l'apprentissage de la nomenclature anatomique: (lignes 1-7) τῶν νέων τοῖς κατὰ λόγοις εἰς | τὸ ἰατρεύειν προσάγουσιν, ὦ Δημό|σθενες, πρώτ[ο]υ̣ καὶ ἀναγκαιοτάτο[υ] | πρὸς

ou à celui du début d'un discours. On connaît en effet l'importance de la rhétorique dans la pratique médicale dès l'époque classique[32], et son emprise grandissante, dans tous les domaines, à l'époque romaine[33].

Bibliographie

Sources primaires

Pline, *Histoire naturelle*, éd., trad. et comment. A. Ernout, Paris 1956.

Quintilien, *Institution oratoire*. Tome I. Livre I. Texte établi et traduit par Jean Cousin, Paris 1975.

Sources secondaires

Andorlini, I., I papiri e la tradizione medievale nella recettazione dei testi medici tardoantichi, dans A. Garzya (éd.), *Tradizione e ecdotica dei testi medici tardoantichi e bizantini. Atti del Convegno internazionale, Anacapri, 29-31 ottobre 1990* (Collectanea 5), Napoli 1992, 13-27.

Andorlini, I., La ricetta medica dell'Anonimo Londinese (P. Brit. Libr. inv. 137v = Suppl. Arist. III 1, p. 76 Diels), dans *Galenos* 4 (2010), 39-45.

Barras, V. et al., *Galien. L'âme et ses passions. Les passions et les erreurs de l'âme. Les facultés de l'âme suivent les tempéraments du corps. Introduction, traduction et notes*, Paris 1995.

Boudon-Millot, V., *Galien. Tome I. Introduction générale. Sur l'ordre de ses propres livres. Sur ses propres livres. Que l'excellent médecin est aussi philosophe*, Paris 2007.

Boudon-Millot, V., *Galien de Pergame. Un médecin grec à Rome*, Paris 2012.

Bowman, A.K. et al., *Oxyrhynchus. A city and its texts*, London 2007.

Cavallo, G., Pratiche di scrittura come rappresentazione. Qualche traccia, dans C. Leonardi, M. Morelli et F. Santi (éd.), *Modi di scrivere. Tecnologie e pratiche della scrittura dal manoscritto al CD-ROM. Atti del Convegno di studio della Fondazione Ezio Franceschini e della Fondazione IBM Italia. Certosa del Galluzzo, 11-12 ottobre 1996*, Spoleto 1997, 5-15.

Coste, J., D. Jacquart, et J. Pigeaud, *La rhétorique médicale à travers les siècles. Actes du colloque international de Paris, 9 et 10 octobre 2008*, Genève 2012.

[εἰ]σαγωγὴν ὑπάρχοντος τοῦ δι|ακατασχεῖν τῶν ἐπὶ τοῖς ἐντός τε | καὶ ἐκτὸς τόποις τοῦ σώματος κε[ι]|μένων ὀνομάτων (...), "Pour ceux des jeunes qui abordent la médecine dans l'ordre logique, Démosthène, la première et la plus importante des choses pour l'introduction étant de retenir les noms attribués aux régions internes et externes du corps (...)".

32 Jouanna, *Hippocrate*.

33 Petit, *Galien* (avec bibliographie antérieure).

de Boer, W., *Galeni De propriorum animi cuiuslibet affectuum dignotione et curatione. De animi cuiuslibet peccatorum dignotione et curatione. De atra bile*, Leipzig-Berlin 1937.

Del Corso, L., Ercolano e l'Egitto: pratiche librarie a confronto, dans *Cronache Ercolanesi* 43 (2013), 139-60.

Del Corso, L., Le scritture di Dioscoro, dans J.-L. Fournet et C. Magdelaine (éd.), *Les archives de Dioscore d'Aphrodité cent ans après leur découverte. Histoire et culture dans l'Égypte byzantine. Actes du colloque de Strasbourg (8-10 décembre 2005)*, Paris 2008, 89-115.

Dorandi, T., Den Autoren über die Schulter geschaut: Arbeitsweise und Autographie bei den antiken Schriftstellern, dans *Zeitschrift für Papyrologie und Epigraphik* 87 (1991), 11-33.

Dorandi, T., *Le stylet et la tablette. Dans le secret des auteurs antiques*, Paris 2000.

Dorandi, T., *Nell'officina dei classici. Come lavoravano gli autori antichi*, Roma 2007 (édition italienne, revue et corrigée, de Dorandi, *Le stylet*).

Dorandi, T., Per l'autografia di PLitLond 165, dans *Zeitschrift für Papyrologie und Epigraphik* 91 (1992), 50-1.

Fournet, J.-L., *Hellénisme dans l'Égypte du VIe siècle. La bibliothèque et l'œuvre de Dioscore d'Aphrodité*, Le Caire 1999.

Fournet, J.-L., Un papyrus médical byzantin de l'Académie des Inscriptions et Belles-Lettres, dans *Travaux et Mémoires. Centre de Recherches d'histoire et de civilisation byzantines* 12 (1994), 309-22.

Fournet, J.-L. et C. Magdelaine (éd.), *Les archives de Dioscore d'Aphrodité cent ans après leur découverte. Histoire et culture dans l'Égypte byzantine. Actes du colloque de Strasbourg (8-10 décembre 2005)*, Paris 2008.

Fressura, M., Tipologie del glossario virgiliano, dans M.-H. Marganne and B. Rochette (éd.), *Bilinguisme et digraphisme dans le monde gréco-romain: l'apport des papyrus latins. Actes de la Table Ronde internationale (Liège, 12-13 mai 2011)*, Liège 2013, 71-116.

Froschauer H. et C. Römer (éd.), *Zwischen Magie und Wissenschaft. Ärzte und Heilkunst in den Papyri aus Ägypten*, Wien 2007.

Garzya A. (éd.), *Tradizione e ecdotica dei testi medici tardoantichi e bizantini. Atti del Convegno internazionale, Anacapri, 29-31 ottobre 1990*, Napoli 1992.

Hanson, A.E., Introduction, dans L.C. Youtie, *P. Michigan XVII. The Michigan medical codex (P. Mich. 758 = P. Mich. inv. 21)*, Atlanta 1996, XV-XXV.

Jouanna, J., *Hippocrate*, Paris 1992.

Jouanna, J., Rhétorique et médecine dans la Collection hippocratique. Contribution à l'histoire de la rhétorique au Ve siècle, dans *Revue des Études Grecques* 97 (1984), 26-44.

Leith, D., The Hippocratic oath in Antiquity and on papyrus, dans H. Froschauer et C. Römer (éd.), *Zwischen Magie und Wissenschaft. Ärzte und Heilkunst in den Papyri aus Ägypten*, Wien 2007, 35-42.

Leith, D. et al., *The Oxyrhynchus papyri. Volume LXXIV (Nos 4968-5019)*, London 2009.

Leonardi, C., M. Morelli et F. Santi (éd.), *Modi di scrivere. Tecnologie e pratiche della scrittura dal manoscritto al CD-ROM. Atti del Convegno di studio della Fondazione Ezio Franceschini e della Fondazione IBM Italia. Certosa del Galluzzo, 11-12 ottobre 1996*, Spoleto 1997.

Littré, E., *Œuvres complètes d'Hippocrate* 9, Paris 1861.

Mac Coull, L.S.B., *Dioscorus of Aphrodito. His works and his world*, Berkeley-Los Angeles-London 1988.

Manetti, D., *Anonymus Londiniensis De medicina*, Berlin-New York 2011.

Manetti, D., Autografi e incompiuti: il caso dell'Anonimo Londinese P. Lit. Lond. 165, dans *Zeitschrift für Papyrologie und Epigraphik* 100 (1994), 47-58.

Manetti, D., Doxographical deformation of medical tradition in the report of the Anonymous Londinensis on Philolaus, dans *Zeitschrift für Papyrologie und Epigraphik* 83 (1990), 219-33.

Manetti, D., Note di lettura dell'Anonimo Londinese. Prolegomena ad una nuova edizione, dans *Zeitschrift für Papyrologie und Epigraphik* 63 (1986), 57-74.

Marganne, M.-H., *Le livre médical dans le monde gréco-romain*, Liège 2004.

Marganne, M.-H., *L'ophtalmologie dans l'Égypte gréco-romaine d'après les papyrus littéraires grecs*, Leiden-New York-Köln 1994.

Marganne, M.-H. et B. Rochette (éd.), *Bilinguisme et digraphisme dans le monde gréco-romain: l'apport des papyrus latins. Actes de la Table Ronde internationale (Liège, 12-13 mai 2011)*, Liège 2013.

Mazal, O., *Der Wiener Dioskurides. Codex medicus graecus 1 der Österreichischen Nationalbibliothek*, Graz 1998.

Menu, B. (ed.), *L'organisation du travail en Égypte ancienne et en Mésopotamie. Colloque Aidea (Nice, 4-5 octobre 2004)*, Le Caire 2010.

Pack, R.A., *The Greek and Latin literary texts from Greco-Roman Egypt. Second revised and enlarged edition*, Ann Arbor 1965.

Parca, M.G., *Ptocheia or Odysseus in disguise at Troy (P. Köln VI 245)*, Atlanta (Georgia) 1991.

Parsons, P.J., Copyists of Oxyrhynchus, dans A.K. Bowman et al., *Oxyrhynchus. A city and its texts*, London 2007, 262-70.

Petit, C., Galien et le discours de la méthode. Rhétorique(s) médicale(s) à l'époque romaine (Ier-IIe siècles de notre ère), dans J. Coste, D. Jacquart, et J. Pigeaud (éd.), *La rhétorique médicale à travers les siècles. Actes du colloque international de Paris, 9 et 10 octobre 2008*, Genève 2012, 49-75.

Petrucci, A., Minuta, autografo, libro d'autore, dans C. Questa Cesare et R. Raffaelli (éd.), *Atti del convegno internazionale Il libro e il testo, Urbino, 20-23 settembre 1982*, Urbino 1984, 397-414.

Petrucci, A., Autografi, dans *Quaderni di Storia* 63 (2006), 111-25.

Piacentini, P., Les scribes: trois mille ans de logistique et de gestion des ressources humaines dans l'Égypte ancienne, in B. Menu (éd.), *L'organisation du travail en Égypte ancienne et en Mésopotamie. Colloque Aidea (Nice, 4-5 octobre 2004)*, Le Caire 2010, 107-13.

Questa, C. et R. Raffaelli (éd.), *Atti del convegno internazionale Il libro e il testo, Urbino, 20-23 settembre 1982*, Urbino 1984.

Radiciotti, P., Della genuità e delle opere tràdite da alcuni antichi papiri latini, dans *Scrittura e Civiltà* 24 (2000), 259-373.

Radiciotti, P., Ercolano: papiri latini in una biblioteca greca, dans *Studi di Egittologia e di Papirologia* 6 (2009), 103-14.

Ricciardetto, A., La lettre de Marc Antoine (SB I 4224) écrite au verso de l'Anonyme de Londres (P. Brit. Libr. inv. 137 = MP3 2339), dans *Archiv für Papyrusforschung und verwandte Gebiete* 58 (2012), 43-60.

Ricciardetto, A., *L'Anonyme de Londres (P.Lit.Lond. 165, Brit.Libr. inv. 137). Édition et traduction française d'un papyrus médical grec du Ier siècle*, Liège 2014.

Youtie, L.C., *P. Michigan XVII. The Michigan medical codex (P. Mich. 758 = P. Mich. inv. 21)*, Atlanta (Georgia) 1996.

CHAPTER 3

Arabic Holographs: Characteristics and Terminology

Adam Gacek

1 Holograph versus Autograph

According to the *Oxford English Dictionary* (OED), the word "holograph" comes to us from the Late Latin *holographus*, "entirely written by the signer," but originally from the Greek *holographos*. The same source states that the word "autograph" also comes from Late Latin *autographum*, neuter of *autographus*, and again originally from the Greek (*autographos*), meaning "written with one's own hand."

An autograph, defined by *Encyclopaedia Britannica*, is

> any manuscript handwritten by its author, either in alphabetical or musical notation. (The term also refers to a person's handwritten signature.) Aside from its antiquarian or associative value, an autograph may be an early or corrected draft of a manuscript and may provide valuable evidence of the stages of composition or of the "correct" final version of a work.

Webster's New International Dictionary, on the other hand, gives these definitions: a holograph is "a document, as a letter, deed, or will, wholly in the hand of the person from whom it proceeds and whose act it purports to be," while an autograph means "in the author's own handwriting; as, an autograph letter; an autograph will."

It is clear from the above definitions that an autograph can be understood to mean a person's own signature as well as a manuscript (of any kind) in the author's own handwriting. Perhaps it was because of this dual meaning that paragraph 4.7 of the *Anglo-American Cataloguing Rules* (AACR2) recommends instead the use of the word holograph or holographs to denote "manuscripts handwritten by the person(s) responsible for the work(s) contained therein."

In my *Vademecum*, having stated that both words are used interchangeably, I tended to use the word "holograph" for a work written entirely by its author,

 | DOI:10.1163/9789004413177_004

and reserved the usage of "autograph" for an author's signature or a short piece of writing, such as a certificate, ownership statement, or study/reading note, executed in his own hand.[1] We have opted to maintain these distinctions in this volume.

The holograph, therefore, is the author's own intellectual output in the form of either a draft or fair copy. An Arabic holograph can be an original composition (*matn*) in prose or verse, an abridgment of the original (*mukhtaṣar*, *mūjaz*), or a versification (*naẓm*, *manẓūma*) of, or even a systematic commentary (*sharḥ*) or a gloss (*ḥāshiya*) on another scholar's work. Holographs can be signed by the author himself or remain unsigned (anonymous), just as they can be dated or undated. The author's signature (autograph) is usually found in his colophon but can also feature in his reading statements or transmission certificate (*ijāza*).

2 Drafts

Unlike fair copies, drafts are relatively easy to identify. They tend to have a number of distinct features, such as certain types of book structures (loose leaves, notebooks, irregular quires, etc.); a personal, even idiosyncratic hand, often lacking full pointing; an irregularly shaped main text with heavily annotated margins; a messy appearance; numerous cancellations/deletions; frequent additions (interlinear, marginal, and on inserts), and allocated blank spaces for material to be supplied later.[2]

We find this description in the colophon to a copy of Ibn al-Jawzī's *al-Birr wa-l-ṣila* (Chester Beatty Library, MS Arabic 3945), penned by the prominent Ḥanbalī scholar Jamāl al-Dīn Yūsuf al-Surramarī (d. 776/1374) (see fig. 3.1): "The draft in the hand of the author (*musawwada bi-khaṭṭ al-mu'allif*) was full of errors (*saqam*) [and had] numerous cancellations (*ḍurūb*), glosses (*ḥawāshin*), and additions (*ilḥāqāt*) between lines and on the front and back of the quires (*bayna al-suṭūr wa-wujūh al-ajzā' wa-ẓuhūrihā*)."[3]

A good example of a draft may be found in a manuscript preserved in Princeton (MS Garrett 3520Y), namely a didactic poem, *Naẓm al-durar al-saniyya fī l-siyar al-zakiyya* by Zayn al-Dīn ʿAbd al-Raḥīm al-ʿIrāqī (d. 806/1404). This

1 Gacek, *Vademecum* 14–5.

2 For more on the way drafts were prepared and the working method of Muslim scholars, see Witkam, Les Autographes; Bauden, Maqriziana I; Bauden, Maqriziana II; Gardiner and Bauden, Recently discovered.

3 Ibn al-Jawzī died in 597/1200. The colophon carries the date 20 Shawwāl 735/1335.

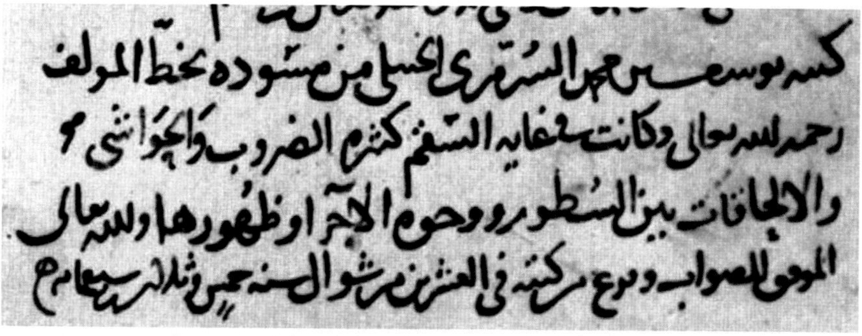

FIGURE 3.1 MS Arabic 3945, fol. 137[b]
DUBLIN, CHESTER BEATTY LIBRARY

draft was corrected in the presence of students, who read and audited it in a number of sessions, in Medina in the Mosque of the Prophet (near his tomb) in ca. 791/1387 (see fig. 3.2). It displays most of the features of a draft as mentioned above. Another excellent example is the draft of *Taṣḥīḥ al-taṣḥīf wa-taḥrīr al-taḥrīf* by Ṣalāḥ al-Dīn al-Ṣafadī (d. 764/1363) (see below, p. 69).

Unlike regular compositions, glosses or comments were usually inscribed in the margins or between the lines (or both) of the author's original text or in a copy of a work by another author. They were gathered, if copious, into an independent composition, thus creating a fair copy of the original draft, be it a systematic commentary (*sharḥ*) or a gloss (*ḥāshiya*). Occasional glosses incorporated in the margins of copies made from the holograph are known as authorial glosses (*minhiyāt*, from the word *minhu*, "from him"),[4] and the process of copying these glosses into new codices is known in Arabic as *tajrīd* (from *jarrada*—"to peel, strip, divest, isolate," etc.)—hence the noun *mujarrid*, for a person engaged in this process.[5]

There is a very interesting manuscript in the Chester Beatty Library (MS Arabic 3456) which illustrates this process of glossing a text. It contains a colophon (see fig. 3.3), dated Damascus 679/1281, as a form of authorial approbation, copied in the hand of the commentator Jamāl al-Dīn Abū Bakr Muḥammad al-Sharīshī l-Mālikī l-Naḥwī (d. 685/1286). The work in question is a commentary on *al-Durra al-alfiyya* (a metrical Arabic grammar) composed by Abū Zakariyyā' Yaḥyā l-Zawāwī (d. 628/1231). Al-Sharīshī completed it at the instance of the copyist of the manuscript Badr al-Dīn Abū ʿAbdallāh Muḥam-

4 Gacek, *Glossary. Supplement* 74.
5 See Gacek, *Glossary* 22. For instance, Walī l-Dīn Jār Allāh al-Rūmī (Carullah) (d. 1151/1738), an Ottoman scholar and collector of manuscripts, was a well-known *mujarrid*.

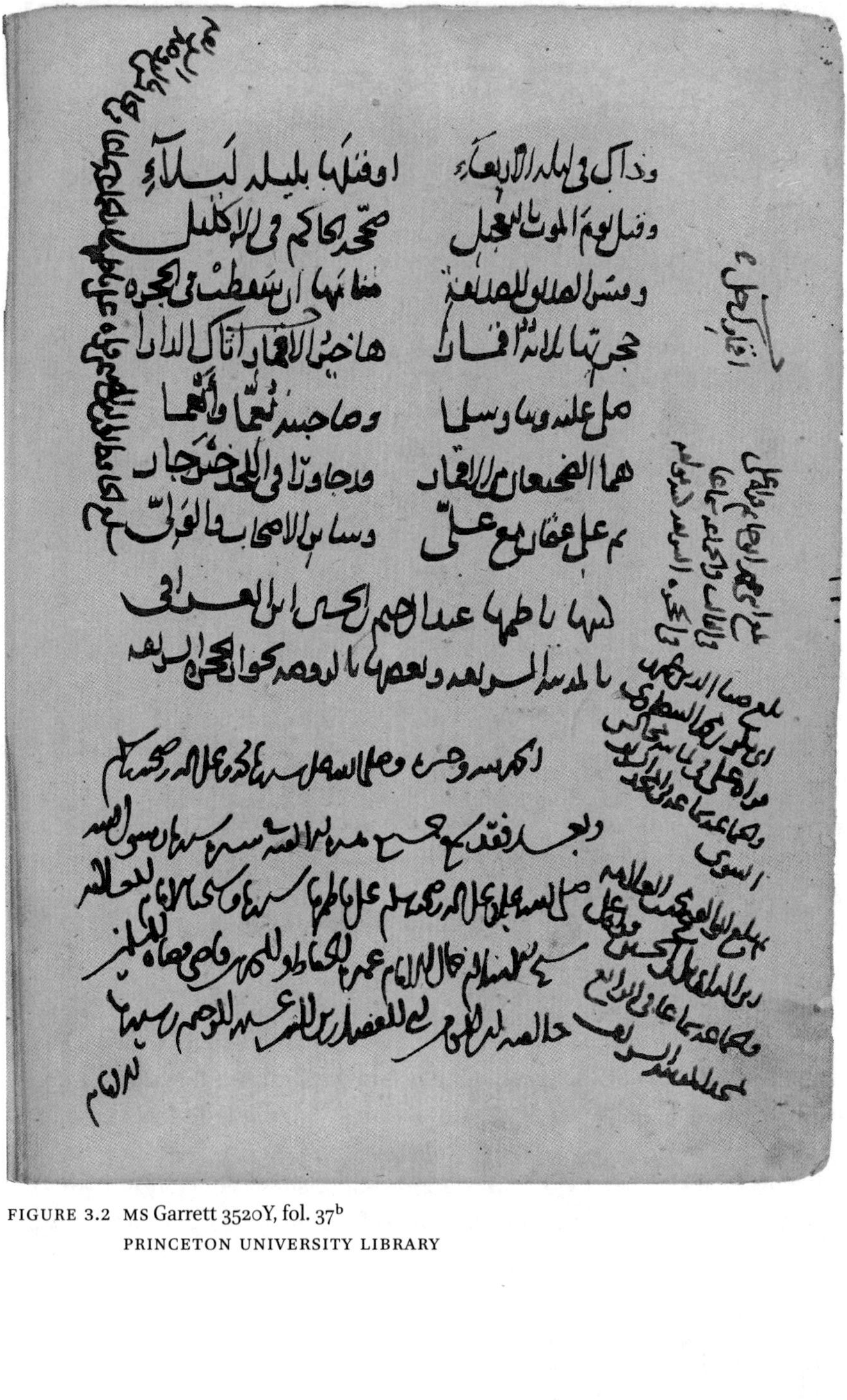

FIGURE 3.2 MS Garrett 3520Y, fol. 37b
PRINCETON UNIVERSITY LIBRARY

FIGURE 3.3 MS Arabic 3456, fol. 225b
DUBLIN, CHESTER BEATTY LIBRARY

mad al-Ḥalabī l-Tādifī, a well-known calligrapher who died in 705/1305. The commentator begins his statement by saying,

> This is the end of the commentary (*sharḥ*) which I entitled *al-Taʿlīqāt al-wāfiya bi-sharḥ al-Durra al-alfiyya* since it consists of various notes (*taʿlīqāt*) I jotted down (*ʿallaqtuhā*) during the recitation of the *Durra* in my presence. I forgot about them but when Badr al-Dīn Muḥammad b. Ayyūb al-Ḥalabī, known as al-Tādifī, became acquainted with them (*waqafa ʿalayhā*), he urged me to collect them and arrange them by chapters for those who will read and profit from them, and I responded to his suggestion and made it an urgent task …

The note ends with: *qāla hadhā wa-katabahu bi-khaṭṭihi muʾallif hadhā l-sharḥ al-faqīr ilā llāh taʿālā Muḥammad b. Aḥmad b. Muḥammad al-Bakrī l-Sharīsī ghafara llāh lahu.*

Another manuscript worth mentioning here is a copy of *Ḥall mushkilāt al-Ishārāt*, a commentary composed by Naṣīr al-Dīn al-Ṭūsī (d. 672/1274) on the *Ishārāt* of Ibn Sīnā (d. 428/1037) but copied by the famous scholar Quṭb al-Dīn al-Rāzī l-Taḥtānī (d. 766/1364), the author of *Muḥākamāt bayna sharḥay al-Ishārāt* (MS Carullah 1310M). There are two statements in this manuscript that attest to the fact that it is indeed a copy in the hand of Quṭb Dīn al-Rāzī. The manuscript has numerous glosses, some signed with abbreviations (such as ش = Sharaf al-Dīn al-Khurāsānī and ق = Quṭb al-Dīn al-Shīrāzī) and others unsigned, all in the same hand as the main body of the text. Everything (style of writing, numerous quotations from other relevant works, etc.) points to the fact that this indeed could be a private copy of Quṭb al-Dīn al-Rāzī with his extensive unsigned glosses in the margins.

3 Fair Copies

In contrast to drafts, fair copies may be difficult to authenticate as they often have far fewer corrections and additions, if any, while their appearance is much more polished and the style of writing has been made more legible or even formal. Those without additions and corrections may be clean copies made by authors for their patrons and unless there is at least another authenticated specimen of that author's hand, it may be impossible to ascertain if that work was really executed by him.[6]

Here I discuss two examples of clean or almost clean fair copies made for patrons. The first is *Qalāʾid al-ʿiqyān* (in praise of the Ottomans) by al-Karmī (d. 1033/1623) (Dublin, Chester Beatty Library, MS Arabic 4731; see fig. 3.4) for a patron named Sulaymān Āghā, and the second, a supergloss on Sirāj al-Dīn al-Urmawī's *Maṭāliʿ al-anwār*, was penned by its author Muḥammad b. Pīr Aḥmad al-Shahīr bi-Arghūn al-Shīrāzī for the library of the Ottoman Sultan Selim II; it was executed in Bursa in 918/1512, the year of his accession to the throne (Baltimore, Walters Art Museum, MS 591; see fig. 3.5). Both manuscripts are written in elegant hands but, except for the fact that the styles of writing and the material supports correspond roughly to the periods and regions where the authors produced them or where they originated, there is very little else that can be said, since no authenticated samples of their writing have yet come to light.

Another interesting example here may be a fair copy of *Sharḥ al-Mulakhkhaṣ fī l-hayʾa* by Qāḍī-zādah al-Rūmī (d. after 830/1487) (Süleymaniye, MS Ayasofya 2662).[7] The codex was executed by the author himself six years after the date of composition—this being 814/1411, whereas the date of copying (*naskh*!) is the end of Jumādā II 820/1417, or approximately six years later.[8] The beginning of the colophon reads (see fig. 3.6): *faragha min naskhihi muʾallifuhu l-faqīr ilā llāh al-Ghanī Mūsā b. Muḥammad b. Maḥmūd al-maʿrūf bi-Qāḍī-zādah al-Rūmī* ...

5 Arabic Terminology

In Arabic the generic terms for holographs are *aṣl* and *umm*, although these two words can also mean "exemplar" or "archetype."[9] Then there are more specific terms that relate to drafts and fair copies. For drafts, the terms *sawād*

6 Another connected issue here are simple ownership statements, whether just names or short ex libris (*min kutub*), which may have been penned by a librarian on behalf of a given author. This may be the case of the signature of Naṣīr al-Dīn al-Ṭūsī on a copy of *Kitāb al-Bayān* by al-Ḥaṣṣār (Univ. of Pennsylvania, LJS 293) executed in elegant Iranian *taʿlīq* script.

7 This is a commentary on the *Mulakhkhas fī l-hayʾa* by Maḥmūd b. ʿUmar al-Jaghmīnī (d. after 618/1221).

8 Interestingly, the commentator gives first the date of copying (i.e., fair copy) as 820 and then on the left in a chronostichon we read وارخوا به (*wāw alif rāʾ khāʾ wāw alif bāʾ hāʾ* = 821!).

9 Gacek, *Glossary* 7, 8.

كتاب قلائد العقيان
في فضائل سلاطين بني عثمان
رقمه بخط مصنفه الفقير ورسمه بنفسه مولفه الحقير
برسم سيدنا اعز خواص الحضرة السلطانيه
واجل جلسا الصفوة الخاقانيه معتمد السلاطين
الكرام وموتمن الخواقين العظام الفخام
مولانا سليمان اغا
لا زال صاحب اسرار الملوك ساحب اذيال القبول
في مراتب السلوك مقبول سلطان الزمان
مامون اسكندر العصر والاوان امين امين

FIGURE 3.4 MS Arabic 4731, fol. 2[a]
DUBLIN, CHESTER BEATTY LIBRARY

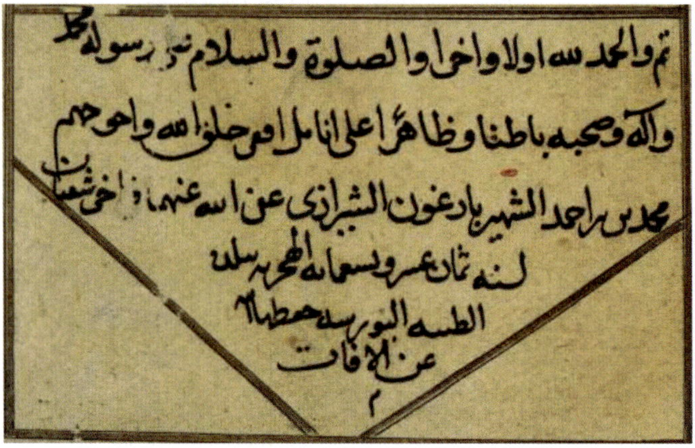

FIGURE 3.5 MS W 591, fol. 78a
BALTIMORE, WALTERS ART MUSEUM

(*taswīd*, *musawwada*) and *dustūr*; for fair copies, the terms *bayāḍ* (*tabyīḍ*, *mubayyaḍa*) are used.[10]

Furthermore, in authorial colophons we encounter, as part of the author's signature, a variety of verbs and verbal nouns expressing a mode of writing. These verbs and verbal nouns may or may not be helpful in the establishment of an authentic holograph since they are also used in various periods and regions for the simple process of copying. They are *kataba*, *ʿallaqa*, *zabara*, *nasakha*, *qayyada*, *dawwana*, *ḥabbara*, *ḥarrara*, *nammaqa*, *naqala*, *raqama*, etc.[11] For instance, the above-mentioned Qāḍī-zādah al-Rūmī uses *nasakha* for a fair copy, Zayn al-Dīn al-ʿIrāqī uses *kataba* for a draft, but the same verb *kataba* is used by Jamāl al-Dīn Yūsuf al-Surramarī to denote the copying of Ibn al-Jawzī's *al-Birr wa-l-ṣila*.

Two of these terms, however, originally had a more clearly defined usage, namely, *taʿlīq* (from the verb *ʿallaqa*), for a draft and *taḥrīr* (from the verb *ḥarrara*), for a fair copy. In its original meaning *ʿallaqa* is a synonym of *kataba*, i.e., "to write." However, it came to be associated, especially in the middle period, with informal writing characterized by the unconventional joining of letters and assimilations/contractions. Indeed, in many texts, *ʿallaqtuhu* means "I jotted down/wrote a quick note." Hence, *taʿlīqāt* are notes, glosses, or annotations.[12] The words *ḥarrara* and *taḥrīr*, on the other hand, tend to be associated

10 Ibid. 16, 46, 73.
11 Gacek, *Glossary*, see under relevant roots.
12 See above the case of al-Sharīshī and his note. See also ibid. 101–2 and Gacek, *Glossary. Supplement* 55.

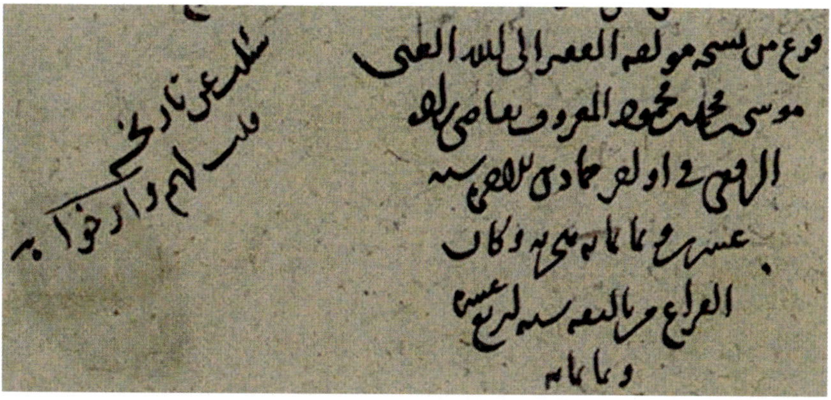

FIGURE 3.6 MS Ayasofya 2662, fol. 69[a]
ISTANBUL, SÜLEYMANIYE KÜTÜPHANESI

with careful, even elegant writing. In the early Islamic period *muḥarrir* was a penman/calligrapher, often working in the state chancery.[13]

Even such expressions as *ʿalā yad al-muʾallif* ("in the hand of the author"), *katabahu muʾallifuhu bi-khaṭṭih* ("the author wrote it in his own hand"), etc., may not be of much help in terms of establishing the authenticity of a holograph, as these could easily have been copied by a scribe who neglected to record his own name.

5 Fraudulent and Authentic Attestations

Moreover, the difficulty of properly identifying a holograph may be compounded by statements in manuscripts which claim that a given hand belongs to such and such a person. Such claims have to be carefully evaluated. Some of these assertions, made by scribes and former owners, are certainly questionable. What one sees is not necessarily what one gets. There is a tendency to take such statements in manuscripts at their face value. This, however, is contrary to the principle of detection that should be one of the main characteristics of the codicologist and paleographer. Some of these statements are undoubtedly true, but some may be categorized at best as wishful thinking or at worst outright forgery.[14] Here are a few examples.

13 Gacek, *Glossary* 30 and idem, *Glossary. Supplement* 15.
14 On forgeries in manuscripts, see idem, *Vademecum* 108–10.

FIGURE 3.7 MS Damad Ibrahim Paşa 822, fol. 354b
ISTANBUL, SÜLEYMANIYE KÜTÜPHANESI

The McGill Mamlūk Qur'ān (RBD A22) has an inscription in a clumsy hand stating that this is the handwriting of Ibn Muqla (d. 328/940) expressed as *ḥarraru huwa Ibn Muqla al-Wazīr al-Aʿẓam*! There is no doubt, however, that this manuscript was copied in an elegant *naskh* script, probably in Egypt in the eighth/fourteenth century.

MS Damad Ibrahim Paşa 822, a copy of Ibn Sīnā's *al-Shifā'*, has a collation note supposedly in the hand of the author himself, dated 412/1021–2 (see fig. 3.7); however, Ibn Sīnā composed this work in 420/1029 and died in 428/1037. Moreover, the style of writing does not fit the period in which the author lived, rather it is probably attributable to the seventh/thirteenth century.

There are three attestations in the National Library of Iran MS 1153, a copy of *Ḥall mushkilāt al-Ishārāt* by Naṣīr al-Dīn al-Ṭūsī (d. 672/1274), claiming that this manuscript is in the hand of the commentator, that is, Naṣīr al-Dīn himself. These statements (see fig. 3.8) belong to Ẓahīr al-Dīn al-Dabbūsī (dated Ṣafar 776/1374), Ḥaydar Āmulī (fl. eighth/fourteenth century) and a certain Muḥammad b. Raḍī l-Dīn Riḍawī. This manuscript, with an introduction by Sayyid Muḥammad ʿImādī Ḥā'irī, was published in Tehran in 2011 with the sub-title "A facsimile edition of the author's copy."[15]

On close examination, however, one comes to the conclusion that these statements cannot be true. The extant copy consists of three parts by three different hands, including a very late last leaf (without a colophon). The earliest part, although copied probably in the late seventh/thirteenth or early eighth/fourteenth century, has corrections and glosses in the same hand as the body of the text. These corrections include textual variants (خ = *nuskha*) and conjectures (ظ = *ẓāhir*), while some of the glosses are superscript by the abbreviation ق, understood to indicate Naṣīr al-Dīn's favorite pupil Quṭb al-Dīn al-Shīrāzī (d. 710/1311).

15 An unsigned portion of this work may have survived in the University of Tehran (Dānishgāh-i Tihrān), MS 1912.

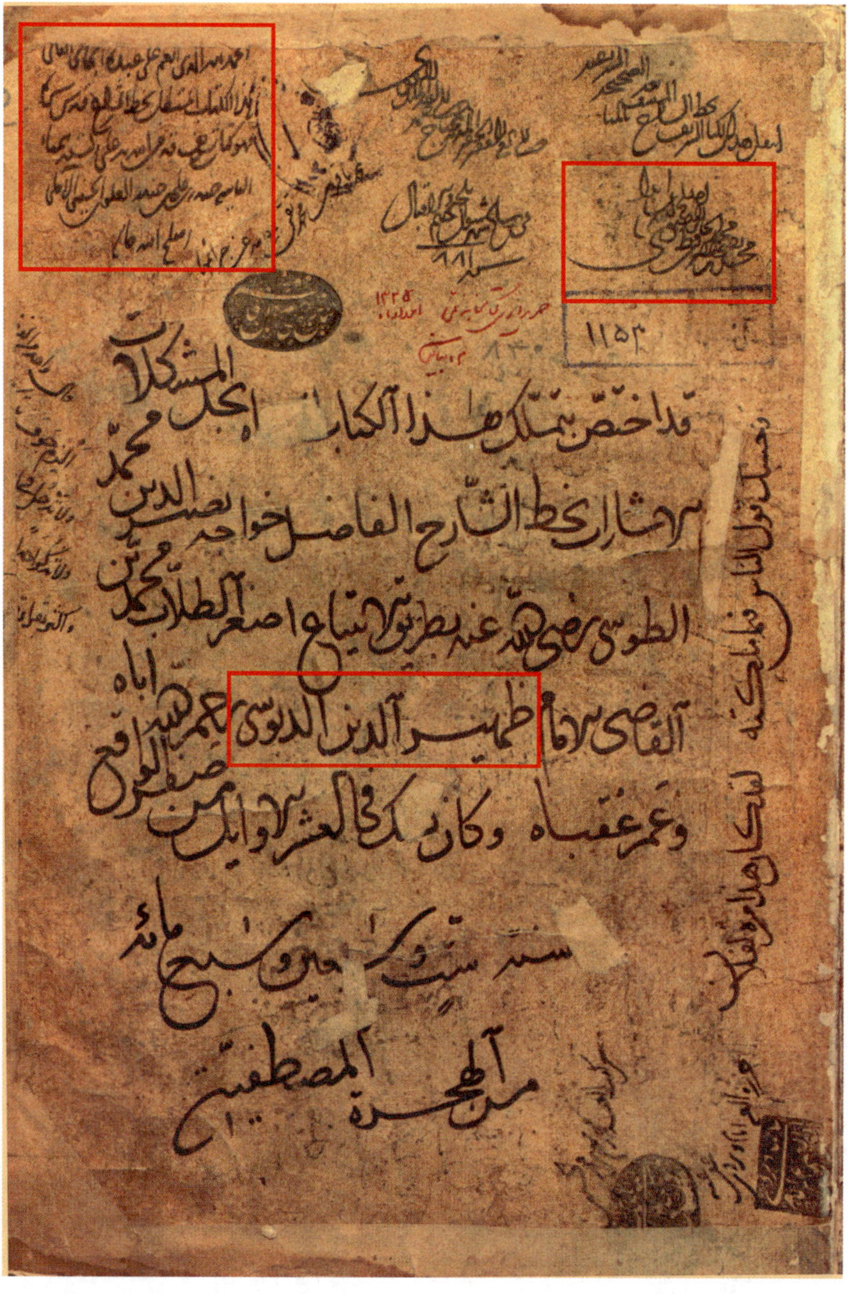

FIGURE 3.8 MS 1153, fol. 1[a]
TEHRAN, KITĀBKHĀNA-YI MILLĪ-I JUMHŪRĪ-I ISLĀMĪ-I ĪRĀN

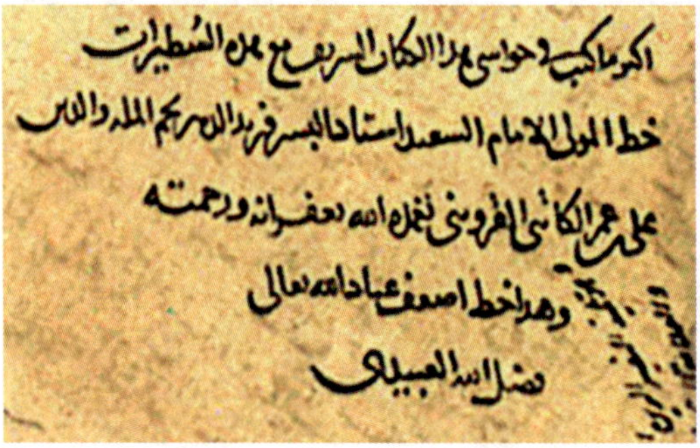

FIGURE 3.9
MS Yeni Cami 763, fol. 198[b]
ISTANBUL, SÜLEYMANIYE KÜTÜPHANESI

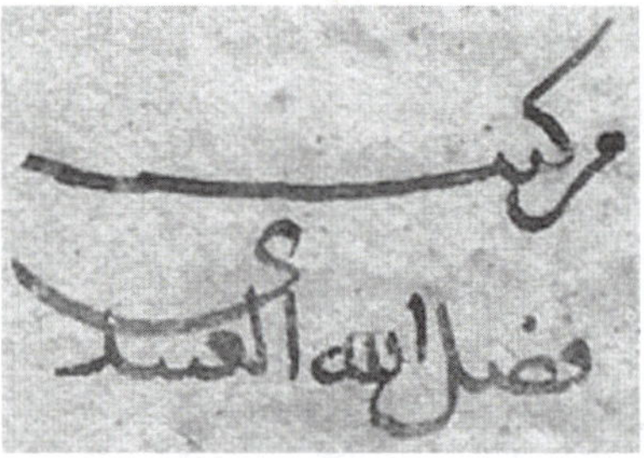

FIGURE 3.10
MS Or. 7969, fol. 3[a]
LONDON, BRITISH LIBRARY

Naturally, not all such attestations in Arabic manuscripts are false. We can cite two examples of statements that can be corroborated by external evidence. The MS Yeni Cami 763 is another copy of the above-mentioned *Ḥall mushkilāt al-Ishārāt* by Naṣīr al-Dīn al-Ṭūsī, collated in Jumādā II 661/1263. It has a note (see fig. 3.9) by [Jalāl al-Dīn] Faḍl Allāh al-ʿUbaydī (d. 750/1350), the commentator of *al-Mulakhkhaṣ fī l-hayʾa* by Maḥmūd al-Jaghmīnī (d. after 618/1221), stating that most of the marginal glosses are by Najm al-Dīn ʿAlī b. ʿUmar al-Kātibī l-Qazwīnī (d. 675/1276). Is this statement really in the hand of Faḍl Allāh al-ʿUbaydī? And are those glosses indeed in the hand of Najm al-Dīn al-Kātibī? The answer to both questions is yes. Faḍl Allāh's signature is also visible in MS Or. 7969 (British Library; see fig. 3.10) and other examples of the handwriting of Najm al-Dīn can likewise be found in MS Fazıl Ahmed Paşa 1618 (Köprülü Yazma Eser Library; see fig. 3.11) and MS Rağıp Paşa 792 (see fig. 3.12), two books known with certainty to have been copied by him.

From the later period there is, for instance, the work *al-Liwāʾ al-marfūʿ fī ḥall mabāḥith al-mawḍūʿ* by the great Ottoman scholar Ṭāshkūbrī-zādah (d. 968/1560). The MS Carullah 1442 (Süleymaniye Library) has a note below the title on the front of the textblock which reads (see fig. 3.13): *bi-khaṭṭ muʾallifihi Ṭāshkūbrī-zādah yadull ʿalayhi mā kutiba fī ākhir al-risāla* ("in the hand of its author Ṭāshkūbrī-zādah as it is indicated at the end of the work"). Is this work in

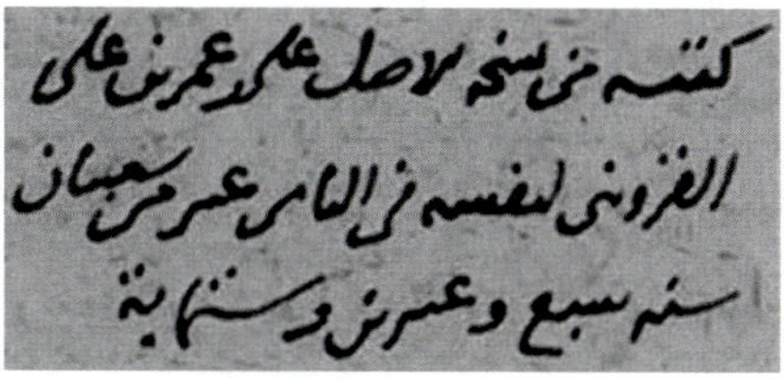
كتبه من نسخة الاصل علي عمر بن علي
القزويني لنفسه في الثاني عشر من شعبان
سنة سبع وعشرين وستمائة

FIGURE 3.11
MS Fazıl Ahmed Paşa 1618, fol. 43[a]
ISTANBUL, KÖPRÜLÜ KÜTÜPHANESI

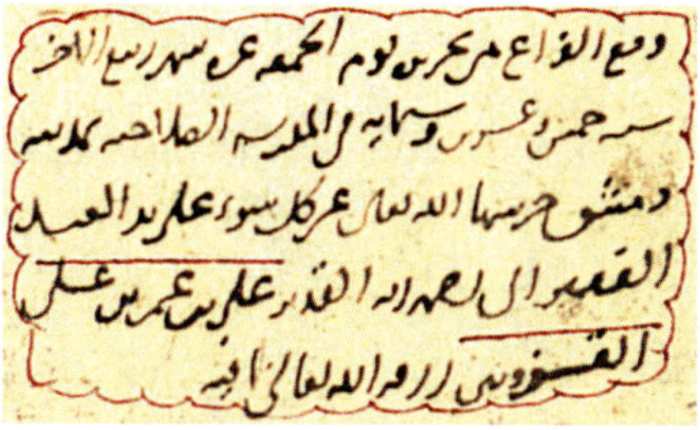
وقع الفراغ من تحريره يوم الجمعة عن شهر ربيع الآخر
سنة خمس وعشرين وستمائة في المدرسة الصلاحية بمدينة
دمشق حرسها الله تعالى عن كل سوء على يد العبد
الفقير الى رحمة الله القدير علي بن عمر بن علي
القزويني [illegible]

FIGURE 3.12
MS 792, fol. 214[a]
ISTANBUL, RAĞIB PAŞA KÜTÜPHANESI

the hand of its author? The colophon certainly implies it. It reads (see fig. 3.14): *najiza taḥrīruhu fī l-thālith ʿashar min shahr Ramaḍān … min shuhūr sanat tisʿ wa-arbaʿīn wa-tisʿimiʾa* (*fī baldat Qusṭanṭiniyya al-maḥmiyya ṣaḥḥa*—insertion marked with a dotted line) *wa-anā muʾallifuhu l-faqīr ilā ʿafw rabbih al-jalīl Aḥmad b. Muṣṭafā b. Khalīl arshadahu llāh taʿālā ilā l-maʿārif al-zākhira* … By carefully examining the whole manuscript, we can conclude that indeed, this appears to be a fair copy of the original, with a few additions, executed in an informal but clear Turkish *taʿlīq* (*nastaʿlīq*) with a slant to the right.

6 Some Questions to Consider

The fact that a colophon or some other statement says that such and such a person wrote or copied a given work has to be corroborated by internal and external evidence. But how can such evidence be corroborated?

Here are some questions that need to be addressed before a verdict can be reached. For instance, How much do we know about the life of a given author? Where and when did he live? What was his upbringing and formation? Do we know, from existing sources, anything about the quality of his handwriting? What script or scripts were used in his time and the region where he was active? Does the script in question match the period and the region in which he lived? Are there extant samples of his handwriting, such as reading notes, ownership statements, transmission certificates (*ijāzāt*) or extant copies of works by other scholars but copied by him or attributed to him? How do they compare? If there

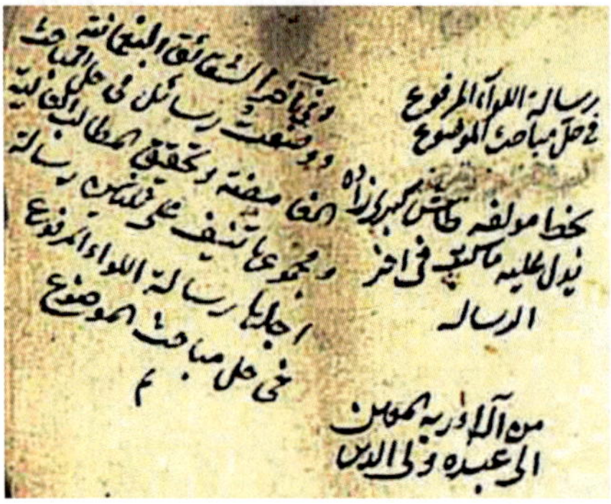

FIGURE 3.13
MS Carullah 1442, fol. 1[a]
ISTANBUL, SÜLEYMANIYE KÜTÜPHANESI

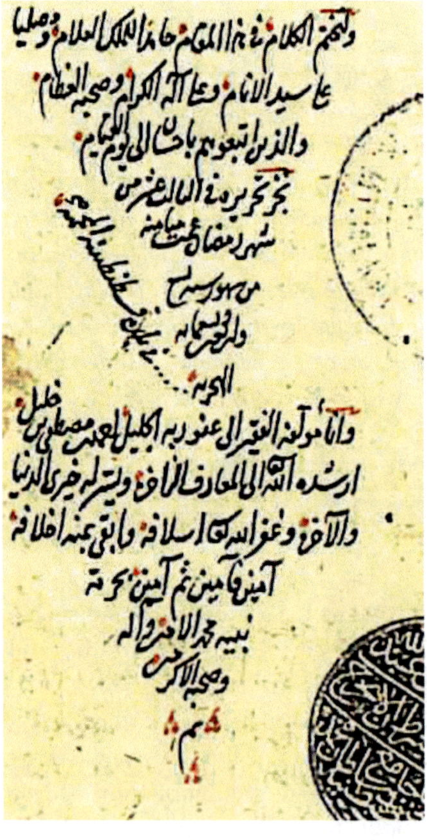

FIGURE 3.14
MS Carullah 1442, fol. 51[b]
ISTANBUL, SÜLEYMANIYE KÜTÜPHANESI

is an authenticated piece of his writing, what are the main features of his hand, such as ductus, aspect, characteristic way of writing specific letterforms, the use of ligatures, evidence of assimilation/contraction, unconventional joining of letters, etc.? Is his handwriting influenced by another style, and if so, which one? With regard to his name, how does he introduce himself and what invocations, if any, does he use after his name? And finally, is the writing surface (especially in the case of paper), binding, etc. contemporaneous with the style of writing?

7 Ṣalāḥ al-Dīn al-Ṣafadī and His Holographs

One of the most remarkable figures in Arabic literature is Ṣalāḥ al-Dīn al-Ṣafadī (d. 764/1363), who received his training and worked in the Mamlūk chancery, authored many books on diverse subjects, and copied and illuminated many of his and other authors' works, a good number of which are extant. One of those works is his *Taṣḥīḥ al-taṣḥīf wa-taḥrīr al-taḥrīf*, which has survived in both a draft and a fair copy (MS Ayasofya 4732).[16] Neither the draft nor the fair copy has a colophon. However, the draft is accompanied by an *ijāza* in the hand of the author (see fig. 3.15). The certificate states that the draft was read in Aleppo in sixteen sessions and that the last session took place on Tuesday, 10 Dhū l-Qaʿda 759/1358. It was recited by Shams al-Dīn Abū ʿAbdallāh Muḥammad al-ʿUmarī, in the presence of the author and a number of auditors including al-Ṣafadī's two sons (Muḥammadān), his daughter Fāṭima, and his Turkish slave Asan Buġā. The signature reads, *wa-kataba Khalīl b. Aybak al-Ṣafadī bi-Ḥalab al-maḥrūsa* and the handwriting shows a heavily influenced *tawqīʿ*, the chancery script *par excellence* with which al-Ṣafadī was very familiar, given his training as a secretary in the Mamlūk chancery. Furthermore, his draft has the following salient characteristics: cancellations by means of single lines across the canceled group of words, additions (*mulḥaqāt*) either in the margins or, for longer ones, on inserts linked to the main text by means of numbers or a dotted line, and blank spaces in between segments of text.

Another of his holographs is *Ṣarf al-ʿayn* (MS Or. oct. 3806, Berlin), a self-help manual of the genre "Every man his own doctor."[17] The manuscript has no colophon and no date but it does feature the title and the author's name on the front of the textblock executed by another scribe-illuminator (see fig. 3.16).

---

16 This codex was printed in facsimile by Fuat Sezgin in 1985.

17 The full title is *Ṣarf al-ʿayn ʿan ṣarf al-ʿayn fī waṣf al-ʿayn*. For more information on this work, see Sellheim, *Materialien* i, no. 54.

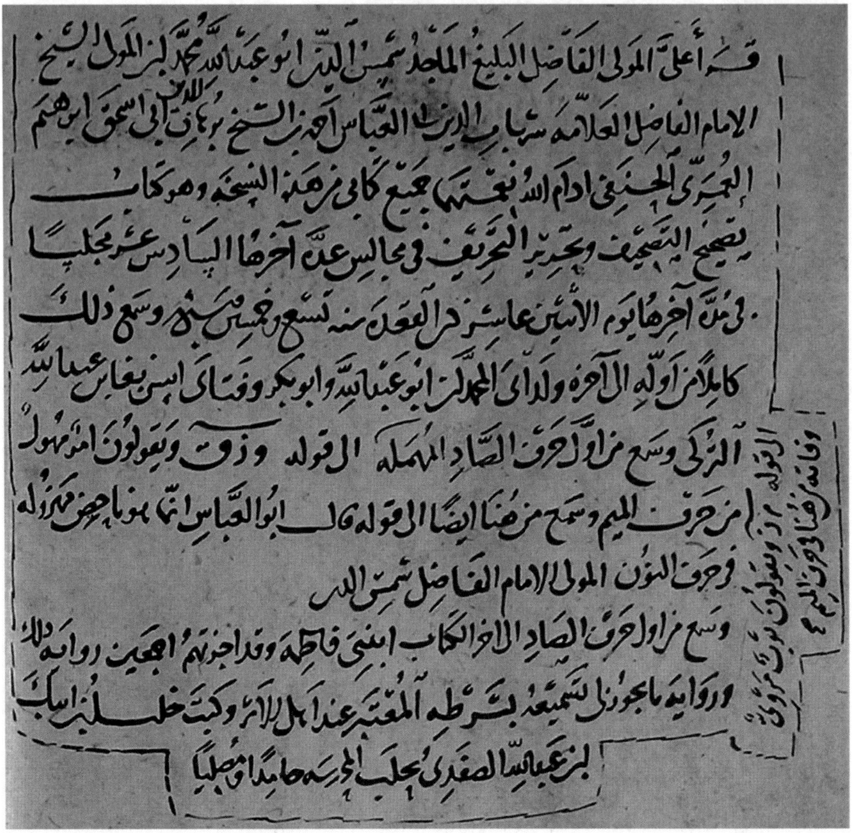

FIGURE 3.15 MS Ayasofya 4732, fol. Ab
ISTANBUL, SÜLEYMANIYE KÜTÜPHANESI

The author's name, in a lobed ornament, is given as *ta'līf al-adīb al-fāḍil Khalīl al-Ṣafadī*. It exhibits, moreover, all the characteristics of the handwriting employed in the draft of *Taṣḥīḥ al-taṣḥīf*.

Among the many surviving manuscripts that Ṣalāḥ al-Dīn al-Ṣafadī transcribed is the Copenhagen *al-Maqāmāt al-Ḥarīriyya* by al-Qāsim b. ʿAlī l-Ḥarīrī (d. 516/1122). This copy was also illuminated and glossed by him in Ṣafad 720/1320 (Royal Library, MS Cod. Arab. Add. 83). The colophon reads (see fig. 3.17): *katabahā wa-dhahhabahā wa-raqama ḥawāshiyahā … al-ʿabd al-faqīr ilā llāh taʿālā Khalīl b. Aybak bi-Ṣafad al-maḥrūsa* … The manuscript was studied in class on a number of occasions; this is attested in transmission certificates in the hand of Ṣalāḥ al-Dīn himself. The main text is penned in an elegant Mamlūk *naskh* script influenced by *tawqīʿ*, whereas the chapter headings are chrysographed in a formal calligraphic *tawqīʿ*.[18]

18 See Gacek, Copenhagen ms.

FIGURE 3.16 MS Or. Oct. 3806, fol. 1a
BERLIN, STAATSBIBLIOTHEK

FIGURE 3.17 MS Arab. Add. 83, fol. 154[a]
COPENHAGEN, KONGELIGE BIBLIOTEK

8 The Author's Signature

Contrary to what one might expect, the author does not have to introduce his name by adjectives of humility and his name does not have to be followed by an invocation, though this was often the custom in the manuscript age.

Also, the fact that the name is preceded by such adjectives as *ʿabd*, *faqīr*, and the like, and is followed by a prayer, does not necessarily speak for the authenticity of the signature. In fact, copies made from holographs but lacking scribal colophons often repeat *verbatim* the original authorial statement. Nevertheless, it is very important to discover the way various authors presented their names, in order to use that knowledge to authenticate holographs. Here, for instance, the case of Quṭb al-Dīn Maḥmūd al-Shīrāzī (d. 710/1311) is interesting. In all extant examined manuscripts Quṭb al-Dīn al-Shīrāzī always introduces himself by the phrase "*aḥwaj khalq Allāh ilayhi*" (see e.g., MS Yeni Cami 763, Süleymaniye Library; MS Fazıl Ahmed Paşa 867, Köprülü Library; see fig. 3.18). He also normally follows his name with the expression "*aṣlaḥa llāh aʿmālahu*" but changed it, probably in old age, to "*khatama llāh lahu bi-l-ḥusnā.*"

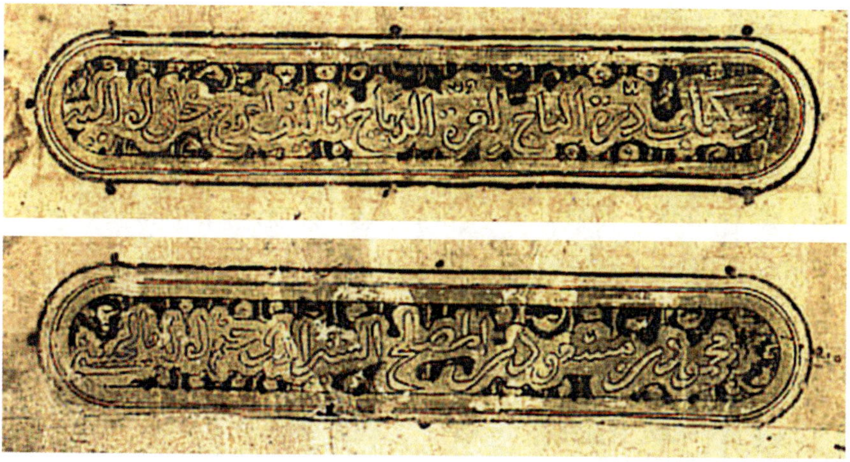

FIGURE 3.18 MS Fazıl Ahmed Paşa 867, fol. 1[a]
ISTANBUL, KÖPRÜLÜ YAZMA ESER KÜTÜPHANESI

Furthermore, most authors, such as Ṣalāḥ al-Dīn, Quṭb al-Dīn, Naṣīr al-Dīn, Badr al-Dīn, never use honorifics as part of their signatures. This is the case with the above-mentioned Ṣalāḥ al-Dīn al-Ṣafadī who in all examined instances gives his name as Khalīl b. Aybak, and not Ṣalāḥ al-Dīn or his earlier honorific Ghars al-Dīn, bestowed on him when he was a fledgling scholar. These were given to him by his contemporaries in recognition of his great learning. If such honorifics are used at the beginning of the name and even in such a statement as "known as," they have to be looked at with suspicion.

There is a statement in a copy of Naṣīr al-Dīn al-Ṭūsī's *Ḥall mushkilāt al-Ishārāt* (MS Or. 95, Leiden Library) to the effect that Jamāl al-Dīn (!) Muḥammad b. al-Muṭahhar al-Ḥillī collated this manuscript with the author's original. His name is preceded by the expression "*afqar ʿibād Allāh.*" This is certainly a false statement. Muḥammad was the son of Ḥasan b. Yūsuf who died in 726/1326 and was known as Jamāl al-Dīn. Muḥammad's authentic signature can be found in a copy of *Nahj al-mustarshidīn* by his father Ḥasan b. al-Muṭahhar (MS 4, Marʿashī Library, Qum) where he styles himself simply as Muḥammad b. Muṭahhar. In another codex (University of Tehran, MS 2301, dated Sulṭāniyya 4 Jumādā II 710/1310), also containing his father's work *Marāṣid al-tadqīq wa-maqāṣid al-taḥqīq*, his signature reads, Muḥammad b. Ḥasan b. Yūsuf b. ʿAlī b. al-Muṭahhar al-Ḥillī. In addition, there is no comparison between those two specimens and the Leiden Or. 95 manuscript. They are simply two completely different hands.[19]

19 For discussion of this statement in Leiden 95 see also ʿImādī, Nuskhahā 185–9.

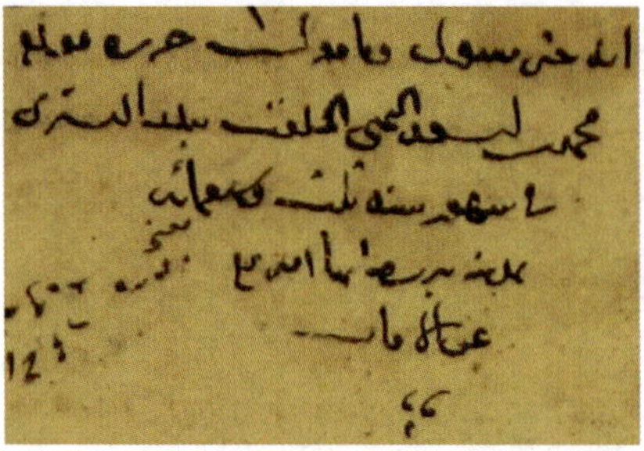

FIGURE 3.19
MS Fazıl Ahmed Paşa 831, fol. 142[a]
ISTANBUL, KÖPRÜLÜ YAZMA ESER KÜTÜPHANESI

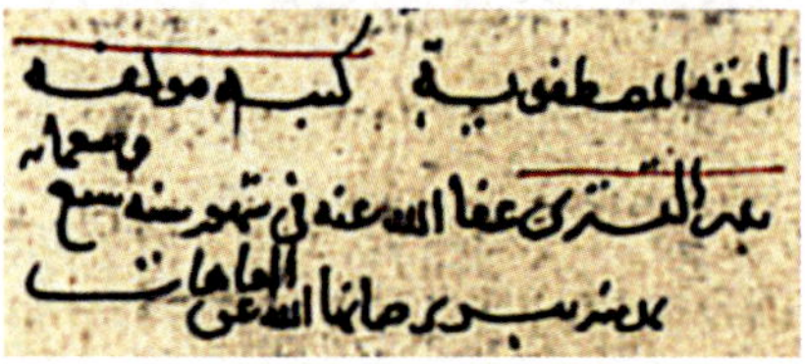

FIGURE 3.20
MS 781, fol. 229[a]
ISTANBUL, RAĞIB PAŞA KÜTÜPHANESI

Based on the information supplied in the colophons, some might consider another two manuscripts genuine holographs. The two works are commentaries by Badr al-Dīn al-Yamanī l-Tustarī (d. 732/1332) on *Ṭawāliʿ al-anwār* by al-Bayḍāwī (MS Fazıl Ahmed Paşa 831, Köprülü Library) and *Maṭāliʿ al-anwār* by Sirāj al-Dīn al-Urmawī (d. 682/1283) (MS Rağıb Paşa 781). The first one is dated 703/1303–4 and the second 705/1305–6; both were supposedly composed in Tabrīz.

The commentary on the *Ṭawāliʿ* has a colophon (see fig. 3.19) beginning *ḥarrararu muʾallifuhu Muḥammad b. Asʿad al-Yamanī l-mulaqqab bi-Badr al-Tustarī*, while the colophon of the commentary on the *Maṭāliʿ* reads, *ʿallaqahu muʾallifuhu l-faqīr al-muḥtāj ilā raḥmat Rabbih al-Ghanī Muḥammad b. Asʿad al-Yamanī l-madʿū bi-Badr al-Tustarī* … The work *Sharḥ al-Maṭāliʿ* also has a reading note by al-Tustarī (see fig. 3.20), who introduces himself with the phrase "*yaqūlu l-faqīr al-ḥaqīr Muḥammad b. Asʿad al-Yamanī l-mushtahir bi-Badr al-Tustarī*" and signs the note "*katabahu muʾallifuhu Badr al-Tustarī ʿafā llāh ʿanhu.*" Could both be al-Tustarī's holographs? The verbs *ʿallaqa* and *ḥarrara* are not of much help here. In both cases the style of writing is very similar but does not seem to reflect, as one might expect, an Iranian ductus of the period. Both manuscripts appear to be copies made from a holograph by an anonymous copyist who did not, for whatever reason, inscribe his name. More importantly, we have to ask the question: Would al-Tustarī speak of himself as "called (or known as) Badr al-Tustarī"?

As food for thought, there are two extant manuscripts of an *ijāza* granted by the Iranian scholar Jalāl al-Dīn al-Dawānī (d. 908/1502) to Muʾayyad-zāda

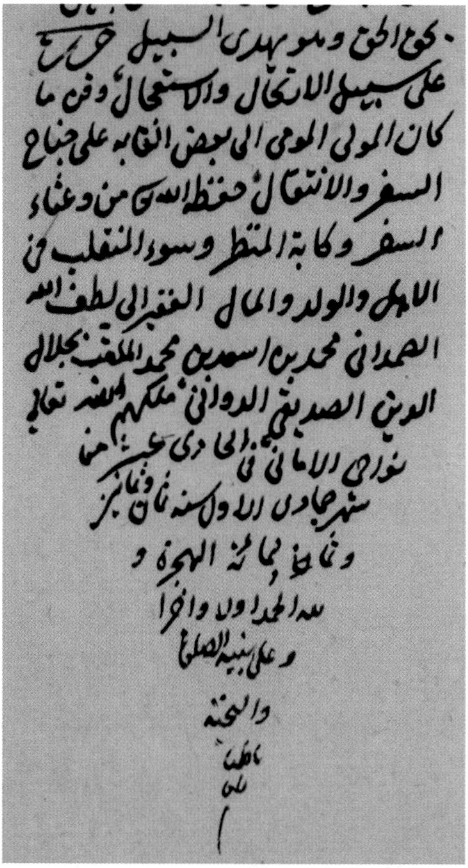

FIGURE 3.21
MS Esad Efendi 3733, fol. 47[a]
ISTANBUL, SÜLEYMANIYE KÜTÜPHANESI

ʿAbd al-Raḥmān Efendī (d. 922/1516), namely MS Esad Ef. 3733 (Süleymaniye Library; see fig. 3.21) and MS Escorial 687. In both cases the name Jalāl al-Dīn is given as "*al-faqīr ilā luṭf Allāh al-Ṣamadānī Muḥammad b. Asʿad b. Muḥammad al-mulaqqab bi-Jalāl al-Dīn al-Ṣiddīqī l-Dawānī.*" Nevertheless, both were copied by Ottoman Turkish scribes using two different styles of Ottoman *taʿlīq* (*nastaʿlīq*). They are certainly copies of the original and not authentic. The authentic signature of al-Dawānī can be found in MS 12388 (Marʿashī Library, Qum), written in an informal Iranian *shikastah*, where the author gives his name (see fig. 3.22) as "*al-faqīr Muḥammad b. Asʿad b. Muḥammad al-Ṣiddīqī l-Dawānī.*" Here we see clearly that the introductory phrase and the expression "*al-mulaqqab bi-*," followed by the honorific Jalāl al-Dīn, are absent.[20]

20 For more on this see Pfeiffer, Teaching.

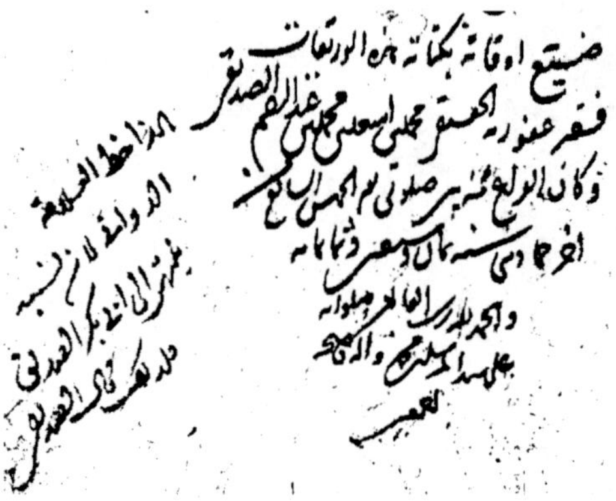

FIGURE 3.22
MS 12388, fol. 190[a]
QUM, MAR'ASHĪ KITĀBKHĀNAH

9 In Conclusion

There are many authentic, noteworthy examples of holographs in various collections around the world that have not yet received the attention they deserve. Much research has yet to be done on various authorial practices. Authorial statements and attestations by former owners of Arabic manuscripts should never be taken at their face value. Very often the only way to authenticate a holograph, or a piece of writing attributed to an author, is to compare it, if possible, with other extant samples of that author's writing. In order to do that, there is an urgent need for a database of images with signed specimens of well-known scholars and authors.

Bibliography

Bauden, F., Maqriziana I. Discovery of an autograph manuscript of al-Maqrīzī: Towards a better understanding of his working method: Description: Section 1, in *Mamlūk Studies Review* 7, no. 2 (2003), 21–68.

Bauden, F., Maqriziana II. Discovery of an autograph manuscript of al-Maqrīzī: Towards a better understanding of his working method: Analysis, in *Mamlūk Studies Review* 12, no. 1 (2008), 51–118.

Gacek, A., *Arabic manuscripts: A vademecum for readers*, Leiden 2009.

Gacek, A., *The Arabic manuscript tradition: A glossary of technical terms and bibliography*, Leiden 2001.

Gacek, A., *The Arabic manuscript tradition: A glossary of technical terms and bibliography—Supplement*, Leiden 2008.

Gacek, A., The Copenhagen manuscript of the *Maqāmāt al-Ḥarīriyya*, copied, illuminated and glossed by the Mamluk litterateur Ṣalāh ad-Dīn aṣ-Ṣafadī, in R.M. Kerr and Th. Milo (eds.), *Writings and writing: Investigations in Islamic text and script in honour of Januarius Justus Witkam*, Cambridge 2013, 143–66.

Gardiner, N., and F. Bauden, A recently discovered holograph fair copy of al-Maqrīzī's *al-Mawāʿiẓ wa-al-iʿtibār fī dhikr al-khiṭaṭ wa-al-āthār* (Michigan Islamic MS 605), in *Journal of Islamic Manuscripts* 2, no. 2 (2011), 123–31.

ʿImādī, Ḥā'irī Sayyid Muḥammad, Nuskhahā-yi kuhan az Sharḥ-i Ishārāt-i Ṭūsī: nisbat-i ānhā bā nuskha'i mu'allif va nuktahā-yi dar bāb-i sunnat-i taʿlīm va taʿallum-i aṣar, in *Āyina'i Mīrāṣ* 50 (2013), 179–234.

Pfeiffer, J., Teaching the learned: Jalāl al-Dīn al-Dawānī's *Ijāza* to Mu'ayyadzāda ʿAbd al-Raḥmān Efendi and the circulation of knowledge between Fārs and the Ottoman Empire at the turn of the sixteenth century, in M.A. Pomerantz and A. Shahin (eds.), *The heritage of Arabo-Islamic learning. Studies presented to Wadad Kadi*, Leiden and Boston 2015 [2016], 284–332.

Sellheim, R., *Materialien zur arabischen Literaturgeschichte*, 2 vols., Wiesbaden-Stuttgart 1976–87.

Witkam, J.J., Les Autographes d'al-Maqrīzī, in A.C. Binebine (ed.), *al-Makhṭūṭ al-ʿarabī wa-ʿilm al-makhṭūṭāt* (= *Le manuscrit arabe et la codicologie*), Rabat 1994, 89–98.

CHAPTER 4

"Bi-khaṭṭ mu'allifihi"... Vraiment ?! L'apport de l'analyse judiciaire d'écritures à l'étude des manuscrits arabes

Méthodes et étude de cas : la recension égyptienne des Mille et une Nuits

Élise Franssen

> *Assuredly Nature would prompt every individual to have a distinct sort of writing, as she has given a peculiar countenance – a voice – and a manner.*
>
> D'ISRAELI, *A second series* 208

∴

Nous avons tous fait l'expérience de reconnaître au premier coup d'œil l'écriture de l'un de nos proches sur une enveloppe et donc de savoir qui nous a écrit avant même d'avoir ouvert ou lu le message[1]. Mais nous sommes tous en peine d'expliquer précisément ce qui nous permet d'identifier si aisément les écritures familières. D'ailleurs, il nous arrive de douter, de nous tromper… Dès lors, même si de nombreux chercheurs habitués à l'écriture de l'auteur qu'ils étudient disent pouvoir la reconnaître entre toutes et de manière infaillible[2], il serait bon de mettre au point une méthode scientifique d'identification des écritures, des outils qui nous permettraient de justifier une attribution, arguments à l'appui, de dépasser la subjectivité et d'aller au-delà de la première impression, rarement neutre, générée par une écriture, une méthode qui permettrait au chercheur moins habitué à une certaine écriture de l'identifier également.

Un domaine où l'objectivité est primordiale et où l'identification d'une main peut avoir de lourdes conséquences est le domaine judiciaire. Il y a très

1 Cet article présente un approfondissement du chapitre six de la première partie de ma thèse de doctorat, v. Franssen, *Les Manuscrits* 97-116.

2 Ou presque : des exemples d'erreurs sont connus et soulignés, v. par ex. Bauden, Maqriziana IX 160, n. 5.

 | DOI:10.1163/9789004413177_005

longtemps qu'une écriture identifiée par un expert peut servir de preuve au cours d'un procès : l'empereur byzantin Justinien (r. 527-565) mentionne déjà ce cas de figure dans ses *Novelles*, sa dernière œuvre juridico-législative, qui passera à l'Europe[3]. C'est toujours le cas aujourd'hui et il n'est pas rare que des experts en écriture soient appelés à la barre[4]. D'abord nommée "graphologie", la discipline a été scindée en deux branches distinctes, différant tant par leurs objectifs que par leurs méthodes : la graphologie désigne actuellement l'"étude de l'écriture manuscrite, considérée comme révélatrice du caractère, des aptitudes d'une personne"[5], tandis que la seconde, appelée désormais "expertise en écriture", s'est débarrassée des considérations psychologiques pour se concentrer sur l'identification des scripteurs et la discrimination des faux[6]. Cette branche de la discipline s'est rationalisée et, dès la fin du XXe siècle, plusieurs méthodologies s'inspirant des principes de la méthode scientifique, ont été publiées[7]. Cependant, aucune étude générale dans le domaine des écritures arabes n'est connue à ce jour[8]. Dès lors, comme en paléographie, il faut se tourner vers les travaux des experts en écritures "occidentales", plus précisément en alphabet latin, et adapter leurs pratiques aux particularités de l'alphabet arabe. C'est ce que nous tenterons de faire ici, en exposant théoriquement l'une de ces méthodes et sa transposition à l'arabe, puis en la testant sur un groupe de manuscrits, la première phase de la recension égyptienne des *Mille et une Nuits*.

Une telle démarche, scientifique, la plus objective possible, est préférable par nature ; elle permet de dépasser préjugés et *a priori*, condition *sine qua non* de toute analyse scientifique. Il est plusieurs cas où elle se révèle particulièrement utile. D'abord, une telle méthode systématique serait profitable à tout

3 Sur les *Novelles* et leur importance en droit moderne, v. Coffinières, *Analyse* 187 partic. pour ce qui concerne la preuve par l'identification d'une écriture donnée et les précautions à prendre à ce sujet, notamment la nécessité de corroborer cette preuve par le témoignage de trois personnes "dignes de foi". L'importance des *Novelles* dans la reconnaissance de l'écrit comme moyen d'identification d'une personne a déjà été soulignée par Guiral, *La valeur* et citée par Münch, *L'Expertise* 10, parmi d'autres exemples.

4 L'affaire Dreyfus est un triste exemple en la matière, de même que l'affaire dite du petit Grégory (v. Michel, *40 ans* 46-57).

5 *Dictionnaire de l'Académie*, 9e édition.

6 Pour un rappel concis et clair des différences entre les deux disciplines : Gervais, Expertise ; v. aussi Huber et Headrick, *Handwriting* 351-92, et les entrées respectives du glossaire de Münch, *L'Expertise* 183, 185. v. aussi Sedeyn, *Méthode SHOE* 9-11 (partic.).

7 Buquet, *L'Expertise* ; Buquet, *Manuel* ; Ellen, *Scientific Examination* ; Guiral, *La valeur* ; Günther et Ludwig, *Schrift* ; Huber et Headrick, *Handwriting* ; Münch, *L'Expertise* ; Rück, *Methoden* ; Sedeyn, *Méthode SHOE* ; ...

8 Seuls quelques articles traitant d'un point particulier, surtout de signatures, ont été publiés. v. par exemple Al-Haddad et al., Examination ; Al-Musa Alkahtani et Platt, Relative difficulty.

chercheur qui, commençant un travail sur un auteur particulier, voudrait rapidement être en mesure d'identifier les manuscrits ou notes holographes[9] de celui-ci, sans passer à côté des manuscrits non signés ou lacunaires, et sans devoir se fier à des attributions réalisées par d'autres. Par ailleurs, ces attributions n'étant pas toujours convaincantes, ce même chercheur devrait pouvoir étayer ses dires.

Deuxièmement, certains scripteurs respectent si bien le modèle scolaire que leur écriture, régulière et lisible, présente à première vue peu de particularités personnelles et se distingue difficilement des autres écritures normées. C'est le cas des scribes professionnels talentueux, des calligraphes et des secrétaires de chancellerie, dont les activités supposent une telle écriture[10].

Troisièmement, quand on suspecte qu'un document ou une note serait un faux, qu'un colophon ne serait pas relatif au manuscrit en présence mais à son modèle – la copie des colophons étant monnaie courante, surtout si celui-ci est prestigieux, que ce soit en raison du ou des nom(s) mentionné(s), de la date de copie ou du modèle –,[11] il convient de le (dé)montrer, *a fortiori* si cette affirmation va à l'encontre de l'avis de tiers. Si le faux est réalisé avec soin et si les scribes sont habiles, rapprocher deux échantillons d'écriture peut ne pas suffire.

Ensuite, l'écriture varie au cours du temps (une même main, jeune, mature ou à l'aube de la mort, n'est pas identique[12]) et en fonction des circonstances (on est souvent malhabile quand il fait froid, par exemple), de l'état physique (fatigue et maladie altèrent le trait) et mental (l'angoisse, l'inquiétude, rendent une graphie plus saccadée)[13]. Mais l'écriture d'une même main conserve des

---

9 Par exemple, des notes de lecture, d'emprunt, des *ex-libris*, des commentaires, etc. Attention toutefois à l'étendue de l'échantillon : plus le texte est long, plus il offrira de données utiles à l'identification de la main qui l'a tracé. Notez cependant que dans certains textes courts et souvent tracés, comme les signatures, par exemple, on observe des singularités très caractéristiques et très personnelles, v. Huber et Headrick, *Handwriting* 73-4 et *infra* p. 94.

10 Khalīl b. Aybak al-Ṣafadī et sa belle main régulière, même dans ses notes personnelles, sont la parfaite illustration de ce cas de figure. V. aussi la contribution d'Adam Gacek à ce volume, p. 69.

11 V. encore la contribution d'Adam Gacek à ce volume, p. 63 : "Even such expressions as *'alā yad al-mu'allif* ("in the hand of the author"), *katabahu mu'allifuhu bi-khaṭṭihi* ("the author wrote it in his own hand"), etc., may not be of much help when it comes to establishing the authenticity of a holograph, as these could have easily been copied by a scribe who did not mention his own name."

12 V. le chapitre 5 de ce volume, p. 136-231.

13 Sedeyn, *Méthode SHOE* 6, 72 ; Beit-Arié et Pasternak, Comfort ; Münch, *L'Expertise* 37.

singularités personnelles[14] qu'il convient de déceler et de décrire. Ainsi, des manuscrits qui, au premier coup d'œil, pourraient sembler avoir été copiés par différentes mains, se révèlent parfois être l'œuvre d'une seule et même personne à des moments différents de sa vie[15].

Enfin, un cas où l'identification des graphies revêt une importance particulière est celui des textes sans auteur. Identifier – avec un degré de certitude satisfaisant – une main revient parfois à identifier un compilateur et à préciser les conditions de naissance de la tradition en présence. Ce dernier cas sera abordé ici, à travers l'exemple de la recension égyptienne des *Mille et une Nuits*.

1 Méthode SHOE de Marie-Jeanne Sedeyn

Plusieurs chercheurs s'y sont essayés[16], mais Marie-Jeanne Sedeyn, expert honoraire près la Cour d'Appel de Paris, est à ma connaissance celle qui est allée le plus loin dans cet effort d'objectivation de l'analyse des écritures occidentales et, surtout, c'est la seule qui ait publié une véritable méthode pratique[17] : sa méthode SHOE (Standard Handwriting Objective Examination).

Après avoir défini l'écrit, à la fois message et trace, objectivation (au sens propre) du passage d'un vivant, forme et mouvement, objet physique, culturel et affectif, elle préconise tout d'abord une approche neutre et impartiale : l'on ne voit que ce que l'on s'attend à voir[18], ou, pire, ce que l'on espère voir. Dès lors, pour contourner cet obstacle, il convient de rassembler le plus d'observations neutres possible, au sujet du (ou des) écrit(s) à étudier. Sedeyn propose un ensemble de 381 critères à observer systématiquement. Cette liste est le résul-

---

14 Sedeyn, *Méthode SHOE* 9, 99-104 *et passim* ; Huber et Headrick, *Handwriting* 298-302 et 321 ; Kapoor et al., Study ; Lester et al., Differences.

15 À cet égard, analyser les écritures d'un scripteur qui change de style d'écriture au cours de sa vie, comme par exemple Ibn Khaldūn (Tunis 732/1332-Le Caire 808/1406), formé dans son enfance à l'écriture *maghribī*, puis, avec l'âge, se rapprochant de plus en plus des modèles d'écriture orientaux, serait des plus intéressants. Sur l'écriture d'Ibn Khaldūn, v. la contribution de R. Hashizume dans ce volume, p. 300-22.

16 V. n. 7, p. 79.

17 Huber et Headrick, *Handwriting* est un ouvrage très complet ; cependant, il n'est pas facile d'usage. Organisé sous forme de questions-réponses pratiques et exclusivement tournées vers le domaine judiciaire, il s'agit plus d'un ouvrage à consulter ponctuellement pour obtenir une information précise que d'une méthode. Notons tout de même que les auteurs citent 21 "discriminating elements", classés en trois groupes (éléments de style, d'exécution, liés aux habitudes d'écriture, p. 90-139), qui sont intéressants mais difficilement utilisables en pratique pour notre sujet.

18 V. introduction de Sedeyn, *Méthode SHOE* 8, 9, 11-4 surtout.

tat de sa longue expérience, mais ne doit pas être vue comme fermée, chaque "praticien" étant invité à l'amender ou à l'augmenter en fonction de la réalité à laquelle il est confronté. Au terme de l'examen, on obtient donc une description de l'écriture étudiée, que l'on peut dès lors comparer aux autres écrits à authentifier ou sur lesquels porte l'analyse: points communs et différences apparaissent clairement. Mais ces critères sont à pondérer: certains sont caractéristiques de groupes (ainsi, les écritures anglo-saxonnes ont des caractéristiques communes et étrangères aux écritures francophones, par exemple, ou les scripteurs lettrés ont une graphie différente des personnes qui écrivent peu[19]) et ne reflètent donc pas un individu. Ensuite, et comme en tout, rien ne remplace l'expérience[20].

Un écueil fréquent dans lequel il ne faut pas tomber est celui de s'attacher au détail en perdant de vue l'ensemble. L'observer à distance, de biais, à l'envers, ou encore dans un miroir donne une "vision globale" de l'écrit et permet d'exprimer les caractéristiques les plus saillantes de celui-ci[21]. Dans le cas d'écrits volontairement falsifiés, des détails peuvent être facilement reproduits, sans que l'ensemble des caractéristiques de l'écriture ne concorde avec le modèle.

Plusieurs instruments sont nécessaires à l'examen des écrits: des instruments de mesure (règle, compas, rapporteur), le plus utile étant certainement le calque ou transparent millimétré, puisqu'il donne des informations sur les mesures, les angles, les orientations, etc.[22] Il faut aussi plusieurs feuilles de papier calque, des feutres de couleurs et de quoi prendre des notes. Si possible, le mieux est de travailler conjointement sur le document original et sur une reproduction, à l'échelle 1/1, que l'on pourra annoter.

La méthode s'articule autour de 12 chapitres comprenant chacun une liste de critères à examiner accompagnée d'explications détaillées. Voici un aperçu des critères qui s'appliquent à notre propos et quelques précisions[23]. Tout d'abord, le support, l'instrument et l'encre utilisés doivent être observés et décrits (p. 20-2). En effet, ils sont susceptibles de modifier le tracé. En ce qui concerne les manuscrits arabes, l'instrument utilisé est en grande majorité le calame, mais il ne présente pas toujours la même forme et il est intéressant d'au

19 À cet égard, v. l'étude de Verjans, *Écritures*; v. aussi Huber et Headrick, *Handwriting* 175-86, 243, 297-98.

20 Sedeyn, *Méthode SHOE* 15.

21 Sedeyn, *Méthode SHOE* 16 *et passim.*

22 Sedeyn, *Méthode SHOE* 16.

23 J'avais pensé joindre en annexe les fiches synthétiques établies par M.-J. Sedeyn et reprenant les critères à analyser, mais celle-ci a préféré que le lecteur intéressé s'en remette à sa publication.

moins préciser s'il est biseauté ou coupé en pointe, comme c'est l'usage au Maghreb[24]. Pour ce qui est du support, se limiter aux catégories générales suffira : papier oriental ou européen, parchemin, papyrus. Une indication concernant l'apprêt nous semble également à ajouter : un papier mal apprêté absorbe l'encre, ce qui modifie l'apparence du tracé[25].

Le deuxième chapitre concerne l'ordonnance et l'utilisation de l'espace (p. 23-34). Après des considérations générales (l'écriture est-elle parallèle à la longueur ou à la largeur du papier, diagonale, présente sur les deux faces ou non, et si non, sur laquelle ?), il convient de s'intéresser aux espaces laissés vierges, qu'il s'agisse des marges ou d'éventuels alinéas, et aux ajouts ou additions. L'auteure précise que ce ne sont pas des mesures absolues qu'il faut noter, mais plutôt des indications relatives par rapport au reste du document : "... il s'agit d'évaluer en quelque sorte l'équilibre des masses entre la partie écrite et les espaces blancs qui l'entourent."[26] Une feuille de papier calque, de la même taille que le document examiné et pliée de manière à former des demis, des quarts et des tiers, dans les deux sens, et en outre des huitièmes, verticalement, est donc utile pour répondre à ces questions. Les marges sont évaluées en fonction du texte qu'elles pourraient contenir : une marge supérieure ou inférieure réduite ne peut pas abriter de texte, une grande marge est égale ou plus grande que deux ou trois interlignes, et une marge moyenne se situe entre les deux. Pour ce qui est des marges latérales, elles sont dites faibles ou absentes si elles ne peuvent abriter plus d'une ou deux lettres, petites si elles sont moins larges qu'un huitième de la largeur de la feuille, moyennes si elles sont comprises entre un quart et un huitième de la largeur de la feuille, larges si elles se déploient entre le quart et le tiers de la feuille et enfin très larges si elles atteignent ou excèdent le tiers de la largeur de la page. Leur régularité est également à décrire. Elles peuvent être régulières ou non, verticales ou plus ou moins progressives (c'est-à-dire croissantes) ou régressives (décroissantes). Une marge irrégulière peut être inégale, régressive, progressive ou ondulante, c'est-à-dire à la fois progressive et régressive, d'abord l'un ou l'autre. Les marges gauches et droites sont à distinguer. Pour notre propos, il faut évidemment inverser l'ordre des informations s'appliquant à l'une ou

---

24 V. Houdas, *Essai* 96 ; Déroche et al., *Manuel* 113-4 ; Déroche, *Le Livre* 79-80 ; Déroche et al., *Islamic codicology* 104-6 ; Gacek, *Vademecum* 42. Sur la préparation des calames, v. Levey, *Medieval* 13-4.

25 Sur l'apprêt dans les manuscrits arabes, v. Pedersen, *The Arabic book* 66 ; Levey, *Medieval* 39-40 ; Déroche et al., *Manuel* 59-60 ; Humbert, La fabrication 45-6 ; Déroche et al., *Islamic codicology* 53 ; Gacek, *Vademecum* 7, 188.

26 Sedeyn, *Méthode SHOE* 27.

à l'autre. Pour ce qui est de la marge située en fin de ligne, il est important de noter si elle est existante, volontaire et régulière, ou non, et si les lignes d'écriture présentent des tassements, des mots coupés, ou au contraire des blancs ou des étirements de mots en fin de ligne. L'emplacement des éventuels ajouts est également à décrire à ce stade ; se situent-ils dans les marges (laquelle) ou entre les lignes ? En pratique, tracer au feutre de couleur, sur la reproduction des feuillets étudiés, un trait rejoignant la fin de la dernière lettre de chacune des lignes écrites permet de dépasser l'impression de rectilinéarité souvent donnée par un texte justifié.

Le troisième chapitre s'intéresse aux axes des lettres (p. 35-42). Il est important de les décrire en termes de parallélisme, d'orientation et d'homogénéité. Pour ce faire, le calque ou transparent millimétré est encore très utile : il suffit de choisir un *alif* ou *lām*, par exemple, comme référent, et d'y superposer une verticale du papier millimétré ; cela permet de vérifier si les autres hampes*[27] sont parallèles à celle de la lettre choisie. Il y a plusieurs cas de figure possibles, allant du parallélisme constant et régulier à l'anarchie, en passant par de légères inégalités ou des lettres parallèles entre elles mais selon un axe différent de celui d'autres lettres. Pour ce qui est de l'orientation, elle sera dite verticale dans le cas de lettres formant un angle de 90° par rapport à la ligne d'écriture, inclinée ou légèrement inclinée si cet angle est de 54° ou plus, et très inclinée dans le cas contraire (moins de 54°). Si l'écriture présente des orientations très différentes, il convient de mesurer les extrêmes. Enfin, le dernier critère concerne l'homogénéité : l'écriture présente-t-elle les mêmes caractéristiques tout du long, ou y a-t-il des "trains d'écriture" : "des phrases entières, de une à plusieurs lignes, dont l'orientation relativement régulière diffère nettement du texte qui précède ou qui suit"[28] ?

Le critère suivant concerne la ligne d'écriture ; stabilité, direction générale et homogénéité sont à scruter (p. 39-43). Ainsi, une ligne de base* peut être rectiligne ou très instable (inégalités d'une lettre à l'autre), en passant par stable (groupes de 4-5 lettres alignées) ou instable (2 ou 3 lettres alignées maximum). Un guide (papier ligné, ou traces de *misṭara*, par exemple) n'aide pas à écrire droit, tout juste à respecter un certain interligne[29] ; les diverses méthodes de réglures du papier ne sont donc d'aucune utilité à cet égard. La direction générale de la ligne de base doit ensuite être définie. Elle peut être horizontale,

---

27 Les mots marqués d'un astérisque sont repris sur le schéma explicatif, v. fig. 4.1. Pour un glossaire anglais très complet, v. Huber et Headrick, *Handwriting* 394-411 ; Gacek, *Vademecum* 141-3 offre le vocabulaire principal.

28 Sedeyn, *Méthode SHOE* 38.

29 Sedeyn, *Méthode SHOE* 40.

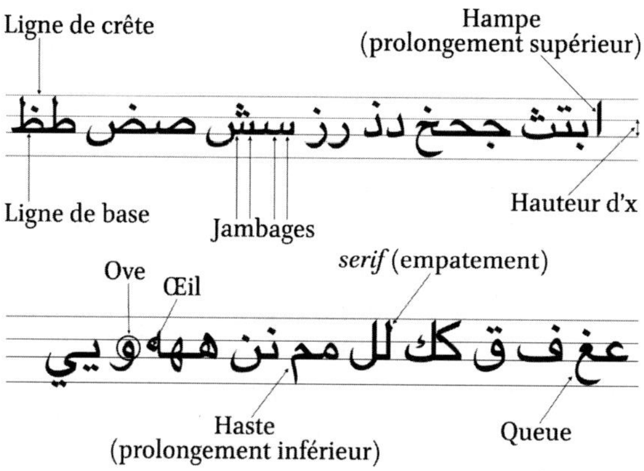

FIGURE 4.1 Schéma et lexique de description des graphies

légèrement ou très ascendante ou descendante, chuter en fin de parcours, être plutôt convexe ou concave, onduler (en commençant par monter ou par descendre), ou encore présenter plusieurs mouvements successivement ascendants ou descendants, elle est alors dite "chevauchante en montant/descendant". Les lignes sont-elles rigoureusement parallèles, ou y a-t-il des inégalités ? Quand les lignes suivent des directions irrégulières, il faut noter si elles présentent de fortes inégalités ou carrément une absence totale d'homogénéité. En pratique, tracer quelques lignes de base théoriques au feutre de couleur, c'est-à-dire suivre la partie inférieure de chacune des lettres devant s'y trouver (en omettant donc les lettres faisant partie d'une ligature) permet de visualiser cette ligne de base.

Le cinquième chapitre s'intéresse aux dimensions et proportions des lettres (p. 43-50). C'est évidemment un chapitre qui a dû être adapté pour l'appliquer à l'alphabet arabe ; il a notamment fallu choisir des lettres étalons. D'après la méthode, les critères à prendre en compte sont : la régularité, le calibre général, les minuscules surélevées, la largeur des lettres, les proportions hauteur-largeur, les hampes* et hastes*, et enfin, deux critères qui, *a priori*, ne nous concernent pas (mais nous verrons que cette opinion est à nuancer) : les doubles lettres et les majuscules. Une écriture est régulière lorsque "... les petites lettres d'un mot peuvent s'inscrire entre deux parallèles, que ces parallèles soient rectilignes ou non."[30] En arabe, les petites lettres sont les *bāʾ*, *tāʾ*, *thāʾ*, *ʿayn*, *ghayn*, *sīn*, *shīn*, *mīm*, *nūn* et *yāʾ* dans leurs formes initiale et médiane, ainsi que le *hāʾ* isolé, c'est-à-dire toutes les lettres dont le corps est intégrale-

30 Sedeyn, *Méthode SHOE* 46.

ment inscrit entre la ligne de base et la ligne directement au-dessus, délimitant la hauteur d'x*[31]. Si l'écriture en présence n'est pas régulière, plusieurs cas sont possibles : parfois, des lettres distinctes qui devraient avoir la même taille sont systématiquement de tailles différentes ; ou une même lettre est tantôt haute, tantôt basse ou épaisse et maigre ; ou une tendance au gladiolement (hauteurs décroissantes des lettres) ou, au contraire, au grossissement, est observée au sein des mots, voire des syllabes ; enfin, la ligne de crête peut onduler. Le calibre général de l'écriture, son module, sont à estimer à partir d'une lettre étalon, le *mīm* initial, par exemple (pour remplacer le "a" latin). S'il mesure 2 mm, le calibre est petit, 3 mm, moyen et 4 mm ou plus, grand. Certaines écritures peuvent présenter un tassement systématique des lettres en fin de ligne ou une alternance de tassement et étalement apparemment sans lien avec la position du texte sur la ligne, qu'il convient de noter. Le rapport entre la hauteur et la largeur des lettres est à décrire également. Pour ce faire, il suffit d'observer les *dāl/dhāl* et *ʿayn/ghayn* initiaux et de vérifier s'ils s'inscrivent dans un carré ou dans un rectangle, debout ou couché. Les hampes* et hastes*, prolongements supérieurs et inférieurs verticaux des lettres, sont également à observer, mesurer et comparer, entre elles et par rapport aux petites lettres. Les tiges des *alif*, *lām*, *ṭāʾ/ẓāʾ* sont-elles de dimensions égales ? Sont-elles courtes (moins de la hauteur de deux *mīm* initiaux), moyennes ou longues (plus de deux *mīm* et demi) ? Pour ce qui est des prolongements inférieurs, je suggère de mesurer et de comparer les *raʾ* et *wāw*, d'une part, et les *lām* et *kāf* finaux, d'autre part, et de mesurer les *yāʿ* finaux ainsi que les *mīm maqlūba musbala*[32] (c'est-à-dire à queue verticale), s'il y en a. Il s'agit ensuite de comparer ces mesures à celles des prolongements supérieurs, particulièrement pour les lettres qui comprennent les deux (comme les *lām* finaux). Marie-Jeanne Sedeyn passe ensuite à l'examen des lettres doubles, qui ne concerne pas à proprement parler l'arabe puisque c'est par l'usage de la *shadda* que l'écriture indique le redoublement d'une lettre. Cependant, si l'on omet les points diacritiques, il arrive assez fréquemment que deux lettres de *rasm* (forme) identique se suivent, ce qui fait que les observations au sujet des lettres redoublées nous concernent tout de même. Il faudra noter si elles sont toutes les deux de même hauteur, si la première ou la deuxième est plus haute que l'autre et si cela est récurrent ou si ces proportions relatives varient sans qu'il soit possible d'en déduire une logique. Après

31 V. Gacek, *Vademecum* 142-143.

32 Pour une illustration de ce type de *mīm* final, v. Gacek, *Vademecum* 319 (appendix II, num. 38).

des remarques quant aux majuscules, hors de propos pour nous, l'auteure conclut que, s'il nous est facile d'écrire grand ou petit, "... les proportions, qui résultent de mouvements inconscients, ne peuvent pas être modifiées avec la même facilité"[33]. Voilà donc une caractéristique véritablement personnelle.

Le sixième critère d'analyse de la méthode SHOE s'intitule "liaison – parcours du geste" (p. 51-7) et concerne donc le mouvement qui donne naissance à l'écriture examinée. Il a évidemment été nécessaire d'adapter ce chapitre d'analyse également puisque l'écriture arabe présente par nature un degré de liaison très élevé. Ce chapitre reste cependant d'une importance capitale pour la description des écritures en alphabet arabe, leur comparaison et leur classement. Un premier critère à examiner est celui des ligatures abusives, c'est-à-dire des ligatures entre des lettres qui devraient normalement être séparées. Sont-elles fréquentes[34]? Si oui, l'écriture peut être dite "hyperliée", qualificatif s'appliquant *a fortiori* aux graphies présentant des liens occasionnels entre les mots. Le type de liaison est ensuite abordé. Dans l'ensemble, s'agit-il d'une écriture plutôt anguleuse ou plutôt arrondie? Pour répondre à cette question, il est conseillé de regarder l'écrit à une certaine distance, ou dans un miroir. D'autre part, s'agit-il d'une écriture progressive – dont les mouvements, c'est-à-dire les traits, sont principalement orientés dans le sens de l'écriture, vers la gauche pour nous – ou, au contraire, régressive? La façon dont les éléments circulaires des lettres – les oves* – sont formés est très instructive. Les lettres à observer sont les *mīm*, *wāw*, *fāʾ* et *qāf*; tous leurs oves sont-ils formés de la même façon, indépendamment de leur point d'attaque (et si non, préciser)? Une même lettre est-elle toujours formée par le même geste? Si non, les différences sont-elles liées à l'environnement de la lettre? Où débute le geste traçant les oves: en haut, à droite ou à gauche, au niveau de la base, avec un recouvrement? Celui-ci comporte-t-il un trait d'attaque? L'ove est-il toujours fermé ou reste-t-il ouvert, et si oui, où: au sommet? à droite? à gauche? à la base? Sa fermeture se fait-elle par un trait supplémentaire? Marie-Jeanne Sedeyn propose ensuite de s'attarder sur la lettre "o", aux multiples possibilités de tracés, et de l'utiliser comme cas d'étude, lettre que je suggère de remplacer par le *hāʾ* (ou *tāʾ marbūṭa*) isolé pour l'arabe. De la même manière, je propose de remplacer les remarques concernant les "m" et "n" par des observations au

33 Sedeyn, *Méthode SHOE* 50.

34 Marie-Jeanne Sedeyn ne définit pas le terme "fréquent"; pour ma part, je considère que si des ligatures abusives sont constatées dans plus de la moitié des cas sur une page, celles-ci peuvent être dites fréquentes.

sujet des *sīn/shīn*. Leur tracé[35] est-il anguleux, arrondi ou imprécis (ondulation, voire trait horizontal) ? Présentent-ils toujours la même forme ou celle-ci dépend-elle de leur environnement ? Le dernier critère qui nous concerne cherche à définir l'existence d'une certaine continuité entre les mots : le début du premier trait d'un mot est-il au même niveau que la fin du dernier trait du précédent ?

Le chapitre sept concerne la pression exercée par la main pour tracer l'écriture (p. 58-64). Elle peut s'évaluer à l'aune de la couleur de la page (pâle, moyenne ou forte), même si celle-ci est évidemment influencée par les instruments utilisés et l'état de conservation du document, voire de la qualité de sa reproduction. La puissance d'appui est visible au verso du texte inscrit, sur l'original ou sur photo prise en lumière rasante, quand le support utilisé est assez fin pour permettre l'apparition d'un foulage (inexistant, moyen ou fort). La fermeté du trait est un critère moins évident, qui nous donne des indications sur l'assurance de la main. Pour l'évaluer, il convient d'examiner les traits descendants : sont-ils droits, courbes, en torsion, tremblés ou hachés ? L'épaisseur du trait, bien que dépendant également en partie de l'instrument utilisé, donne des informations sur la pression exercée aussi, puisqu'une pression forte donne un trait d'autant plus épais. Marie-Jeanne Sedeyn propose les mesures suivantes : le trait est fin lorsqu'il mesure moins de 0,2 mm d'épaisseur, moyen lorsque sa largeur est comprise entre 0,3 et 0,5 mm, assez épais quand il est de 0,5 à 1 mm, et très épais quand il mesure plus de 1,5 mm de large. Les yeux des lettres (observer les *wāw*, *fā'*, *qāf*...) sont-ils épargnés ou remplis d'encre ? Il convient ensuite d'examiner la netteté du trait, si nécessaire à la loupe ou en agrandissant la reproduction du document. Les contours sont-ils nets (d'un ou des deux côtés), flous (les 2 bords des traits sont imprécis) ou baveux ? S'ils sont baveux, cela peut aussi résulter d'un mauvais apprêt du papier, qui se comporte à la manière d'un buvard. L'appui est-il uniforme, ou présente-t-il un léger relief (traits ascendants plus clairs et descendants plus encrés), un relief marqué (différence claire entre les pleins et déliés, qui, encore une fois, peut être due à l'instrument, un calame très biseauté, notamment), une pression déplacée (c'est-à-dire plus forte sur les traits régressifs), s'agit-il d'une écriture moirée (à déterminer en observant la page dans son ensemble : des lettres, groupes de lettres, ou mots entiers apparaissent plus foncés que d'autres) ? Enfin, l'examen des finales, plus précisément de leur longueur (de suspendues, c'est-à-dire inachevées, à prolongées, éventuellement uniquement en fin

35 Seul le *rasm* est à examiner : la forme et la position des points diacritiques seront abordées ultérieurement.

de ligne, en passant par courtes, moyennes et longues, lorsqu'elles sont plus longues qu'une largeur de lettre), de leur direction (ascendante, horizontale, descendante ou arrondie), de leur forme (en crochet, supérieure et/ou inférieure, ou en "queue de renard") et de leur appui (effilées, pointues, arrondies, épaissies et éventuellement prolongées en fin de ligne), clôt ce chapitre.

Viennent ensuite des considérations sur le rythme et la vitesse d'écriture (p. 65-9), critères difficiles à objectiver, mais importants puisqu'une même main ne produit pas exactement la même écriture si elle écrit vite ou lentement : plus le rythme est lent, plus le trait est lourd et épais, plus le modèle scolaire est respecté et moins les courbes sont souples. Marie-Jeanne Sedeyn propose la classification suivante : rythme très lent, lent, moyen ("main bien exercée, écrivant sans précipitation"), rapide (caractérisé par une grande souplesse des courbes, une fermeté des traits droits, mais des inégalités de tracé et une perte en lisibilité), ou précipité (avec des traits parfois exagérés)[36]. Ces critères variant en fonction des circonstances, ils ne peuvent être un argument décisif permettant l'identification d'un scripteur.

Ensuite, le chapitre neuf nous enjoint d'observer la densité du texte et les espacements (p. 69-74) sur la page en général, puis entre les mots et entre les lignes. La description de la densité globale du texte doit se faire à une certaine distance, ou à travers un miroir. Cette observation peut révéler un texte compact ou aéré, homogène ou disparate. En effet, des blancs peuvent apparaître sur la page examinée ; s'agit-il de trous, de "cheminées" verticales, obliques ou en v, et où sont-ils situés (partie droite, gauche, centrale ou répartis) ? La page semble-t-elle divisée en deux parties distinctes par ces blancs, et si oui, plutôt verticalement, horizontalement ou en diagonale ? Les espaces entre les mots et les interlignes sont ensuite à examiner. La régularité des blancs séparant les mots et leur largeur, évaluée à l'aune d'une largeur de lettre (faibles, ils occupent la largeur d'une à deux lettres et larges, plus de trois lettres) sont à noter. Pour les interlignes aussi, régularité et mesures (petits, moyens, grands ou très grands) sont à évaluer, de même que leur netteté : y a-t-il des enchevêtrements et quelle est leur fréquence ? Noter sur un calque millimétré les départs de chacune des lignes rend cette analyse aisée. Un interligne est "normal" s'il est possible d'y inclure une ligne de petites lettres, c'est-à-dire une hauteur d'x*, il

36 Pour estimer la régularité du rythme d'une écriture, Marie-Jeanne Sedeyn préconise de tracer les "axes des lettres" sous la ligne d'écriture, sans tenir compte des lettres larges (comme les *sīn/shīn*, *ṣād/ḍād*, … par exemple), puis d'estimer s'ils sont régulièrement espacés ou non, les inégalités pouvant se manifester sur un mot ou une ligne. L'éventuel tassement de l'écriture en fin de ligne pour respecter une marge ou à l'approche de l'extrémité du papier sera dès lors observable également. Sedeyn, *Méthode SHOE* 67.

est "grand" lorsqu'il est double (il peut abriter une ligne d'écriture complète) et "très grand" s'il peut en contenir deux. Les enchevêtrements, c'est-à-dire les conflits entre les descendantes d'une ligne et les ascendantes de la suivante, sont occasionnels quand ils ne sont observés qu'à deux ou trois reprises sur une même page; ils sont par contre généralisés quand ils sont si fréquents qu'ils entravent la lisibilité du texte[37]. Si la densité d'écriture est assurément une caractéristique individuelle, elle n'est cependant pas constante et ce critère ne peut donc être le seul argument en faveur de l'identification, ou de la réfutation d'identité d'une main[38].

Le dixième chapitre s'intéresse à la morphologie (p. 75-80). Il se rapproche dès lors des pratiques des paléographes occidentaux qui se constituent un alphabet, modèle auquel comparer les graphies étudiées. Les premiers critères concernent le type d'écriture (capitales, script, cursive, ...) et ne s'appliquent pas à l'arabe, sauf si un style calligraphique précis est représenté. La distance par rapport au modèle scolaire, le degré de lisibilité, les éventuels idiotismes et déteriorations morphologiques sont à observer. Le respect du modèle scolaire peut présenter six degrés, de la conformité absolue virant à l'impersonnalité, jusqu'à la création de formes compliquant le graphisme, en passant par une proximité plus relative par rapport au modèle, une différenciation lisible, des formes très originales, ou très simplifiées. Pour évaluer la lisibilité du texte, il est utile d'isoler les mots, pour que le contexte n'interfère pas dans notre capacité à reconnaître les formes des lettres et, donc, à lire le mot en présence. En matière de détériorations morphologiques, on peut citer des courbes cabossées, des tremblements, des fractionnements, ou des spasmes et saccades. Toutes ces déformations peuvent être dues à l'âge, à la maladie, ou encore au contexte: effort, froid, émotions...[39] Les lettres présentant toujours une forme singulière sont à décrire et éventuellement à reproduire (v. Tableau 4.2).

L'avant-dernier chapitre concerne les habitudes graphiques (p. 80-6). Il s'agit d'un chapitre capital, même si certains critères abordés ne nous sont d'aucune utilité (date, abréviations, ponctuation, majuscules non justifiées) car il aborde "... les petits gestes que nous exécutons [...] sans y penser"[40] et c'est bien là que résident les caractéristiques les plus personnelles d'un scripteur donné. Ces habitudes graphiques sont appelées par d'aucuns "coups de plume indiciaires"[41]. Ils sont si caractéristiques que certains experts privilé-

37 Ce critère de lisibilité est cependant quelque peu subjectif.

38 Sedeyn, *Méthode SHOE* 72.

39 Beit-Arié et Pasternak, Comfort; Sedeyn, *Méthode SHOE* 78; Münch, *L'Expertise* 11, 129-36.

40 Sedeyn, *Méthode SHOE* 83.

41 Buquet, *L'Expertise* 56-7, 65.

gient leur analyse, au détriment d'autres critères[42]. Pour l'arabe, l'étude de la forme et de la localisation des points diacritiques peut donner de bons résultats. En effet, l'écriture arabe en est abondante et ceux-ci font partie des signes tracés "sans y penser". Les conseils de Marie-Jeanne Sedeyn concernant l'étude des points sur le "i" et des accents sont une bonne source d'inspiration (p. 81, 84). Il convient donc d'observer la localisation des points isolés par rapport à la lettre (dans l'axe, en avant ou en arrière, variable) et par rapport à la hauteur d'x* (sont-ils tracés tout contre la lettre ou très haut/bas par rapport à celle-ci, c'est-à-dire plus haut que le sommet des ascendantes ou plus bas que les hastes les plus longues ?), en différenciant les points diacritiques placés au-dessus de ceux placés en dessous des lettres qu'ils complètent. Pour les points diacritiques multiples, il faut ajouter à cette description des indications sur leur localisation relative (le deuxième point est-il toujours/régulièrement au même niveau que le premier ?) et décrire la forme résultant éventuellement de leur ensemble, d'autant plus quand ils ne sont pas distincts mais reliés par un même trait (deux traits obliques convergents en forme d'accent circonflexe pour les points triples, trait horizontal/oblique pour les doubles, par exemple). Leur forme individuelle peut être circulaire, en forme d'accent, de virgule, de losange, en flèche, de façon systématique ou non, et pas toujours en lien avec l'instrument utilisé. Les signes rubricateurs, notamment utilisés pour séparer les hémistiches d'un vers, doivent être décrits à ce stade-ci également. Les soulignements sont intégrés dans ce chapitre aussi. En arabe, il s'agit de surlignements et il peut être utile d'y prêter attention ; sont-ils utilisés en complémentarité de l'encre rouge, ou pour la remplacer en cas d'oubli, ou pour accentuer encore l'emphase que son utilisation produit ? Sont-ils proches du texte, coupent-ils les ascendantes, s'interrompent-ils pour ne pas les couper ou sont-ils simplement placés plus haut que celles-ci ? Ces caractéristiques sont-elles systématiques ?

Le dernier chapitre concerne la signature (p. 87-92). S'il n'est pas utile pour le propos actuel – les noms apparaissant dans les colophons étant généralement notés de la même manière que le reste du texte –, il peut l'être pour l'étude des notes paratextuelles présentes sur les manuscrits, comme les ex-libris, par exemple. Voici donc, pour mémoire, les critères retenus par Marie-Jeanne Sedeyn qui pourraient s'appliquer à ces marques. Tout d'abord, il convient de définir le type de signature (complète ou abrégée et préciser). Ensuite, la lisibilité est à caractériser (la signature est-celle claire, inutilement

42 V. les conseils reçus d'Anne-Marie Verjans, expert judiciaire en écritures près la cour de Liège, lors de son intervention au colloque *Autograph/Holograph and Authorial manuscripts*, Liège, 10-11 octobre 2013.

compliquée, illisible? ...), de même que sa position par rapport au texte (critère peu utile pour nous, s'appliquant dans le cas de lettres), les axes des lettres (parallélisme, divergence ou convergence, tendance verticale/inclinée/renversée), la ligne de base (stabilité et direction générale horizontale/ascendante/descendante) et les dimensions (conformes/plus grandes ou plus petites que les lettres du texte principal?). Les éventuelles particularités de fin de signature sont à noter aussi (point, soulignement, ajout d'un paraphe avec extrémité finale vers la droite, vers la gauche ou encore plongeante), de même que l'aspect global du schéma, anguleux ou courbe (relier les points extrêmes de la signature et voir si elle s'inscrit dans un oval ou polygone). Enfin, le tracé est-il régulier ou inégal, lent, posé ou rapide-précipité, sans levée de plume ou avec levée(s) de plume entre des groupes de lettres, ou présente-t-il des lettres séparées? Est-il globalement anguleux ou arrondi?

Enfin, des remarques concernant l'application de la méthode closent l'ouvrage. L'auteure explique l'importance de réaliser des études sur des groupes d'individus, afin de mieux connaître les habitudes graphiques socio-culturelles et ainsi de mieux pouvoir cerner les caractéristiques individuelles de chaque scripteur[43]. Elle donne ensuite des conseils aux aspirants experts en écriture sur la manière de construire leur démarche, sur la nécessité d'analyser de la façon la plus complète possible les pièces étudiées et les éléments de comparaison. Elle attire notamment à nouveau l'attention sur le fait que si l'on se contente d'isoler des lettres, on perd la vision globale du document alors que celle-ci est justement un élément primordial pour l'expertise. L'auteure note "... c'est *l'absence* de différences significatives entre deux écrits qui justifie leur attribution à une seule et même personne. Par contre, une seule différence irréductible suffit pour différencier un scripteur d'un autre scripteur."[44] Mais qu'est-ce qu'une "différence irréductible"? C'est toute la difficulté de l'exercice puisqu'il faudra juger, au cas par cas, si les différences observées peuvent être expliquées par des circonstances particulières, ou si elles révèlent l'existence de deux scripteurs différents. C'est cela qui amène Marie-Jeanne Sedeyn au paragraphe sur l'imitation ou le déguisement (p. 99-104), chapitre éminemment utile puisqu'il "... cherch[e] à établir des règles générales sur le degré de difficulté que représente la modification de chacune des caractéristiques graphiques..."[45], soit ce qu'il est plus ou moins difficile de falsifier, c'est-à-dire, en

43 Ces habitudes collectives, sortes de caractéristiques nationales des graphies, sont aussi abordées par Huber et Headrick, *Handwriting* 175-86 (par pays); Verjans, *Écritures*.

44 Sedeyn, *Méthode SHOE* 97.

45 Ibid. 100.

miroir, ce qui relève de l'inconscient, ce qui est personnel à un individu donné, donc les critères qui doivent peser le plus dans notre analyse. Ainsi,

- la disposition du texte répond souvent à des "habitudes inconscientes qui risquent de réapparaître" ;
- il faut prêter une attention particulière au parallélisme des axes et définir l'angle formé par ceux-ci par rapport à la ligne de base ;
- la stabilité de la ligne de base est importante ;
- les attaques, variations de pression et finales sont symptomatiques ;
- la densité du texte est impossible à imiter ; il faut donc porter son attention sur les interlignes, les espaces entre les mots, etc. ;
- en termes d'habitudes graphiques, les différences sont toujours plus significatives que les similitudes ;
- d'une manière générale, les différences de proportion, de densité de texte, de pression et certaines habitudes graphiques sont significatives.

Voici donc les quelques critères dont l'observation est particulièrement opportune. Si, comme on l'a vu, la disposition du texte répond à des pratiques scribales stéréotypées, le parallélisme des axes est par contre un critère spécifique et assez facile à observer, de même que la stabilité de la ligne de base ou l'espacement des mots/au sein des mots dans le texte, sur la ligne d'écriture et sur la page. Pour ce qui est de la pression, tout dépend de la nature du document de travail et de la qualité de la reproduction disponible. Identifier les habitudes graphiques spécifiques peut prendre plus de temps. Donc, même si Marie-Jeanne Sedeyn insiste à plusieurs reprises sur le fait que sa méthode peut sembler fastidieuse, il est primordial de ne rien négliger, car ce n'est qu'en fin de recherche que l'on découvre ce qui est *vraiment* significatif dans le cas concret en présence[46] : privilégier les critères précités au détriment des autres peut donner de bons résultats, comme on va le voir.

2 Paléographie 2.0[47]

Avant de passer à l'application pratique de la méthode exposée, quelques considérations pratiques s'imposent. En effet, la plupart des bibliothèques

---

46 Cette importance fondamentale de conserver une vision globale de l'écrit est constamment martelée, v. Sedeyn, *Méthode SHOE* 16, 19, 71, 72, 74, 76, 79, 91 et surtout 97 : "La méthode qui consiste à rapprocher des formes de lettres ne peut [...] être considérée comme valable [...] ; en portant l'attention sur la morphologie des lettres, en les isolant, on perd la vision globale, qui est un élément très important de l'expertise."

47 Sur les apports des "digital humanities" pour notre propos, v. l'introduction à ce volume,

conservant des manuscrits arabes proposent aujourd'hui des reproductions numériques de ceux-ci ou de leurs microfilms. Il est possible d'acheter, ou de disposer gratuitement, de ces reproductions sous forme de fichier PDF ou de fichiers images (.jpg ou .tif, généralement). Les qualités proposées sont très variables, ce qui complique le travail de comparaison des graphies. En outre, en raison de leur piètre qualité, certains documents nécessitent un "lissage" préalable à toute étude[48]. Malheureusement, aucune d'entre elles ne présente d'échelle, ce qui complique la tâche dès le début puisque l'établissement de l'échelle est un préalable indispensable à toute analyse. Par ailleurs, dans le cadre d'études paléographiques, il peut être utile d'isoler des éléments du manuscrit, qu'il s'agisse de lettres particulières pour illustrer une description, ou, mieux, de passages plus longs où l'écriture se déploie naturellement et où l'environnement des lettres, leur agencement les unes par rapport aux autres et leur disposition sur la ligne de base sont visibles. Bien que peu indiqué pour Marie-Jeanne Sedeyn, comme on vient de le voir[49], un tel fractionnement se révèle toutefois utile pour vérifier les conclusions de l'analyse de l'écriture ou tout simplement pour en faire voir un aspect, car comme le dit Colette Sirat "… one cannot *prove* that two texts are penned by the same hand. The only way to persuade other people that it is so is to show them."[50] Enfin, certains mots courts et très fréquents ne sont plus à proprement parler un enchaînement de lettres, mais deviennent presque des symboles unitaires, caractéristiques[51], qu'il est intéressant d'isoler. Un bon programme de traitement d'image est dès lors de la plus grande utilité : en plus de rendre possible l'amélioration générale des images, en jouant sur les contrastes de couleurs ou en gommant les parasites, il permet de sélectionner précisément, copier et coller ces éléments significatifs, de manière à les rapprocher les uns des autres, voire à les superposer, et à pouvoir ainsi les comparer très finement (v. fig. 4.2).

Par ailleurs, cela fait plusieurs années que des informaticiens travaillent sur un programme qui permettrait d'identifier automatiquement des mains[52].

---

p. 1-37, et Fischer et al., *Kodikologie*, partic. ii, 229-339 ; Bausi et al., *Comparative* 12-34, 364-6, 531-7, 570-80 ; Muhanna, *Digital humanities*, partic. 1-9, 65-91, 151-73.

48 Les reproductions de microfilms de la Dār al-Kutub égyptienne sont particulièrement difficiles, parfois impossibles, à utiliser en raison des nombreuses traces d'usure, griffes et trous polluant le texte.

49 V. n. 46, p. 93.

50 Sirat, *Writing* 493. V. aussi Münch, *L'Expertise* 80-1 (même si l'auteur écrit qu'il est parfois possible d'identifier une main "hors de tout doute raisonnable", p. 61 et 90 ; cité par Patenaude, Chronique, 423).

51 Huber et Headrick, *Handwriting* 73-4.

52 Nikolaj Serikoff en parlait déjà en 2001, v. Serikoff, Image 55-66.

Ainsi, une équipe de recherche pluridisciplinaire de l'Université publique de Saint-Pétersbourg s'y consacre[53], mais d'après les dernières informations reçues, aucun algorithme performant n'a été mis au point à ce jour. Le traitement statistique des données relatives aux écritures arabes a également été mis en œuvre avec quelque succès, semble-t-il, à la fin du XXe siècle, mais n'a eu que peu de postérité[54]. Les récents progrès de l'OCR laissent entrevoir une possibilité de reconnaissance de caractères arabes manuscrits, réalisés en entraînant les ordinateurs à lire[55]. Enfin, Marie-Jeanne Sedeyn a le projet de faire informatiser sa méthode, mais elle n'a pas encore trouvé l'informaticien qui mènerait cette entreprise à bien.

3 Cas d'étude : les manuscrits de la recension égyptienne des *Mille et une Nuits*

Passons désormais au volet pratique de cette étude, consacré à l'analyse des graphies des manuscrits d'une recension particulière des *Mille et une Nuits*. L'appellation "mille et une nuits" regroupe des textes de nature et d'origine chronologiques et géographiques très diverses, leurs points communs étant la division en nuits de récits enchâssés dans le conte-cadre de Shéhérazade qui, chaque nuit, raconte une histoire au roi Shāhriyār, s'interrompant avec l'aube à un moment critique de la narration dans l'espoir de sauver sa vie, d'éviter l'exécution matinale infligée à toutes les femmes précédentes du roi misogyne, puisque celui-ci voudra connaître la suite de l'histoire. L'ouvrage s'est répandu en Occident grâce à l'adaptation française d'Antoine Galland (1646-1715), commencée à la fin du XVIIe siècle et publiée à Paris de 1704 à 1717, les deux derniers volumes étant posthumes[56]. Le recueil a rapidement suscité un enthousiasme

53 Équipe dirigée par les professeurs Redkin, Bernikova, Shalymov et Granichin, comprenant en outre plusieurs doctorants, v. l'article http://english.spbu.ru/news/883-spbu-scientists-and-scholars-mathematics-and-sociolinguistics-a-new-insight-into-the-origin-of-islam, où l'affirmation d'identification d'un holographe des *Khiṭaṭ* d'al-Maqrīzī est cependant très exagérée, pour ne pas dire fausse.

54 V. les études de Rezvan et Kondybaev, New Tool et Rezvan et Kondybaev, The ENTRAP software.

55 Le programme d'OCR développé par Benjamin Kiessling (Leipzig University) fonctionne déjà sur cette base, v. la présentation du corpus OpenITI, développé par Sarah Savant, Maxim Romanov et Matthew Miller, dans le cadre du Kitab Project : http://kitab-project.org/corpus/ et v. l'introduction de ce volume, p. 1-37.

56 *Les Mille et une nuit* (*sic*). Le texte de Galland ne constitue pas une traduction au sens où on l'entend aujourd'hui, mais plutôt une adaptation au goût français du siècle des Lumières ; sur ce point précis, v. notamment Hagège, Traitement ; Larzul, *Les Traductions* 20-119 ; Marzolph et al., *The Arabian Nights* 556-60 (spéc. 559).

extraordinaire dans le monde francophone et au-delà, le texte de Galland ayant été traduit à son tour en de nombreuses langues[57]. Cependant, Galland a été confronté à un problème majeur : le manuscrit qu'il traduit[58] est incomplet ; il ne compte pas mille et une nuits – mais ce titre ne doit pas être compris de manière comptable[59] –, et il s'arrête abruptement, au cours du conte de Qamar al-Zamān et Budūr[60], dont il ne présente pas la fin. Il ne comporte pas non plus le dénouement du conte-cadre. Pour obtenir un texte cohérent selon les critères de son époque, qui présenterait autant de nuits qu'annoncé dans le titre, Galland a modifié la division en nuits, ajouté des contes issus d'autres sources, manuscrites ou orales, et inventé une conclusion pour le conte-cadre[61]. L'attrait exceptionnel suscité par ce recueil, mais aussi le malaise provoqué par le flou régnant autour du texte et de l'intervention de Galland, firent que, bientôt, tout voyageur européen en Orient chercha à se procurer une version authentique du texte, non modifiée et intégrale, un manuscrit complet des *Nuits*. Jusque dans les dernières années du XVIIIe siècle, tous rentrèrent bredouilles[62], puis plusieurs manuscrits du même type apparurent soudainement et concommitamment, formant ce que l'on appelle aujourd'hui la tradition ou recension égyptienne des *Nuits*, ou encore la recension égyptienne de Zotenberg, du nom de l'orientaliste qui la décrivit le premier[63].

Derrière cette apparition soudaine et si à propos se trouve un homme qui a rassemblé des contes, histoires, anecdotes et romans d'origines diverses,

57 Y compris en arabe (!), v. la liste dans Chauvin, *Bibliographie* iv, 25-81 ; Marzolph et al., *The Arabian Nights* 724-7.

58 Paris, BnF, MS Arabe 3609-3611 ; en ligne sur Gallica depuis 2011 : [ark:/12148/btv1b8433372b]. McGuckin de Slane, *Catalogue* 619.

59 "Mille et un" étant utilisé pour signifier "beaucoup" ; à cet égard, v. par exemple Bencheikh et Miquel, Préface xlii.

60 Chauvin, *Bibliographie* v, n° 120, 204-12 ; Marzolph et al., *The Arabian Nights* 341-5.

61 Il a également modifié le début du conte-cadre. V. Zotenberg, *Histoire* 10-5, 28-33 ; Marzolph et al., *The Arabian Nights* 556-60 ; Bauden et al., *Journal* 84-90 (spéc. 88), 290 (surtout n. 365), 321-2, 327-30, 331-4, 335-8, 343-6, 347-52, 353-7, 358-63, 363-7, 369-72, 373-6 ; Bauden et al., *Journal II* 253-4, 302.

62 V. par exemple le témoignage de Jean Jacques Antoine Caussin de Perceval, dans Galland et Caussin de Perceval, *Les Mille et une Nuits* viii, V : "Les manuscrits complets des *Mille et une Nuits* sont rares, non seulement en Europe, mais même en Orient", ou celui d'un autre fameux traducteur des *Nuits*, Josef von Hammer-Purgstall, qui indique, au sujet de livres de contes : "Les Arabes sont extrêmement avares de tous les ouvrages de ce genre. [...] Leur avarice [...] vient surtout de ce qu'il leur serait très-difficile à eux mêmes de se procurer ces ouvrages complets. On peut en avoir facilement des fragments déchirés et dépareillés, mais il est très-rare qu'on soit assez heureux pour en trouver dans toute leur intégrité", dans von Hammer-Purgstall et Trébutien, *Contes inédits* i, XVI-XVII.

63 Zotenberg, *Histoire* 44-7.

pas uniquement issus des traditions précédentes des *Nuits*[64], les a divisés en mille et une nuits, les a ceint dans un conte-cadre complet, les a copiés en 4 volumes, toujours selon la même répartition de texte par volume, le même ordre, la même mise en page, toujours sur le même type de papier, avec les mêmes encres et dans le même niveau de langue. Cet homme a signé certains volumes et s'appelle ʿAlī l-Anṣārī[65]. Le groupe compte aujourd'hui quatorze manuscrits[66] ; ceux-ci ne sont pas tous signés de la même main et certains des manuscrits sont plus tardifs de plusieurs années. Tout cela, ainsi que d'autres arguments développés ailleurs[67], laisse entrevoir l'existence de deux sous-traditions. L'étude actuelle se concentre sur la première phase chronologique de la recension, représentée par sept manuscrits conservés à ce jour à la Bibliothèque ALPHA de Liège Université (Lg), à la British Library (L), à la BnF (P1, P2 et P3), à l'Institute of Oriental Manuscripts de Saint-Pétersbourg (SP), à la Bayerische Staatsbibliothek de Munich (Mu) et chez un particulier (v. la liste en annexe 1, p. 115-6)[68].

Lors d'une précédente recherche sur les graphies des manuscrits de ce groupe, alors que je ne connaissais pas encore les travaux de Marie-Jeanne Sedeyn, les critères d'analyse avaient été choisis empiriquement, d'une part, et en m'inspirant des recommandations des quelques auteurs s'étant penchés sur la question, d'autre part[69]. Ces critères comprenaient des considérations d'ordre général, comme le module de l'écriture (en pratique, la hauteur de ligne des manuscrits avait été retenue), sa compacité (rapport entre le nombre de mots par ligne et la hauteur de ligne), sa linéarité (l'écriture se déploie-t-elle suivant une ligne droite ou est-elle mouvante par rapport à la ligne de base ?), la direction de ses hampes, la présence ou non de ligatures et d'empattements. Plusieurs de ces critères se rapprochent donc de ceux de Marie-Jeanne Sedeyn.

64 La liste des contes compris dans les différentes traditions des *Nuits* est donnée dans Marzolph et al., *The Arabian Nights*, Appendix 1, 743-82.

65 Malheureusement non identifié à ce jour.

66 Seuls treize d'entre eux étaient connus jusqu'en octobre 2016 et la vente aux enchères d'un quatorzième ensemble, apparemment complet, à Londres, v. Christie's, *Arts* 38. Notez que le manuscrit a atteint des sommets inattendus en termes de prix : il a été adjugé à 10.625 £ ! Pour une liste complète des manuscrits des *Nuits* connus avant cela, v. Akel, Liste (bien que les datations des manuscrits manquent parfois de précision) ; le corpus détaillé de la recension égyptienne avant cette découverte figure dans Franssen, Les Manuscrits 332-5.

67 Franssen, *Les Manuscrits* ; une monographie tirée de ce travail est en préparation.

68 L'analyse des graphies des autres manuscrits du groupe sera publiée ultérieurement, dans la monographie en préparation.

69 Gacek, *Vademecum* 242 ; Déroche, *Catalogue* 17-8, 35-47 ; Polosin, Arabic manuscripts ; Rezvan et Kondybaev, New tool.

L وادرك شهرزاد الصباح فسكتت عن الكلام المباح

Lg وادرك شهرزاد الصاح نسكت عن الكلام المباح

P3 وادرك شهرزاد الصباح فسكتت عن الكلام المباح

SP وادرك شهرزاد المصباح فسكتت عند الكلام المباح

P2 وادرك شهرزاد الصباح سكتت عن الكلام المباح

Mu وادرك شهرزاد الصباح فسكتت عن الكلام المباح

P1 واوركـ شهرزاد الصباح فسكتت عن الكلام المباح

FIGURE 4.2 Comparaison de formules introductives des *Nuits*

Note: Dans un souci de concision, les manuscrits sont désignés par leur acronyme, tant dans cette illustration que dans le texte. Manuscrits et acronymes figurent en annexe 1, sous forme de liste et de tableau récapitulatif, v. p. 115. Les extraits de texte comparés ici proviennent tous du vol. 2, sauf dans le cas de P3 (dont le vol. 2 est manquant), v. *infra*, n. 72, p. 100.

En outre, quelques lettres au tracé franchement caractéristique avaient été scrutées plus attentivement, comme le font les paléographes occidentaux: l'*alif*, les oves des *fāʾ*, *qāf* et *wāw*, ou le degré d'ouverture des *dāl/dhāl*. Mais comme on l'a déjà souligné, l'arabe est une écriture intrinsèquement cursive dont la forme des lettres dépend grandement de leur environnement: un tel alphabet modèle ne suffisait pas pour aborder la morphologie des lettres. J'y avais donc ajouté la comparaison d'une formule entière identique (v. fig. 4.2, où seuls Mu et P1 sont de la main de ʿAlī l-Anṣārī).

Dans le cadre de cet article, j'ai donc décidé d'appliquer la méthode SHOE, en l'adaptant aux particularités de l'arabe. Je dois reconnaître que j'ai eu beaucoup de mal à observer les espaces blancs superflus au sein du texte. D'après Marie-Jeanne Sedeyn, consultée à ce sujet, c'est une question de pratique.

Par ailleurs, plusieurs critères de la méthode se sont révélés peu pertinents dans le cadre de l'analyse de ces manuscrits, et le sont de manière générale pour l'analyse de manuscrits arabes copiés par des scribes. Ainsi, les données relatives au support, à l'instrument et aux encres étaient identiques et n'ont donc fourni aucune information utile. Une analyse plus fine de ces critères, surtout des encres, ferait certainement apparaître des divergences, sans qu'elles soient nécessairement significatives non plus – rien n'empêche un même copiste d'utiliser différents types d'encres… Les critères concernant l'ordonnance et l'utilisation de l'espace ont également été peu opportuns, l'utilisation du papier, le sens de l'écriture et la proportion de la page laissée en marge correspondant à des habitudes de scribes très courantes. Par contre, la linéarité des marges fait apparaître différents groupes de manuscrits et est donc intéressante à première vue, mais se revèle peu pertinente dans un deuxième temps; en effet, les différences par rapport à la verticale sont peu affirmées (plus ou moins une lettre) et sont à corréler à la vitesse d'exécution. Ainsi, bien que tracés par la même main, les marges de SP, rédigé avec soin et à un rythme posé, sont bien plus rectilinéaires que celles de Lg, copié plus rapidement. Dans le chapitre "dimensions et proportions", seul le critère de la proportion hauteur-largeur a donné des résultats, les autres critères étant soit trop peu précis, soit trop conditionnés par le modèle d'écriture, que ces scribes professionnels maîtrisent évidemment, ce qui explique également que les critères de pression, vitesse et morphologie soient eux aussi peu pertinents.

Pour résumer, les éléments d'analyse de la méthode SHOE qui se sont révélés judicieux concernent: les axes des lettres, la ligne de base, les proportions hauteur-largeur des lettres, les degré, type et système de liaison, la densité du texte et les espacements au sein de celui-ci et, enfin, les habitudes graphiques. Remarquons que ces critères sont précisément ceux que Marie-Jeanne Sedeyn désigne comme étant les plus pertinents[70].

Cette démarche nouvelle, alliant certains critères de la méthode SHOE adaptés à la situation en présence et des critères dont l'utilité a été empiriquement établie, a donc été appliquée aux manuscrits de la première phase de la recension égyptienne des *Mille et une Nuits*. Un échantillon de 3 pages[71] a été soumis à l'analyse et, en cas de doute, d'autres feuillets ont été consultés. Dans un premier temps, ce sont principalement des feuillets issus du deuxième volume

70 V. *supra*, p. 93.

71 Sur l'étendue de texte à examiner pour pouvoir conduire une analyse, v. Huber et Headrick, *Handwriting* 249-50.

de chacun des ensembles qui ont été analysés[72]. Les résultats de l'analyse ne concordant pas toujours avec les informations issues des colophons signés, des feuillets d'autres volumes ont à leur tour été examinés, ce qui a mis au jour le fait que tous les volumes d'un même ensemble n'avaient pas toujours été copiés par la même main. Cette deuxième phase du travail a profité de la première, puisque seuls les critères vraiment pertinents ont été étudiés, à savoir ceux qui concernent le degré de liaison et le parcours du geste (particulièrement le système de liaison et le tracé des oves) et les habitudes graphiques, notamment les points diacritiques (bien que les conclusions que l'on peut tirer de ces observations soient moins claires).

Les résultats de ces analyses, présentés sous forme de tableaux (v. 4.2-4.3), indiquent que deux mains sont responsables de la copie d'au moins vingt-cinq des vingt-huit volumes qui constituent le corpus[73]. Si l'une d'entre elles, le copiste des manuscrits L, Lg, SP et Christie's (au moins du vol. 4) et des vols. 1, 3 et 4 de P1, 2 et 3 de P2, 1 et 4 de P3, reste anonyme (on l'appelera scribe 1), l'autre, un certain ʿAlī l-Anṣārī b. al-shaykh Ibrāhīm al-Anṣārī, a signé trois colophons : ceux du vol. 2 de P1, du vol. 4 de P2 et du vol. 4 de Mu et est identifiable sur cinq autres volumes (vol. 1 de P2, vol. 3 de P3 et vols. 1-3 de Mu).

Les caractéristiques qui permettent de différencier les deux scripteurs sont multiples (cf. les fig. 4.3-4.5 : scribe 1 et 4.6-4.7 : ʿAlī l-Anṣārī). La ligne de base des écrits du scribe 1 est instable, alors que celle de ʿAlī l-Anṣārī est rectiligne. Les proportions hauteur-largeur diffèrent également : les *dāl* et *ʿayn* initiaux du scribe 1 s'inscrivent dans un carré, contrairement à ceux de ʿAlī l-Anṣārī, qui sont plus élancés – ils s'inscrivent dans un rectangle vertical. L'aspect général des liaisons est aussi très différent : celles de ʿAlī l-Anṣārī donnent une impression anguleuse, alors qu'elles sont arrondies, car elles sont réduites à l'extrême ; autrement dit, les lettres de ʿAlī l-Anṣārī sont plus proches les unes des autres que celles du scribe 1. De la même manière, les espaces entre les mots sont très réduits, chez ʿAlī l-Anṣārī, à tel point qu'ils ne sont que rarement plus importants que ceux pouvant exister au sein des mots, ce qui complique parfois la lecture et ce qui accroît l'impression que le texte est un bloc uniforme.

72 Sauf dans le cas de P3, dont le volume 2 est perdu. L'explication de ce choix est simplement pragmatique : ayant édité un conte issu du deuxième volume, je disposais principalement de reproductions de ce volume précis.

73 Les volumes 1, 2 et 3 de Christie's n'ont pas pu être analysés, leur acquéreur restant à ce jour inconnu (le vendeur aussi, du reste). Les responsables de la vente chez Christie's ont été contactés à plusieurs reprises, mais n'ont jamais donné suite à mes questions ; je suppose que l'acheteur n'a pas désiré se faire connaître.

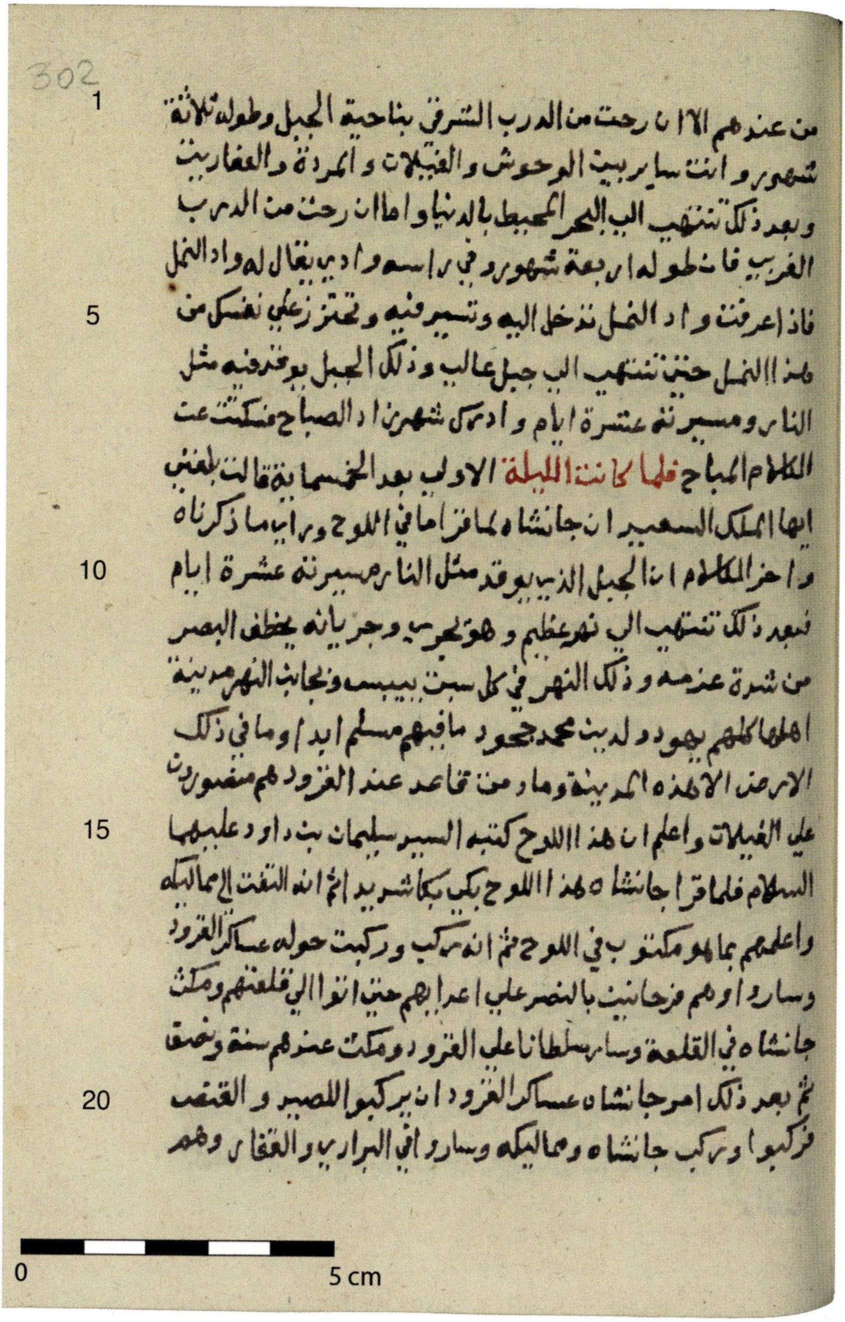

302

من عندهم الا ان رحت من الدرب الشرقي بناحية الجبل وطوله ثلاثة
شهور وانت ساير بين الوحوش والغيلات والمردة والعفاريت
وبعد ذلك تنتهي الى البحر المحيط بالدنيا واما ان رحت من الدرب
الغربي فان طوله اربعة شهور وفي راسه وادي يقال له واد النمل
فاذا عرفت واد النمل تدخل اليه وتسير فيه وتحترز على نفسك من
هذا النمل حتى تنتهي الى جبل عالي وذلك الجبل يوقد فيه مثل
النار ومسيرته عشرة ايام وادرك شهرزاد الصباح فسكتت عن
الكلام المباح فلما كانت الليلة الاولى بعد الخمسماية قالت بلغني
ايها الملك السعيد ان جانشاه لما قرا ما في اللوح ورايما ذكرناه
واخر الكلام ان الجبل الذي يوقد مثل النار مسيرته عشرة ايام
فبعد ذلك تنتهي الى نهر عظيم وهو يجري وجريانه يخطف البصر
من شدة عزمه وذلك النهر في كل سبت ييبس وبجانب النهر مدينة
اهلها كلهم يهود ولدين محمد جحود ما فيهم مسلم ابدا وما في ذلك
الارض الا هذه المدينة وما دمت قاعد عند القرود هم منصورون
على الغيلات واعلم ان هذا اللوح كتبه السيد سليمان بن داود عليهما
السلام فلما قرا جانشاه هذا اللوح بكى بكا شديدا ثم انه التفت الى مماليكه
واعلمهم بما هو مكتوب في اللوح ثم انه ركب وركبت حوله عساكر القرود
وساروا وهم فرحانين بالنصر على اعدايهم حتى اتوا الى قلعتهم ومكث
جانشاه في القلعة وسار سلطانا على القرود ومكث عندهم سنة ونصف
ثم بعد ذلك امر جانشاه عساكر القرود ان يركبوا للصيد والقنص
فركبوا وركب جانشاه ومماليكه وساروا في البراري والقفار وهم

FIGURE 4.3 Scribe 1 (MS B-1114, vol. 2, f. 302)
SAINT-PÉTERSBOURG, INSTITUTE OF ORIENTAL MANUSCRIPTS. PHOTO: IOM, SAINT-PÉTERSBOURG

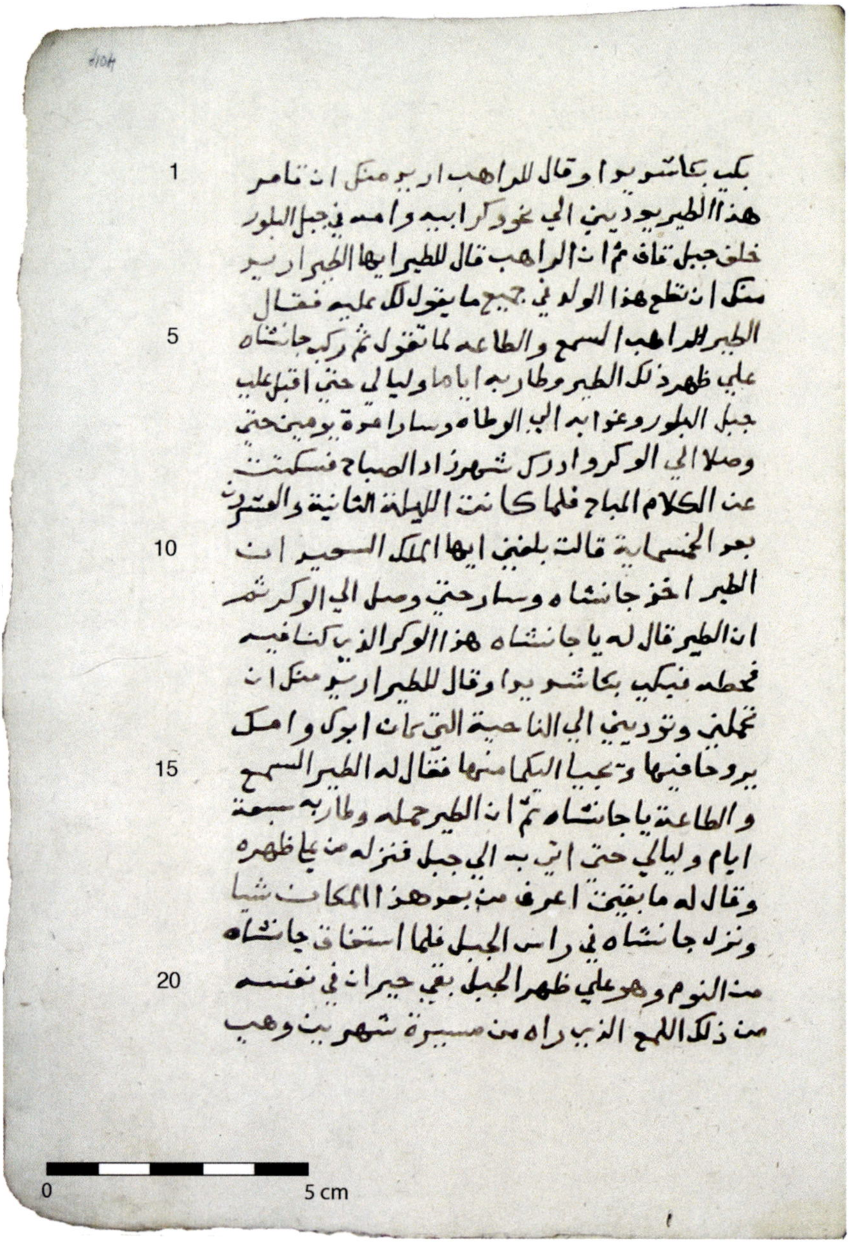
بكي بكاشتو بوا وقال للراهب اريد منك ان تامر
هذا الطير يوديني الي نحو وكر ابيه وامه في جبل البلور
خلف جبل قاف ثم ان الراهب قال للطير ايها الطير اريد
منك ان تطلع هذا الولد في جميع ما يقول لك عليه فقال
الطير للراهب السمع والطاعه لما تقول ثم ركب جانشاه
علي ظهر ذلك الطير وطار به اياما وليالي حتي اقبل علي
جبل البلور وغاب به الي الوطاه وسار امه يومين حتي
وصلا الي الوكر وادرك شهرزاد الصباح فسكتت
عن الكلام المباح فلما كانت الليلة الثانية والعشرين
بعد الخمسماية قالت بلغني ايها الملك السعيد ان
الطير اخذ جانشاه وسار حتي وصل الي الوكر ثم
ان الطير قال له يا جانشاه هذا الوكر الذي كنا فيه
محطه فبكي بكاشتو بوا وقال للطير اريد منك ان
تحملني وتوديني الي الناحية التي كان ابوك وامك
يروحا فيها وتجيا البكا منها فقال له الطير السمع
والطاعة يا جانشاه ثم ان الطير حمله وطار به سبعة
ايام وليالي حتي اتي به الي جبل فنزله من علي ظهره
وقال له ما بقيت اعرف من بعد هذا المكان شيا
ونزل جانشاه في راس الجبل فلما استفاق جانشاه
من النوم وهو علي ظهر الجبل بقي حيران في نفسه
من ذلك اللمح الذي راه من مسيرة شهرين وهب

FIGURE 4.4 Scribe 1 (MS 2241, f. 404)
LIÈGE, LIÈGE UNIVERSITÉ, BIBLIOTHÈQUE D'ARCHITECTURE, LETTRES, PHILOSOPHIE, HISTOIRE ET ARTS. PHOTO É.F.

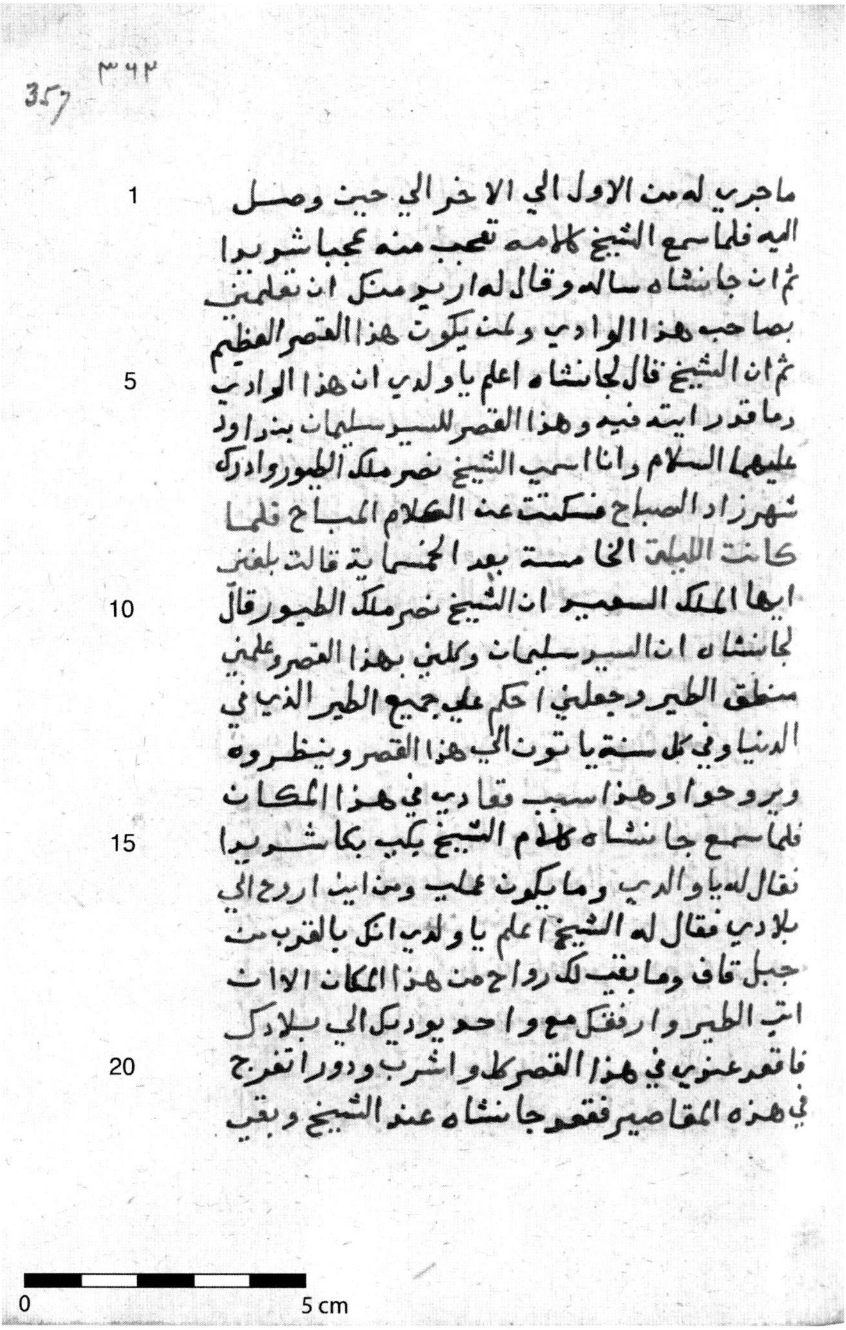

٣٦٢
357

ماجرى له من الاول الي الاخر الي حين وصل
اليه فلما سمع الشيخ كلامه تعجب منه عجبا شديدا
ثم ان جانشاه ساله وقال له اريد منك ان تعلمني
بصاحب هذا الوادي ولمن يكون هذا القصر العظيم
ثم ان الشيخ قال لجانشاه اعلم يا ولدي ان هذا الوادي
وما قد رايته فيه وهذا القصر للسيد سليمان بن داود
عليهما السلام وانا اسمي الشيخ نصر ملك الطيور وادرك
شهرزاد الصباح فسكتت عن الكلام المباح فلما
كانت الليلة الخامسة بعد الخمسماية قالت بلغني
ايها الملك السعيد ان الشيخ نصر ملك الطيور قال
لجانشاه ان السيد سليمان وكلني بهذا القصر وعلمني
منطق الطير وجعلني احكم علي جميع الطير الذي في
الدنيا وفي كل سنة يا تون الي هذا القصر وينظروه
ويروحوا وهذا سبب قعادي في هذا المكان
فلما سمع جانشاه كلام الشيخ بكي بكا شديدا
فقال له يا والدي وما يكون عملي ومن اين اروح الي
بلادي فقال له الشيخ اعلم يا ولدي انك بالقرب من
جبل قاف وما بقي لك رواح من هذا المكان الا ان
اتي الطير وارفقك مع واحد يوديك الي بلادك
فاقعد عندي في هذا القصر كل واشرب ودور اتفرج
في هذه المقاصير فقعد جانشاه عند الشيخ وبقي

0 5 cm

FIGURE 4.5 Scribe 1 (MS Or. 2917, f. 57)
LONDON, BRITISH LIBRARY. PHOTO: BL

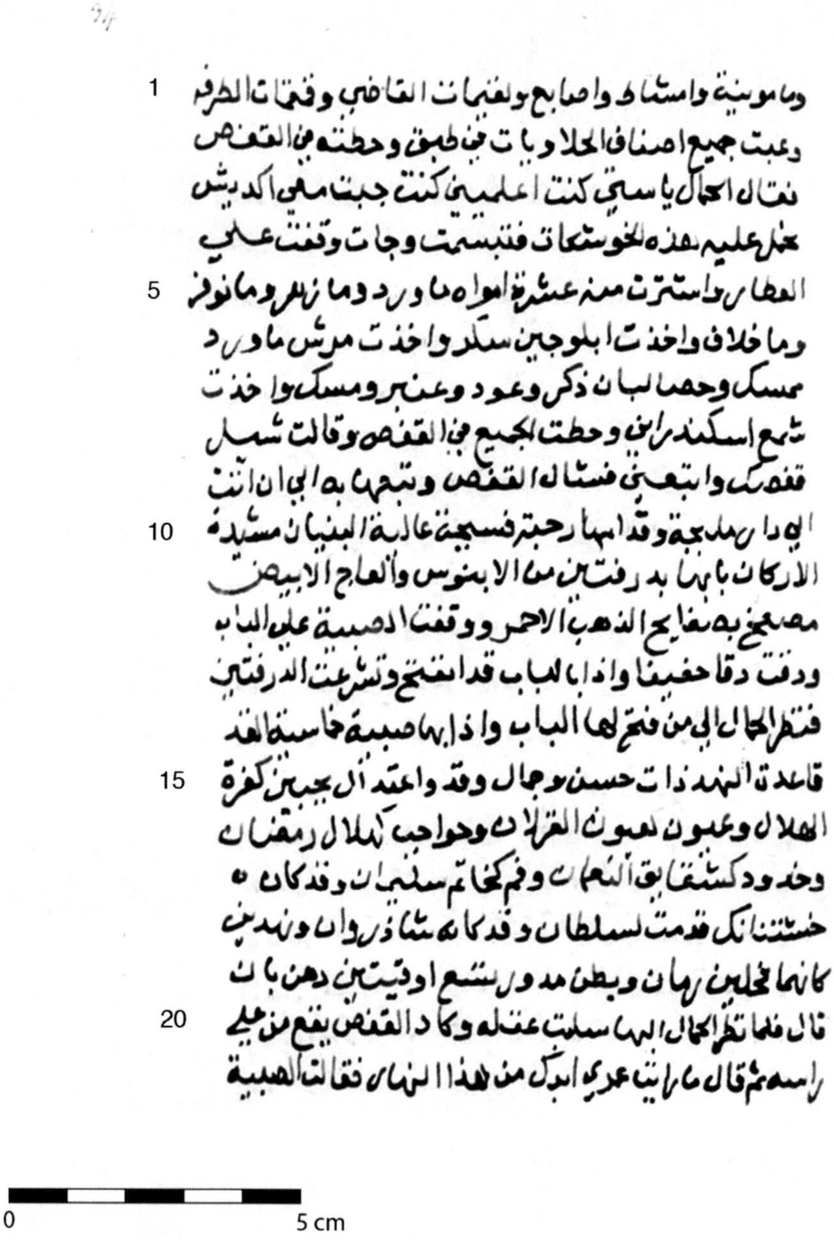

FIGURE 4.6 ʿAlī l-Anṣārī (MS Ar. 3602, f. 34)
PARIS, BNF. PHOTO: BNF

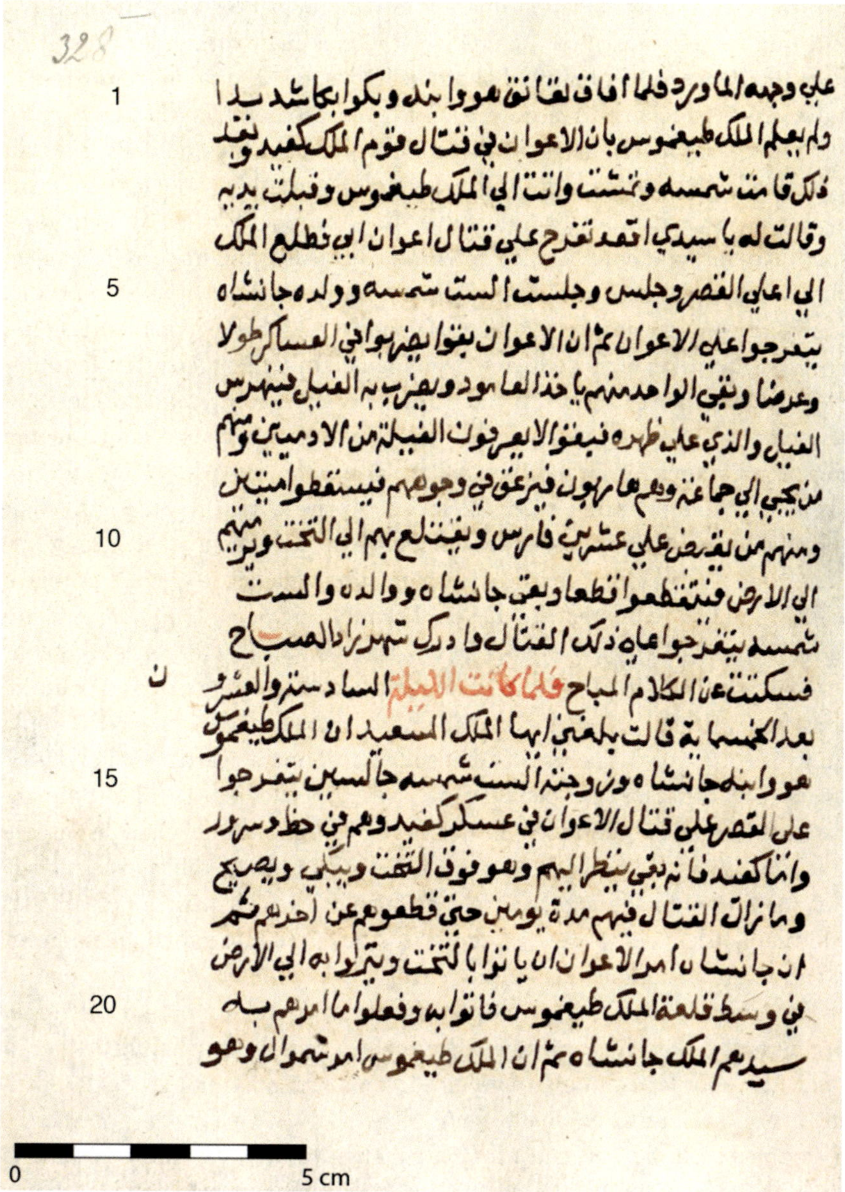

FIGURE 4.7 ʿAlī l-Anṣārī (MS Cod. ar. 624, f. 328)
MUNICH, BAYERISCHE STAATSBIBLIOTHEK. PHOTO BSB

Mais le critère principal permettant de différencier les deux mains est le parcours du geste. Le scribe 1 a une façon bien à lui de former les oves : il les trace toujours en deux temps, d'abord la boucle, en partant du sommet de la lettre vers la gauche, puis la suite, avec un recouvrement dans la partie droite de la lettre, recouvrement parfois incomplet, laissant un vide dans la partie droite de l'ove (v. par exemple fig. 4.3, l. 2 : *shuhūr* et plus loin, *al-wuḥūsh*, et fig. 4.4, l. 18 : *aʿrifu*, et fig. 4.2), alors que ʿAlī l-Anṣārī les forme d'un seul geste continu démarrant dans la partie inférieure de l'ove. Toujours dans le chapitre du parcours du geste, une différence notable entre les deux écritures que nous analysons concerne les *sīn*/*shīn*. Sous la main de ʿAlī l-Anṣārī, deux cas de figure sont possibles : soit leurs denticules sont bien marqués, soit ils sont volontairement lissés (v. par ex. fig. 4.6, l. 5 : *ʿashara* et fig. 4.7, l. 21 : *sayyiduhum*) ; pour le scribe 1, ces lettres présentent toujours des denticules et ceux-ci sont toujours très peu marqués (v. par ex. fig. 4.5, l. 15 : *al-shaykh* ou fig. 4.4, l. 21 : *masīra*). Un point commun entre les deux scribes concerne le tracé de l'*alif*, qui se fait (presque) toujours de haut en bas, même s'il est rattaché à la lettre le précédant. Dans ce cas, le scribe trace la liaison entre cette lettre et l'*alif*, puis lève son calame pour commencer l'*alif* par le haut (v. fig. 4.4, l. 4 : *fa-qāla*, ou l. 19 : *Jānshāh*, fig. 4.5, l. 11 : *Sulaymān* et fig. 4.6, l. 1 : *al-qāḍī*, où la forme et la couleur du trait, plus épais et plus foncé en haut, ne laissent aucune place au doute ; v. aussi fig. 4.2). Chez ʿAlī l-Anṣārī, dans certains cas, ce trait de liaison est si ample qu'il n'est presque pas nécessaire d'ensuite tracer un trait vertical pour l'*alif* (v. fig. 4.7, l. 12 : *al-ṣabāḥ*). Les deux personnages respecteraient-ils les recommandations des traités théoriques sur l'écriture préconisant une analogie entre le tracé de l'*alif* et la chute de l'Homme sur Terre[74] ? C'est possible, mais ce tracé est plus vraisemblablement à corréler au fait que les traits tirés sont plus faciles à former que les traits poussés[75], cette façon de faire s'illustrant d'ailleurs pour d'autres lettres, comme nous allons le voir.

En termes de morphologie, plusieurs formes de lettres sont particulières et permettent de distinguer les deux scripteurs[76]. En suivant l'alphabet, après l'*alif*, déjà abordé, il faut mentionner les *bāʾ*/*tāʾ*/*thāʾ* qui sont particulièrement incurvés dans leur forme finale, chez ʿAlī l-Anṣārī (v. fig. 4.7, l. 13 : *fa-sakatat*, à comparer à la fig. 4.5, l. 2 : *taʿajjaba* ; v. aussi fig. 4.2). Le scribe 1 forme la tête des *jīm*/*ḥāʾ*/*khāʾ* en un seul trait, qu'il soit ondulant (une sorte de volute, v. fig. 4.5, l. 15 : *Jānshāh*) ou droit et oblique, laissant dès lors la tête de la lettre ouverte (v. fig. 4.2, particulièrement Lg), alors que ʿAlī l-Anṣārī la trace à

74 Comme suggéré dans Atanasiu, Le rétroencrage 34 pour expliquer ce genre de pratique.

75 Cette règle des "pushed" et "pulled strokes" est exposée dans Gumbert, The Pen 14.

76 Seules les lettres et parties de lettres caractéristiques sont abordées.

l'aide de deux traits, lui donnant une apparence plus anguleuse (fig. 4.6, l. 12 : *al-aḥmar*). Les *dāl*/*dhāl* du scribe 1 sont très ouverts (v. fig. 4.5, l. 21 : *ʿind* ou fig. 4.3, l. 14 : *al-qurūd*) – ils forment un angle de 90-100° – alors que ceux de ʿAlī l-Anṣārī sont plutôt fermés (v. fig. 4.7, l. 1 : *wa-radda*) – angle de 70-90° (v. aussi fig. 4.2). La queue du *sīn* final du scribe 1 est dans le prolongement de la ligne d'écriture (fig. 4.3, l. 12 : *yaybasu*), quand celle tracée par ʿAlī l-Anṣārī descend sous la ligne d'écriture d'autant que celle du *rāʾ* (fig. 4.6, l. 6 : *mirashsh*). Les *ṭāʾ*/*ẓāʾ* du scribe 1 sont systématiquement formés en deux temps, la hampe n'étant tracée qu'après l'ove, de haut en bas, comme l'*alif* (v. fig. 4.5, l. 7 : *al-ṭuyūr*), alors que ceux de ʿAlī l-Anṣārī sont tracés en un mouvement, de haut en bas, leur hampe étant légèrement inclinée (v. fig. 4.6, l. 1 : *amshāṭ*).

Les têtes des *ʿayn*/*ghayn* sont assez différentes aussi d'un scribe à l'autre ; à l'initiale, le trait inférieur de celles de ʿAlī l-Anṣārī s'arrête toujours légèrement plus loin que l'amorce du trait supérieur (v. fig. 4.7, l. 19 : *al-aʿwān*), leur donnant un air incliné dans le sens de l'écriture, tandis que celles du scribe 1 sont droites, les deux traits se trouvant au même niveau (v. fig. 4.5, l. 5 : *iʿlam*). Dans leur forme médiane et finale, elles sont plutôt arrondies, couchées sur la ligne d'écriture et obliques dans le sens de l'écriture chez le scribe 1 (v. fig. 4.5, l. 12 : *jamīʿ* ou fig. 4.4, l. 15 : *al-samʿ*) et en forme de triangle sur pointe chez ʿAlī l-Anṣārī (fig. 4.7, l. 20 : *Ṭīghmūs*). Les *lām-alif* de ʿAlī l-Anṣārī sont toujours du type *mukhaffafa marshūqa*[77] (fig. 4.6, l. 11 : *al-abnūs*), quand ceux du scribe 1 sont *warrāqiyya*[78] (fig. 4.5, l. 1 : *al-awwal*), avec la singularité supplémentaire (fréquente, surtout après un *kāf*) d'une ligature à droite ressemblant à un *lām* supplémentaire (v. fig. 4.3, l. 10 : *al-kalām* ou fig. 4.5, l. 2 : *kalāmahu* et fig. 4.2, surtout Lg et SP). Chez ʿAlī l-Anṣārī, la queue des *kāf* et *lām* finaux n'est pas horizontale, mais arrondie et très concave, et ne descend que peu sous la ligne de base (fig. 4.6, l. 7 : *misk* et fig. 4.7, l. 2 : *qitāl*). La tête du *mīm* initial varie également d'un scribe à l'autre. Très arrondie, petite et donc souvent remplie d'encre chez le scribe 1 (pochage, v. fig. 4.3, l. 14 : *manṣūrūna*), elle est au contraire fine et anguleuse chez ʿAlī l-Anṣārī (fig. 4.7, l. 18 : *muddat yawmayn*). En position médiane et finale, elle se trouve sous la ligne d'écriture pour l'un (fig. 4.3, l. 15 : *Sulaymān*) et posée dessus pour l'autre (ʿAlī l-Anṣārī, fig. 4.7, l. 3 : *Shamsa*). De la même manière que la queue du *sīn* final est dans le prolongement de la ligne d'écriture, le *nūn* final du scribe 1 est si peu incurvé qu'il ne descend que peu (ou pas) sous la ligne d'écriture et qu'il ressemble parfois à un *bāʾ* portant son point au-dessus de lui (v. fig. 4.3, l. 2 : *sāyirīn* [*sic*] ou fig. 4.4,

77 Gacek, *Vademecum* 319-20 (appendix II, num. 62).

78 Ibid. (appendix II, num. 59).

l. 10 : *inna* et fig. 4.2, surtout P3 et Lg) ; sous le calame de ʿAlī l-Anṣārī, il est bien incurvé et son point diacritique est parfois dans son prolongement direct, et non centré (v. fig. 4.7, l. 14 : *inna* et fig. 4.6, l. 17 : *kāna*).

Venons-en au *hāʾ*, qui était à scruter particulièrement dans notre compréhension de la méthode SHOE, et ce, par analogie au "o" latin ; chez le scribe 1, le *hāʾ* isolé adopte la forme d'une goutte d'eau dont la pointe est légèrement décentrée sur la droite (fig. 4.4, l. 12 ou fig. 4.5, l. 3 : *Jānshāh* dans les deux cas), tandis que chez ʿAlī l-Anṣārī, il est arrondi (fig. 4.7, l. 11 : *Jānshāh* ou fig. 4.6, l. 4 : *hādhihi*), son trait d'attaque étant vertical et placé en haut à droite de la lettre (et non au centre). Le *hāʾ* initial prend toujours la forme d'un *hāʾ* médian *mashqūqa*, avec deux boucles, ce qui fait de lui un *hāʾ mulawwaza*[79] (fig. 4.3, l. 6 : *hādhā*), chez le scribe 1, alors qu'il est plus conforme au modèle pour ʿAlī l-Anṣārī (c'est-à-dire *wajh al-hirr*[80], v. fig. 4.7, l. 16 : *hum*), dont le *hāʾ* médian est de type *mudghama*[81] (fig. 4.6, l. 10 : *quddāmahā*). Enfin, le *yāʾ* final ou isolé du scribe 1 est particulièrement couché sur la ligne d'écriture (fig. 4.3, l. 11 : *yajrī*, fig. 4.4, l. 21 : *hiya*[82] ou fig. 4.5, l. 12 : *al-ladhī*)[83].

L'observation des points diacritiques n'a pas donné autant de résultat qu'escompté ; cependant, les trois points du *shīn* ou du *thāʾ* permettent de différencier les scripteurs : ʿAlī l-Anṣārī les trace d'un seul geste, leur conférant une forme particulière caractéristique (v. fig. 4.7, l. 1 : *shadīdan*, ou l. 11 : *Janshāh*, ou l. 12 : *Shamsa*, ou fig. 4.6, l. 5 : *ʿashara*, ou l. 8 : *shīl* [*sic*]), alors que chez le scribe 1, ceux-ci sont la plupart du temps différenciés (fig. 4.3, l. 1 : *thalātha* ou fig. 4.5, l. 5 : *thumma* et *al-shaykh*) ou alors, de formes variées (fig. 4.5, comparer *al-shaykh* l. 15 et l. 17 et fig. 4.2).

Enfin, il est manifeste que ʿAlī l-Anṣārī a apporté plus de soin à la copie des manuscrits que le scribe 1, dont le rythme de travail apparaît en général plus rapide[84]. La rectilinéarité plus ou moins affirmée des marges, point déjà abordé, va dans ce sens. C'est aussi l'opinion formulée par von Hammer, qui compara trois manuscrits certainement copiés par le scribe 1 (SP, le ms. de

79 Ibid. (appendix II, num. 45, 48).

80 Ibid. (appendix II, num. 46).

81 Ibid. (appendix II, num. 47).

82 D'autant plus couché ici que le mot est le dernier de la ligne et qu'il faut remplir tout l'espace restant.

83 Les prépositions se terminant en *yāʾ* (*fī*) ou en *alif maqṣūra* (*ʿalā*, *ilā*) n'ont pas été prises en compte car elles sont si courtes et fréquentes qu'elles peuvent être considérées comme des symboles monolitères et non comme des mots constitués de plusieurs lettres. À cet égard, v. p. 94 et n. 51.

84 Dommage que les colophons ne présentent pas d'information sur la durée de travail nécessaire pour terminer une copie complète de cette recension des *Nuits*.

Clarke and Crisps, aujourd'hui perdu, et le ms. de Varsy, parfois identifé à P2[85]) à sa copie personnelle, aujourd'hui disparue, signée ʿAlī l-Anṣārī : "Aucun de ces trois manuscrits ne peut être comparé avec le nôtre sous le rapport de la netteté et de l'élégance de l'écriture ; car il est en même temps aussi beau que correct et lisible"[86]. Un faisceau d'éléments concordants désigne donc ʿAlī l-Anṣārī comme étant le père de la recension égyptienne. Pour répondre à la demande insistante et constante de tant d'Occidentaux, ce lettré – comme son écriture rapide et assurée et sa désignation comme "shaykh fils de shaykh" et descendant d'un compagnon du Prophète, si l'on en croit son *laqab* – réalise donc un manuscrit modèle, dont il fera plusieurs copies lui-même, avec soin, qu'il datera et signera. La demande ne tarissant pas, il se fera seconder d'un scribe professionnel, très vraisemblablement payé à la copie et non à l'heure, si l'on en croit la vitesse à laquelle il semble travailler, et moins concentré sur le texte, travaillant sans doute sur plusieurs ensembles à la fois, puisque des hiatus et erreurs dans les numéros de nuits d'un volume à l'autre apparaissent dans ses manuscrits. La demande restant importante, leur travail sera complété par d'autres scribes, formant ensuite la deuxième phase de la recension et, encore plus tard, vers 1840, une autre recension[87].

4 En guise de conclusion

L'idée d'appliquer une méthode rationnelle d'identification des écritures avait fait naître de grands espoirs et des éléments d'analyse nouveaux et intéressants ont été mis en évidence. On reste évidemment loin d'une méthode miracle, rapide et efficace dans tous les cas de figures : l'œil exercé et l'expérience demeurent incontournables – comment aurait-il pu en être autrement ? ... –, mais de grands pas sont franchis dans la direction d'une rationalisation des études paléographiques arabes.

En effet, il ressort de notre analyse que plusieurs nouveaux critères, outre les formes particulières de lettres, sont pertinents pour les études de mains arabes. Ainsi, les axes des lettres sont intéressants, bien que ce critère doive être couplé à d'autres et ne puisse, seul, entraîner l'identification (ou la réfu-

85 Elisséeff, *Thèmes* 61.

86 von Hammer-Purgstall et Trébutien, *Contes inédits* III et XXXVIII. Pour l'analyse du texte et la fréquence légèrement accrue de plusieurs marques du Moyen Arabe dans les copies du scribe 1, v. Franssen, *Les Manuscrits* i, 220-228, et ii.

87 Représentée par le manuscrit Reinhardt, v. Marzolph et al., *The Arabian Nights* 20 ; Chraïbi, *Contes*.

tation) formelle d'un scripteur. Il en va de même pour les conclusions tirées de l'étude de la ligne de base, des proportions hauteur-largeur des lettres (les *dāl/dhāl* et *ʿayn/ghayn* servant d'étalon), et de la linéarité des marges, qui donne une idée de la rapidité d'exécution de la copie en présence. Quant aux éléments révélateurs du système de liaison, ils sont véritablement distinctifs et se sont montrés décisifs pour ce cas d'étude. Les habitudes graphiques, particulièrement l'usage des points diacritiques, ne sont pas à négliger non plus, même si une seule caractéristique manifeste est apparue dans ce cas d'étude. Les critères de densité et d'espacement au sein du texte sont certainement importants, mais plus difficiles à maîtriser pour le novice.

Nous sommes donc bien loin de l'étude exigeante et chronophage des 381 critères de la méthode SHOE. Et tant mieux: nos documents de travail sont d'une ampleur autrement plus importante que ceux sur lesquels se penchent généralement les experts judiciaires. Par ailleurs, les conséquences d'une erreur de notre part sont beaucoup moins graves que pour un expert judiciaire. Enfin, nous sommes rarement confrontés à des documents de faussaires qui déguiseraient volontairement leur écriture. Dès lors, en dépit du credo de Marie-Jeanne Sedeyn sur la vision globale des documents, il n'est à mon sens ni réaliste, ni nécessaire de prendre en compte tous les critères de la méthode pour chaque étude. Par contre, observer la petite dizaine de données pertinentes mises en évidence ici n'est pas trop fastidieux et permet tout de même de tester une intuition et d'asseoir plus fermement une attribution.

Outre cette avancée théorique pour les études d'écritures, l'analyse détaillée des deux graphies représentées dans les manuscrits de la première phase chronologique de la recension égyptienne des *Mille et une Nuits* précise le statut des manuscrits en présence: modèles pour ceux d'al-Anṣārī et reproductions pour ceux du scribe 1. D'ailleurs, l'analyse philologique des textes confirme cette déduction[88]. En outre, l'attention fine portée aux mains a montré que, contrairement aux autres, les ensembles de la BnF (P1, P2 et P3) étaient particulièrement hétérogènes en termes de mains (v. annexe 1 et tableau 4.1). En effet, tous les autres ensembles complets sont intégralement de la même main: du scribe 1 pour L et SP et de ʿAlī l-Anṣārī pour Mu. Il semble possible de reconstituer trois ensembles homogènes avec les volumes de Paris et celui de Liège, l'un de la main de ʿAlī l-Anṣārī et deux de celle de son scribe. Ainsi, on doit à ʿAlī l-Anṣārī un ensemble constitué de vol. 1 = P2 (nuits 1-214), vol. 2 = P1 (nuits 215-536), vol. 3 = P3 (nuits [537]-771[89]), vol. 4 = P2 (nuits 771-1001). Les deux ensembles de scribe 1 se composent comme suit: vol. 1 = P1 (nuits 1-214) et P3

88 V. Franssen, *Les Manuscrits* i, 220-228, et ii.

89 Acéphale, la première nuit numérotée est la cinq-cent-quarante-neuvième; la comparai-

(nuits 1-220)[90], vol. 2 = P2 et Lg (nuits 218-536)[91], vol. 3 = P1 et P2 (nuits 537-771), vol. 4 = P1 et P3 (nuits 771-1001).

Enfin, la systématisation que suppose cette méthode ne peut qu'être positive ; elle est particulièrement utile dans le cadre de l'étude de manuscrits holographes. Une connaissance précise des caractéristiques personnelles de l'écriture d'un auteur permettrait certainement l'identification d'autres holographes, tout en faisant avancer la recherche sur les variations de l'écriture avec le temps et l'âge du scripteur. Ces données enregistrées sur un formulaire type seraient à joindre à la base de données des manuscrits arabes holographes que nous préconisons de créer (comme indiqué dans l'introduction, p. 9), dans un champ dédié sur la fiche personnelle des auteurs.

Bibliographie

Al-Haddad, A., P.C. White, and D.M. Cole, Examination of a collection of Arabic signatures, dans *Journal of the American Society of Questioned Document Examiners* 12-1 (2009), 35-52.

Al-Musa Alkahtani, A., and A.W.G. Platt, Relative difficulty of freehand simulation of four proportional elements in Arabic signatures, dans *Journal of the American Society for Questioned Document Examiners* 12-2 (2009), 69-75.

Akel, I., Liste des manuscrits arabes des *Nuits*, dans A. Chraïbi (dir.), *Arabic manuscripts of the Thousand and One Nights. Presentation and critical editions of four noteworthy texts. Observations on some Osmanli translations*, Paris 2016, 65-114.

Atanasiu, V., Le Rétroencrage. Analyse du ductus des écritures d'après le dégradé du coloris des encres, dans *Gazette du Livre médiéval* 37 (2000), 34-42.

Aumer, J., *Die arabischen Handschriften der K. Hof- und Staatsbibliothek in Muenchen*, Munich 1866.

Bauden, F., *Al-Maqrīzī's collection of opuscules : An introduction*, Leiden-Boston (à paraître).

Bauden, F., *Catalogue of the Arabic, Persian and Turkish manuscripts in Belgium. Vol. 1: Handlist. Part 1: Université de Liège*, Leiden-Boston 2017.

---

son avec le texte de Mu indique qu'il manque deux quinions et que le texte du volume commençait plus que probablement à la cinq-cent-trente-septième nuit.

90 Comme le volume 2 de Mu, qui a donc servi de modèle pour la copie de ce volume.

91 À l'exception de P1 et de sa copie L, qui commencent à la nuit 220, tous les volumes 2 de cette première phase de la recension débutent à la nuit 218, indépendamment du numéro de la dernière nuit de leur premier volume (celui-ci étant variable : 214, 215, 216 ou 220). Des flottements dans la numérotation des nuits de la fin du volume 1 sont manifestes et des tentatives de corrections sont observées (notamment dans SP).

Bauden, F., Maqriziana IX: Should al-Maqrīzī be thrown out with the bath water? The question of his plagiarism of al-Awḥadī's *Khiṭaṭ* and the documentary evidence, dans *Mamlūk Studies Review* XIV (2010), 159-232.

Bauden, F. et al., *Le Journal d'Antoine Galland (1646-1715). La période parisienne*, 4 vol., Louvain, Paris and Walpole 2011-5.

Bausi, A. et al., *Comparative Oriental manuscript studies: An introduction*, Hamburg 2015.

Beit-Arié, M., and N. Pasternak, Comfort of reading, comfort of writing: some reflections on line management, dans *Gazette du Livre médiéval* 31 (1997), 9-21.

Bencheikh, J.E., and A. Miquel, Préface, in *Les Mille et une Nuits*, Paris 2005, vol. 1, i-xlvi.

Boiarov, A. et al., Arabic manuscript author verification using deep convolutional networks (inédit).

Buquet, A., *L'Expertise des écritures manuscrites*, Paris 1991.

Buquet, A., *Manuel de criminalistique moderne et de police scientifique*, Paris 2011.

Chauvin, V., *Bibliographie des ouvrages arabes ou relatifs aux Arabes publiés dans l'Europe chrétienne de 1810 à 1885*, 12 vol., Liège-Leipzig 1892-1922.

Chraïbi, A., *Contes nouveaux des* 1001 Nuits. *Étude du manuscrit Reinhardt*, Paris 1996.

Chraïbi, A. (dir.), *Arabic manuscripts of the* Thousand and One Nights. *Presentation and critical editions of four noteworthy texts. Observations on some Osmanli translations*, Paris 2016.

Christie's, *Arts and textiles of the Islamic and Indian Worlds. [Auction at] South Kensington, 21 October 2016*, London 2016.

Coffinières, A.-S.-G., *Analyse des* Novelles *de Justinien, conférées avec l'ancien droit français et le Code Napoléon*, Paris 1805.

Déroche, F., *Catalogue des manuscrits arabes. Deuxième partie: Manuscrits musulmans. Tome I, 1: Les manuscrits du Coran. Aux origines de la calligraphie coranique*, Paris 1983.

Déroche, F., *Le Livre manuscrit arabe. Préludes à une histoire*, Paris 2004.

Déroche, F. et al., *Islamic codicology: An introduction to the study of manuscripts in Arabic script*, London 2005.

Déroche, F. et al., *Manuel de codicologie des manuscrits en écriture arabe*, Paris 2000.

Dictionnaire de l'Académie française, 9e édition (1986-…), en ligne http://atilf.atilf.fr/academie9.htm

D'Israeli, I., *A second series of curiosities of literature: Consisting of researches in literary, biographical, and political history of critical ans philosophical inquiries; and of secret history*, 3 vols., London 1824 (2e éd.).

Ellen, D., *Scientific examination of documents: Methods and techniques*, Boca Raton-New York 2012 (3rd ed.).

Elisséeff, N., *Thèmes et motifs des* Mille et une Nuits: *Essai de classification*, Beyrouth 1949.

Fischer, F. et al., *Kodikologie und Paläographie im Digitalen Zeitalter/Codicology and palaeography in the digital age*, 2 vol., Norderstedt 2010.

Franssen, É., *Les Manuscrits de la recension égyptienne des* Mille et une Nuits: *Étude codicologique, avec édition critique, traduction et analyse linguistique et littéraire du conte de Jānšāh*, Thèse de doctorat, sous la direction du Prof. F. Bauden, 3 vol., Liège Université 2012.

Franssen, É., Les Manuscrits ZER des *Mille et une Nuits*: le point sur leur support. Papiers filigranés européens de la fin du XVIIIe et du début du XIXe siècle, dans *Acta orientalia Belgica* XXV (2012), 329-343.

Gacek, A., *Arabic manuscripts: A vademecum for readers*, Leiden-Boston 2009.

Galland, A., and J.J.A. Caussin de Perceval, *Les Mille et une Nuits, contes arabes, traduits en français par M. Galland, membre de l'Académie des Inscriptions et Belles-Lettres, Professeur de langue arabe au Collège royal; continués par M. Caussin de Perceval, Professeur de langue arabe au Collège impérial*, Paris 1806.

Garcin, J.-Cl., *Pour une lecture historique des* Mille et Une nuits, Paris 2013.

Gervais, S.-L., Expertise en écriture et graphologie: deux pratiques bien distinctes, dans *Journal du Village des Notaires* 32 (2012), en ligne (http://www.village-notaires.com/Expertise-en-ecriture-et).

Guiral, M., *La Valeur de la preuve dans l'expertise des écritures*, Lyon 1927.

Gumbert, J.P., The pen and its movement: some general and less general remarks, dans *Gazette du Livre médiéval* 40 (2002), 14-24.

Günther, H., and O. Ludwig, *Schrift und Schriftlichkeit. Ein interdisziplinäres Handbuch internationaler Forschung*, Berlin-New York 1994.

Hagège, C., Traitement du sens et fidélité dans l'adaptation classique: sur le texte arabe des "Mille et Une Nuits" et la traduction de Galland, dans *Arabica* 27 (1980), 114-39.

Huber, R.A., et A.M. Headrick, *Handwriting identification: Facts and fundamentals*, Boca Raton-New York 1999.

Humbert, G., La fabrication du papier, in M.-G. Guesdon et A. Vernay-Nouri (éd.), *L'Art du livre arabe. Du manuscrit au livre d'artiste*, Paris 2001, 45-51.

Kapoor, T.S., M. Kapoor, and G.P. Sharma, Study of the form and extent of natural function of age, dans *Journal of the Forensic Science Society* 25 (1985), 371-5.

Khalidov, A.B., *Arabskie rukopisi Instituta Vostokovedeniya: kratkiĭ katalog*, Moskow 1986.

Larzul, S., *Les Traductions françaises des* Mille et Une Nuits: *Étude des versions Galland, Trébutien et Mardrus*, Paris 1996.

Lester, D., N. Werling, and N.H. Heinle, Differences in handwriting as a function of age, dans *Perceptual and Motor Skills* 57 (1983), 738-41.

Levey, M., *Medieval Arabic bookmaking and its relation to early chemistry and pharmacology*, Philadelphia 1962.

Marzolph, U., R. van Leeuwen, and H. Wassouf (collab.), *The Arabian Nights encyclopedia*, Santa Barbara (CA) – Denver (CO) – Oxford (England) 2004.

McGuckin de Slane, W., *Catalogue des manuscrits arabes*, Paris 1883-95.

Les Mille et une nuit [sic], contes arabes traduits en françois par M. Galland, 12 vol., Paris 1704-17.

Les Mille et une nuits, trad. J.E. Bencheikh and A. Miquel, 4 vol., Paris 2005-6.

Michel, P., *Quarante ans d'affaires criminelles 1969-2009*, Paris 2009.

Muhanna, E.I., *The Digital humanities and Islamic & Middle East studies*, Berlin 2016.

Münch, A., *L'Expertise en écritures et en signatures*, Québec 2000.

Patenaude, P., [Chronique bibliographique] L'Expertise en identification d'écritures et de signatures [Critique de l'ouvrage de A. Münch, Sillery, Septentrion, 2000], dans *Revue de droit de l'Université de Sherbrooke* 30 (2000), 423-4.

Pedersen, J., *The Arabic book*, Princeton 1984.

Polosin, V., Arabic manuscripts: Text density and its convertibility in copies of the same work, dans *Manuscripta Orientalia* 3-2 (1997), 3-17.

Rezvan, E.A., and N.S. Kondybaev, New tool for analysis of handwritten script, dans *Manuscripta Orientalia* 2-3 (1996), 43-53.

Rezvan, E.A., and N.S. Kondybaev, The ENTRAP software: Tests results, dans *Manuscripta Orientalia* 5-2 (1999), 58-64.

Rieu, Ch., *Supplement to the Catalogue of Arabic manuscripts [acquired since 1872]*, London 1894.

Rück, P., *Methoden der Schriftbeschreibung: Historische Hilfwissenschaften*, Stuttgart 1999.

Sedeyn, M.-J., *Délits d'écrits*, Paris 2002.

Sedeyn, M.-J., *Introduction à l'examen objectif des écritures manuscrites, Méthode SHOE à l'usage des médecins, sociologues, chercheurs, experts en écritures*, Meyreuil 1999.

Sedeyn, M.-J., Un dialogue constructif: archiviste paléographe et expert en écritures, dans P. Rück (éd.), *Methoden der Schriftbeschreibung: Historische Hilfwissenschaften*, Stuttgart 1999, 413-6.

Serikoff, N., Image and letter: "Pace" in Arabic script (a thumb-nail index as a tool for a catalogue of Arabic manuscripts: Principles and criteria for its construction), dans *Manuscripta Orientalia* 7-4 (2001), 55-66.

Sirat, C., *Writing as handwork: a history of handwriting in Mediterranean and Western culture*, Turnhout 2006.

von Hammer-Purgstall, J., and G.-St. Trébutien, *Contes inédits des Mille et Une Nuits*, 3 vol., Paris 1828.

Zotenberg, H., *Histoire d''Alâ al-Dîn ou la Lampe merveilleuse. Texte arabe publié avec une Notice sur quelques manuscrits des* Mille et Une Nuits *et la traduction de Galland*, Paris 1888.

Annexe 1 : Liste des manuscrits

a) Liège, Liège Université, Bibliothèque d'Architecture, Lettres, Philosophie, Histoire et Arts, MS 2241 (Lg)[92]
Incomplet : uniquement vol. 2 ; non daté, non signé ; 422 ff., de 228 × 163 mm, 21 l./p., lignes longues. Nuits 218 à 536. Examen détaillé des ff. 369, 384, 404. Scribe 1.

b) London, British Library, MS Or. 2916-2919 (L)[93]
Complet, non daté, non signé ; vol. 1 : 531 ff. de 240 × 168 mm, nuits 1-214 ; vol. 2 : 399 ff. de 236 × 171 mm, nuits 215-536 ; vol. 3 : 414 ff. de 214 × 154 mm, nuits 537-771 ; vol. 4 : 428 ff. de 224 × 156 mm, nuits 771-1001. 21 l./p., lignes longues. Examen détaillé des ff. 344, 352, 357 du vol. 2. Scribe 1.

c) Paris, BnF, MS Ar. 3598-3601 (P^1)[94]
Complet, non daté, vol. 2 signé ʿAlī l-Anṣārī b. al-shaykh Ibrāhīm al-Anṣārī ; vol. 1 : 532 ff. de 216 × 157 mm, nuits 1-214 ; vol. 2 : 334 ff. de 227 × 167 mm, nuits 215-536 ; vol. 3 : 368 ff. de 230 × 156 mm, nuits 537-771 ; vol. 4 : 392 ff. de 226 × 159 mm, nuits 771-1001. 21 l./p., lignes longues. Examen détaillé des ff. 291, 298 et 304 du vol. 2. Vol. 1 : scribe 1 ; vol. 2 : ʿAlī l-Anṣārī ; vol. 3 : scribe 1 ; vol. 4 : scribe 1.

d) Paris, BnF, MS Ar. 3602-3605 (P^2)[95]
Complet, non daté, vol. 4 signé ʿAlī l-Anṣārī b. al-shaykh Ibrāhīm al-Anṣārī ; vol. 1 : 481 ff. de 212 × 160 mm, nuits 1-214 ; vol. 2 : 408 ff. de 220 × 157 mm, nuits 218-536 ; vol. 3 : 414 ff. de 214 × 157 mm, nuits 537-771 ; vol. 4 : 345 ff. de 214 × 155 mm, nuits 771-1001. 21 l./p., lignes longues. Examen détaillé des ff. 356 et 357 du vol. 2. Vol. 1 : ʿAlī l-Anṣārī ; vol. 2 : scribe 1 ; vol. 3 : scribe 1 ; vol. 4 : ʿAlī l-Anṣārī.

e) Paris, BnF, MS Ar. 3606-3608 (P^3)[96]
Incomplet (manque vol. 2), non daté (*terminus ante quem* 1222/1807-8, v. empreinte de sceau datée sur le f. 72b du vol. 2), non signé ; vol. 1 : 548 ff. (555 avec annexes non contemporaines) de 230 × 162 mm, nuits 1-220 ; vol. 3 : 279 ff. de 218 × 164 mm, nuits 549-771 ; vol. 4 : 416 ff. de 218 × 154 mm, nuits 771-1001. 21 l./p., lignes longues. Examen détaillé des ff. 50, 359 et 436 du vol. 1. Vol. 1 : scribe 1 ; vol. 3 : ʿAlī l-Anṣārī ; vol. 4 : scribe 1.

---

92 Bauden, *Catalogue* 21.
93 Rieu, *Supplement* 738.
94 McGuckin de Slane, *Catalogue* 618-9.
95 Ibid. 619.
96 Ibid.

f) Saint-Pétersbourg, Institute of Oriental Manuscripts, MS B-1114 (SP)[97]
Complet, non daté, non signé ; vol. 1 : 495 ff. de 206 × 154 mm, nuits 1-216 ; vol. 2 : 338 ff. de 205 × 153 mm, nuits 218-536 ; vol. 3 : 326 ff. de 204 × 152 mm, nuits 537-771 ; vol. 4 : 382 ff. de 204 × 152 mm, nuits 771-1001. 21 l./p., lignes longues. Examen détaillé des ff. 296, 302, 318 du vol. 2. Scribe 1.

g) Munich, Bayerische Staatsbibliothek, MS Cod. ar. 623-636 (Mu)[98]
Complet, vol. 4 daté du 3 *Muḥarram* 1221/23 mars 1806 et signé ʿAlī l-Anṣārī b. al-shaykh Ibrāhīm al-Anṣārī ; vol. 1 : 498 ff. de 225 × 157 mm, nuits 1-220 ; vol. 2 : 339 ff. de 215 × 160 mm, nuits 218-536 ; vol. 3 : 316 ff. de 229 × 161 mm, nuits 537-771 ; vol. 4 : 340 ff. de 216 × 162 mm, nuits 772-1001. 21 l./p., lignes longues. Examen détaillé des ff. 296, 312 et 338 du vol. 2. ʿAlī l-Anṣārī.

h) Christie's[99]
Complet (? en tout cas, 4 volumes conservés), non daté, non signé. Pas consulté à ce jour, mais d'après les images disponibles, scribe 1.

97 Khalidov, *Arabskie rukopisi* i, 414, ii, 202.
98 Aumer, *Die arabische Handschriften* 272.
99 Christie's, *Arts* 38.

TABLEAU 4.1 Reconstitution de trois ensembles complets fondée sur l'analyse des graphies

	Ensemble ʿAlī l-Anṣārī		**Ensemble scribe 1 – 1**		**Ensemble scribe 1 – 2**	
	MSS	**Nuits**	**MSS**	**Nuits**	**MSS**	**Nuits**
vol. 1	BnF Ar. 3602	1-214	BnF Ar. 3598	1-214	BnF Ar. 3606	1-220
vol. 2	BnF Ar. 3599	215-536	BnF Ar. 3603	218-536	Lg	218-536
vol. 3	BnF Ar. 3607	537-771	BnF Ar. 3600	537-771	BnF Ar. 3604	537-771
vol. 4	BnF Ar. 3605	771-1001	BnF Ar. 3601	771-1001	BnF Ar. 3608	771-1001

TABLEAU 4.2 Tableau d'analyse des graphies[100]

	Lg ALPHA 2241, ff. 369, 384, 404	L vol. 2 BL 2916-2919, ff. 344, 352, 357	P3 vols. 1, 4 BnF 3606-3608
Support-instrument			
Support	Papier blanc, filigrané (motif dans le pli de reliure), apprêt ok	Papier blanc, apprêt très inégal, parfois très mauvais	Papier blanc, apprêt ok
Instr.	calame biseauté	calame biseauté	calame biseauté
Couleur de l'encre	noire brunâtre/grisâtre, rouge claire-rouille	noire et rouge	noire et rouge
Ordonnance-utilisation espace – générale			
Sens de l'écriture	normal (// largeur)	normal	normal
Utilisation papier	r/v	r/v	r/v
Ordonnance-utilisation espace – distances verticales			
Marge sup.	grande	grande	grande
Marge inf.	grande	grande	grande
Ordonnance-utilisation espace – distances horizontales			
Marge int.	petite, ondulante (+/- une lettre) d'abord progressive	petite, en dents de scie +/- affirmées	petite, en dents de scie +/- affirmées
Marge ext.	large, volontaire	large, volontaire, régulièrement fin de mot dans la marge après un espace de 3-4 mm, ondulante d'abord régressive	large, volontaire
Alinéas	∅ Lignes longues justifiées	∅ Lignes longues justifiées	∅ Lignes longues justifiée
Additions	corrections en surcharge dans le texte ou juste après erreur, barrée; un cas dans la marge; un cas de mot fini dans marge int. après petit espace	∅	dans la marge int., en oblique

100 Dans les tableaux qui suivent, plusieurs abréviations sont utilisées : d. (droite), g. (gauche), horiz. (horizontal.e), inf. (inférieur.e), l. (ligne), sup. (supérieur.e), vertic. (vertical.e).

vol. 2 M B-1114	P2 vols. 2-3 BnF 3602-3605	Mu vol. 1-4 BSB Cod. ar. 623-626	P1, vol. 2 BnF 3598-3601	Conclusions
pier blanc, apprêt	Papier blanc, apprêt ok	Papier blanc, apprêt ok	Papier blanc, apprêt ok	pas pertinent
ame biseauté	calame biseauté	calame biseauté	calame biseauté	pas pertinent
re et rouge	noire et rouge	noire et rouge	noire et rouge	pas pertinent
rmal	normal	normal	normal	pas pertinent
	r/v	r/v	r/v	pas pertinent
nde	grande	grande	grande	pas pertinent
nde	grande	grande	grande	pas pertinent
ite (? pli reliure !), tiligne	petite (? pli reliure !), en dents de scie +/- affirmées	moyenne, rectiligne	petite, rectiligne	Lg-L-P2-P3 / SP-Mu-P1
ge, volontaire	large, volontaire	large, volontaire, régulièrement fin de mot dans la marge après un espace de 3-4 mm	large, volontaire, régulièrement fin de mot dans la marge après un espace de 3-4 mm	pas pertinent
ignes longues jus- ées	∅ Lignes longues justifiées	∅ Lignes longues justifiées	∅ Lignes longues justifiées	pas pertinent
	∅ ?	∅ ?	∅ ?	pas pertinent

TABLEAU 4.2 Tableau d'analyse des graphies (*suite*)

	Lg ALPHA 2241, ff. 369, 384, 404	L vol. 2 BL 2916-2919, ff. 344, 352, 357	P3 vols. 1, 4 BnF 3606-3608
Axes des lettres			
Parallélisme	sensiblement parallèles (constant, avec très légères inégalités)	sensiblement parallèles (constant, avec très légères inégalités)	sensiblement parallèles (constant)
Orientation générale	légèrement inclinés à d. (70°)	très légèrement inclinés à d. (75°)	verticaux
Homogénéité	oui	oui	oui
Ligne de base			
Stabilité	instable	instable	sensiblement rectiligne
Dir. gén.	horiz.	horiz.	horiz.
Homogénéité	régulière	régulière	faibles inégalités
Dimensions et proportions			
Régularité	régulière	régulière	régulière
Calibre général	petit	petit	petit
Largeur des lettres	sensiblement régulière (tassement ou étalement occasionnel en fin de ligne pour respecter "linéarité" de la marge)	sensiblement régulière (tassement ou étalement occasionnel en fin de ligne pour respecter "linéarité" de la marge)	sensiblement régulière (tassement ou étalement occasionnel en fin de ligne pour respecter "linéarité" de la marge)
Proportions hauteur-largeur	*dāl* et *'ayn* s'inscrivent dans un carré	*dāl* et *'ayn* s'inscrivent généralement dans un carré	*dāl* et *'ayn* s'inscrivent généralement dans un carré

vol. 2 м B-1114	P2 vols. 2-3 BnF 3602-3605	Mu vol. 1-4 BSB Cod. ar. 623-626	P1, vol. 2 BnF 3598-3601	Conclusions
nsiblement paral- es (constant, avec s légères inégalités)	sensiblement paral- lèles (constant)	sensiblement paral- lèles (constant)	sensiblement paral- lèles (constant)	Lg-L-SP / P3-P2-Mu-P1
rticaux, mais casionnellement ɡèrement obliques rs la d. ou vers la g. ıns logique déce- ɔle)	verticaux, mais occasionnellement légèrement obliques vers la d.	légèrement inclinés à d. (70°-80°)	légèrement inclinés à d. (70°-80°)	Lg-L-Mu-P1 P3-SP-P2
eu près	à peu près	oui	oui	Lg-L-Mu-P1 / P3-SP-P2
table	instable	rectiligne	rectiligne	Lg-L-SP-P2 / P3-Mu-P1
riz.	horiz.	horiz.	horiz.	Lg-L-SP-P2 / P3-Mu-P1
ɔles inégalités	régulière	régulière	régulière	Lg-L-SP-P2 / P3-Mu-P1
ulière	régulière	régulière	régulière	pas pertinent
it	petit	petit	petit	identique
ısiblement régu- e (tassement ou lement occasion- en fin de ligne ır respecter "linéa- " de la marge), fins mots = régulière- nt dans la marge, ès espace	sensiblement régu- lière	sensiblement régu- lière (tassement ou étalement occasion- nel en fin de ligne pour respecter "linéa- rité" de la marge), fins de mots = parfois dans la marge, après espace	sensiblement régu- lière (tassement ou étalement occasion- nel en fin de ligne pour respecter "linéa- rité" de la marge, v. f. 291!), fins de mots = régulièrement dans la marge, après espace	identique
et *'ayn* s'inscrivent ıs un carré	*dāl* et *'ayn* s'inscrivent généralement dans un carré	*dāl* et *'ayn* s'inscrivent dans un rectangle debout	*dāl* et *'ayn* s'inscrivent généralement dans un rectangle debout (moins clair pour le *dāl*)	Lg-L-P2- P3-SP / Mu-P1

TABLEAU 4.2 Tableau d'analyse des graphies (*suite*)

	Lg **ALPHA 2241, ff. 369, 384, 404**	**L vol. 2** **BL 2916-2919, ff. 344, 352, 357**	**P3 vols. 1, 4** **BnF 3606-3608**
Prolongements supérieurs	**égaux, moyen** (*mīm* = 2 mm, *alif* etc. = 5 mm)	**égaux, moyen** (*mīm* = 2 mm, *alif* etc. = 5 mm)	**égaux, moyen** (*mīm* = 2 mn *alif* etc. = 5 mm)
Prolongements inférieurs	*rāʾ* et *wāw* égaux = 2 mm sous la ligne d'écriture, *lām/kāf* finaux = 1 mm sous l., *yāʾ* = à peine 1 mm, *mīm maqlūba musbala* = 3-4 mm. → **plus courts que prolongements sup.** *Nūn* et *yāʾ* finaux descendent très peu sous la l., = presque sur la ligne	*rāʾ* et *wāw* égaux = 2 ou 3 mm sous la ligne d'écriture, *lām/kāf* finaux = 1 mm sous l., *yāʾ* = à peine 1 mm ou même posé sur la l. de base, id. *nūn, mīm maqlūba musbala* = 3-4 mm. → **plus courts que prolongements sup.**	*rāʾ* et *wāw* égaux = 1 ou 2 m sous la ligne d'écriture, *lām* finaux = 2 mm sous l, *kāf* finaux = 1 mm sous la l., *yāʾ* = à peine 1 mm ou même posé sur la l. de base, id. *nū* *mīm maqlūba musbala* = 2-3 mm. → **plus courts que prolongements sup.**
Liaisons-parcours du geste			
Degr. de liaison	normal	normal	normal
Type de liaison, aspect général	plutôt arrondie, sauf avant *alif/lām*: angle droit; écriture progressive	plutôt arrondie, sauf avant *alif/lām*: angle droit; écriture progressive	plutôt arrondie, sauf avant *alif/lām*: angle droit; écritu progressive
Système de liaison	lettres à oves en position initiale = tracées de haut en bas, d'abord la boucle puis la suite de la lettre, avec trait recouvert à droite de l'œil, l'ove reste parfois ouvert à d. Pas de continuité entre les mots	lettres à oves en position initiale = tracées de haut en bas, d'abord la boucle puis la suite de la lettre, avec trait recouvert à droite de l'œil, l'ove reste parfois ouvert à d., surtout quand la suite du mot n'est pas dans le prolongement, ou dans le cas des *wāw* isolés. Pas de continuité entre les mots	lettres à oves en position initiale = tracées de haut e bas, d'abord la boucle puis la suite de la lettre, avec tr recouvert à droite de l'œil, l'ove reste parfois ouvert à d. Pas de continuité entre l mots

vol. 2 M B-1114	P2 vols. 2-3 BnF 3602-3605	Mu vol. 1-4 BSB Cod. ar. 623-626	P1, vol. 2 BnF 3598-3601	Conclusions
ıux, moyen (*mīm* .5 mm, *alif* etc. = ım)	**égaux, moyen** (*mīm* = 2 mm, *alif* etc. = 5 mm (sauf *alif* isolé : 4 mm)	**égaux, moyen** (*mīm* = 2 mm, *alif* etc. = 4-5 mm)	**égaux, moyen** (*mīm* = 2 mm, *alif* etc. = 4-5 mm)	identique
et *wāw* égaux = 2 3 mm sous la ligne criture, *lām/kāf* aux = 1 mm sous l., = à peine 1 mm ou me posé sur la l. base, id. *nūn, mīm qlūba musbala* très ırts, = 2-3 mm. → **ıs courts que pro-gements sup.**	*rā’* et *wāw* égaux = 2 ou 3 mm sous la ligne d’écriture, *lām/kāf* finaux = 1 mm sous l., *yā’* = à peine 1 mm ou même posé sur la l. de base, id. *nūn, mīm maqlūba musbala* très courts, = 2-3 mm. → **plus courts que pro-longements sup.**	*rā’* et *wāw* égaux = 3 ou 4 mm sous la ligne d’écriture, *lām/kāf* posés sur la l. de base, *yā’* = 1 ou 2 mm sous la l. de base, *nūn* = quasi posés sur la ligne de base, ou dépassent de 1 mm, *mīm maqlūba musbala* très courts, = 4-5 mm. → **égaux aux prolongements sup.**	*rā’* et *wāw* égaux = 3 ou 4 mm sous la ligne d’écriture, *lām/kāf* posés sur la l. de base, *yā’* = 1 ou 2 mm sous la l. de base, *nūn* = quasi posés sur la ligne de base, ou dépassent de 1 mm, *mīm maqlūba musbala* très courts, = 4-5 mm. → **égaux aux prolongements sup.**	identique
rmal	normal	normal	normal	id.
ıtôt arrondie, sauf ınt *alif/lām* : angle it ; écriture pro-ssive	plutôt arrondie, sauf avant *alif/lām* : angle droit ; écriture pro-gressive	plutôt arrondies, mais donnent impression anguleuse car très réduites ; écriture pro-gressive	plutôt arrondies, mais donnent impression anguleuse car très réduites ; écriture pro-gressive	Lg-L-P3-SP-P2 / Mu-P1
res à oves en ition initiale = tra-s de haut en bas, bord la boucle puis uite de la lettre, c trait recouvert à ite de l’œil, l’ove e parfois ouvert à as de continuité re les mots	lettres à oves en position initiale = tra-cées de haut en bas, d’abord la boucle puis la suite de la lettre, avec trait recouvert à droite de l’œil, l’ove reste parfois ouvert à d. Pas de continuité entre les mots	Lettres à ove tra-cées en un seul geste continu. Impression de continuité entre les mots car espaces très réduits	Lettres à ove tra-cées en un seul geste continu. Impression de continuité entre les mots car espaces très réduits	Lg-L-P3-SP-P2 / Mu-P1

TABLEAU 4.2 Tableau d'analyse des graphies (*suite*)

	Lg ALPHA 2241, ff. 369, 384, 404	L vol. 2 BL 2916-2919, ff. 344, 352, 357	P3 vols. 1, 4 BnF 3606-3608
	Hāʾ initial = médian : boucle démarrant au niveau de la ligne d'écriture, vers le bas, puis 1/2 cercle dont centre serait sur la l. de base, puis boucle repartant sur la l. de base. *Hāʾ* final = comme une goutte d'eau, tracé du haut vers la d., boucle puis remonte et trait remontant s'arrête souvent légèrement après le trait descendant, sécant, ou peu avant : boucle pas fermée. *Alif* = tracés de haut en bas → trait stoppé pour repartir du haut	*Hāʾ* initial = médian : boucle démarrant au niveau de la ligne d'écriture, vers le bas, puis 1/2 cercle dont centre serait sur la l. de base, puis boucle repartant sur la l. de base. *Hāʾ* final = comme une goutte d'eau, tracé du haut vers la d., boucle puis remonte et trait remontant s'arrête souvent légèrement après le trait descendant, sécant, ou peu avant : boucle pas fermée. *Alif* = tracés de haut en bas → trait stoppé pour repartir du haut	*Hāʾ* initial = médian : boucl démarrant au niveau de la ligne d'écriture, vers le bas, puis 1/2 cercle dont centre serait sur la l. de base, puis boucle repartant sur la l. de base. Plus allongé que mss Lg et L2. *Hāʾ* final = comme une goutte d'eau, tracé du haut vers la d., boucle puis remonte. *Alif* = tracés de haut en bas → trait stoppé pour repartir du haut. Par contre, recouvrement pour *kāf* médians
	Sīn et *shīn* : denticules très peu marqués.	*Sīn* et *shīn* : denticules très peu marqués.	*Sīn* et *shīn* : denticules très peu marqués.
Pression			
Coloration d'ensemble	Forte	Forte	Forte (?) (microfilm)
Épaisseur du trait	assez épais ; pochages fréquents (oves remplis d'encre, boucles pleines)	assez épais ; pochages fréquents	assez épais ; pochages fréquents
Puissances d'appui	?	?	?
Contours	nets des deux côtés	nets des deux côtés	nets des deux côtés (?)
Fermeté du trait	traits descendants (*mīm* final) légèrement courbes : *mudghama* (*muʿallaqa*) *mukhtāla*	traits descendants rectilignes	traits descendants rectilig
Variation de l'appui	uniforme, très léger effet moiré car reprises de plume	uniforme	uniforme

vol. 2 M B-1114	P2 vols. 2-3 BnF 3602-3605	Mu vol. 1-4 BSB Cod. ar. 623-626	P1, vol. 2 BnF 3598-3601	Conclusions
ʾ initial = médian : ucle démarrant niveau de la ligne écriture, vers le s, puis 1/2 cercle nt centre serait la l. de base, puis ucle repartant sur . de base. *Hāʾ* final comme une goutte au, tracé du haut s la d., boucle puis nonte	*Hāʾ* initial = médian : boucle démarrant au niveau de la ligne d'écriture, vers le bas, puis 1/2 cercle dont centre serait sur la l. de base, puis boucle repartant sur la l. de base. *Hāʾ* final = comme une goutte d'eau, tracé du haut vers la d., boucle puis remonte	*Hāʾ* initial = rond, différent du médian (mais le médian est moins allongé dans ce ms). Final = ouvert (2 traits en sens inverses) ou fermé (une goutte plus ou moins grande) sans logique décelable. Isolé, il est très rond, souvent ouvert aussi (trait de départ presque vertical), trait final pas toujours assez arrondi pour fermer la boucle	*Hāʾ* initial = rond, différent du médian (mais le médian est moins allongé dans ce ms). Final = ouvert (2 traits en sens inverses) ou fermé (une goutte plus ou moins grande) sans logique décelable. Isolé, il est très rond	Lg-L-P3-SP-P2 / Mu-P1
et *shīn* : denticules s peu marqués.	*Sīn* et *shīn* : denticules très peu marqués.	*Sīn* et *shīn* : denticules bien marqués ou volontairement lissés	*Sīn* et *shīn* : denticules bien marqués ou volontairement lissés	Lg-L-P3-SP-P2 / Mu-P1
rte	Forte	Forte	Forte	id. pas pertinent
ez épais ; pochages quents	assez épais ; pochages fréquents	assez épais ; pochages fréquents	assez épais ; pochages fréquents	id. pas pertinent
	?	?	?	?
s des deux côtés	nets des deux côtés	nets des deux côtés	nets des deux côtés	id. pas pertinent
its descendants tilignes	traits descendants rectilignes	traits descendants rectilignes	traits descendants rectilignes	id. pas pertinent
iforme	uniforme	uniforme	uniforme	id. pas pertinent

TABLEAU 4.2 Tableau d'analyse des graphies (*suite*)

	Lg ALPHA 2241, ff. 369, 384, 404	L vol. 2 BL 2916-2919, ff. 344, 352, 357	P3 vols. 1, 4 BnF 3606-3608
Finales	ni allégées, ni alourdies, courtes mais parfois prolongées en fin de ligne, extrémité arrondie	courtes, extrémité arrondie	courtes, extrémité arrondie
Vitesse et rythme			
Allure générale	rapide	rapide	rapide
Régularité	régulier	régulier	régulier
Densité du texte – espacements			
Aspect général	Compact, disparate	compact, disparate	Compact, disparate
Espaces blancs superflus dans le texte	non	pas vraiment, mais certaines lignes plus étalées donnent aspect + aéré à certains endroits	pas vraiment, mais certaines lignes plus ondulan[tes] donnent aspect + aéré à ce[r]tains endroits
Espaces entre les mots	assez réguliers, faibles	assez réguliers, faibles	assez réguliers, faibles
Interlignes	réguliers, petits, nets	réguliers, petits, nets	assez réguliers, petits, enc[h]evêtrements occasionnels
Différences de densité	régulièrement, mais pas systématiquement, interligne(s) +grand(s) au milieu de la p.	certaines lignes plus étalées donnent aspect + aéré à certains endroits, surtout en milieu de page	certaines lignes + ondulan[tes] donnent aspect + aéré à ce[r]tains endroits
Morphologie			
Détériorations morpho	/	/	/
Distance modèle scolaire	Assez proche	Assez proche	Assez proche

vol. 2 M B-1114	P2 vols. 2-3 BnF 3602-3605	Mu vol. 1-4 BSB Cod. ar. 623-626	P1, vol. 2 BnF 3598-3601	Conclusions
urtes, extrémité ondie	courtes, extrémité arrondie	courtes, extrémité arrondie	courtes, extrémité arrondie	id. pas pertinent
sé	normal	très rapide (lien entre lettres pas toujours ok ; se laisse emporter par son geste et ligature avec *alif*)	très rapide	pas pertinent car professionnels
gulier	régulier	régulier	régulier	pas pertinent car professionnels
mpact, disparate	Compact, disparate	Compact, homogène	Compact, homogène	Lg-L-P3-SP-P2 / Mu-P1
n	non	non	non	? v. avis Sedeyn
ez réguliers, faibles	assez réguliers, faibles	assez réguliers, (très) faibles	assez réguliers, (très) faibles	id.
ez réguliers, petits, hevêtrements oc- ionnels en fin de l.	réguliers, petits, nets	assez réguliers, petits, enchevêtrements occasionnels en fin de l.	assez réguliers, petits, enchevêtrements occasionnels en fin de l.	Lg-L-P2 / P3-SP-Mu-P1
hevêtrements de de l. et élongation nnent aspect irré- ier	non	enchevêtrements occasionnels en fin de l. donnent aspect légèrement irrégulier	enchevêtrements occasionnels en fin de l. donnent aspect légèrement irrégulier	? avis Sedeyn
	/	/	/	
ez proche	Assez proche	Assez proche	Assez proche	pas pertinent car professionnels

TABLEAU 4.2 Tableau d'analyse des graphies (*suite*)

	Lg **ALPHA 2241, ff. 369, 384, 404**	**L vol. 2** **BL 2916-2919, ff. 344, 352, 357**	**P3 vols. 1, 4** **BnF 3606-3608**
Lisibilité	Claire	Claire	Claire
Formes partic.	v. tableau 4.3	v. tableau 4.3	v. tableau 4.3
Habitudes graphiques			
Accents et points	séparateurs de vers : *hāʾ* finaux, avec souvent petite queue vers le haut = prolongement du trait final.	séparateurs de vers: *hāʾ* finaux, avec souvent petite queue vers le haut = prolongement du trait final.	séparateurs de vers: *hāʾ* finaux mais plus fins
	Un point diacritique **dessus** : centré au-dessus de la lettre ou légèrement plus à g., **dessous** : bien centré. **Proche de la lettre** : à 1,5 ou 2 mm	Un point diacritique **dessus** : centré au-dessus de la lettre ou légèrement plus à g., **dessous** : bien centré. **Proche de la lettre** : à 1,5 ou 2 mm	Un point diacritique **dessu** centré au-dessus de la lett ou légèrement plus à g., **de sous** : bien centré. **Proche la lettre** : à 1,5 ou 2 mm
	2 points diacritiques **dessus** : 2e toujours + haut que 1er, souvent décalés vers la g., **dessous** : idem. **Proches de la lettre** (à 1 ou 1,5 mm de la lettre) ; quand plusieurs lettres à 2 points, la 1re porte les points + hauts	2 points diacritiques **dessus** : au même niveau, **dessous** : idem. **Proches de la lettre** (à 1 ou 1,5 mm de la lettre) ; quand plusieurs lettres à 2 points, la 1re porte les points + hauts	2 points diacritiques **dessus** : au même niveau (ou, rarement, le 1er est plus ba **dessous** : idem. **Proches d la lettre** (à 1 ou 1,5 mm de lettre)
	3 points diacritiques forment des triangles d'apparence très variable (petit v ou au contraire triangle sur base). 1er point = toujours le plus bas. **Proches de la lettre** : à 1 ou 1,5 mm	3 points diacritiques forment des triangles d'apparence très variable (petit v ou au contraire triangle sur base). 1er point = toujours le plus bas. **Proches de la lettre** : à 1 ou 1,5 mm	3 points diacritiques form des triangles sur base. 1er point = toujours le plus ba **Proches de la lettre** : à 1 o 1,5 mm
Soulignements	/	/	/

vol. 2 M B-1114	P2 vols. 2-3 BnF 3602-3605	Mu vol. 1-4 BSB Cod. ar. 623-626	P1, vol. 2 BnF 3598-3601	Conclusions
ıire	Claire	Assez lisible mais espaces réduits entre les mots compliquent parfois lecture	Assez lisible mais espaces réduits entre les mots compliquent parfois lecture	pas pertinent car professionels
ableau 4.3	v. tableau 4.3	v. tableau 4.3	v. tableau 4.3	
arateurs de vers : ' finaux, avec sount petite queue vers haut = prolongeent du trait final.	?	séparateurs de vers : *hā'* finaux, avec souvent petite queue vers le haut = prolongement du trait final.	séparateurs de vers : *hā'* finaux, avec souvent petite queue vers le haut = prolongement du trait final.	pas pertinent, idem
point diacritique ssus : centré aussus de la lettre ou èrement plus à g., ssous : 3 positions ssibles : bien centré, légèrement plus ., ou légèrement ıs à d. **Proche de la tre** : à 1,5 ou 2 mm	Un point diacritique **dessus** : décalé à g., à 2-3 mm de la lettre, **dessous** : centré, ou légèrement plus à g., à 1 ou 2 mm	Un point diacritique **dessus** : centré ou légèrement à g., à 1,5 ou 2 mm ; **dessous** : idem	Un point diacritique **dessus** : centré ou légèrement à g., à 1,5 ou 2 mm ; **dessous** : idem	Lg-L-P3 / SP / P2 / Mu-P1
oints diacritiques ssus : au même eau, ou le 1er est s haut, **dessous** : au me niveau, ou le 1er plus bas. **Proches la lettre** (à 1 ou nm de la lettre)	2 points diacritiques **dessus** : centrés ou à g., le 1er étant plus bas ; **dessous** : idem. **Proches de la lettre** (à 2 ou 3 mm de la lettre)	2 points diacritiques **dessus** : 3 positions possibles (centré, légèrement à d. ou à g.), le 1er = toujours le plus haut ; **dessous** : dessous, le 1er = le plus haut. **Proches de la lettre** : à 1,5-3 mm	2 points diacritiques **dessus** : 3 positions possibles (centré, légèrement à d. ou à g.), le 1er = toujours le plus haut ; **dessous** : dessous, le 1er = le plus haut. **Proches de la lettre** : à 1,5-3 mm	Lg-L-P3 / SP / P2 / Mu-P1
oints diacritiques ment des triangles base. 1er point = fois le plus bas. **ches de la lettre** : à ı 1,5 mm	3 points diacritiques forment des triangles sur base. 1er point = le plus bas. **Proches de la lettre** : à 1 ou 1,5 mm	3 points = trait arrondi d'en bas à d. vers haut milieu (sorte de *dāl* inversé), **Proches de la lettre** : à 1 ou 1,5 mm	3 points = trait arrondi d'en bas à d. vers haut milieu (sorte de *dāl* inversé), **Proches de la lettre** : à 1 ou 1,5 mm	Lg-L / P3-P2-(SP ?) Mu-P1
	/	occasionnels, audessus de ligature	/	pas pertinent

TABLEAU 4.3 Tableau d'analyse de lettres spécifiques

	Lg	L vol. 2	P3 vol. 1, 4
alif			
	toujours de haut en bas	toujours de haut en bas	souvent de haut en bas
bā', tā', thā'			
	habituel	habituel	habituel
jīm, ḥā', khā'			
initial	volute ou ouvert	volute ou ouvert	volute ou ouvert
médian	lettre le précédant souvent suscrite (ligature), toujours attaqué par le haut	lettre le précédant souvent suscrite (ligature), toujours attaqué par le haut	lettre le précédant souvent su crite (ligature), toujours attaq par le haut
dāl, dhāl			
	mukhtalasa (habituel), très ouverts (90-100°), // *rā'/zāy* ou *wāw*: verticale courte, trait horizontal = oblique et part sous la l. de base	*mukhtalasa* (habituel), très ouverts (90-100°), // *rā'/zāy* ou *wāw*: verticale courte, trait horizontal = oblique et part sous la l. de base	*mukhtalasa* (habituel), très ouverts (90-100°), // *rā'/zāy* ou *wāw*: verticale courte, trait horizontal = oblique et part sc la l. de base
rā', zāy			
	mabsūṭa (habituel), queue oblique ne descendant pas très bas, mais allant parfois loin vers la g.	*mabsūṭa* (habituel), queue oblique ne descendant pas très bas	*mabsūṭa* (habituel), queue oblique ne descendant pas trè bas
sīn, shīn			
	denticules peu marqués, queue longue presque horizontale	denticules peu marqués	denticules peu marqués
ṭā', ẓā'			
	en 2 mouvements, ove puis hampe	en 2 mouvements, ove puis hampe	en un trait (?)

vol. 2	P2 vol. 2, 3	Mu vol. 1-4	P1 vol. 2
rfois de haut en bas, ais pas systématique	parfois de haut en bas, mais pas systématique	le plus souvent de haut en bas mais pas toujours. Parfois arrondi en fin de mot (vitesse)	le plus souvent de haut en bas mais pas toujours. Parfois arrondi en fin de mot (vitesse)
bituel	finaux/isolés: très profonds	finaux/isolés: très profonds	
ute	volute ou ouvert	ouvert, anguleux (pas de volute)	ouvert, anguleux (pas de volute)
tre le précédant souvent crite (ligature), tou- rs attaqué par le haut	lettre le précédant souvent suscrite (ligature), toujours attaqué par le haut	fin de la lettre le précédant suscrite, tête très anguleuse	fin de la lettre le précédant suscrite, tête très anguleuse
khtalasa (habituel), its par rapport aux res lettres (90-100°)	*mukhtalasa* (habituel), très ouvert (90-105°?), arrondi, petit (surtout la verticale)	*mukhtalasa* (habituel), taille normale, fermé (70-90°), anguleux	*mukhtalasa* (habituel), taille normale, fermé (70-90°), anguleux
dghama	*mabsūṭa* (habituel), queue oblique ne descendant pas très bas, mais allant parfois loin vers la g.	*mabsūṭa* (habituel) ou *mudghama*	*mabsūṭa* (habituel) ou *mudghama*
ticules peu marqués	denticules peu marqués	denticules marqués, finaux/isolés: queue courte, pas plus longue qu'un *wāw*, très incurvée	denticules marqués, finaux/isolés: queue courte, pas plus longue qu'un *wāw*, très incurvée
	en 2 mouvements, ove puis hampe (sauf initial)	en un trait, hampe courbe à l'initiale (d.-g.)	en un trait, hampe courbe à l'initiale (d.-g.)

TABLEAU 4.3 Tableau d'analyse des lettres spécifiques (*suite*)

	Lg	L vol. 2	P3 vol. 1, 4
ʿayn, ghayn			
initial	arrondi concave presque fermé, traits sup. et inf. au même niveau	arrondi concave presque fermé, traits sup. et inf. au même niveau	arrondi concave, trait inf. se pr longe un peu plus loin que trai sup.
médian	couché sur la ligne, plein (pochage), oblique dans le sens d'écriture	couché sur la ligne, plein (pochage), oblique dans le sens d'écriture	comme un triangle (bas), plein (pochage), tête plate
final	tête couchée sur la l., pleine, oblique, queue en 1/2 cercle, max. 3 mm de long, ne dépasse pas la tête en largeur	tête couchée sur la l., pleine, oblique, queue en 1/2 cercle, max. 3 mm de long, ne dépasse pas la tête en largeur	tête couchée sur la l., pleine, oblique, queue dépasse de la tête en largeur, par un trait ho zontal, max. 3 mm de long
fāʾ, qāf, wāw			
	en 2 mouvements, ove restant parfois ouverte sur la d.	en 2 mouvements, ove restant parfois ouverte sur la d.	en 2 mouvements, ove restant parfois ouverte sur la d.
kāf			
médian	trait vertical puis oblique, angle 120°, ou parfois *mabsūṭa* (titre nuit ou pour remplir une l.)	trait vertical puis oblique, angle 115-120° ou parfois *mabsūṭa* (titre nuit ou pour remplir une l.)	trait vertical, puis oblique, ang 100-120° ou parfois *mabsūṭa* (titre nuit ou pour remplir un l.)
final	forme médiane = *mashkūla* (*mashqūqa*)	forme médiane = *mashkūla* (*mashqūqa*)	forme médiane = *mashkūla* (*mashqūqa*), queue étroite
lām			
final	descend peu sous l. de base (max 1,5 mm)	descend peu sous l. de base (max 1,5 mm)	queue étroite

vol. 2	**P2 vol. 2, 3**	**Mu vol. 1-4**	**P1 vol. 2**
ondi concave presque mé, traits sup. et inf. au ème niveau	arrondi, ouvert	arrondi, concave mais reste ouvert, trait inf. se prolonge légèrement plus loin que trait sup.	arrondi, concave mais reste ouvert, trait inf. se prolonge légèrement plus loin que trait sup.
mme un triangle (bas), ut de tête ronde	comme un triangle (bas), haut de tête ronde	tête plate sur le dessus, en triangle sur le dessous	tête plate sur le dessus, en triangle sur le dessous
e couchée sur la l., ine, oblique, queue 1/2 cercle, max. 3 mm long, ne dépasse pas la e en largeur	tête arrondie sur le dessus, légèrement oblique dans le sens d'écriture, queue dépasse un peu la largeur de la lettre	tête plate sur le dessus, légèrement oblique dans le sens d'écriture, queue dépasse la largeur de la lettre horizontalement	tête plate sur le dessus, légèrement oblique dans le sens d'écriture, queue dépasse la largeur de la lettre horizontalement
2 mouvements, ove restant parfois ouverte sur la *fā'* final ou isolé aussi ncave qu'un *qāf*	en 2 mouvements, ove restant parfois ouverte sur la d.	un seul geste continu	un seul geste continu
it vertical, puis oblique, gle 108-120°. Barre ique très longue, égale sup. à verticale	trait vertical puis oblique, angle 100-115° ou parfois *mabsūṭa* (titre nuit ou pour remplir une l. ET devant *alif*)	trait vertical puis oblique, angle 110-120°	trait vertical puis oblique, angle 110-120°
me médiane, queue oite	forme médiane ou *mabsūṭa*	forme médiane = *mashkūla* (*mashqūqa*), fin de queue concave	forme médiane = *mashkūla* (*mashqūqa*), fin de queue concave
cend peu sous l. de e (max 1,5 mm)	descend généralement peu sous l. de base, queue étroite	descend peu sous l. de base (max 1,5 mm), queue = oblique + retour vertical ou oblique opposé	descend peu sous l. de base (max 1,5 mm), queue = oblique + retour vertical ou oblique opposé

TABLEAU 4.3 Tableau d'analyse des lettres spécifiques (*suite*)

	Lg	L vol. 2	P3 vol. 1, 4
mīm			
initial	arrondi, pochage, en un trait, parfois progressif, parfois régressif…	arrondi, pochage, en un trait, parfois progressif, parfois régressif…	arrondi, pochage, en un trait, parfois progressif, parfois régressif…
médian	sous l. de base, tracé depuis le haut, vers la d.	sous l. de base, tracé depuis le haut, vers la d.	sous l. de base, tracé depuis le haut, vers la d.
final	*musbala* (queue verticale) ou *mukhtāla* (queue vers la droite)	*musbala* (queue verticale) ou *mukhtāla* (queue vers la droite)	*musbala* (queue verticale) ou *mukhtāla* (queue vers la droite)
hāʾ			
initial	*mashqūqa* (forme médiane)	*mashqūqa* (forme médiane)	*mashqūqa* (forme médiane)
final	2 formes, en un geste ou 2 : goutte, reste souvent ouvert	2 formes : un seul trait, ouvert, OU en goutte fermée	2 formes : un seul trait, ouvert, OU en goutte fermée
isolé	goutte, trait de droite dépasse parfois	goutte, trait de droite dépasse parfois	goutte, très rond
yāʾ			
final	presque sur la l. de base	à peine 1 mm ou même posé sur la l. de base	couché sur l. de base
lām-alif			
	lien sous ligne de base ; après un *kāf mashkūla* (*mashqūqa*, normal), ligature à d. ressemble à *lām* supplémentaire	lien sous ligne de base ; après un *kāf mashkūla* (*mashqūqa*, normal), ligature à d. ressemble à *lām* supplémentaire	lien sous ligne de base ; ligature à d. ressemble à un *lām* supplémentaire
serifs			
	non	rares	occasionnels
compacité			
	0,9	1,3	1,4

vol. 2	P2 vol. 2, 3	Mu vol. 1-4	P1 vol. 2
ondi, pochage, en un it, parfois progressif, rfois régressif…	arrondi, pochage fréquent, en un trait, progressif	anguleux et reste souvent ouvert	anguleux et reste souvent ouvert
us l. de base, tracé puis le haut, vers la d.	sous l. de base, tracé depuis le haut, vers la d.	sur l. de base, du haut vers la d.	sur l. de base, du haut vers la d.
sbala (queue verticale)	*mukhtāla* (queue vers la d.)	*musbala* (queue verticale)	*mukhtāla* (queue vers la d.)
shqūqa (forme diane)	*mashqūqa* (forme médiane)	initial : *wajh al-hirr*; médian : *mudghama* (zigzag)	initial : *wajh al-hirr*; médian : *mudghama* (zigzag)
ormes : un seul trait, vert, OU en goutte mée. souvent pas de chage	2 formes : un seul trait, ouvert, OU en goutte fermée	2 formes : un seul trait, ouvert, OU en goutte fermée avec dépassement fréquent	2 formes : un seul trait, ouvert, OU en goutte fermée avec dépassement fréquent
tte, très rond	goutte	goutte	goutte avec parfosi trait(s) dépassant
fois *rājiʿa* en fin de ne ; couché sur la ligne base	à peine 1 mm ou même posé sur la l. de base	*rājiʿa* en fin de ligne, 1 ou 2 mm sous la l. de base	*rājiʿa* en fin de ligne, 1 ou 2 mm sous la l. de base
n sous ligne de base ; ès un *kāf mashkūla* *ashqūqa*, normal), ligae à d. ressemble à *lām* plémentaire	posé sur la ligne de base, ligature à d. ressemble parfois à un *lām* supplémentaire	PARFOIS ligature à d. ressemble à un *lām* supplémentaire	PARFOIS ligature à d. ressemble à un lām supplémentaire
, SAUF : systématique *ām* de l'article, dans *nalik*	non	occasionnels	non
	1,3	1,3	1,5

CHAPTER 5

Maqriziana XV: The Characteristics of al-Maqrīzī's Handwriting

Frédéric Bauden

> *Habet enim singularum ut vox ita manus quoque quiddam suum et peculiare*
>
> ERASMUS, *De recta pronuntiatione*[1]

•••

> Genuine handwriting had become the material embodiment of the immaterial spirit of the individual.
>
> CHARTIER, *From the author's hand* 10

1 Introduction

The identification of one of al-Maqrīzī's holograph manuscripts in the holdings of the Liège University was a key moment in my life as a researcher: its nature (a notebook) was an irresistible, though challenging, invitation to examine al-Maqrīzī's methodology as a scholar. Since then, I have devoted several studies to his working method and other issues related to his holograph manuscripts as well as his œuvre in general.[2] The discovery also led me to realize that, if al-Maqrīzī's works were largely available in print, sometimes with several editions for a single text, most editors did not rely on his holograph manuscripts despite

1 "Just as individual voices differ, so does every handwriting have something unique about it". Erasmus, The right way 391.

2 The following are among my works on al-Maqrīzī: al-Maqrīzī; Maqriziana I; Maqriziana II; Maqriziana IV; Maqriziana VIII; Maqriziana IX; Maqriziana X; Maqriziana XI; Maqriziana XII; Maqriziana XIII; Maqriziana XIV; Taqī al-Dīn Aḥmad ibn ʿAlī al-Maqrīzī; Vers une archéologie du savoir.

 | DOI:10.1163/9789004413177_006

their huge number. Moreover, whenever some of these editors considered the holograph copy, they did not pay attention to al-Maqrīzī's editorial work (e.g., the nature and place of his corrections and emendations). This statement of fact induced me to conceive the *Bibliotheca Maqriziana* project, which aims to publish critical editions based on his holograph or authorial manuscripts (with a reproduction in facsimile) and takes into consideration al-Maqrīzī's editorial process and methodology as a copyist and an author. Each edition is accompanied by an annotated translation facing the Arabic text and a thorough study by a specialist of the field to which the edited text belongs.[3]

I identified al-Maqrīzī's notebook in 1997 in a fortunate stroke of serendipity. In April of that year, I attended an international conference in London. As usual, a few local institutions had displayed some of their most recent publications. Among them, the al-Furqān Foundation presented Ayman Fu'ād Sayyid's recently released edition of the draft of al-Maqrīzī's *al-Mawāʿiẓ wa-l-iʿtibār fī dhikr al-khiṭaṭ wa-l-āthār* (henceforth *al-Khiṭaṭ*).[4] The dust jacket of the book featured a leaf from the holograph manuscript on which the edition was made, while several additional leaves were reproduced on glossy paper at the end of the introduction. Passing by the table, I could not help but to be attracted to the image: it contained two elements that reminded me of a manuscript that I had catalogued in the collection of the Liège University a few years before.[5] The first, and most conspicuous given the size of the image, was a combination of two different handwritings: one line, written in large characters in a calligraphic style comparable to *thulth*, appeared in the middle of a text in smaller characters deftly arranged around the former.[6] The second element—in terms

3 The series is composed of two sections: the *Opera minora*, which includes al-Maqrīzī's opuscules on a wide variety of subjects, and the *Opera maiora*, which is devoted to al-Maqrīzī's major works. So far, three volumes have been published in the *Opera minora* section (see al-Maqrīzī, *Ḍaw' al-sārī*; al-Maqrīzī, *al-Maqrīzī's Trakat*; al-Maqrīzī, *Caliphate and kingship*) and two volumes in the *Opera maiora* section (*al-Maqrīzī's al-Ḫabar*, vol. V, sections 1–2: The Arab thieves, and section 4: Persia and its kings). In addition to *al-Khabar ʿan al-bashar*, the following major works are currently being edited and translated: *Ittiʿāẓ al-ḥunafā'*, *al-Sulūk*, and *al-Muqaffā*. For a similar approach regarding the medieval Jewish philosopher Maimonides, see Sirat and Di Donato, *Maïmonide*, which also includes an analysis of his handwriting by the expert in handwriting identification M.-J. Sedeyn.

4 Al-Maqrīzī, *Musawwadat*.

5 The handlist was published in 2017: Bauden, *Catalogue*. In a presentation of the most significant Arabic manuscripts preserved in Belgium (published in 1993, shortly after the cataloguing work was finished) and well before the identification of al-Maqrīzī's handwriting, I had correctly dated the manuscript to the ninth/fifteenth century and identified the place of production as Egypt. See Bauden, Les Manuscrits 151.

6 It turned out that these inscriptions belong to Mamlūk chancery documents that al-Maqrīzī

of chronology too—that drew my attention was the particular handwriting of the person who penned the main text around the *thulth* inscription. Before I could say Jack Robinson, I had the intuition that a manuscript I had described in the catalogue in Liège a few years earlier was a holograph of al-Maqrīzī. Upon my return to Liège a few days later, with a copy of Sayyid's edition in hand, I went to the Manuscripts Reading Room and asked for MS 2232 (Lg).[7] The comparison of the two elements—the writings in larger characters and the handwriting around them—which were critical for the flash of remembrance led me to conclude that the manuscript in Liège was indeed a manuscript in al-Maqrīzī's handwriting and that it had the same characteristic as the draft of *al-Khiṭaṭ* edited by Sayyid: it was partly written on reused Mamlūk chancery documents.[8]

I am sharing the circumstances of this discovery for the first time for several reasons. First, the identification was the result of pure serendipity. Second, to emphasize the significance of visual memory; even after several years, I retained a recollection of the distinctive and critical features, and this allowed for an identification. Third, the identification was made possible through comparison (i.e., of the same kind of reused paper; handwriting). Fourth, to highlight that the identification was confirmed based on a philological analysis (a comparison of the contents of the notebook with al-Maqrīzī's works). Indeed, comparison and philological analysis remain the main means of certifying that a manuscript is in the hand a specific scholar. In the mid-nineteenth century, when the Dutch scholar Reinhart Dozy (1820–83) wanted to establish that three volumes held in the collections of the University of Leiden (L1–3) were holograph copies of al-Maqrīzī's *al-Tārīkh al-kabīr al-muqaffā* (from now on *al-Muqaffā*), he used the same methods.[9] He first noticed that the three volumes shared some characteristics, for example, numerous additions in the margins and on inserts were in the same handwriting as the main text, a feature the

---

reused as scrap paper. In my 1993 article, I referred to that by pointing out that the documents reused in the Liège notebook were from al-Ṣāliḥ Ismāʿīl's reign (743–6/1342–5). See Bauden, Les Manuscrits 151. On these documents, see Bauden, The recovery; id., Diplomatic entanglements; id., Yemeni-Egyptian diplomatic exchanges.

7 Henceforth, I refer to al-Maqrīzī's manuscripts with the abbreviations listed in the appendix at the end of this chapter.

8 I announced the discovery a year later with a paper entitled: À propos du ms. 2232 de l'Université de Liège: découverte d'un nouvel autographe d'al-Maḳrīzī?, which was read at the *7th International Colloquium on Egypt and Syria in the Fatimid, Ayyubid and Mamluk Eras* (Leuven, 12–13 May 1998).

9 The three volumes had already been identified as containing one of al-Maqrīzī's work. See Dozy, Découverte 9.

Leiden manuscripts shared with a copy of *al-Muqaffā* known to be a holograph (P).[10] At that time, there were only two ways to verify whether or not a manuscript was in the hand of a given scholar: to ask another person or institution to send a manuscript considered to be a holograph or to share a facsimile of a sample of the handwriting. Though the first option was still widely practiced until the beginning of the twentieth century, Dozy opted for the second option.[11] Dozy sent a facsimile to Charles Defrémery (1822–83), a French Orientalist who frequently reviewed Dozy's publications for the French audience. Defrémery, in turn, shared a facsimile of P. Both scholars reached the same conclusion, that the handwriting was identical. Dozy also confirmed that L1–3 and P were part of the same work, i.e., *al-Muqaffā*.

One last, and perhaps less expected, impact of my discovery relates to two additional holographs that have been identified since then.[12] Undoubtedly, the

10 Dozy, Découverte 13–4.

11 The color facsimile was reproduced by Dozy, Découverte, after p. 28, to permit the comparison with two other presumed holograph manuscripts held in Gotha (G1 and G2). See Dozy, Découverte 14.

12 In this respect, it is worth mentioning that two of al-Maqrīzī's holograph manuscripts remained unnoticed for some time, though they had been described in old catalogues.

(1) The first one, Al, is now in the holdings of the Bibliotheca Alexandrina, which incorporated the collections of the Municipal Library (al-Maktaba al-Baladiyya), where the manuscript was previously preserved. It was first described in 1955 by al-Shandī, *Fihris* 15, under the title *Qiṭaʿ tārīkhiyya*. Al-Shandī identified the MS as a holograph that corresponds to preparatory drafts (*musawwadāt taḥḍīriyya*) for *al-Tārīkh al-kabīr* (i.e., *al-Muqaffā*) and various notes on a wide range of topics that are briefly described in his catalogue. A few years later, the Institute of Arabic Manuscripts in Cairo microfilmed the most significant manuscripts in this library, including al-Maqrīzī's holograph. These were then described in the catalogue of microfilmed manuscripts published by the Institute: see *Fihris al-makhṭūṭāt al-muṣawwara: al-Tārīkh*, part 2, 165. This manuscript was first mentioned in a scientific publication in 1990: ʿIzz al-Dīn ʿAlī, *al-Maqrīzī* 76 (no. 39: *nubadh tārīkhiyya*) and Muṣṭafā, *al-Tārīkh al-ʿarabī* 3, 149 (no. 19: *nubadh tārīkhiyya*). After its incorporation in the Bibliotheca Alexandrina holdings, the manuscript was briefly described in Zaydān, *Fihris* 19 and 83–4 (no. 59). The manuscript is the subject of a thorough description in my Maqriziana VII.

(2) The second one, Da, is a manuscript that was first mentioned in the old catalogue of the Ẓāhiriyya Library in Damascus under the title *Dhikr bināʾ al-Kaʿba al-bayt al-ḥarām* and thereafter referred to in *GAL* ii, 675 (no. 17). In the subsequent years, it was mentioned in other Syrian catalogues like al-ʿIshsh, *Fihris* 105 (*Bināʾ al-Kaʿba*) and al-Rayyān, *Fihris* 647. Though the volume opens with a text composed by al-Maqrīzī, entitled, as the title page witnesses, *al-Juzʾ fī bināʾ al-Kaʿba al-ḥarām*, it also contains some thirty additional leaves with his various notes that essentially make the whole volume another example of one of his notebooks. The manuscript was first mentioned in a study in 1990: Muṣṭafā, *al-Tārīkh al-ʿarabī* 3, 149 (no. 26: *Dhikr bināʾ al-Kaʿba wa-l-bayt al-ḥarām*).

notice has drawn the attention of scholars from around the world, and consequently increased their awareness of some of the above-mentioned features.

In a 2002 catalogue of a selection of manuscripts held at the National Library of Dushanbe (Tajikistan), the authors described a so far unnoticed holograph manuscript of al-Maqrīzī. It consists of selections (*mukhtār*) al-Maqrīzī took from Ibn Ḥabīb al-Ḥalabī's (d. 779/1377) *Durrat al-aslāk fī dawlat al-Atrāk*, a chronicle of the Mamlūk sultanate from its beginning until the year 777/1375. In the colophon (fol. 179^b), al-Maqrīzī specifies that he completed his work on Monday, 20 Rabīʿ I 824/25 March 1421.[13] Thanks to this note, identifying this manuscript as a holograph was fairly straightforward for the cataloguers and it could be corroborated by consulting some reproductions of al-Maqrīzī's handwriting.

The next identification was made in 2010 at the University of Michigan (Ann Arbor). In April of the same year, Noah Gardiner, then a third-year graduate student taking part in the cataloguing of a poorly known collection of roughly 1,100 Islamic manuscripts,[14] started to look at MS Isl. 605, identified on the title page as the third volume of al-Maqrīzī's *al-Khiṭaṭ*. Gardiner noticed that the manuscript was unusual because it included blank spaces in the text, probably left for later inclusions, in addition, there were several pasted-in inserts with additions in the manuscript's primary hand—both features that usually set off alarms for cataloguers. Just as Dozy had done in the mid-nineteenth century, Gardiner compared the manuscript's handwriting with the reproductions he found in some of my articles, and concluded that they were a perfect match, something that he asked me to confirm by sharing some pictures of the manuscript.[15]

These stories tellingly illustrate that al-Maqrīzī's holographs are firstly identified on the basis of a personal impression. This personal impression is linked to one's ability to recognize specific physical characteristics (the presence of features commonly associated with drafts, reused chancery paper, handwrit-

13 See Bahramiyān and Yūnus Āf, *Fihrist* 91. In 2006, the author published a short study about this manuscript: Bahramiyān, Atharī nāshinākhtah.

14 The catalogue as well as the digitization of the whole collection are now complete. It can be consulted online (https://search.lib.umich.edu/catalog?filter.collection=Islamic+Manuscripts&filter.location=Special+Collections&library=All+libraries&sort=date_asc).

15 The discovery was officially announced in the newsletter of the University of Michigan Department of Near Eastern Studies in August of the same year. The text is now available online (https://www.lib.umich.edu/international-studies/news/autograph-al-maqrizis-khitat-revealed-university-michigan-library). Subsequently, we published together an article presenting the finding and its significance for al-Maqrīzī's methodology. See Gardiner and Bauden, A recently discovered holograph fair copy.

ing). Several scholars are now able to establish, with some confidence, whether or not a handwriting is that of al-Maqrīzī. Nonetheless, even if they are convinced of the soundness of their expertise—and this is generally trusted—, they are hardly able to demonstrate that their identification is beyond doubt. As Colette Sirat put it: "It is obvious that one cannot *prove* that two texts were penned by the same hand. The only way to persuade other people that this is so is to *show* them, to give them the *feeling* that it is the same hand."[16] The only way to reach this goal is to objectivize, to distance onseself from the object because nothing is worse than the absolute desire to detect—sometimes at all costs—a scholar's handwriting on a manuscript.[17] One can rightly ask if it is really al-Maqrīzī's handwriting. The quantity of preserved material—some 5,000 leaves from twenty-five manuscripts[18]—and its variety (notebooks, sketches, drafts, fair copies), together with philological and paleographical analyses, are helpful to rule out the hypothesis that it could be in someone else's handwriting. Other features strengthen the assumption that a work could be that of al-Maqrīzī, for example, the way he writes his name on the title pages or in the colophons (the *laqab* is always neglected, as it should be) or includes an invocation after his name.[19] Al-Maqrīzī also left numerous consultation notes on manuscripts that he accessed for his work and these are useful for comparison.[20] Combined with other elements grasped from a codicological analysis, paleography allows scholars to develop great insight and enables them to accurately describe a handwriting and point to its idiosyncrasies. The contribution of other disciplines, fields, and techniques, like philology, expertise in handwriting, diplomatics and the digital humanities can only enhance the way we look at and describe a handwriting, and, can in fact, help us refine the analysis.

16 Sirat, *Writing* 493 (author's emphasis).

17 See the interesting case reported by Griffel, Is there an autograph. The author shows that a license of transmission found at the end of a copy of al-Ghazālī's *al-Wajīz fī l-fiqh* preserved at Yale (MS Landberg 318) and presented by the editors of one of his texts as a unique example of al-Ghazālī's handwriting is in fact a copy of an original found in another manuscript. Apparently the editors neglected the fact that the colophon of the manuscript is dated after al-Ghazālī's death (d. 505/1111): 570/1175 (not 507/1114 as Griffel reported on the basis of the cataloguer's reading (ibid., 174)). In any case, this means that, even though the editors wanted to see al-Ghazālī's hand in this license, the intention of the person who penned it was pure. For other examples, see chapter 3 in this volume.

18 See next section.

19 See chapter 3 in this volume, 72. As the author states, these elements are not definitive proof of the identification. They must be considered together with other external and internal elements.

20 On these, see Bauden, Maqriziana XVIII. Once again, consultation notes can also be faked, but their number helps to dismiss such an hypothesis.

Why does it matter? The identification of al-Maqrīzī's handwriting not only counts for the owners—nowadays usually public libraries—who can boast about a precious item, but first and foremost for the historian who wants to ascertain whose work he is considering and to know that the words he is reading were penned by this scholar. Even more importantly, an irrefutable identification also relates to consultation notes that a specific scholar left in the books he consulted and, sometimes, notes or even criticisms he jotted down in the books he read and excerpted passages from.[21] From the philological point of view, the editor needs to verify all the handwriting on the page; for instance, if a copyist copied a text of al-Maqrīzī, but al-Maqrīzī intervened in some way (an authorial manuscript), can the editor identify the hand of the copyist versus that of al-Maqrīzī.[22] These are critical matters for significant issues like the accusations of plagiarism raised by some of al-Maqrīzī's contemporaries. When I found twenty leaves in a different handwriting in one volume of his draft of *al-Khiṭaṭ* (IT2), I approached them in light of the words expressed by al-Maqrīzī's colleague and friend, Ibn Ḥajar (d. 852/1449), and later repeated by the latter's student, al-Sakhāwī (d. 902/1497), in which he stated that al-Maqrīzī had taken advantage of his colleague and neighbor's manuscript and had appropriated it. The neighbor in question was al-Awḥadī (d. 811/1408), who had been working for years on a book detailing the history of the city of Cairo from an architectural point of view. According to al-Sakhāwī, al-Awḥadī's manuscript was in part a fair copy and al-Maqrīzī, added material to it, greatly expanding the original work, but essentially availed himself of the work without naming its original author. I resorted to a paleographical and philological analysis in order to demonstrate that the hand that penned the twenty leaves still found in al-Maqrīzī's draft was that of al-Awḥadī.[23] Al-Awḥadī's handwriting is preserved in just a few consultation notes jotted down on the title pages of books he consulted for his work or in ownership marks. Enough specimens have been preserved to allow a fair comparison, though the size of these specimens, by definition, is limited.[24] The study of the text also revealed that al-Maqrīzī could not have written it because the author of the lines described some persons

21 On this, see Bauden, Maqriziana XVIII.

22 This is particularly true for the edition of his opuscules preserved in L5, most of which are in someone else's hand but revised by al-Maqrīzī. See Bauden, *Al-Maqrīzī's collection*, as well as the opuscules so far published in the *Bibliotheca Maqriziana*: al-Maqrīzī, *Ḍawʾ al-sārī*; al-Maqrīzī, *Al-Maqrīzī's Traktat*; al-Maqrīzī, *Caliphate and kingship*.

23 See Bauden, Maqriziana IX.

24 In the case of the consultation notes, they include his name, the place where he read the text, and the date. The note is introduced by a verb that indicates the nature of the

FIGURE 5.1 Handwriting identified as al-Awḥadī's (MS Emanet Hazinezi 1405, fol. 83b)
ISTANBUL, TSMK

FIGURE 5.2 al-Maqrīzī's handwriting at the age of 28 (MS Murat Molla 575, fol. 3b)
ISTANBUL, SÜLEYMANIYE KÜTÜPHANESI

as his masters, some people with whom al-Maqrīzī never studied. Despite the evidence presented, Ayman Fu'ād Sayyid, the editor of *al-Khiṭaṭ*, rejected the identification of al-Awḥadī's handwriting (see fig. 5.1), instead, he considered it to be al-Maqrīzī's handwriting and explained the large number of discrepancies between the two hands as due to the fact that that part of the manuscript was penned in his youth, as witnessed, for instance, by IM, copied when al-Maqrīzī was twenty-eight years old (see fig. 5.2).[25]

---

consultation, i.e., if he only read it, or read it and took notes. Since the publication of my Maqriziana IX, I have identified two additional marks: one consultation note and one ownership mark.

25 Fu'ād Sayyid, *al-Maqrīzī* 90–1. A comparison between these handwritings cannot be tackled in the framework of this study (nevertheless, see below, 196, for at least two discrepancies). This issue will be scrutinized in a forthcoming study devoted to al-Awḥadī and his book. However, I can certainly respond to the issue of the masters. Fu'ād Sayyid tried to invalidate my argument by demonstrating that the two masters with whom al-Maqrīzī did not study were in fact part of his curriculum. Unfortunately, with regard to the first master, he cites a name that I specifically indicated as having been al-Maqrīzī's master (al-Bulqīnī; see Bauden, Maqriziana IX 184). Regarding the second master (al-Bilbaysī), he refers to two places (there are in fact three) in the *Khiṭaṭ* where al-Maqrīzī characterizes him as *shaykhunā*. As for the first two places (al-Maqrīzī, *al-Mawāʿiẓ wa-l-iʿtibār*, Fu'ād Sayyid ed., iv/2, 582 and 677), the passages appear in the twenty leaves that I identified as being in al-Awḥadī's hand. Al-Maqrīzī left out both passages in his final version (for the first see, al-Maqrīzī, *al-Mawāʿiẓ wa-l-iʿtibār*, Būlāq ed., ii, 394; for the second, al-Maqrīzī ignored the whole entry for the *madrasa*). Finally, the third quotation (al-Maqrīzī, *al-Mawāʿiẓ wa-l-iʿtibār*, ed. Fu'ād Sayyid, iv/2, 729) is found in al-Maqrīzī's hand in the first version of the *Khiṭaṭ* (IT2, fol. 111b), but al-Maqrīzī cancelled it in his final version too (ibid., Būlāq ed., ii, 415). This final passage is further proof that the first version of the *Khiṭaṭ* is largely a fair copy of al-Awḥadī's text, as I suggested in Bauden, Maqriziana IX 209–12. Al-Maqrīzī faithfully copied al-Awḥadī's text (mostly a draft), and even included personal particulars that could only be related to al-Awḥadī. He only left out these particulars after he expanded the original text.

Before addressing al-Maqrīzī's handwriting in the framework of a fact-based and empirical analysis, I first consider elements that may have impacted his way of writing. First, I outline the main facts related to his life and his output as a scholar, I then detail the quantity, the quality, and the variety of the corpus constituted by the holographs preserved, particularly those aspects that are germane to a paleographical study. Finally, I tackle the issue of al-Maqrīzī's training in writing and, probably, in calligraphy.

2 A Prolific Author and Copyist[26]

Born in 766/1364–5 in the Barjawān quarter of the Fatimid district of Cairo, Aḥmad b. ʿAlī b. ʿAbd al-Qādir al-Maqrīzī (d. 845/1442) was raised in a family of scholars on his father's and mother's sides. After moving from Damascus, where he was born, to Cairo, al-Maqrīzī's father (d. 779/1378) cultivated a strong relationship with one of the most influential amirs of that time in the capital; thus, he secured his nomination to a position of secretary at the chancery. Married to the daughter of a prominent scholar, Ibn al-Ṣāʾigh (d. 776/1375), al-Maqrīzī's father also took advantage of his father-in-law's standing and favor at court, as the latter had the privilege, in his capacity as *muftī*, of sitting at the supreme court at the citadel. Even though al-Maqrīzī lost his maternal grandfather and his father when he was barely a teenager, he continued his education in the religious sciences, until he reached his majority and received his first positions. In his early twenties, treading in his father's steps, he joined the chancery as a secretary, then started a career in the judiciary, and occupied various positions, like market inspector (*muḥtasib*). During these years, he enjoyed a privileged relationship with the military and ruling elite. In his early fifties, he decided not to run for office and to retire from public service to devote himself entirely to writing, especially the history of his homeland, Egypt.[27]

In some fifty years of scholarship, al-Maqrīzī produced some of the most significant works ever written in the field of history, covering the full span of time, from the pre-Islamic period to his own time. His interests covered a wide range of disciplines, from economy to law and *ḥadīth*, from metrology to gemmology, and other fields. According to his own testimony, his works (*muṣannafāt*) exceeded two hundred large volumes.[28] The adjective "large" (*kibār*) implies

26 For al-Maqrīzī's life, see Bauden, Taqī al-Dīn Aḥmad ibn ʿAlī al-Maqrīzī 161–7.

27 For a similar pattern regarding al-Nuwayrī—this is clearly not a topos—, see chapter 6 in this volume.

28 Al-Sakhāwī, *al-Ḍawʾ al-lāmiʿ* ii, 23.

at least 200–250 leaves—the average number of leaves in the preserved holograph manuscripts of his personal works—, which means that he would have copied between 40,000–50,000 leaves. In total, including his drafts and notebooks, he must have penned over 100,000 leaves.[29] As al-Sakhāwī stressed, al-Maqrīzī wrote copiously in his own hand (*khaṭṭa bi-khaṭṭihi l-kathīr*);[30] the remains of his writing activity corroborate this: among the twenty-five volumes, representing the various stages of his scholarship (drafts, fair copies, notebooks, summaries), twenty-four are holographs.[31] In sum, al-Maqrīzī controlled the whole process of creation, from reading, excerpting, and summarizing sources to drafting and preparing the fair copy of his works. One exception relates to his collection of opuscules (MS L5), composed at various periods in his life, which he gathered toward the end of his life and gave to a scribe whom he probably hired to prepare a fair copy of them. The reason behind this exceptional behavior is clear if we note his activities at that time: he was too busy with his last major work to copy the opuscules himself.[32] Al-Maqrīzī indeed devoted himself to voluminous works. Those works that have reached us include, by order of size: *al-Muqaffā* (sixteen volumes), *Imtāʿ al-asmāʿ* (six volumes), *al-Khabar* (six volumes), *al-Sulūk* (five volumes), *al-Khiṭaṭ* (four volumes), and *Durar al-ʿuqūd al-farīda* (four volumes), i.e., forty-one volumes in all.[33] Each of these works also involved at least two stages: a rough draft or first version, and a fair copy or last version. Of this prolific activity, about 5,000 leaves have been preserved, representing only the tip of the iceberg.

---

29 On the writing pace in general, see Déroche, Copier des manuscrits. For the specific case of al-Nuwayrī, see chapter 6 in this volume. In his biography of his master Ibn Ḥajar (*al-Jawāhir wa-l-durar* i, 167–9), al-Sakhāwī reports (under the heading "the hurriedness of [Ibn Ḥajar's] nevertheless nice handwriting" [surʿat al-kitāba maʿa ḥusnihā]) several anecdotes related to his master's prowess as a copyist.

30 Al-Sakhāwī, *al-Ḍawʾ al-lāmiʿ* ii, 22.

31 For the list of al-Maqrīzī's holograph and authorial manuscripts, see the appendix at the end of this chapter.

32 The collection of opuscules was copied by the scribe before Shaʿbān 841/February 1438, which is when al-Maqrīzī started to revise the scribe's work. At that time, al-Maqrīzī was trying to complete *al-Khabar ʿan al-bashar*, a six-volume work devoted to the history of humankind before Islam. See Bauden, Maqriziana XIV; id., *Al-Maqrīzī's collection*.

33 With the exception of *al-Khabar*, the information regarding the number of volumes for each work is given by the Meccan historian Ibn Fahd (d. 885/1480), who studied with al-Maqrīzī and read his books during his last two pilgrimages to Mecca (834–5/1431 and 838–40/1435–6). See Ibn Fahd, *Muʿjam al-shuyūkh* 66. For *al-Khabar*, Ibn Fahd refers to two volumes because at the time of al-Maqrīzī's last pilgrimage the work was not yet complete. It now stands at six volumes, of which five holograph volumes have been preserved (see appendix: IA, IF1, IF2, IF3, IF4).

3 A Dated/Datable and Mixed Corpus

These leaves provide us with unique material, both in terms of chronology and variety. The corpus is indeed helpful to characterize al-Maqrīzī's handwriting as it covers a period of some fifty years, i.e., the majority of his life as a scholar, starting in 795/1392–3, when he was twenty-eight years old, and ending with the year of his death in 845/1442 at the age of seventy-seven. In fig. 5.3, I present a timeline of his holograph and authorial manuscripts. This timeline helps to visualize the periods when al-Maqrīzī completed some of these copies.[34] The dating, whether it is precise or estimated, is based on several internal and external elements. In the case of the independent summaries[35] (C, Du, IM), al-Maqrīzī revealed in the colophon the precise date of the completion of his work.

In other cases, the analysis of al-Maqrīzī's working method allows me to state that whenever he consulted and took notes from a source, he added a consultation note in the source manuscript, stating that he had taken advantage of it (*istafāda minhu*), by which he meant that he took notes from it, or that he prepared a summary (*intaqā*) (see fig. 5.4).[36] These notes are critical to date other summaries for which al-Maqrīzī neglected to write a colophon as well as some parts of his works that are based on material he selected from his summaries. For example, as his consultation note attests (see fig. 5.4), he read and prepared a résumé of Ibn Faḍl Allāh al-ʿUmarī's (749/1349) *Masālik al-abṣār* in 831/1427–8. Some parts of this résumé are now found in one of his notebooks (Lg).[37] The study of these résumés demonstrates that they were made by al-Maqrīzī on the spot, i.e., while reading the source,[38] a method that we can now assume he used for his résumés of other sources. In the case of *Masālik al-abṣār*, the résumé can thus be dated accordingly, i.e., to 831/1427–8, which corresponds to the date he consulted this source (see fig. 5.4). Moreover, al-Maqrīzī sometimes reused the material selected in his résumés in his own works. In such cases, the relevant

34 I must stress that this timeline does not attempt to date the point when al-Maqrīzī started to compose these books. This is a different issue that I hope to tackle in the future.

35 By independent summaries, I mean those that stand as a single unit in one volume, that is, not those found in al-Maqrīzī's notebooks. In the case of the notebooks, al-Maqrīzī does not say when he completed the summary.

36 Bauden, Maqriziana II 72–3. Since this article was published, eight additional consultation notes have been identified and must be added to the list of consultation notes (twenty-five volumes representing seven works) found in appendix 2 of that study (ibid. 117–8). These consultation notes will be the subject of my Maqriziana XVIII.

37 Bauden, Maqriziana I-1 63–4; Bauden, Maqriziana I-2 135.

38 Bauden, Maqriziana II 60–7.

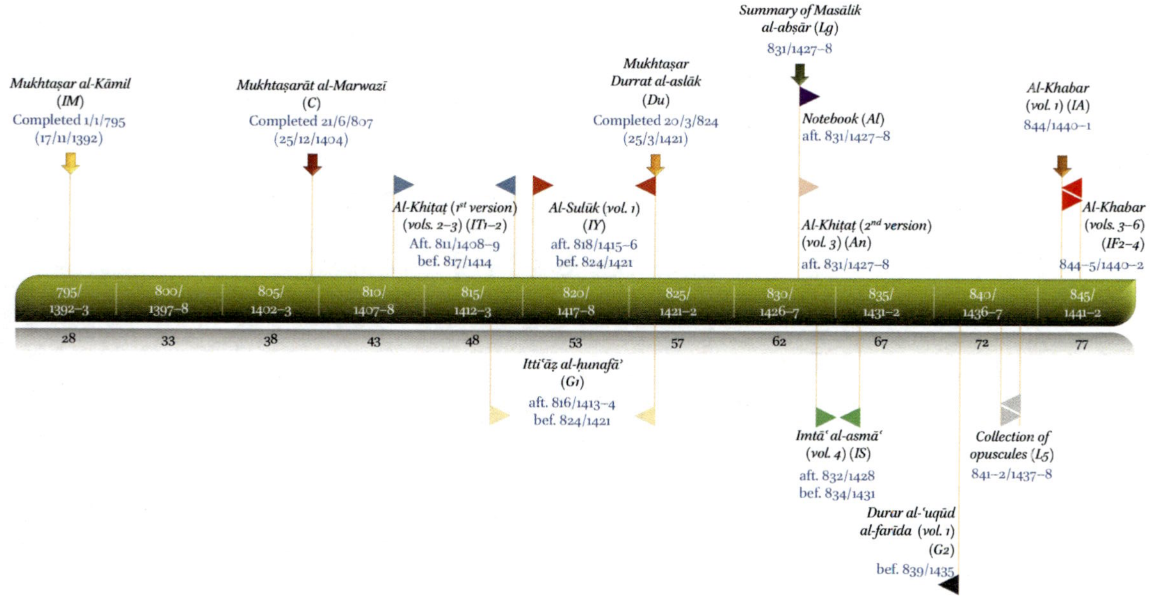

FIGURE 5.3 Timeline of al-Maqrīzī's holograph and authorial manuscripts
Note: The timeline is divided in periods of five *hijra* years with indications of al-Maqrīzī's age (according to CE years) beneath each reference point. An arrow indicates that the manuscript was dated by al-Maqrīzī in the colophon or can be dated precisely thanks to other factors (e.g., date of consultation notes of the source on which the summary is based). The dates of the titles between flags are tentative and based on data collected either in the manuscript or elsewhere (e.g., a dated consultation note of a source on which the work is based). For the details that are useful to fix *termini ante quem* and *post quem*, see the appendix.

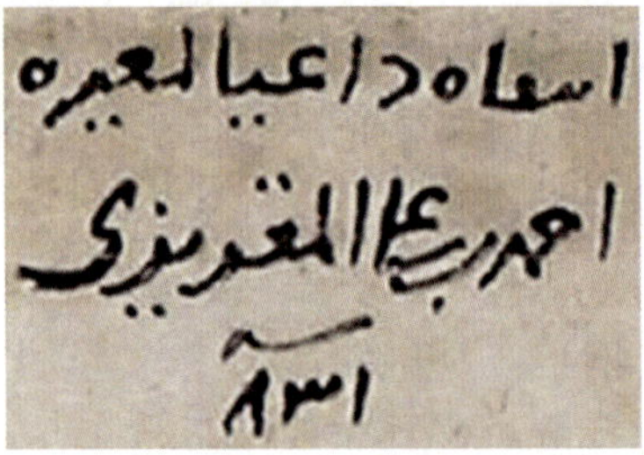

FIGURE 5.4
Al-Maqrīzī's consultation note in Ibn Faḍl Allāh al-ʿUmarī's *Masālik al-abṣār*, vol. 3 (MS Ayasofya 3416, fol. 1[a])
Note: It reads: *intaqāhu dāʿiyan li-muʿīrihi / Aḥmad b. ʿAlī l-Maqrīzī / sanat 831.*
ISTANBUL, SÜLEYMANIYE KÜTÜPHANESI

sections in these works can also be dated appropriately, like the section on the Mongol *Yāsa* (book of laws) in *al-Khiṭaṭ*, which is taken entirely from *Masālik al-abṣār* via the résumé found in Lg.[39] The last version of *al-Khiṭaṭ*, represented by a single manuscript (An), which includes the relevant section, was thus written down after 831/1427–8, most probably shortly after that date.

Al-Maqrīzī's reuse of chancery documents is also helpful to place his manuscripts—in full when the whole manuscript is made of the same document or, when that is not the case, some sections of it only—on the timeline when the original documents can be reconstructed and dated.[40]

In other circumstances, the holograph manuscripts can be dated based on an internal reference, like vol. 1 of *al-Khabar* (IA), where al-Maqrīzī specifies that a practice he describes in his text is contemporaneous, i.e., in 844/1440–1.[41]

The variety of the corpus is also quite uncommon. Al-Maqrīzī's writing activity represents all the circumstances by which a writer commits to paper his or someone else's words, i.e., a combination of the activity of a writer and a copyist. As a writer composing his own work—in his particular case, given that he was mostly a compiler, his work was based on information he gathered from sources in résumés and notebooks—, his first sketches are the result of a cre-

39 On this see, Bauden, *Trusting the source*.

40 A section of *al-Khabar* (the one on Alexander the Great and Aristotle; IF3, fols. 115[a]–31[b]) could only have been composed after 819/1416–7, as it was penned on a document that reached Cairo that year. In this case, it is clear that al-Maqrīzī took that section from a previous work, presumably lost, as it fitted well in *al-Khabar*, which is dated to the years 844–5/1440–2. It partly relies on a résumé al-Maqrīzī made based on Ibn Abī Uṣaybiʿa's (d. 668/1270) *ʿUyūn al-anbāʾ*, which is preserved in Lg (unfortunately undated). Part of the same text had already been used in *al-Khiṭaṭ*. The difference between the handwriting of this section on Alexander the Great and that of the remainder of the manuscript also confirms that it was penned earlier in al-Maqrīzī's life. See Bauden, Maqriziana I–1 29–33; al-Maqrīzī, *Al-Maqrīzī's al-Ḫabar* 5/4, 10–1, 399–434. For the reconstructed document, see Bauden, Yemeni-Egyptian diplomatic exchanges.

41 See Bauden, Maqriziana XIV.

ative process in which he chose his words and rephrased his source, if any. As a copyist preparing a fair copy from his drafts, he paid attention to every word and collated the result to ascertain that he did not make mistakes typical of copyists (*saut du même au même* and homeoteleuton being the most frequent phenomena). The aspects of the composition and copy usually indicate the various circumstances that may influence a scholar's handwriting.

The corpus is representative of those diverse circumstances in many respects. Some manuscripts correspond to summaries based on sources that al-Maqrīzī consulted. I have established, through an analysis of his working method, that the summarizing process was taking place while he was reading.[42] As indicated, his summaries can be found in independent volumes or were inserted in notebooks, depending on their size. Other manuscripts may contain first sketches of his personal works. These first sketches may be the result of his personal testimonies collected over time and compiled to create a text that he jotted down in a single moment. These first sketches are typically found in his notebooks and on slips of paper inserted in his fair copies. In other cases, the manuscript is already the result of a rough draft that was copied into a neater copy, which he still intended to emend and enlarge.[43] Medieval authors usually referred to these copies as drafts (*musawwada* or *muswadda*).[44] However, the fair copy (*mubayyaḍa* or *mubyaḍḍa*) rarely remained fair: authors continued to modify their texts with rewordings, additions, corrections, cancellations, etc. All of al-Maqrīzī's manuscripts that can be described as fair copies are full of such alterations, including pasted inserts and replaced leaves. Even the evidence left by al-Maqrīzī that he collated the copy is not a sufficient distinction because this evidence does not always appear, particularly in the final version.[45] In conclusion, most, if not all, of his manuscripts that consist of copies of his personal works must be regarded as fair or working copies; al-Maqrīzī's later revisions do not change their status as fair or working copies.[46]

---

42 See Bauden, Maqriziana II 113.

43 This is typically the case of IT1 and IT2 (two volumes containing parts of *al-Khiṭaṭ*), a copy of a previous rough draft attributable to al-Awḥadī. We know that al-Maqrīzī knew that this was not the definitive fair copy because he recycled chancery scrap paper for both these volumes.

44 See chapter 3 in this volume.

45 Al-Maqrīzī uses the word *balagha* (for *balagha muqābalatan*, "he reached [this place] in the collation") in the following manuscripts: IA, IF1, IF2, IF3, IF4, IY, IT1, IT2. This phrase does not appear in An, G1, G2, and IS, which should nevertheless be considered fair copies. Note that these collation notes were usually in the margins (inner or outer), in most cases close to the edge, and they were trimmed when the manuscript was bound. On these collation notes, see Bauden, *Al-Maqrīzī's collection*.

46 See Sirat, *Writing* 479; Bauden, Maqriziana X–1. In the case of al-Maqrīzī, we know that the

All in all, with the exception of the first sketches, the majority of al-Maqrīzī's manuscripts may be characterized as copies, as they are the result of a writing activity that was a process of copying: his eyes moved from the text he was copying to the blank page where he wrote it.

4 Al-Maqrīzī's Training in Writing and Calligraphy

The training that al-Maqrīzī received in his younger days is another factor that must be taken into consideration. As noted by paleographers and handwriting specialists, children who are trained as scribes and taught to write usually adopt common shapes that were elaborated and taught over the course of centuries.[47] Furthermore, in modern times, it has been demonstrated that children who are first taught how to write with unconnected letters in the Latin alphabet develop cursive handwriting between the ages of 7 and 15, when the need to write more quickly arises. It is also during this period that children develop idiosyncratic shapes that diverge from the standard models they were taught when they were young. These idiosyncrasies are among the elements that make their handwriting personal;[48] therefore, in this respect, it is worth investigating whether or not al-Maqrīzī received a specific education and how it might have impacted his handwriting.

Despite al-Maqrīzī's fame and in comparison with some of his contemporaries like Ibn Ḥajar, little is known of al-Maqrīzī's primary education, aside from the fact that his maternal grandfather mainly took care of it.[49] Born in a propitious context—into a family of scholars on both his mother's and father's sides—, al-Maqrīzī went through the classical education of that time which began with memorizing the Qurʾān at the age of four or five.[50] Reading and writing the holy text were also part of the curriculum.[51] Before reaching puberty

final fair copy was produced by a copyist based on al-Maqrīzī's working copy that corresponded to the last stage of his work. This corresponds to the moment when the work was published, i.e., made public.

47 Beit-Arié, Stéréotypies 201–2, speaks of the Hebrew tradition and also stresses that the would-be scribe would imitate his master's handwriting until his own writing matches it, thus the student reproduces what becomes a standardized handwriting.

48 Wing, Étude 134.

49 Ibn Ḥajar, *Inbāʾ al-ghumr* iv, 187.

50 By way of comparison, note that al-Sakhāwī attended a Qurʾānic school (*maktab*) at the age of four and his master, Ibn Ḥajar, at five. See Guérin du Grandlaunay, *Iršād al-ġāwī* i, respectively 198 and 79. Al-Sakhāwī's first teacher was a copyist (*nāsikh*). Ibid. 199.

51 Hirschler, *The written word* 91–9. As stated by Sirat, *Writing* 88: "To give an adequate

(*bulūgh*)—generally between the age of eight and twelve—, a student was expected to have memorized the whole text; this accomplishment was usually celebrated by a public recitation, which also tallied with the end of the primary education.[52] Al-Maqrīzī was unique, as he was only seven when he memorized the whole Qur'ān,[53] a fact that corroborates that he received a good primary education.[54] As noted, his father worked as a secretary at the state chancery, which means that he must have practiced calligraphy, which was a prerequisite for a secretary.[55] Once his secondary education was complete, around the age of twenty, we know that al-Maqrīzī followed in his father's steps by entering the state chancery[56] and that he was quickly assigned to oversee the department of secretaries (*mubāsharat al-tawqīʿ*).[57] Thus, al-Maqrīzī must have received

account of Muslim schools is an impossible task, for two reasons: First, the Muslim cultural sphere penetrated vast stretches of Asia, Africa, and Europe. Each country had its own traditions of schooling and they cannot be treated as a whole. Second, we know almost nothing about how most of these schools taught Arabic writing." On the teaching of writing and calligraphy in the Mamlūk period, see now Behrens-Abouseif, *The book* 108–13. Moreover, we have a precise description of the teaching of writing for the beginning of the eighth/fourteenth century in Egypt. In his *Nihāyat al-arab*, al-Nuwayrī (d. 733/1333), who was known for his excellent handwriting, explains that writing was taught in two steps: primary training provided the pupil with the fundamentals of writing, followed by secondary training, where calligraphy was taught (see *Nihāyat al-arab* ix, 218–23). On this text, see also chapter 6 in this volume as well as Gacek, Al-Nuwayrī's classification, for a translation of the last part of the section referred to above.

52 In the case of Ibn Ḥajar, the public recitation took place when he was twelve, while for al-Sakhāwī it was before he turned thirteen. Guérin du Grandlaunay, *Iršād al-ġāwī* i, 189 and 204 respectively. This event was sometimes celebrated with even greater solemnity by allowing the pupil to recite the entire Qur'ān throughout the full month of Ramadan. See ibid. 189–91.

53 Ibn Fahd, *Muʿjam al-shuyūkh* 64.

54 This is all Ibn Ḥajar says when he states that al-Maqrīzī *"nasha'a nash'a ḥasana."* See Ibn Ḥajar, *Inbā' al-ghumr* iv, 187.

55 Wiet, Les Classiques, 45. Prerequisite refers to the ability to write in one of the styles used by the chancery. Some obviously had more skill than others and therefore they were asked to pen the most significant documents. See below, n. 57.

56 Al-Maqrīzī personally affirms his activity at the chancery when he says that he wrote (*katabtu*) there. See al-Maqrīzī, *Durar al-ʿuqūd al-farīda* ii, 49.

57 During the Mamlūk period, the state chancery employed two categories of secretaries. The first category included the *kuttāb al-dast* or *al-muwaqqiʿūn*. These secretaries attended the sessions held in the sultan's presence, in which petitions were presented, and notes were written down (*tawqīʿ*) to record the decision taken during these sessions. According to al-Qalqashandī, this category of secretaries increased in number in the eighth/fourteenth century, rising from three to about ten by the third quarter of the same century, and continued increasing progressively until there were twenty by the end of the century, when al-Maqrīzī headed the department. Initially, the second category, the *kuttāb al-darj*, were

some training in calligraphy, though this is not clear from the list of his masters,[58] with one notable exception.

We would know nothing of his training in calligraphy if he had not mentioned, *en passant*, that one of the most important calligraphers of his time was his master: ʿAlī b. Muḥammad al-Sinjārī, known as ʿUṣfūr (d. 808/1406). ʿUṣfūr, who was of Syrian origin, settled in Cairo later in life to become a secretary at the chancery.[59] Ibn Ḥajar depicts him as a calligrapher who wrote the pro-

responsible for issuing all categories of documents. This group also increased in number until they exceeded one hundred thirty at the end of the eighth/fourteenth century. Yet, the tasks they performed decreased at that time, as they only issued documents of the lower categories, while the *muwaqqiʿūn* took over the preparation of the most significant documents. Al-Qalqashandī underlines that some *kuttāb al-darj* were asked to issue some more important documents, provided they had nice handwriting; this means that most of the *kuttāb al-darj* at that time had not mastered the various styles used for the issuance of the documents of the highest categories. This also implies that all of the *muwaqqiʿūn* had. Considering that al-Maqrīzī was the supervisor of this category of secretaries, it corroborates the claim that he had also studied how to pen documents. See al-Qalqashandī, *Ṣubḥ al-aʿshā* i, 137–8. Behrens-Abouseif (*The book* 114) emphasizes that "… the bureaucracy, notably the chancery, was the main domain for recruiting calligraphers. Prominent calligraphers were sought after by the chancery and other administrative offices." For a lavish example of the kind of manuscripts a secretary (*kātib al-darj* in this case) could produce, see MS Garrett no. 12G (PUL): the text, *Idrāk al-sūl fī musābaqat al-khuyūl*, was composed and copied by al-Ḥusayn b. Muḥammad al-Ḥusaynī in 729/1329 for the library of the reigning sultan, al-Nāṣir Muḥammad.

58 Al-Jalīlī argues that for most of his life and until his death al-Maqrīzī worked at the chancery (*Durar al-ʿuqūd al-farīda* iv, 43–52 (52: "fa-yabdū anna l-Maqrīzī baqiya fī dīwān al-inshāʾ ḥattā qabl wafātihi fī 845h")). Al-Jalīlī's assumption is based on his interpretation of passages in which al-Maqrīzī specifies that he had a close relationship with each of the secretaries of state from the reigns of Barqūq and his successors, and he means precisely that. Al-Maqrīzī did not state that he worked for them. The only clear indication that al-Maqrīzī worked at the chancery, like his father, is given by al-Maqrīzī himself, who states that he was employed at the *dīwān al-inshāʾ* until the 790s/early 1390s: "I sat in it [the hall of the vizier which is in the vicinity of the chancery], by the judge Badr al-Dīn Muḥammad b. Faḍl Allāh al-ʿUmarī [who was the secretary of state, for the second time, from 786/1385 to 792/1390], when I was supervising the sultanic bureau that oversaw the issuance of official documents (*tawqīʿ*) until about the 790s [/1390]" ("wa-anā jalastu bi-hā [qāʿat al-ṣāḥib bi-jiwār dīwān al-inshāʾ] ʿind al-qāḍī Badr al-Dīn Muḥammad b. Faḍl Allāh al-ʿUmarī ayyām mubāsharatī l-tawqīʿ al-sulṭānī ilā naḥw al-tisʿīn wa-l-sabʿimiʾa"). See al-Maqrīzī, *al-Mawāʿiẓ wa-l-iʿtibār* iii, 730 (Būlāq ed., ii, 225); Bauden, The recovery 74–5. *Ṣāḥib* initially referred to the vizier, a position that fell into disuse in the eighth/fourteenth century. The term was then used to designate the secretary of state as well as the hall where the secretaries worked and the archives were kept (*qāʿat al-ṣāḥib*).

59 His full name was ʿAlāʾ al-Dīn ʿAlī b. Muḥammad b. ʿAbd al-Naṣīr al-Sinjārī l-Dimashqī. In the biography of another master calligrapher, al-Ziftāwī (on whom see below), al-Maqrīzī (*Durar al-ʿuqūd al-farīda* iii, 119) reveals that he was his master: "I met him [al-Ziftāwī] at

portionate styles (*al-mansūb*) according to Yāqūt al-Mustaʿṣimī (d. 696/1298), though he followed the Syrian school in this respect. Ibn Ḥajar also mentions that a large number of notables (*aʿyān*) learned calligraphy from him.[60] In addition to ʿUṣfūr, al-Maqrīzī also may have studied under Muḥammad b. Aḥmad b. ʿAlī l-Ziftāwī (d. 806/1403), to whom he devoted an entry in the biographical dictionary of his contemporaries.[61] There al-Maqrīzī underlines that al-Ziftāwī followed the school of Ibn al-ʿAfīf (d. 736/1336)[62] and that al-Ziftāwī authored a short treatise on calligraphy.[63] Al-Maqrīzī also stressed that he and al-Ziftāwī attended the classes (*majlis*) of ʿUṣfūr in Cairo[64] and that al-Ziftāwī dedicated himself to teaching calligraphy to many Egyptians.[65] Al-Maqrīzī also reckons that al-Ziftāwī was an authority for his knowledge of the proportionate styles, such that he was able to identify the calligrapher of any piece of writing presented to him.[66] He also reports that al-Ziftāwī boasted that he could write a proportionate script with the iron cubit (*al-dhirāʿ al-ḥadīd*) used by merchants to measure fabrics the same way he used a reed pen.[67] If it is established that al-Maqrīzī studied the art of writing with ʿUṣfūr, it remains to be demonstrated that al-Ziftāwī also taught him his art. In any case, it is clear that al-Maqrīzī was acquainted with two of the most prominent calligraphers of his time.

The question of his age when this training took place is central to the development and evolution of one's writing. Unfortunately, al-Maqrīzī remains

---

the classes of our master, the most unique of his time, ʿAlāʾ al-Dīn ʿAlī b. ʿUṣfūr" (ijtamaʿtu bihi fī majlis shaykhinā awḥad al-zamān ʿAlāʾ al-Dīn b. ʿUṣfūr). Even though he calls him "our master," al-Maqrīzī did not deem it necessary to devote an entry to ʿUṣfūr in his *Durar al-ʿuqūd al-farīda*. On him see also Ibn Ḥajar, *Inbāʾ al-ghumr* ii, 341 (no. 21); al-Sakhāwī, *al-Ḍawʾ al-lāmiʿ* v, 316–7 (no. 1045); Behrens-Abouseif, *The book* 132–3 (what she states on p. 132 regarding his teaching ("He seems to have been associated with the aristocracy, which might have prevented him from teaching") is contradicted by the above-mentioned quotation where his *majlis* is evoked).

60 Ibn Ḥajar, *Inbāʾ al-ghumr* ii, 341.

61 Al-Maqrīzī, *Durar al-ʿuqūd al-farīda* iii, 119 (no. 1004). On him see also Ibn Ḥajar, *al-Majmaʿ al-muʾassis* iii, 255–6, no. 630; al-Sakhāwī, *al-Ḍawʾ al-lāmiʿ* vii, 24.

62 On him, see Behrens-Abouseif, *The book* 135.

63 Al-Ziftāwī, *Minhāj al-iṣāba*. Al-Maqrīzī knew the treatise because he quotes its full title.

64 According to Ibn Ḥajar, *Inbāʾ al-ghumr* ii, 341, he was ʿUṣfūr's friend.

65 In *al-Sulūk* iv, 23, al-Maqrīzī refers to him as the dean of calligraphers (*shaykh al-kuttāb*).

66 Al-Maqrīzī, *Durar al-ʿuqūd al-farīda* iii, 119; repeated by Ibn Ḥajar, *al-Majmaʿ al-muʾassis* iii, 256, no. 630.

67 Al-Maqrīzī, *Durar al-ʿuqūd al-farīda* iii, 119. See also Behrens-Abouseif, *The book* 136. In Cairo at that time the length of the iron cubit (also known as the *dhirāʿ al-bazz* or *al-qumāsh*) was 58.187 cm. See Hinz, *Islamische Masse* 56 and 58. Al-Ziftāwī probably used a long instrument (with which to trace the characters on paper) for the monumental stone inscriptions then carved on buildings.

silent on the circumstances that led him to attend ʿUṣfūr's classes. From al-Maqrīzī's statement that it was there that he struck up an acquaintance with al-Ziftāwī, who was already a master calligrapher, we might deduce that this took place during his teenage years (al-Ziftāwī was fifteen years older than al-Maqrīzī).[68] To get a more precise answer, we must turn to al-Maqrīzī's contemporaries. In fact, we know that al-Maqrīzī's colleague and friend Ibn Ḥajar was first trained in calligraphy after he completed his primary education, around thirteen,[69] and afterward proceeded to study with another master, who allowed him to write in the style of calligraphers.[70] Al-Sakhāwī, who belonged to the following generation, started to study calligraphy (*al-kitāba*) at about the same time.[71] These two cases might help us to speculate when al-Maqrīzī began to attend ʿUṣfūr's classes, i.e., around the age of thirteen to fifteen, when al-Ziftāwī, an accomplished calligrapher whom he met during the same classes,[72] was already in his late twenties.

Be that as it may, al-Maqrīzī abandoned his career at the chancery in his mid-twenties and calligraphy was not required in the other positions he filled until his late forties. Unlike other scholars who spent their whole working lives employed at the chancery (e.g., al-Ṣafadī, d. 764/1363), or those who earned a living by copying their own texts or those of others (like al-Nuwayrī),[73]

---

68 He was born in 750/1349–50. See al-Maqrīzī, *Durar al-ʿuqūd al-farīda* iii, 119.

69 See al-Sakhāwī, *al-Jawāhir wa-l-durar* i, 167. His first master was Nūr al-Dīn ʿAlī b. ʿAbd al-Raḥmān al-Badamāṣī (d. 802/1399–1400). On him see Ibn Ḥajar, *al-Majmaʿ al-muʾassis* i, 185, no. 555; al-Maqrīzī, *Durar al-ʿuqūd al-farīda* ii, 553 (no. 871); al-Sakhāwī, *al-Ḍawʾ al-lāmiʿ* v, 438. According to Ibn Ḥajar, ibid., he was a skilled calligrapher (*māhir fī ṣināʿat al-khaṭṭ*) who taught the proportionate styles (*al-mansūb*), had nice handwriting (*kataba l-khaṭṭ al-malīḥ*), and was also proficient in the art of the bookbinding (*ʿarafa ṣināʿat al-wirāqa*).

70 See al-Sakhāwī, *al-Jawāhir wa-l-durar* i, 167 (*adhina lahu fī an yaktub ʿalā ṭarīqat al-kuttāb*). In this context *kuttāb* does not mean secretaries, but calligraphers, as in the expression *shaykh al-kuttāb* seen above (see n. 65). The second master was al-Ziftāwī, under whom al-Maqrīzī also may have learned calligraphy. Contrary to Behrens-Abouseif's assertion (*The book* 111), Ibn Ḥajar did not study under Ibn al-Ṣāʾigh (d. 845/1442), the author of a treatise on calligraphy (see Ibn al-Ṣāʾigh, *Tuḥfat ūlī l-albāb*). She quotes the same reference as above, where al-Sakhāwī simply indicates that al-Ziftāwī was Ibn al-Ṣāʾigh's master and that he, al-Sakhāwī, studied under the latter for a short period.

71 Guérin du Grandlaunay, *Iršād al-ġāwī* i, 20, 120; ii, 439, 506 (n. 8), and 525 (n. 5). In general, scholars rarely detail the dates they studied under a specific master, a fact that complicates the historian's quest to know precisely when they were tutored in a given discipline.

72 Al-Ziftāwī may have followed the teachings of ʿUṣfūr because the latter had been trained according to the Syrian school. Perhaps al-Ziftāwī wanted to enhance his calligraphic prowess and further develop his own style.

73 See chapter 6 in this volume, pp. 232–259.

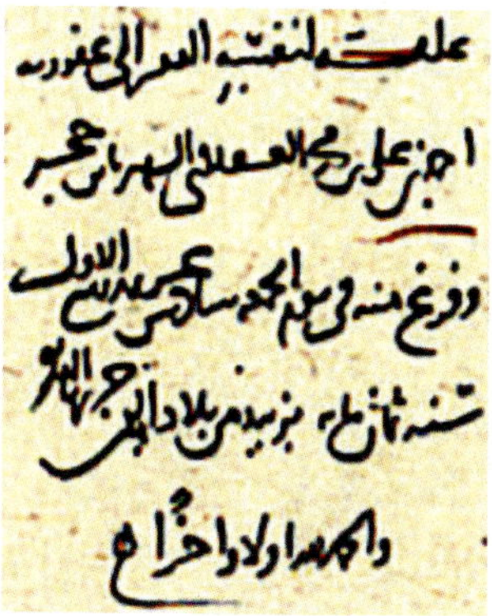

FIGURE 5.5
Abū Dāwūd, *al-Sunan* (MS Fazıl Ahmed Paşa 294, fol. 327[a]), Ibn Ḥajar's colophon
ISTANBUL, KÖPRÜLÜ YAZMA ESER KÜTÜPHANESI

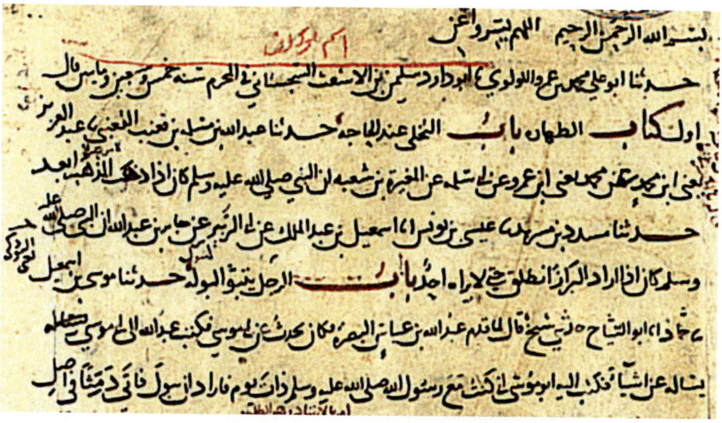

FIGURE 5.6 Abū Dāwūd, *al-Sunan* (MS Fazıl Ahmed Paşa 294, fol. 1[b]), beginning of the text in Ibn Ḥajar's restrained handwriting
ISTANBUL, KÖPRÜLÜ YAZMA ESER KÜTÜPHANESI

al-Maqrīzī no longer needed to practice calligraphy. Thus, his handwriting evolved independently from his training and his personal style developed. We can observe the same process in al-Maqrīzī's colleague and friend, Ibn Ḥajar. Though his master in calligraphy had licensed him to write as a calligrapher, Ibn Ḥajar's handwriting changed when he embarked on a career as a scholar and calligraphy was no longer a necessity. One of the texts (specifically, of *ḥadīths*) that he copied in the framework of his superior education, at the age of twenty-five, demonstrates that while his handwriting was restrained, it could not be identified with any of the proportionate styles used in calligraphy (see figs. 5.5–5.6. Rather, his hand already featured characteristics that make it recognizable and that later blossomed into his own unrestrained writing (see fig. 5.7).

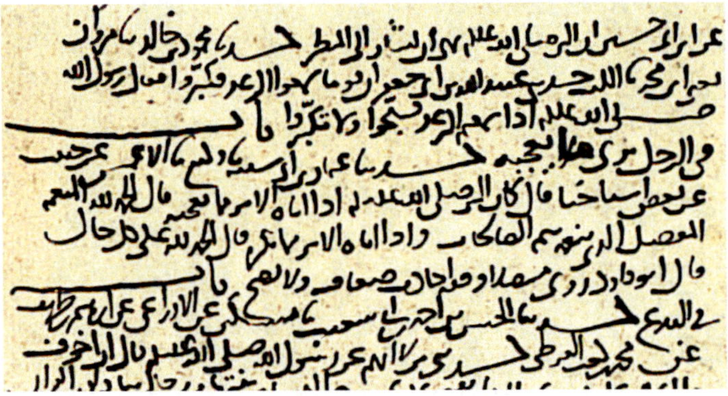

FIGURE 5.7 Abū Dāwūd, *al-Marāsīl* (MS Fazıl Ahmed Paşa 294, fol. 356ª), Ibn Ḥajar's unrestrained handwriting
ISTANBUL, KÖPRÜLÜ YAZMA ESER KÜTÜPHANESI

5 Al-Maqrīzī's Handwriting: Analysis

5.1 *Some Considerations*

Despite the exceptional character of the corpus, most of which has been known for decades, al-Maqrīzī's handwriting has never been thoroughly described and analyzed.[74] Thus far, the only attempt to characterize it was made by Jan Just Witkam, who stated that

> [al-Maqrīzī's handwriting] is quite idiosyncratic. The letters are tilted a little backwards, there is a fairly large number of ligatures, punctuation[75] is rather limited but we can say that the text is, generally speaking, very readable. The handwriting has a very personal aspect. No doubt it is possible to maintain that we can always recognize this handwriting as soon as we have seen it.[76]

---

74 Contrary to what the title indicates, Fu'ād Sayyid's Khuṭūṭ al-Maqrīzī is just a presentation of al-Maqrīzī's holograph and authorial manuscripts known to him. A revised and expanded version of the same article appeared in Fu'ād Sayyid's *al-Maqrīzī* 95–123.

75 By punctuation, Witkam is referring to diacritical dots.

76 Witkam, Les Autographes 92 ("Elle est bien caractéristique. Les lettres s'inclinent un peu en arrière, il y a un assez grand nombre de ligatures, la ponctuation est assez parcimonieuse, mais on peut dire que le texte est, généralement, bien lisible. L'écriture a un air très personnel. Sans doute il est possible de soutenir que l'on peut toujours reconnaître cette écriture dès qu'on l'a vue"). Fu'ād Sayyid's description, in his Khuṭūṭ al-Maqrīzī 140, seems to be an exact copy of Witkam's words: "Either in his drafts or in his fair copies, al-Maqrīzī's handwriting is clear and obvious with distinctive traits: the letters are slightly inclined towards the right; he quite often binds together the [unconnected] letters; he seldom uses the diacritical dots. Generally speaking, it is a handwriting that can easily

This depiction pinpoints some of the main features of the handwriting that are apparent to any scholar with some experience with manuscripts in Arabic script: he reports a general impression of letters leaning to the right, letters connected to the following ones despite the fact that they should remain unjoined, diacritical dots that are not fully indicated, and a degree of legibility. Nevertheless, this description, and the fact that "we can always recognize this handwriting as soon as we have seen it," are far from precise enough to characterize al-Maqrīzī's handwriting beyond doubt. And clearly, several of these features can be noted in the handwriting of other scholars who preceded and followed al-Maqrīzī. In addition, Witkam reduces al-Maqrīzī's writing to basic elements that he observed in a small selection of the corpus, and he does not take into account other factors, like the chronology (did his writing evolve over time, and if so, how?) and the circumstances in which he wrote (typically leading to a fully—or slightly—restrained or unrestrained writing).

In order to characterize al-Maqrīzī's handwriting and help identify it beyond reasonable doubt, we must consider a wide gamut of factors and elements. First and foremost, writing is the result of a tension between two types of habits: those of a prescribed writing system—typically the system one learns at school—and those developed by the writer, which become and reflect his own idiosyncrasies.[77] Such habits must be identified in order to discern between the lucid (learned) and elusive (elements of execution) differences.[78] Several factors may also affect the appearance of a handwriting: the age of the writer, and the process of aging, the circumstances in which the text is produced, the nature of the text being written (personal notes, a copy of someone else's text, a fair copy of a personal text, etc). Depending on the combination of several of these factors, the writer might adopt a more restrained writing characterized by more lucid elements or a less restrained, more automatic, writing that features more elusive components. In this respect, we must analyze the handwriting across a full range of variations, as implied by the above-mentioned factors, and we must consider a broad spectrum of neutral observations. These observations must include the codicological features of the manuscripts produced

be recognized once you have seen it" ("wa-khaṭṭ al-Maqrīzī, sawāʾ fī musawwadātihi aw mubayyaḍātihi, wāḍiḥ wa-jalī, mutamayyiz al-khaṣāʾiṣ, tamīl fīhi l-ḥurūf qalīlan ilā l-khalf wa-yarbuṭu aḥyānan kathīra bayna ḥurūfihi, wa-ʿalāmāt al-tarqīm ʿindahu qalīla. Wa-fī l-ʿumūm, fa-huwa khaṭṭ yumkin al-taʿarruf ʿalayhi bi-suhūla, bi-mujarrad an narāhu").

77 Huber and Headrick call the first type "class characteristics" and the second "individual characteristics." Huber and Headrick, *Handwriting identification* 33.

78 Sirat, *Writing* 495.

by the author (support; layout: justification, alignment, spacing), the orthographical habits and mistakes, and the shapes of individual letters, knowing that the way they are connected within words may take specific and fixed forms. Phenomena, like abusive ligatures and the contraction of the ending of given letters, must not be overlooked to study the issue of control vs. the speed of execution, two factors that should be considered together with the circumstances linked to the writing. Finally, physical and/or mental impairment can reveal the problems a writer encounters with the passing of time. Taken together, all these elements offer a global vision recommended by handwriting experts,[79] one that will be applied, whenever it is useful, to characterize al-Maqrīzī's handwriting.

5.2 *Selection of the Corpus*

To tackle the various issues that I have outlined briefly, it is necessary to rely on a significant and multifarious corpus. As highlighted in the third section above, al-Maqrīzī's legacy in terms of holograph and authorial manuscripts is helpful in this respect: it reflects fifty years of activity,[80] it offers a plethora of material (more than ten thousand pages), and it covers a wide array of categories of texts copied in diverse circumstances. Thus, after six centuries, we can finally scrutinize al-Maqrīzī's handwriting in all its complexities. Paradoxically, the size of the corpus in itself poses a problem: the whole corpus can hardly be grasped in the framework of an analysis that attempts to address all the criteria detailed above. For this reason, I focus my attention on a selection of manuscripts that are dated or datable with some precision and that cover a variety of circumstances. This led me to put aside the manuscripts of *al-Muqaffā* (MSS L1–4, P), a biographical dictionary that al-Maqrīzī composed over a long period, though most of it is already a fair copy. Unlike some of his other texts, it has been impossible to accurately date the fair copy because al-Maqrīzī could add a quire at any time, given the nature of the text, which is alphabetically organized.[81] G2, which contains another biographical dictionary, *Durar al-ʿuqūd al-farīda*, was

---

79 Sirat, *Writing* 499–6 largely based herself on the method developed by M.-J. Sedeyn, *Introduction*. This method is also described in detail in chapter 4 in this volume, see pp. 78–135. For the sake of exhaustiveness, I must also mention Huber and Headrick, *Handwriting identification*.

80 Unfortunately, there remains a big gap between the first witness of his activity as a scholar (IM, dated 795/1392–3 at twenty-eight years old) and the following references available to me (IT1 and IT2, datable between 811/1408–9 and 817/1414, when he was between forty-four and fifty years old). See fig. 5.3.

81 For the dating of some parts, see Bauden, Maqriziana X–1.

set aside for the same reason.[82] Two additional manuscripts were also left out: the Damascene notebook (Da);[83] and C, a dated volume of résumés preserved in Calcutta.[84] In addition, I could not physically examine them, which means that no codicological description is available, particularly regarding the paper.

Apart from these exceptions, I have taken into consideration most of al-Maqrīzī's holographs and authorial manuscripts. These include résumés made while reading (Du, IM and Lg), the first sketches of sections to be included in his already composed works (Al and Lg*[85]), fair copies of previous versions (An, IA, IT1, IT2, IS, IY, G1, G2), and finally, a copy of someone else's work that al-Maqrīzī undertook toward the end of his life (L5).[86]

Unless otherwise stated, for the analysis of the writing that follows, I selected two contiguous pages located at some distance from the beginning of the manuscript.[87] I did this in order to avoid pages where al-Maqrīzī might have paid more acute attention to his writing: in other words, where he would have exercised more control (typically for the first leaves). For tables 5.14 through 5.17, I chose most of the letters and combinations of letters from these two pages, unless I could not find an occurrence there, in which case, I extended my search on the preceding and following pages until I found such an occurrence.[88] Whenever al-Maqrīzī uses allographs, i.e., two shapes for the same letter, I reproduced both in the tables. In addition to this sampling, I also perused the remainder of each text in search of idiosyncratic shapes of combinations of letters or full words. For tables 5.3–5.4, and 5.7 to 5.9, where specific shapes of individual and combined letters are provided according to the number of

82 The only element we know with certainty is that most of it was completed before 839/1435, though al-Maqrīzī added material until shortly before his death.

83 No color reproduction was available to me and the quality of the black and white copy that I have is not good enough for an analysis of this scope. Its physical state is not good either: it was severely damaged by bookworms and several leaves are in pieces.

84 I do not have a high quality color reproduction of this manuscript.

85 To distinguish this section in Lg from the above-mentioned résumé found in the same manuscript, I have appended an asterisk to it.

86 Al-Maqrīzī copied the short text (fols. 1^{a}–14^{b}) in Mecca in 841/1435. Though L5 is included in the timeline (fig. 5.3), this section does not appear there because, according to the definition adopted in this volume, it is neither a holograph nor an authorial manuscript. It is someone else's text in al-Maqrīzī's hand (see the introduction to this volume, particularly pp. 4–6).

87 The pages selected are as follows: Al, fols. 4^{b}–5^{a}; An, pp. 8–9; Du, fols. 37^{b}–38^{a}; G1, fols. 10^{b}–11^{a}; IA, fols. 74^{b}–75^{a}; IM, fols. 8^{b}–9^{a}; IS, fols. 12^{b}–13^{a}; IT2, fols. 16^{b}–17^{a}; IY, fols. 28^{a-b}; MS L5, fols. 10^{a-b}; Lg, fols. 131^{a-b}, Lg*; fols. 188^{a-b}. The reader will find a reproduction of the first of the two pages at the end of this chapter (see figs. 5.26–5.37).

88 In the cases of the first sketches (Al and Lg*), sometimes I was unable to find an occurrence, given the limited number of folios concerned (for instance, the section chosen in Al covers only two pages).

occurrences (for statistical reasons), I counted them on a single page (the first of the two selected), with the exception of manuscripts in a smaller format (Du, IT2). In these cases, I used two pages in order to assess roughly the same quantity of text as for the manuscripts in a larger format.

5.3 *The Pace and Thumbnail Index Method*

In a 2001 article, Nikolaj Serikoff proposed to establish a thumbnail index based on pace for the identification of—particularly informal—hands.[89] Serikoff detailed the criteria as consisting of:[90] (1) a description of the script according to its resemblance to one of the calligraphic styles (e.g., *naskh*-like); (2) the number of lines to the page; (3) the density (Δ) of the text, calculated by multiplying the number of word segments[91] by the number of lines to the page;[92] (4) the ratio between the height of the *alif* and the width of the unconnected *bāʾ*;[93] and (5) the angles of inclination of the connected *alif* (a) and the stroke of the connected *kāf* (k).[94] The whole calculation constitutes the pace of the manuscript; for instance: *naskh*-like; 17; Δ 17 × 31 (530); 1:0.9; a 100°, k 30°. According to Serikoff, each manuscript can be characterized according to its pace and using tables, where such paces are organized on the basis of density, ratio, or angle of the *alif* allows us to quickly find possible matches for another hand. Such a system is presented as an effective tool to compare handwritings and manuscripts with similar features. Comparison is obviously key to the process: identical or evenly matched formulas do not imply that two manuscripts were penned by the same person.[95]

---

89 See Serikoff, Image and letter.

90 Ibid. 57–8.

91 I.e., composed of connected letters (thus the word الأطباق contains three segments), without considering the *wāw* when used as a coordinator or the words written above the line.

92 Serikoff, Image and letter 57, recommends reducing the result to the nearest ten, but in his *Arabic medical manuscripts* 6–7, he seems to have adopted the nearest five.

93 Or *tāʾ* and *thāʾ*.

94 See also fig. 1 in Serikoff, Image and letter 57. Serikoff, *Arabic medical manuscripts* 544, recommends measuring several *alif*s and *kāf*s and giving the average value. He does not say so but he reduces the average of all the measures taken to the nearest five, as the figures in the tables show. We must also emphasize that the angle of the *kāf* can differ greatly according to its shape (either *mabsūṭa* or *mashkūla*). Serikoff does not seem to have taken this into consideration (in Image and letter, his description corresponds to the *kāf mashkūla*). For the sake of precision, I only measured the angle of the *kāf mashkūla*.

95 Serikoff put his method into practice in his catalog of medical manuscripts held at the Wellcome Institute in London: Serikoff, *Arabic medical manuscripts* 6–7, 544–50. As he stresses (ibid. 544): "As average values are used throughout the tables, one and the same pace can describe several different handwriting styles. It is therefore suggested that neigh-

TABLE 5.1 Paces of al-Maqrīzī's manuscripts

MS	Age	No. of lines	Density coeff.	Ratio *alif*:*bāʾ*	*alif*	*kāf*
IM	28	21	525	1:1.5	085	030
IT2	bet. 44–50	20	400	1:1.3	075	035
G1	bet. 49–57	27	620	1:1.25	075	030
IY	aft. 50	27	650	1:1.45	075	035
Du	bet. 51–7	14	400	1:1.25	065	030
Lg	56	21	440	1:1.25	075	030
Lg*	63	17	340	1:1.15	070	035
Al	aft. 63	24	530	1:1.65	070	030
An	aft. 63	27	620	1:1.3	070	030
IS	bet. 64–7	25	550	1:1.4	065	030
L5	71	25	450	1:1.4	065	030
IA	76–7	25	475	1:1.35	070	035

Before accepting or rejecting this method, I first checked to see if it provides significant results when applied to the corpus of al-Maqrīzī manuscripts I had selected. Table 5.1 presents the pace calculated for each of the manuscripts that are part of this corpus, with the data arranged according to the date of production as evidenced in the timeline (see fig. 5.3).[96]

We immediately note the large discrepancies in density and ratio between the manuscripts. Density is calculated based on the number of word segments on one line. This number can vary greatly from one line to the next and according to the nature of the text. Therefore, the factor of density, when calculated this way, is not pertinent. Indeed, while choosing a line at random and multiplying the number of word segments by the number of lines produces a result, this result is hardly representative of a manuscript. But, if we calculate the average of the word segments found on several lines, we would have a better picture of this factor, and it would be a meaningful element in the identification of handwriting. The same assessment can be made with regard to the ratio of the average height of the *alif* to the isolated *bāʾ*: this ratio fluctuates between 1.15 and 1.65, with a majority (eight manuscripts) between 1.25 and 1.4. As for the angle of inclination of the connected *alif* and *kāf*, the results are more stable,

bouring paces are examined and the handwriting styles they describe be compared to that in the manuscript being studied."

96 The calculations were made on the first of the two pages selected, as explained above.

oscillating between 65° and 85° for the first, with a majority between 65° and 75°, and between 30° and 35° for the second, with a majority at 30°. In this case, the average is obtained by measuring five occurrences of each letter. Yet, the variation between each of these occurrences is at times large: for instance in IA, it gives 67°, 68°, 69°, 74°, 84° for the *alif*. Obviously, this sometimes large variation is completely lost in the average result calculated. As for the *kāf*, the variation is somewhat more limited: 28°, 33°, 35°, 36°, 38°.

But the best way to test the method is to apply it to another manuscript penned by al-Maqrīzī and see whether or not it identifies a match in table 5.1. For this I chose IF1, a manuscript belonging to a five-volume set of the same text copied the same year and in the same context as IA. I calculated its pace as 25, 425, 1:1.45, 65°, 30°. With the exception of the angle of the *alif* and the *kāf* and the number of lines to the page, the pace scarcely compares with the one calculated for IA—or with any of the other manuscripts considered: the density, the ratio, and the angle of the *alif* all differ slightly. On the basis of this pace, the manuscript would not be identified as possibly by the same author of IA despite the links that tie it to IF1 (text, period of copy, paper). In conclusion, at least in al-Maqrīzī's case, the pace method and the thumbnail index that relies on it cannot be regarded as a trustworthy and accurate way to identify a handwriting. The one element that may be a sufficiently accurate method of analysis is that of the angle of the *kāf mashkūla*, and to a lesser extent, of the *alif*.

5.4 *A Global Analysis*

5.4.1 Codicological Features

5.4.1.1 *Support*

Table 5.2 lists the formats of each of al-Maqrīzī's manuscripts (size of one leaf, size of the frame within which the text is justified, number of lines to the page, number of leaves, and number of leaves composed of reused documents). The table, divided into three sections on the basis of the number of lines to the page in each manuscript, helps us understand what kind of format al-Maqrīzī used for certain categories of texts. The first section shows that the size of one leaf varies between 140 and 180 in height and 120 to 162 in width, with a number of lines spanning between fourteen and twenty-one lines with an average of twenty to twenty-one. In the second and third sections, the table displays sizes that range between 233 and 255 in height and 152 to 169 in width, with a clear difference for the number of lines between sections 2 and 3 (25 for the first and 27 for the second). The first section is notable for the categories of texts it includes: the three notebooks, two independent résumés, and one draft of one of his texts. As the table shows, the manuscripts belonging to these categories

TABLE 5.2 List of the sizes of al-Maqrīzī's manuscripts[a]

	MS	Title	Size	Justification	No. of lines	No. of fols.	Reused docs. (no. of fols.; %)
1	Du	*Mukhtaṣar Durrat al-aslāk*	140×162	105×125	14	179	107 (60%)
	Da	Notebook	150×120	125×90	17–20	80	2 (2.5%)
	Al	Notebook	155×120	120×95	20 (mostly)	52	0
	IT2	*al-Khiṭaṭ* (draft)	179×141	135×100	20	182	177 (97%)
	IT1	*al-Khiṭaṭ* (draft)	181×144	140×105	20	179	158 (88%)
	Lg	Notebook	165×136	140×100	21 (mostly)	209	85 (41%)
	C	*Mukhtaṣar al-Marwazī*	184×140	145×100	21	131	?
2	IA	*al-Khabar*	233×152	180×110	25	245	2 (1%)
	IF1	*al-Khabar*	233×155	180×110	25	254	0
	IF2	*al-Khabar*	233×155	180×110	25	163	0
	IF3	*al-Khabar*	238×155	180×110	25	265	15 (6%)
	IF4	*al-Khabar*	235×155	180×110	25	276	0
	IS	*Imtāʿ al-asmāʿ*	237×155	180×110	25	211	2 (1%)
	L5	Ibn Ḥabīb, *al-Mukhtalif*	239×154	180×110	25	214[b]	0
	IM	*Mukhtaṣar al-Kāmil*	255×169	190×120	25	215	0
3	L4	*al-Muqaffā*	235×159	190×110	27	550	25 (5%)
	P	*al-Muqaffā*	250×160	190×110	27	260	14 (5.5%)
	L2	*al-Muqaffā*	238×159	195×110	27	287	5 (2%)
	L1	*al-Muqaffā*	255×160	195×110	27	226	9 (4%)
	L3	*al-Muqaffā*	239×160	195×110	27	252	12 (5%)
	IY	*al-Sulūk*	250×166	195×115	27	257	0
	G2	*Durar al-ʿuqūd al-farīda*	245×160	195×115	27	185	3 (2%)
	G1	*Ittiʿāẓ al-ḥunafāʾ*	245×160	200×115	27	58	0
	An	*al-Khiṭaṭ* (fair copy)	245×165	200×115	27	261	0

a The manuscripts are arranged according to the number of lines to the page, then the size of the justified text.

b The text copied by al-Maqrīzī covers fols. 1^a–14^b, the remainder is mostly in someone else's hand.

have smaller formats in comparison with the remainder of the volumes in sections 2 and 3. Their format varies between 140 and 184 in height and 120 to 162 in width. Of these manuscripts, four are mainly composed of reused chancery paper (Du, IT1, IT2, Lg) with the percentage of reused paper ranging from 41 to 97%.[97]

Al-Maqrīzī used discarded chancery paper for an obvious reason: these texts (notebooks, drafts, and résumés) were for personal use and were not meant to survive its author.[98] In this context, the use of a cheaper material was natural. Most chancery documents were issued on scrolls made of sheets of paper pasted one below the other. While the length of the scroll depended on the text to be copied, its width depended on the nature of the document and the rank of the recipient. The sheets used to make the scroll could be kept in their original size for the largest of documents that were for recipients of a higher rank, or cut into smaller sizes for the lower categories. The text was penned in large characters, the size of which depended on the category of the document, with a large interlinear space of several centimeters. Moreover, the writing covered only one side of the scroll.[99] These features explain why these kinds of documents could be reused once they were discarded.[100] Once discarded, the scrolls could be cut into smaller pieces to create quires, where usually only one line of text of the original document would appear on one side of each leaf inside the quire. In light of this, the size of these quires clearly depended on the category of the original document. Of course, this also determined the size of the quires of blank paper that al-Maqrīzī could use to complete a volume composed of reused documents, but also for a volume made entirely from blank paper, as in the case of two of the notebooks (Al and Da).[101] Generally speaking, we can say

97 A copy of C is not yet available to me, thus I have not yet determined whether or not it contains recycled documents.

98 If such manuscripts have been preserved, this is a result of al-Maqrīzī's personality and fame: such objects became collectibles because they were in al-Maqrīzī's hand, something that could still be recognized several centuries after his death. For instance, Lg was part of the library of al-Zabīdī (d. 1205/1790), who knew that the notebook had been penned by al-Maqrīzī though his name is never mentioned in the notebook. For his ownership mark, see Bauden, Maqriziana I–1 25–6.

99 Bauden, Mamluk diplomatics 47–50; Dekkiche, Diplomatics 200–2.

100 These features were not specific to the Mamlūk chancery: they were also applied, though not necessarily in full, by the chanceries of other eastern dynasties, like the Rasulids of Yemen, the Qara Qoyunlu, the Timurids, etc. For the reused chancery documents in al-Maqrīzī's manuscripts, see Bauden, The recovery; Bauden, Diplomatic entanglements; Bauden, Yemeni-Egyptian diplomatic exchanges.

101 Da contains only one bi-folio from a reused document.

that al-Maqrīzī saved quires of a smaller format for the category of texts that may be defined as his *Nachlass* (texts not meant to be published).[102]

When al-Maqrīzī prepared a fair copy of one of his texts—and in one case made a copy of someone else's text (L5)—, he opted to use blank paper.[103] All the manuscripts listed in sections 2 to 3 share the same characteristics: the support is an Oriental laid paper that is creamy and rather thick with some imperfections (e.g., undissolved pieces of fabric, like pills and fibers, and unevenly distributed paste that produces thinner or thicker areas in the sheet) that are visible to the naked eye; its surface was unevenly sized; the chain lines are grouped in twos and, like the laid lines, they are sometimes askew.[104]

With regard to the number of lines, the difference that we note between manuscripts of sections 2 and 3—25 and 27 lines respectively—should not be attributed to the small increase in the size of leaves between the two sections. Some manuscripts of section 2 share similar measurements with some of section 3 and vice versa (compare IM with L1 and L4 with IF4).[105] We must find the reason in the tool (called *misṭara*) al-Maqrīzī used to imprint a blind ruling of lines on the sheet he used. Interestingly, with the exception of IM, all the manuscripts in section 2 were produced after 832/1428, while those in section 3 that can be dated were made after 816/1413–4 and shortly after 831/1427–8. This chronological shift in the number of lines to the page provides us with a significant piece of data: around his mid-sixties, al-Maqrīzī opted for a smaller number of lines to the page. It is difficult to argue why he would have needed to reduce this number. A decrease of two lines does not amount to a lot and can hardly be related to old age. Whatever the case may be, if we could confirm this pattern of using a 25-line *misṭara* after the age of 65, it would help us date the other manuscripts in section 3 (L1, L2, L3, L4, P, G2) to before the 830s/1426–7.

5.4.1.2 *Layout*

In this section, I consider the right and left margins, the alignment, and the interword and intraword spacings. To determine the most minor variations, I added a grid to the figures on which this section is based (see figs. 5.26–5.37).

---

102 One exception to this rule is IM, a résumé al-Maqrīzī made at the beginning of his career entirely on blank paper. In this case, he used the usual format of paper that gives an in-quarto volume.

103 As noted in table 5.2, reused documents also feature in fair copies, but in smaller quantities (between 1 and 6 percent) and always for later additions.

104 Humbert, Un papier, describes this kind of paper. She gives the size of the sheet, after trimming, as being between 466–532 × 320–364.

105 These differences in size are attributable to trimming which, sometimes, took place more than once during the life of a manuscript.

The observation of the right margin shows that in most cases it moves progressively a few millimeters toward the left, usually around the middle (IM, G1, Lg*, IY, Du, An, L5, IA). We notice that it is clearly regressive in only three cases (IT2, Lg, IS).[106] As for the inner margin, IM is the only manuscript with an almost rectilinear alignment; it is closely followed by G1. In both cases, al-Maqrīzī pays more attention to the justification than he does in most of the other manuscripts that follow them chronologically. In the other cases, the left margin is mostly irregular, and sometimes regressive. In order to keep the ending of lines aligned with the others a system was applied: the final part of the word was written above the last segment (see IM, l. 25: *al-Shāfiʿī*) or at some space in the inner margin (see IM, l. 22: *al-Shāfiʿī*), and the last letter was extended (see IM, l. 15: *māta*). These phenomena are all visible in IM, the manuscript in which the justification to the left is aligned most evenly, in comparison with the other manuscripts.

The study of the alignment of lines with the baseline also reveals interesting features. While in IM and Lg lines tend to descend slightly toward the end,[107] in all the other manuscripts, by contrast, the lines tend to slope upward. This is partly, but not fully, explained by the tendency to end the last word or part of it somewhat above the baseline, a practice commonly observed in documents produced in the Mamlūk chancery, and justified by the need to avoid breaking the last word at the end of the line. Moreover, in four cases, some lines look concave with the central part clearly at a lower level in comparison with the beginning and ending of the line: the impression is that the line snakes up and down and then up again. This feature can be observed in Lg* (ll. 7, 16–7), An (ll. 7–8, 21, 24–5), IS (ll. 10–6, 24), and L5 (ll. 9–10). In all these cases, the handwriting shows a wavy writing line.

The spacing between words and within words is irregular, with the exception of IM. Moreover, unlike IM, all the other manuscripts reflect a system in which the beginning of a word is usually written above the end of the preceding word. This system explains why the spacing between words is narrower, giving the writing a more compact aspect (see fig. 5.8).

5.4.2 Orthography

Issues linked to the way an author writes specific words must be addressed. Some traits or habits can help in the identification of an author's handwriting. Unfortunately, such features are rarely scrutinized and analyzed for authors

106 Al is not considered here because the leaf is clearly not aligned on the picture and this gives a false impression of regressive movement, i.e., toward the right margin.

107 Here again, Al is set aside for the same reason invoked in the preceding note.

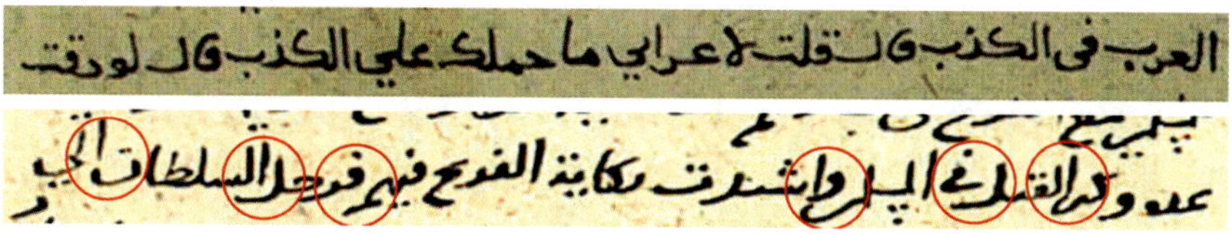

FIGURE 5.8 Spacing between words and the overlapping of words (above: IM [MS 575], fol. 20, l. 9, 47 letters; below: IY [MS Şehit Ali Paşa 1847], fol. 28 a, l. 19, 57 letters)
ABOVE: ISTANBUL, MURAT MOLLA KÜTÜPHANESI; BELOW: ISTANBUL, SÜLEYMANIYE KÜTÜPHANESI

in the Islamic world. The text editors pay scant attention to these characteristics and, in the majority of cases, standardize the orthography without noting details about the readings in the holograph. In a study based on a large part of Lg, I was able to list a series of orthographical, morphological, and syntactical phenomena when I worked on the assumption that Lg is a notebook composed of résumés made on the spot, first sketches, and personal notes. Examining a text in this way might reveal more of such phenomena that appear when an author is not just copying but writing, in the sense of composing or summarizing. In such conditions, my presupposition was that he might pay less attention to the way he writes some words.[108] As I noted then, some of the phenomena I identified result from archaic orthography still found in the Qurʾān, like disregarding the *alif* as the mark of the long vowel *ā* within certain categories of personal and common names (like *Sulaymān*, *ʿUthmān*, *qiyāma*, *thalāth* written سليمن، عثمن، قيمة، ثلث). Others are more idiosyncratic, and reflect what is now defined as Middle Arabic or Mixed Arabic, e.g., the support of the *hamza* (*ruʾūs* written روس for instance) or the use of the *alif otiosum* almost systematically at the end of words ending with a *wāw* (e.g. *banū* written بنوا). These phenomena, as interesting as they may be, are not necessarily characteristic of a way of writing and a writer as they can be observed in many other cases in holograph and non-holograph manuscripts.

Here, other cases that are less often observed in the hand of other authors are more pertinent to the issue. For example, al-Maqrīzī tends to drop the initial *alif* for the word *ithnān* and its various forms (feminine, different cases, in annexation; see fig. 5.9). This phenomenon appears in several of his holographs, indicating that this is his usual practice, one that should not be identified only in his notebooks. Another idiosyncrasy relates to the word *allafa*, which he writes systematically in its past form with two *lām*s (see fig. 5.10). I spotted no fewer than seven occurrences in Lg and one in IY; this indicates that it is his

108 Bauden, Maqriziana VIII.

FIGURE 5.9 The word *ithnān* in Lg, fol. 166^{a}, l. 17 (MS 2232, left: *thnān*) and IF3 (MS Fatih 4340), fol. 117^{a}, l. 2 (right: *thnatay*)
LEFT: LIÈGE, LIÈGE UNIVERSITÉ, BIBLIOTHÈQUE D'ARCHITECTURE, LETTRES, PHILOSOPHIE, HISTOIRE ET ARTS; RIGHT: ISTANBUL, SÜLEYMANIYE KÜTÜPHANESI

FIGURE 5.10 The word *allafa* in Lg (MS 2232), fol. 8^{b}, l. 20 (left: *allafahā*) and IY (MS Şehit Ali Paşa 1847), fol. 4^{a}, marginal addition, last line (*fa-allaftu*)
LEFT: LIÈGE, LIÈGE UNIVERSITÉ, BIBLIOTHÈQUE D'ARCHITECTURE, LETTRES, PHILOSOPHIE, HISTOIRE ET ARTS; RIGHT: ISTANBUL, SÜLEYMANIYE KÜTÜPHANESI

very personal way of writing this specific word.[109] Other cases can be found in his other holographs too. Even though this orthographic habit concerns a very specific word that does not appear frequently in his writings, it constitutes one peculiar element that is helpful for those seeking to identify his handwriting.

5.4.3 Handwriting

5.4.3.1 *Letters*

Handwriting specialists stress that writing is not the result of a regular combination of calibrated independent letters. Children are first taught how to write individual, separate letters, then they learn to combine them with other letters,[110] to join them together with specific ligatures, and eventually, some create their own ligatures. This process implies that short words and combinations of letters reveal more about a handwriting than the study of independent letters because each word is a shape in itself: ligatures and spaces are considered more personal than the shapes of letters themselves.[111] Despite the fact that Arabic script is predominantly composed of connected letters (i.e., with ligatures,

109 This systematic phenomenon cannot be associated with letter stutter, where the repetition of a letter in handwriting is considered accidental.

110 In medieval Islam too according to al-Nuwayrī's description (*Nihāyat al-arab* ix, 218–9).

111 Berrichon-Sedeyn, Acte mécanique 221, 224 (no written element taken separately can be significant), 227 (similitudes and discrepancies noted in the shapes of letters are not significant in themselves); Sirat, *Writing* 492; and chapter 4 in this volume.

which makes the analysis of letters taken independently less pertinent),[112] I maintain that it is still useful to look at the shape of each letter, connected as well as unconnected, when the handwriting is an informal one.[113] As we will see, these letters present features that are already characteristic of a person's age and the circumstances in which this person is writing. Here the caveat outlined by handwriting specialists is countered by the large chronological span of time during which one person may be writing. When considered in relation to the issue of the connections, which is dealt with in the following sub-sections on ligatures, idiosyncratic forms, and cursivity, they reveal features and trends that demonstrate the validity of this approach. In what follows, I describe the main attributes of each letter—or homograph—and focus on its evolution with the passing of time. My description is based on the occurrences gathered in tables 5.14–5.17 placed at the end of this chapter, where the manuscripts are arranged in chronological order based on the timeline (fig. 5.3).

5.4.3.1.1 *alif* (Table 5.14)

When unconnected, the letter is traced from top to bottom without a head-serif. The shaft generally consists of a dash that tends to be thick at the top and fades away to a thin line at the bottom. Largely vertical in IM (see table 5.1, where the average angle is 85°), it starts to slant slightly to the right with an angle that can vary up to fifteen degrees, the angle increasing a bit toward the end of al-Maqrīzī's life.

In its connected form, the letter is written from bottom to top, with the upper part of the shaft sloping toward the right. In one particular case (the word *qāla* not preceded by another connecting letter), the top of the *alif* curves above the *qāf* as if it took the place of the diacritical dots of that letter (that is always dotless in this case).[114]

5.4.3.1.2 *bāʾ-tāʾ-thāʾ* (Table 5.14)

Isolated, it is similar to the *mawqūfa* shape of the letter, i.e., with the initial stroke leaning moderately to the left followed by a long stroke on the baseline and the ending faintly above it.[115] In its initial form, the letter consists of a small

112 Déroche, Analyser 4.

113 Scholars who want to analyze formal handwritings face more difficulties. See, for instance, the recent study of Ben Azzouna, *Aux origines du classicisme*, especially chap. 3, where the author discusses her study of Yāqūt al-Mustaʿṣimī's style and where discrepancies can be identified in the shape of a single letter, like the *alif*.

114 On the possible link of this idiosyncratic shape of the word with cursivity, see the following sub-section.

115 Gacek, *Vademecum* 318 (no. 5).

FIGURE 5.11 Examples of the use of *matres lectionis* and of diacritical dots to specify the phonological value of a letter: Lg (MS 2232), fol. 64ª, l. 12 (left: *laḥiqū*); An (MS Isl. 605), p. 8, l. 18 (center: *al-ʿaskar*); IF3 (MS Fatih 4340), fol. 125ª, l. 5 (right: *ʿarīb*)
LEFT: LIÈGE, LIÈGE UNIVERSITÉ, BIBLIOTHÈQUE D'ARCHITECTURE, LETTRES, PHILOSOPHIE, HISTOIRE ET ARTS; CENTER: ANN ARBOR, UNIVERSITY OF MICHIGAN, SPECIAL COLLECTIONS LIBRARY; RIGHT: ISTANBUL, SÜLEYMANIYE KÜTÜPHANESI

and usually low stroke that is originally vertical, then, from IY, presents a slant toward the right. In its median form, one notices that the blank space left below the denticle disappears starting with G1, giving the letter a flat base.

5.4.3.1.3 *jīm-ḥāʾ-khāʾ* (Table 5.14)

In its unconnected position, the letter corresponds to the *mursala* shape with its curved descender.[116] The curve is plainly round in IM but tends to become more angular later. The initial part of the letter can have a *tarwīs*, i.e., a small serif, or not. For the median position, al-Maqrīzī uses two allographs: one form with or without *tarwīs*, the latter starting sometimes below the base of the letter (IT2). In its final position, the letter looks quite peculiar in IM, at the beginning of al-Maqrīzī's career as a scholar: the stroke before the descender goes well toward the right, somewhat excessively. He soon abandoned this shape for a more conventional form that presents the same tendency for the angular curve noted in the isolated form, to such an extent that the letter looks almost like an isolated *ʿayn*. It is noteworthy that al-Maqrīzī adds, from time to time, a small *ḥāʾ* as a *mater lectionis* to specify when the phonological value of the letter is that of a *ḥāʾ* (see fig. 5.11, left).

5.4.3.1.4 *dāl-dhāl* (Table 5.14)

This letter is initially (IM) written with a clearly curved shape, with the axis of the curve close to the line or the ligature of the preceding letter. In its isolated form, the axis starts to rise from IT2 until it reaches its apex (45°) with IA. The upper part of the letter is also sometimes provided with a kind of *tarwīs*.[117] Once connected, the curve of the letter tends to become flatter (IT2, G1, IY, Lg, Al, An, LG*), until it completely vanishes (Du, IS, L5, IA): the letter is then reduced to a straight oblique stroke.

---

116 Ibid. 318 (no. 9).

117 This feature is studied in the sub-section on cursivity.

5.4.3.1.5 *rāʾ-zāy* (Table 5.14)

In its isolated position, the letter is initially written with a slight curve, with the descender parallel to the baseline.[118] Like for the *dāl-dhāl*, the curve starts to decrease until it becomes a straight stroke (IA). For the connected form, al-Maqrīzī uses two allographs: in addition to the *mabsūṭa* form, he sometimes opts for the contracted shape (*mudghama*) where the descender adopts an ending like a hook.[119] This second allograph seems to fall in disuse at the end of al-Maqrīzī's life.

5.4.3.1.6 *sīn-shīn* (Table 5.14)

The denticles of the letter are all clearly distinguished, and rise somewhat above the baseline in all the positions, but are never sharply pointed, rather rounded. However, from IS onward, the height of these denticles is much smaller and they barely look like dents anymore. Very early on, after IT2, the blank space below the denticles fades away, and the base of the letter flattens. When the letter ends with its bowl, the curve is almost a half circle (at the beginning of al-Maqrīzī's career). Then the final part of the curve remains well below the baseline and somewhat angular. In many cases, al-Maqrīzī favors the *muʿallaqa sīn* (i.e., a straight line with no denticles) in the median position only. From time to time, he also writes three dots beneath the letter in the same position to specify that the letter represents a *sīn* and not a *shīn* (see fig. 5.11, center).

5.4.3.1.7 *ṣād-ḍād* (Table 5.15)

Initially (IM), this letter adopts a curly and rounded shape in all its positions. The upstroke at the junction of the end of the loop is clearly marked. From IT2 onward, the loop is elongated and slightly flattened. The upstroke at the junction tends to fade away with time and the curve of the bowl, as with the preceding letter, remains under the baseline with an angular hook in some cases.

5.4.3.1.8 *ṭā-ẓāʾ* (Table 5.15)

In its isolated position, this letter is penned in one or two strokes, starting with the stem that may or may not reach the baseline before tracing the loop. When connected, it is usually the loop that follows the ligature with the stem added afterward. In some cases, particularly in the final position, the letter is written

118 The shape is called *mabsūṭa*: Gacek, *Vademecum* 318 (no. 14).

119 For the link between this shape and cursivity, see sub-section 5.4.3.3.

in one stroke, as it is in isolation, but it nevertheless connects to the ligature from the preceding letter. The stem is vertical in IM but starts to slant to the right from IT2.

5.4.3.1.9 *ʿayn-ghayn* (Table 5.15)

Unconnected, the letter is characterized by its two curls, the first one almost closed, while the second one, the descender, is round, with its extremity pointing toward the baseline (IM).[120] From IT2, the first curl opens up and becomes in some cases more angular, exactly like the descender which takes the shape already observed for the *jīm-ḥāʾ-khāʾ*. In its median position, the head of the letter is either flat or round with or without counter. In very rare cases, al-Maqrīzī places a small *ʿayn* as *mater lectionis* below the letter to specify that its phonological value is that of a *ʿayn* (see fig. 5.11, right).

5.4.3.1.10 *fāʾ-qāf* (Table 5.15)

Both letters can be written with or without counter. The unconnected *fāʾ* is written on the baseline with a curly ending (*majmūʿa*). This curly ending disappears from IT2 and is replaced with a flat ending (without a curl at the end), as it is in its final position (*mawqūfa*).[121] In its initial position, the letter is written like a small round with a closed counter, while in the median position, it is sometimes harder to distinguish it from the median *ʿayn-ghayn*, the top of the letter being somewhat flat and large. The *qāf* retains its curve. Over time, both letters tend to adopt a shape that is oblique to the baseline.

5.4.3.1.11 *kāf* (Table 5.16)

Al-Maqrīzī makes use of the two allographs available: the *kāf mabsūṭa* and *kāf mashkūla*. The first one, also described as the 's'-shaped *kāf*[122] or the 'hairpin' *kāf*,[123] is written in one stroke, beginning with the upper part of the bar. The angle between the bar and the body can be sharp-cornered or wavy (IM), but over time, it has more of the first type. After IM, the base of the body is separated from the baseline, adopting an oblique angle. The allograph (*kāf mashkūla*) is usually traced in two steps, starting with the shaft and its ligature or ending and followed by the upper bar written from the left, with an average angle of 30° (with a maximum of 35°). In the final position, the shaft slants to the right (Lg*, and more particularly at the end of al-Maqrīzī's life: IS, L5, IA). The bar

120 This is referred to as *makhṭūfa*. See al-Ṭayyibī, *Jāmiʿ maḥāsin* (ed. al-Māniʿ), fol. 5^{b}.

121 Gacek, *Vademecum* 318 (no. 32).

122 Gacek, *The Arabic manuscript tradition* 8.

123 Déroche, Analyser 6.

remains sometimes unconnected or goes through the shaft, a feature probably linked to a question of rhythm. Al-Maqrīzī writes both allographs over time but not consistently and generally as table 5.9 shows. When it is unconnected, al-Maqrīzī largely favors the *mabsūṭa* form, thus conforming to the calligraphic rule set by al-Qalqashandī.[124]

5.4.3.1.12 *lām* (Table 5.16)

Generally speaking, the letter presents a straight vertical shaft with an angled stroke. The descender is parallel to the baseline, particularly when the letter is unconnected, while it becomes curvy when in final position. Over time, the angle of the shaft slants toward the right in all its positions.

5.4.3.1.13 *mīm* (Table 5.16)

In IM, the body of the *mīm* is traced according to calligraphic rules. The letter is traced from the top, going down toward the baseline and then rising toward the top to form a circle with or without counter. After IM, the round shape of the letter vanishes in favor of a small dot, sometimes hardly distinguishable from the ligature. If it is connected on both sides, al-Maqrīzī adopts a ligature that descends and immediately turns to the left, leaving the trace of a small dot (*mulawwaza*).[125] In its unconnected or final position, beside the shape of the letter with a descender slightly curved toward the right (*mukhtāla*),[126] al-Maqrīzī favors a stroke that remains on the baseline.[127] Such a shape is not described in calligraphic treatises and is thus idiosyncratic. It seems to have been part of his early training. While it may completely disappear for the unconnected form after IM, there remains a trace of it in the final position: the descender is either parallel to the baseline or curvy. When it is curvy, most of the descender is oblique. While the letter can still present a counter in IM, it vanishes immediately after that.

5.4.3.1.14 *nūn* (Table 5.16)

In its unconnected and joined forms, the bowl is well rounded in IM. Afterward, the depth of the bowl shortens while its ending becomes angular as the bowl is

---

124 "The *kāf mashkūla* is used when joined in initial and median positions. It can definitely not be unconnected" (*fa-lā takūn illā murakkaba wa-mawḍiʿuhā l-ibtidāʾāt wa-l-wusaṭ wa-lā tanfarid al-batta*). Al-Qalqashandī, *Ṣubḥ al-aʿshā* iii, 84–5.

125 Al-Ṭayyibī, *Jāmiʿ maḥāsin* fol. 7ᵃ.

126 Gacek, *Vademecum* 319 (no. 41).

127 In IM, I counted seventeen occurrences of this horizontal *mīm* versus just two for the one with a descender on one leaf.

traced more obliquely. In certain circumstances, in its final position the letter adopts two different shapes: either a long straight and oblique stroke or a wavy one.[128]

5.4.3.1.15 *hāʾ* (Table 5.17)

Unconnected, the letter is traced like a *mīm*, from the top, with a large counter (*muʿarrāt*).[129] In his seventies, al-Maqrīzī started the letter closer to the baseline, on the left, giving the letter a flatter shape. Two allographs are attested for this letter in its initial position: it resembles a cat face (*wajh al-hirr*)[130] or it is split and wrapped (*malfūfa*).[131] Al-Maqrīzī definitely prefers the first; the second features more in drafts, résumés, and first sketches (IT2, Lg*, Du). For the median position, al-Maqrīzī uses three allographs: mostly the *mudghama* shape (roughly like a 'v'), which he largely preferred to the following one split lengthwise (*mashqūqa ṭūlan*)[132] or, even more rarely, the *wajh al-hirr*. For the final position, al-Maqrīzī initially (IM) wrote the letter with a counter (*mardūfa*), but quickly switched to the *makhṭūfa* shape, which consists of a small stroke with an acute or wavy angle.

5.4.3.1.16 *wāw* (Table 5.17)

Mostly written without counter, the descender of the letter is rather horizontal to the baseline in IM, then leans toward an oblique position. The head of the letter, round in most cases, became more angular when al-Maqrīzī was in his seventies.

5.4.3.1.17 *yāʾ* (Table 5.17)

Considered here only in its unjoined and its final position, the letter is represented by two allographs: the 'duck'-shaped *yāʾ* (*majmūʿa*) and the one that turns back (*rājiʿa*),[133] where the bowl is replaced by a horizontal stroke going backward and parallel to the baseline. For the former shape, we note that its bowl in the unconnected position is well rounded in IM, while its depth is reduced later, as the letter adopts a more oblique angle. In Lg*, the letter can be reduced to a long stroke that also represents the word *ibn* in other circum-

---

128 These shapes are reviewed in the sub-section on cursivity.

129 Gacek, *Vademecum* 319 (no. 53). In IM, he also uses the shape where the stroke crosses at the head of the letter, a shape known as *murabbaʿa* (ibid. 319 (no. 52)).

130 Ibid. 319 (no. 46).

131 Al-Ṭayyibī, *Jāmiʿ maḥāsin* fol. 7b.

132 Gacek, *Vademecum* 319 (no. 45); al-Ṭayyibī, *Jāmiʿ maḥāsin* fol. 7b.

133 Gacek, *Vademecum* 319 (nos. 64–5).

TABLE 5.3 Comparative table of occurrences of *lām-alif* (unconnected and connected)

MS	Age			Total			Total	
IM	28	8	3	11 (92%)	1	0	1 (8%)	0 (0%)
IT2	bet. 44–50	10	0	10 (71%)	2	2	4 (29%)	0 (0%)
G1	bet. 49–57	27	5	32 (86%)	0	5	5 (14%)	0 (0%)
Lg*	aft. 50	12	1	13 (30%)	29	2	31 (70%)	0 (0%)
IY	bet. 51–7	24	2	26 (60%)	2	15	17 (40%)	0 (0%)
Du	56	13	0	13 (81%)	1	2	3 (19%)	0 (0%)
Lg	63	15	2	17 (100%)	0	0	0 (0%)	0 (0%)
Al	aft. 63	28	0	28 (78%)	5	3	8 (22%)	0 (0%)
An	aft. 63	24	2	26 (79%)	1	6	7 (21%)	0 (0%)
IS	bet. 64–7	2	0	2 (8%)	0	11	11 (44%)	12 (48%)
L5	71	0	0	0 (0%)	0	4	4 (29%)	10 (71%)
IA	76–7	0	0	0 (0%)	0	11	11 (30%)	26 (70%)
	Total	163 (67%)	15 (20%)	178 (56%)	41 (17%)	61 (80%)	102 (32%)	40 (16%)[a]

a Note that this figure is taken into account for the total number of occurrences together with the two other shapes, but not for the calculation of the sub-total for each of the two other shapes.

stances. As table 5.8 demonstrates, al-Maqrīzī does not use allographs indiscriminately. At the beginning of his career (IM), he favors the 'duck'-shaped *yā'*. Later, with the exception of Du and IY, he clearly prefers the *rāji'a*.

5.4.3.1.18 *lām-alif* (Table 5.17)

In their unjoined form, the combination of the two letters can be rendered with one or two independent strokes. In the latter case, both strokes are traced from top to bottom where they connect.[134] With just one stroke, the letter is traced with an intersection on the baseline that is angular (*warrāqiyya*) or curved (*muḥaqqaqa*).[135] Al-Maqrīzī does not seem to have used the shape with two strokes: rather he wrote the two forms with the intersection, with a marked preference for the *lām-alif muḥaqqaqa* as table 5.3 reveals (67%). By contrast, for the connected form of the *lām-alif*, he used the *marshūqa* form (80%) for an obvious reason: it allowed him to pen the *lām* from the ligature and reach the baseline, then raise the pen to add the *alif*. As for the *lām-alif muḥaqqaqa*, he had to stop the ligature and raise his hand to trace the intersected stroke, resulting in a ligature that is sometimes quite long (see table 5.17). We must also

134 It corresponds to the *marshūqa* and *musbala* shapes. See Gacek, *Vademecum* 319 (nos. 62–3).

135 Ibid. (nos. 59 and 60–1).

note that, toward the end of his life (from IS; see table 5.3), al-Maqrīzī adopted a slightly modified form for the *lām-alif* (whether connected or not) that seems to derive from the *muḥaqqaqa* shape, in which the combination is traced in one stroke, starting on the left with a curved *alif*, without the angular or curved intersection on the baseline.

5.4.3.2 *Ligatures and Idiosyncratic Forms*

If the analysis of the shapes of letters and the way they evolve over time reveals several idiosyncrasies that help characterize al-Maqrīzī's handwriting and allow the corroboration or confirmation of identifications, handwriting specialists (both paleographers and experts in handwriting identification) insist that such an analysis must also consider how the letters are connected and what shape specific repetitive words may take. In what follows, before studying three repetitive words, I consider the ligatures between specific letters, and distinguish between the usual and the abusive ones.

5.4.3.2.1 The Usual Ligatures: The Case of the Homograph ح

Among the letters of the Arabic alphabet, the homograph for *jīm*, *ḥā'*, *khā'* is one of the most problematic because its shape forces the writer to raise his pen and move it to the left to start to trace the letter. This is of course the case if the writer wants to stay on the baseline. Ligatures are indeed available to bypass the difficulty posed by this letter: this involves writing the preceding letter or letters slightly above the baseline in order to reach the baseline with the homograph or the end of the word. Al-Maqrīzī follows this practice.[136] Interestingly, when the homograph is preceded by a *lām* or the homograph ٮ, the way he treats the ligature changed between two periods: the beginning of his career (IM) and the remainder of his life (from IT2). In the first case, the *lām* or the homograph ٮ is written perpendicular to the ح.[137] In the following years, they generally take the shape of an oblique stroke.[138]

5.4.3.2.2 Abusive Ligatures

The abusive ligatures mainly involve four letters, among which two homographs each represents two sounds, which cannot be connected to the following letter and thus do not offer any ligature, compelling the writer to raise his

136 See, for instance, IM, lines 2 (*ṣaḥīḥ*), 5 (*al-mujālasa*), 14 (*shaykhan*).

137 See IM, lines 6 (*bi-l-ḥadīth*), 7 (*la-ḥalaftu*).

138 For instance see IT2, lines 1 (*bi-ḥāra*), 10 (*al-khalīfa*); G1, l. 23 (*al-ḥarb*); IY, l. 2 (*al-khalīfa*); Lg, l. 3 (*taḥt*); Al, l. 1 (*takhāṣamū*); An, l. 5 (*al-jūdariyya*); IS, l. 2 (*tazwīj*); L5, l. 25 (*wa-l-Ḥārith*); IA, l. 3 (*al-Ḥasan*).

hand to trace the successive letter. These abusive ligatures are attested in the formal writing styles developed by calligraphers[139] and were elaborated in the framework of the chancery. Unsurprisingly, al-Maqrīzī was aware of their existence and used them in certain circumstances. Statistically, the most frequently observed cases concern the final *dāl/dhāl* or *rā'/zāy* followed by the *hā'* (see table 5.4). In such combinations, al-Maqrīzī wrote the *hā'* as an extension of the *dāl/dhāl* or *rā'/zāy*, giving it the shape of a small circle that closes down inside the preceding letter. As for the *wāw*, al-Maqrīzī sometimes connected it to a final *nūn*.[140] Other abusive ligatures relate to any of the four letters (and for two of them, two homographs) above, as well as the *alif* in connection with other letters: the *alif* with the homograph ب,[141] the *dāl/dhāl*,[142] the *rā'/zāy*,[143] the *sīn/shīn*,[144] the *lām*,[145] or the *nūn*;[146] the *dāl/dhāl* with the final *yā'*;[147] the *rā'/zāy* with the homograph ب,[148] and ح,[149] the *dāl/dhāl*,[150] the *ṣād/ḍād*,[151] or the *yā'*;[152] the *wāw* with the homograph ب,[153] and ح,[154] the *rā'/zāy*,[155] or the *hā'*.[156] The majority of these cases feature in two manuscripts only: IT2, Lg* but first and foremost in the latter (see fig. 5.12). Abusive ligatures can also affect two words that are connected, but this only appears sporadically.[157]

5.4.3.2.3 The Contraction (*idghām*)/Curtailment (*ikhtilās*) of the *rā'* and *nūn*

Treatises on calligraphy specify that the descender of the *rā'* and the bowl of the *nūn* can be given a specific shape. In the first case, the descender can be contracted (*mudghama*), meaning that a wavy move is added to give it

139 Déroche, Analyser 6.
140 For example, see G1, l. 4 (*ya'tamidūn*).
141 Lg*, l. 4 (*Ghurāb*).
142 Lg*, l. 14 (*'āda*).
143 IT2, l. 7 (*wa-arba'īn*).
144 IT2, l. 20 (*Ismā'īl*); Lg*, l. 1 (*wa-istaqarra*).
145 IT2, l. 14 (*bi-l-qabr*); Lg*, l. 14 (*wa-'āda*).
146 Lg*, l. 17 (*anna*).
147 An, l. 8 (*al-ladhī*).
148 IT2, l. 15 (*al-kurab*).
149 Lg, l. 8 (*juriḥa*).
150 Lg*, l. 11 (*bi-mufradihi*).
151 Lg*, l. 7 (*al-maraḍ*).
152 IT2, l. 12 (*al-ṭarīq*).
153 Lg*, l. 9 (*wa-thamāni mi'a*).
154 Lg*, l. 12 (*tawajjaha*).
155 Lg*, l. 15 (*al-umūr*), l. 17 (*mashūratihi*).
156 Al, l. 11 (*ja'alūhu*).
157 Like *thamāni mi'a* (Lg*, lines 9 and 13).

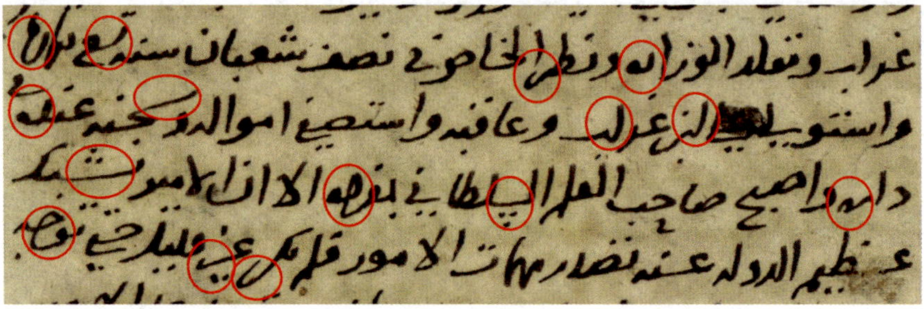

FIGURE 5.12 Occurrences of abusive ligatures, contractions, and *sīn/shīn muʿallaqa* in Lg* (MS 2232)
LIÈGE, LIÈGE UNIVERSITÉ, BIBLIOTHÈQUE D'ARCHITECTURE, LETTRES, PHILOSOPHIE, HISTOIRE ET ARTS

TABLE 5.4 Number of occurrences of abusive ligatures and contractions

MS	Age	Abusive ligatures			Contractions		
		ده	ره	ون	بن	من	ين
IM	28	2 (6)	0 (3)	0 (2)	5 (13)	0 (6)	0 (5)
IT2	bet. 44–50	3 (3)	8 (8)	2 (3)	2 (3)	1 (3)	2 (4)
G1	bet. 49–57	2 (2)	3 (3)	3 (8)	0 (2)	6 (13)	0 (6)
Lg*	aft. 50	3 (3)	2 (2)	0 (0)	3 (4)	2 (3)	6 (7)
IY	bet. 51–7	6 (6)	3 (3)	4 (5)	0 (0)	5 (10)	4 (7)
Du	56	2 (2)	3 (3)	0 (1)	10 (14)	0 (4)	2 (10)
Lg	63	1 (1)	7 (7)	0 (1)	0 (0)	1 (11)	0 (1)
Al	aft. 63	2 (2)	0 (0)	2 (2)	0 (0)	8 (10)	3 (3)
An	aft. 63	5 (5)	6 (7)	3 (4)	0 (7)	2 (6)	1 (1)
IS	bet. 64–7	2 (2)	1 (6)	0 (0)	3 (3)	3 (10)	0 (1)
L5	71	0 (0)	0 (0)	0 (0)	42 (78)	0 (0)	0 (0)
IA	76–7	0 (6)	0 (2)	0 (11)	1 (3)	7 (12)	1 (4)

a hook-like ending.[158] The shape of the letter is also distinguished from its other allograph by its connection to the preceding one in such a way that the passage of one letter to the other is imperceptible. Hence the use of the Arabic word *idghām* to express the coalescence or the fact that two things come together to form one mass. For the *nūn*, a similar phenomenon is documented

158 See Gacek, *Vademecum* 318 (no. 13); Gacek, *The Arabic manuscript tradition* 24.

TABLE 5.5 Some examples of contraction (*idghām*) and curtailment (*ikhtilās*)

سعر	ير	من	عن	ين
Lg, l. 8	Lg*, l. 12	IY, l. 24	IS, l. 9	Lg*, l. 1

but with two possible shapes, called *mudghama* and *mukhtalasa*. While in its contracted form (*mudghama*), the *nūn* takes a shape quite similar to the *rā' mudghama*, though a bit longer, the curtailed *nūn* (*mukhtalasa*) does not feature the hook-like ending: its descender is a long oblique stroke.[159] In his *opus magnum*, al-Qalqashandī specifies that the contraction of the *nūn* can only apply after three letters of a distinct shape: *mīm muʿallaqa*, *ʿayn mulawwaza*, and *kāf mashkūla*.[160]

Al-Maqrīzī uses these shapes in other circumstances too (see fig. 5.13. For the *rā'*, it appears in the middle of a word or at its end.[161] He seems to prefer the *nūn*, mostly the *mudghama* form, when preceded by a *yā'* and in some repetitive words, like *ibn*, *min*, and *ʿan*. The word *ibn* is sometimes reduced to a single oblique stroke (see table 5.17). The same phenomenon can be observed for the word *ʿan* in a text mainly composed of traditions.[162] Such idiosyncratic forms result from a simplified writing similar to stenography.[163] The reason he sometimes adopts the *mudghama/mukhtalasa* form remains to be investigated, but is likely a result of his desire to write more economically by eliminating unnecessary strokes but preserving legibility (see table 5.4 and next sub-section).

5.4.3.2.4 Fixed Shapes

Depending on the genre of text being written or copied, some words are given a particular shape that can be, essentially, regarded as characteristic, though not specific of a given person. One of those frequently used words is certainly *qāla*. In al-Maqrīzī's hand, the word often takes a specific shape in which the

159 See Gacek, *Vademecum* 318 (nos. 43–4); Gacek, *The Arabic manuscript tradition* 22.

160 Al-Qalqashandī, *Ṣubḥ al-aʿshā* iii, 92–3. Al-Ṭayyibī, *Jāmiʿ maḥāsin*, fol. 7[b], gives an example of *sīn* followed by a *nūn mudghama*.

161 In the latter case, it can sometimes even be followed by a final *hā'* with an abusive ligature detailed above.

162 In IS, where twenty of twenty-two occurrences on a page take this shape.

163 Wing, Étude 128.

TABLE 5.6 Comparative table of the word *ḥattā*

IM, fol. 11^{a}, l. 17	IT2, fol. 9^{b}, l. 8	G1, fol. 6^{b}, l. 14	IY, fol. 10^{b}, l. 22	Du, fol. 12^{a}, l. 3	Lg, fol. 161^{a}, l. 17	Lg*, fol. 187^{a}, l. 4	Al, fol. 5^{a}, l. 7	An, p. 9, l. 12	IS, fol. 15, l. 21	L5	IA, fol. 74^{b}, l. 13

alif is curved with its upper part extending toward the right, topping the letter *qāf* (see table 5.17). Such a fixed shape is rather typical of texts composed of *ḥadīth*s where *qāla* is repeated several times on the same page.[164] As already noted by Déroche,[165] this fixed form could play the role of a visual sign that helps to quickly navigate through the text. This is certainly true of *ḥadīth* works. Al-Maqrīzī, who was educated in *ḥadīth*, certainly learned this fixed form that appears several times per page in IM. In his other manuscripts, the habit was well-established enough to repeat itself even though the nature of the texts changed.

Of course, al-Maqrīzī's propensity for the use of the *yāʾ rājiʿa* in all circumstances, after IM, as evidenced above, determines the way words ending with this letter can be rendered. The repetition of some of these words can explain why their shape became characteristic, in a way, of al-Maqrīzī's hand. The following example is certainly one of the most striking. Table 5.6 lists several occurrences of the word *ḥattā* found in each manuscript considered in this study, save for L5.[166] The list shows some interesting features: the rather long ligature that connects the *ḥāʾ* with the following letter, the *tāʾ*, which has the shape of a pointed stroke, sometimes faintly indicated; and finally the *yāʾ rājiʿa*.

Also composed of a final *yāʾ*, the word *fī* offers another case in point. The maximum number of occurrences spotted on a single page in our sample is thirteen (see table 5.8). In the majority of cases listed (88 percent), al-Maqrīzī writes the word with a *yāʾ rājiʿa*, which is perfectly understandable given his preference for this shape after IM. Nevertheless, it is once again characteristic with its 'snake'-like shape.

164 There are other similar fixed forms relating to other words frequently found in those texts, like *ḥaddathanā*, *akhbaranā*, etc.

165 See Déroche, Analyser 6.

166 The text deals with the genealogy of Arab tribes and is almost exclusively composed of names. So no occurrence of *ḥattā* could be found in the fourteen leaves.

5.4.3.3 *Cursivity*

Cursivity is an ambiguous term when applied to the Arabic script. It usually refers to a script, e.g., Latin, in which several elements of a letter or a word are written in one move, as opposed to a variation (e.g., printed Latin) that does not offer this possibility. Typically, cursivity is used in relation to a Latin script in which letters are connected one to the other in contrast with the variety of the script in which each letter is written separately. In its essence, Arabic is a cursive script with ligatures for most of the letters and these ligatures have always existed.[167] In this sub-section, I use the term in its etymological sense (meaning, 'to run') in order to address the issue of speed and how it may have impacted al-Maqrīzī's handwriting.

Despite the existence of numerous ligatures to connect letters to each other, Arabic has six letters that cannot normally be joined to the following letter. While limited in number, the frequency of these letters represents about 30 percent of all letters found in a text, with the *alif* alone accounting for 18 percent.[168] Each time the pen needs to be raised from the baseline to trace such a letter, the writer's movement is consequently slowed. It is not surprising that the chancery—and the calligraphers who elaborated the styles used in this context—tried to increase writing speed by creating various tactics, such as the abusive ligatures. Such tactics were also deployed to limit the number of strokes or moves necessary to write the other letters: for the most part, these included the cancellation of the denticles of the *sīn/shīn*, the contraction (*idghām*) of the *rā'/zāy* and *nūn*, and the backward descender for the *yā'* (*yā' rājiʿa*). However, as Déroche emphasized, calligraphers adopted these shapes with a different intent[169] (aesthetics, variety, rhythm, etc.). We know that al-Maqrīzī was educated in calligraphy and that he had a high position in the chancery at the beginning of his career. Thus, it is legitimate to wonder if he used any of the above-mentioned tactics as a way to write more quickly or simply because he had learned them and they were part of his training. I have adopted a statistical approach to address this issue and better identify the reasons that may lie behind his use of the alternative shapes.

We have seen that al-Maqrīzī resorted to the abusive ligatures in a variety of circumstances. The cases most often represented involve the combination of the *dāl* and *rā'* with the final *hā'*. Table 5.4 shows that the combination with

---

167 See Déroche, Analyser 5.

168 The figures are given in Atanasiu, *De la fréquence* 154 and 156 (*alif*: 18.06%, *wāw*: 7.74%, *rā'*: 3.81%, *dāl*: 1.82%, *dhāl*: 1.52%, *zāy*: 0.5%, *lām-alif*: 1.57%). This calculation is based on the Qur'ān.

169 See Déroche, Analyser 5.

the *dāl* is present from the beginning (IM), though less often in comparison with the following manuscripts, where it seems to be systematic (that is, all the occurrences of the combination have the abusive ligature), and before it vanishes at the very end of his life (IA).[170] The same comment applies to the *rāʾ*. The fact that al-Maqrīzī used these abusive ligatures with parsimony or not at all in IM, where his handwriting is the closest to his calligraphic training, and then almost systematically until his late sixties, is an indication that he perceived these abusive ligatures as a way to hasten his writing.[171] We can draw the same conclusion for the *wāw* joined to the final *nūn*: the phenomenon is not attested in IM, but it is in some other manuscripts he wrote before his seventies.

In light of the elements described above, which are clearly linked to the concept of cursivity, we may wonder if the use of the contraction of the *rāʾ* and the *nūn* (*idghām*) can be regarded as another way to increase writing speed. The samples collected on one leaf for each manuscript of the corpus (see table 5.4) show that their interpretation is more difficult. The percentage of occurrences of contractions in combinations like *ibn*, *min*, *īn-ayn* is definitely higher in Lg*, IT2, and Al, implying that al-Maqrīzī had recourse to these forms for reasons of speed, but in specific circumstances (in the case of Lg* and Al the first sketches, and the draft for IT2). In the other manuscripts, which largely consist of fair copies, the percentage of their use is lower. However, depending on the number of combinations to be written on one leaf, al-Maqrīzī implemented the contraction, though not in a systematic way: for example, in the words *ibn* in Du, IS, L5 and *min* in G1, IY, IA. The contraction of the *nūn* in the group *īn-ayn* is not conclusive in this respect. It is perfectly understandable that repetitive words like *ibn* and *min* would be contracted. Notwithstanding this, we must note that even in a text with almost eighty occurrences of *ibn* (L5), only half of them are contracted. From this, we might conclude that we have another proof of cursivity that depends on the context. Indeed, the manuscript with the most restrained handwriting, that is closest to the school model (IM), does not include any of these contractions for the words *min* and the ending group *īn-ayn*. If al-Maqrīzī knew these contractions, he did not apply them in this early manuscript.

Other examples support this impression. As indicated in sub-section 5.4.3.2.1., when al-Maqrīzī joined the lām or the homograph ـر with the homograph ـح, he always did this at a 90° angle in IM. In all the other manuscripts, he largely opted to incline each of the two letters that are represented by an

170 There are examples of this abusive ligature in IA but they are clearly less frequent when compared to the preceding manuscripts (I could find only one case of a *rāʾ* with a final *hāʾ* out of several leaves, and no case for the *dāl*; see table 5.17).

171 As we see below, their disappearance in his seventies might be related to his aging.

oblique stroke.[172] The *yāʾ rājiʿa* is another case in point (see table 5.8) with its move backward, implying fewer hand movements: while this is seldom used in IM (only 12 percent), it is overwhelming in all the other manuscripts (69 percent of the total of occurrences).[173] The same is true for another repetitive word (*fī*), which he almost systematically writes with a *yāʾ rājiʿa* after IM (in 88 percent of the total of occurrences). In this respect, we must also pay attention to the *kāf*. In its *mabsūṭa* shape, this letter requires the highest number of hand movements in different directions. As Déroche observed, the use of this shape decreases in writings of a medium or ordinary quality.[174] Al-Maqrīzī (see table 5.9) favors the *kāf mabsūṭa* in IM (64 percent), then the *mashkūla* shape takes the lead from IT2,[175] and in Lg* (first sketch) he overwhelmingly (100 percent) overturns the calligraphic rule that specifies that in its unconnected form the *kāf* must always be *mabsūṭa*.[176] The letter *sīn/shīn*, with the allographs with or without denticles, also indicates the level of cursivity of a handwriting.[177] Its relevance in this respect can be gauged by comparing the number of occurrences of each shape in the same text (see table 5.7). While in IM al-Maqrīzī always uses denticles, it represents 77 percent in Lg* (first sketch) and 43 percent in IT2 (draft). In all the other manuscripts, the *muḥaqqaqa* shape is massively represented (85 percent of the total of occurrences).[178] These figures confirm al-Maqrīzī's preference for the *sīn muʿallaqa* in unrestrained or less restrained contexts.

All these elements (specific allographs, contraction, inclination) are clearly linked to the issue of cursivity (i.e., speed of execution), as the occurrences listed demonstrate. Not all of them are necessarily applied in all circumstances, as we see, but a perusal of the number of occurrences is helpful to identify what these circumstances are (first sketches, drafts). In what follows, I tackle the issue of identifying the circumstances in which al-Maqrīzī's handwriting is more or less restrained.

---

172 This inclination, also observable in the beginning of words starting above the baseline (with an average angle of 5–10°), is another criteria of cursivity as observed by Déroche, Analyser 5.

173 In some cases, al-Maqrīzī clearly restrains his handwriting: for example, in IY and Du, the number of *yāʾ mabsūṭa* is proportionately inverted in comparison with the remainder (respectively 47 percent and 65 percent).

174 Déroche, Analyser 6.

175 Here again, al-Maqrīzī exerts a greater control of his handwriting, like in IS, where both shapes are equally used.

176 See above 173.

177 See Déroche, Analyser 5.

178 Even in Al, which is a first sketch though different in nature than Lg*, as al-Maqrīzī is composing the text based on one of his résumés. Thus, in this case, he is largely copying the text.

TABLE 5.7 Comparative table of occurrences of *sīn/shīn muḥaqqaqa* and *muʿallaqa*

MS	Age		
IM	28	41 (100%)	0 (0%)
IT2	bet. 44–50	16 (57%)	12 (43%)
G1	bet. 49–57	41 (100%)	0 (0%)
Lg*	aft. 50	7 (23%)	23 (77%)
IY	bet. 51–7	45 (80%)	11 (20%)
Du	56	48 (92%)	4 (8%)
Lg	63	43 (96%)	2 (4%)
Al	aft. 63	66 (99%)	1 (1%)
An	aft. 63	34 (97%)	1 (3%)
IS	bet. 64–7	27 (73%)	10 (27%)
L5	71	26 (87%)	4 (13%)
IA	76–7	34 (87%)	5 (13%)
	Total	444 (85%)	77 (15%)

TABLE 5.8 Comparative table of occurrences of *yāʾ mabsūṭa* and *rājiʿa* and of the two shapes of *fī*

MS	Age				
IM	28	23 (88%)	3 (12%)	2 (100%)	0 (0%)
IT2	bet. 44–50	7 (33%)	21 (67%)	1 (17%)	5 (83%)
G1	bet. 49–57	11 (25%)	33 (75%)	1 (7%)	13 (93%)
Lg*	aft. 50	4 (11%)	32 (89%)	1 (8%)	12 (92%)
IY	bet. 51–7	16 (47%)	18 (53%)	2 (18%)	9 (82%)
Du	56	17 (65%)	9 (35%)	1 (13%)	7 (87%)
Lg	63	3 (12.5%)	21 (87.5%)	1 (17%)	5 (83%)
Al	aft. 63	6 (33%)	12 (67%)	0 (0%)	6 (100%)
An	aft. 63	16 (36%)	29 (64%)	1 (8%)	11 (92%)
IS	bet. 64–7	6 (12%)	43 (88%)	1 (14%)	6 (86%)
L5	71	10 (30%)	23 (70%)	2 (13%)	13 (87%)
IA	76–7	3 (9%)	30 (91%)	0 (0%)	10 (100%)
	Total	122 (31%)	274 (69%)	13 (12%)	97 (88%)

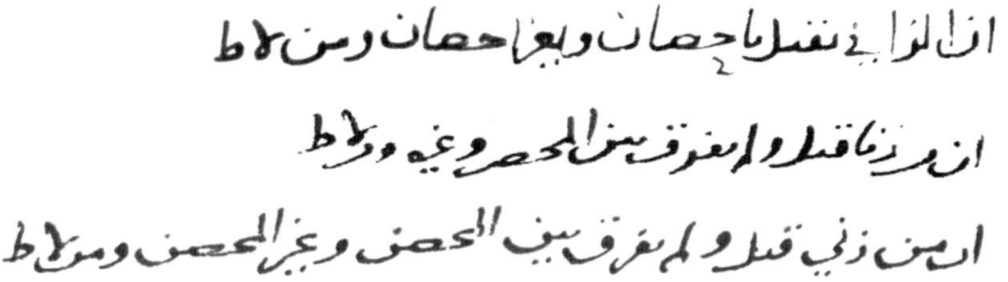
1
2
3

FIGURE 5.13 An almost similar line in three different manuscripts
Note: 1: Lg, fol. 162^{a}, l. 7; 2: Al, fol. 5^{a}, l. 1; An, p. 471, ll. 13–4. The text reads:

1) ان الزاني يقتل باحصان وبغير احصان ومن لاط
2) ان من زنا قتل ولم يفرق بين المحصن وغيره ومن لاط
3) ان من زنى قتل ولم يفرق بين المحصن وغير المحصن ومن لاط.

5.4.3.4 *Circumstances*

The nature of the text being written is one of the factors that impacts writing. If the writer is composing a literary piece, he is involved in a reflexive and creative process, while if he is writing a personal letter, he is calling upon his emotional expression.[179] When he limits himself to copying a text (a fair copy or someone else's text), his writing will be the result of a mechanical process, one in which he can better control his hand.[180] In al-Maqrīzī's case, we have a variety of circumstances in which he is composing a personal text, summarizing a source, producing a draft, preparing a fair copy, or even just copying someone else's text. Rhythm and pressure are elements that reveal a great deal about these circumstances.

As for rhythm, we can consider three interrelated texts that reflect three different processes: (1) a résumé that al-Maqrīzī wrote while reading the source (Lg); (2) a sketch of a text he produced on the basis of the résumé (Al); (3) the fair copy of the section based on the sketch (An). In order to compare similar examples, I selected a succession of words that are similar in the three texts (see fig. 5.13).

In step 1 (Lg), the writing can be characterized as restrained: the words are largely written on the baseline, the shafts (*alif*, *lām*) slant slightly to the right, the text is devoid of abusive ligatures and includes just one contraction (*rāʾ* in final position in *wa-bi-ghayr*; the *nūn* in the *min* is not affected). In step 2 (An), the phrasing changes a bit and the general look of the writ-

179 Berrichon-Sedeyn, Acte mécanique 223.
180 Ibid., 225.

TABLE 5.9 Comparative table of occurrences of *kāf mabsūṭa* (left) and *mashkūla* (right)

MS	Age			ک		
		Connected with following letter	Connected with both letters	Connected with preceding letter	Unconnected	Total
IM	28	9 (39%)	12 (86%)	5 (100%)	3 (100%)	29 (64
IT2	bet. 44–50	4 (33%)	3 (43%)	0 (0%)	1 (100%)	8 (35
G1	bet. 49–57	7 (33%)	8 (40%)	1 (8%)	0 (0%)	16 (29
Lg*	aft. 50	0 (0%)	0 (0%)	0 (0%)	0 (0%)	0 (0%
IY	bet. 51–7	5 (22%)	4 (27%)	6 (100%)	2 (100%)	17 (37
Du	56	1 (8%)	0 (0%)	0 (0%)	1 (100%)	2 (7%
Lg	63	0 (0%)	2 (40%)	0 (0%)	2 (100%)	4 (20
Al	aft. 63	10 (38.5%)	7 (58%)	3 (37.5%)	0 (0%)	20 (43
An	aft. 63	4 (12%)	0 (0%)	0 (0%)	1 (100%)	5 (9%
IS	bet. 64–7	3 (37.5%)	9 (64%)	1 (33%)	0 (0%)	13 (52
L5	71	7 (54%)	2 (67%)	1 (8%)	1 (100%)	11 (38
IA	76–7	10 (45%)	6 (55%)	0 (0%)	1 (100%)	17 (39
	Total	60 (28%)	53 (39%)	17 (20%)	12 (86%)	142 (32

nnected with llowing letter	Connected with both letters	 Connected with preceding letter	Unconnected	Total
4 (61%)	2 (14%)	0 (0%)	0 (0%)	16 (36%)
8 (67%)	4 (57%)	3 (100%)	0 (0%)	15 (65%)
4 (67%)	12 (60%)	12 (92%)	1 (100%)	39 (71%)
2 (100%)	15 (100%)	5 (100%)	1 (100%)	33 (100%)
8 (78%)	11 (73%)	0 (0%)	0 (0%)	29 (63%)
0 (92%)	5 (100%)	11 (100%)	0 (0%)	26 (93%)
9 (100%)	3 (60%)	4 (100%)	0 (0%)	16 (80%)
6 (61.5%)	5 (42%)	5 (62.5%)	0 (0%)	26 (57%)
0 (88%)	15 (100%)	5 (100%)	0 (0%)	50 (91%)
5 (62.5%)	5 (36%)	2 (67%)	0 (0%)	12 (48%)
6 (46%)	1 (33%)	11 (92%)	0 (0%)	18 (62%)
2 (55%)	5 (45%)	10 (100%)	0 (0%)	27 (61%)
4 (72%)	83 (61%)	68 (80%)	2 (14%)	307 (68%)

ing betrays some tension: the line is striking in its inclination, an impression strengthened by the fact that some words begin above the baseline and the shaft of some *alifs* slant significantly to the right; the text presents a case of abusive ligature (*wa-ghayrihi*) and two contractions (two *mins* and at the end of *al-muḥṣin*); the compactness of the line is conspicuous (this is achieved by starting new words above the endings of the previous ones); the *lām-alif* features a kind of *tarwīs* to the left. In the third step (An), in which al-Maqrīzī is preparing the fair copy, we note that even though the beginning of some words starts above the line, the words stick more closely to the baseline; the shafts of the *alif*s and *lām*s lean slightly toward the right; the contractions of the *nūn* have vanished, apart from the presence of contractions in the *rā*ʾ (two cases); and the words are more spaced out, making the line less compact.

Step 2 clearly demonstrates that when he is involved in a creative process, al-Maqrīzī paid less attention to his handwriting even though, in this case, it is a composition of a first sketch on the basis of a résumé; thus, he is largely copying material he had already, in a sense, digested. Lg*, which consists of a biographical notice of one of his contemporaries, definitely tallies more closely with what could be defined as a personal text, one in which he is largely drawing inspiration from personal recollections (see fig. 5.37). We have already noted that this text presents the highest number of abusive ligatures and other phenomena identified with speed of execution.[181]

These circumstances reveal situations in which al-Maqrīzī's hand is less restrained. There are other traces that help to assess the rhythm of his writing. Some of the cases of abusive ligatures that are identified in Lg* certainly contribute to our understanding of this issue (see fig. 5.12). Another element that helps us to appreciate his rhythm relates to the stroke that precedes unconnected letters with heads that start above the baseline and require that the pen be raised (typically the *dāl/dhāl* and the *lām-alif*). When these letters are preceded by another letter that requires a downward move, one notices that in the move that brings the pen from below the baseline up to the point where the head of the letter must be traced, it touches the surface earlier and leaves a somewhat long stroke in the case of the *lām-alif* and a shorter one for the *dāl/dhāl* (see table 5.10). Although we cannot find this example in IM, the first example to the left illustrates how the move impacted the way al-Maqrīzī lengthened the descender of the *wāw* almost to the point that it joined the *alif*.

181 See above 182.

TABLE 5.10 Examples of *lām-alif* and of *dāl* with a hanging stroke

IM, fol. 2^{a}, l. 24 (*wa-lā*)	**IT2, fol. 7^{a}, l. 4 (*awlād*)**	**IT2, fol. 6^{b}, l. 6 (*wilāyatihi*)**	**Lg, fol. 7^{b}, l. 21 (*thalāth*)**	**Lg, fol. 7^{b}, l. 16 (*wa-yaruddu*)**
	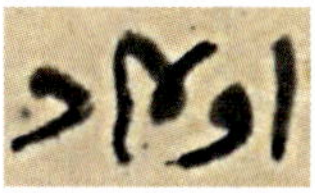			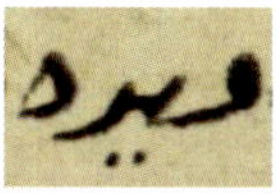

TABLE 5.11 Examples of pressure causing the widening of the nib

IT2, fol. 94^{b}, l. 12.	**L5, fol. 2^{b}, l. 10**
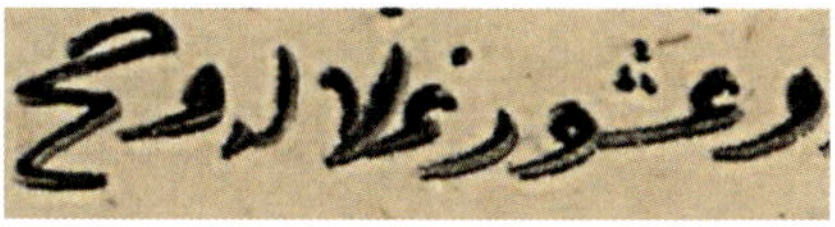	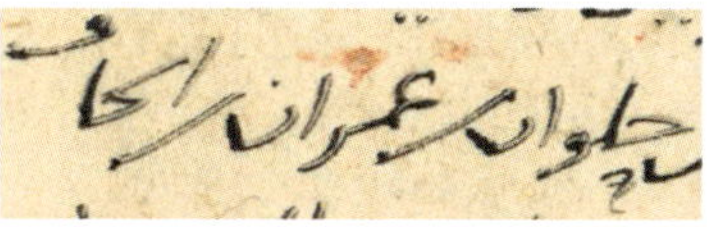

These features reveal that al-Maqrīzī was writing with a certain energy. In addition, they are idiosyncratic of his handwriting in certain circumstances.[182]

Pressure can also betray the circumstances and the conditions in which al-Maqrīzī wrote. In the case of haste, the pressure the hand exerted on the reed pen widens the two parts of the nib. This widening leaves a white line between the two sides of the letters, as evidenced in table 5.11. This phenomenon is notably, but not exclusively, conspicuous in IT2 (a draft copied when al-Maqrīzī was in his mid-fifties) and L5 (a text copied by al-Maqrīzī when he was in his early seventies).

5.4.3.5 *Aging*

The aging process usually impacts a person's writing, though this depends on the state of health of the subject. In the analysis of writing, a number of factors should be taken into account: illness, visual disorders, joint problems, and shaking. Among the phenomena observed, scholars have identified examples of micrography, in which smaller letters are used at the beginning and ending of

182 We could also consider how the bar of the *kāf mashkūla* is added in a second move: the connection of the bar to the body can vary (i.e., be connected, unconnected, or cut through it).

lines, or the lines are not straight.[183] Writing specialists insist that these factors do not inevitably follow a downward curve, and that the analysis of handwriting must consider any variation that may be linked to any of these factors.[184]

Given our corpus, which includes large samples of al-Maqrīzī's writing activity in his seventies, we are in a good position to observe if phenomena linked to some of these factors can be shown. We do not know if he had visual problems that required spectacles at such an advanced age.[185] But we do know that he is said to have died after a long illness.[186] Whatever this illness may have been, apparently, it did not impair his ability to write, as he managed to complete the fair copy of his last major opus—three volumes totaling some seven hundred leaves—during the last eight months of his life.[187] The results of the comparison of several of the elements outlined in the preceding sub-sections reveal that around age sixty-five (from IS) al-Maqrīzī's movements became hampered.

First, his words are not aligned with the baseline: the beginning of several words in the line are written at an angle between 10 and 15°. Most letters adopt the same angle.[188] This general trend is accompanied by a slant toward the right for letters with a shaft (*alif*, *lām*). The axis of the curve of the isolated *dāl/dhāl*, which begins to rise with IT2, reaches its apex from IS up to IA. Letters with a curve (connected *dāl/dhāl*, connected and unconnected *rāʾ-zāy*) see this curve reduced to a stroke that becomes straighter from IS. The denticles of the *sīn-shīn* hardly ascend from the flat base of the letter.

Al-Maqrīzī seems to experience more difficulty with long curves too. This is noticeable in the bowls of the *sīn*/*shīn*, *ṣād*/*ḍād*, *qāf*, *nūn*, and *yāʾ* in their unconnected or final positions: the curve is characterized by an angular shape at the end of the bowl. Instead of closing the bowl with the second part of the curve once he reaches the lower part of the descender, al-Maqrīzī completes it with a straight stroke going upward (see the *nūn* in table 5.11, right). The same observation can be made regarding the *lām-alif*: al-Maqrīzī drops the *warrāqiyya* and the *muḥaqqaqa* shapes in favor of a shape derived from the former, as if he wanted to avoid the round intersection at the level of the

183 See Stiennon's remark, in Sirat et al., *L'Écriture* 75–6.

184 See, for instance, Berrichon-Sedeyn, Acte mécanique 223.

185 Spectacles were known in Egypt and Syria from the eighth/fourteenth century. They were imported from Europe where they were produced. See Mazor and Abbou Hershkovits, Spectacles.

186 Al-Sakhāwī, *al-Ḍawʾ al-lāmiʿ* i, 25 (*baʿd maraḍ ṭawīl*).

187 See the appendix. Besides his copying activity, al-Maqrīzī continued to hold sessions at home, to transmit texts, up to one month before his death. See Bauden, *Al-Maqrīzī's collection*, chap. 1.

188 See tables 5.14–17, all the letters with elongated bodies.

TABLE 5.12 Examples of coordination problems

L5, fol. 1b, l. 10	L5, fol. 1b, l. 9	L5, fol. 2a, l. 11	L5, fol. 2a, l. 9

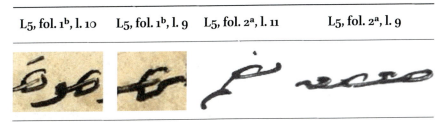

baseline. The final *hā'* connected to a *rā'/zāy* with an abusive ligature confirms that al-Maqrīzī, at that point, had a problem with round shapes or loops: the *hā'* is traced in three moves, instead of just one, giving the letter a quadrangular shape. In any case, such abusive ligatures for the *dāl/dhāl* and *rā'-zāy* were no longer the norm at the very end of his life, as they tended to fall into disuse (see table 5.17 for IA). With its curves, the *hā'* (unconnected, initial, and medial positions) represented a challenge for an old man. Several samples demonstrate that al-Maqrīzī struggled with the circular movements. In its unconnected position, we have seen that the *hā'* becomes flatter, with the circle sometimes remaining open. For the initial and median positions (see table 5.12), al-Maqrīzī tried to solve the problem of the multiple curves indicated by the cat face allograph by first tracing an imperfect—often incomplete—circle, then raising the pen to trace the central stroke whose extension constitutes the ligature for the next letter. Another interesting case relates to the fragmentation of a word into several segments instead of writing it with one stroke. Two examples containing the letter *ṣād/ḍād* (table 5.12) are meaningful. In the first case (*bi-ḍamm*), al-Maqrīzī first traced the first two letters, stopping at the juncture of the flat loop of the *ḍād*. He then raised the pen and put it down at the end of the *ḍād* to trace the final letter. In the second case (*Ṣaʿṣaʿa*), we can observe the same move: he wrote the first *ṣād* with a long extension to the second *ṣād*. The medial *ʿayn* was added in a second move, like an inverted 'L'. Finally, in one move, he added the last two letters, shaping the second *ʿayn* in a normal way. All these features betray a problem in coordination that can be typical of old persons.

Trembling, another factor that can go along with aging, can also affect handwriting. Tremors produce dents, particularly in long strokes. Despite the coordination problem described above, al-Maqrīzī's hand was not shaky, not even in the manuscripts he copied at the end of his life. We do not have evidence of this because of the absence of long strokes in most manuscripts selected from the corpus. Nevertheless, we can spot at least one case in L5 (see fig. 5.35), copied when he was seventy-one years old, where the initial letter (*ḥā'*) of the first word on l. 4, written in red ink, shows some undulation. The most telling exam-

TABLE 5.13 Examples of tremor

G2, fol. 60[a], l. 9	G2, fol. 53[b], l. 1	G2, fol. 143, l. 1

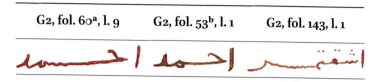

ples of tremor can be found in G2—which was not incorporated in the corpus because we lack a precise date. The text consists of biographies, some of which al-Maqrīzī added at the very end of his life, with the first name usually written in red ink with long strokes between some letters. For a biography penned earlier in his life (table 5.13, center), the elongation is steady, but in two other cases (table 5.13 left and right), dents are conspicuous all along the long stroke. Despite the body of evidence provided by the large number of manuscripts for the late period, these examples prove that al-Maqrīzī's hand was shaky at the end of his life and that he had difficulties controlling this impairment when he had to trace long straight lines.

5.4.3.6 *The Characteristics of al-Maqrīzī's Handwriting*

We can outline some common characteristics of al-Maqrīzī's handwriting. One regards the average angle of the bar for the *kāf mashkūla* which almost invariably corresponds to 30° (with a maximum of 35°). The formats of the volumes indicate some habits. Two formats are concerned: (1) one for the notebooks, drafts, independent résumés, mostly but not exclusively composed of reused chancery paper, with a justification from 140 to 180 in height × from 120 to 160 in width and with chiefly twenty lines to the page; and (2) one for the (fair or working) copies with a justification from 180 to 200 in height × from 110 to 120 in width with twenty-seven lines to the page before 832/1428 and twenty-five afterward. Some orthographic habits, like the stutter of the *lām* in the past form of the verb *allafa*, are idiosyncratic.

With the exception of these common characteristics, the earliest manuscript (IM) clearly stands apart from the rest of the corpus. The handwriting in IM can be described as a controlled and careful one, in which al-Maqrīzī pays attention to the outcome: the text is taut with letters like guardsmen on parade. The shaft of tall letters (*alif*, *ṭāʾ*/*ẓāʾ*, *lām*) is mostly perpendicular to the baseline. Letters with bowls have almost perfect half circles. The words are generally aligned with the baseline and regularly spaced. In the case of a word containing the homograph ح, the word starts above the line, but remains aligned horizontally with the baseline. Al-Maqrīzī also uses abusive ligatures, but in limited circumstances. Contractions are not utilized. In his early years, he definitely favored the *yā' mabsūṭa* over the *yā' rājiʿa* and the *kāf mabsūṭa* over the *kāf mashkūla*. These features demonstrate that al-Maqrīzī maintained the models he studied at school in his childhood and during his secondary education when he learned calligraphy, and even though early on his handwriting can be described as individual, it shares some characteristics with the traits we recognize in al-Maqrīzī's later manuscripts.

In his late forties (with IT2), in the interval that separates IM from IT2, we can note that al-Maqrīzī's handwriting clearly underwent some developments. These were accompanied by an evolution in his handwriting, one that was characteristic until the end of his life. The alignment of the words with the baseline tends toward an oblique angle, with the beginning of words written at some distance above the baseline, and the ending joining it. The beginning of words frequently starts at the ending of the preceding word, strengthening an impression of compact lines and tilting in the handwriting. The slant to the right of stems (*alif*, *ṭā'/ẓā'*, *lām*) adds to the obliqueness of other letters (*bā'/tā'/thā'*, *dāl/dhāl*, *sīn/shīn*, *ṣād/ḍād*, *qāf*) increased with the passage of time and also contributes to this impression. Al-Maqrīzī also shows his preference for some allographs, like the *yā' rājiʿa* that almost becomes the norm (with the exception of IY and Du). He also favors the *lām-alif muḥaqqaqa* when unconnected and the *lām-alif marshūqa* when joined. The *kāf mashkūla* also seems to be the norm, except when it is in an unconnected position; in this circumstance, al-Maqrīzī maintains the calligraphic model that imposes the *kāf mabsūṭa*. In its final position, the *hā'* is written in the *makhṭūfa* shape, i.e., like a circumflex. The connection of a *lām* or of the homograph ٮـ with the homograph ح largely came to be written like an oblique stroke and not more at a 90° angle, like in IM. Al-Maqrīzī also had greater recourse to abusive ligatures as well as contractions (*idghām*) for the *rā'/zāy* and final *nūn*, and to the *sīn muʿallaqa* (without denticles), though these phenomena tend to diminish in his late seventies. Quite often, two letters (the *alif* in the *lām-alif* combination and the *dāl/dhāl*) are preceded by a stroke generated by the movement of the pen coming from below the baseline, in the wake of the preceding letter (typically with a descender).

The nature of the text may also have impacted the handwriting. Drafts (IT2) and first sketches (Lg*, Al) contain more examples of abusive ligatures and contractions than any other manuscripts. In such cases, the handwriting is less restrained and shows the effects of pressure where the sides of the nib widens, leaving a blank line in the middle of the stroke that composes the letter.

In his seventies, al-Maqrīzī faced health problems that hindered his movements. Curves tend to become more angular (this is conspicuous in the way he writes the *dāl/dhāl*, *rā'/zāy*, the bowls of the *sīn/shīn*, *ṣād/ḍād*, *nūn*). Al-Maqrīzī encountered difficulties in tracing circular movements, like full loops (he gave up the two shapes of *lām-alif* that he used throughout his career, opting instead for a new shape that is easier to write; the initial *hā'* is written in two steps with a broken circle; the abusive ligatures and the contraction of the ending of the *rā'/zāy* and the *nūn* fall into disuse). Words are also written progressively, in small segments. The long straight horizontal strokes also reveal tremors.

5.5 *The Future*

In the preceding section, I tried to delineate, in an empirical and analytical way, the main characteristics of al-Maqrīzī's handwriting in the widest gamut of circumstances. In so doing, I hope to make it easier for others to ascertain whether or not a given manuscript or note can be attributed to this author with some certainty. A sample of his handwriting can now be straightforwardly compared to the physical and material features just outlined. At the same time, my description is also intended to allow others to verify the validity of my identifications, which can be challenged on the basis of objective elements. In this respect, the contributions of the digital humanities are worth considering. In this matter, as in many others, the future seems to be upon us. Face recognition systems by artificial intelligence are a reality. Researchers validly argue that if computers can identify a human face in a crowd, they can certainly also differentiate between two handwritings. Over the last decade, computer scientists have developed various systems based on algorithms that are designed to authenticate handwriting in medieval manuscripts.[189] Unfortunately, the results garnered to date are far from satisfying, to say the least.

In Spring 2015, Alexander Knysh (University of Michigan) put me into contact with a team of Russian computer scientists who had created a program to verify whether or not a manuscript is in the handwriting of a specific author. They wanted to work more specifically on al-Maqrīzī's writing, particularly given the holograph that had been identified in the holdings of the University of Michigan a few years before. In contrast to the programs developed so far, the Russian algorithm created by Andrei Boiarov and Alexander Senov involves deep learning and works with a convolutional network on the basis of an analysis of consecutive patches. Two types of patches are taken into consideration: connected components, i.e., groups of letters, and a fixed-size sliding window, i.e., an image split into patches of fixed-size cells (see fig. 5.14).[190]

189 See the references quoted in the introduction to this volume, as well as in Boiarov et al., Arabic manuscript 1, notes 2–6.

190 Boiarov et al., Arabic manuscript 1.

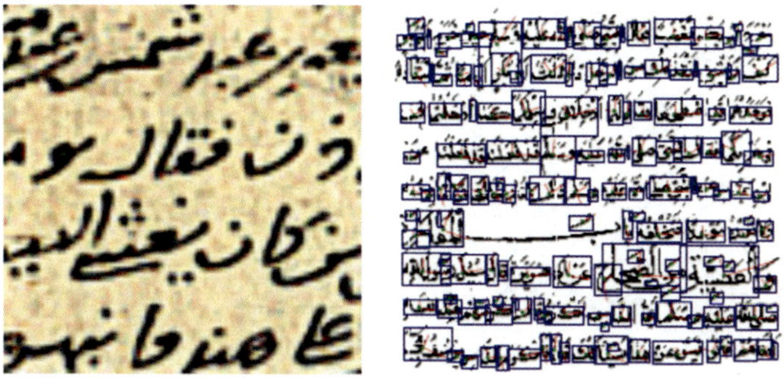

FIGURE 5.14 A sliding window patch (left) and patches of connected components (right)
BOIAROV ET AL., ARABIC MANUSCRIPT 3, FIGS. 3–4

The algorithm was first trained with twenty-six pages of An and a negative set of seven pages selected from five manuscripts that are not in al-Maqrīzī's hand, but are contemporaneous with him (ninth/fifteenth century). It was then tested with fourteen pages of An and another set of seven pages from three contemporaneous manuscripts by another hand and different from the manuscripts used in the first training step. I also shared several reproductions of some of al-Maqrīzī's other holographs. Once tested, the algorithm analyzed pages of An and compared that with the same corpus used in the testing level. It appeared that the level of accuracy for the sliding window patch was higher than for the connected components (87 percent against 80 percent). The former gave a result of 94 percent of probability that An was in al-Maqrīzī's hand and of 0.85 percent for another manuscript, corroborating that An is in al-Maqrīzī's hand. With some correction, the authors of the study concluded that the algorithm identified the handwriting with a precision of 99 percent. An analysis of the connected components revealed that the method was less credible, as it generated "many false positive predictions."[191] Nevertheless, the results were deemed promising for future developments.

The level of accuracy of the authentication of An was clearly thrilling. For the first time, an algorithm was apparently able to corroborate my identification. I thus wanted to push the analysis further by using some leaves from the draft of *al-Khiṭaṭ* (IT2) that are not in al-Maqrīzī's hand, leaves that I consider to be in al-Awḥadī's hand, on the basis of external (paleography) and internal (masters) elements.[192] I asked Andrei Boiarov to submit some of those leaves

191 Ibid. 3–4.
192 See above, 142.

FIGURE 5.15 The word *madrasa* penned by al-Awḥadī (MS Emanet Hazinesi 1405, fol. 96^{b}, l. 10 (left); fol. 98^{b}, l. 1 (right))
ISTANBUL, TSMK

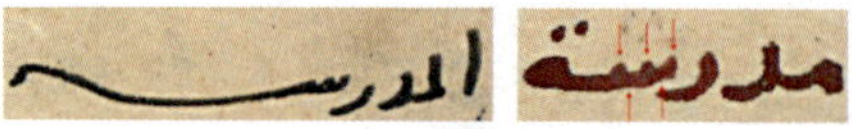

FIGURE 5.16 The word *madrasa* penned by al-Maqrīzī (right) (MS Emanet Hazinesi 1405, respectively fol. 97^{a}, l. 12 (left); fol. 96^{b}, l. 9 (right))
ISTANBUL, TSMK

and I advised him that the handwriting of both scholars sometimes features on the same leaf. The result was quite astonishing to me: according to the algorithm, both handwritings were attributed to al-Maqrīzī with a very high level of accuracy (more than 90 percent). The differences that I could see in the two handwritings were apparently not critical for the algorithm. I drew Boiarov's attention to the particular features that help me to distinguish between the two handwritings. I pointed to the noticeable difference that one can observe in the writing of the word *madrasa*, which appears more that thirty times in the twenty leaves in question. In most cases (see fig. 5.15, left), al-Awḥadī writes the word with a elongated *sīn* devoid of its denticles (*muʿallaqa*) and ends it with a *hāʾ* in the shape of a drop. In rare cases (see fig. 5.15, right), the word is written in a more controlled way: in such cases, the denticles of the *sīn* are well delineated, thin, and pointed, while the *hāʾ* takes the shape of a triangle (*mardūfa*). The first form is obviously idiosyncratic of the person who penned those lines and was never identified in any of al-Maqrīzī's other holographs.

When he wrote the word on these twenty leaves, al-Maqrīzī used both shapes, but with conspicuous differences: in the case of the elongated *sīn* (see fig. 5.16, left), the denticles are clearly traced with a final *hāʾ* that looks like a hook (*makhṭūfa*) while in the other more restrained example (see fig. 5.16, right), the shape of the final *hāʾ* is round with a closed counter. In both cases, the denticles of the *sīn* are not pointed, as they are in al-Awḥadī's case. Compared with al-Awḥadī's *sīn* (fig. 5.15, right), we can also see that the base of al-Maqrīzī's *sīn* is, in both cases, flat on the baseline and does not present the characteristic indentations. The average angle of the *kāf mashkūla* also reveals a neat discrepancy: 40° for al-Awḥadī versus 30° to 35° for al-Maqrīzī.[193]

193 See above, 162.

To further challenge the program, in mid-July 2016 I requested that a wider sample of handwritings be analyzed. I specifically selected some handwritings that differ significantly from those of al-Maqrīzī and al-Awḥadī, and I added some handwritings that were closer to al-Awḥadī's handwriting. The sample was anonymized, i.e., I submitted the reproductions without communicating the identity of the writers. The sample was composed of nine manuscripts (see figs. 5.17–5.25).

A few days later, I was informed of the following results: A = 97 %, B = 79 %, C = 100 %, D = 12 %, E = 82 %, F = 0 %, G = 72 %, H = 0 %, I = 50 %, with the percentage indicating the probability that a text is in al-Maqrīzī's hand.[194] These results call for some remarks. First, A, which is in al-Awḥadī's hand, is considered, with a very limited margin of doubt (3 percent), to be in al-Maqrīzī's hand, like C, which is truly a holograph of al-Maqrīzī (100 percent). Then, three manuscripts (D, F, and H) are rejected even though the leaf selected in H (0 percent) contains seven lines in al-Maqrīzī's hand. The analysis of E is of greater concern: copied by an unkwown copyist, but not al-Maqrīzī, it is considered, with a high probability, to be a holograph of al-Maqrīzī (82 percent). Finally, the algorithm considered I, which is entirely in al-Maqrīzī's hand, dubious (with a probability of 50 percent).[195] These results demonstrate that while the algorithm can be trusted in some cases, it is entirely unreliable in others. In order to refine the analysis of the algorithm, the programmer should take into consideration several factors, among them, the width of the nib, certain connected letters with idiosyncratic shapes (like the *lām-alif*), and even the average angle of the stroke of the *kāf*.

In my mind, there remains little doubt that, once they are well trained and refined, such programs will be able to identify (within a small margin of error) handwritings in manuscripts. But there are caveats that indicate that entirely replacing human expertise may never be possible. The samples of someone's handwriting must be large and varied enough to avoid erroneous identifications or rejections, something that is possible in the case of al-Maqrīzī (both in terms of age and variety of circumstances), but not in the case of al-Awḥadī (we have twenty leaves dating from the same period and a few words in a limited number of ownership marks and consultation notes). In other words, the critical mass of data is central to the process. Even if we have numerous holographs from the Islamic world, there are few cases in which we have a varied and

194 Personal communication in email dated 20 July 2016.

195 The analysis also gives a lower result for B and G (under 80 percent) even though both manuscripts are al-Maqrīzī's holographs.

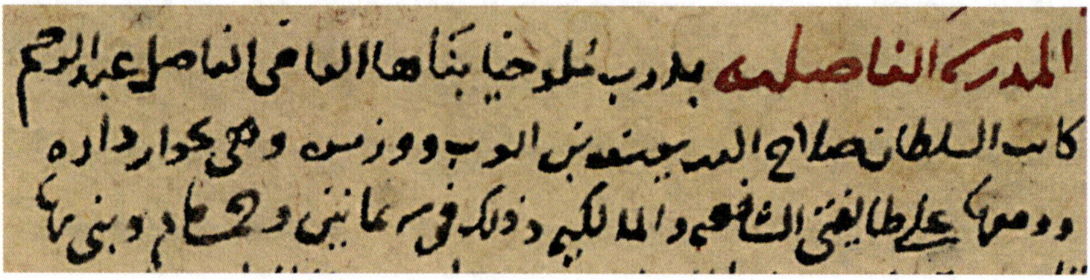

FIGURE 5.17 A: IT2 (MS Emanet Hazinesi 1405), fol. 83[a] (with the exception of two words added in the margin by al-Maqrīzī, the leaf, contains nineteen lines in al-Awḥadī's hand)
ISTANBUL, TSMK

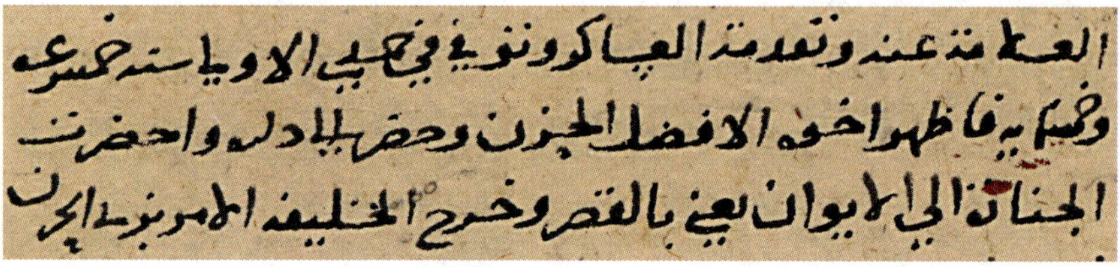

FIGURE 5.18 B: IT1 (MS Emanet Hazinesi 1405), fol. 54[b] (entirely in al-Maqrīzī's hand)
ISTANBUL, TSMK

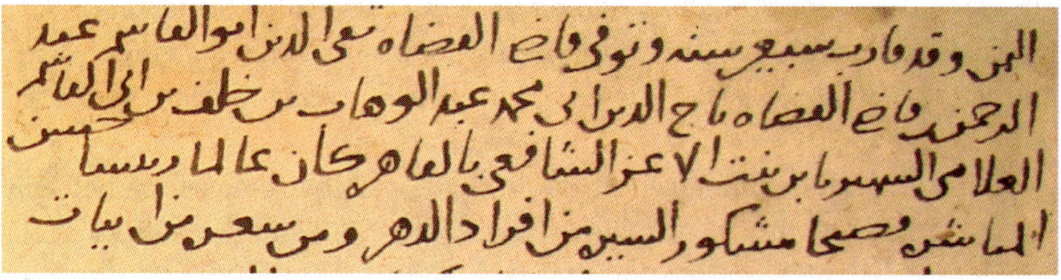

FIGURE 5.19 C: Du (MS 1790), fol. 77[b] (entirely in al-Maqrīzī's hand)
DUSHANBE, KITOBHONA-I MILLI-I TODJIKISTON

rich corpus like al-Maqrīzī's. In addition, whenever two different handwritings appear on the same leaf (H), the program is apparently unable to distinguish between them. This weakness is problematic, if one wants to authenticate a marginal note or just a few words in the hand of a given scholar. Moreover, such programs cannot analyze some material features that are key to the identification process, such as the paper (structure) and the pressure of the pen, unless they are provided by the researcher. This means that, ultimately, the human eye remains the best tool in this field, though clearly, confirmation from a program will be helpful, particularly in cases where an expert is not (anymore) at hand.

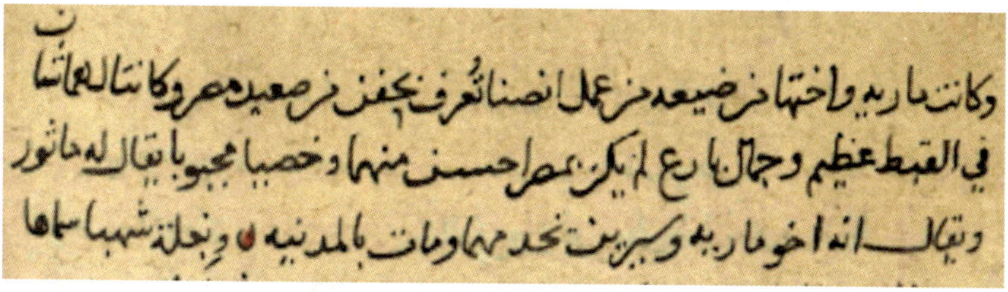

FIGURE 5.20 D: MS 702, fol. 2b (*al-Dhakhāʾir wa-l-tuḥaf*, entirely in Ibn Duqmāq's hand)
AFYON KARAHISAR, GEDIK AHMET PAŞA KÜTÜPHANE

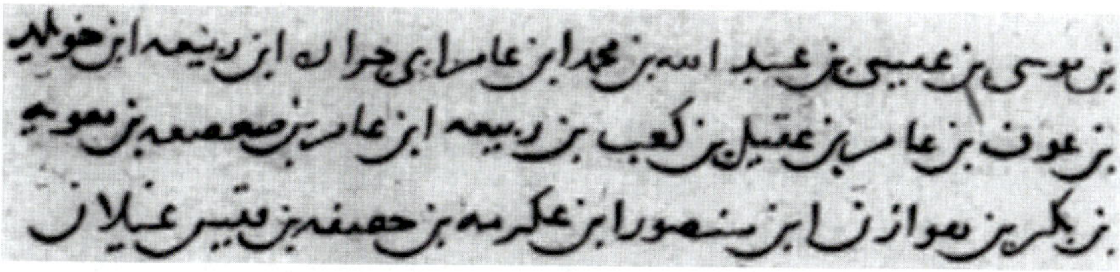

FIGURE 5.21 E: MS cod. ar. 437, fol. 3a (Ibn Duqmāq, *Naẓm al-jumān fī ṭabaqāt aṣḥāb imāminā l-Nuʿmān*, unknown copyist)
MUNICH, BAYERISCHE STAATSBIBLIOTHEK

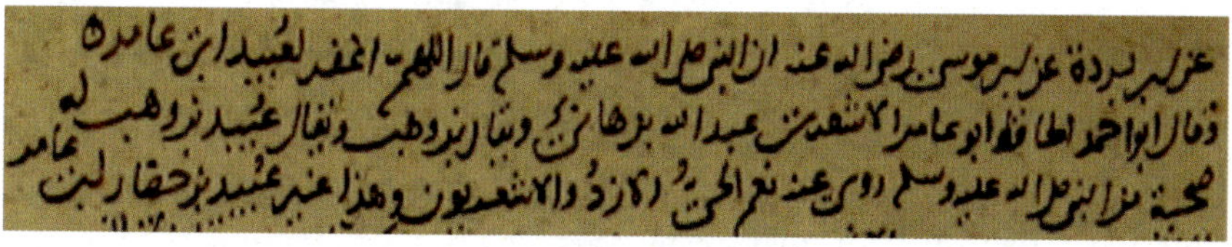

FIGURE 5.22 F: MS Fazıl Ahmed Paşa 242, fol. 39b (Ibn Manda, *al-Tārīkh al-mustakhraj min kutub al-nās*, unknown copyist, seventh/thirteenth c.)
ISTANBUL, KÖPRÜLÜ YAZMA ESER KÜTÜPHANESI

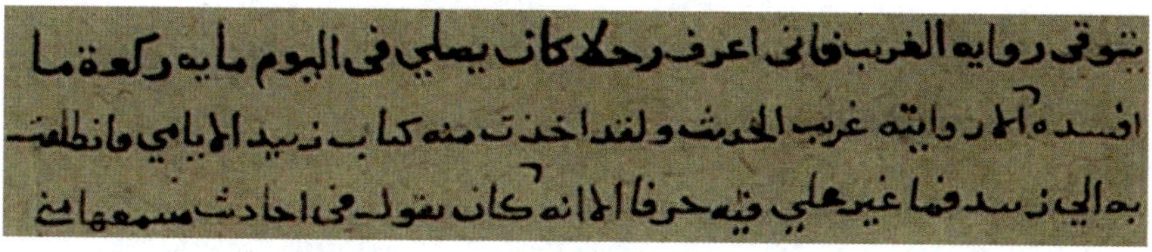

FIGURE 5.23 G: IM (MS 575), fol. 21a (entirely in al-Maqrīzī's hand)
ISTANBUL, MURAT MOLLA KÜTÜPHANESI

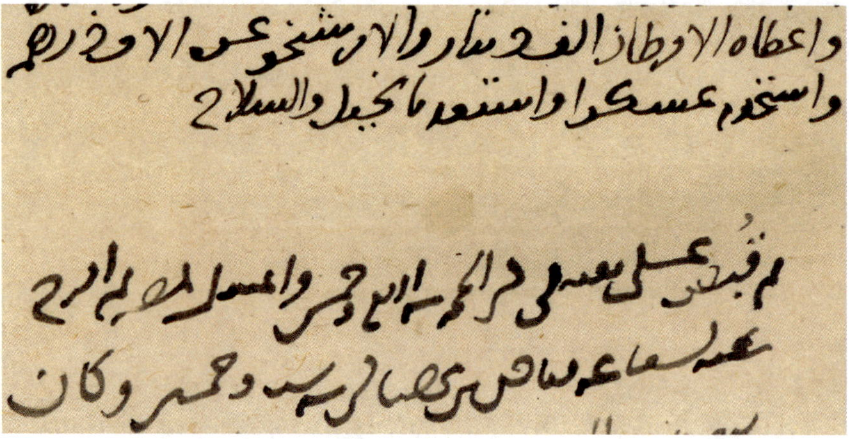

FIGURE 5.24 H: L4 (MS Or. 14533), fol. 348[a] (seven lines in al-Maqrīzī's hand (top), ten lines in Ibn Ḥajar's hand (bottom))
LEIDEN, UNIVERSITEIT LEIDEN, UNIVERSITEITSBIBLIOTHEEK

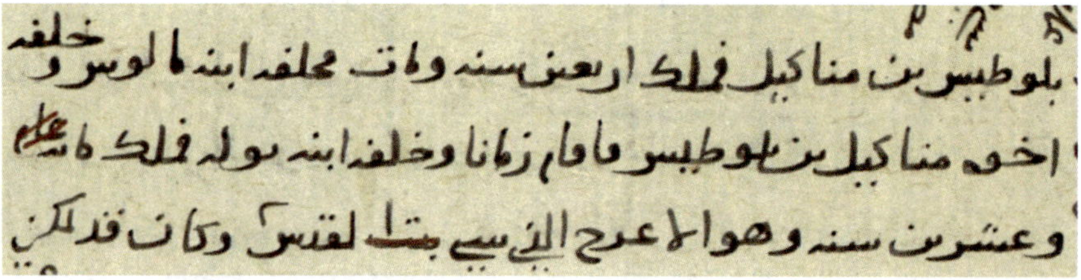

FIGURE 5.25 I: Lg (MS 2232), fol. 48[b] (entirely in al-Maqrīzī's hand)
LIÈGE, LIÈGE UNIVERSITÉ, BIBLIOTHÈQUE D'ARCHITECTURE, LETTRES, PHILOSOPHIE, HISTOIRE ET ARTS

5 Conclusion

The starting point of this study was based on the need 'to show' how al-Maqrīzī's handwriting can be identified and describe how 'to give the feeling' that the same hand is at play in several manuscripts considered his holographs or authorial manuscripts. The global analysis applied to a wide corpus covering an almost uninterrupted fifty years of activity and some 5,000 leaves, yielded tangible results that must not, however, be read in a linear way, rather, we must assess them according to the nature of the written text, the circumstances that led to its writing, and al-Maqrīzī's age when he penned it.[196] Some

196 As Jażdżewski emphasized, though it is paradoxical, that "a writer is free to use some personal 'hands' and he should not be identified with his 'hand.'" See Jażdżewski, Identifizierungsprobleme 326.

general characteristics could be identified, both in codicological and paleographical terms. Other features relate to some categories of texts only. All in all, for the first time, this study offers a fact-based detailed analysis of a scholar's handwriting over time. The idiosyncrasies I have outlined will prove helpful to identify al-Maqrīzī's hand in still unknown manuscripts that have yet to be discovered in libraries around the world (three volumes were located during the last two decades). Hopefully, the global approach applied in this specific case will also offer key elements for further analyses of other scholars' hands. While the expert's 'eye' remains crucial for the identification of a given hand, in the near future, Artificial Intelligence (AI) will certainly contribute to the analysis of scholars' hands in the frame of the digital humanities. Though at present the programs developed do not fully satisfy the paleographer's desires, I am convinced that these programs, once they will have been refined, will provide us with an accurate tool. At the same time, we hope that their progress will not stymie the development of paleographical studies, particularly the informal handwritings of scholars, which have so far drawn little attention. To improve the analysis and knowledge of these handwritings, paleographers and computer programmers will have to establish a framework of mutual cooperation.

TABLE 5.14 Comparative table of letters *alif-sīn*

MS	Age	ا		ب				ح				د		ر		س			
		ا	ـا	ب	بـ	ـبـ	ـب	ح	حـ	ـحـ	ـح	د	ـد	ر	ـر	س	سـ	ـسـ	ـس
IM	28																		
IT2	bet. 44–50																		
G1	bet. 49–57																		
Lg*	aft. 50																		
IY	bet. 51–7																		
Du	56																		
Lg	63																		

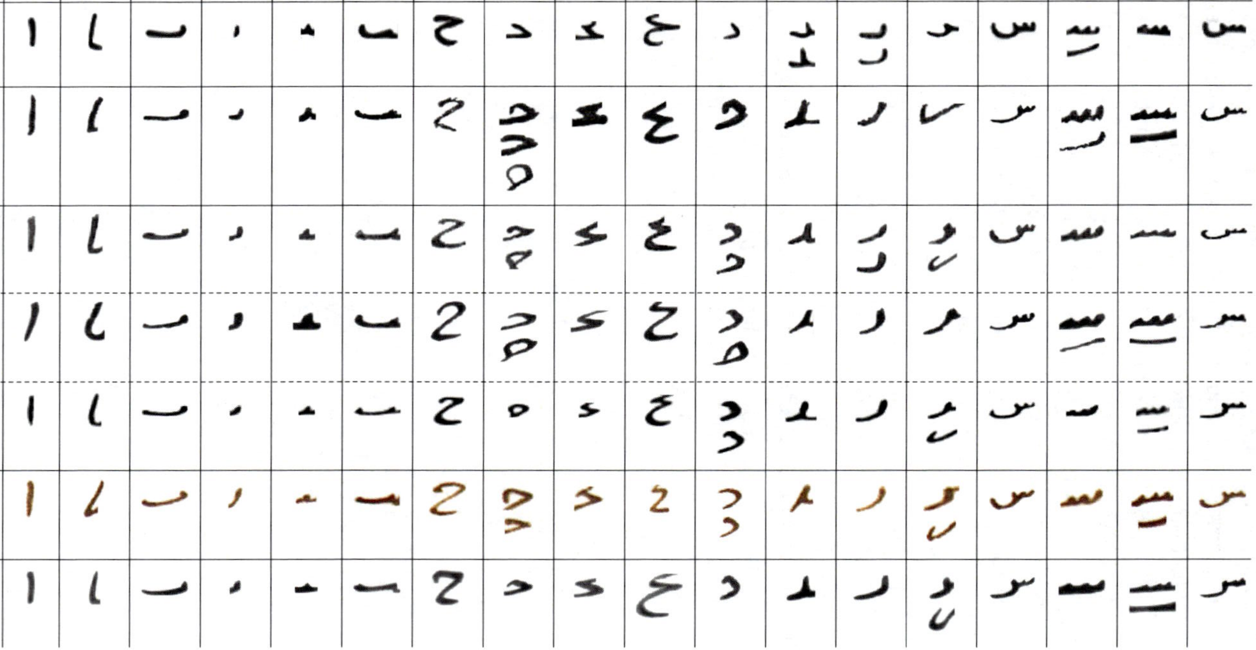

TABLE 5.14 Comparative table of letters *alif-sīn* (*cont.*)

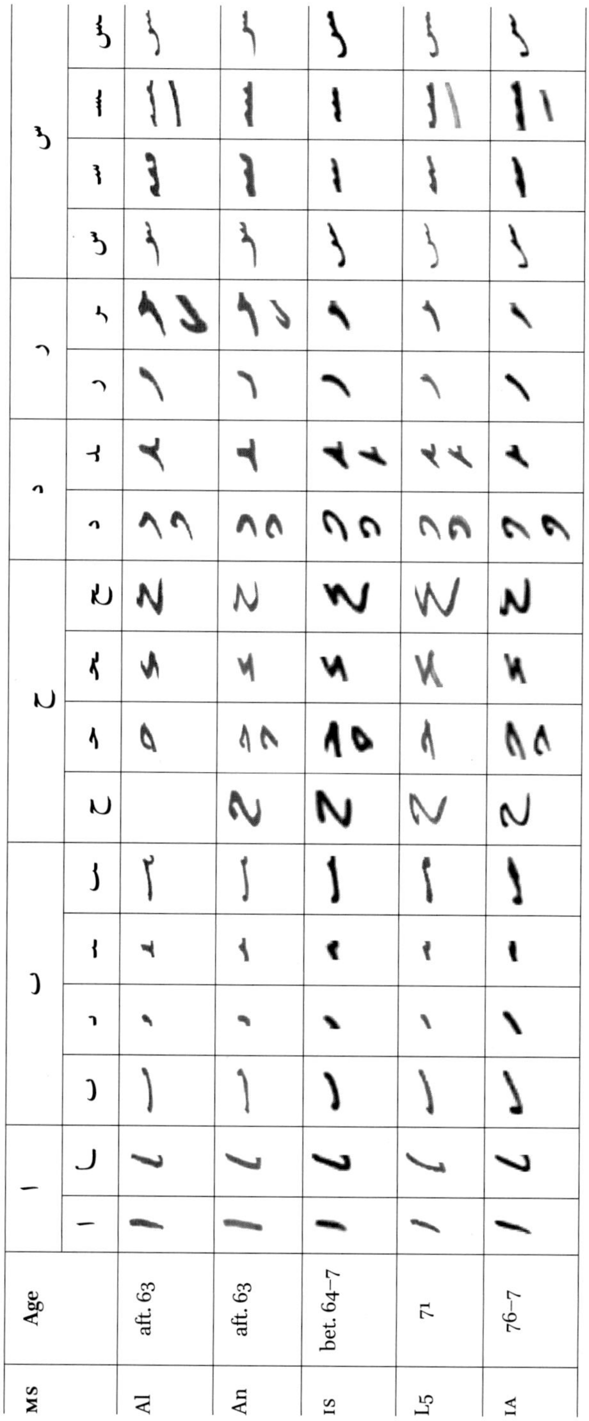
MS
Age
Al
aft. 63
An
aft. 63
IS
bet. 64–7
L5
71
IA
76–7

TABLE 5.15 Comparative table of letters *ṣād-qāf*

MS	Age	ص				ط			ع				ف				ق	
		ص	صـ	ـصـ	ـص	ط	ـطـ	ـط	ع	عـ	ـعـ	ـع	ف	فـ	ـفـ	ـف	ق	ـق
IM	28																	
IT2	bet. 44–50																	
G1	bet. 49–57																	
Lg*	aft. 50																	
IY	bet. 51–7																	
Du	56																	
Lg	63																	
Al	aft. 63																	

TABLE 5.15 Comparative table of letters *ṣād-qāf* (*cont.*)

MS	Age	ص				ط			ع				ف				ق	
		ص	صـ	ـصـ	ـص	طـ	ـطـ	ـط	ع	عـ	ـعـ	ـع	ف	فـ	ـفـ	ـف	ق	ـق
An	aft. 63																	
IS	bet. 64–7																	
L5	71																	
IA	76–7																	

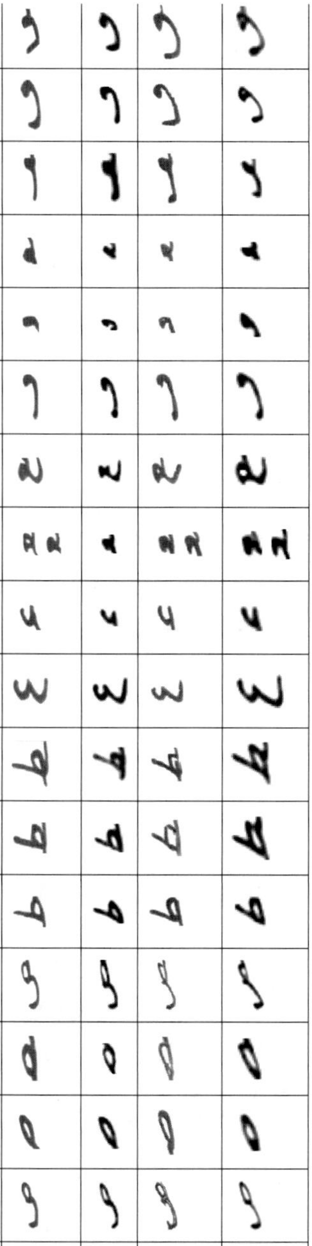

TABLE 5.16 Comparative table of letters *kāf-nūn*

MS	Age	ك				ل				م				ن	
		ك	كـ	ـكـ	ـك	ل	لـ	ـلـ	ـل	م	مـ	ـمـ	ـم	ن	ـن
IM	28														
IT2	bet. 44–50														
G1	bet. 49–57														
Lg*	aft. 50														
IY	bet. 51–7														
Du	56														

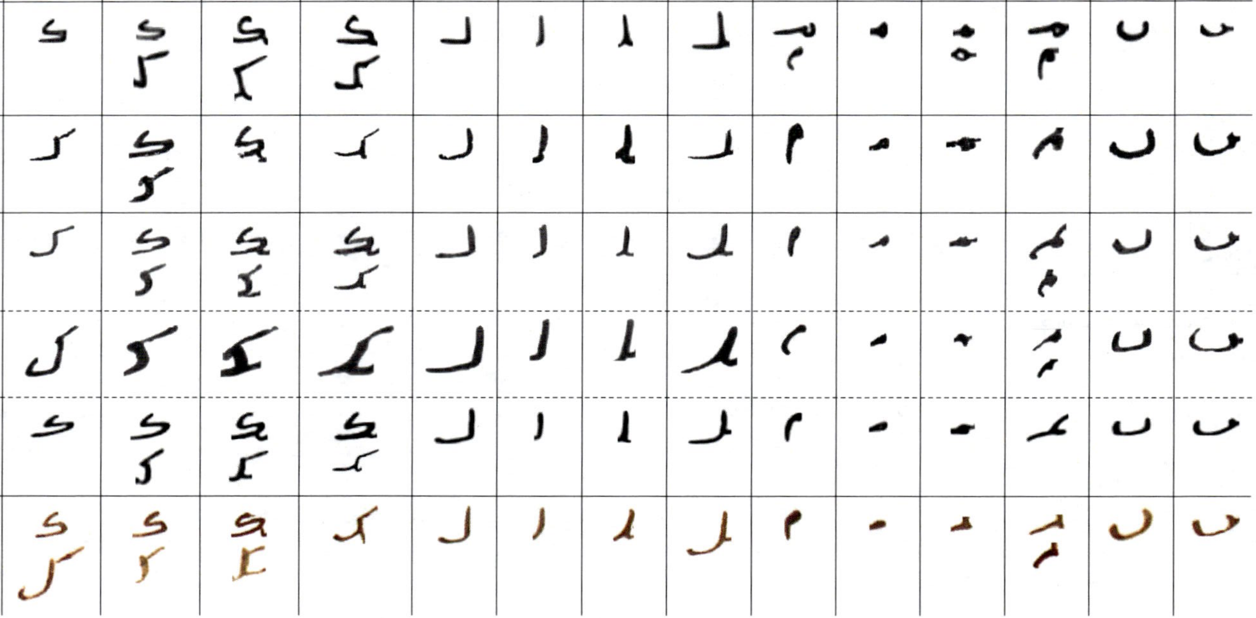

TABLE 5.16 Comparative table of letters *kāf-nūn* (*cont.*)

MS	Age	ك				ل				م				ن	
		ك	كـ	ـكـ	ـك	ل	لـ	ـلـ	ـل	م	مـ	ـمـ	ـم	ن	ـن
Lg	63														
Al	aft. 63														
An	aft. 63														
IS	bet. 64–7														
L5	71														
IA	76–7														

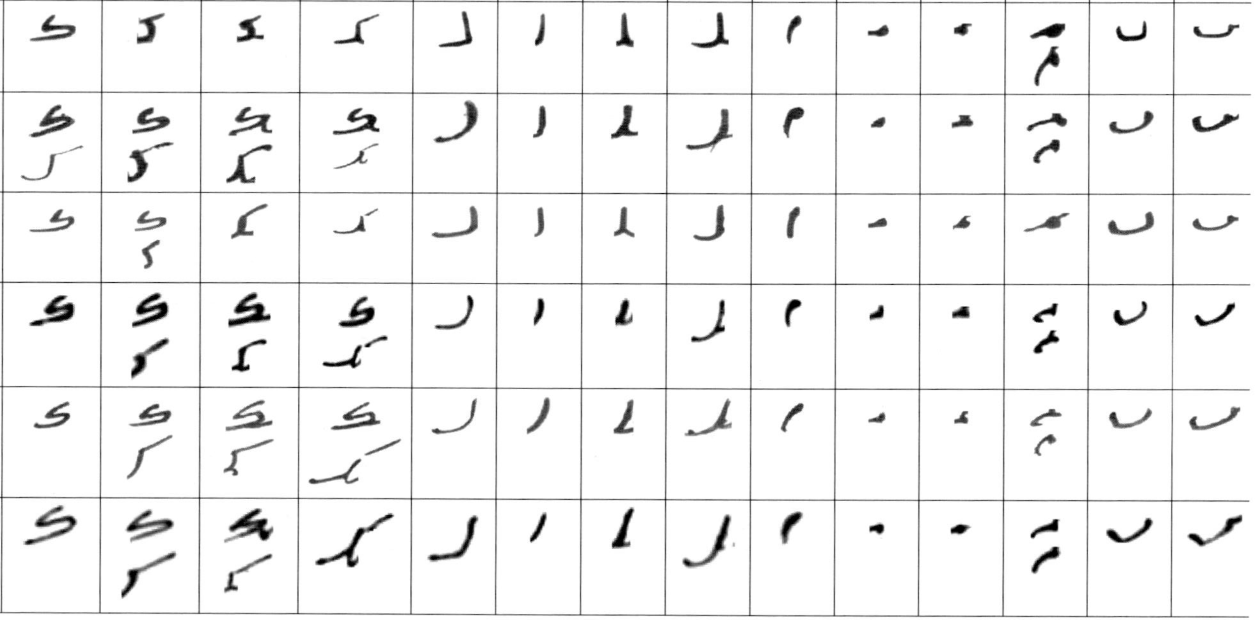

TABLE 5.17 Comparative table of letters *hāʾ-yāʾ* and of some ligatures in specific combinations

MS	Age	ه				و		ي		لا		ـها	بن	في	ده	ره	قال
		ه	هـ	ـهـ	ـه	و	ـو	ى	ـى	لا	ـلا						
IM	28																
IT2	bet. 44–50																
G1	bet. 49–57																
Lg*	aft. 50																
IY	bet. 51–7																
Du	56																

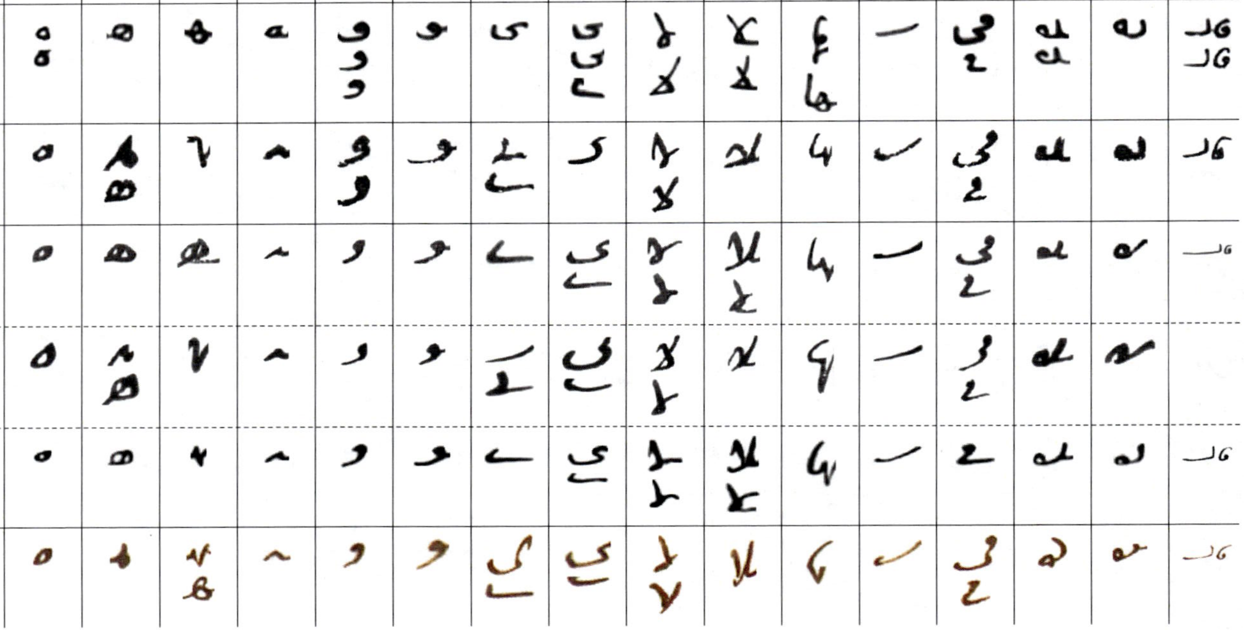

TABLE 5.17 Comparative table of letters *hāʾ-yāʾ* and of some ligatures in specific combinations (*cont.*)

MS	Age	ه				و		ي		لا		ـها	بن	في	ده	ره	قال
		ه	هـ	ـهـ	ـه	و	ـو	ى	ـى	لا	ـلا						
Lg	63																
Al	aft. 63																
An	aft. 63																
IS	bet. 64–7																
L5	71																
IA	76–7																

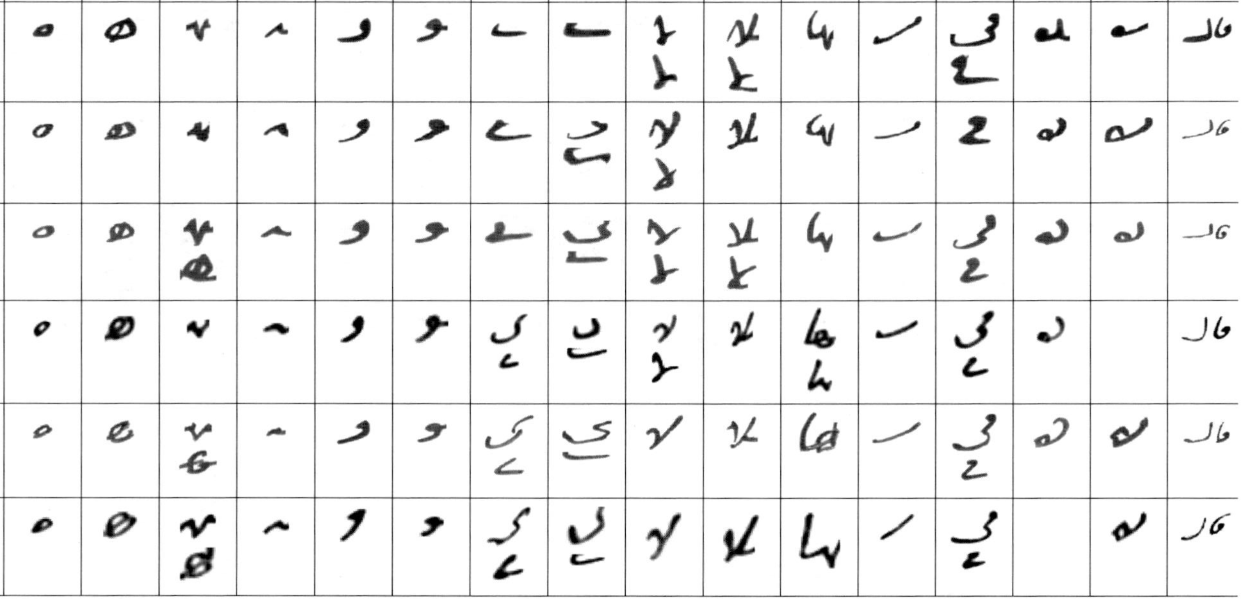

FIGURE 5.26 MS Al (MS 2125 dāl Tārīkh), fol. 4[b]
ALEXANDRIA, BIBLIOTHECA ALEXANDRINA

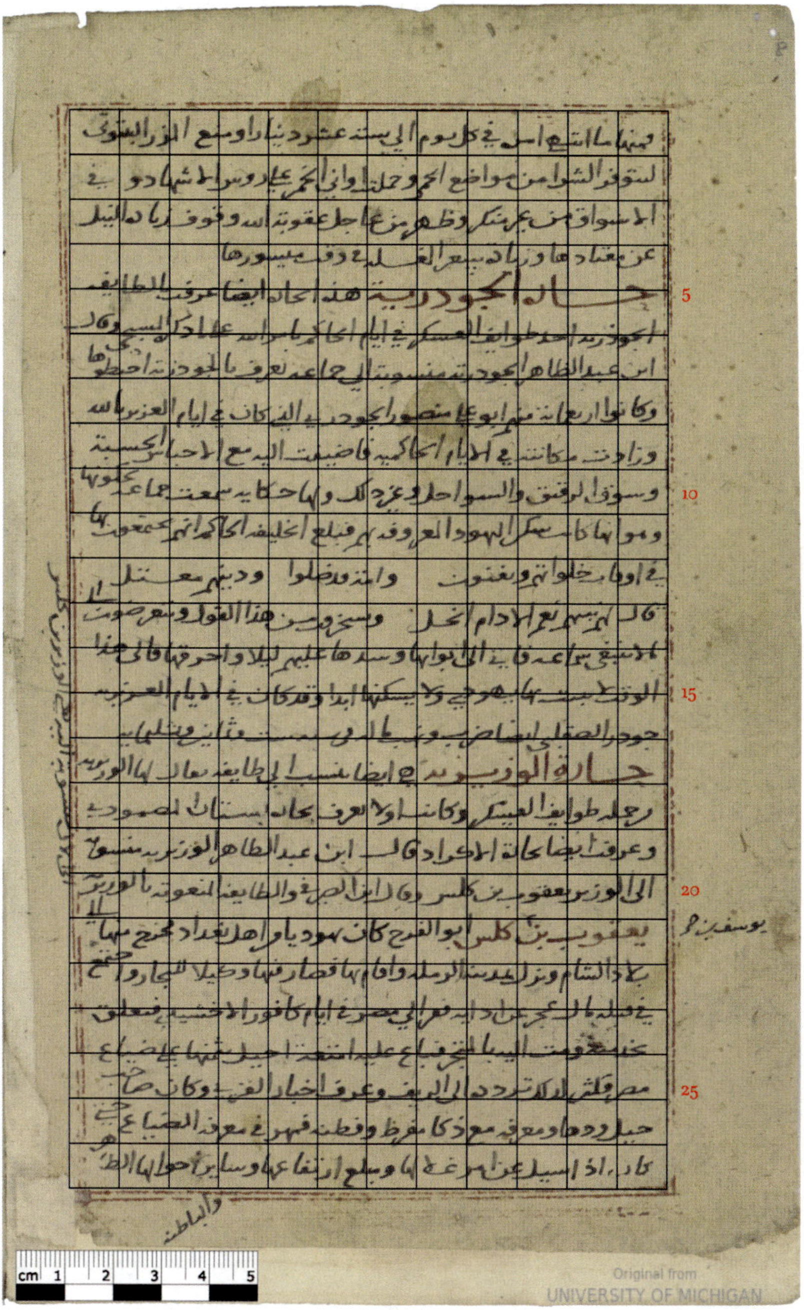

FIGURE 5.27 MS An (MS Isl. 605), p. 8
ANN ARBOR, UNIVERSITY OF MICHIGAN, SPECIAL COLLECTIONS LIBRARY

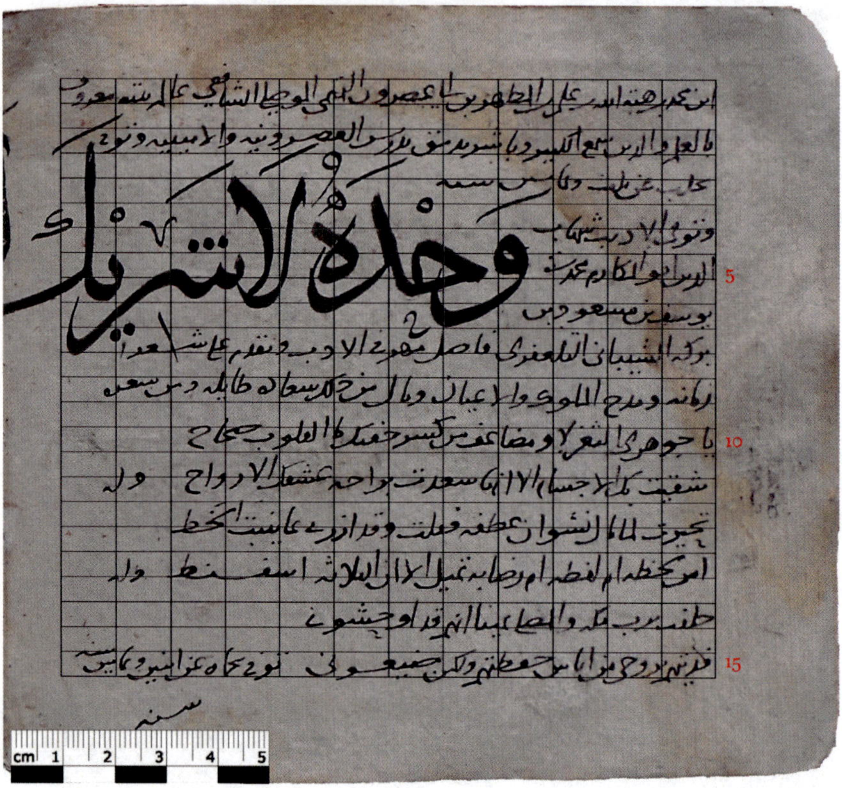

FIGURE 5.28 MS Du (MS 1790), fol. 37b
DUSHANBE, KITOBHONA-I MILLI-I TODJIKISTON

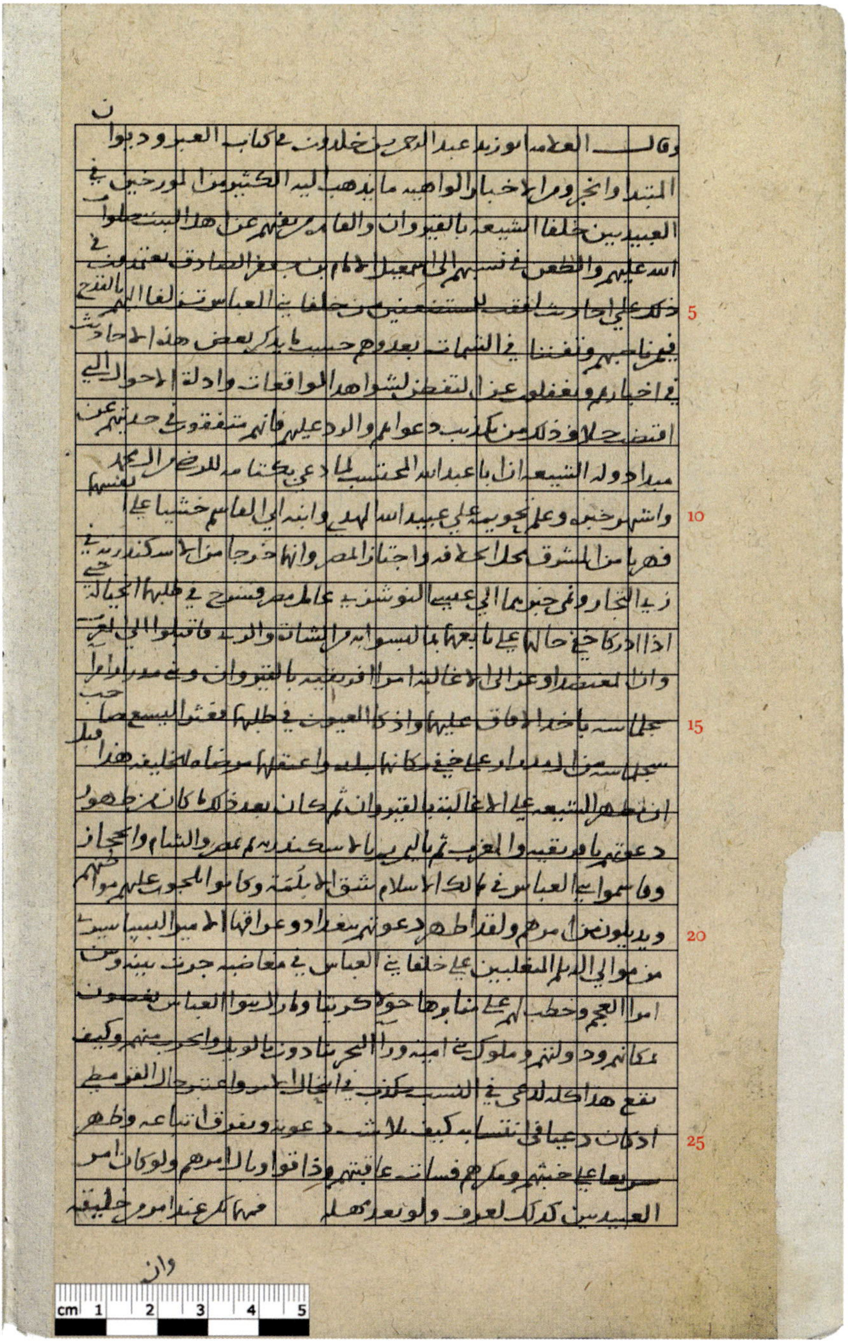

FIGURE 5.29 MS G1 (MS Ar. 1652), fol. 10b
GOTHA, FORSCHUNGS- UND LANDESBIBLIOTHEK

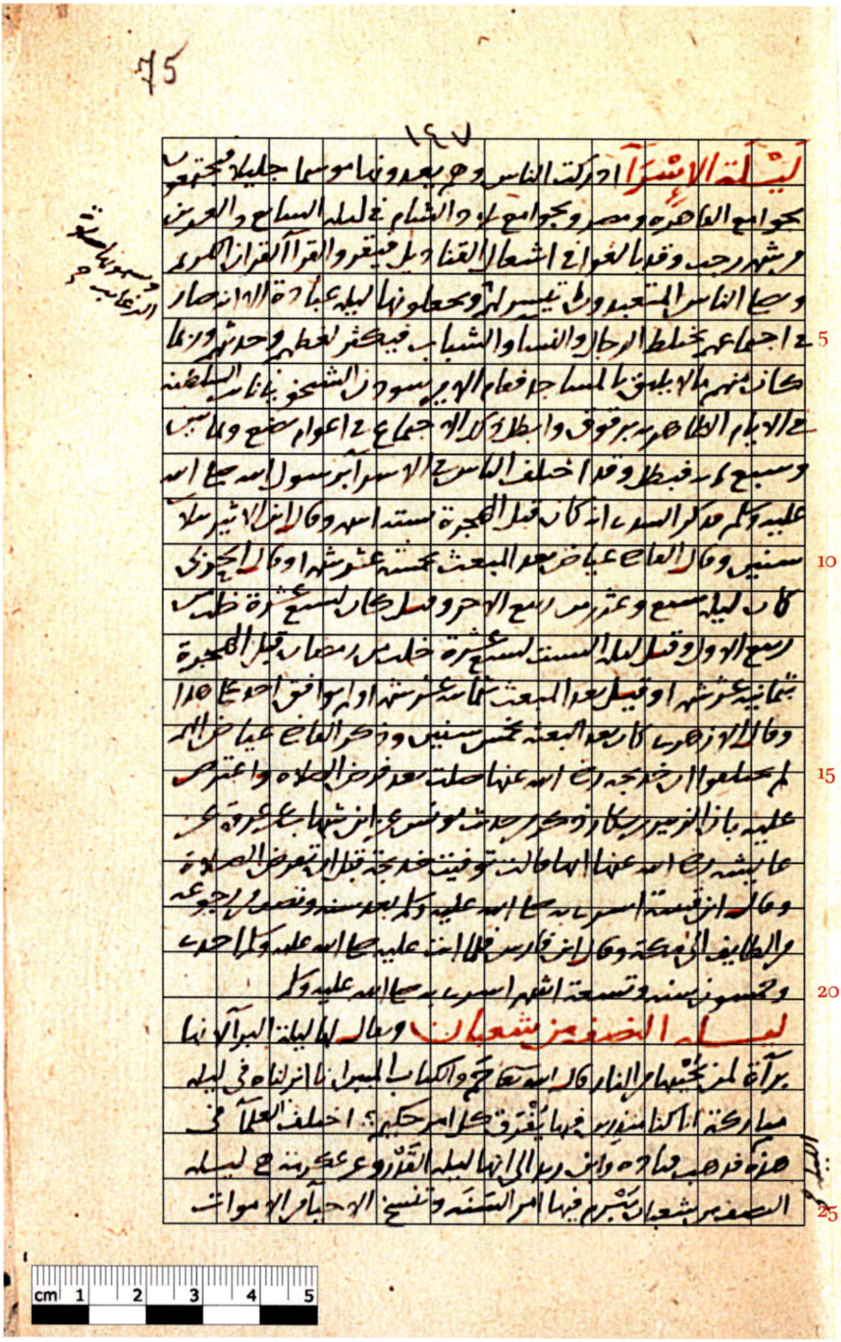

FIGURE 5.30 MS IA (MS Ayasofya 3362), fol. 74b
ISTANBUL, SÜLEYMANIYE KÜTÜPHANESI

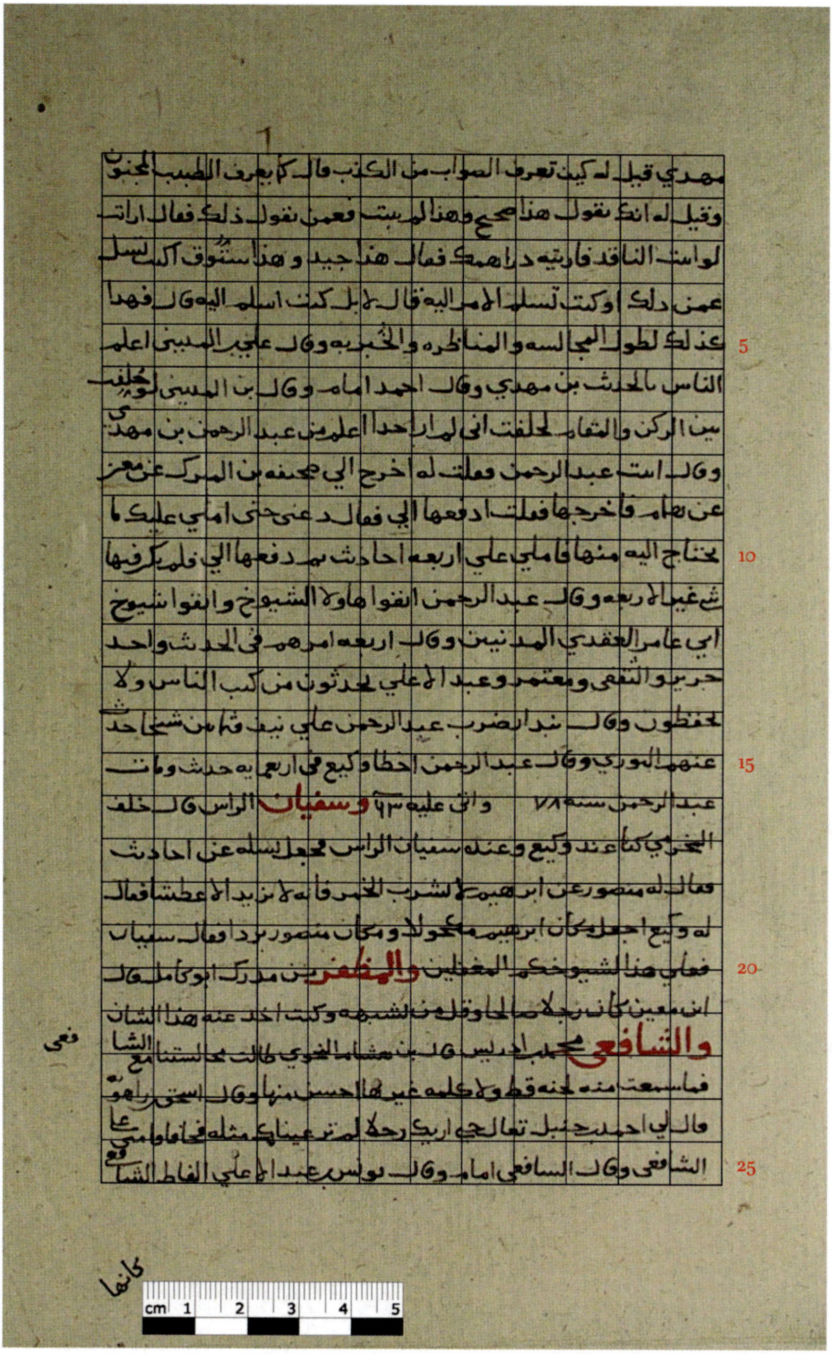

FIGURE 5.31 MS IM (MS 575), fol. 15b
ISTANBUL, MURAT MOLLA KÜTÜPHANESI

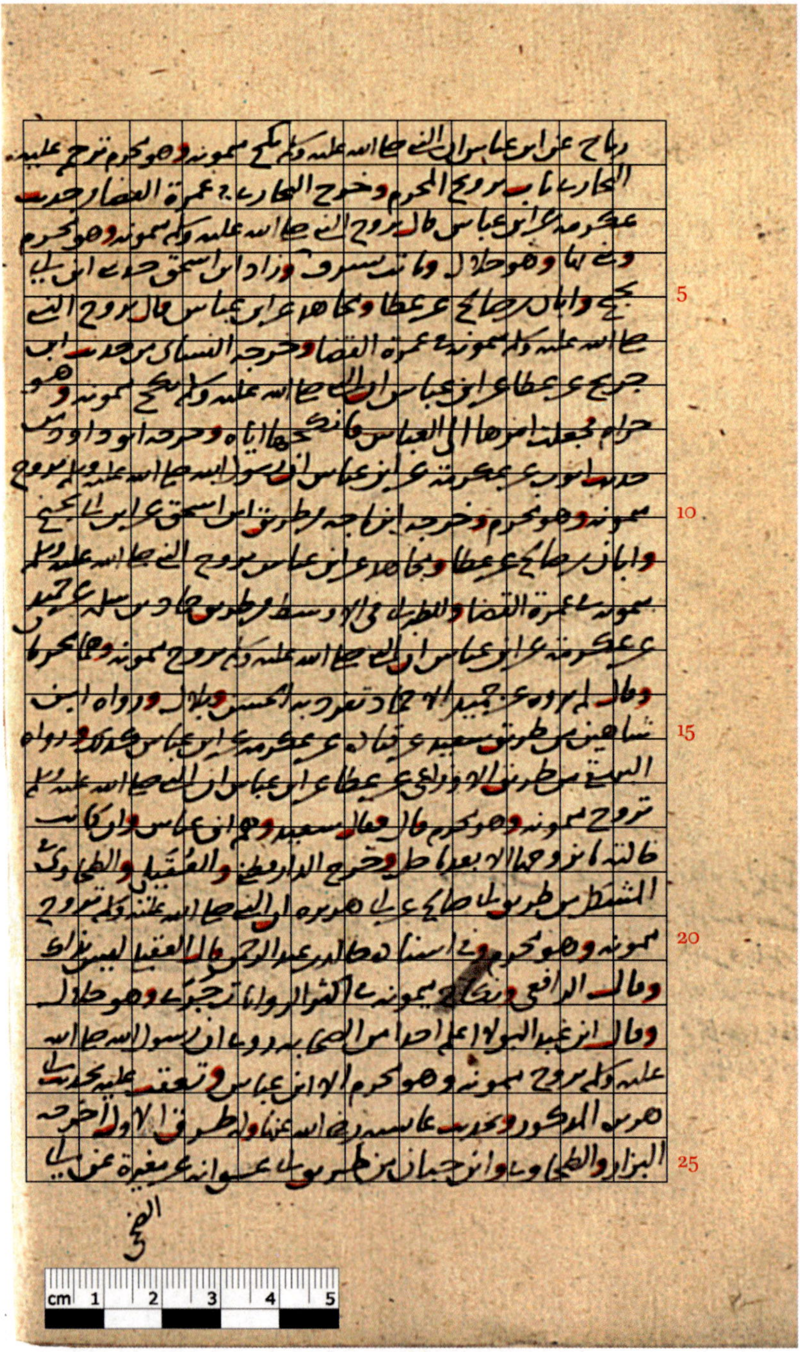

FIGURE 5.32 MS IS (MS Şehit Ali Paşa 1847), fol. 12b
ISTANBUL, SÜLEYMANIYE KÜTÜPHANESI

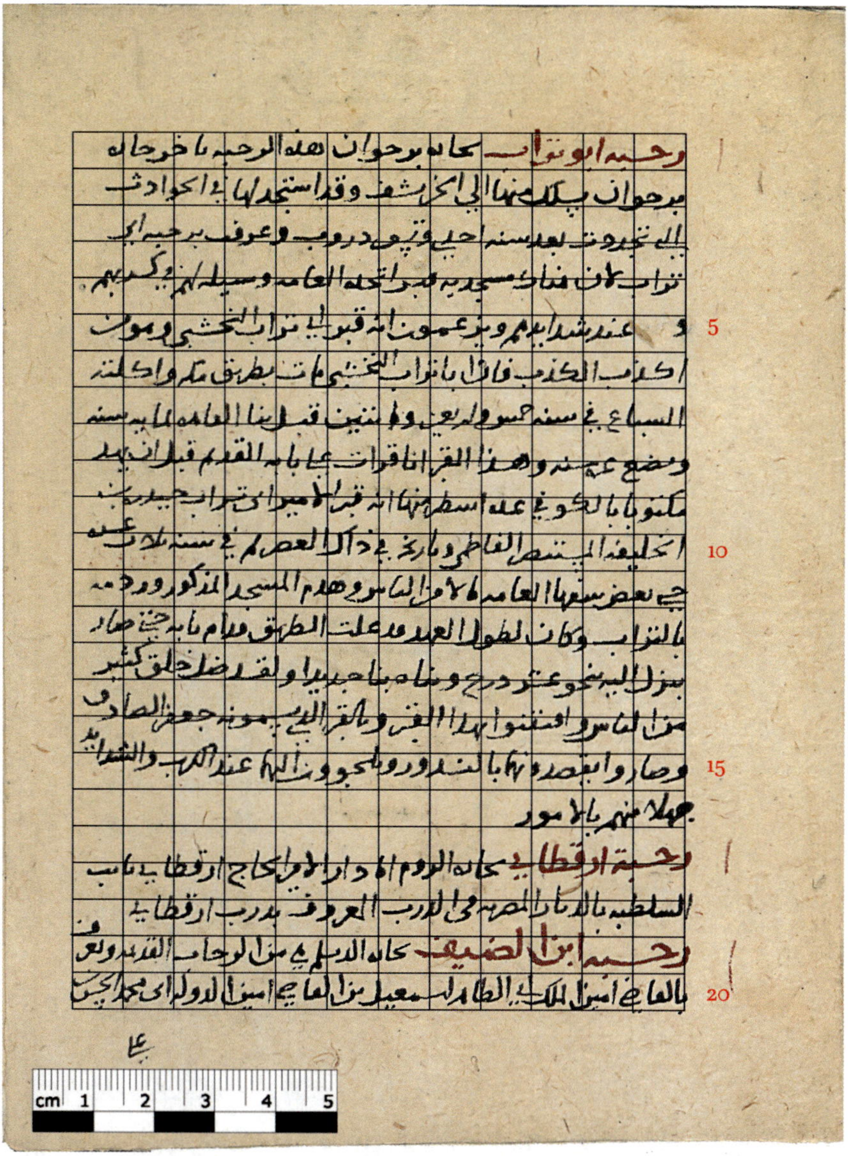

FIGURE 5.33 MS IT2 (MS Emanet Hazinesi 1405), fol. 16b
ISTANBUL, TSMK

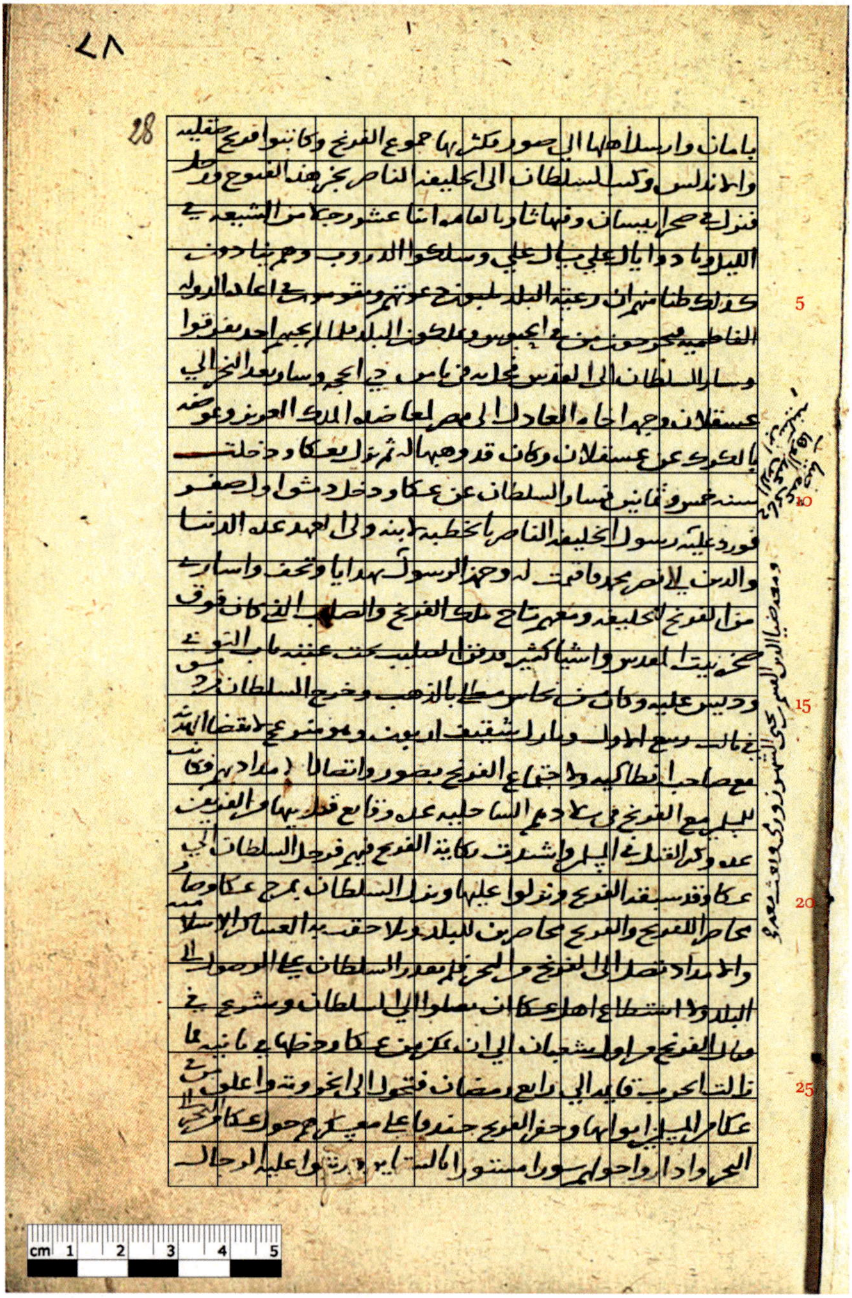

FIGURE 5.34 MS IY (MS Yeni Cami 887), fol. 28ª
ISTANBUL, SÜLEYMANIYE KÜTÜPHANESI

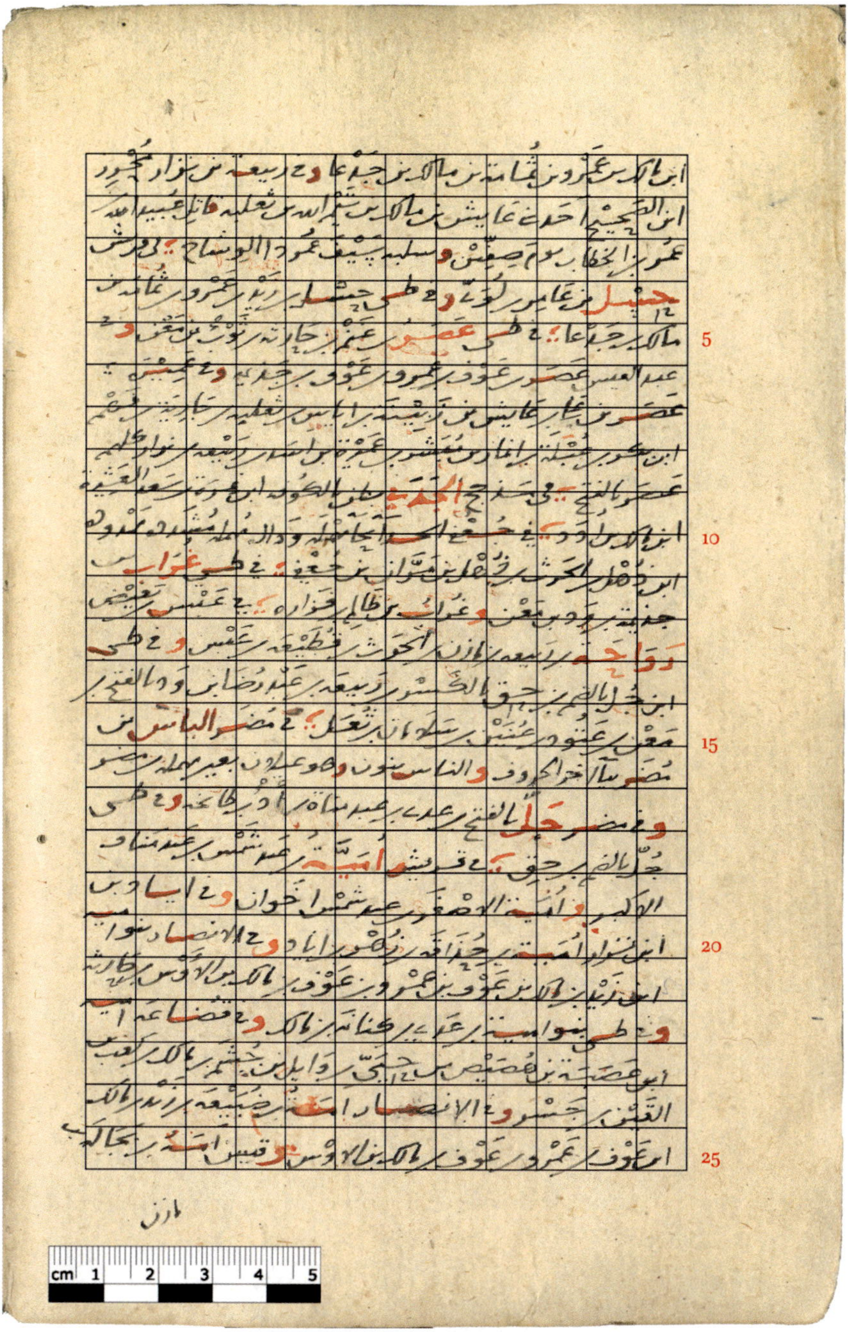

FIGURE 5.35 MS L5 (MS Or. 560), fol. 9b
LEIDEN, UNIVERSITEIT LEIDEN, UNIVERSITEITSBIBLIOTHEEK

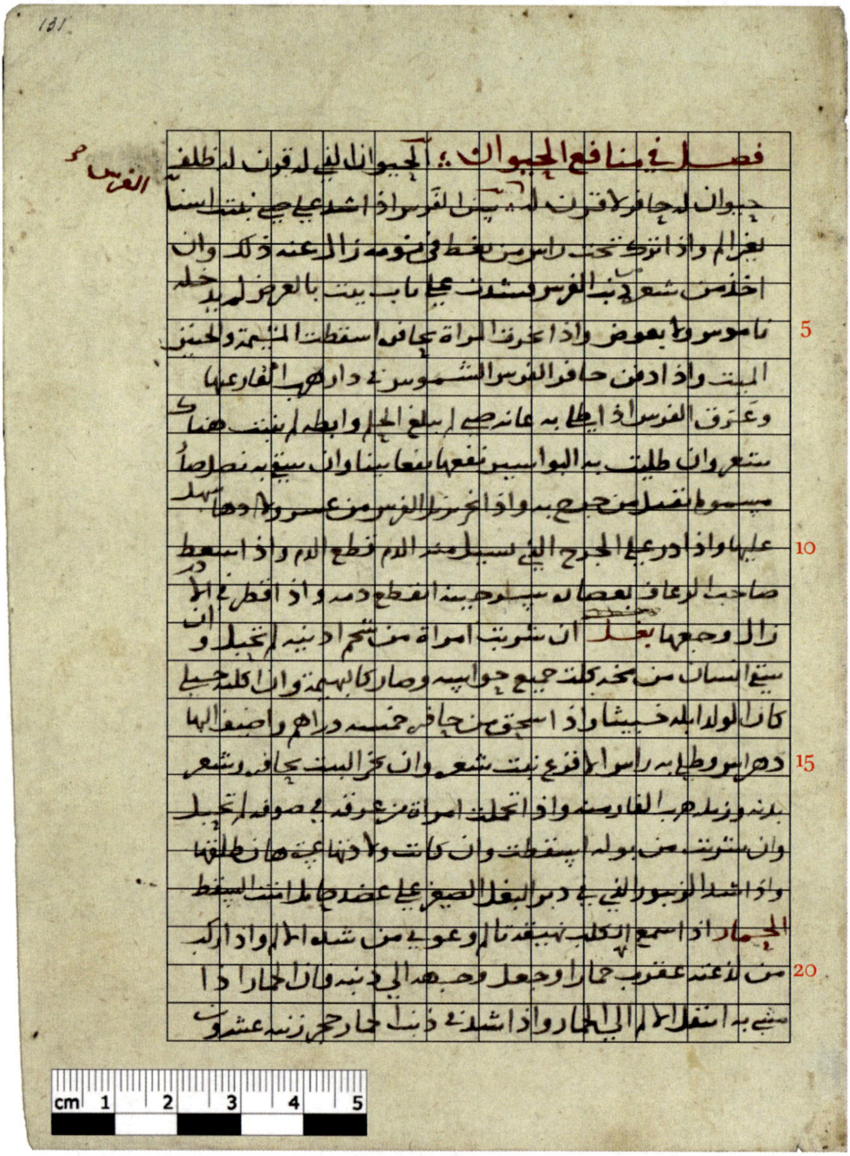

FIGURE 5.36 MS Lg (MS 2232), fol. 131[a]
LIÈGE, LIÈGE UNIVERSITÉ, BIBLIOTHÈQUE D'ARCHITECTURE, LETTRES, PHILOSOPHIE, HISTOIRE ET ARTS

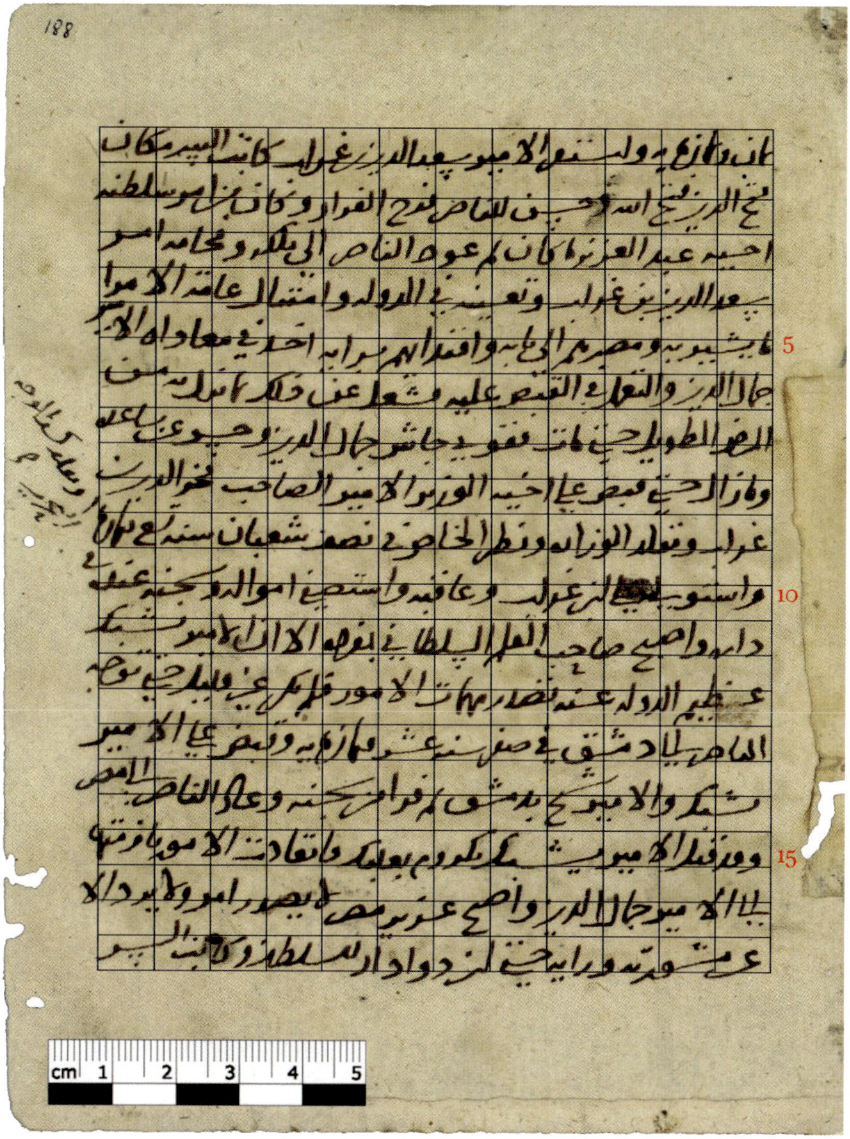

FIGURE 5.37 MS Lg* (MS 2232), fol. 188[a]
LIÈGE, LIÈGE UNIVERSITÉ, BIBLIOTHÈQUE D'ARCHITECTURE, LETTRES, PHILOSOPHIE, HISTOIRE ET ARTS

Bibliography

Primary Sources

Erasmus, *Literary and educational writings* 4, *De pueris instituendis, De recta pronuntiatione*, ed. J.K. Sowards, Toronto, Buffalo, and London 1985.

Ibn Fahd, *Muʿjam al-shuyūkh*, ed. M. al-Zāhī and Ḥ. al-Jāsir, Riyadh 1982.

Ibn Ḥajar, *Inbāʾ al-ghumr bi-abnāʾ al-ʿumr*, ed. Ḥ. Ḥabashī, Cairo 1969–72, 4 vols.

Ibn Ḥajar, *al-Majmaʿ al-muʾassis lil-muʿjam al-mufahris*, ed. Y. ʿA. al-R. al-Marʿashlī, Beirut 1992–4, 4 vols.

Ibn al-Ṣāʾigh, *Tuḥfat ūlī l-albāb fī ṣināʿat al-khaṭṭ wa-l-kitāb*, ed. H. Nājī, Tunis 1981; ed. F. Saʿd, Beirut 1997.

Al-Maqrīzī, *Al-Maqrīzī's al-Ḫabar ʿan al-bašar*. Vol. V, Section 4: Persia and its kings, Part I, ed. J. Hämeen-Anttila, Leiden and Boston 2018.

Al-Maqrīzī, *Al-Maqrīzī's al-Ḫabar ʿan al-bašar*. Vol. V, Sections 1–2: The Arab thieves, ed. and trans. P. Webb, Leiden and Boston 2019.

Al-Maqrīzī, *Al-Maqrīzī's Traktat über die Mineralien: Kitāb al-Maqāṣid al-saniyyah li-maʿrifat al-aǧsām al-maʿdiniyyah*, ed. and trans. F. Käs, Leiden and Boston 2015.

Al-Maqrīzī, *Caliphate and kingship in a fifteenth-century literary history of Muslim leadership and pilgrimage: al-Ḏahab al-masbūk fī ḏikr man ḥaǧǧa min al-ḫulafāʾ wa-l-mulūk*, ed. and trans. J. Van Steenbergen, Leiden and Boston 2016.

Al-Maqrīzī, *Ḍawʾ al-sārī li-maʿrifat ḫabar Tamīm al-Dārī: On Tamīm al-Dārī and his waqf in Hebron*, ed. and trans. Y. Frenkel, Leiden and Boston 2014.

Al-Maqrīzī, *Durar al-ʿuqūd al-farīda fī tarājim al-aʿyān al-mufīda*, ed. M. al-Jalīlī, Beirut 2002, 4 vols.

Al-Maqrīzī, *al-Mawāʿiẓ wa-l-iʿtibār bi-dhikr al-khiṭaṭ wa-l-āthār*, Būlāq 1853, 2 vols.

Al-Maqrīzī, *al-Mawāʿiẓ wa-l-iʿtibār bi-dhikr al-khiṭaṭ wa-l-āthār*, ed. A. Fuʾād Sayyid, London 2013, 6 vols.

Al-Maqrīzī, *Musawwadat Kitāb al-Mawāʿiẓ wa-l-iʿtibār fī dhikr al-khiṭaṭ wa-l-āthār*, ed. A. Fuʾād Sayyid, London 1995.

Al-Maqrīzī, *al-Sulūk li-maʿrifat duwal al-mulūk*, ed. M.M. Ziyāda and S. ʿA. al-F. ʿĀshūr, Cairo 1934–73, 4 vols.

Al-Nuwayrī, *Nihāyat al-arab fī funūn al-adab*, 33 vols., Cairo 1923–97.

Al-Qalqashandī, *Ṣubḥ al-aʿshā fī ṣināʿat al-inshāʾ*, ed. M. ʿA. al-R. Ibrāhīm, Cairo 1963, 14 vols.

Al-Sakhāwī, *al-Ḍawʾ al-lāmiʿ li-ahl al-qarn al-tāsiʿ*, Cairo 1934–6, 12 vols.

Al-Sakhāwī, *al-Jawāhir wa-l-durar fī tarjamat shaykh al-Islām Ibn Ḥajar*, ed. I.B. ʿAbd al-Ḥamīd, Beirut 1999, 3 vols.

Al-Ṭayyibī, *Jāmiʿ maḥāsin kitābat al-kuttāb wa-nuzhat ūlī l-baṣāʾir wa-l-albāb*, ed. ʿA. al-ʿA. b. N. al-Mānīʿ, Riyadh 2015.

Al-Ziftāwī, *Minhāj al-iṣāba fī maʿrifat al-khuṭūṭ wa-ālāt al-kitāba*, ed. H. Nājī, in H. Nājī, Nuṣūṣ fī l-khaṭṭ al-ʿarabī, in *al-Mawrid* 15/4 (1986), 157–316.

Secondary Sources

Atanasiu, V., *De la fréquence des lettres et de son influence en calligraphie arabe*, Paris and Montréal, 1999.

Atanasiu, V., *Le Phénomène calligraphique à l'époque du sultanat mamluk: Moyen-Orient, XIIIe–XVIe siècle*, PhD dissertation, École pratique des Hautes Études, Paris 2003.

Bahrāmiyān, ʿA., Atharī nāshinākhtah az Maqrīzī (*Muntakhab Durrat al-aslāk fī dawlat al-Atrāk* az majmūʿah-yi Khwājah Muḥammad Pārsā), in *Nāmah-yi Bahāristān* 11–12 (2006), 211–6.

Bahrāmiyān, ʿA. and ʿA.A. Yūnus Āf, *Fihrist nuskhahā-yi khaṭṭī kitābkhānah-yi millī-i Tājikistān*, vol. 1, Qom and Tehran 2002.

Bauden, F., al-Maqrīzī, in R.G. Dunphy (ed.), *Encyclopedia of the Medieval Chronicle*, Leiden and Boston 2010, 1074–6.

Bauden, F., al-Maqrīzī, in D. Thomas, and A. Mallett (eds.), *Christian-Muslim relations: a bibliographical history*, vol. 5 (1350–1500), Leiden and Boston 2013, 380–95.

Bauden, F., *Al-Maqrīzī's collection of opuscules: an introduction*, Leiden and Boston (forthcoming).

Bauden, F., *Catalogue of the Arabic, Persian and Turkish manuscripts in Belgium. Volume 1: Handlist. Part 1: Université de Liège*, Leiden and Boston 2017.

Bauden, F., Diplomatic entanglements between Tabriz, Cairo, and Herat: a reconstructed Qara Qoyunlu letter datable to 818/1415, in F. Bauden, and M. Dekkiche (eds.), *Mamluk Cairo: a crossroads for embassies*, Leiden and Boston 2019, 410–83.

Bauden, F., Mamluk diplomatics: The present state of research, in F. Bauden, and M. Dekkiche (eds.), *Mamluk Cairo: A crossroads for embassies*, Leiden and Boston 2019, 1–104.

Bauden, F., Les Manuscrits arabes dans les bibliothèques publiques belges: une introduction, in J.L.Y. Chan, and B.W. Lee (eds.), *International Association of Orientalist Librarians, Ninth general meeting at the 34 ICANAS, 24–25 August 1993, Hong Kong, Proceedings*, Hong-Kong 1993, 149–70.

Bauden, F., Maqriziana I: Discovery of an autograph manuscript of al-Maqrīzī: towards a better understanding of his working method, description: section 1, in *Mamlūk Studies Review* VII (2003), 21–68.

Bauden, F., Maqriziana I: Discovery of an autograph manuscript of al-Maqrīzī: towards a better understanding of his working method, description: section 2, in *Mamlūk Studies Review* X (2006), 81–139.

Bauden, F., Maqriziana II: Discovery of an autograph manuscript of al-Maqrīzī: towards a better understanding of his working method, analysis, in *Mamlūk Studies Review* XII/1 (2008), 51–118.

Bauden, F., Maqriziana IV. Le Carnet de notes d'al-Maqrīzī: l'apport de la codicologie à une meilleure compréhension de sa constitution, in F. Déroche, and F. Richard (eds.), *Scripts, page settings and bindings of Middle-Eastern manuscripts. Papers of the Third International Conference on Codicology and Paleography of Middle-Eastern Manuscripts (Bologna, 4–6 October, 2000)*, Part 2, *Manuscripta Orientalia*, St. Petersburg 2003, 24–36.

Bauden, F., Maqriziana VIII: Quelques remarques sur l'orthographe d'al-Maqrīzī (m. 845/1442) à partir de son carnet de notes: peut-on parler de moyen arabe?, in J. Lentin, and J. Grand'Henry (eds.), *Moyen arabe et variétés mixtes de l'arabe à travers l'histoire. Actes du Premier Colloque International (Louvain-la-Neuve, 10–14 mai 2004)*, Louvain-la-Neuve 2008, 21–38.

Bauden, F., Maqriziana IX: Should al-Maqrīzī be thrown out with the bathwater? The question of his plagiarism of al-Awḥadī's *Khiṭaṭ* and the documentary evidence, in *Mamlūk Studies Review* XIV (2010), 159–232.

Bauden, F., Maqriziana X: al-Maqrīzī and his *al-Tārīkh al-Kabīr al-Muqaffā li-Miṣr*, part 1: An inquiry into the history of the work, in S. Massoud (ed.), *Studies in Islamic historiography: essays in honour of Professor Donald P. Little*, Leiden and Boston 2020, 66–124.

Bauden, F., Maqriziana X: al-Maqrīzī and his *al-Tārīkh al-Kabīr al-Muqaffā li-Miṣr*, part 2: The fortunes of the work and of its copies, in *Quaderni di Studi Arabi* 15 (2020) (forthcoming).

Bauden, F., Maqriziana XI. Al-Maqrīzī et al-Ṣafadī: Analyse de la (re)construction d'un récit biographique, in F. Bauden (éd.), *Les Méthodes de travail des historiens en Islam, Quaderni di Studi Arabi, Nuova serie*, Rome 2009, 99–136.

Bauden, F., Maqriziana XII. Evaluating the sources for the Fatimid period: Ibn al-Ma'mūn al-Baṭā'iḥī's *History* and its use by al-Maqrīzī (with a critical edition of his résumé for the years 501–515 A.H.), in B.D. Craig (ed.), *Ismaili and Fatimid studies in honor of Paul E. Walker*, Chicago 2010, 33–85.

Bauden, F., Maqriziana XIII: An exchange of correspondence between al-Maqrīzī and al-Qalqashandī, in Y. Ben-Bassat (ed.), *Developing perspectives in Mamluk history: Essays in honor of Amalia Levanoni*, Leiden and Boston 2017, 201–29.

Bauden, F., Maqriziana XIV: al-Maqrīzī's last opus (*al-Khabar ʿan al-bashar*) and its significance for the historiography of the pre-modern islamicate world (forthcoming).

Bauden, F., Maqriziana XVIII: al-Maqrīzī as a reader (forthcoming).

Bauden, F., Taqī al-Dīn Aḥmad ibn ʿAlī al-Maqrīzī, in A. Mallett (ed.), *Medieval Muslim historians and the Franks in the Levant*, Leiden and Boston 2014, 161–200.

Bauden, F., The recovery of Mamlūk chancery documents in an unsuspected place, in M. Winter, and A. Levanoni (eds.), *The Mamluks in Egyptian and Syrian politics and society*, Leiden and Boston 2004, 59–76.

Bauden, F., *Trusting the source as far as it can be trusted: al-Maqrīzī and the Mongol book of laws (Maqriziana VII)* (forthcoming).

Bauden, F., Vers une archéologie du savoir en Islam: la méthode de travail d'al-Maqrīzī, historien du XVe siècle, in *Comptes rendus de l'Académie des Inscriptions et Belles-Lettres* 2009 (2010), 97–111.

Bauden, F., Yemeni-Egyptian diplomatic exchanges about the Meccan Sharifate: A reconstructed Rasulid letter addressed to al-Mu'ayyad Shaykh in 817/1415, in F. Bauden (ed.), *The Mamluk sultanate and its periphery*, Leiden and Boston 2020 (forthcoming).

Behrens-Abouseif, D., *The book in Mamluk Egypt and Syria (1250–1517): Scribes, libraries and market*, Leiden and Boston 2018.

Beit-Arié, M., Stéréotypies et individualités dans les écritures des copistes hébraïques du Moyen Âge, in Sirat, C., J. Irigoin, and E. Poulle (eds.), *L'Écriture: le cerveau, l'œil et la main*, Turnhout 1990, 201–19.

Ben Azzouna, N., *Aux Origines du classicisme: calligraphes et bibliophiles au temps des dynasties mongoles (les Ilkhanides et les Djalayirides, 656–814/1258–1411)*, Leiden and Boston 2018.

Berrichon-Sedeyn, M.-J., Acte mécanique ou présence vivante, in C. Sirat, J. Irigoin, and E. Poulle (eds.), *L'Écriture: le cerveau, l'œil et la main*, Turnhout 1990, 221–35.

Boiarov, A., A. Senov, and A. Knysh, Arabic manuscript author verification using deep convolutional networks, in *1st International Workshop on Arabic script analysis and recognition* (ASAR) *(Nancy, 3–5 April 2017)*, s.l. 2017, 1–5 (available online: https://ieeexplore.ieee.org/document/8067750).

Brockelmann, C., *Geschichte der arabischen Litteratur*, Leiden, 1937–2, 2 vols. and 3 vols. of supplement.

Chartier, R., *From the author's hand to the printer's mind: Who is an author in early modern Europe?*, San Diego 2013.

Dekkiche, M., Diplomatics, or another way to see the world, in F. Bauden, and M. Dekkiche (eds.), *Mamluk Cairo: A crossroads for embassies*, Leiden and Boston 2019, 185–213.

Déroche, F., Analyser l'écriture arabe: remarques sur la "cursivité", in *Manuscripta orientalia* 9/3 (2003), 4–7.

Déroche, F., Copier des manuscrits: remarques sur le travail du copiste, in *REMMM* 99–100 (2002), 133–44.

Dozy, R.P.A., Découverte de trois volumes du Mokaffá d'al-Makrízí, in Dozy, *Notices sur quelques manuscrits arabes*, Leiden 1847, 8–16.

Fu'ād Sayyid, A., Khuṭūṭ al-Maqrīzī, in Y. Zaydān, *al-Makhṭūṭāt al-muwaqqaʿa: aʿmāl al-muʾtamar al-duwalī l-thānī li-Markaz al-Makhṭūṭāt (Abrīl 2005)*, Alexandria 2008, 123–40.

Fu'ād Sayyid, A., *al-Maqrīzī wa-kitābuhu l-Mawāʿiẓ wa-l-iʿtibār fī dhikr al-khiṭaṭ wa-l-āthār*, London 2013.

Gacek, A., Al-Nuwayrī's classification of Arabic scripts, in *Manuscripts of the Middle East* 2 (1987), 126–30.

Gacek, A., *The Arabic manuscript tradition: A glossary of technical terms and bibliography. Supplement*, Leiden and Boston 2008.

Gacek, A., *Arabic manuscripts: A vademecum for readers*, Leiden and Boston 2009.

Gardiner, N., and F. Bauden, A recently discovered holograph fair copy of al-Maqrīzī's *al-Mawāʿiẓ wa-al-iʿtibār fī dhikr al-khiṭaṭ wa-al-āthār* (Michigan Islamic MS 605), in *Journal of Islamic Manuscripts* 2/2 (2011), 123–31.

Griffel, F., Is There an Autograph of al-Ghazālī in MS Yale, Landberg 318?, in Griffel (ed.), Islam and rationality: The impact of al-Ghazālī. Papers collected on his 900th anniversary, 2 vols., Leiden and Boston 2016, 2:168–85.

Guérin du Grandlaunay, R., *Iršād al-ġāwī bal isʿād al-ṭālib wa-l-rāwī li-l-iʿlām bi-tarǧamat al-Saḫāwī. Édition et analyse de la première partie de l'autobiographie d'al-Saḫāwī (831–902/1428–1497)*, PhD dissertation, Paris 2015, 3 vols.

Hinz, W., *Islamische Masse und Gewichte*, Leiden 1955.

Hirschler, K., *The written word in the medieval Arabic lands: A social and cultural history of reading practices*, Edinburgh 2012.

Huber, R.A., and A.M. Headrick, *Handwriting identification: Facts and fundamentals*, Boca Raton FL, London, New York, and Washington, DC 1999.

Humbert, G., Un papier fabriqué vers 1350 en Égypte, in M. Zerdoun Bat-Yehouda (ed.), *Le Papier au Moyen Âge: Histoire et techniques*, Turnhout 1999, 61–73.

Al-ʿIshsh, Y., and Kh. al-Rayyān, *Fihris makhṭūṭāt Dār al-Kutub al-Ẓāhiriyya: Al-Tārīkh wa-mulḥaqātuhu*, Damascus 1947.

ʿIzz al-Dīn ʿAlī, M.K. al-D., *al-Maqrīzī muʿarrikhan*, Beirut 1990.

Jahdani, A., À propos d'un traité mamelouk de calligraphie, in F. Déroche and F. Richard (eds.), *Scripts, page settings and bindings of middle-eastern manuscripts: Papers of the Third International Conference on Codicology and Paleography of Middle-Eastern Manuscripts (Bologna, 4–6 October, 2000), part 2*, St. Petersburg 2003, 61–4.

Jażdżewski, K.K., Identifizierungsprobleme bei Schreiberhänden, in H. Härtel, and W. Milde (eds.), *Probleme der Bearbeitung mittelalterlicher Handschriften*, Wiesbaden 1986, 325–6.

Mazor, A., and K. Abbou Hershkovits, Spectacles in the Muslim world: New evidence from the mid-fourteenth century, in *Early Science and Medicine* 18/3 (2013), 291–305.

Muṣṭafā, Sh., *al-Tārīkh al-ʿarabī wa-l-muʾarrikhūn*, Beirut 1983–94, 4 vols.

Al-Rayyān, Kh., *Fihris makhṭūṭāt Dār al-Kutub al-Ẓāhiriyyah: Al-Tārīkh wa-mulḥaqātuhu. Al-Juzʾ al-thānī*, Damascus 1973.

Sedeyn, M.J., *Introduction à l'examen objectif des écritures manuscrites. Méthode "SHOE" (Standard Handwriting Objective Examination)*, Meyreuil 1999.

Serikoff, N., *Arabic medical manuscripts of the Wellcome Library: A descriptive catalogue of the Ḥaddād collection*, Leiden and Boston 2005.

Serikoff, N., Image and letter: "pace" in Arabic script (a thumb-nail index as a tool for a catalogue of Arabic manuscripts. Principles and criteria for its construction), in *Manuscripta orientalia* 7/4 (2001), 55–66.

Al-Shandī, M. al-B., *Fihris al-tārīkh wa-mulḥaqātihi*, in al-Shandī, *Fihris baʿḍ al-makhṭūṭāt al-ʿarabiyya al-mūdaʿa bi-Maktabat Baladiyyat al-Iskandariyya mundhu inshāʾihā sanat 1892m. ilā sanat 1930m.*, vol. 2, Alexandria 1955.

Sirat, C., *Writing as handwork: A history of handwriting in Mediterranean and Western culture*, Turnhout 2006.

Sirat, C., and S. Di Donato, *Maïmonide: Les brouillons autographes du Dalâlat al-ḥâʾirīn (Guide des égarés)*, Paris 2011.

Sirat, C., J. Irigoin, and E. Poulle (eds.), *L'Écriture: le cerveau, l'œil et la main*, Turnhout 1990.

Wiet, G., Les Classiques du scribe égyptien au XVe siècle, in *Studia Islamica* 18 (1963), 41–80.

Wing, A.M., Étude sur la variabilité dans la forme spatiale de l'écriture cursive, in C. Sirat, J. Irigoin, and E. Poulle (eds.), *L'Écriture: le cerveau, l'œil et la main*, Turnhout 1990, 127–37.

Witkam, J.J., Discovery of a hitherto unknown section of the *Kitāb al-Muqaffā* by al-Maqrīzī, in *Quaerendo* 9 (1979), 353–4.

Witkam, J.J., Les Autographes d'al-Maqrīzī, in A.-C. Binebine, *Le Manuscrit arabe et la codicologie*, Rabat 1994, 88–98.

Zaydān, Y., *Fihris makhṭūṭāt Baladiyyat al-Iskandariyya. al-Juzʾ al-thālith: al-Tārīkh wa-mulḥaqātuhu*, Alexandria 1999.

Appendix 1: *List of al-Maqrīzī's holograph, autograph, and authorial manuscripts*

Al Alexandria, Bibliotheca Alexandrina, MS 2125 *dāl* Tārīkh
52 fols., 155×120 (120×95), mostly 20 lines.
A notebook gathering summaries from a variety of sources as well as the first sketches of some of al-Maqrīzī's writings. One of the first sketches can be dated to shortly after 831/1427–8 because it is entirely based on a source that al-Maqrīzī consulted that year.[197]

An Ann Arbor, University of Michigan, Special Collections Library, MS Isl. 605
261 fols., 245×165 (200×115), 27 lines.
The text corresponds to the second, and final, version of the third volume of *al-Mawāʿiẓ wa-l-iʿtibār fī dhikr al-khiṭaṭ wa-l-āthār*. The text can be dated to after 831/1427–8 because it includes the first version of a section found in Al which was based on a source al-Maqrīzī consulted that year.[198]

C Calcutta, The Asiatic Society, MS I 774
131 fols., 184×140 (145×100), 21 l.
The manuscript is composed of three summaries: *Mukhtaṣar Kitāb Qiyām al-layl, Mukhtaṣar Kitāb Qiyām Ramaḍān, Mukhtaṣar Kitāb al-Witr*. The three original texts were authored by Muḥammad b. Naṣr al-Marwazī (d. 294/906). Al-Maqrīzī indicates in the colophon that he completed his summaries on Thursday 21 Jumādā II 807/25 December 1404.

Da Damascus, Maktabat al-Asad, MS 4805 *ʿāmm*
80 fols., 150×120 (125×90), 17 and 20 lines.
A notebook composed of the first version of one of al-Maqrīzī's opuscules and various other notes.

Du Dushanbe, Kitobhona-i milli-i Todjikiston, MS 1790
179 fols., 140×162 (105×125), 14 lines.
The summary al-Maqrīzī made from Ibn Ḥabīb al-Ḥalabī's (d. 779/1377) *Durrat al-aslāk fī dawlat al-Atrāk*. The colophon is dated Monday 20 Rabīʿ I 824/25 March 1421.

G1 Gotha, Forschungs- und Landesbibliothek, MS Ar. 1652
58 fols., 245×160 (200×115), 27 lines.
The text corresponds to the beginning of the fair copy of *Ittiʿāẓ al-ḥunafāʾ bi-akhbār al-khulafāʾ* (the end is missing). This copy can be dated to before the year

197 See Bauden, Maqriziana XII 70.
198 See Gardiner and Bauden, A recently discovered holograph 127; Bauden, Maqriziana XII 70.

824/1421, when he consulted a source which he mentions in the margin,[199] and after 816/1413–4, when al-Maqrīzī completed the first version of *al-Khiṭaṭ*.

G2 Gotha, Forschungs- und Landesbibliothek, MS Ar. 1771
185 fols., 245×160 (195×115), 27 lines.
The manuscript contains the beginning of the first volume of the fair copy of *Durar al-ʿuqūd al-farīda fī tarājim al-aʿyān al-mufīda* (the end of the volume is missing). Most of the manuscript predates the year 839/1435, when it was consulted by a scholar who left a consultation note on the title page.

IA Istanbul, Süleymaniye Kütüphanesi, MS Aya Sofya 3362
245 fols., 233×152 (180×110), 25 lines.
The manuscript contains the first volume of the fair copy of *al-Khabar ʿan al-bashar*. In a passage, al-Maqrīzī discusses an event that he describes as still taking place at the time of the copy, which he gives as the year 844/1440–1.

IF1 Istanbul, Süleymaniye Kütüphanesi, MS Fatih 4338
254 fols., 235×155 (180×110), 25 lines.
The third volume of the fair copy of *al-Khabar ʿan al-bashar*. The colophon indicates that al-Maqrīzī completed the copy on Thursday 25 Dhū l-Ḥijja 844/17 May 1441.

IF2 Istanbul, Süleymaniye Kütüphanesi, MS Fatih 4339
163 fols., 235×155 (180×110), 25 lines.
The fourth volume of the fair copy of *al-Khabar ʿan al-bashar*. Given the date of MS IF1, this volume and the subsequent ones (IF3, IF4) can be dated between the end of 844/May 1441 and al-Maqrīzī's death in Ramaḍān 845/January 1442.

IF3 Istanbul, Süleymaniye Kütüphanesi, MS Fatih 4340
265 fols., 238×155 (180×110), 25 lines.
The fifth volume of the fair copy of *al-Khabar ʿan al-bashar*. For the dating, see MS IF2.

IF4 Istanbul, Süleymaniye Kütüphanesi, MS Fatih 4341
276 fols., 235×155 (180×110), 25 lines.
The sixth volume of the fair copy of *al-Khabar ʿan al-bashar*. For the dating, see MS IF2.

IM Istanbul, Murat Molla Kütüphanesi, MS 575
215 fols., 255×169 (190×120), 25 lines
The manuscript contains a summary of Ibn ʿAdī's (d. 365/976) *al-Kāmil fī ḍuʿafāʾ al-rijāl* which al-Maqrīzī completed on 1 Muḥarram 795/17 November 1392.

IS Istanbul, Süleymaniye Kütüphanesi, MS Şehit Ali Paşa 1847
211 fols., 237×155 (180×110), 25 lines.

---

199 See Maqriziana XII 70.

The manuscript holds the fourth volume of the fair copy of *Imtāʿ al-asmāʿ*. The copy can be dated between 832/1428, when al-Maqrīzī started the fair copy, and 834/1431, when this volume was read aloud to al-Maqrīzī during his stay in Mecca (as several marginal notes confirm).[200]

IT1 Istanbul, TSMK, MS Hazine 1472
179 fols., 181×144 (140×105), 20 lines.
This is the second volume of the first version (draft) of *al-Mawāʿiẓ wa-l-iʿtibār fī dhikr al-khiṭaṭ wa-l-āthār*. This copy can be dated after 811/1408–9, if one accepts that al-Maqrīzī started to work on this subject once he acquired al-Awḥadī's (d. 811/1408–9) work, and 816/1416, given that additions were made later, on the years 817–8/1414–6.[201]

IT2 Istanbul, TSMK, MS Emanet Hazinesi 1405
182 fols., 179×141 (135×100), 20 lines.
This manuscript contains the third volume of the first version (draft) of *al-Mawāʿiẓ wa-l-iʿtibār fī dhikr al-khiṭaṭ wa-l-āthār*. Its dating can be narrowed on the basis of the evidence provided by the preceding manuscript (MS IT1).

IY Istanbul, Süleymaniye Kütüphanesi, MS Yeni Cami 887
257 fols., 250×166 (195×115), 27 lines.
This is the first volume of the fair copy of *al-Sulūk li-maʿrifat duwal al-mulūk*. This volume can be dated after 818/1415–6 on the basis of one of the sources used by al-Maqrīzī (Ibn al-Furāt) whose work he accessed that year, and before 824/1421 on the basis of another source which he consulted that year and from which he added biographies (on slips of paper) to this manuscript.[202]

L1 Leiden, Universiteit Leiden, Universiteitsbibliotheek, MS Or. 1366a
226 fols., 255×160 (195×110), 27 lines.
This manuscript contains the fair copy of what must have been the first volume of *al-Tārīkh al-kabīr al-muqaffā*.

L2 Leiden, Universiteit Leiden, Universiteitsbibliotheek, MS Or. 1366c
287 fols., 238×159 (193×110), 27 lines.
The manuscript corresponds to the fair copy of what must have been the third volume of *al-Tārīkh al-kabīr al-muqaffā*.

L3 Leiden, Universiteit Leiden, Universiteitsbibliotheek, MS Or. 3075
252 fols., 239×160 (195×110), 27 lines.
The manuscript contains the fair copy of what must have been the second volume of *al-Tārīkh al-kabīr al-muqaffā*.

---

200 See Bauden, *Al-Maqrīzī's collection*.
201 See Bauden, Maqriziana II 205–12.
202 See Bauden, Maqriziana X/1.

L4 Leiden, Universiteit Leiden, Universiteitsbibliotheek, MS Or. 14533
550 fols., 235×159 (188×110), 27 lines.
This manuscript corresponds to the fair copy of what must have been the fourth and possibly fifth volume of *al-Tārīkh al-kabīr al-muqaffā*.

L5 Leiden, Universiteit Leiden, Universiteitsbibliotheek, MS Or. 560
214 fols., 239×154 (180×110), 25 lines.
This authorial manuscript is a collection of opuscules, the majority of which were composed by al-Maqrīzī. Most of the texts are in someone else's hand (probably a scribe he hired for this purpose), while only a few are in al-Maqrīzī's handwriting. The texts copied by the scribe were collated by al-Maqrīzī between 841 and 842/1438.[203]

Lg Liège, Liège Université, Bibliothèque d'Architecture, Lettres, Philosophie, Histoire et Arts, MS 2232
209 fols., 165×136 (140×100), mostly 21 lines (in some cases 20, 18, 17 lines).
A notebook that includes several summaries from a wide variety of sources. One of these sources (Ibn Faḍl Allāh al-ʿUmarī's *Masālik al-abṣār*) was consulted in 831/1427–8. This enables us to date several parts of the notebook accordingly.[204]

P Paris, BnF, MS Arabe 2144
260 fols., 250×160 (190×110), 27 lines.
The manuscript contains the fair copy of what must have been one of the last volumes of *al-Tārīkh al-kabīr al-muqaffā*.

---

203 See Bauden, *Al-Maqrīzī's collection*.
204 See Bauden, *Maqriziana VII*.

CHAPTER 6

The Art of Copying: Mamlūk Manuscript Culture in Theory and Practice

Elias Muhanna

The study of manuscript culture in the Islamic world is a subject that has attracted much scholarly attention in recent decades, even if the evolution and diversity of copying practices remains fairly little understood.[1] Less is known about the strategies of collation, edition, and source management used to produce large compilations. In the Mamlūk period, such works were composed in great quantity and drew upon hundreds of sources, swelling in physical size and thematic scope. The material conditions of book production during this age of bibliomania remain relatively obscure. What working methods did copyists use to assemble multi-volume manuscripts? How did one distinguish one's own copies of authoritative texts from those of other copyists? What kind of training was necessary to become a successful copyist?

In the case of the Egyptian encyclopedist Shihāb al-Dīn al-Nuwayrī (d. 733/1333), we have an opportunity to explore such questions on the basis of several sources of evidence. First, al-Nuwayrī's copying prowess is discussed by his biographers, who mention how many pages he produced each day and how much money he commanded for his manuscripts. Second, several holograph volumes of his universal compendium of knowledge, *Nihāyat al-arab fī funūn al-adab* ("The Ultimate Ambition in the Arts of Erudition", henceforth, *Nihāya*), have been preserved in manuscript libraries in Leiden, Paris, Berlin, and Istanbul. These texts are valuable for what they reveal about the production of fair copies and about the range of calligraphic scripts at al-Nuwayrī's disposal, a subject he discusses in the *Nihāya* itself. Third, al-Nuwayrī was noted for making fine copies of al-Bukhārī's canonical *ḥadīth* collection, which he sold while working on the *Nihāya*. I have discovered what appears to be one of these copies, which tells us something about an author's approach to copying his own work as opposed to a work by a different author, in addition to the differences between copying *ḥadīth* manuscripts and other types of works.

---

1 See in particular Gacek, *Glossary*; id., *Vademecum*; Déroche, *Islamic Codicology*; Rosenthal, *The Technique*. A slightly modified version of this contribution appears in Muhanna, *World*, chapter 5.

 | DOI:10.1163/9789004413177_007

Finally, al-Nuwayrī addresses the education and practice of the copyist in his chapter on secretaryship (*kitāba*), which lies at the heart of the *Nihāya* and, in certain ways, is its *raison d'être*. I will treat each of these sources of evidence in this essay with the aim of exploring aspects of al-Nuwayrī's working method and shedding some light on the theory and practice of the all-important craft of copying.

1 A Master Copyist

Born in 677/1279 in Akhmīm, a town in Upper Egypt, Aḥmad b. ʿAbd al-Wahhāb al-Nuwayrī spent his childhood in Qūṣ and moved to Cairo at the age of nineteen, where he got a job in the Mamlūk imperial administration.[2] Over the next decade, al-Nuwayrī would rise in the ranks, becoming a close confidant of the sultan al-Nāṣir Muḥammad.[3] By the time he retired in the mid-710s/mid-1310s, he had held important positions in a number of scribal bureaus: managing the sultan's properties in Syria, overseeing the Nāṣiriyya madrasa and the Manṣūrī hospital in Cairo, and serving as head of the chancery and superintendent of army finances in Tripoli. As he tells his readers in the preface to the 31-volume *Nihāya*, al-Nuwayrī left a lucrative career in the empire's administrative elite in order to immerse himself in a world of books and humanistic learning. The eventual product of this decision was the *Nihāya* itself, a massive concatenation of poetic and prose excerpts from hundreds of authoritative sources, arranged thematically into five principal divisions: (1) the cosmos; (2) the human being; (3) the animal world; (4) the plant world; (5) a universal history.

In an age of big books, the *Nihāya*'s enormous size was unexceptional. However, the fact that al-Nuwayrī produced more than one copy of this 9,000-page book while making and selling several copies of al-Bukhārī's *Ṣaḥīḥ* was noteworthy even by Mamlūk standards. As his acquaintance Kamāl al-Dīn Jaʿfar b. Thaʿlab al-Udfuwī (d. 748/1347) recounts in his biographical dictionary:

> He wrote a great deal, copying al-Bukhārī several times, and compiled a large history in thirty volumes ... He held numerous scribal offices: he was Supervisor of Army Revenues (*nāẓir al-jaysh*) in Tripoli and he oversaw the bureau of al-Daqahliyya and al-Murtāḥiyya. He was intelligent,

2 On Qūṣ's Baḥrī period, when it witnessed its height as a provincial capital, military base, and center for scholars and poets, see Garcin, *Qūṣ* 181–410, esp. 287–357.

3 Al-Nāṣir Muḥammad reigned with two brief interruptions from 693/1293 to 741/1341. For a study of al-Nuwayrī 's administrative career, see Muhanna, *Encyclopaedism*, chapter 2.

> handsome, noble, and generous, and loving to his friends. He fasted for Ramaḍān during the year that he died, and he recited the Qur'ān assiduously. Each day after the afternoon prayers he would commence reading the Qur'ān until sunset. He was afflicted with pain in the ends of his fingers, which was the cause of his death. He died on the 21st of Ramaḍān in the year 733 [5 June 1333], and he was the author of some decent poetry and prose. He was my friend. May God have mercy on him.[4]

Al-Udfuwī's description of the *Nihāya* as "a large history in thirty volumes" provides an indication of its contemporary classification, as well as a sign that the work circulated *in toto* within a few years of al-Nuwayrī's death and was not broken up into its constituent parts. Ṣalāḥ al-Dīn Khalīl b. Aybak al-Ṣafadī (d. 764/1363) includes al-Nuwayrī in his *Aʿyān al-ʿaṣr wa-aʿwān al-naṣr*, a biographical dictionary comprised of al-Ṣafadī's contemporaries. The two men, however, do not appear to have met, as al-Ṣafadī bases his biography of al-Nuwayrī almost entirely on al-Udfuwī, with the exception of the following report:[5]

> He copied al-Bukhārī's *Ṣaḥīḥ* eight times. He would draft a copy, collate it, copy the audition notes (*al-ṭibāq*), bind it, and sell it for between 700 or 1,000 *dirhams*, and he sold his work of history once to Jamāl al-Kufāt for 2,000 *dirhams*. He would fill three manuscript quires (*karārīs*) in a day.[6]

The quires of the *Nihāya*'s holographs are quinions, which suggests that al-Nuwayrī could copy sixty pages in a single day. That he could get such a significant sum for a copy of al-Bukhārī's *Ṣaḥīḥ* (a widely available text) speaks to his talents as a copyist. On the other hand, it is interesting that he would part with a copy of his own 31-volume magnum opus for only twice the price of the single-volume *ḥadīth* collection. If this report is correct, then the comparatively less expensive cost of the *Nihāya* may be explained by al-Nuwayrī's status as a lesser-known author during his own lifetime.

---

4 See al-Udfuwī, *al-Ṭāliʿ al-saʿīd* 96–97. Note the incorrect name of al-Nuwayrī's grandfather (who was Muḥammad b. ʿAbd al-Dāʾim), as well as his incorrect birthplace (which was Akhmīm and not Qūṣ).

5 Al-Ṣafadī, *Aʿyān al-ʿaṣr* i, 83. Ibn Ḥajar al-ʿAsqalānī (d. 852/1449) draws his biography of al-Nuwayrī from al-Ṣafadī's account; see Ibn Ḥajar, *al-Durar al-kāmina* i, 209.

6 Ibn al-Wardī (d. 749/1349) may be the source of the report about al-Nuwayrī's ability to copy three quires; see Ibn al-Wardī, *Tārīkh* ii, 303.

Al-Ṣafadī writes in his larger biographical dictionary, *al-Wāfī bi-l-wafayāt*, that he had seen a copy of the *Nihāya*,[7] as did the Syrian jurist Ibn Ḥabīb al-Ḥalabī (d. 779/1377) who described the work as "a book on *adab* and history in thirty volumes ... [entitled] *Muntahā l-arab fī ʿilm al-adab*". Ibn Ḥabīb states that he examined, copied, and benefited from it.[8] Ibn Kathīr (d. 774/1373) called al-Nuwayrī a "master copyist" (*nāsikh muṭīq*) and a rarity of his age, but mistakenly claimed that he had composed two thirty-volume collections: one on *adab* and another on history.[9] It is possible that Ibn Kathīr was confused by an earlier report from the Coptic historian Mufaḍḍal b. Abī l-Faḍāʾil (fl. 759/1358), who writes that al-Nuwayrī sold two copies of the *Nihāya* for 1,200 dirhams each, which, as we will see, tallies with the manuscript evidence.[10] The work's correct title first appears in al-Maqrīzī's (d. 845/1442) *Kitāb al-Tārīkh al-kabīr al-muqaffā*, a biographical dictionary about prominent Egyptians.[11] Al-Maqrīzī's account rehearses some of the previous material from al-Udfuwī and al-Ṣafadī, but also provides some important additions, notably the description of al-Nuwayrī's history as "famous" (*mashhūr*).

The biographical literature, then, provides several interesting glimpses of al-Nuwayrī's working method. It suggests that he produced two copies of the *Nihāya* over the course of about twenty years, that he could copy about three quires or sixty pages a day, and that he also made several expensive copies of al-Bukhārī's *ḥadīth* collection while working on his own book. It is little wonder that he was known as a master copyist or that he should have suffered from pain in the ends of his fingers. What these descriptions elide, however, is the great amount of work that went into producing the fair copies that were sold. Most of the extant holograph manuscripts, as we will see, are very fine specimens. There is hardly a slip of the pen across their hundreds of pages, which testifies to al-Nuwayrī's great skill as a master calligrapher but also to the fact that these fair copies would have been preceded by a draft copy of the text, abstracted from the hundreds of books that al-Nuwayrī consulted while composing the *Nihāya*. In other words, the production of the two 30-volume copies that his biographers mention represented the culmination of a much larger process of copying, collating, and editing.

7 Al-Ṣafadī, *al-Wāfī* vii, 165.
8 Ibn Ḥabīb, *Tadhkirat al-nabīh* ii, 246.
9 Ibn Kathīr, *al-Bidāya* xiv, 164.
10 Ibn Abī l-Faḍāʾil, *al-Nahj al-sadīd* 55.
11 Al-Maqrīzī, *al-Muqaffā* 521–2. See also id., *al-Sulūk* ii, 363, which has a brief death notice for al-Nuwayrī ("the author of the work of history").

2 The Art of Copying

At the end of Book II of the *Nihāya*, al-Nuwayrī devotes a lengthy chapter to secretaryship and its different branches and duties. These included chancery writing (*kitābat al-inshāʾ*), bureaucratic and financial secretaryship (*kitābat al-dīwān wa-qalam al-taṣarruf*), legal secretaryship (*kitābat al-ḥukm wa-l-shurūṭ*), the copying of manuscripts (*kitābat al-naskh*), and the teaching of reading and writing (*kitābat al-taʿlīm*).[12] While the whole chapter provides an important window on scribal practice in the early fourteenth century, it is the fourth subchapter on the copying of manuscripts that is of special relevance here, particularly the following passage on copying scholarly texts (*naskh al-ʿulūm*).[13]

> As for he who copies [works of] the sciences, such as jurisprudence, philology, the principles of jurisprudence and other things, it is most fitting and suitable for him not to begin writing anything until he has surveyed the subject, reading and familiarizing himself with it. This is so that he may be free from errors, copying mistakes, and substitutions, and so that he may know where to move from one chapter to another, from a question to an answer, from one section to another, from a fundamental principle to a derivative principle or vice versa, from an exception to an illustration or a digression that is unrelated to an important principle, or to the speech of a speaker, or the question of a questioner, or the objection of an objector, or the critique of a critic.
>
> The copyist must know what he is saying and where he is heading, separating each quote with a dividing mark that indicates its completion, and highlighting the statement of someone other than himself with a mark indicating its significance. If he does not do this, he will be like a wood-gatherer at night, not knowing when the morning will suddenly dawn on

12 This chapter (§ 2.5.14) may be found at al-Nuwayrī, *Nihāyat al-arab* vii, 1-ix, 221. The subchapters' page ranges are as follows: *kitābat al-inshāʾ* (vii, 1-viii, 191); *kitābat al-dīwān wa-qalam al-taṣarruf* (viii, 191–305); *kitābat al-ḥukm wa-l-shurūṭ* (ix, 1–160); *kitābat al-naskh* (ix, 160–218); *kitābat al-taʿlīm* (ix, 218–21). The end of the third subchapter is missing from the manuscript, as is the beginning of the fourth subchapter.

13 Part of this sub-chapter has unfortunately been lost. It begins *in media res* with an excerpt from *Kitāb al-Muʾtalif wa-l-mukhtalif* by ʿAbd al-Ghanī b. Saʿīd al-Azdī (d. 410/1019), followed by a second excerpt of the same author's *Mushtabah al-nisba*, two works that treat the similarities in the names of different *ḥadīth* transmitters. This suggests that al-Nuwayrī was mainly concerned here with the copying of *ḥadīth* manuscripts, given the greater space he devotes to this subject in comparison with the material on *naskh al-ʿulūm*.

him, or the sailor in a storm who does not know the difference between morning or evening.

As for copying historical works, one must know the names of the kings, their sobriquets, personal names, and patronymics, especially the kings of the Persians, Turks, Khwārizmīs, and Tatars, for most of their names are foreign and cannot be ascertained except through oral transmission. The copyist, when he writes these names, must specify them by using diacritics, markings, and notes that indicate [their correct pronunciation]. The same is true for names of cities, towns, villages, fortresses, rural areas, districts, provinces, and climes. He must indicate such instances in which the spelling [of two place names] is the same but the pronunciation is different, or instances where the spelling and pronunciation are the same but the referent is different, as in the case of Marw and Marw. The first one is Marw al-Rūdh and the other is Marw al-Shāhijān. Or, for example, al-Qāhira and al-Qāhira. The first is al-Qāhira al-Muʿizziyya [Cairo], and the second is the fortress al-Qāhira which was built in Zawzan by Mu'ayyid al-Mulk, the ruler of Kirmān. If the copyist refers to al-Qāhira without distinguishing it by its place and full title, the mind of the listener will rush to al-Qāhira al-Muʿizziyya because of its unsurpassed fame.

And as for the names of men, such as ʿUbayd Allāh b. Ziyād and ʿUbayd Allāh b. Ziyād, the first of them is ʿUbayd Allāh b. Ziyād b. Abīhi, [whose father] Ziyād was the son of Sumayya, and whom Muʿāwiya b. Abī Sufyān appointed after his father ... This ʿUbayd Allāh was governor of Iraq after his father until the days of Marwān b. al-Ḥakam, while the second was ʿUbayd Allāh b. Ziyād b. Ẓabyān. Their story is similar to one of those circular arguments in logic, as ʿUbayd Allāh b. Ziyād b. Abīhi was killed by al-Mukhtār b. Abī ʿUbayd al-Thaqafī, who was killed by Muṣʿab b. al-Zubayr, who was killed by ʿUbayd Allāh b. Ziyād b. Ẓabyān. If each of these two individuals is not distinguished by his grandfather and his lineage, the matter would remain confusing for the listener, insofar as he does not have a knowledge of the facts or a grasp of the historical reports. The copyist is responsible for clarifying such matters, and the same is true for the names of the Battle Days of the Arabs ... and other things as well. He must point out all of this, using the appropriate indications.

As for he who copies poetry, he cannot do this without the knowledge of its meters, for that will help him to copy it faithfully according to the original, as it was first copied. He must be knowledgeable about the Arabic language and about prosody so that he can determine the meter of a verse when its scansion is problematic. Thereby he may learn whether the poem is in its original form and order, or whether it contains a change in

> meter due to omissions or additions. After correcting it, he should recognize the correction and mark it in its place, for its alteration changes the meaning and corrupts it, diverting it from the intended meaning.
>
> If the copyist masters these skills, correctly applies these principles, clarifies these names, traces these lineages, [he will have achieved][14] the desired objective of his learning and secretaryship. At that point, let him deploy his pen widely in copying scholarly texts, setting down prose and poetry.[15]

As a branch of secretaryship, al-Nuwayrī considered the copying of scholarly manuscripts (*naskh al-ʿulūm*) to be a specialized craft that required an understanding of a discipline's principles, conventions, and authorities before one could embark upon copying its texts. This raises the question of what, precisely, *naskh* meant. Why should a scribe be expected to understand the subject matter of a work, rather than copying it as he found it? Even allowing for a degree of idealization in depictions of scribal practice, al-Nuwayrī's discussion suggests that *naskh* involved more than mere replication of exemplar manuscripts.[16] Some level of editing and mark-up was not only considered acceptable, but was expected from a good scribe.

This editing might have taken two forms. At a basic level, a master copyist was assumed to be within his rights when correcting mistakes or making small changes to material copied from an exemplar. This could be as simple as replacing a word in a poem based on a flaw in its meter, clarifying the orthography of a foreign name, or glossing an ambiguous toponym. The copyist, al-Nuwayrī says, "is responsible for clarifying such matters" so that the reader would not be led astray, and the author's intention would be preserved from the corruption of time and human error.

However, the second dimension of *naskh* is more thoroughgoing than mere correction or glossing. As al-Nuwayrī states in the beginning of the passage, the scribe must know "where to move from one chapter to another, from a question to an answer, from one section to another," and so forth. Here, he may simply be referring to the conventions of *mise-en-page* observed by different disciplines, such as drawing attention to the structural divisions in a manuscript by using different calligraphic styles, colors, text sizes, symbols, and blank space. However, al-Nuwayrī's statement that the "copyist must know what he is saying and where he is heading" indicates that there was more at stake in this practice

14 There is a lacuna in the manuscript here; this is my suggested replacement.

15 Al-Nuwayrī, *Nihāyat al-arab* ix, 214–8.

16 On the idealization of the *kātib*, see Carter, The Kātib; van Berkel, al-Qalqashandī.

than neatening up the page layout and highlighting elements already present in the original manuscript. Rather, the activity of the copyist likely also involved the introduction of structural elements into works that previously did not contain them, differentiating questions from answers, critiques from illustrations, chapters from sub-chapters, and so on and so forth.

One wonders, in fact, whether al-Nuwayrī considered the broader activity of compilation itself—which depends upon the selective quotation, embellishment, and rearrangement of older materials into new forms—to be a species of *naskh*. Translating the term *nāsikh* as "copyist" may be problematic in this regard, for what differentiates the person described in the passage above from what we would call an "editor," "anthologist," or "compiler" today? In fact, these are distinctions that are frequently difficult to draw in the world of Mamlūk letters. While al-Nuwayrī clearly had a sense of the importance of maintaining the integrity of transmitted material, he saw little contradiction between this *desideratum* and a parallel interest in serving his contemporary audience by making manuscripts more reader-friendly.[17]

3 The *Nihāya*'s Holographs

Scholars of medieval texts usually regard the existence of a single preserved holograph manuscript of a given work as a stroke of good fortune. In the case of al-Nuwayrī's *Nihāya*, we are confronted with an embarrassment of riches. A survey of several manuscript libraries yields a list of thirty volumes of the *Nihāya* that have been attributed to al-Nuwayrī himself: Leiden University Library and the Bibliothèque nationale de France hold thirteen of these volumes; sixteen are held by various Istanbul libraries; and there is a single volume at the Staatsbibliothek in Berlin. Most of the Istanbul holographs were microfilmed by Aḥmad Zakī Pāshā around the turn of the twentieth century and brought to Egypt to be used as the basis for Dār al-Kutub al-Miṣriyya's edition of the *Nihāya*, along with many other volumes copied in later centuries.

I have examined the Leiden and Paris manuscripts, and they contain among them what I believe to be a previously unidentified holograph (Leiden Or. 2d),

17 A final dimension of the term *naskh* that may be useful in this discussion is the concept of *naskh* as transcription rather than copying. If one bears in mind that *naskh al-ʿulūm* often took place while sitting with a teacher and transcribing a book as it was read aloud (rather than copying a manuscript in a library or private study), one may appreciate more fully the relative fluidity of textual composition as the product of this mode of knowledge transmission.

as well as two manuscripts that may have been erroneously attributed to al-Nuwayrī (Leiden Or. 19b and BnF Arabe 1579, which I discuss below). As I have not had the opportunity to consult the remaining manuscripts, I have relied upon the work of other scholars, editors, and cataloguers for their descriptions and attributions of these volumes to al-Nuwayrī, recognizing that a comprehensive study of all the surviving manuscripts would be necessary to confirm the authenticity of the presumed holographs. In order to facilitate such a study, I have assembled a list of the relevant manuscripts in Table 6.1.

TABLE 6.1 Manuscripts of the *Nihāyat al-arab* attributed to al-Nuwayrī[18]

Vol.[19]	Shelfmark	Date	Evidence for attribution
1	DKM 551	20 Dhū l-Qaʿda 721/11 December 1321	Signed colophon[20]
4	DKM 551	Undated	Signed colophon[21]
5	DKM 551	22 Rabīʿ I 722/10 April 1322	Signed colophon[22]

18 The manuscripts with the shelfmark DKM 551 are microfilms held at Dār al-Kutub al-Miṣriyya. According to a note by the editor of the seventeenth manuscript volume of the *Nihāyat al-arab*, the original manuscripts are held at the Ayasofya library in Istanbul, which contains a complete set of 31 holographs (see Nuwayrī, *Nihāyat al-arab* xix, 5–6). However, according to *Ayasofya Kütüphanesi* 210, there are only seventeen manuscripts of the *Nihāyat al-arab* held in the collection (shelfmarks 3511–27; note the error in *GAL* ii, 140, who gives 3511–37), some of which are duplicate volumes. This casts some doubt on the *Nihāyat al-arab* editors' claims that all of the manuscripts microfilmed under shelfmark DKM 551 were holographs. Furthermore, the information regarding the identification of holographs is often incomplete: sometimes the text of a signed colophon is supplied in the edition, while at other times an editor simply states that the edition was based upon a holograph without explaining how they authenticated it. It may be that some of the manuscripts listed in the table are not in fact holographs, just as it is possible that there are some holograph manuscripts extant that are not identified above.

19 Note that this column refers to the manuscript volume, which does not always correspond to the edition volume. The volume numbers of manuscript and edition are in sync from volumes 1–6. Between volumes 7–13, they begin to deviate, with the following correspondence between manuscript and edition: 7 = 7–8:101; 8 = 8:101–9:223; 9 = 9:224–10; 10 = 11–12; 11 = 13–14:81; 12 = 14:82–15:80; 13 = 15:81-end of 15. From manuscript vol. 14 to vol. 31, the correspondence is regular, with the edition numbering always two ahead of the manuscript. Thus, the 31-volume manuscript corresponds to a 33-volume edition.

20 Al-Nuwayrī, *Nihāyat al-arab* i, 416.

21 Ibid. iv, 423.

22 Ibid. v, 339. Note the error in Jamāl al-Dīn, *al-Nuwayrī* 113, who gives the month as Jumādā I rather than Rabīʿ I.

TABLE 6.1 Manuscripts of the *Nihāyat al-arab* attributed to al-Nuwayrī (*cont.*)

Vol.	Shelfmark	Date	Evidence for attribution
10	DKM 551	Jumādā I 722/May–June 1322	Signed colophon[23]
10	Berlin We. 86	Undated	Signed colophon[24]
11	DKM 551	Undated	Handwriting; no colophon (fragment)[25]
12	DKM 551	Undated	Signed colophon[26]
13	DKM 551	Undated	Signed colophon[27]
13	BnF Arabe 1573	Undated	Handwriting; no colophon[28]
14	Leiden Or. 2d[29]	Undated	Handwriting; colophon likely added later[30]
15	DKM 551	7 Ramaḍān 722/19 September 1322	Signed colophon[31]

23 Al-Nuwayrī, *Nihāyat al-arab* ii, III–IV. Note that the editor states in the preface that this printed volume's edition was based on three manuscripts, one of which was attributed to the author and dated Jumādā I 922 (*sic*). I am assuming that this is a typographical error, and that the holograph is dated 722 AH. Curiously, however, the editor of vol. 12 of the printed edition (which should correspond to the same manuscript volume as vol. 11) states that this volume's edition was based on two manuscripts rather than three, one of which was an undated holograph (see al-Nuwayrī, *Nihāyat al-arab* xii, III–IV). Direct consultation of the manuscripts or microfilms would be necessary to sort out this puzzle.

24 Ahlwardt, *Die Handschriften* v, 482–3 (no. 6202).

25 The editor of print vol. 13 states in the preface that his edition was based on three manuscripts: two complete volumes copied in 966/1558–9 and a fragment of a third manuscript attributed to al-Nuwayrī based on its script. See al-Nuwayrī, *Nihāyat al-arab* xiii, III–IV.

26 Ibid. xv, 80, fn. 2.

27 Ibid. xv, 434–5.

28 This manuscript is missing about eight folios and has forty folios out of order, as remarked by de Slane, *Catalogue* 296–7, who says that the manuscript "est considéré comme autographe," presumably on the basis of its script; cf. Sauvan & Balty-Guesdon, *Catalogue* 122, who says it is "probablement autographe". I am not fully convinced of this identification, and would propose that the hand resembles that of Leiden Or. 2c, which has not been identified as a holograph.

29 Some of the Leiden manuscripts have two volumes bound together under a single shelfmark. In the case of Or. 2d and Or. 2f, the two volumes were copied by different individuals; in the case of Or. 2i and Or. 2l, the copyist is the same.

30 On the basis of a colophon (fol. 254^{b}) dated 972 AH and signed by the copyist ʿAbd al-Ḥāfiẓ al-Ḥalabī this manuscript was not considered a holograph; see De Goeje & Houtsma, *Catalogus* 14; Voorhoeve, *Handlist* 252; Witkam, *Inventory* 13. However, the colophon is in a very different hand from the main text, which is more or less identical to the hand of several manuscripts attributed to al-Nuwayrī (in particular, Or. 2f, which has a signed colophon).

31 Al-Nuwayrī, *Nihāyat al-arab* xvii, 379; cf. Jamāl al-Dīn, *al-Nuwayrī* 113, who mistakenly identifies this as volume 17, which corresponds to the printed edition's numbering rather than the manuscript volume numbering.

TABLE 6.1 Manuscripts of the *Nihāyat al-arab* attributed to al-Nuwayrī (*cont.*)

Vol.	Shelfmark	Date	Evidence for attribution
16	DKM 551	27 Ramaḍān 722/9 October 1322	Signed colophon[32]
16	Leiden Or. 2f	Dhū l-Qaʿda 716/January–February 1317	Signed colophon and handwriting[33]
17	DKM 551	Undated	n/a[34]
19	DKM 554	9 Jumādā II 718/8 August 1318	Signed and dated colophon[35]
21	TSMK EH 1369	25 Ṣafar 724/22 February 1324	Signed and dated colophon[36]
21	BnF Arabe 1574	Undated	Handwriting[37]
22	BnF Arabe 1575	719/1319–20	Signed colophon and handwriting[38]
22	TSMK n/a	Undated	Handwriting[39]
23	BnF Arabe 1576	Undated	Handwriting[40]
24	Leiden Or. 2i	Undated	Signed colophon and handwriting[41]

32 Al-Nuwayrī, *Nihāyat al-arab* xviii, 407. Jamāl al-Dīn, *al-Nuwayrī* 113, mistakenly identifies this as volume 18; see previous note.

33 The colophon of this manuscript is undated. However, while discussing an important relic thought to belong to the Prophet Muḥammad, al-Nuwayrī states that it remained in the possession of its owners "until the present time, which is the last tenth of Dhū l-Qaʿda, in the year 716" (see Leiden Or. 2f, fol. 140ᵇ).

34 Al-Nuwayrī, *Nihāyat al-arab* xix, 5–6.

35 Ibid. xxi, 540, fn. 1. Note that the editor gives the shelfmark of this volume as DKM 554 rather than 551, which is puzzling given what the editor of manuscript volume 17 (printed volume 19, pp. 5–6) says about the Ayasofya microfilms being held together under shelfmark 551. See also Jamāl al-Dīn, *al-Nuwayrī* 113, who does not make the same numbering mistake with this volume that she does with vols. 15 and 16 (see above).

36 Al-Nuwayrī, *Nihāyat al-arab* xxiii, 5–7.

37 De Slane, *Catalogue* 297; Sauvan & Balty-Guesdon, *Catalogue*, 123–4.

38 The colophon of this manuscript is undated. However, while discussing the Merinid sultan ʿUthmān b. Yaʿqūb on fol. 68ᵃ, al-Nuwayrī states that he "is the current king at our present time, in the year 719." See al-Nuwayrī, *Nihāyat al-arab* xxiv, 352.

39 Ibid. xxiv, 1–3. The edition of this volume was based on three manuscripts, one of which is held in the TSMK (with a microfilm copy at the library of the Institute of Arabic Manuscripts in Cairo). The editor does not provide the shelfmark of the TSMK manuscript; he identifies it as a holograph based upon a comparison of the script with a copy of Abū Hilāl al-ʿAskarī's *Dīwān al-maʿānī* that is held at al-Maktaba al-Ẓāhiriyya in Damascus and is apparently in al-Nuwayrī's hand. I have not had the chance to examine either manuscript.

40 De Slane, *Catalogue* 297; Sauvan & Balty-Guesdon, *Catalogue*, 123–4.

41 De Goeje & Houtsma, *Catalogus* 16; Voorhoeve, *Handlist* 253; Witkam, *Inventory* 14. The colophon on fol. 100ᵃ is undated. Interestingly, there is a lacuna in the colophon where the number of the next volume would be, indicating that al-Nuwayrī was still working out the volume numbering of the entire work at this stage.

TABLE 6.1 Manuscripts of the *Nihāyat al-arab* attributed to al-Nuwayrī (*cont.*)

Vol.	Shelfmark	Date	Evidence for attribution
25	Leiden Or. 2i	714/1314–5	Signed colophon and handwriting[42]
26	Leiden Or. 2l	Undated	Handwriting; no colophon[43]
27	Leiden Or. 2l	Undated	Handwriting; incomplete colophon[44]
27	TSMK?	Undated	n/a[45]
28	DKM 551	29 Dhū l-Ḥijja 725/6 December 1325	Signed colophon[46]
28	BnF Arabe 1578	Undated	Handwriting; no colophon[47]
29	BnF Arabe 1578	after Jumādā II 726/May 1326	Handwriting; colophon by later copyist[48]

42 De Goeje & Houtsma, *Catalogus* 16; Voorhoeve, *Handlist* 253; Witkam, *Inventory* 14. The colophon on fol. 205^b is undated, however there are two places in the manuscript where al-Nuwayrī makes reference to the year in which he is writing (see fol. 129^b and 142^a, corresponding to al-Nuwayrī, *Nihāyat al-arab* xxvii, 114, 162). As with the previous volume (which is bound together with this one under the same shelfmark), there is a lacuna in the colophon where the number of the next volume would be, which indicates that al-Nuwayrī had not yet determined the final numbering of the *Nihāyat al-arab* at this stage. The colophon reads: *kamula l-juzʾ ʿalā yad muʾallifihi faqīr raḥmat rabbihi / yatlūhu in shāʾa llāh taʿālā fī awwal al-juzʾ* [*lacuna*] *al-bāb al-thānī ʿashar* [...].

43 De Goeje & Houtsma, *Catalogus* 16; Voorhoeve, *Handlist* 253; Witkam, *Inventory* 14.

44 De Goeje & Houtsma, *Catalogus* 16; Voorhoeve, *Handlist* 253; Witkam, *Inventory* 14. The colophon (p. 427) is incomplete, stating only: *najiza l-sifr* [lacuna] *min Nihāyat al-arab fī funūn al-adab*. As with the two manuscripts bound in Leiden Or. 2i, it appears that al-Nuwayrī had not yet settled on the volume numbering at this stage.

45 Al-Nuwayrī, *Nihāyat al-arab* xxix, 5–6. The edition of this volume was based on a single non-holograph manuscript until the editor found a microfilm of a presumed holograph in the library of the Institute of Arabic Manuscripts. Given that the previous two Institute of Arabic Manuscripts microfilms were taken from the Treasury Collection at TSMK, I would speculate that this may have come from that collection as well.

46 Ibid. xxx, 401.

47 De Slane, *Catalogue* 298 mistakes this manuscript to be the twenty-fifth volume, while Sauvan & Balty-Guesdon, *Catalogue* 125–6 consider it to be the twenty-ninth volume. In fact, BnF Arabe 1578 contains both volumes 28 and 29. The end of volume 28 falls at fol. 104^b, where there is no colophon.

48 The final 18 fols. of this manuscript (including a colophon) were added by a later copyist in 814/1412, but the earlier fols. are in al-Nuwayrī's hand. With regard to dating the holograph portion, al-Nuwayrī makes a reference to the appointment of Qaraṭāy al-Ṣāliḥī as governor of Tripoli and says that he remained in this position until "he was removed from it in Jumādā II, 726" (see fol. 117^b). In the printed edition, however, (see al-Nuwayrī, *Nihāyat al-arab* xxxi, 59), al-Nuwayrī says that Qaraṭāy was the governor "up until the time that we wrote this volume, and that was at the end of Rajab, 725." In other words, we can be certain that al-Nuwayrī made at least two copies of this volume: one in Rajab 725 (which reflects the text of the printed edition), and this copy, made one year later and updated to reflect the latest developments in the political arena.

TABLE 6.1 Manuscripts of the *Nihāyat al-arab* attributed to al-Nuwayrī (*cont.*)

Vol.	Shelfmark	Date	Evidence for attribution
29	BnF Arabe 1579	18 Ṣafar 726/24 January 1326	Signed colophon[49]
31	Leiden Or. 19b	After 730/1330	Comment on flyleaves in a different hand[50]

There are different types of evidence for the attribution of a manuscript to a copyist. The most direct evidence (which is not necessarily decisive) is the identification of the copyist in the manuscript itself. Other types of evidence include the copyist's handwriting, the way in which he is introduced in the work, the presence or absence of honorifics and certain supplications accompanying his signature, the types of paper and styles of script common to the region in which the copyist lived, etc.[51] In al-Nuwayrī's case, the question of attribution is further complicated because of his noted skill as a copyist and his mastery of different kinds of scripts.[52]

If we set aside for the time being the problem of authenticating holographs, what can we learn from such a large collection of manuscripts produced by a single copyist? For the purposes of studying working methods, one would ideally like to have draft copies and fair copies to compare. All of the *Nihāya* holographs that I have consulted are fair copies, with scarcely a word out of place. However, even such spotless exemplars have things to tell us about a copyist's practice and I will briefly address two issues of relevance to the case of al-Nuwayrī: composition schedule and the problem of different scripts.

49 De Slane, *Catalogue* 298; Sauvan & Balty-Guesdon, *Catalogue* 126–7. This manuscript has been attributed to al-Nuwayrī on the basis of a signed colophon, and yet the script, page layout, rubrication, and paper of this volume are very different from all the other manuscripts attributed to him, with the exception of Leiden Or. 19b. See below for a discussion of both manuscripts.

50 De Goeje & Houtsma, *Catalogus* 17; Voorhoeve, *Handlist* 253; Witkam, *Inventory* 16. The dating of this manuscript is based on the fact that it chronicles the years 721/1321 to 730/1330. It is in a very different hand from the other presumed holographs with the exception of BnF Arabe 1579. The attribution to al-Nuwayrī is not in a colophon but rather in a comment written on the flyleaves (*tārīkh Nuwayrī* [*sic*] *bi-khaṭṭ al-muṣannif*) in a different hand. See below for a discussion of both Leiden Or. 19b and BnF Arabe 1579.

51 See Chapter 3 in this volume.

52 Gacek, *Al-Nuwayrī's classification*.

3.1 *Composition Schedule*

As we see in fig. 6.1, there are two sources of evidence to consider with regard to the question of when al-Nuwayrī composed the *Nihāya*. First, there are nine manuscripts that have signed and dated colophons.[53] Second, there are five manuscripts that can be dated based on references to specific events or individuals in the text.[54] Putting the two sets of dates together, we can construct the following timeline:

Amīna Jamāl al-Dīn has suggested that al-Nuwayrī made two copies of the *Nihāya*: one begun before 718/1318, and another started in 721/1321.[55] She proposed that a single manuscript from the first set survives (DKM 554, vol. 19), while four other dated holographs belong to the purported second set and were copied within a ten-month span between 721/1321 and 722/1322 (DKM 551, vols. 1, 4, 15, and 16).[56] Table 6.2 contains several additional manuscripts that Jamāl al-Dīn was unable to consult, and they seem to substantiate her hypothesis. There is, however, the question of how to explain the earliest manuscript in the group: Leiden Or. 2i, vol. 25. This volume covers the history of the Saljūq, Khwārizmid, and Chingisid states, and there are two places in the text where al-Nuwayrī identifies 714/1314 as the year in which he is writing.[57] Could it be that this manuscript belongs to a third, even earlier set of the *Nihāya*? Or perhaps al-Nuwayrī wrote this volume before he knew where it might fit within an anticipated larger collection.

As we have already seen, the colophons of both volumes of Leiden Or. 2i have blank spaces where the volume numbers would have been written, as does vol. 27 of Leiden Or. 2l.[58] This suggests to me that these three volumes were in fact written at an early stage in the *Nihāya*'s compilation, before al-Nuwayrī knew how many volumes he would devote to the sections on the cosmos, the human being, the animal world and the plant world. We have another example of this practice in the table of contents of the *Nihāya*, where al-Nuwayrī describes chapter 5.5.12, which covers the political history of Egypt "up until our composition of this work in the year seven hundred and [lacuna]" (*ilā*

53 These are DKM 551, vols. 1, 5, 10, 15, 16, 28; DKM 554, vol. 19; TSMK EH 1369; BnF Arabe 1579.

54 These are Leiden Or. 2f, vol. 16; BnF Arabe 1575; Leiden Or. 2i, vol. 25; BnF Arabe 1578, vol. 29; and Leiden Or. 19b. See the footnoted annotation for each manuscript for an account of how I arrived at the copy date.

55 Jamāl al-Dīn, *al-Nuwayrī* 111–4.

56 Note that Jamāl al-Dīn mistook the 7 Ramaḍān and 27 Ramaḍān manuscripts as being volumes 17 and 18, respectively, rather than 15 and 16. See Jamāl al-Dīn, *al-Nuwayrī* 113.

57 See note 42.

58 See notes 41, 42, and 44.

TABLE 6.2 A Timeline of al-Nuwayrī's Compilation of the *Nihāyat al-arab*

Date	Manuscript volume	Shelfmark
714/1314	Volume 25	Leiden Or. 2i
Dhū l-Qaʿda 716/January–February 1317	Volume 15	Leiden Or. 2f
9 Jumādā II 718/8 August 1318	Volume 19	DKM 554
719/1319–20	Volume 22	BnF Arabe 1575
20 Dhū l-Qaʿda 721/11 December 1321	Volume 1	DKM 551
22 Rabīʿ I 722/10 April 1322	Volume 5	DKM 551
Jumādā I 722/May–June 1322	Volume 10	DKM 551
7 Ramaḍān 722/19 September 1322	Volume 15	DKM 551
27 Ramaḍān 722/9 October 1322	Volume 16	DKM 551
25 Ṣafar 724/22 February 1324	Volume 21	TSMK EH 1369
29 Dhū l-Ḥijja 725/6 December 1325	Volume 28	DKM 551
18 Ṣafar 726/24 January 1326	Volume 29	BnF Arabe 1579
After Jumādā II 726/May 1326	Volume 29	BnF Arabe 1578
After 730/1330	Volume 31	Leiden Or. 19b

ḥīn waḍʿinā li-hādhā l-taʾlīf fī sanat [lacuna] *wa-sabʿimiʾa*).[59] Given that the Dār al-Kutub al-Miṣriyya edition of this first volume was based on the 721/1321 holograph, this lacuna in the text is interesting. It may suggest that al-Nuwayrī planned to go back and fill in the composition date after he finished the historical section, so as to provide an accurate *terminus ante quem* for chapter 5.5.12 in the table of contents. As it happened, al-Nuwayrī did not go back and pencil in the date, and perhaps neglected to do so in the first version of the work as well, since two later copies of the manuscript preserve the lacuna in the same spot.[60]

It is difficult, then, to establish exactly when al-Nuwayrī began compiling the *Nihāya* or the order in which he produced the volumes. The holographs suggest that he may have begun with certain volumes that he later decided to insert toward the end of the work, as his vision for it grew more ambitious. The *Nihāya*'s textual architecture and extensive cross-referencing demand that al-Nuwayrī would have had to establish the overall plan for the work before he

59 Al-Nuwayrī, *Nihāyat al-arab* i, 25.

60 See BnF Arabe 5050, fol. 10^b; Leiden Or. 273, fol. 3^b; Muhanna, *Encyclopaedism* 60.

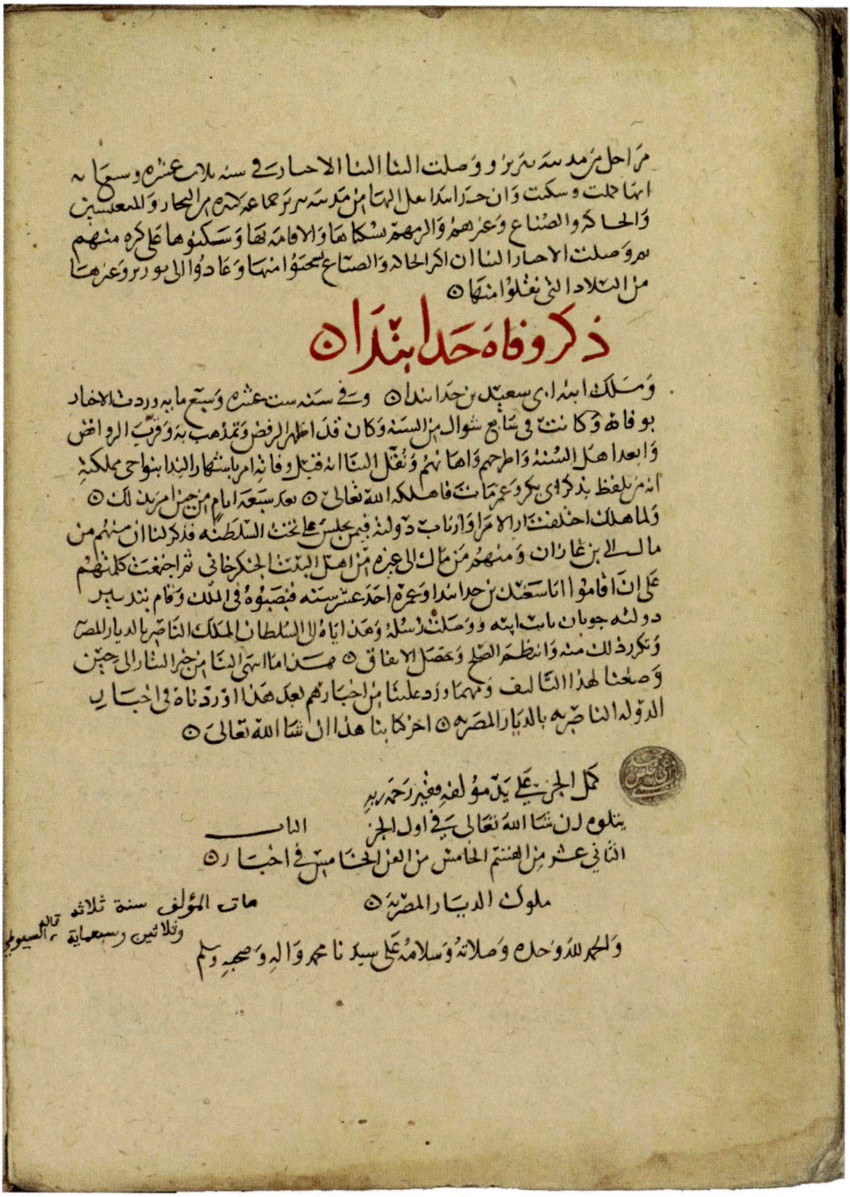

FIGURE 6.1 Volume 25 of al-Nuwayrī's *Nihāyat al-arab fī funūn al-adab*. Note that the colophon identifies this manuscript as a holograph, and also shows a lacuna where the number of the next volume would be, suggesting that al-Nuwayrī had not yet established the final ordering of volumes in this copy of the work. (MS Or. 2i)
LEIDEN UNIVERSITY LIBRARY

produced his first fair copy. However, he may not have known exactly how many volumes each *fann*, *qism*, and *bāb* would encompass, even if their general order and contents were clear to him from the start.[61]

3.2 *Different Scripts*

It is often very difficult to identify a manuscript as a holograph purely on the basis of its script. Unless a copyist has a distinctive hand, one frequently finds oneself hazarding impressionistic guesses as to whether an unsigned manuscript might be a holograph. Most of the manuscripts of the *Nihāya* that I have consulted have very similar scripts, rubrication patterns, page layouts, colophons, and chapter titles, and running headers. Two volumes, however, look nothing like the others and strongly resemble each other: BnF Arabe 1579 (vol. 29) and Leiden Or. 19b (vol. 31). The former has a signed colophon identifying the copyist as al-Nuwayrī and the copy date as 18 Ṣafar 726/24 January 1326. The latter is unsigned and was copied between 730–3/1329–33; it seems to have been attributed to al-Nuwayrī on the basis of a comment made in a different hand on the flyleaves of the manuscript.

As al-Nuwayrī was a master of many scripts, one might propose that the difference between Leiden Or. 19b/BnF Arabe 1579 and the other Leiden and Paris holographs was the result of a conscious decision to use a different script in his manuscript copies toward the end of his life. Al-Udfuwī remarked in his biography that al-Nuwayrī "was afflicted with pain at the end of his fingers, which was the cause of his death." Might these manuscripts reflect a debilitating condition that prevented him from producing the very fine specimens he copied a decade earlier? I would think not, given that we have a second copy of volume 29 (BnF Arabe 1578) produced at least a few months after BnF Arabe 1579, which is in the same hand as the other Leiden and Paris holographs. Alternatively, one might speculate that the manuscripts were produced by a different copyist and passed off as holographs, or perhaps were copied by an amanuensis.[62] Further analysis of these manuscripts and comparison with other copies of the *Nihāya* would be necessary to solve this puzzle.

61 Muhanna, *Encyclopaedism* chap. 3.

62 A final possibility, suggested to me by Adam Gacek, is that Leiden Or. 19b and BnF Arabe 1579 are the true holographs while the rest of the manuscripts held at Leiden and Paris are forgeries.

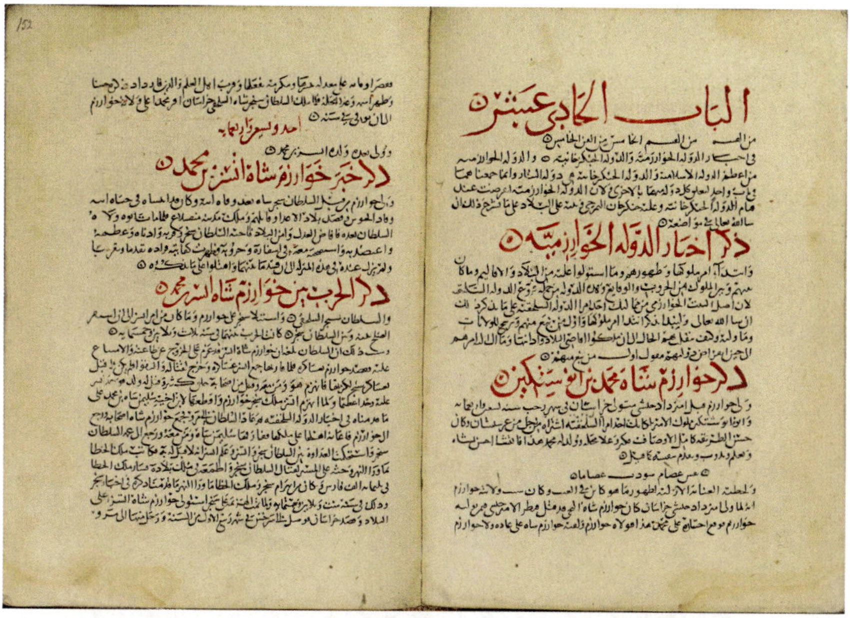

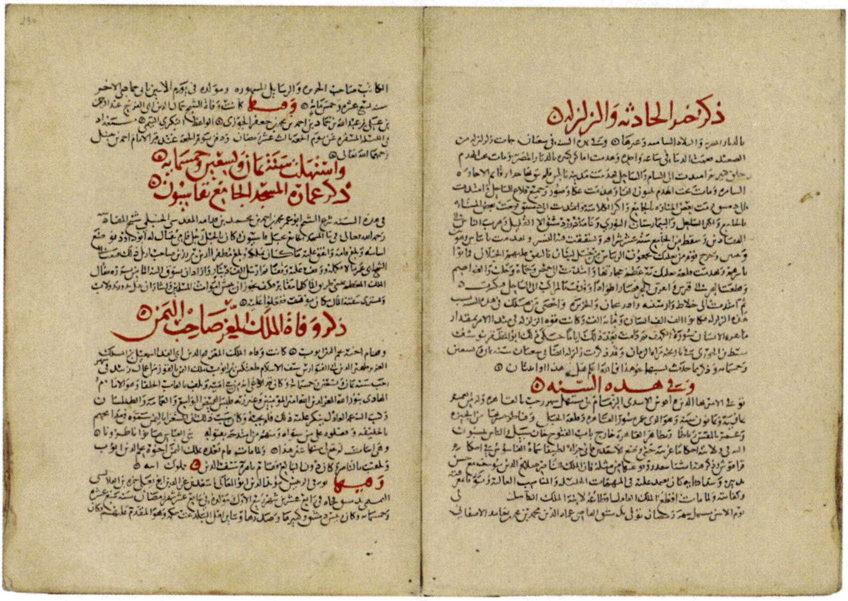

FIGURE 6.2 MSS Or. 2i (top) and Or. 2l (bottom), representing al-Nuwayrī's *Nihāyat al-arab fī funūn al-adab*, volumes 24–25 and 26–27, respectively. These volumes are both presumed holographs.
LEIDEN UNIVERSITY LIBRARY

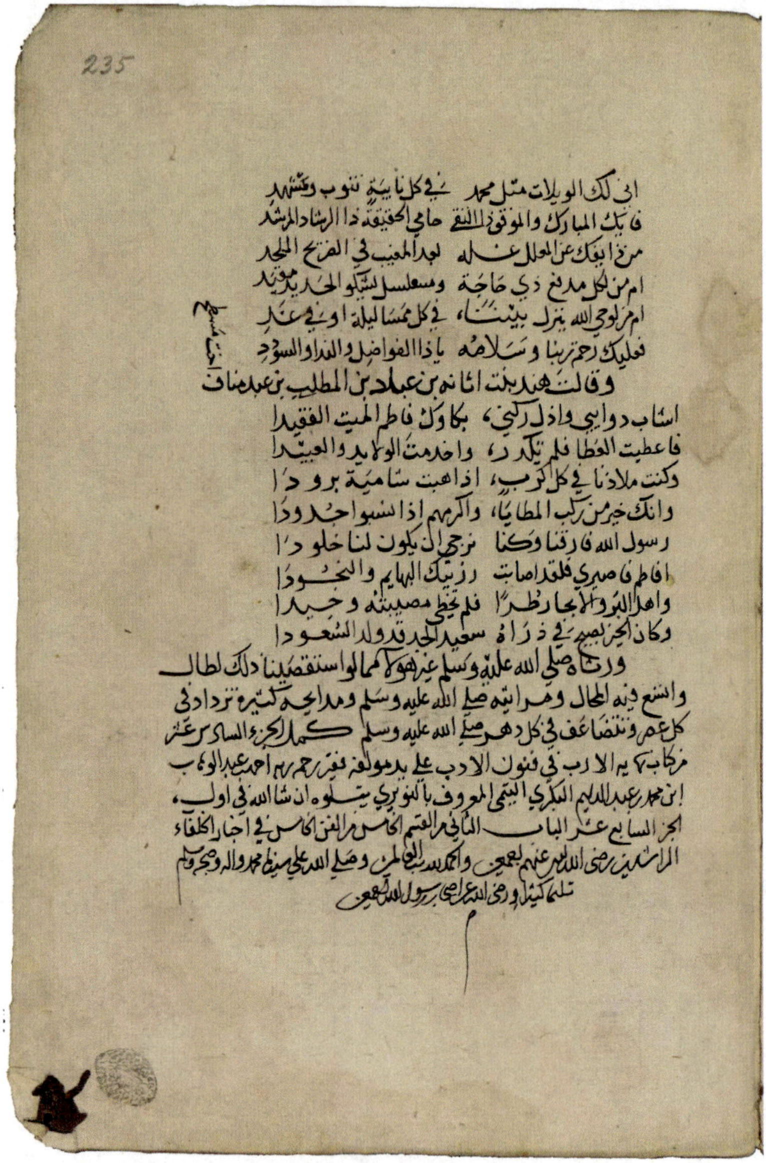

FIGURE 6.3 Colophon of al-Nuwayrī's *Nihāyat al-arab fī funūn al-adab*, signed by the author. MS Or. 2f
LEIDEN UNIVERSITY LIBRARY

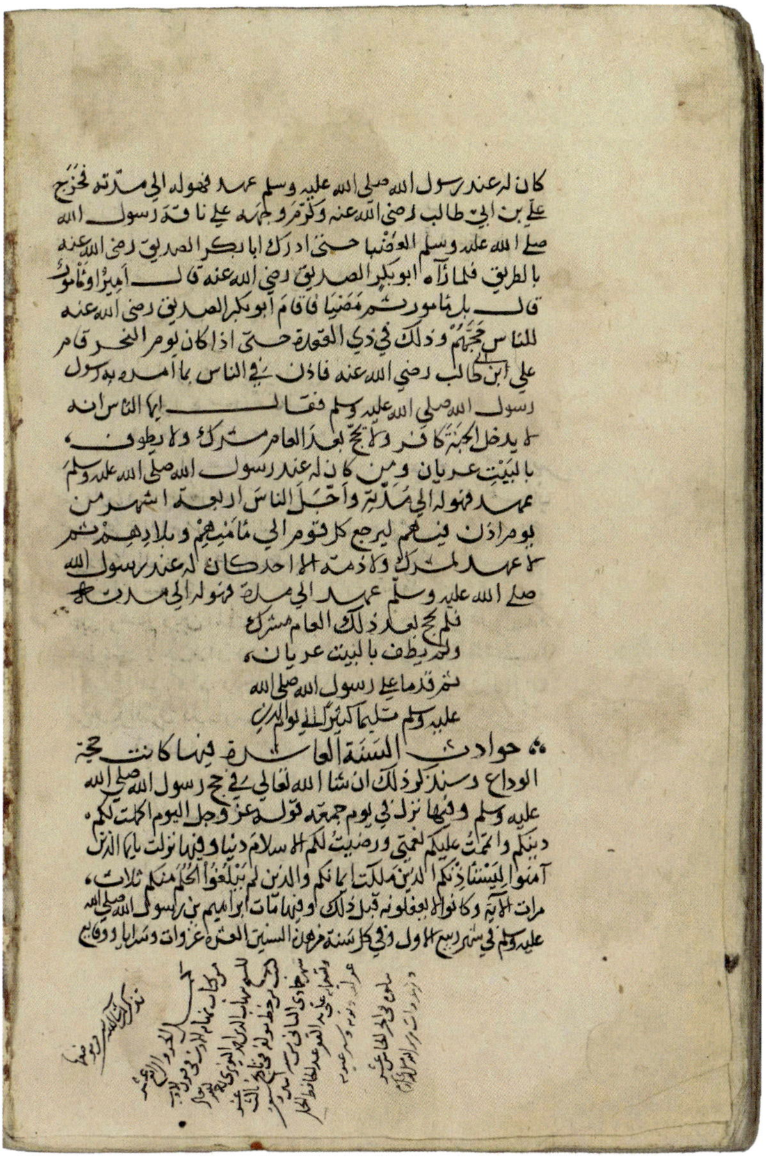

FIGURE 6.4 Last page of MS Or. 2d, which contains a colophon added by a later copyist. The script of the colophon and the main text do not match; the latter is identical to Or. 2f (see fig. 6.3), a presumed holograph. This leads me to propose that the final folios of Or. 2d may have been originally part of a different holograph manuscript, and were stitched into a copy produced by the 10th-century (AH) copyist mentioned in the colophon, who was responsible for the earlier part of the volume.
LEIDEN UNIVERSITY LIBRARY

4 An Important *Ḥadīth* Manuscript in al-Nuwayrī's Hand?[63]

As his biographers inform us, al-Nuwayrī supported himself during the period in which he composed the *Nihāya* by making and selling copies of al-Bukhārī's *al-Jāmiʿ al-ṣaḥīḥ*. I have found what seems to be one of these copies, a manuscript held in the Fazıl Ahmed Paşa collection at the Köprülü Manuscript Library in Istanbul (MS Fazıl Ahmed Paşa 362) (see figs. 6.5–6.7).[64] Dated to Jumādā I 725/April–May 1325, the manuscript contains 316 folios of compact script with ample marginal annotations. The title page indicates that it was commissioned for the library of a high official in the Mamlūk administration.[65] This may be further evidence of the esteem in which al-Nuwayrī's manuscript copies were held; one presumes that institutional commissions were reserved for very fine copies.[66]

The value of this particular manuscript, however, may have had as much to do with the nature of its contents as the quality of the copy itself. As we learn from the final pages of the work (fol. 296ᵇ), the manuscript was copied from an exemplar that had been authorized by Sharaf al-Dīn ʿAlī b. Muḥammad al-Yūnīnī (d. 701/1302), the older half-brother of the historian Quṭb al-Dīn al-Yūnīnī, whose chronicle *Dhayl Mirʾāt al-zamān* was one of al-Nuwayrī's main sources for Book V of the *Nihāya*. Sharaf al-Dīn al-Yūnīnī's redaction of al-Bukhārī's *Ṣaḥīḥ* was a marvel of philological scholarship, an attempt to reconstruct the original text of this canonical *ḥadīth* collection several centuries after it was composed. He performed this task by collating the recensions of several important transmitters and making notes of the variants he encountered, labeling them with abbreviations in the margins much like a modern critical edition.

Perhaps as a result of this philological zeal, al-Yūnīnī's redaction (known as the Yūnīniyya) "was less suited for transmission by reading and listening" than other manuscripts of the *Ṣaḥīḥ*, and so his careful work was mostly neglected by

---

63 I am grateful to Adam Gacek and Joel Blecher for their insights on the subject matter of this section.

64 Şeşen, *Fihris* i, 183.

65 Probably the chief of the chancery as the title *al-ṣāḥibī* could imply (i.e. *ṣāḥib dīwān al-inshāʾ*). The title page (fol. 19ᵃ) states in ornamental script: *bi-rasm al-khizāna al-ʿāliya al-mawlawiyya al-sayyidiyya al-mālikiyya al-makhdūmiyya al-ṣāḥibiyya.*

66 The first sixteen folios of the manuscript contain a detailed table of contents that is almost surely a later addition. The contents are organized in a tabular format, with five columns of twenty-three rows on each page. Each cell has a short title for the *ḥadīth* in question and its chapter (*bāb*) number. The foliation (also surely a later addition) restarts in the main portion of the work, on the folio following the title page.

FIGURE 6.5 The Yūnīniyya recension of al-Bukhārī's *Kitāb al-Jāmiʿ al-ṣaḥīḥ*, copied by al-Nuwayrī in 725/1325. MS Fazıl Ahmed Paşa 362, fols. 17^{b}–18^{a} (title page).
ISTANBUL, KÖPRÜLÜ YAZMA ESER KÜTÜPHANESI

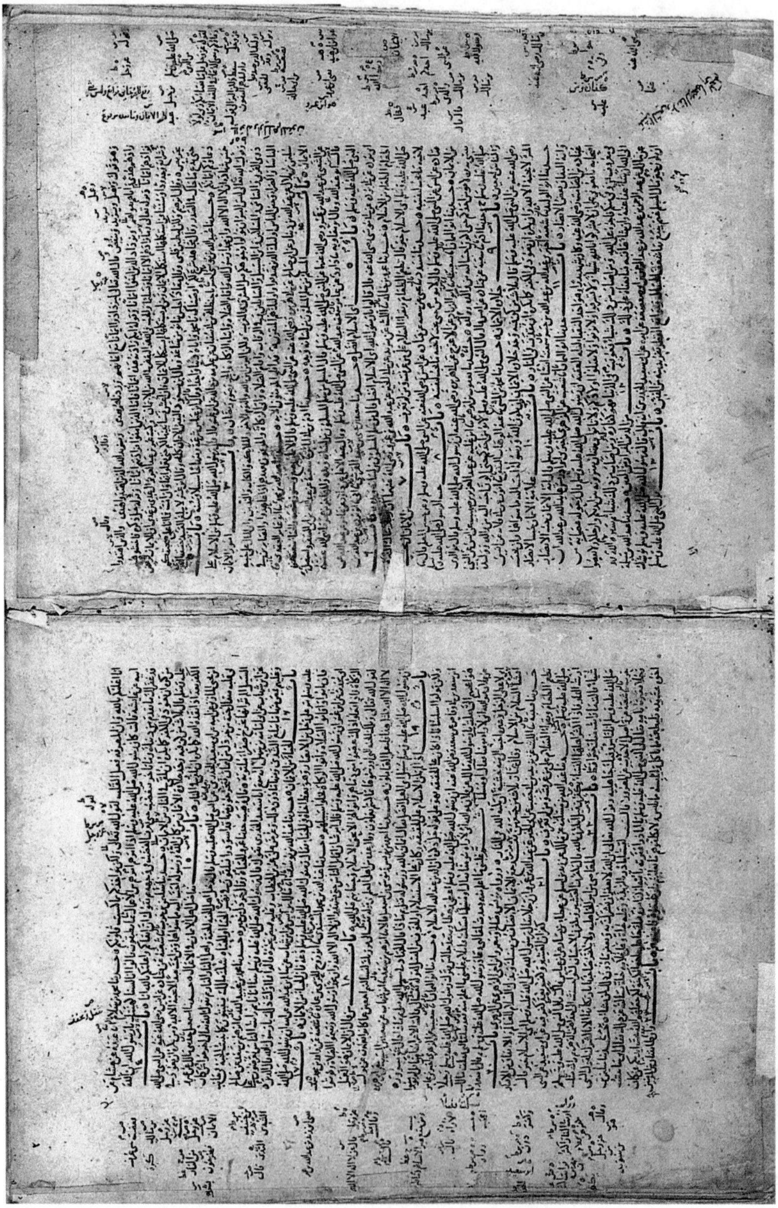

FIGURE 6.6 MS Fazıl Ahmed Paşa 362, fols. 19^b–20^a.
ISTANBUL, KÖPRÜLÜ YAZMA ESER KÜTÜPHANESI

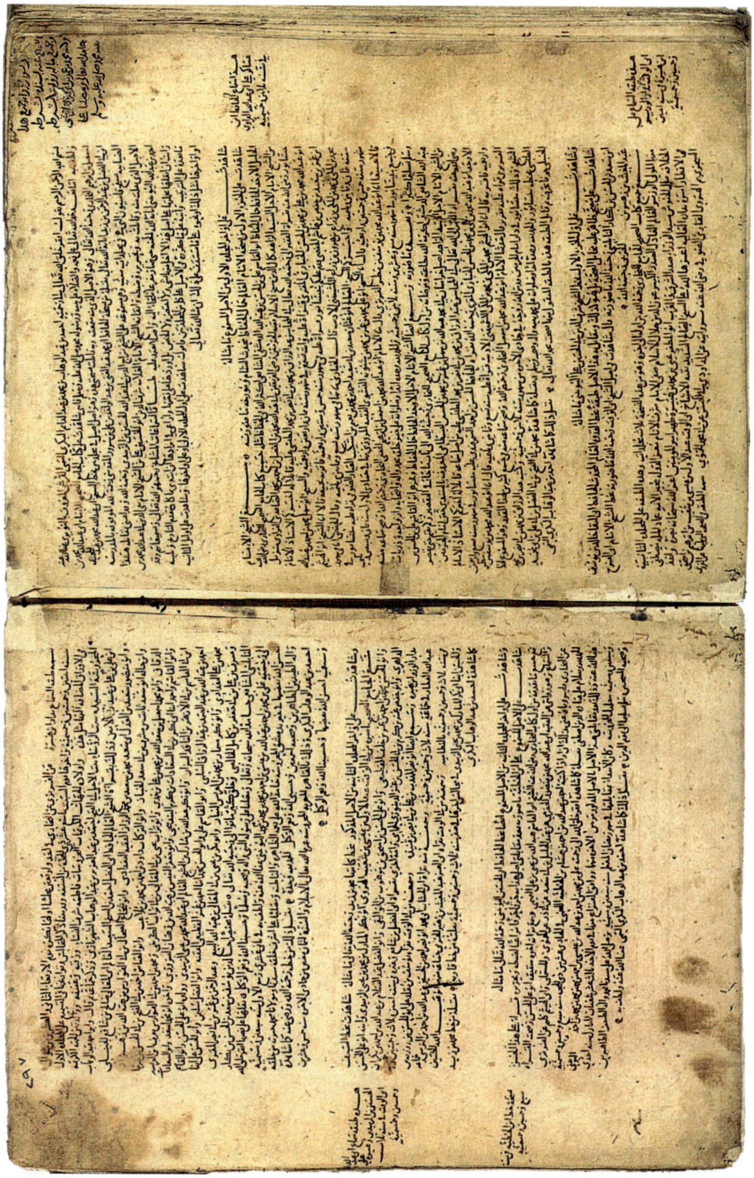

FIGURE 6.7 Final pages of the Yūnīniyya manuscript, containing audition statements and identifying the copyist as al-Nuwayrī. MS Fazl Ahmed Paşa 362, fols. 314[b]–315[a].
ISTANBUL, KÖPRÜLÜ YAZMA ESER KÜTÜPHANESI

later *ḥadīth* commentators, with the exception of al-Qasṭallānī (d. 923/1517).[67] After al-Yūnīnī's death, his personal copy of the *Ṣaḥīḥ* with its precious annotations was sold, then lost, then found again, and eventually made its way to Istanbul, where it was held in an Ottoman library. According to Fuat Sezgin, the sultan ʿAbd al-Ḥamīd II sent it to Cairo in 1895–6 to be printed, after which it disappeared permanently.

In al-Nuwayrī's obituary of Sharaf al-Dīn al-Yūnīnī in the *Nihāya*, he states: "He concerned himself with al-Bukhārī's *Ṣaḥīḥ* in all of its channels, and he exactingly edited his own copy, giving each channel its own abbreviation, and adding correct marginal annotations. I have copied al-Bukhārī's *Ṣaḥīḥ* from his model seven times, and I edited it just as he did, and collated it against his own model, which was the model upon which I performed my audition with al-Ḥajjār and Wazīra."[68] These last two figures were al-Nuwayrī's principal teachers of *ḥadīth*, Abū l-ʿAbbās Aḥmad b. Abī Ṭālib al-Ḥajjār and Sitt al-Wuzarāʾ Umm Muḥammad Wazīra bt. ʿUmar al-Tanūkhī.[69] Like al-Yūnīnī, both of these teachers had studied *ḥadīth* with Ibn al-Zabīdī when they were young, which is why al-Nuwayrī felt he could collate the Yūnīniyya against the model of his own audition with al-Ḥajjār and Wazīra, as they both derived from the same source. He explains his methodology in detail in the last few pages of the *Ṣaḥīḥ* manuscript:

> I have seen the *Kitāb al-Jāmiʿ al-ṣaḥīḥ* by the imam … al-Bukhārī … and it is the model that I heard (*samiʿtu*) and collated this copy against. It is an authentic model in two volumes, in the hand of the shaykh Abū ʿAbdallāh Muḥammad b. ʿAbd al-Majīd b. Abī l-Faḍl b. ʿAbd al-Raḥmān b. Zayd, may God distinguish him. He copied it from the copy of al-Ḥāfiẓ Abū Muḥammad ʿAbd al-Ghanī b. ʿAbd al-Wāḥid b. ʿAlī b. Surūr al-Maqdisī, may God have mercy upon him, which is held in the Ḍiyāʾiyya *madrasa*, at the foot of Mount Qāsiyūn. It is in six volumes, and was audited by (*masmūʿa ʿalā*) the shaykh Sirāj al-Dīn Abū ʿAbdallāh al-Ḥusayn Ibn al-Zabīdī. The former manuscript, which I copied and collated against, was audited by the shaykh, imam, and great scholar Sharaf al-Dīn Abū l-Ḥusayn ʿAlī, son of the shaykh and imam Taqī l-Dīn Abū ʿAbdallāh Muḥammad b. Aḥmad b. ʿAbdallāh al-Yūnīnī, may God reveal Paradise to him. He occupied him-

67 Quiring-Zoche, How al-Bukharī's 212.

68 Al-Nuwayrī, *Nihāyat al-arab* xxxii, 16–17.

69 Al-Nuwayrī received his *ijāza* to transmit al-Bukhārī's *Ṣaḥīḥ* from them in the Manṣūriyya *madrasa* in Cairo in Jumādā I 715 (August 1315), as he states in the introduction to the manuscript (fol. 19b).

> self greatly with the collation, editing, correction, and perfection of that manuscript, such that it would become an arbiter to which one could have recourse, and a model upon which one could depend ... I have decided to copy it in its entirety from the exemplar without forsaking, summarizing, or abbreviating any part of it. Rather, I determined to present it according to its original text ...[70]

Al-Nuwayrī was careful to copy all of the reading and auditing statements at the end of the exemplar, and it seems that he took the same care in preserving al-Yūnīnī's editorial apparatus, listing variants in the margins of the text. For this reason, this manuscript would appear to deserve careful study by scholars working on the history of the transmission of al-Bukhārī's *Ṣaḥīḥ* during the medieval period. For the purposes of the present article, the Yūnīniyya manuscript represents an interesting comparandum to the holograph manuscripts of the *Nihāya*. It underscores the importance that al-Nuwayrī placed on maintaining the integrity of an exemplar in the course of copying it, as we discussed earlier, and it provides an example of how a copyist approached a work by a different author rather than his own work.

However, the Yūnīniyya manuscript also raises some interesting issues concerning the problems of authenticating holographs. The handwriting is very different from that of the Leiden and Paris holographs; it is much more compact and the text block has more lines per page, in addition to being uninterrupted by line breaks. This may have been due to al-Nuwayrī's desire to fit the entire work within a single volume. The exemplar had been in two volumes (and was itself based on another manuscript in six volumes), while this manuscript is squeezed into 300-odd folios. On the other hand, one cannot help but noting that the script is somewhat similar (again, impressionistically speaking) to that of the two problematic "holographs" of the *Nihāya*, Leiden Or. 19b and BnF Arabe 1579. Could it be that the Yūnīniyya and those two other manuscripts are the real holographs? Or perhaps there were amanuenses involved? Again, a broader survey of manuscripts would be necessary to settle these interesting puzzles.

70 Köprülü Kütüphanesi, MS Fazıl Ahmed Paşa 362, fol. 296b.

5 Conclusions

The aim of this essay has been to explore aspects of the copying of Arabic manuscripts in the Mamlūk period through the study of a single figure's work. Al-Nuwayrī is a rare example of a medieval author whose copying practices might be analyzed from such a wide range of perspectives. We have the testimony of his biographers to consider along with his own views on the education and practice of the model copyist; these textual sources alone constitute a valuable window on the production of medieval encyclopedic texts. Added to this documentary evidence, however, is the considerable codicological and paleographical evidence represented by at least thirty presumed holographs of the *Nihāya*, as well as one of several copies of al-Bukhārī's *Ṣaḥīḥ* that al-Nuwayrī was known to have made. In light of this enormous cache of materials, it is difficult to think of a Mamlūk-era figure better suited to the study of holograph manuscripts.

Bibliography

Primary sources

Ibn Abī l-Faḍāʾil, *al-Nahj al-sadīd wa-l-durr al-farīd*, ed. S. Kortantamer, Freiburg im Breisgau 1973.
Ibn Ḥabīb al-Ḥalabī, *Tadhkirat al-nabīh fī ayyām al-Manṣūr wa-banīh*, 3 vols., Cairo 1982.
Ibn Ḥajar al-ʿAsqalānī, *al-Durar al-kāmina fī aʿyān al-miʾa al-thāmina*, ed. M.S. Jād al-Ḥaqq, 5 vols., Cairo 1966–67.
Ibn Kathīr, *al-Bidāya wa-l-nihāya*, 14 vols., Cairo 1932.
Ibn al-Wardī, *Tārīkh Ibn al-Wardī*, Cairo 1868.
Al-Maqrīzī, *Kitāb al-Muqaffā l-kabīr*, ed. M. al-Yaʿlāwī, 8 vols., Beirut 1991.
Al-Maqrīzī, *Kitāb al-Sulūk li-maʿrifat duwal al-mulūk*, ed. M.M. Ziyāda and S.ʿA. al-F. ʿĀshūr, 4 vols., Cairo 1934–73.
Al-Nuwayrī, *Nihāyat al-arab fī funūn al-adab*, 33 vols., Cairo 1923–97.
Al-Ṣafadī, *Aʿyān al-ʿaṣr wa-aʿwān al-naṣr*, ed. ʿA. Abū Zayd et al., 6 vols., Beirut 1998.
Al-Ṣafadī, *Kitāb al-Wāfī bi-l-wafayāt*, ed. H. Ritter et al., 30 vols., Leipzig 1931–2010.
Al-Udfuwī, *al-Ṭāliʿ al-saʿīd al-jāmiʿ asmāʾ nujabāʾ al-Ṣaʿīd*, Cairo 1996.

Secondary sources

Ahlwardt, W., *Verzeichniss der arabischen Handschriften*, 10 vols., Berlin 1887–99.
Carter, M., The *Kātib* in fact and fiction, in *Abr Nahrain* 11 (1971), 42–55.
Defter-i Kütüphane-i Ayasofya, Dersaadet 1886.
De Goeje, M.J., and M.Th. Houtsma, *Catalogus codicum arabicorum Bibliothecae Academiae Lugduno-Batavae* i, Leiden 1888.

Déroche, F. (ed.), *Islamic codicology: An introduction to the study of manuscripts in Arabic script*, London 2006.
de Slane, W. McGuckin, *Catalogue des manuscrits arabes*, Paris 1883–95.
Gacek, A., Al-Nuwayrī's classification of Arabic scripts, in *Manuscripts of the Middle East* 2 (1987), 126–30.
Gacek, A., *Arabic manuscripts: A vademecum for readers*, Leiden 2009.
Gacek, A., *The Arabic manuscript tradition: A glossary of technical terms and bibliography*, Leiden 2008.
Garcin, J.-Cl., *Un centre musulman de la Haute-Égypte médiévale: Qūṣ*, Cairo 1976.
Jamāl al-Dīn, A.M., *al-Nuwayrī wa-kitābuhu Nihāyat al-arab fī funūn al-adab: maṣādiruhu l-adabiyya wa-ārā'uhu l-naqdiyya*, Cairo 1984.
Muhanna, E., *Encyclopaedism in the Mamluk period: The composition of Shihāb al-Dīn al-Nuwayrī's (d. 1333)* Nihāyat al-arab fī funūn al-adab, Ph.D. diss., Harvard University 2012.
Muhanna, E., *The World in a Book: al-Nuwayri and the Islamic Encyclopedic Tradition*, Princeton 2018.
Quiring-Zoche, R., *Arabische Handschriften* iii, Stuttgart 1994.
Quiring-Zoche, R., How al-Bukhārī's *Ṣaḥīḥ* was edited in the Middle Ages: ʿAlī l-Yunīnī and his *Rumūz*, in *BÉO* 50 (1998), 191–222.
Rosenthal, F., *The Technique and approach of Muslim scholarship*, Rome 1947.
Sauvan, Y., and M.-G. Balty-Guesdon, *Catalogue des manuscrits arabes, Bibliothèque nationale, Département des manuscrits* v, Paris 1995.
Şeşen, R., *Fihris makhṭūṭāt Maktabat Kūprīlī*, Istanbul 1986.
van Berkel, M., A Well-Mannered man of letters or a cunning accountant: Al-Qalqashandī and the historical position of the *Kātib*, in *Al-Masāq* 13 (2001), 87–96.
Voorhoeve, P., *Handlist of Arabic manuscripts in the Library of the University of Leiden and other collections in the Netherlands*, Leiden 1980.
Witkam, J.J., *Inventory of the Oriental manuscripts of the Library of the University of Leiden* i, Leiden 2007.

CHAPTER 7

The Holograph Notebooks of Akmal al-Dīn Muḥammad b. Mufliḥ (d. 1011/1603)

Kristina Richardson

In this essay I identify and discuss three manuscripts authored by the Damascene judge and compiler Akmal al-Dīn Muḥammad b. Mufliḥ (d. 1011/1603). The earliest of the three, MS Pococke 26 (Oxford, Bodleian Library), is listed in both the online *Fihrist* catalogue and in the 1787 print catalogue as an untitled, anonymous miscellany, but handwriting analysis and autobiographical clues in the text point to an identification of the scribe as Ibn Mufliḥ. The second oldest, MS We 408 (Berlin, Staatsbibliothek),[1] is a miscellany. One entry is signed by Akmal al-Dīn b. Mufliḥ. The most recent volume, MS 1004 (American University of Beirut), is the only one with a title page that identifies it as the fifteenth volume of *al-Tadhkira al-akmaliyya al-mufliḥiyya* (Al-Akmal [b.] al-Mufliḥ's Commonplace Book). While only the Beiruti manuscript has a positively identified title, I argue that the Berlin and Oxford manuscripts are likely portions of other volumes of Ibn Mufliḥ's *Tadhkira*.

For the most part these *tadhkira* volumes consist of book excerpts and reading notes; this places the work squarely within the medieval Arabic scholarly genres of commentary, summarization, and compilation, i.e., encyclopedias, commonplace books, manuals, and abridgments, which proliferated in this period. In all of the volumes, Ibn Mufliḥ includes details about his family. Here I investigate the potential of these *tadhkira* volumes as archives of family history.

1 Biography of Akmal al-Dīn b. Mufliḥ

Akmal al-Dīn Muḥammad b. Ibrāhīm b. ʿUmar b. Ibrāhīm b. Muḥammad b. ʿAbdallāh b. Mufliḥ al-Ḥanbalī was known to his contemporaries as al-Qāḍī Akmal, or Judge Akmal.[2] He was one of the last surviving members of the

1 Ahlwardt no. 8467.
2 Al-Ghazzī, *Luṭf al-samar* i, 73.

 | DOI:10.1163/9789004413177_008

prestigious Mufliḥ clan, whose male members served as Ḥanbalī and Ḥanafī judges throughout Syria. He was born near Bāb Tūmā in Damascus in 930/1524 and later studied with his father and such luminaries of the period as Ibn Ṭūlūn (d. 953/1546). In his professional life, he served as a court witness and eventually as a judge in Baalbek, the village of Zabadān, Damascus, Karak, Beirut, and Sidon. Sometime between 991/1583 and 997/1588–9, he accompanied Sulaymān b. Qubād (d. Rajab 997/May 1589), the Ottoman viceroy of Syria (*mālik al-umarāʾ*), to Istanbul and remained there for four years.[3] Once back in Damascus, he befriended amir Muḥammad Bak b. Manjak (d. 1032/1623), who was appointed superintendent of Sultan Sulaymān's Syrian *waqf*s in Shawwāl 997/1589.[4] As superintendent, Ibn Manjak paid Ibn Mufliḥ twenty *ʿuthmānī*s per day to oversee the architectural expansion of al-Takiyya al-Sulaymāniyya. Their relationship eventually soured due to unexplained circumstances.[5]

According to Ibn Ayyūb al-Anṣarī, one of his biographers, he possessed a thorough knowledge of documents and records. This same biographer noted that Akmal al-Dīn studied the verbal patterns and formulaic expressions of earlier judges. So, he knew how his contemporaries and historical figures back to the fourth/tenth century would likely have expressed praise for God. Ibn Ayyūb al-Anṣarī said: "He used to hear a phrase and be able to say 'this is what so-and-so used to say.'"[6]

In addition to this reputation for fastidious observation, Akmal al-Dīn was also known for more frivolous interests. Al-Ghazzī noted that by night, he gathered with others for fun and play. He was known for his debauchery and reportedly had a relationship with a young Egyptian man named Jaʿfar, and Syrians composed poems that mocked them. He partook of an addictive opium mixture called *barsh*. People also claimed that he manipulated official records, altering them in such a way that his relative was a *waqf* founder; thus he gave himself these endowments. People mocked him, saying: "O, Qadi, you have many ancestors!" He died in 1011/1603 in Damascus.[7]

One can also supplement the data in biographical dictionaries with information gleaned from manuscript colophons, *marginalia*, and ownership notes. Ibn Mufliḥ transcribed the works of many other authors, including two copies

3 Ibid.; Ibn Ayyūb, *Das* Kitāb ar-rauḍ al-ʿāṭir 107 (Arabic pagination). Ibn Qubād's death is mentioned in the *marginalia* of MS Or. A. 114 (Gotha), fol. 3ª. In MS We. 408 (Berlin), fol. 256ª, Ibn Mufliḥ mentions that he received an *ijāza* in 992/1584 from a judge in western Istanbul.

4 Ibn Ayyūb, *Das* Kitāb ar-rauḍ al-ʿāṭir 107 (Arabic pagination); El-Zawahreh, *Religious endowments* 111–3.

5 Ibn Ayyūb, *Das* Kitāb ar-rauḍ al-ʿāṭir 107 (Arabic pagination).

6 Ibid. 106–7 (Arabic pagination).

7 Al-Ghazzī, *Luṭf al-samar* i, 74–7; Winter, Ottoman *qaḍī*s 98.

of a commentary on a *qaṣīda* by Abū l-Fatḥ al-Bustī (d. 400/1010), and single copies of Abū l-Faraj b. al-Jawzī's (d. 597/1201) critique of twenty-one *ḥadīths* and of Ibn al-ʿAfīf al-Tilimsānī's (d. 688/1289) sermon on *taqlīd*.[8] He added ownership statements to at least three manuscripts: al-Ābī's (d. 421/1030) anthology of prose and verse, al-Qazwīnī's (d. 682/1283) *Āthār al-bilād*, and al-Harawī's (d. 401/1011) treatise on difficult words in the Qurʾān.[9] His annotations are also found on very many of Ibn Ṭūlūn's holograph drafts, namely MS Majmūʿa Taymūr 79 (Cairo, Dār al-Kutub al-Miṣriyya, *al-Thaghr al-bassām fī dhikr man wulliya qaḍāʾ al-Shām*) and MS Garrett 196B (PUL, miscellaneous fragments).

It is unclear how many of his authored works have survived, as they may lie unidentified or uncatalogued in archives. According to Ibn al-Shaṭṭī (d. 1379/1959), Ibn Mufliḥ wrote the following:

1. a history from Adam to the reign of Sultan Qāyitbāy,
2. an excerpt of *Taʾrīkh Dimashq*,
3. a book on those who were appointed Ḥanbalī judges in Cairo,
4. a treatise on prophetic histories from Adam to our prophet Muḥammad,
5. a treatise on the caliphal period after the prophet,
6. a treatise on the affairs of the Egyptian kings,
7. an abridgment of Abū Shāma's *Kitāb al-Rawḍatayn*, and
8. other works of commentaries, useful notes, poetry, literature, and history.[10]

Additionally, he planned a *Dhayl* to Quṭb al-Dīn al-Nahrawānī's tenth-/sixteenth-century history of Mecca and Yemen, as well as continuations of al-Nuʿaymī's and Ibn Ṭūlūn's histories. "On his own, he undertook a multi-volume

8 The poetic commentaries are found in MS 0520 (Leipzig) and MS ʿIlm ʿarabī 125 (Cairo, Dār al-Kutub al-Miṣriyya; a digitized copy is available at http://www.wdl.org/en/item/14240), pp. 41–89. Ibn al-Jawzī's work on *ḥadīth* is found on pp. 89–98 of the aforementioned Cairene manuscript (a digitized copy is available at http://www.wdl.org/en/item/14241). Note that the Dār al-Kutub manuscripts are paginated. Ibn al-ʿAfīf al-Tilimsānī's work is MS Spr. 1962 (Berlin, Staatsbibliothek; Ahlwardt no. 3953).

9 MS 0593 (Leipzig), MS Or. 3623 (London, British Library), and MS We.71 (Berlin: Ahlwardt no. 696).

10 Shaṭṭī, *Mukhtaṣar* 104. I believe that a holograph portion of the second listed work survives. Gotha Ms. or. A1778 is an abridgement of volume 54 of Ibn ʿAsākir's *Taʾrīkh Dimashq*. It is not a copy of Ibn Manẓūr's *Taʾrīkh madīnat Dimashq*. The manuscript begins on fol. 1[a] in the middle of a biographical entry for Muḥammad b. Wāsiʿ b. Jābir b. al-Akhnas b. ʿĀʾid b. Khārija b. Ziyād b. Shams. A later writer inscribed a *bismillāh* above this line to make it look as though it were the beginning of a treatise. This same writer also appended the erroneous title "Taʾrīkh Ibn Iyās" to the upper margin of fol. 1[a]. The manuscript ends with a biography of Hārūn b. ʿImrān b. Yazīd in the right margin of fol. 200[b].

Tadhkira, following Ibn Ṭūlūn's organization of day, month, year, in which he assembled many inappropriate things about people's faults that were unrelated to illness."[11] Ibn Mufliḥ's *Tadhkira* was a self-initiated project that was inpired by the example of his esteemed teacher.

2 *Tadhākir* and Notebooks as Literary Genres in Mamlūk and Ottoman Arab Lands

Between the eighth/fourteenth and eleventh/seventeenth centuries, Arab scholars commonly used notebooks and commonplace books to record impressions, book passages or to copy documents. Let the following stand as an overview of the practice. The historian al-Ṣafadī (d. 764/1363) compiled a *Tadhkira* of at least 49 volumes, in which he copied passages that interested him and could be incorporated into other works.[12]

Al-Burhān b. Jamāʿa (d. 790/1388) served as chief judge in both Cairo and Damascus. His *Tadhkira* has survived as fragments in other individuals' works, for instance in Ibn Ṭūlūn's *al-Multaqaṭ min al-Tadhkira* (Dublin, Chester Beatty Library, MS Ar. 3101, fols. 274–307), which consists entirely of excerpts from this *tadhkira*, and in Akmal al-Dīn b. Mufliḥ's MS We. 408 (Berlin), fol. 135^{a}.

The notebooks used by al-Maqrīzī (d. 845/1442) in composing his Cairene chronicles and topographies have been analyzed extensively. Frédéric Bauden has identified the paper used as scrap chancery documents, ascertained al-Maqrīzī's reading habits and compilation methods, and even found evidence in the notebooks that he had plagiarized one of his contemporaries. Bauden's series of *Maqriziana* articles serve as models for codicological and historical investigations of notebooks and *tadhākir*.

Ibn Qāḍī Shuhba (d. 851/1448) used notebooks to record excerpts (*muntaqā*) from other authors' works, and then used these to compile his histories. Each notebook was a long excerpt from a single work. David Reisman has identified three in manuscript: a *muntaqā* of the histories of Ibn al-Furāt, Ibn Duqmāq, and al-Dhahabī.[13] Ibn Qāḍī Shuhba himself mentioned that he had written a *Muntaqā* of *Taʾrīkh Dimashq* in two volumes. MS We. 134 (Berlin; Ahlwardt no. 9783), fols. 1^{b}–29^{a}, is a treatise entitled *Taʾrīkh bināʾ madīnat*

11 Ibn Ayyūb, *Das* Kitāb ar-rauḍ al-ʿāṭir 106.

12 Bauden, A neglected reservoir; Franssen, Aṣ-Ṣafadī. MS Ar. 3861 (Dublin, Chester Beatty Library) contains volumes 14, 24, 25, and 26 of al-Ṣafadī's *Tadhkira*, for which see Arberry, *A Handlist* iv, 40. Élise Franssen is currently working on al-Ṣafadī's *Tadhkira*.

13 Reisman, A holograph 26–7.

Dimashq wa-maʿrifat man banāhā wa-ṭaraf min akhbārihā. In the colophon, the scribe, Ibrāhīm b. Muḥammad b. Ibrāhīm al-Shāfiʿī (d. 920/1514), wrote that this is a copy of what he had found in the handwriting of Ibn Qāḍī Shuhba on 2 Dhū l-Ḥijja 913/3 April 1508. Someone, perhaps the scribe himself, used red ink to cross out his statement that it was a *muntaqā* from Ibn ʿAsākir's *Taʾrīkh Dimashq*.[14]

Shihāb al-Dīn Aḥmad al-Ḥijāzī (d. 875/1471), a Cairene poet, composed a *tadhkira* filled with poetic excerpts from other authors. A later copy of it survives as MS 0620 (Leipzig).

In late Mamlūk and early Ottoman Syria one finds several surviving specimens of notebooks. Ibn Ṭūlūn (d. 953/1546) included the title *al-Ḥalāwa al-ṣābūniyya fī l-tadhkira al-ṭūlūniyya* in a list of his completed works, but its whereabouts are currently unknown.[15] Ibn Ayyūb al-Anṣarī (d. 1000/1591) wrote *al-Tadhkira al-ayyūbiyya*, consisting of biographies of famous men from all historical periods. Two volumes are known to scholars. The first volume, MS Spr. 252 (Berlin; Ahlwardt 9887), was completed in 998/1590 in Damascus, and al-Ziriklī claimed to have seen the second in Damascus (currently Maktabat al-Asad).[16] A fragment of an Aleppan silk-weaver's notebook (Forschungsbibliothek Gotha, MS Or. A114), dateable to 997–8/1589–90, has been recently identified and edited.[17] The diaristic notebook of the Aleppan scholar Muḥammad Fatḥ Allāh al-Baylūnī (d. 1042/1632–3) consists mostly of entries about current events and people.[18] Najm al-Dīn al-Ghazzī (d. 1061/1651) maintained a notebook, wherein he jotted down poetry and notes on a variety of subjects.[19]

Tamar El-Leithy has recently called for scholars of medieval Islamdom, who often assume that no legal archives have survived from the period, to think more creatively about what could constitute an archive. He has found that surviving document repositories tend to reside in politically marginal communities, such as the collection of *fatwā*s preserved with the monks of St. Catherine's monastery in the Sinai, and the Cairo Genizah maintained in a Jewish synagogue. Accordingly, during regime changes or political upheavals, their properties were not targeted for seizure or destruction. El-Leithy has also shown

14 Berlin, MS We. 134, fol. 29ª. On the scribe, see al-Ghazzī, *al-Kawākib al-sāʾira* i, 100; and Ibn al-ʿImād, *Shadharāt al-dhahab* viii, 13.

15 Ibn Ṭūlūn, *al-Fulk al-mashḥūn* 98.

16 Ibn Ayyūb, *Das* Kitāb ar-rauḍ al-ʿāṭir 6.

17 Liebrenz and Richardson, *Notebook*.

18 Al-Asad Library MS 4325; Schwarz, Ich erzähle.

19 BnF MS Ar. 5046.

that extralegal details, such as interest-bearing loans, are found in the notary Ibn Ṭawq's (d. 915/1509) journal, but absent from official records.[20]

Here, I propose to "investigate the social logic of archival strategies" in Ibn Mufliḥ's notebooks, focusing on his passages related to his family. As a public figure accused of manipulating family records, I propose that these private records may have served as a defense against the claims or even as a purposeful falsification of family history to support his efforts to seize *waqf*s. Secondly, before the advent of systematically and centrally maintained birth and death records, collective memory, family lore, and personal records were the most common forms of record-keeping in pre-modern Islamdom. Ibn Mufliḥ's records were even cited in the works of such later historians as al-Ghazzī in his *al-Kawākib al-sāʾira* and al-Najdī in his *al-Suḥub al-wābila*.

3 First *Tadhkira*: MS Pococke 26 (Oxford, Bodleian Library) (fig. 7.4)

MS Pococke 26 appears to be the earliest of the three Ibn Mufliḥ manuscripts. In the text, the author mentions contemporaneous events that took place between 982/1574 and 991/1584. The 179-folio volume was apparently in four parts when the Oxfordian Edward Pococke acquired it in Aleppo between 1630 and 1633, approximately thirty years after Ibn Mufliḥ's death. As I was only able to examine a microfilm of this manuscript, I could not make a full codicological survey of this codex. It was later combined into a single volume. This process of recombination and rebinding likely accounts for this large range of dates. The folios may have originated from several older notebooks or *tadhākir*.

3.1 *Identification of MS Pococke 26*

I found this manuscript while pursuing a separate project on Ibn Ṭūlūn's autograph fragments at Princeton University. A search of the term "Ṭūlūn" in the *Fihrist* database brought up MS Pococke 26, a miscellany with many Damascene topics (*madrasas*, Umayyad history, and most tellingly an anecdote on fol. 89^{b} from Ibn Ṭūlūn's paternal uncle Jamāl al-Dīn Yūsuf). I ordered a microfilm of the manuscript, hoping that it was a Ṭūlūnid fragment and found a text in a script I recognized from the margins of Ibn Ṭūlūn's holograph manuscripts. It was the hand of his student Akmal al-Dīn b. Mufliḥ, who had annotated many of his teacher's works. In fact, his relative al-Niẓām b. Mufliḥ figures among the anecdote's chain of transmitters.

20 El-Leithy, Living documents.

In MS Pococke 26 itself, Akmal left clues about authorship. Across the top of fol. 113[a] is written, "What is in this extract comes from the handwritten works of my paternal great-grandfather, the Chief Judge Ibrāhīm b. al-Akmal b. Mufliḥ." Several couplets that I have been unable to identify follow. And there is a transcribed *ijāza* on fol. 62[b] that closes with the following statement: "I, Muḥammad b. Ibrāhīm b. ʿUmar b. Ibrāhīm b. Muḥammad b. Mufliḥ, wrote it in early Jumādā II 982 [September 1574]." Based on the familial names, the script, and the date of the letter, there can be little doubt that this manuscript is one of the *tadhākir* of Akmal al-Dīn b. Mufliḥ. Even the known topics on which he wrote accord with many of the topics in the notebook.

The manuscript is in a single hand. There are no notes of ownership, reading or collation; this could simply be due to the missing leaves. Or more likely, it was intended for private consumption.

4 Second *Tadhkira*: MS We. 408 (Berlin) (fig. 7.2)

This second manuscript is the next oldest, as the dated entries range from 992/1584 to 1006/1598.[21] The Berlin cataloguer Wilhelm Ahlwardt identified this manuscript as a mostly holograph miscellany by Akmal al-Dīn b. Mufliḥ, and based the authorial and scribal attribution on Ibn Mufliḥ's dated signature on fol. 69[a].[22] (On folio 203[a], a later hand has written the names of prominent scholars, and noted a death in 1044/1634–5, decades after Ibn Mufliḥ's own death.) The manuscript consists of 256 leaves, measuring 21×13.5 cm each, of mostly poems, biographies, and historical extracts. Of the three manuscripts under discussion here, this one contains the greatest number of references to current events and family.

Ibn Mufliḥ noted that Ibn Ṭūlūn issued an oral *ijāza* and that he had received another *ijāza* in 992/1584 from a judge in western Istanbul.[23] On 3 Dhū l-Ḥijja 1003/9 August 1595, he attended a burial at al-Muʿaẓẓama *madrasa* on Mount Qāsiyūn in al-Ṣāliḥiyya, Damascus, and described the relative positions of several seventh/thirteenth and eighth-/fourteenth-century tombs and their inscriptions.[24]

---

21 On fol. 69[a] Ibn Mufliḥ signed and dated an entry "mid-Ṣafar 992," [1584] and on fol. 256[a], an *ijāza* was issued in Rajab 992/July 1584. The most frequently mentioned year is 1003/1595 (fols. 110[b], 199–200, 255[b]). The year 1006/1598 is mentioned on fol. 254[b].

22 Ahlwardt, *Verzeichnis* vii, 440–2.

23 MS We. 408, fols. 11[b], 256[a].

24 Ibid., fol. 110[b].

Ibn Mufliḥ also reproduced many of his ancestors' writings. He copied a letter from his paternal uncle Sharaf al-Dīn Abū Muḥammad ʿAbdallāh b. Mufliḥ to the *muftī* of the time, Kamāl Pāshāzādah, on 26 Muḥarram 935/15 October 1528.[25] He also has an excerpt on bathers written by his ancestor Shams al-Dīn Abū ʿAbdallāh Muḥammad b. Mufliḥ (d. 763/1362).[26] Additionally, al-Akmal found a five-line poem by al-Shāfiʿī in the handwriting of his great-grandfather al-Burhān Ibrāhīm b. Mufliḥ and reproduced it here.[27] His grandfather Najm al-Dīn ʿUmar b. Mufliḥ had noted a *ḥadīth* related on the authority of ʿAlī b. Abī Ṭālib.[28] More cryptically, Akmal al-Dīn wrote an anonymized account of an event in Najm al-Dīn's life. He noted:

> I saw a page in the hand of someone I did not know. This person related that the Ḥanbalī judge was in Cairo, his presence having been requested by the sultan. He was anguished by it. In his sleep one night, he heard someone recite verses. He memorized them. Even after he was released, what happened to him remained with him, and he feared it.[29]

The six verses quoted after this paragraph were composed by the imam al-Shāfiʿī (d. 204/820) and they urge those suffering through trials to turn to God for succor and refuge.[30] The identity of the Ḥanbalī judge in this excerpt remains anonymous, but the summons to Cairo and the judge's anguish are certainly suggestive of Najm al-Dīn b. Mufliḥ's own summons to Cairo to appear before the sultan in 888/1483. He had been accused of abusing the *waqf* of the ʿUmariyya *madrasa* in Damascus.[31] Several factors suggest that this may be an anonymized account of the aftermath of that earlier incident. Akmal al-Dīn quoted extensively from his ancestors' personal letters, *fatwā*s, and notebooks in his *Tadhākir*, demonstrating that he was knowledgeable about his family's history. He would have learned about al-Najm's ordeal not only as family lore, but also from Ibn Ṭūlūn. Though Akmal al-Dīn maintained lengthy notebooks on various subjects, family members seem to have been spared

25 Ibid., fol. 138ᵃ.
26 Ibid., fols. 61ᵃ–63ᵃ.
27 Ibid., fol. 40ᵇ.
28 Ibid., fol. 242ᵃ.
29 Ibid., fol. 1ᵇ.
30 Al-Shāfiʿī, *Dīwān* 52–3.
31 Ibn al-Ḥimsī, *Ḥawādith al-zamān* i, 185, 188; Ibn Ṭūlūn, *Mufākahat al-khillān* i, 60; idem, *al-Qalāʾid al-jawhariyya* ii, 269; al-Malaṭī, *Nayl al-amal* vii, 346; al-Sakhāwī, *al-Ḍawʾ al-lāmiʿ* vii, 170–1.

such exposure.[32] Anonymizing the account of his grandfather's summons to Cairo may have been Akmal al-Dīn's chosen method of preserving a particular legacy for his family. Secondly, Akmal al-Dīn later recorded in this same *Tadhkira* volume another poem by al-Shāfiʿī that he had found in his father's handwriting; this suggests a familial interest in al-Shāfiʿī's poetry.[33] If Akmal al-Dīn indeed anonymized his grandfather's experiences of 887–8/1482–3, then it can be read as an interesting impulse to preserve a dignified legacy for the Mufliḥ clan.

5 Third *Tadhkira*: MS 1004 (American University of Beirut) (fig. 7.3)

The title page of MS 1004 reads "*al-sifr al-khāmis ʿashara min al-Tadhkira al-akmaliyya al-mufliḥiyya Muḥammad Akmal al-Dīn b. Ibrāhīm b. ʿUmar b. Mufliḥ al-Maqdisī.*" The folios measure 21.5 × 11.5 cm, which are nearly the same dimensions of MS We. 408. This handwriting is the same as that throughout this 249-folio manuscript. It is the author's holograph work and consists of poems and fragments of literary prose, though many leaves may be out of order and the volume may certainly be missing folios. The catchword at the bottom of fol. 248^b is not reproduced on the subsequent page, and a note in the bottom left corner of fol. 249^a in Akmal al-Dīn's hand records the total number of pages in the volume as 345. The year most frequently mentioned in the text is 1003/1594–5, and the latest date I have found in the *Tadhkira* is 1005/1596–7, six years before the author's death. At least two owner's notes are still legible: Muḥammad al-Maghribī, dated 1208/1793–4, on fol. 2^b, and Ḥusayn al-Labatī, dated 1040/1630–1, on fol. 249^a.

On fols. 7^b and 9^a–10^a, Ibn Mufliḥ outlined his family tree (see fig. 7.1). The interpolated leaf, fols. 8^a and 8^b, interrupts what would have been a flowing narrative about the Mufliḥ clan. The eighth page features anecdotes from the historian al-Masʿūdī (d. 346/957), the Mālikī jurist al-Khazrajī (d. 671/1272), and the Sufi leader Ibn Qawwām al-Bālisī (d. 658/1260), so the pages seem to have been bound slightly out of order. The following is a translation of the family passages from fols. 7^b and 9^a–10^a.

> (Fol. 7^b) The author of *al-Furūʿ* is my most prestigious ancestor, Shams al-Dīn Muḥammad b. Mufliḥ b. Mufarraj b. Muḥammad al-Rāmīnī. His

32 Ibn Ayyūb, *Das* Kitāb ar-rauḍ al-ʿāṭir 106 (Arabic pagination).

33 MS We. 408, fol. 40^b.

children were chief judge Burhān al-Dīn Ibrāhīm, the scholar of Muslims Sharaf al-Dīn ʿAbdallāh, Shihāb al-Dīn Aḥmad, and Muwaffaq al-Dīn ʿAbd al-Raḥmān.

As for Burhān al-Dīn, he had two honorifics: Burhān al-Dīn and Taqī l-Dīn. He is a major scholar. His children were chief judge Niẓām al-Dīn ʿUmar and chief judge Ṣadr al-Dīn Abū Bakr. Niẓām al-Dīn had a son by the name of Shams al-Dīn Muḥammad. Ṣadr al-Dīn's son, chief judge ʿAlāʾ al-Dīn ʿAlī, was appointed to the judgeship of Syria, then Aleppo. He died in the year [blank].

As for Sharaf al-Dīn ʿAbdallāh, his children were Akmal al-Dīn Muḥammad, ʿAbd al-Kāfī, and Rashīd al-Dīn ʿAbd al-Jabbār. Akmal al-Dīn's son ʿAlī l-Alāʾ was chief judge and head of the Ḥanbalīs. [His other son was] Burhān al-Dīn Ibrāhīm, author of *al-Mubdiʿ sharḥ al-Muqniʿ*, and he died in the year 884/1479–80. His father Akmal al-Dīn was a *nāʾib* of Syria and Egypt. He died in the year [blank]. His father Sharaf al-Dīn ʿAbdallāh died in the year 834/1430–1, and Burhān al-Dīn b. Akmal al-Dīn had a son, who was my paternal grandfather, chief judge Najm al-Dīn ʿUmar, and he died in the year 919/1513–4.

As for the children of ʿAlāʾ al-Dīn b. Ṣadr al-Dīn, they are Badr al-Dīn Ḥasan, ʿAbd al-Munʿim, Kamāl al-Dīn Muḥammad, and Shihāb al-Dīn Aḥmad. They are buried in al-Rawḍa cemetery, except for ʿAlāʾ al-Dīn and his son ʿAbd al-Munʿim, who both died in Aleppo.

(Fol. 9[a]) As for Najm al-Dīn ʿUmar and his children, Sharaf al-Dīn ʿAbdallāh [was] chief judge in Damascus. He died in Istanbul in the year 955/1548–9. He was given a female slave (*jāriya*) who was called Aḥad Aḥad. Shams al-Dīn Muḥammad was Ḥanafī and was deputy to the chief judge Walī l-Dīn b. al-Farfūr, then to his brother Sharaf al-Dīn, then to Damascene judge Ibn Isrāfīl, and to others [aside from them]. He was a minor figure (*khāmil*) until he died in 970/1562–3. He was buried in Bāb al-Farādīs cemetery, and left behind four sons: Najm al-Dīn ʿUmar, Walī l-Dīn Yaḥyā, Muwaffaq al-Dīn ʿAbd al-Raḥmān, and Raḍī l-Dīn Aḥmad. They died after their father in the year [blank] and were buried with him.

Muḥyī l-Dīn ʿAbd al-Qādir, a Ḥanbalī, was appointed to a position in al-Ṣāliḥiyya, Damascus, in al-Maydān, and in Qanāt al-ʿAwnī, and he died in 957/1550–1. He was also buried at the Bāb al-Farādīs cemetery. He had a son named Maḥmūd who was murdered in 955/1548–9. He was buried in al-Farādīs.

My father Burhān al-Dīn Ibrāhīm was a renowned, perfect Ḥanbalī scholar who issued *fatwā*s. Among his teachers was the scholar Aḥmad al-Shuwaykī. He was appointed a position in the Damascene courts, but

> not in al-Ṣāliḥiyya. He taught at al-Jawziyya, Dār al-Ḥadīth, al-Ṣāḥibiyya, al-Yūnusiyya, Abū ʿUmar *madrasa*, the Umayyad Mosque, and al-Zāwiyya al-ghazāliyya. He was best known as the head of the Ḥanbalīs, and he was glorified by scholars, princes, judges, elites, and commoners until he died in Shaʿbān 969/April 1562 and was buried with his father. (Fol. 9b) All of his children moved away before his death, except for the author of this work, Muḥammad al-Akmal, Abū l-Suʿūd Muḥammad, and a daughter. As for those who passed away before his death. Ṣalāḥ al-Dīn Ṣāliḥ died in 953/1546–7 or 952/1545–6. Quṭb al-Dīn Aḥmad was Mālikī, meritorious, intelligent, and generous. He was trampled by his father's mule in a garden in a cedar grove, and he died in 961/1553–4. Karīm al-Dīn ʿAbd al-Raḥīm was Ḥanafī. He lived a beautiful life and copied documents in the Buzūriyyīn quarter. He, and others, died suddenly in the year 964/1556–7. They were buried in the Bāb al-Ṣaghīr Cemetery. Ṣalāḥ [al-Dīn] and Karīm al-Dīn had no children. Quṭb al-Dīn left two daughters. One died after him in the year [blank], leaving her son by Aḥmad b. Mubārak al-Ṣāliḥī. The second daughter had a son and a daughter from Aḥmad b. Manṣūr b. Muḥibb al-Dīn. As for the writer of this work and his brother [Abū l-Suʿūd Muḥammad], they are under the favors of God. May He protect them.
>
> (Fol. 10a, left margin) On Wednesday morning, 23 Muḥarram 1005/15 September 1596, a male child was born to the author. The slave mother (*mustawlada*) was Ḥaram bt. ʿAbdallāh. … After evening prayers, I named him Muḥammad, out of piety and [?] with the name of the chosen one (*al-muṣṭafā*).

The passage reads straightforwardly like a patrilineal family tree. When Ibn Mufliḥ wrote the main passages on fols. 7b, 9a, and 9b, he and his brother Abū l-Suʿūd Muḥammad were childless. The marginal update on fol. 10a allows me to date the manuscript prior to the start of 1005/September 1596, which accords with our preliminary dating of the composition to approximately 1003/1594.

It is also worth noting that in this long passage, the only women named are slaves: Sharaf al-Dīn ʿAbdallāh's slave Aḥad Aḥad and Akmal al-Dīn's *umm walad* Ḥaram. Free Muslim daughters and sisters remain anonymous, only identified through their relations to husbands, fathers, sons, or brothers.

These preliminary identifications of portions of Akmal al-Dīn b. Mufliḥ's holograph notebooks will hopefully spur future research into his literary and incidental output. Investigating family lore and local histories through scholars' notes and notebooks is a necessary first step in understanding how family records were maintained in the absence of centralized bureaucracies that tracked births, marriages, and deaths. Additionally, historians must recognize the importance of notebooks and commonplace books for understanding how people read, which literary topics captured readers' imaginations, and what constituted useful knowledge at a given time.

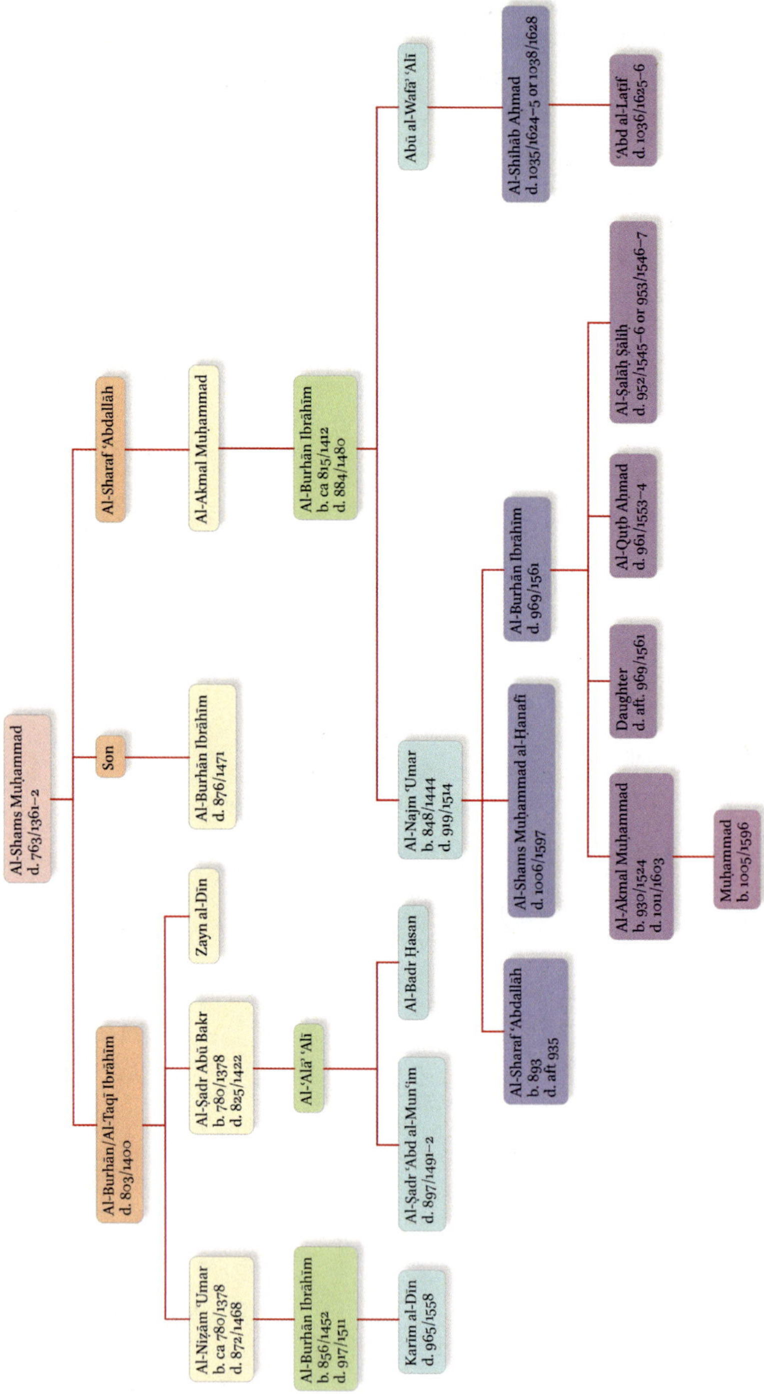

FIGURE 7.1 The Banū Mufliḥ Family Tree
Note: Cf. the Ibn al-Mufliḥ genealogy given in Mandaville, *The Muslim judiciary* 125.

FIGURE 7.2 MS We. 408, fol. 99ª
BERLIN, STAATSBIBLIOTHEK

FIGURE 7.3 MS 1004, fols. 9ᵇ–10ᵃ
BEIRUT, AMERICAN UNIVERSITY OF BEIRUT LIBRARY

FIGURE 7.4 MS Pococke 26, fols. 62b–63a
OXFORD, OXFORD UNIVERSITY LIBRARY

Bibliography

Primary Sources

Al-Ghazzī, *al-Kawākib al-sāʾira bi-aʿyān al-miʾa al-ʿāshira*, ed. J.S. Jabbūr, 3 vols., Beirut 1945.

Al-Ghazzī, *Luṭf al-samar wa-qaṭf al-thamar*, ed. M. Shaykh, 2 vols., Damascus 1981–2.

Ibn Ayyūb, *Das* Kitāb ar-rauḍ al-ʿāṭir *des Ibn-Aiyūb: Damaszener Biographien des 10./16. Jahrhunderts, Beschreibung und Edition*, ed. A.H. Güneş, Berlin 1981.

Ibn al-Ḥimsī, *Ḥawādith al-zamān wa-wafayāt al-shuyūkh wa-l-aqrān*, ed. ʿU.ʿA. al-S. Tadmūrī, 3 vols., Sidon and Beirut 1999.

Ibn al-ʿImād, *Shadharāt al-dhahab fī akhbār man dhahab*, 10 vols., Damascus and Beirut 1986.

Ibn Ṭūlūn, *al-Fulk al-mashḥūn fī aḥwāl Muḥammad b. Ṭūlūn*, ed. M.Kh.R. Yūsuf, Beirut 1996.

Ibn Ṭūlūn, *Mufākahat al-khillān fī ḥawādith al-zamān: taʾrīkh Miṣr wa-l-Shām*, ed. M. Muṣṭafā, 2 vols., Cairo 1964.

Ibn Ṭūlūn, *al-Qalā'id al-jawhariyya fī ta'rīkh al-Ṣāliḥiyya*, ed. M.A. Dahmān, 2 vols., Damascus 1980–1.

Al-Malaṭī, 'Abd al-Bāsiṭ b. Khalīl al-Ḥanafī, *Nayl al-amal fī dhayl al-duwal*, ed. 'U.'A. al-S. Tadmūrī, 9 vols., Sidon 2002.

Al-Sakhāwī, *al-Ḍaw' al-lāmi' li-ahl al-qarn al-tāsi'*, 12 vols., Beirut 1966.

Al-Shāfi'ī, *Dīwān al-Imām al-Shāfi'ī*, ed. 'A. al-R. al-Muṣṭawī, Beirut 2005.

Shaṭṭī, Jamīl, *Mukhtaṣar Ṭabaqāt al-ḥanābila*, ed. F. Zimrilī, Beirut 1986.

Secondary Sources

Ahlwardt, W., *Verzeichniss der arabischen Handschriften der Königlichen Bibliothek zu Berlin*, 10 vols., Berlin 1887–99.

Arberry, A.J., *A Handlist of Arabic manuscripts*, 8 vols., Dublin 1955–69.

Bauden, F., A neglected reservoir of Mamlūk literature: al-Ṣafadī and his *Tadhkirah*, talk presented at the *International Conference on Mamlūk Literature*, 29 April 2012, Chicago, 2012.

El-Leithy, T., Living documents, dying archives: Towards a historical anthropology of medieval Arabic archives, in *Al-Qanṭara* 32, no. 2 (2011), 389–434.

El-Zawahreh, T., *Religious endowments and social life in the Ottoman province of Damascus in the 16th and 17th Centuries*, Karak (Jordan) 1995.

Franssen, É., Aṣ-Ṣafadī: His personality, methodology, and literary tastes approached through the 44th volume of his *Tadhkirah*, talk presented at the Ninth Islamic Manuscript Conference: *Manuscripts of the Mamlūk Sultanate and Its Contemporaries*, 2 July 2013, Cambridge, England, 2013.

Liebrenz, B. and K. Richardson (eds.), *Notebook of the 16th-century Aleppine silk-weaver Kamāl al-Dīn*, Beirut, forthcoming.

Mandaville, J.E., *The Muslim judiciary of Damascus in the late Mamluk period*, PhD dissertation, Princeton University 1969.

Reisman, D., A holograph MS of Ibn Qāḍī Shuhbah's *'Dhayl'*, in *Mamlūk Studies Review* II (1998), 19–50.

Schwarz, Fl., 'Ich erzähle nichts als die Wahrheit!' Erlebnis und Erinnerung im Notizheft und im *Dīwān* von Muḥammad Fatḥallāh al-Bailūnī aus Aleppo (gest. 1632), in S. Reichmuth and Fl. Schwarz (eds.), *Zwischen Alltag und Schriftkultur: Horizonte des Individuellen in der arabischen Literatur des 17. und 19. Jahrhunderts*, Würzburg 2008, 81–99.

Winter, M., "Ottoman *Qāḍī*s in Damascus in the 16th–18th centuries," in R. Shaham (ed.), *Law, custom, and statute in the Muslim world: Studies in honor of Aharon Layish*, Leiden 2007, 87–109.

CHAPTER 8

Al-ʿAynī's Working Method for His Chronicles: Analysis of His Holograph Manuscripts

Nobutaka Nakamachi

1 Introduction

According to the two major Mamlūk biographical dictionaries, al-Sakhāwī's *al-Ḍaw' al-lāmiʿ* and Ibn Taghrī Birdī's *al-Manhal al-ṣāfī*, Badr al-Dīn al-ʿAynī (762–855/1361–1451) was so well known for his skilled penmanship and quick writing that "he wrote [the book of] al-Qudūrī in one night."[1] This statement suggests how much al-ʿAynī's handwriting impressed his contemporary intellectuals, although it is difficult for us to evaluate the aesthetics of his penmanship. Fortunately, modern scholars can access dozens of extant holograph manuscripts by al-ʿAynī, including the holographs of his famous chronicle, *ʿIqd al-jumān fī ta'rīkh ahl al-zamān*.

Since the nineteenth century, several scholars have highlighted the existence of al-ʿAynī's holographs. Otto Spies was the first scholar to mention al-ʿAynī's holographs preserved in the Beyazıt National Library (MSS Veliyyüddin 2390 and 2392).[2] Fehmi Edhem Karatay, who edited the catalogue of the TSMK, stated that a dozen volumes of *ʿIqd al-jumān* in the Ahmet III collection were written in the author's hand.[3] Another manuscript in the Süleymaniye Library, Esad Efendi 2317, can be added to this list. Thus, fifteen holograph manuscripts labeled *ʿIqd al-jumān* are known to exist (see table 8.1).[4]

Are these manuscripts definitely holographs of *ʿIqd al-jumān*? If we observe the time span of the last three volumes on the list in table 8.1, we find overlaps between volumes 17 and 18, and between volumes 18 and 19. Therefore, these manuscripts cannot be considered a coherent version of *ʿIqd al-jumān*.

On the other hand, some scholars have studied the interrelationships between al-ʿAynī and his contemporary historians, the most famous among them being al-Maqrīzī. Thus, it is not clear who wrote the more primary descriptions.

1 Al-Sakhāwī, *al-Ḍaw' al-lāmiʿ* x, 133; Ibn Taghrī Birdī, *al-Manhal al-ṣāfī* xi, 197.
2 Spies, *Beiträge* 88.
3 Karatay, *Topkapı* iii, 392–5.
4 See also Nakamachi, Al-ʿAynī's chronicles 143.

 | DOI:10.1163/9789004413177_009

TABLE 8.1 Holograph manuscripts of *ʿIqd al-jumān*

Catalogue no.	Volume (contents)	Completion date (AH/AD)
MS A2911/A1 (TSMK)	Vol. 1	30.01.825/24.01.1422
MS A2911/A2 (TSMK)	Vol. 2	10.04.825/02.04.1422
MS A2911/A3 (TSMK)	Vol. 3 (–10/631–2)	27.07.825/17.07.1422
MS A2911/B6 (TSMK)	Vol. 6 (61/680–1–95/713–4)	26.06.828/15.05.1425
MS A2911/B7 (TSMK)	Vol. 7 (96/714–5–150/767–8)	n.d.
MS A2911/A8 (TSMK)	Vol. 8 (151/768–9–225/839–40)	30.01.830/30.11.1426
MS A2911/A9 (TSMK)	Vol. 9 (226/840–1–330/941–2)	24.08.830/19.06.1427
MS A2911/A10 (TSMK)	Vol. 10 (331/942–3–430/1038–9)	03.02.831/22.11.1427
MS Esad Efendi 2317 (SK)	Vol. 11 (431/1039–40–520/1126–7)	10.05.831/26.02.1428
MS A2911/A12 (TSMK)	Vol. 12 (521/1127–8–578/1182–3)	08.09.831/22.06.1428
MS Veliyyüddin 2390 (BK)	Vol. 13 (579/1183–4–620/1223–4)	28.01.832/06.11.1428
MS Veliyyüddin 2392 (BK)	Vol. 15 (689/1290–1–707/1307–8)	n.d.
MS A2911/A17 (TSMK)	Vol. 17 (725/1324–5–745/1344–5)	n.d.
MS A2911/A18 (TSMK)	Vol. 18 (727/1326–7–835/1431–2)	n.d.
MS A2911/A19 (TSMK)	Vol. 19 (799/1396–7–849/1445–6)	n.d.

For instance, ʿAbd al-Razzāq al-Ṭanṭāwī l-Qarmūṭ, the editor of *ʿIqd al-jumān*, remarks that al-ʿAynī frequently borrowed from al-Maqrīzī, while Sami Massoud postulates the exact opposite, i.e., al-Maqrīzī borrowed from al-ʿAynī.[5] Donald P. Little, who evaluated al-ʿAynī's fundamental importance as a source for the Baḥrī period, does not undertake a strict source analysis between these two historians.[6]

This article focuses on al-ʿAynī's three holograph manuscripts that describe his lifetime (the early Circassian Mamlūk period); these are preserved in the TSMK and the BnF. This comparison clarifies al-ʿAynī's working method, and illustrates the textual relationship among several recensions of al-ʿAynī's chronicles. This article also clarifies the textual relationship between al-ʿAynī and his rival historians, in order to answer the question: Who borrowed from whom?

5 Al-ʿAynī, *ʿIqd al-jumān* ii, 28; Massoud, *The chronicles* 160–1.
6 Little, *An introduction*; idem, A comparison.

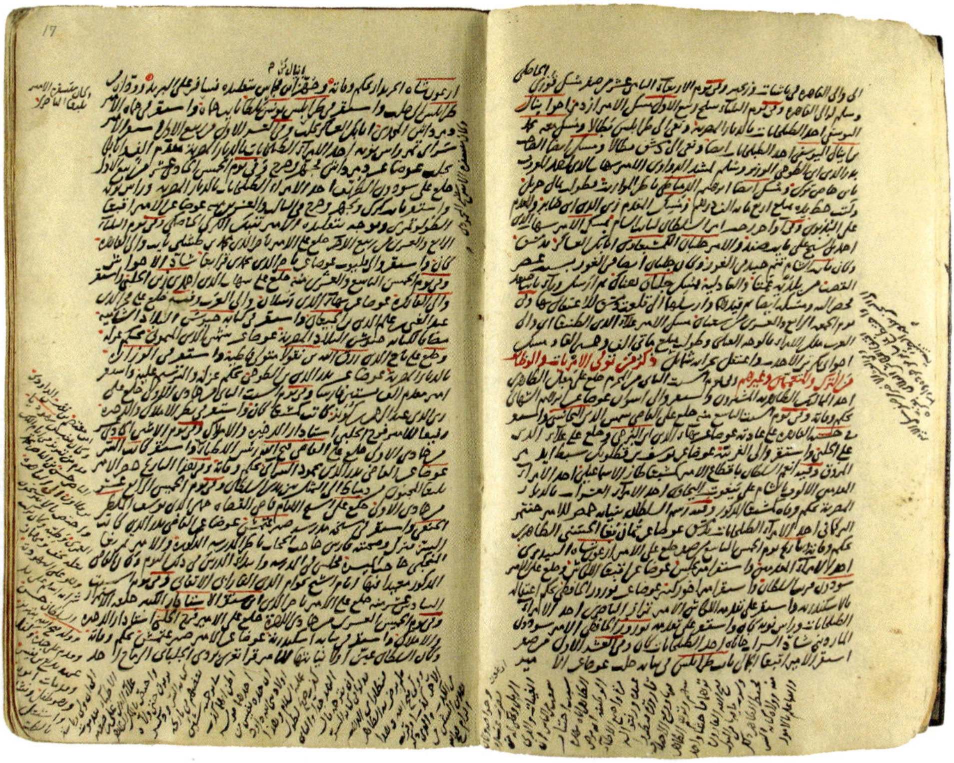

FIGURE 8.1 MS A2911/A18, fols. 16b–17a
ISTANBUL, TSMK

2 Codicological Data

As seen in table 8.1, the TSMK preserves most of the holographs of *ʿIqd al-jumān* in the Ahmet III collection. Among these, volumes 18[7] and 19 cover the early Circassian period. The manuscripts share certain features: right-inclined *naskh* handwriting, a 30-line layout, and 27 cm × 18 cm size (fig. 8.1).

One manuscript, however, has a 31-line layout and 25 × 16 cm size and also covers the early Circassian period, from 799/1396–7 to 832/1428–9. It is MS Arabe 1544 (Paris, BnF), which consists of three persons' handwriting (table 8.2). William McGuckin de Slane, the compiler of the BnF catalogue, identified handwriting A as that of Shihāb al-Dīn al-ʿAynī, al-ʿAynī's younger

7 Karatay numbered this manuscript "A18," although the catalogue kept in the reading room of the TSMK marked it "B2," according to my survey in March 2004. This article follows the numbering in the published catalogue.

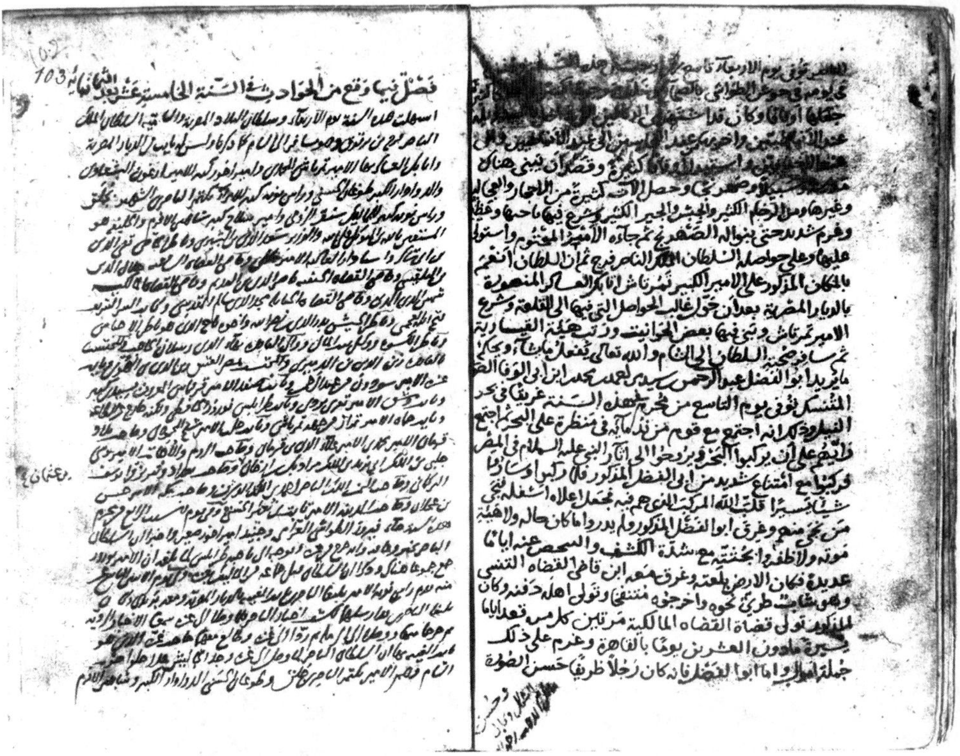

FIGURE 8.2 MS Arabe 1544, fols. 102b–103a
PARIS, BNF

TABLE 8.2 Handwritings in MS Ar. 1544 (BnF)

	Folios	Covering period
Handwriting A	1b–102b, 117b–167b	799/1396–7–814/1411–2, 820/1417–8–827/1423–4
Handwriting B	103a–117	815/1412–3–819/1416–7
Handwriting C	168a–186b	828/1424–5

brother.[8] Handwriting B, although not mentioned by de Slane, can clearly be attributed to al-ʿAynī himself based on a comparison with the TSMK manuscripts (fig. 8.1). Handwriting C is attributed to a disciple of al-ʿAynī, Bahāʾ al-Dīn Aḥmad b. ʿAlī, whose name is not found in any of the biographical dictionaries.

8 De Slane, *Catalogue*, 291. See also Nakamachi, Life 98.

Although de Slane labeled this manuscript a volume of *ʿIqd al-jumān*, its contents differ from the text of the version of *ʿIqd al-jumān* edited by al-Qarmūṭ, based on volume 19 of MS A2911.

Thus, these three manuscripts differ in their contents, although all of them cover the same time period. Consequently, al-ʿAynī wrote three recensions for this era in his own hand. This raises the question: What stage does each of these manuscripts represent?

3 Sample Test

In this article, we analyze the two annals, 801/1398–9 and 816/1413–4, as samples. Tables 8.3 and 8.4 show all the paragraphs, events (*ḥawādith*), and obituaries (*wafayāt*) for each year, listing whether they are contained in each manuscript. The topic order in the tables follows the one found in MS A2911/A19 (TSMK), while the numbers in the tables indicate the order of equivalent paragraphs appearing in the other manuscripts. As these tables roughly show, MS A2911/A19 has the most detailed descriptions of the three, and MS A2911/A18 (TSMK) has the fewest details.[9]

A comparison between MSS A2911/A18 and A19 simply demonstrates that the text of MS A2911/A18 is an excerpt (*mukhtaṣar*) of MS A2911/A19; we base this on the following reasons. First, all of the paragraphs in MS A2911/A18 are included in MS A2911/A19. Second, the topic order of MS A2911/A18 is identical to that of MS A2911/A19. Third, the narratives of MSS A2911/A18 and A19 contain similar material.

Although MS Arabe 1544 (BnF) has fewer descriptions than MS A2911/A19, it cannot be regarded as merely another excerpt of MS A2911/A19 text. First, the narrative of MS Arabe 1544 differs more from that of MS A2911/A19 than that of MS A2911/A18 does. The BnF text also contains some original information not found in MS A2911/A19. Second, the topics in the *ḥawādith* part of MS Arabe 1544 follow a strict chronological order, while those in MS A2911/A19 are arranged by common themes (such as "amirs who are under arrest and titleholders who have been dismissed," "death of the sultan Barqūq," and "past events of Syria"). Therefore, the text of MS Arabe 1544 should not be regarded as merely an excerpt from the TSMK series, but as an independent work.

Which, then, is an older recension: MS Arabe 1544 or MS A2911/A19? Closer textual comparisons focusing on a single event illustrate the relationship

9 See also the quantitative data in table 8.5.

TABLE 8.3 Descriptions of the year 801/1398–9

Topics	Date (MM/DD)	MS A2911/ A19	MS A2911/ A18	MS Ar. 1544
List of officials and rulers		1	1(+)	1
Arrest of *amīr*s and dismissal of titleholders				
Karīm al-Dīn b. Shams al-Dīn's dismissal	01/02	2		2
Shams al-Dīn al-Bajānisī as *muḥtasib*	01/09	3	2	3
Ibn al-Ḥarīrī as *kāshif* of Lower Egypt	01/28	4		4
ʿAlībāy's brothers' crucifixion	01/16	5	3	44(-)
Nāṣir al-Dīn Muḥammad al-Dimashqī as chief secretary in Damascus	01/10	6		
Sūdūn al-Ḥamzāwī executed	01/20	7	4	
Īnāl, a treasurer of Tānībak, arrested	02/01	8		
A report of Baklamish's death	02/09	9		
Nawrūz al-Ḥāfiẓī arrested	02/13	10	5(-)	5(-)
Qūzī l-Khāṣṣakī arrested	02/18	11	6	
Īnāl al-Yūsufī's family arrested	03/30	12	7	7, 17(-)
Arrest of Syrian *amīr*s	07/30	13		8(-)
Arrest of governor of Arabs in Upper Egypt	08/24	14		32(+)
Āqbughā l-Lukāsh arrested in Gaza	02/30	15		6
Appointment of Turks and Turbans				
Muqbil al-Ẓāhirī as viceroy of Aswan	01/02	16		
An appointment to *muḥtasib*	01/09	17		
Jāntamur al-Turkmānī as viceroy of Hims	01/09	18		
Arghūnshāh al-Baydamurī as *amīr majlis*	02/09	19		9
Āqbughā l-Jamāʿī as viceroy of Aleppo	02/10	20		10
Appointment to viceroys of Tripoli and Hama	02/10	21		11(-)
Sarāytamur as *atabeg* of Aleppo	03/10	22		13
Sūdūn al-Ẓarīf as viceroy of al-Karak	03/11	23	8	12
Nāṣir al-Dīn Muḥammad al-Tashlī as governor of Qalyūb	04/24	24		
Shihāb al-Dīn b. Zayn al-Ḥalabī as governor of Cairo	04/29	25	9	14
Ibn al-Jīʿān as secretary and Tāj al-Dīn Nūqūlā as *wazīr*	04/23	26	10(-)	15, 16

TABLE 8.3 Descriptions of the year 801/1398–9 (*cont.*)

Topics	Date (MM/DD)	MS A2911/ A19	MS A2911/ A18	MS Ar. 1544
Zayn al-Dīn b. Kuwayz as *nāẓir*	05/02	27		18
An episode regarding Fatḥ Allāh al-Dāwūdī	05/11	28	11(-)	19(-)
Fatḥ Allāh as chief secretary	05/11	29	11	
Yalbughā l-Majnūn's visit from Damietta	05/11	30		20
Jamāl al-Dīn Yūsuf as master of the *madrasa* of Ṣarghitmish	05/14	31	12(-)	21(-)
Nāṣir al-Dīn b. Sunqur as *ustādār*	05/16	32		22
Faraj al-Ḥalabī as viceroy of Alexandria	06/20	33		23
Kamāl al-Dīn ʿAbd al-Raḥmān b. Ṣaghīr as head doctor	06/24	34		24
Yalbughā l-Aḥmadī receiving *iqṭāʿ*	07/06	35	13	25
al-Maqrīzī as *muḥtasib*	07/11	36	14	26
Ṣadr al-Dīn al-Munāwī as chief Shāfiʿī *qāḍī*	07/15	37	15(-)	27
Yalbughā l-Majnūn as *ustādār*	07/22	38	16	28
Faraj al-Ḥalabī departing to Alexandria	07/22	39		28
Yalbughā l-Sālimī as *nāẓir* of the *madrasa* of Shaykhūn	08/02	40	17	29(-)
Alṭunbughā l-ʿUthmānī as viceroy of Ṣafad	08/00	41		30
Asīl al-Dīn al-Shāfiʿī as chief Shāfiʿī *qāḍī* in Damascus	08/23	42	18	31
Wazīr Tāj al-Dīn b. Nūqūlā receiving a robe	09/01	43		34
Ibn Khaldūn as chief Mālikī *qāḍī*	09/15	44	19	36
Sharaf al-Dīn b. Ghurāb as head of *dīwān al-mufrad*	09/19	45		37
Rukn al-Dīn ʿUmar al-Kūrānī as governor of Fusṭāṭ	09/22	46		39
Ibn al-Kuwayz and Ibn Samʿ as supervisors	09/29	47		40
Appointment of Ẓāhirī *amīr*s	04/20	48	h2	43(-)
Wazīr Tāj al-Dīn Rizq Allāh receiving a mule	06/29	49		47
ʿUmar b. al-ʿAdīm receiving a robe of chief *qāḍī* in Aleppo	08/10	50		
Commanders of thousands receiving robes	08/10	51		
Amīn al-Dīn b. al-Ṭarābulusī as *qāḍī l-ʿaskar*	03/02	52		
Rest of the events before the death of Barqūq				
Birth of the prince Ibrāhīm b. Barqūq	09/02	53		35

TABLE 8.3 Descriptions of the year 801/1398–9 (*cont.*)

Topics	Date (MM/DD)	MS A2911/ A19	MS A2911/ A18	MS Ar. 1544
Confiscation of the property of Aḥmad b. al-Shaykh ʿAlī	09/20	54		38
Ibn al-Shaykh ʿAlī as viceroy of Ṣafad	10/10	55	20	42
Ibn al-Shaykh ʿAlī as commander of one thousand	10/10	56	20(+)	
Disposal of the sultan's mules	02/10	57		45
Summons of Badr al-Dīn b. al-Tūkhī	06/14	58		46
Artisans leaving for Jerusalem	07/15	59	55	48
Baybars al-Dawādār's wedding	07/18	60		49
Al-Qudsī and Ibn Mufliḥ were appointed as chief *qāḍī*s in Damascus	07/01	61		
Tīmūr invaded India		62		51
Tuqtamish encounters the Ottomans		63		52
Repair of Jerusalem wall	08/15	64		53
A stranger in the stable	04/25	65		
Revolt of Arabs	05/30	66		
ʿAlāʾ al-Dīn b. al-Ṭablāwī's release	09/27	67		
al-Ṭablāwī departs for al-Karak and Jerusalem	10/06	68	21	41(-)
A solar eclipse	02/28	69		
A lunar eclipse	08/14	70		
Arrest of a *sharīf* in Damascus	09/00	71		
Obituary of the Sultan Barqūq				
Omen of death	09/30	72		54
Physical disorder	10/05	73	22	55(-)
Leaving a will		74	23(-)	55(-)
Almsgiving		75	24(-)	56
Civil disturbance	10/13	76		57
Summons for the *khalīfa* and *qāḍī*s	10/14	77		58
An oath of notables		78		
His death and burial	10/15	79	25(-)	59

TABLE 8.3 Descriptions of the year 801/1398–9 (*cont.*)

Topics	Date (MM/DD)	MS A2911/ A19	MS A2911/ A18	MS Ar. 1544
His race and age		80	26(-)	60
Episode of accession to *atabeg*		81		
Episode of accession to sultan		82		
His character 1		83	27	61
His character 2		84	28	62
His achievement		85	29(-)	63, 64
His children		86	30	73(-)
Viceroys of Egypt		87		65
Viceroys of Damascus		88		
Viceroys of Aleppo		89		
Viceroys of Tripoli		90		
Viceroys of Hama		91		
Viceroys of Ṣafad		92		
Viceroys of al-Karak		93		
Viceroys of Gaza		94		
*Ustādār*s		95		67
*Dawādār*s		96		68
*Amīr ākhūr*s		97		69
Chief secretaries		98		70
Nāẓir al-jaysh		99		71
Nāẓir al-khawāṣṣ		100		
Chief *qāḍī*s of the Shāfiʿīs		101		72
Chief *qāḍī*s of the Ḥanafīs		102		
Chief *qāḍī*s of the Mālikīs		103		
Chief *qāḍī*s of the Ḥanbalīs		104		
Chief *qāḍī*s of the Shāfiʿīs in Damascus		105		
*Wazīr*s		106		66
His inheritance		107	31(-)	

TABLE 8.3 Descriptions of the year 801/1398–9 (*cont.*)

Topics	Date (MM/DD)	MS A2911/ A19	MS A2911/ A18	MS Ar. 1544
Elegy 1		108		
Elegy 2		109		
Appointment of *kāshif* in Lower Egypt and governor of Qūṣ	08/24			33
Decline in grain prices				50
"Enthronement of Faraj b. Barqūq"	10/15	110	32	74
An episode regarding his title "al-Nāṣir"		111		75
Summon of *amīr*s after his enthronement	10/15	112		76(+)
"Appointment of Aytamish as *niẓām al-mulūk*"		113	33(-)	77(-)
Dispatching messengers to viceroys in Syria	10/16	114	34	78
Arrest of *amīr*s				
Arrest of Sūdūn, the *amīr ākhūr*	10/12	115	35	79
Āqbāy al-Karakī and Quṭlūbughā l-Karakī receive robes of honor	10/19	116		80
Arrest of Aristāy and Tamurāz al-Nāṣirī	10/21	117	36	81
Transfer of Qarākusk al-Khāṣṣakī to Tripoli	10/25	118		82
Appointment of *amīr*s				
Nāṣir al-Dīn Sunqur as an *ustādār*	10/23	119	37	83
Salary for the Ẓāhiriyya	10/23	120	38	84(-)
Quṭlūbughā l-Karakī as *shādd sharābkhāna*	10/25	121	39	85
A false report of revolt	10/25	122		86
Sharaf al-Dīn ʿĪsā l-Turkumānī as governor of Cairo	10/27	123	40	87
Alṭunbughā l-Murādī as governor of Aswan	10/28	124		88
Advancement of the Ẓāhiriyya	11/02	125	41	89
Duqmāq al-Khāṣṣakī, a man of the viceroy of Damascus, arrested	11/05	126	42	90
Appointment of Dunkuzbughā l-Khuṭaṭī and etc.	11/09	127	43	91
Shaykh al-Islām as shaykh of the *khānqāh* in Siryāqūs	11/14	128		92
Transfer of Yalbughā l-Majnūn to Alexandria	11/15	129	44	93

TABLE 8.3 Descriptions of the year 801/1398–9 (*cont.*)

Topics	Date (MM/DD)	MS A2911/A19	MS A2911/A18	MS Ar. 1544
Rest of the events				
Appointment of the *khalīfa* and three *qāḍī*s	11/16	130		94
Aqbāy al-Karakī as *khāzindār*	11/17	131	45	95
Arghūn Shāh as *nāẓir* of the Mosque of Shaykhūn	11/19	132	46(-)	96
Sūdūn al-Ṭayyār as *amīr ākhūr*	11/21	133	47	97
Shihāb al-Dīn b. Qutayna as *wazīr*	11/23	134	48	98
ʿAlam al-Dīn Sulaymān as governor of Fusṭāṭ	11/24	135		99
Jarkas al-Qāsimī as lesser *dawādār*	11/25	136		100
Tāj al-Dīn b. al-Baqarī as governor of Alexandria	11/28	137		101
al-ʿAynī as *muḥtasib* and Ibn Khaldūn as chief *qāḍī*	12/01	138	49	102(-)
Nūr al-Dīn al-Bakrī as *muḥtasib* of Fusṭāṭ	12/07	139	50	103
Fakhr al-Dīn b. Ghurāb as *wazīr*	12/09	140	51	104
Dispatch of Tamurbughā l-Mashṭūb to Damascus	12/15	141		105(+)
Sūdūn al-Ṭayyār inspects troops	12/13	142		106
Transfer of Nawrūz to Damietta	12/00	143	52	
Dispatch of ʿAlāʾ al-Dīn b. al-Ṭablāwī to Damascus	11/30	144		
Abolition of taxes	12/00	145		
Information about the Ottoman Bāyazīd		146	53	
Fulfillment to the Nile		147		
Pilgrimage		148	54	107
Obituaries				
Q. Badr al-Dīn Maḥmūd b. ʿAbdallāh al-Kastanī	05/10	1	1(-)	2
Sh. Qunbur al-Sabzawārī l-Shāfiʿī	07/02	2	2	19
Q. Nāṣir al-Dīn Muḥammad b. Muḥammad al-Tūnisī	09/01	3	3	18(-)
Q. Shihāb al-Dīn Aḥmad al-ʿIbādī	04/19	4		
Q. Shihāb al-Dīn Aḥmad b. Ibrāhīm al-Mawṣilī	04/00	5		
Q. Shihāb al-Dīn Aḥmad b. ʿAlī b. Ṣāliḥ al-Adhraʿī	02/00	6		
Q. Shihāb al-Dīn Aḥmad b. Sulaymān b. Muḥammad	12/00	7		

TABLE 8.3 Descriptions of the year 801/1398–9 (*cont.*)

Topics	Date (MM/DD)	MS A2911/ A19	MS A2911/ A18	MS Ar. 1544
Q. ʿImād al-Dīn Aḥmad b. ʿĪsā l-Muqayrī l-Karakī	03/17	8	4	
Tāj al-Dīn Aḥmad b. Muḥammad al-Bīlisī	03/00	9		
Sh. Khalīl b. ʿUmar b. ʿAbd al-Raḥmān al-Muqriʾ	03/00	10	5	
Jamāl al-Dīn ʿAbdallāh al-Saksūnī l-Mālikī	04/00	11		
Nūr al-Dīn ʿAlī b. Muḥammad al-Mīqātī l-Munajjim	01/00	12	6	
Shams al-Dīn Muḥammad b. Saʿd al-Kāzarūnī		13		
Qāsim b. al-Ashraf Shaʿbān	03/12	14		3
A. Baklamish al-ʿAlāʾī	02/01	15	7	4
A. Arghūn Shāh al-Khāzindār al-Ibrāhīmī	03/01	16	10(-)	5
A. Azdamur al-ʿIzzī, *amīr* of forty	04/27	17	11(-)	6
A. Tamurbughā l-Qūjawī	05/10	18		7
A. Ṣarghitmish al-Khāṣṣakī	06/15	19	12(-)	8
A. Ḥusām al-Dīn al-Kujukunī	07/03	20	13(-)	9
A. Shaykh al-Ṣafawī l-Khāṣṣakī	04/01	21	8	10
A. Kumushbughā l-Ḥamawī	09/30	22	9	11
A. Mankalībughā l-Qarājā l-Ẓāhirī	07/16	23	14(-)	12
Muʿallim Muḥammad al-Ṭūlūnī l-Muhandis	07/25	24		13
Zayn al-Dīn Ṣandal al-Ṭawāshī l-Manjakī	09/23	25	17	14
A. Ḥājj b. Mughulṭāy	02/15	26	15(-)	20
A. Urunbughā l-Ḥāfiẓī	11/15	27	16(-)	21
al-Manṣūr Muḥammad b. al-Muẓaffar Ḥājjī	01/09	28	20	1
Sh. Aḥmad b. ʿAbdallāh al-Zuhūrī	02/01	29	19	15
Sh. ʿAlāʾ al-Dīn al-Kalāmī, *khalīfat* al-Shaykh Ḥusayn	04/02	30	18	16
Sh. Khalaf b. ʿAbdallāh al-Sutūḥī	04/00	31		
Nūr al-Dīn ʿAlī b. Aybak al-Dimashqī		32		
Nāṣir al-Dīn Muḥammad b. Yalbughā		33		
Q. Karīm al-Dīn b. al-Bahār al-Kārimī	02/30			17

A.= *al-Amīr*, Q.= *al-Qāḍī*, Sh.= *al-Shaykh*

TABLE 8.4 Descriptions of the year 816 /1413–4

Topics	Date (MM/DD)	MS A2911/ A19	MS A2911/ A18	MS Ar. 1544
List of officials and rulers		1	1(-)	1
Qurqumās leaving for Syria	01/20	2	2	2(-)
Ṣadr al-Dīn b. al-ʿAjamī as *nāẓir al-mawārīth al-ḥashriyya*	02/30	3	3	3(-)
Execution of Fatḥ Allāh	01/15	4	4	
Famine and Epidemic in Egypt	01/02	5	5	4
Execution of Fāris al-Muḥammadī	03/07	6	6	5(-)
Arrest of Khusraw	03/07	7	7	
Shihāb al-Dīn al-Umawī as *chief qāḍī* of the Mālikīs	04/12	8	8	6
Fulfillment to the Nile	05/04	9		7
Tāj al-Dīn b. Haytham as *wazīr*	05/05	10	9	8
ʿAlam al-Dīn b. Kuwayz as *nāẓir al-jaysh*	05/08	11	10	9(-)
Execution of Muḥammad b. Shaʿbān, the *muḥtasib*	05/10	12	11	10
Ṣadr al-Dīn b. al-Ādamī as *muḥtasib*	05/12	13	12	11
Submission of Jānibak al-Ṣūfī and Taghrībirdī	05/12	14	13(-)	11/2
"Ṭūghān al-Ḥasanī leaving"	05/17	15	14	12
Turbulence among the people	05/17	16	15	13
Ṭūghān going to Alexandria	05/20	17	16	14
Arrest of Sūdūn al-Ashqar and Kumushbughā l-Īsawī	05/21	18	17	15
Execution of viceroy of Jerusalem	05/22	19	18	16
Distribution of the *iqṭāʿ* of the arrested *amīrs*	05/23	20	19	17
Īnāl al-Ṣaṣlāʾī as *amīr majlis*	05/23	21	20	18
Jānibak as *dawādār*	05/28	22	21	19
Fakhr al-Dīn b. Abī l-Faraj as *ustādār*	05/30	23	22	20
Visit of Jārqutlū, the *atabeg* of Damascus	07/06	24	23	21
Prince Ibrāhīm's wedding	07/08	25		22
Qurqumās and Taghrībirdī as viceroys of Ṣafad and Gaza	07/12	26	24	23(-)
Return of envoys from Sinop	07/19	27		24(-)
Manklibughā l-ʿAjamī as *muḥtasib*	07/20	28	25	25(-)

TABLE 8.4 Descriptions of the year 816 /1413–4 (*cont.*)

Topics	Date (MM/DD)	MS A2911/ A19	MS A2911/ A18	MS Ar. 1544
Revolt of viceroys	08/01	29		26,28
"Viceroy of Aleppo, Damurdāsh's visit"	09/01	30	26	29
Ṣadr al-Dīn al-ʿAjamī as *shaykh* of a mosque and dispatch of Āqbughā Buzq	09/06	31	27	30
Transfer of Sūdūn al-Ashqar and Kumushbughā l-ʿĪsawī to Damietta	09/06	32	28(-)	31
Transfer of Sūdūn al-Qāḍī	09/07	33		32
Arrest of two *amīr*s in Ramaḍān	09/02	34	29	33
Suppression of Taghrībirdī	09/10	35	30(+)	35
Nāṣir al-Dīn al-ʿAdīm as chief *qāḍī* of the Ḥanafīs	09/10	36	31	34
Qānibāy as viceroy of Damascus	09/13	37	32	36
Badr al-Dīn Ḥasan receives a robe	10/06	38	33	37
Sultan going to Giza	10/06	39		38
The *atabeg* Yalbughā going to Syria	10/06	40		39
Ṣadr al-Dīn al-ʿAjamī as *nāẓir al-mawārīth al-ḥashriyya*	10/21	41		27,40
Death of Taghrībirdī and execution of Ḥusām al-Dīn al-Ahwal	10/07	42	34	
Regulations for Jews and Christians	11/19	43	36	41(-)
Inspection of troops	11/25	44	35	42
Departure of viceroys of Aleppo and Gaza	11/25	45	37	43
Campaign to Syria	12/17	46	38	44
Accession of *khalīfa* al-Muʿtaḍid	12/17	47	39	45
A bonus for *mamlūk*s	12/17	48	40	46
Departure of Sūdūn min ʿAbd al-Raḥmān and Sūdūn al-Qāḍī	12/20	49	41	47
Departure of Qānibāy	12/20	50	42	
Shams al-Dīn al-Tabbānī as Ḥanafī *qāḍī* in Damascus	12/20	51	43	48(-)
Departure of the sultan	12/27	52	44	49
Wazīr Tāj al-Dīn b. Hayṣam beaten	12/28	53	45	50
Events in Syria				
Murder of al-ʿAjl b. Nuʿayl, the *amīr al-ʿArab*	03/24	54		

TABLE 8.4 Descriptions of the year 816 /1413–4 (*cont.*)

Topics	Date (MM/DD)	MS A2911/ A19	MS A2911/ A18	MS Ar. 1544
ʿUthmān the stranger appeared in ʿAjlūn	03/00	55		
Rumaytha, *amīr al-ʿArab*, in Mecca	06/00	56		
al-Harawī as chief *qāḍī* of the Shāfiʿīs in Damascus	07/00	57		
Prices				
Price rise	01/30	58		4
Decline of grain prices	08/00	59		
Pilgrimage		60	46	51
Obituaries				
Sh. Shihāb al-Dīn Aḥmad b. Ḥijjī l-Ḥusbānī		1	3	
Q. Shihāb al-Dīn Aḥmad b. Naṣr b. Khalīfa al-Nāṣirī l-Bāʿūnī	01/04	2	2	
Sh. Ḥusām al-Dīn Ḥasan b. ʿAlī l-Ābiyurdī		3		
Sh. Ibrāhīm b. Muḥammad Ibn Zuqqāʿa	12/15	4	1	
Sh. Fakhr al-Dīn ʿUthmān b. Ibrāhīm al-Birmāwī	08/07	5		4
Q. Nūr al-Dīn ʿAlī b. ʿAbdallāh al-Miṣrī l-Qarāfī	09/00	6	8	
Q. Ṣadr al-Dīn ʿAlī b. Muḥammad al-Dimashqī, Ibn al-Ādamī	09/08	7	4	5
Sh. Shams al-Dīn Muḥammad b. Aḥmad al-ʿArrāqī	08/05	8	5	3
Q. Shams al-Dīn Muḥammad b. Muḥammad al-Ikhnāʾī l-Saʿdī	07/00	9	6	6
Sīdī ʿUmar b. al-Muʾayyad	02/25	10		1
Q. Fatḥ Allāh b. Mustaʿṣim, *kātib al-sirr*	03/05	11	7	2
Bint al-Muʾayyad	03/09	12		
A. ʿAlāʾ al-Dīn Altunbughā l-Mihmandār	08/25	13		10
A. Mubārak Shāh al-Ẓāhirī	09/00	14	9	8
Q. Tāj al-Dīn Rizq Allāh, ʿAbd al-Razzāq		15		
A. Taghrībirdī, Sīdī Ṣaghīr	10/07	16		9
A. Qurqumāsh, Sīdī Kabīr		17		
Q. Shihāb al-Dīn al-Qarāfī	09/20			7
A. Jaqmaq al-Aḥmadī	05/30			11

TABLE 8.5 Number of topics in al-ʿAynī's chronicles

	801/1398–9			816/1413–4		
	Ḥawādith	*Wafayāt*	Sum	*Ḥawādith*	*Wafayāt*	Sum
MS Ar. 1544 (BnF)	107	21	128	51	11	62
MS A2911/A19 (TSMK)	148	33	181	60	17	77
MS A2911/A18 (TSMK)	55	20	75	46	9	55

between these texts. The first example concerns famine and high prices in Egypt in 816/1413. As presented in table 8.6, MS A2911/A19 has two paragraphs that each, separately, addresses epidemics and high prices. MS A2911/A18 contains a *verbatim* repetition of the first paragraph (on epidemics) of MS A2911/A19 and no equivalent paragraph to its last paragraph (on high prices). MS Arabe 1544 has only one paragraph that addresses both epidemics and high prices. By comparing the texts of MS A2911/A19 and MS Arabe 1544, we can identify two possibilities about al-ʿAynī's writing process: al-ʿAynī wrote the mixed paragraph in MS Arabe 1544 first and then divided it into two paragraphs and enlarged each of them in MS A2911/A19, or he wrote the two separate paragraphs in MS A2911/A19 first and then later combined and summarized them.

The next example is taken from the descriptions of the death of Sultan Barqūq in 801/1399, as shown in table 8.7. In this case also, MS A2911/A19 has the most detailed descriptions; however, it not only lacks chronological order but also duplicates some information. MS Arabe 1544, on the other hand, follows a strict chronological order. For example, in MS A2911/A19, al-ʿAynī reports the rumor of Barqūq's death on 13 Shawwāl and his summons of the notables on 14 Shawwāl (lines D and E), and then reports the same events again in a different form (lines H and I). This duplication shows that al-ʿAynī was confused while writing the text of MS A2911/A19; no such confusion is reflected in the writing of MS Arabe 1544. We can explain this by assuming the following: When al-ʿAynī wrote the text of MS A2911/A19, he may have copied several phrases from other sources and inserted them into the proto-text and carelessly, for unknown reasons, failed to delete previous phrases. If this is the case, the text of MS Arabe 1544 should be regarded as the pre-insertion prototext.

To conclude, al-ʿAynī's writing process can be reconstructed as follows: First, al-ʿAynī wrote the text of BnF Arabe 1544. Second, he incorporated it into the text of MS A2911/A19. Finally, he reproduced an excerpt of it: i.e., MS A2911/A18.

TABLE 8.6 Famine and high price in Egypt in 816/1413

MS A2911/19, fols. 126b, 129b	*MS A2911/18, fol. 171a*	*MS Ar. 1544, fol. 107b*
وفي أواخر المحرم وأوائل صفر، وقوي الفناء بمصر والقاهرة، وتزايد الطاعون. فبلغ الموتى في كل يوم مائة وعشرين، وعز البطيخ الصيفي حتى بيعت واحدة بخمسمائة درهم. وفي أواخر صفر، ارتفع الفناء عن المسلمين برحمة الله ولطفه.	وفي أواخر المحرم وأوائل صفر، قوي الفناء بمصر والقاهرة، وتزايد الطاعون، فبلغ الموتى في كل يوم مائة وعشرين وعزّ البطيخ الصيفي حتى بيعت واحدة بخمسمائة درهم. وفي أواخر صفر، ارتفع الفناء عن المسلمين برحمة الله	وقوي الفناء في القاهرة في أواخر المحرم، وبلغ عدة الموتى إلى مائة وعشرين نفس وأكثر، وتحسنت الأسعار جدا. فأصرف الدينار من الذهب المصري مبلغ مائتين وأربعين، وعومل بمائتين وخمسين. والمشخص الأفرنتي مبلغ مائتين وثلاثين والناصري بمبلغ مائتين وعشرة. والرطل المصري من العسل بيع بأربعة عشر درهما، وكذا الرطل من السمن ومن الزيت بثمانية،
وفي أواخر المحرم، وتحسنت الأسعار جدا. فبلغ الأفرنتي إلى مائتين وثلاثين درهما فلوسا، والناصري إلى مائتين وعشرة، ودينار المصري إلى مائتين وأربعين. وفي المعاملة بالقماش ونحوه كل واحد يزائد عشرة على ما ذكرنا. والرطل من العسل المصري إلى أربعة عشر درهما، وكذا من السمن ومن الزيت إلى ثمانية		

4 Classification of the Manuscripts

These three recensions seem to represent the three histories (*taʾrīkh*s) described by al-Sakhāwī in his biographical dictionary: "[Al-ʿAynī has] a large history in nineteen volumes, of which I saw the final part, which ends in [8]50 [AH]. And [he has] the middle (*mutawassiṭ*) [version] in eight [volumes] and has also excerpted it (*ikhtaṣarahu*) in three [volumes]."[10]

It is clear that MS A2911/A19 is a holograph of his "large history," *ʿIqd al-jumān*, and MS A2911/A18 may also be an excerpt of it. Therefore, does MS Arabe

10 Al-Sakhāwī, *al-Ḍawʾ al-lāmiʿ* x, 134. See also Ibn Taghrī Birdī, *al-Manhal al-ṣāfī* xi, 197.

TABLE 8.7 Death of Sultan Barqūq in 801/1399

		MS A2911/19, fols. 19^{a}–20^{b}	MS A2911/18, fol. 115^{a}	MS Ar. 1544, fols. 16^{b}–17^{a}
A	In the end of Ramaḍān, astrologers circulated the idea that something serious would happen to Barqūq.	1	/	1
B	On 5 Shawwāl, Barqūq had pain in his head and heart and he stopped [tending to] his affairs.	/	/	2
C	On 5 Shawwāl, Barqūq ate *kahtāwī* honey and got diarrhea and a fever. The matter [continued to] worsen until 9 Shawwāl.	2	1	/
D	On 13 Shawwāl, Barqūq [developed a] death rattle and a rumor of his death spread. The governor of Cairo settled the confusion.	3	2	/
E	On 14 Shawwāl, Barqūq summoned the *khalīfa*, the four *qāḍīs*, and the *amīrs* to dictate a will (long statement)	4	3	/
F	Only *jamdāriyya* and the eunuchs could meet with him and the *qāḍī* Fatḥ Allāh stayed by during his treatment	5	/	3
G	On 10 Shawwāl, Barqūq ordered the *amīr* Sūdūn to donate 15 thousand *afrantī* to the poor.	6	4	4
H	On 13 Shawwāl, there was a rumor of a revolt by the *amīr* Arstāy and the governor of Cairo settled the confusion.	7	/	5
I	On 14 Shawwāl, Barqūq realized his end and summoned the *khalīfa*, the *atābak*, all the *amīrs*, and the *qāḍīs* in order to dictate a will.	8	/	6

1544 correspond to "the middle version," i.e., another of al-ʿAynī's chronicles, *Taʾrīkh al-Badr fī awṣāf ahl al-ʿaṣr*?

To determine this, we must consult another manuscript, one that is copied by al-ʿAynī's younger brother, Shihāb al-Dīn. The manuscript, MS Süleymaniye 830, which is preserved in the Süleymaniye Library and labeled as *ʿIqd al-jumān*, seems to have features in common with MS Arabe 1544: they share the same handwriting, line numbers, and size (see fig. 8.3). While the Süleymaniye manuscript ends in the year 798/1395–6, MS Arabe 1544 text starts in the year 799/1396–7. Therefore, these two manuscripts can be regarded as a continuous series. As I pointed out in a previous article,[11] the title page of MS Süleymaniye 830 reads: "volume 9 of (*al-*)*Taʾrīkh al-Badr*(*ī*)." Therefore, MS Arabe 1544 should be labeled as volume 10 of *Taʾrīkh al-Badr*.

11 Nakamachi, Al-ʿAynī's chronicles 146.

FIGURE 8.3 MS Süleymaniye 830, fols. 216b–217a
ISTANBUL, SÜLEYMANIYE KÜTÜPHANESI

The TSMK also preserves several holographs of *Taʾrīkh al-Badr* (the manuscripts written by the elder al-ʿAynī), one of which has a colophon showing that it was written in 799/1396.[12] Al-ʿAynī's younger brother Shihāb al-Dīn copied them in 813/1410, as shown in the colophon of the Süleymaniye manuscript.

As for *ʿIqd al-Jumān*, some of the holographs in the TSMK have colophons, which we can see were first written in 825/1422. Furthermore, MS A2911/A19 seems to have been written after 838/1434.[13] Thus, their date of writing also clearly demonstrates that *Taʾrīkh al-Badr* preceded *ʿIqd al-jumān*.

12 MS A2911/D1. This manuscript was also erroneously labeled *ʿIqd al-jumān*. See Nakamachi, A historiographical analysis 46.

13 This manuscript can be separated into two parts with a *basmala* attached to the beginning of the year 838/1434–5, written on fol. 217b. See ibid. 43–4.

5 The Interrelationship between al-ʿAynī and al-Maqrīzī

We must now address the issue of the interrelationship between al-ʿAynī and al-Maqrīzī. Table 8.8 shows the information of the *kātib* Fatḥ Allāh b. Nafīs,[14] who was appointed head secretary (*kātib al-sirr*) in 801/1399. The body of the text in MS Arabe 1544 and MS A2911/A19, both holographs, shows the same simple descriptions of Ibn Nafīs's appointment; it states only the date and names of the persons involved. However, MS A2911/A19 has a long and revealing insertion in its margin that describes his family history, origin, and secret to success.

Al-Qarmūṭ, the editor of *ʿIqd al-jumān*, pointed out that al-ʿAynī cited this marginal annotation from al-Maqrīzī's chronicle, *al-Sulūk*, and mentioned that "some of them say" (*dhakara baʿḍuhum*). For example, al-ʿAynī describes, in the margin, the career of Fatḥ Allāh's Jewish grandfather, who came to Cairo from Tabrīz and who advanced through the favor of an amir (superscript A). These descriptions are obviously a *verbatim* copy from *al-Sulūk*. Thereafter, al-ʿAynī criticizes his source for reporting that Fatḥ Allāh was a descendant of the Prophet David (superscript B) and was appointed head secretary despite another candidate's attempt to procure this position with a bribe (superscript C). Rather, al-ʿAynī asserts that Fatḥ Allāh was favored by the sultan because he drank his urine for medical examinations. Further, al-ʿAynī discredits his informant, al-Maqrīzī, for relating such a false story, and insists that he was a necromancer.[15] Needless to say, al-ʿAynī may have disparaged al-Maqrīzī and his patron Fatḥ Allāh because of a personal rivalry or animosity toward al-Maqrīzī.[16]

However, it is also noteworthy that these three texts share the basic details about Fatḥ Allāh's appointment. Massoud postulated that al-Maqrīzī often borrowed from al-ʿAynī, and in this case, Massoud's postulation is probably correct, although it must be stressed that al-Maqrīzī's reference was restricted to *Taʾrīkh al-Badr*, and did not relate to *ʿIqd al-jumān*.

To summarize, we classify the works of these two historians' chronologically, as follows: al-ʿAynī wrote his minor chronicle *Taʾrīkh al-Badr* after 799/1396. Then al-Maqrīzī wrote *al-Sulūk*, presumably citing *Taʾrīkh al-Badr*. Later, after 838/1434, al-ʿAynī completed *ʿIqd al-jumān*, in which he refers to *al-Sulūk*. The relationship between these two historians may have occurred sequentially, like moves in a chess game, rather than simultaneously.

---

14 Ibn Taghrī Birdī, *al-Manhal al-ṣāfī* viii, 375–7.

15 Al-ʿAynī, *ʿIqd al-jumān* ii, 574.

16 About the rivalry and animosity between these two historians, see Broadbridge, Academic rivalry.

TABLE 8.8 Appointment of Fatḥ Allāh b. Nafīs in 801/1399

MS Ar. 1544, fol. 14[a]
وفي يوم الاثنين الحادي عشر من جمادى الأولى، خلع على القاضي فتح الله رئيس الأطباء واستقر كاتب الشريف عوضا عن القاضي بدر الدين محمود السراي بحكم وفاته.
MS A2911/19, fols. 16[b]–17[a] (in the margin)
وفي يوم الاثنين الحادي عشر من جمادى الأولى خلع على القاضي فتح الله رئيس الأطباء ابن معتصم بن نفيس الداودي. // واستقر كاتب السر عوضا عن القاضي بدر الدين محمود السراي بحكم وفاته.   **(وكان نفيس يهوديا قدم من تبريز في أيام الملك الناصر حسن بن الناصر محمد بن قلاون إلى القاهرة، واختص بالأمير شيخون العمري وطيبه، وكان يركب بغل بخف ومهماز وهو على اليهودية، ثم إنه أسلم على يد السلطان حسن، وولد فتح الله بتبريز وقدم على جده، وكفله عمه بديع بن نفيس، وقد مات أبوه وهو طفل ونشأ واشتغل بالطب إلى أن ولي رئاسة الأطباء بعد موت علاء الدين ابن صغير واختص بالملك الظاهر برقوق حتى ولاه كتابة السر**(A)، وذكر بعضهم في تاريخه في ترجمته شيئين، أظن أنهما كذب أحدهما قوله **أن جده نفيس من أولاد نبي الله داود عليه السلام**(B)، وهذا كذب صريح لطول المدة جدا، **والثاني أن مترجمه قال بذلوا في كتابة السر قنطارا من الذهب، فلم يرض به الظاهر وولي فتح الله**(C)، وهذا الآخر كذب أو قريب من الكذب، والذي أكد هذين الشيئين من إلزام فتح الله وخواصه، وكان يضرب عنده الرمل ويحكي له المغيبات. والذي سمعت من الناس أن سبب اختيار الظاهر إياه لهذه الوظيفة، أنه مرض مرة واجتمع الأطباء عنده ودفعوا له قارورة، فنظروا فيها ووقع الاختلاف بينهم وتوهم الظاهر توهما فاحشا، وأخذ فتح الله القارورة وشرب ما فيها من البول، فحفظ الظاهر منه ذلك وولاه كتابة السر والله أعلم بالأمور.)
Al-Maqrīzī, *al-Sulūk*, iii, 927
وفي يوم الاثنين حادي عشره، استدعى الرئيس فتح الدين فتح الله ابن معتصم بن نفيس الداودي—رئيس الأطباء—وخلع عليه، واستقر في كتابة السر عوضا عن بدر الدين محمود الكلستاني بحكم وفاته.

TABLE 8.8 Appointment of Fatḥ Allāh b. Nafīs in 801/1399 (*cont.*)

وفتح الله هذا كان جده نفيس يهوديا[A] من أولاد نبي الله داود عليه السلام[B]، فقدم من توريز في أيام الملك الناصر حسن بن محمد بن قلاون إلى القاهرة، واختص بالأمير شيخو العمري وطبّبه، وصار يركب بغلة بخف ومهماز، وهو على اليهودية. ثم أنه أسلم على يد السلطان حسن، وولد فتح الله بتوريز وقدم على جده، فكفله عمه بديع بن نفيس، وقد مات أبوه وهو طفل، ونشأ وعانى الطب إلى أن ولي رئاسة الأطباء بعد موت شيخنا علاء الدين علي ابن صغير، واختص بالملك الظاهر، فولاه كتابة السر [A]بعدما سئل فيها بقنطار من ذهب، فأعرض عنه، واختار فتح الله[C]، مع علمه ببعده عن معرفة صناعة الإنشاء، وقال "أنا أعلّمه" فباشر ذلك، وشكره الناس.

6 Conclusion

How can we evaluate these three holograph manuscripts of al-ʿAynī? From a historiographical point of view, al-ʿAynī's minor chronicle, *Taʾrīkh al-Badr*, deserves more attention. Since MS A2911/A18 is not *ʿIqd al-jumān* but an excerpt of it, as table 8.1 shows, the part(s) covering the period from 746/1345–6 to 798/1395–6 of *ʿIqd al-jumān* remain(s) unknown. Because copies covering this period have not yet been found, to reconstruct the missing part of volume 18 of *ʿIqd al-jumān*, if there was one, it is necessary to consult both the proto-text of *ʿIqd al-jumān* (that is, *Taʾrīkh al-Badr*), and an excerpt of *ʿIqd al-jumān*.

From a codicological point of view, MS Arabe 1544 has specific characteristics. It must be a draft containing the text of *Taʾrīkh al-Badr*. It was copied by Shihāb al-Dīn first, and then written by al-ʿAynī himself, and thereafter supplemented by Shihāb al-Dīn again. Shihāb al-Dīn was a minor historian whose biography does not appear in any biographical dictionaries. In fact, he was not only a copyist, but also the author of his own chronicle entitled *al-Taʾrīkh al-Shihābī wa-l-qamar*. Based on its descriptions, we can deduce that his chronicle was written after he copied *Taʾrīkh al-Badr*.[17] If this is the case, then who is the author of MS Arabe 1544? We could argue that Shihāb al-Dīn was a co-author of this manuscript. This doubly holograph manuscript is a unique example of the writing history of this era.

17 About Shihāb al-Dīn's life and chronicle, see Nakamachi, Life.

Bibliography

Primary Sources

Al-ʿAynī, Maḥmūd, *ʿIqd al-jumān fī taʾrīkh ahl al-zamān*, ed. ʿA. al-R. al-Ṭanṭāwī l-Qarmūṭ, 2 vols., Cairo 1985–9.

Ibn Taghrī Birdī, *al-Manhal al-ṣāfī wa-l-mustawfī baʿd al-Wāfī*, ed. M.M. Amīn, 12 vols., Cairo 1985–2006.

Al-Maqrīzī, *al-Sulūk li-maʿrifat duwal al-mulūk*, vol. 3, ed. S. ʿA. al-F. ʿĀshūr, Cairo 1972.

Al-Sakhāwī, *al-Ḍawʾ al-lāmiʿ li-ahl al-qarn al-tāsiʿ*, 12 vols., Beirut n.d.

Secondary Sources

Broadbridge, A.F., Academic rivalry and the patronage system in fifteenth-century Egypt: al-ʿAynī, al-Maqrīzī, and Ibn Hajar al-ʿAsqalānī, in *Mamlūk Studies Review* 3 (1999), 85–107.

De Slane, M., *Catalogue des manuscrits arabes de la Bibliothèque nationale*, Paris 1883.

Karatay, F.E., *Topkapı Sarayı Müzesi Kütüphanesi Arapça Yazmalar Kataloğu*, vol. 3, Istanbul 1966.

Little, D.P., A comparison of al-Maqrīzī and al-ʿAynī as historians of contemporary events, in *Mamlūk Studies Review* 7, no. 2 (2003), 205–15.

Little, D.P., *An introduction to Mamluk historiography: An analysis of Arabic annalistic and biographical sources for the reign of al-Malik an-Nāṣir Muḥammad ibn Qalāʾūn*, Wiesbaden 1970.

Massoud, S.G., *The Chronicles and annalistic sources of the early Mamlūk Circassian period*, Leiden 2007.

Nakamachi, N., A historiographical analysis of the four chronicles attributed to Badr al-Dīn al-ʿAynī, in S. Conermann and T. Miura (eds.), *Studies on the history and culture of the Mamluk Sultanate (1250–1517). Proceedings of the First German-Japanese Workshop held at Tokyo, November 5–6, 2016*, Göttingen, forthcoming.

Nakamachi, N., Al-ʿAynī's chronicles as a source for the Bahrī Mamluk period, in *Orient* 40 (2005), 140–71.

Nakamachi, N., Life in the margins: Shihāb al-Dīn Aḥmad al-ʿAynī, a non-elite intellectual in the Mamluk period, in *Orient* 48 (2013), 95–112.

Spies, O., *Beiträge zur arabischen Literaturgeschichte*, Leipzig 1932.

CHAPTER 9

Textual Criticism of the Manuscripts of Ibn Khaldūn's *Autobiography*

Retsu Hashizume

1 Introduction[1]

Several methods are used to identify whether a certain manuscript is, in fact, a holograph. Although the process of revising a given edition of a manuscript and elucidating its lineage is indispensable, in the field of Arabic textual criticism, this is often not undertaken. The edition of Ibn Khaldūn's *Autobiography* (hereafter *al-Taʿrīf*) revised by Muḥammad Ibn Tāwīt is a clear example. The present article examines the holograph of Ibn Khaldūn's autobiography and emphasizes the need to focus on the marginal notes of the manuscripts. Since *al-Taʿrīf* and, of course, *al-Muqaddima*, constitute a part of Ibn Khaldūn's voluminous work, *al-ʿIbar*, the three works should be regarded as a single work and each of these should be examined comprehensively.[2] However, there is not enough material on *al-Muqaddima* and *al-ʿIbar* at my availability. Therefore, I will only focus on *al-Taʿrīf* in this study. In addition, I not only attempt to ascertain which is Ibn Khaldūn's holograph of *al-Taʿrīf*, but I also clearly describe his overall writing activity, because this enables us to understand the interrelationship between the surviving manuscripts of *al-Taʿrīf*, *al-Muqaddima*, and *al-ʿIbar*. Furthermore, this examination elucidates Ibn Khaldūn's intellectual activity as a polestar in the study of Islamic history.[3]

Information on the manuscripts of *al-Taʿrīf* used for this study is provided in the *List of manuscripts* at the end of this chapter. This information is based on the introduction of Ibn Tāwīt's edition as well as on my own research. Of particular importance are MS Ayasofya 3200 (hereafter *Ayasofya*) and MS Ahmet III 2924/13–14 (hereafter *Ẓāhirī*).

1 This work was supported by the Japan Society for the Promotion of Science, KAKENHI Grant no. 24720319.
2 Regarding his three works, see the bibliography.
3 On Ibn Khaldūn's intellectual activity, see Fischel, *Ibn Khaldūn and Tamerlane*; Fischel, *Ibn Khaldūn in Egypt*; Mahdi, *Ibn Khaldûn's Philosophy*.

 | DOI:10.1163/9789004413177_010

2 The Lineage of the *al-Taʿrīf* Manuscripts According to Ibn Tāwīt

Diagram 9.1 presents the lineage of *al-Taʿrīf* manuscripts, based on Ibn Tāwīt's conclusion,[4] including the manuscripts that he utilized, which are enumerated in the *List of manuscripts*. A closer examination of the lineage reveals the ramified process of *al-Taʿrīf*. First, Ibn Khaldūn wrote the original manuscript (*nuskhat al-umm*); this was followed by Archetype 1, which is the copy of the early version of *al-Taʿrīf* (*farʿ qadīm*) created from the original. Second, five manuscripts were copied from Archetype 1 while Archetype 2, which is the copy of the middle version (*farʿ mutawassiṭ*) of *al-Taʿrīf*, was simultaneously made from Archetype 1 (although Ibn Tāwīt did not indicate that Ibn Khaldūn made additions and deletions during this process). Third, three manuscripts were copied from Archetype 2, while Archetype 3, which is the copy of the late version (*farʿ ḥadīth*) of *al-Taʿrīf*, was established on the basis of Archetype 2.[5] Finally, two manuscripts were copied from Archetype 3, while four manuscripts were copied from *Ayasofya*.[6]

According to Ibn Tāwīt, *al-ʿIbar* was derived from three archetypes. The first archetype[7] is the copy presented to the Ḥafṣid ruler—Abū l-ʿAbbās Aḥmad b. Muḥammad al-Mustanṣir (r. 772–96/1370–94)—before Ibn Khaldūn left for Egypt on 15 Shaʿbān 784/24 October 1382 (hereafter the *Ḥafṣī Copy*).[8] The second archetype (*nuskha ukhrā*) is the book that Ibn Khaldūn gave as a gift to the Mamlūk sultan al-Ẓāhir Barqūq (r. 784–91/1382–9, 792–801/1389–99) (hereafter the *Ẓāhirī Copy*).[9] Finally, the third archetype (*nuskha thālitha*) is the copy donated as a *waqf* to the Qarawiyyīn Mosque in Fez during the reign of the Marinid ruler, Abū Fāris ʿAbd al-ʿAzīz (r. 796–9/1394–7) on 799/1396–7 (hereafter the *Qarawiyyīn Copy*).

---

4 See Ibn Tāwīt's explanation and diagram of the manuscripts' lineage in *al-Taʿrīf* 5 (*hā*)-17 (*yāʾ zāy*) of the introduction.

5 In this case as well, Ibn Tāwīt did not indicate whether or not Ibn Khaldūn made any additions or deletions.

6 Regarding this argument, see ibid.

7 According to Ibn Tāwīt, this exemplar is *al-nuskha al-ūlā min kitābihi li-Abī l-ʿAbbās al-Ḥafṣī malik Tūnis* (the first copy copied from Ibn Khaldūn's book for Abū l-ʿAbbās al-Ḥafṣī).

8 Ibn Khaldūn, *al-Taʿrīf* 233, 241, 245. Cf. Cheikha, Los manuscritos 356. Although the details are unclear, Cheikha states that the book presented to the Ḥafṣid ruler was lost after it was used for the *Būlāq* edition.

9 It is likely that the *Ẓāhirī* copy was given to Barqūq during his second reign (792–801/1389–99) since the year written on the last folio of *Ẓāhirī* is 797/1394–5. However, the exact date of the gift is unknown. In 797/1394–5 al-Ẓāhir Barqūq ousted Ibn Khaldūn from public office (Ibn Khaldūn, *al-Taʿrīf* 331, 347).

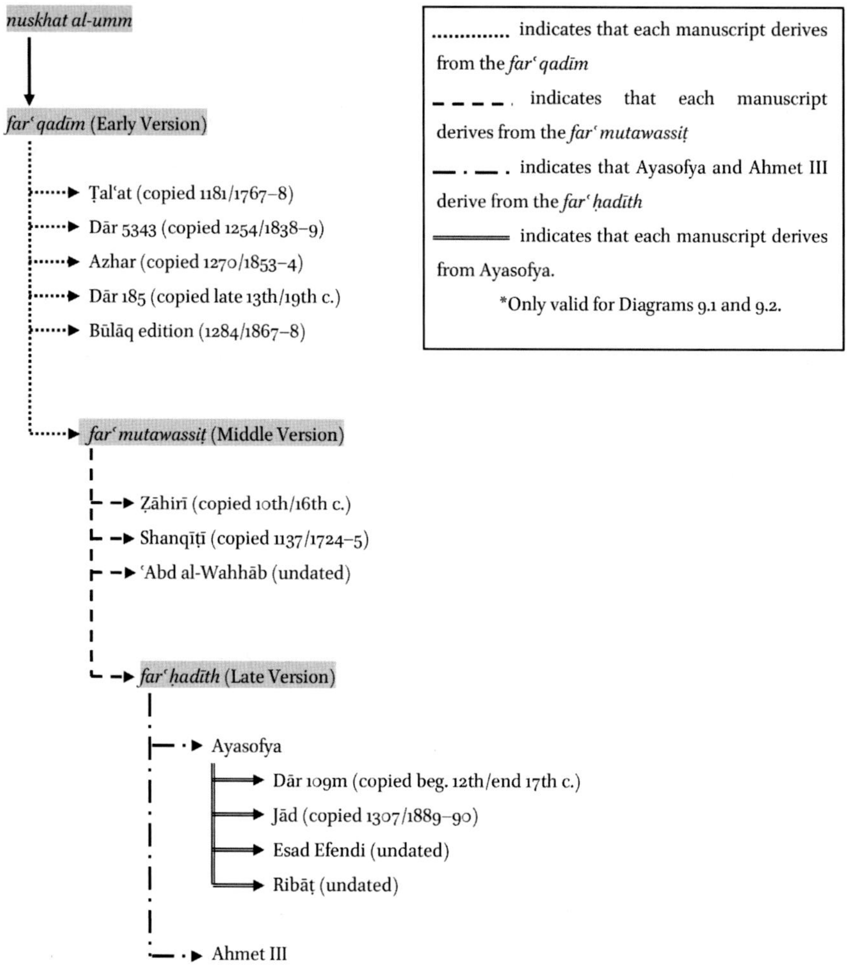

DIAGRAM 9.1 Lineage of *al-Ta'rīf* manuscripts based on Ibn Tāwīt's conclusion

Among these three archetypes, it is assumed that the *Ẓāhirī Copy* is related to the *Ẓāhirī* manuscripts housed in the TSMK (MS Ahmet III 2924). The existence of the copies corresponding to the other two archetypes has not yet been confirmed.[10] Although I cannot substantiate the validity of Ibn Tāwīt's opin-

10 According to Prof. Kentaro Sato at Hokkaido University, Ibn Khaldūn donated several manuscripts of *al-'Ibar* as a *waqf* in 799/1396–7 to the Qarawiyyīn Mosque in Fez; these can still be found in the library of this institution. However, the presence of manuscripts of *al-Ta'rīf* cannot be confirmed by his research conducted in February 2014. In addition, Rosenthal reported that the *Muqaddima* manuscript was lost (Ibn Khaldūn, *The Muqaddimah* i, xciii).

ion, his conclusion has so far to be accepted since there is no alternative. As described in diagram 9.1, Ibn Tāwīt mentions that the extant manuscripts of *al-Taʿrīf* are divided into three versions, which are related to the three aforementioned archetypes of *al-ʿIbar*. Furthermore, Ibn Tāwīt states that manuscripts of *al-Taʿrīf* can be classified into the early version derived from the *Ḥafṣī Copy* and the late version derived from the draft in which Ibn Khaldūn made additions and deletions several months before his death (hereafter the *Ibn Khaldūn's Draft*).

However, there is no mention that *Ibn Khaldūn's Draft* is, in fact, the *Qarawiyyīn Copy* nor does Ibn Tāwīt refer to Archetype 2. According to diagram 9.1, it is clear that the *Ẓāhirī Copy* is included among the manuscripts of Archetype 2,[11] but it is not clear whether or not the *Qarawiyyīn Copy* is included among Archetype 2 or 3, since Ibn Tāwīt does not refer to it at all.

I believe that it may not be included among the manuscripts of Archetype 3 because the *Qarawiyyīn Copy* was made in 799/1396–7 and Archetype 3 can be regarded as *Ibn Khaldūn's Draft* (although Ibn Tāwīt did not say so explicitly in his diagram). On the other hand, it is not clear whether the *Qarawiyyīn Copy* is included in Archetype 2 and whether its contents correspond to the *Ẓāhirī Copy*. Thus, further investigation is necessary.

We can summarize this as follows:

Archetype 1 of *al-Taʿrīf*: *Ḥafṣī Copy*
Archetype 2: unknown (*Ẓāhirī Copy*? or *Qarawiyyīn Copy*?)
Archetype 3: *Ibn Khaldūn's Draft*

Furthermore, Ibn Tāwīt states that all the manuscripts derive from the first original version (*umm ūlā*)—the *Ḥafṣī Copy*. Conversely, the new manuscript (*aṣl ḥadīth*) corresponds to *Ibn Khaldūn's Draft*, which includes additions and deletions made by Ibn Khaldūn himself toward the end of his life.[12] Therefore, Ibn Tāwīt states that in order to create an accurate edition of *al-Taʿrīf*, it is necessary to base it on the new manuscript included in the late version.[13]

11 Judging from the last folio of the *Ẓāhirī*, the end point of the middle version of *al-Taʿrīf*'s content is the same as the early version (see figs. 9.1–9.3). That is, both versions include contents that correspond to pages 1–278 of Ibn Tāwīt's edition. Although he asserts that the middle version is different from the late version because it does not include Ibn al-Khaṭīb's letters (pp. 155–209 in the edition), similarly, the early version does not include these letters. Thus, we must determine whether it is correct to classify *al-Taʿrīf* manuscripts into these two versions.

12 *Al-Taʿrīf* 8(*ḥāʾ*): *wa-l-aṣl al-ḥadīth min hādhihi l-uṣūl huwa lladhī baqiya bayna yaday Ibn Khaldūn ḥattā l-ayyām al-akhīra min ḥayātihi.*

13 See diagram 9.2 for more details.

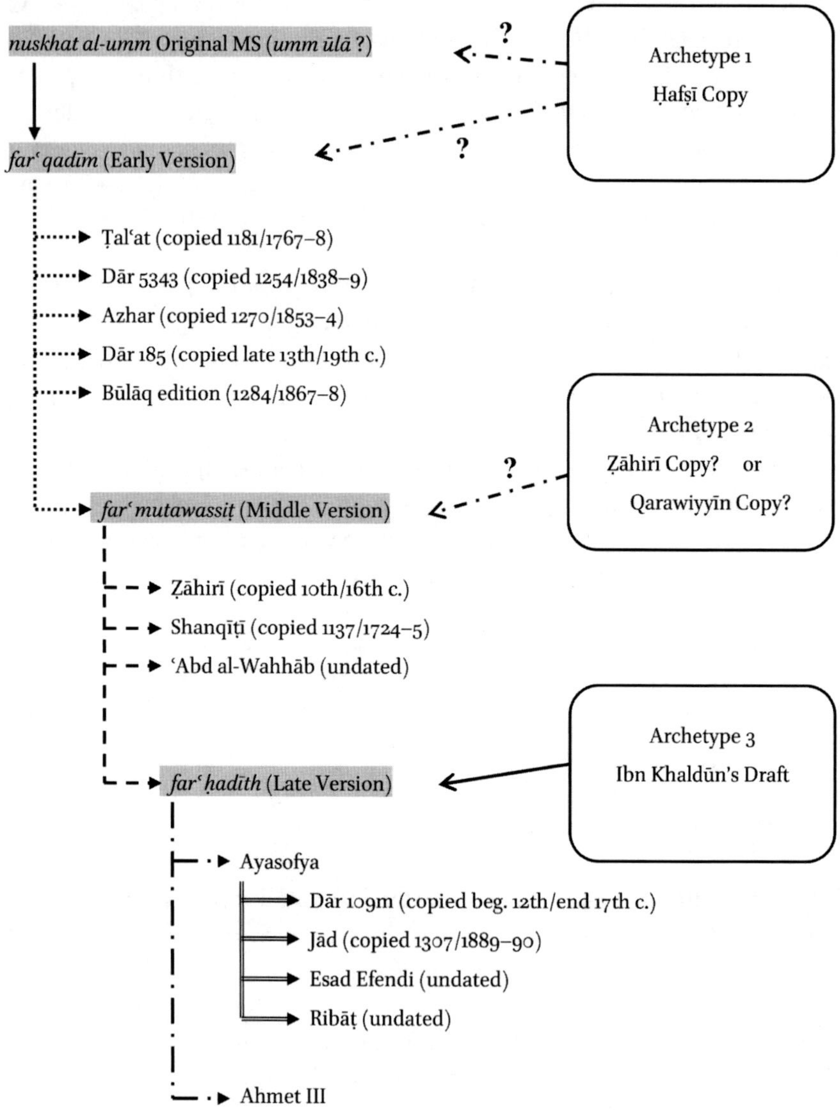

DIAGRAM 9.2 Lineage of *al-Taʿrīf* manuscripts according to the archetypes

3 The Lineage of the *al-Taʿrīf* Manuscripts

According to Ibn Tāwīt, the original manuscript exists, though the archetypes of each version have not been identified. In his opinion, all the manuscripts of *al-Taʿrīf* are derived from the original, which is the *Ḥafṣī Copy*. However, he does not indicate which manuscript is the *Ḥafṣī Copy* (*nuskha umm, umm ūlā* or *farʿ qadīm*).[14]

In addition, Ibn Tāwīt does not indicate which manuscripts correspond to the Archetypes 2 and 3, which he believes were gifts for the rulers (al-Ẓāhir Barqūq and Abū Fāris). If his assumption is correct, then we must accept the idea that Ibn Khaldūn wrote the archetype of the newer version based on the book housed in the ruler's library. However, it is unlikely that Ibn Khaldūn created a new archetype in such a procedure, rather it is possible that there was one identical copy or a draft on which the gift copy was based. Therefore, we may reasonably conclude that Ibn Tāwīt lacked the concept of a draft or fair copy.

Diagram 9.3 presents the lineage of manuscripts of *al-Taʿrīf* based on my study. The difference between this diagram and that of Ibn Tāwīt is the position of *Ibn Khaldūn's Draft*.[15] In my opinion, *Ibn Khaldūn's Draft* is the original, from which Ibn Khaldūn prepared fair complimentary copies (the *Ḥafṣī Copy*, the *Ẓāhirī Copy*, and the *Qarawiyyīn Copy*). This conclusion is much more reasonable than assuming that Ibn Khaldūn made a copy from the manuscript that he gave away as a gift. Moreover, since Ibn Khaldūn frequently modified his text by adding or omitting words and sentences, we assume that there should be some marginal notes in the draft of *al-Taʿrīf* (or *al-ʿIbar*). Moreover, he could not have presented the manuscripts as gifts if they had marginal notes. Therefore, it is valid to conclude that Ibn Khaldūn prepared his fair copies from his personal draft—*Ibn Khaldūn's Draft*.

Based on this conclusion, diagram 9.3 shows that the *Ḥafṣī Copy*, the *Ẓāhirī Copy*, and the *Qarawiyyīn Copy*, as well as all the other manuscripts, were copied from *Ibn Khaldūn's Draft*. In other words, although *Ibn Khaldūn's Draft* is a unique archetype, its contents have been gradually changed according to Ibn Khaldūn's marginal notes.

In addition to Ibn Tāwīt's edition, there are twelve duplicates of the manuscripts of *al-Taʿrīf*: *Ayasofya, Ahmet III, Dār 109 mīm, Esad Efendi, Ṭalʿat, Azhar, Dār 185, Dār 5343, Būlāq,* BN, *Zakiyya*, and *Nuruosmaniye*. Unfortunately, I was

---

14 See diagram 9.2.

15 Compare diagrams 9.2 and 9.3.

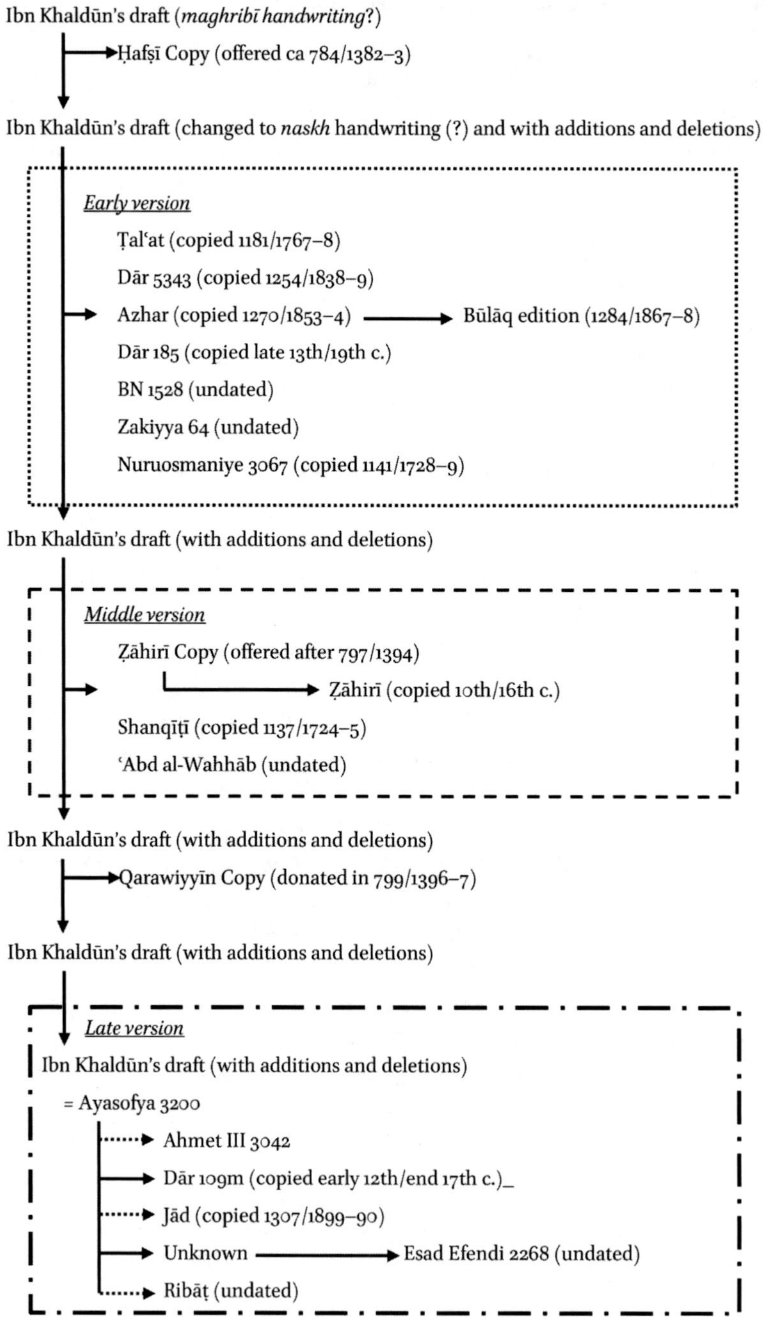

*The line shape of each frame corresponds to each of the three versions as envisaged by Ibn Tāwīt.

DIAGRAM 9.3 Lineage of the *al-Taʿrīf* manuscripts according to Hashizume

not able to analyze manuscripts of *al-Taʿrīf* that Ibn Tāwīt classified as belonging to the middle version.[16]

For this study, I conducted a comparative investigation between the manuscripts of the early and late versions and discovered certain differences between them. Four manuscripts (*Ayasofya, Ahmet III, Dār 109 mīm*, and *Esad Efendi*) are classified as the late version. Conversely, the remaining eight manuscripts (*Ṭalʿat, Azhar, Dār 185, Dār 5343, Būlāq*, BN, *Zakiyya*, and *Nuruosmaniye*) are classified as the early version. These manuscripts cover the period of Ibn Khaldūn's career until his dismissal as the supervisor of Baybars' *Khānqāh* in the year 790/1389, which corresponds to pages 1–278 in the edition. In the process of my research, I discovered the BN, *Zakiyya*, and *Nuruosmaniye* manuscripts, which are not listed in the edition.

As described above, the classification of these versions corresponds to their contents. For comparison, I selected two manuscripts (*Ṭalʿat* and BN) from the early version and three manuscripts (*Ayasofya, Esad Efendi*, and *Dār 109 mīm*) from the late version. Since *Ayasofya* is used in the comparison, it is necessary to provide a reason for emphasizing this particular manuscript. Ibn Tāwīt concludes that the *Ayasofya* is a holograph of *al-Taʿrīf*, based only on the notes from the title pages.[17] However, I believe his conclusion is ill-founded, since these notes are not supported by other evidence. This raises the question of whether there is any other basis on which to judge the *Ayasofya* as a holograph.

The *Ayasofya* includes numerous marginal notes,[18] which are useful for comparing the *al-Taʿrīf* manuscripts. The similarities in the handwriting lead us to conclude that a majority of these notes appear to be written by the same person who composed the main body of *Ayasofya*. According to Fischel, some marginal notes in the *Ayasofya* were written by Ibn Khaldūn himself.[19]

At this point, let us examine four manuscripts (*Ṭalʿat*, BN, *Esad Efendi*, and *Dār 109 mīm*) based on the marginal notes of the *Ayasofya*. The scope of the examination is as follows:

16 Since the TSMK was closed in summer 2013, I was not able to see *Ahmet III* and *Ẓāhirī* (considered as being part of the middle version) housed in the library. In Spring 2017, I was finally able to check both manuscripts but I am still unable to solve a problem related to an argument where these manuscripts are included.

17 See figs. 9.4 and 9.5. There are three notes in a different handwriting; these suggest that this manuscript was written by Ibn Khaldūn himself. Fig. 9.4: *Kitāb riḥlat li-Ibn Khaldūn bi-khaṭṭihi* and *müellif hattıladır*; fig. 9.5: *riḥlat Ibn Khaldūn bi-khaṭṭihi raḥimahu llāh taʿālā*.

18 See figs. 9.6, 9.7, 9.8, 9.16.

19 Cf. Fischel, *Ibn Khaldūn and Tamerlane*, 7–12. See figs. 9.7 and 9.8: long marginal note in *Ayasofya*, fols. 11^b–12^a.

Ayasofya: fols. 1^b–22^a; 62^a–63^a;
Ṭalʿat: fols. 160^b–174^a; 195^b–196^a;
BN: fols. 3^b–15^b; 34^b–36^a;
Esad Efendi: fols. 1^a–23^b; 68^b–69^a;
Dār 109 mīm: pp. 1–36; 107.

As a result of my comparison of the contents of these folios, a majority of the marginal notes in the *Ayasofya* are reflected in *Ṭalʿat*, BN, and *Dār 109 mīm* manuscripts. *Dār 109 mīm* belongs to the late version and thus, it is similar to *Ayasofya*.[20] However, the marginal indications in the *Ayasofya* (which is classified as the late version) are reflected in the main body of *Ṭalʿat* and BN (belonging to the early version);[21] this indicates a strong possibility that *Ayasofya* is the copy from which both manuscripts were made. In other words, it is quite possible that the *Ayasofya* corresponds to *Ibn Khaldūn's Draft* from which *Ṭalʿat* and BN (or their exemplars) were directly copied.

If the indications in the margins of the *Ayasofya* were written after the archetype of the early version was copied, then it would be almost impossible for these indications to be reflected in the main body of *Ṭalʿat* and BN (or their exemplars). In addition, if these manuscripts or the copies from which they were made were copied from the *Ayasofya* toward the end of Ibn Khaldūn's life (or even after his death), then we cannot explain why both manuscripts do not include all the contents of *Ayasofya*.

As stated earlier, *Esad Efendi* belongs to the late version. However, it does not reflect many of the marginal emendations in the *Ayasofya*[22] (among 86 emendations in *Ayasofya*, 26 are not reflected in *Esad Efendi*).[23] This leads us to inquire if there is a direct relationship between the *Esad Efendi* and *Ayasofya* manuscripts. In addition, in the bottom-left margin of *Ayasofya* (fol. 14^a),[24] there is evidence that the sentence "*wa-dhahaba bi-l-aʿyān wa-l-ṣudūr wa-jamīʿ*

20 Compare figs. 9.6 and 9.9–9.12. In fig. 9.6, there are two indications of additions and deletions in the margins of the *Ayasofya* fol. 1^b. Then, see figs. 9.9–9.10. We can see that the sentence '*wa-fīhim Wāʾil hādhā*' is added in the *Dār* 109 m, fol. 2^a and that the sentence '*intahā kalām Ibn Ḥazm … wa-kānat lahum akhbār*' is deleted in the *Dār 109 mīm* p. 2 according to a marginal indication in the *Ayasofya*. In fig. 9.14 (*Esad Efendi*, fol. 2^a), we can see the same difference.

21 See figs. 9.11 (BN) and 9.12–9.13 (*Ṭalʿat*). We can see that the scribes of these manuscripts added the sentence '*wa fīhim Wāʾil hādhā*' and deleted the sentence '*intahā kalām Ibn Ḥazm … wa-kānat lahum akhbār*,' according to marginal indications in the *Ayasofya*.

22 Compare figs. 9.8 and 9.15. The *Esad Efendi* does not indicate the addition of a long marginal note in the *Ayasofya* fols. 11^b–12^a.

23 This result is based on a comparison of the two manuscripts (*Ayasofya*: fols. 1^b–22^a; 62^a–63^a.; *Esad Efendi*: fols. 1^a–23^b; 68^b–69^a).

24 See fig. 9.16.

al-mashyakha" was added. *Esad Efendi* has this sentence, with the exception of the last word (*al-mashyakha*).[25] Based on these two facts, we can conclude that *Esad Efendi* was not copied directly from the *Ayasofya*. In the case of the latter, it is unlikely that the scribe would have failed to copy this explicit indication. Rather, there is at least an intermediate manuscript between the *Ayasofya* and *Esad Efendi*. When *Esad Efendi* was copied from this intermediate manuscript, the scribe may have mistakenly omitted the word *al-mashyakha*. However, since we have not yet discovered this intermediate manuscript, this argument requires further consideration.

According to the aforementioned findings, we can make two conclusions: (1) The *Ayasofya* must be identified as *Ibn Khaldūn's Draft* (holograph), in which he added and deleted certain words and sentences; (2) Ibn Khaldūn made gift copies, i.e., the archetype of each version, from this draft.[26]

4 A Problem of Handwriting Style

Although we have concluded that the *Ayasofya* is a holograph, as described above, one issue remains: his handwriting style. Ibn Khaldūn was born and educated in the Maghrib, so it is believed that his style of handwriting was originally *maghribī*. However, the *Ayasofya* is written in *naskh*.[27] I propose that Ibn Khaldūn could write in *naskh* because, according to his autobiography, he was able to copy a *qaṣīda*, written in *maghribī*, in a *naskh* style so that they (al-Ẓāhir Barqūq and his entourage) could read it easily.[28] Therefore, we may reasonably conclude that he could write in a *naskh* style[29] and, if we assume that this conclusion is correct, we can state that Ibn Khaldūn wrote in *naskh* during his time in Egypt. However, this assumption is not conclusive, since it is based on indirect evidence.[30] Thus, there is room for further investigation.[31]

---

25 See fig. 9.17.

26 See diagram 9.3 for more details.

27 It is a common style of handwriting in the eastern Islamic world, sometimes called *mashriqī*, see the introduction to this volume pp. 13–4, and this chapter, n. 28.

28 Ibn Khaldūn, *al-Taʿrīf* 271: *adhina lī fī naskh al-qaṣīda al-madhkūra bi-l-khaṭṭ al-mashriqī li-tashul qirāʾatuhā ʿalayhim fa-faʿaltu dhālika.*

29 In this case, Rosenthal notes that Ibn Khaldūn "presumably did not do the actual copying himself." However, since Ibn Khaldūn's sentence is written in the first person, I believe that he must have done this himself. Cf. Ibn Khaldūn, *The Muqaddimah* i, xcv–xcvi.

30 Ibid.; Cheikha, Los manuscritos 356, 358–9. They point out that Ibn Khaldūn signed an *ijāza* regarding the qualification to transmit his works for his pupil Ibn Ḥajar who inserted it in his *al-Tadhkirat al-jadīda*; and this signature is in *maghribī* script. Thus, it is possible that Ibn Khaldūn wrote in *maghribī* script routinely.

31 If we are allowed to consider a book that was written from Ibn Khaldūn's dictation or tran-

5 Conclusion

In this study I focus on the issues of Ibn Tāwīt's understanding and use of the manuscripts of *al-Taʿrīf* to present an alternative viewpoint that identifies the *Ayasofya* as a holograph. In addition, I demonstrate a more valid understanding of the lineage of the manuscripts of *al-Taʿrīf*, based on a comparative investigation between them.

Ibn Tāwīt, the author of the revised edition of *al-Taʿrīf*, concluded, based only on the notes of the title page, that the *Ayasofya* is a holograph of *al-Taʿrīf*. In contrast, through the comparative study of the manuscripts of *al-Taʿrīf* and by focusing on the marginal notes in the *Ayasofya*, I demonstrate that the *Ayasofya* is an archetype of all the other manuscripts of *al-Taʿrīf* and that it is a holograph, because those indications were reflected in some form or other in all the subsequent manuscripts of *al-Taʿrīf*. Moreover this study helps us to understand that Ibn Khaldūn kept the draft of *al-Taʿrīf* (or *al-ʿIbar*) at hand, the text of which he frequently modified, and had fair gift copies made from it. I believe that the draft in question must be identified with the *Ayasofya*. Nevertheless, because I was not able to consider all of the manuscripts of *al-Taʿrīf* (of course including *al-ʿIbar* and *al-Muqaddima*), future studies should focus on the manuscripts of the three works (*al-Muqaddima*, *al-ʿIbar*, and *al-Taʿrīf*) to clarify the issue of Ibn Khaldūn's holographs in a broader perspective.

6 List of the Manuscripts of *al-Taʿrīf* with Their Abbreviations

Ayasofya
Manuscript in the Süleymaniye Library, Ayasofya 3200, 83 fols. 25.9 cm × 18.5 cm, 25, 29 lines, *naskh*. It is separated from the manuscript of *al-ʿIbar* and divided into two parts because of the difference in handwriting and the number of lines per folio. The first part consists of fols. 1^b–40^b, 49^a–67^b, while the second part includes the remainder. Based on the handwriting, Ibn Tāwīt assumed that the scribe of the second part is ʿAbdallāh b. Ḥasan b. al-Fakhkhār, who was the scribe of one of the *Muqaddima* manuscripts (MS Yeni Cami 888 in the Süleymaniye Library). However, Ibn Tāwīt's view on the scribe of the first part seems to be uncertain; he states that the scribe was unknown but revises the edition of *al-Taʿrīf* based on the *Ayasofya* as Ibn Khaldūn's holograph. Thus,

scribed by a certain scribe or pupil from his draft written in *maghribī* script (under his supervision) to be a holograph, then it seems reasonable to conclude that the *Ayasofya* is Ibn Khaldūn's holograph.

his statement regarding the manuscripts of *al-Taʿrīf* in his introduction of the edition is extremely dubious.

Ahmet III

Manuscript in the TSMK, Ahmet III 3042/4, 51 fols., 32×51.5cm, 35 lines, n.d., *naskh*. The information about this manuscript offered by Ibn Tāwīt (*al-Taʿrīf yāʾ-yāʾ*) is in all probability wrong; I based this on the folio size and the fact that there is no information about the manuscript with the classifying number "Ahmet 3042/4" in Karatay's catalogue. The correct information about the manuscript, including Ibn Khaldūn's autobiography, is (according to my direct examination of the manuscripts at the TSMK in Spring 2017) the following: Ahmet 3042/b–1–a, fols. 148^{b}–198^{a}, 31.5×22cm, 35 lines (cf. Karatay, *Topkapı* 382, no. 5885).

Ahmet III is attached to the end of the manuscript of *al-ʿIbar*. Ibn Tāwīt assumed that the scribe is Ibn al-Fakhkhār, as mentioned above, and that *Ahmet III* is newer than the *Ayasofya*, since it includes the letter sent from al-Ẓāhir Barqūq to the Ḥafṣid Abū l-ʿAbbās. According to Ibn Tāwīt, he revised the edition of *al-Taʿrīf* on the basis of these two manuscripts.

Dār 109 mīm

Manuscript in the Dār al-Kutub al-Miṣriyya, Taʾrīkh 109 mīm, fols. 1^{a}–75^{b}, 23×17cm, 31 lines, *taʿlīq* (*fārsī*). It was transcribed at the beginning of the twelfth/end of the eighteenth century. Ibn Tāwīt assumed that it is the manuscript derived from the *Ayasofya*, since it shares the same title. Furthermore, it was not used to revise the edition of *al-Taʿrīf* due to the scribe's inability to use Arabic.

Jād (not investigated yet)

Manuscript in a private library (it may be owned by Ibn Tāwīt himself), 128 fols., 25×17.5cm, 19 lines, *naskh*, transcribed in 1307/1889–90. According to Ibn Tāwīt, it was transcribed from the *Ayasofya* by the scribe Muḥammad b. ʿAbd al-Salām b. Jād. Based on the result of Ibn Tawīt's comparison between *Jād* and *Ayasofya*, we will accept for the moment that the former is in fact derived from the latter. Its abbreviation is *jīm* in the edition.

Esad Efendi

Manuscript in the Süleymaniye Library, Esad Efendi 2268, 93 fols., 32.7×15.5cm, 25 lines, *naskh*. The date of transcription and the name of the scribe are unknown. Although Ibn Tāwīt did not state it clearly, he may have concluded that it is derived from the *Ayasofya*, based on the result of a comparison of the contents of the two manuscripts. In addition, it was not used in the revision of the *al-Taʿrīf* edition.

Ribāṭ (not investigated yet)
Manuscript in the Library of Rabat, D1345. Its details are unknown, since Ibn Tāwīt did not describe the manuscript. He assumed that the *Ribāṭ* is derived from the *Ayasofya*, as it has the same title as the *Ayasofya*. In addition, it was not used to revise the *al-Taʿrīf* edition. According to Ibn Tāwīt, the above-mentioned manuscripts that derive from the *Ayasofya* belong to a late version of the manuscript of *al-Taʿrīf*.

According to Ibn Tāwīt, the following manuscripts belong to the middle version:

Ẓāhirī
Manuscript in the TSMK, Ahmet III 2924/13–14, vol. 14, fols. 313^{b}–374^{a}, 27×18.5 cm, 21 lines, *naskh*, transcribed in the tenth/sixteenth century. Ahmet III 2924 contains twelve volumes (vols. 3–14) in six books, but lacks volumes 1 and 2.[32] *Al-Taʿrīf* is contained in the latter part of volume 14 and the set of these manuscripts includes the title, *Kitāb al-Ẓāhirī*. If we accept Karatay's perspective regarding the era in which this manuscript was transcribed, then it is not a holograph and does not correspond to the manuscripts offered to al-Ẓāhir Barqūq. However, Karatay did not give an exact year for its transcription, and there is room for debate about this manuscript.[33]

Shanqīṭī (not investigated yet)
Manuscript in the Library at Chinguetti, Mauritania, Taʾrīkh 1 shīn, 20 fols., 31.4×21.4 cm, 42 lines, *maghribī*. This is the manuscript given as a gift to the ʿAlawid ruler, al-Malik Mawlā Ismāʿīl (r. 1072–1139/1661–1727). According to Ibn Tāwīt, it belongs to the same group as the *Ẓāhirī*.

ʿAbd al-Wahhāb (not investigated yet)
Manuscript in the Dār al-Kutub al-Waṭaniyya in Tunis, 127 fols., 22.2×16.7 cm, 26 lines, transcribed in 1304/1886–7. The owner was Ḥasan Ḥusnī ʿAbd al-Wahhāb Bāshā.

32 Karatay, *Topkapı* 381–4, nos. 5886, 5888–92.
33 It is presumed that the MS Damad Ibrahim 863 in the Süleymaniye Library is equivalent to volume I, i.e. *al-Muqaddima*, of *Ẓāhirī*.

According to Ibn Tāwīt, the following manuscripts belong to the early version:

Azhar
Manuscript in the Azhar University Library (Cairo), Ta'rīkh Abāẓa 6729, fols. 203^b–247^a, 31 lines, *naskh*, transcribed in 1270/1853–4 by the scribe, Aḥmad b. Yūsuf b. Ḥamd b. Turkī l-Shāfiʿī l-Azharī. The *Būlāq* edition is derived from this manuscript.

Ṭalʿat
Manuscript in the Dār al-Kutub al-Miṣriyya (Cairo), Ṭalʿat Ta'rīkh 2106, fols. 160^b–196^a, 31 lines, *maghribī*, transcribed in 1181/1767–8. Originally, it was housed in the library of Aḥmad Bey Ṭalʿat. Ibn Tāwīt stated that there is no difference between this and the *Azhar* (except the scribe). Therefore, it belongs to the same group as the *Azhar* manuscript.

Dār 5343
Manuscript in the Dār al-Kutub al-Miṣriyya (Cairo), Ta'rīkh 5343, fols. 215^b–262^a, 32.7 × 23 cm, 27 lines, *naskh*, transcribed in 1254/1838–9.

Dār 185
Manuscript in the Dār al-Kutub al-Miṣriyya (Cairo), Ta'rīkh 185, fols. 160^b–196^a, 33.2 × 22.8 cm, 29 lines, *maghribī*, transcribed in the thirteenth/nineteenth century. This manuscript, and *Dār 5343* are considered to correspond to the early version, based on a comparison with the *Azhar* and *Ṭalʿat*.

The following three manuscripts are not mentioned in the *al-Taʿrīf* edition:

BN
Manuscript in the BnF (Paris), Arabe 1528, fols. 3^b–36^a, 32 × 21 cm, 33 lines, *maghribī*, possibly transcribed in 1192/1778–9. It is contained in volume III of the *al-ʿIbar* manuscript. Judging from its contents, it may be appropriate to classify it with the early version. However, it must be compared with the manuscripts that belong to the middle version.

Zakiyya
Manuscript in the Dār al-Kutub al-Miṣriyya (Cairo), Zakiyya 64, fols. 189^a–231^a, 30 × 21.5 cm, 31 lines, *maghribī*. It is contained in volume VII of the manuscript of *al-ʿIbar*. It can also be classified with the early version, for the same reason as the *BN*.

Nuruosmaniye

Manuscript in the Nuruosmaniye Library, 3067, fols. 177[a]–204[b], 43 lines, *naskh*, transcribed in 1141/1728–9, by the scribe Shāhīn b. al-Dafrāwī. It can also be classified with the early version, for the same reason as the *BN*.

Bibliography

Primary Sources

Ibn Khaldūn, *Prolégomènes d'Ebn Khaldoun: texte arabe publié d'après les manuscrits de la Bibliothèque impériale*, ed. É. Quatremère, 3 vols., Paris 1858.

Ibn Khaldūn, *Taʾrīkh Ibn Khaldūn al-musammā bi-Kitāb al-ʿIbar*, 7 vols., Beirut 1971.

Ibn Khaldūn, *al-Taʿrīf li-Ibn Khaldūn wa-riḥlatuhu gharban wa-sharqan*, ed. M. b. Tāwīt, Cairo 1951.

Ibn Khaldūn, *The Muqaddimah: An Introduction to History*, trans. F. Rosenthal, 3 vols., Princeton 1967.

Secondary Sources

ʿAbd al-Badīʿ, L., *Fihris al-makhṭūṭāt al-muṣawwara*, Part 2: Taʾrīkh, Cairo 1956.

Cheikha, J., Los manuscritos de Ibn Jaldún y análisis de su escritura, in M.J. Viguera Molins et al. (eds.), *Ibn Jaldún. El Mediterráneo en el siglo XIV: Auge y declive de los Imperios. Exposición en el Real Alcázar de Sevilla, mayo-septiembre 2006*, Granada 2006.

De Slane, McGuckin, *Catalogue des manuscrits arabes*, Paris 1883–95.

Fischel, W.J., *Ibn Khaldūn and Tamerlane: Their historic meeting in Damascus, 1401 A.D. (803 A.H.). A study based on Arabic manuscripts of Ibn Khaldūn's "Autobiography," with a translation into English, and a commentary*, Berkeley 1952.

Fischel, W.J., *Ibn Khaldūn in Egypt: His public functions and his historical research (1382–1406). A study in Islamic historiography*, Berkeley 1967.

Karatay, F.E., *Topkapı Sarayı Müzesi Kütüphanesi Arapça Yazmalar Kataloğu*, vol. 3, Istanbul 1966.

Lévi-Provençal, É., Note sur l'exemplaire du *Kitâb al-ʿIbar* offert par Ibn Khaldûn à la bibliothèque d'al-Ḳarawîyîn à Fès, in *Journal Asiatique* 203 (1923), 161–8.

Mahdi, M., *Ibn Khaldûn's philosophy of history: A study in the philosophic foundation of the science of culture*, London 1957.

الناصري بعد هاسنة احدى وتسعين ولحقت السلطان النكبة التي يحمدها الله فيها واقاله وجعل الى الخير فيها عاقبته وما لبث اعاده الى كرسيه للنظر في مصالح عباده وطوقه القلادة التي البسه كا كانت فاعاد لي ماكان من اجراه من نعمته ولم متكسر البيت ممتعًا بالعافية لا يسا بررد العمر لة عاكنا على قراة العلم وتدريسه لهذا العهد فالح سبع وتسعين واسا يعرفنا عوادف لطفه ويعد علينا طلبتين وختم لنا بصالح الاعمال. وهذا اخر ما انتهينا اليه وتلخـــــا الغرض ما اردنا ايراده في هذا الكتاب واسه الموفق برحمته للصواب والهادي الى الحسن المآب والصلاة والسلام على سيدنا ومولانا محمد وعلى اله والجمع العظيم العاليز.

كمل الغرين مولف الكتاب وبكا لـه كل الجزء الرابع عشر من الكتاب الظاهري في العبر باخبار العرب والعجم والبربر وهو اخر ما الفنا فخرا ايديوانه كله بكماله والحمد لله وحده وصلوا ته على سيدنا ومولانا محمد نبيه وعبده وعلى اله وصبه وسلامه

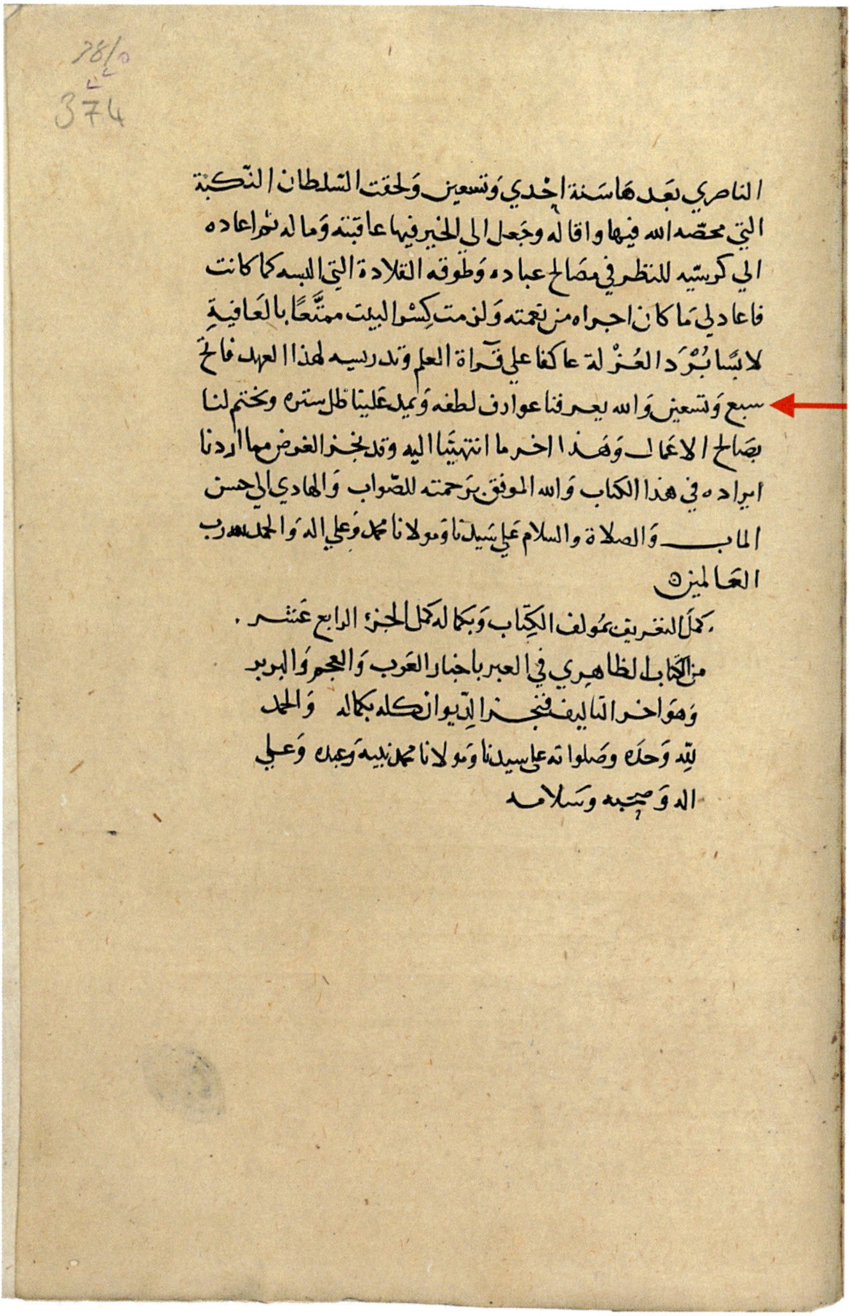

FIGURE 9.1 MS Ahmet III 2924/13–14, fol. 374ᵃ
ISTANBUL, TSMK

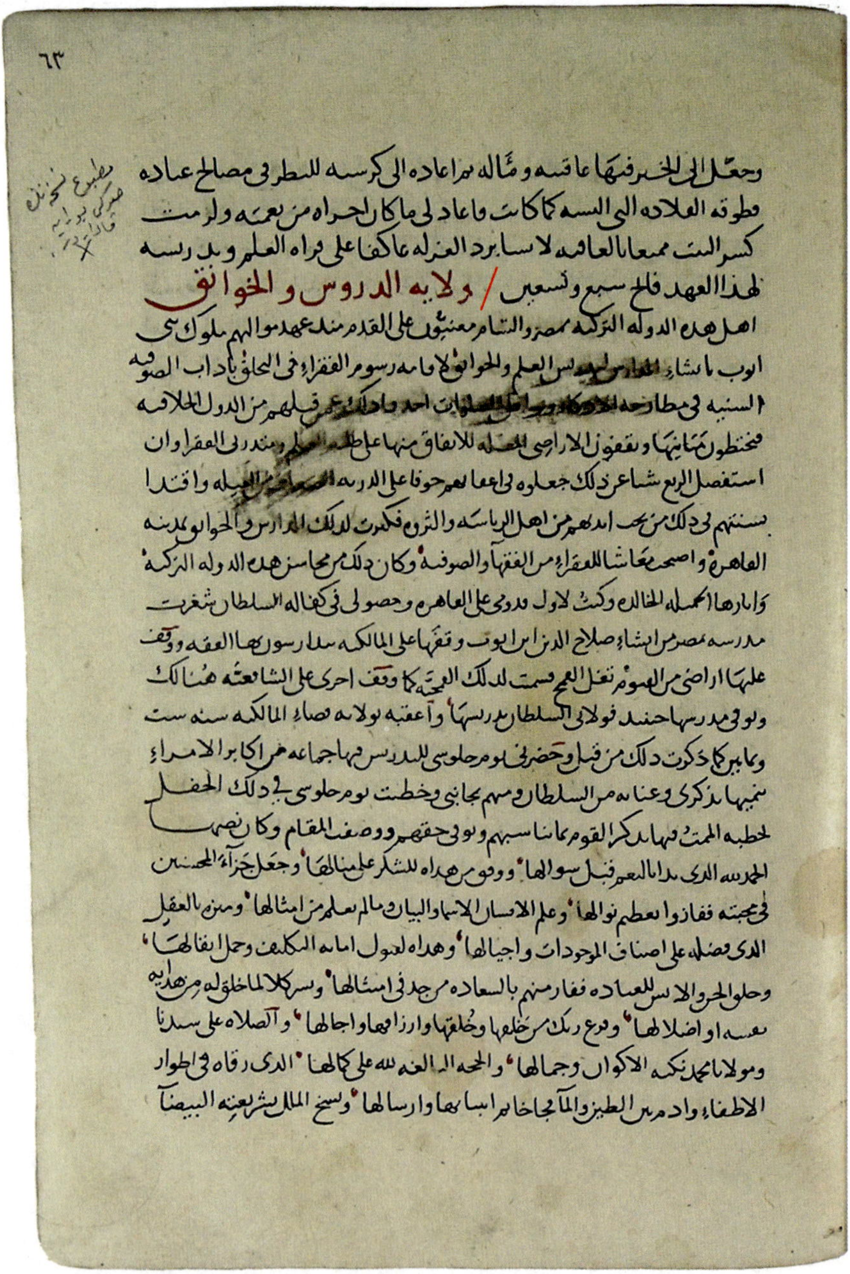

FIGURE 9.2 MS Ayasofya 3200, fol. 63[a]
ISTANBUL, SÜLEYMANIYE KÜTÜPHANESI

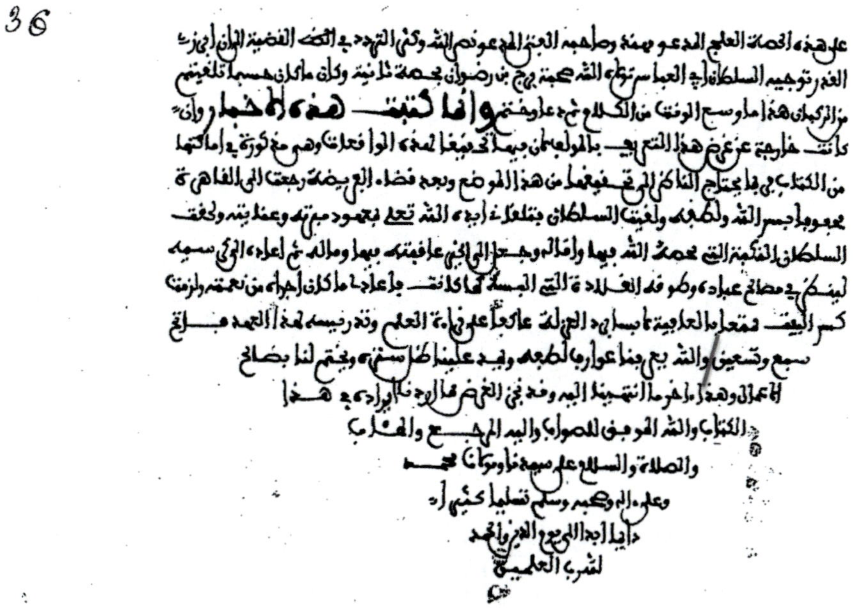

FIGURE 9.3 MS Ar. 1528, fol. 36a
PARIS, BNF

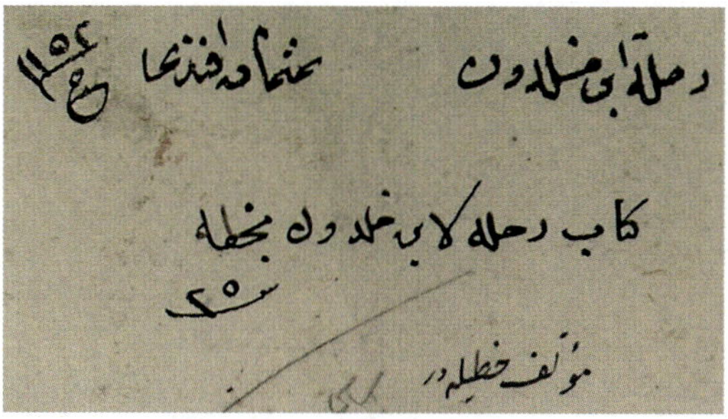

FIGURE 9.4 MS Ayasofya 3200, fol. 1a
ISTANBUL, SÜLEYMANIYE KÜTÜPHANESI

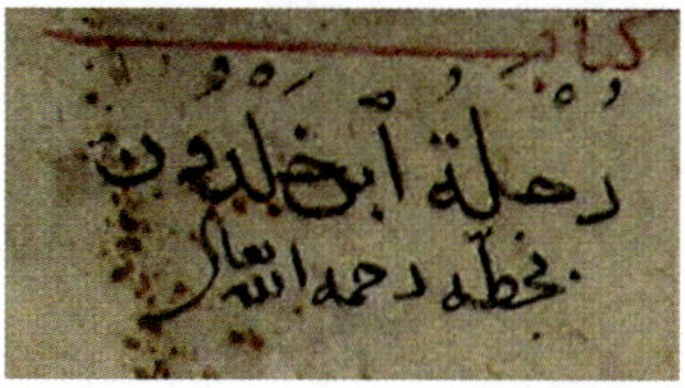

FIGURE 9.5
MS Ayasofya 3200, fol. 1a
ISTANBUL, SÜLEYMANIYE KÜTÜPHANESI

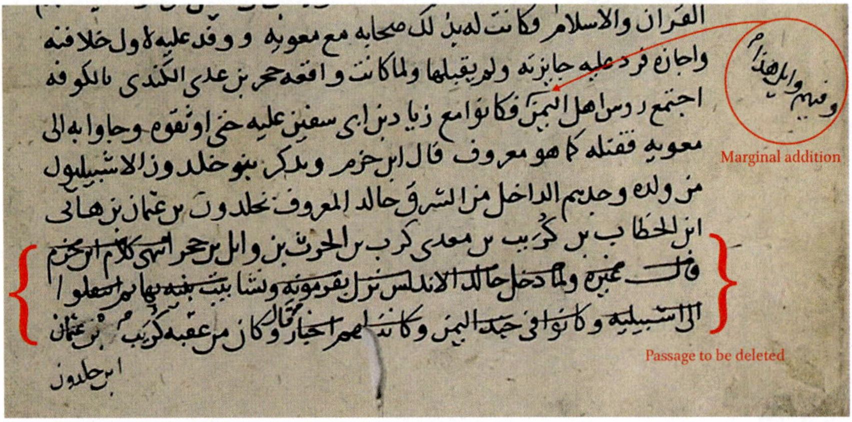

FIGURE 9.6 MS Ayasofya 3200, fol. 1b
ISTANBUL, SÜLEYMANIYE KÜTÜPHANESI

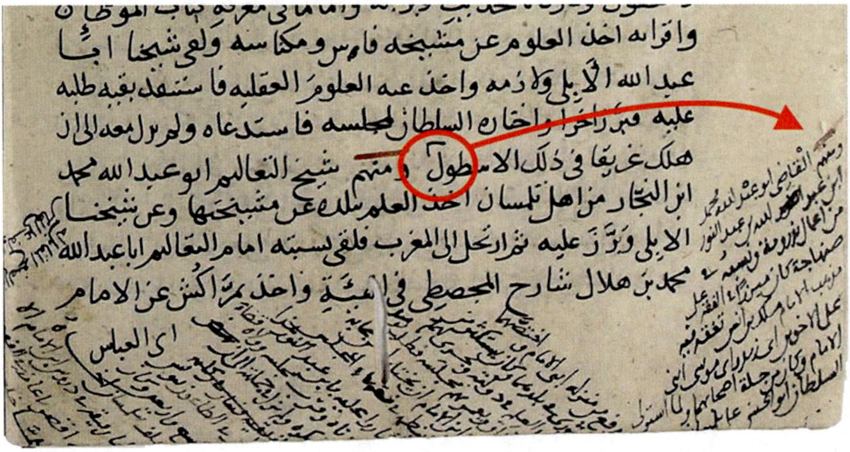

FIGURE 9.7 MS Ayasofya 3200, fol. 11b
ISTANBUL, SÜLEYMANIYE KÜTÜPHANESI

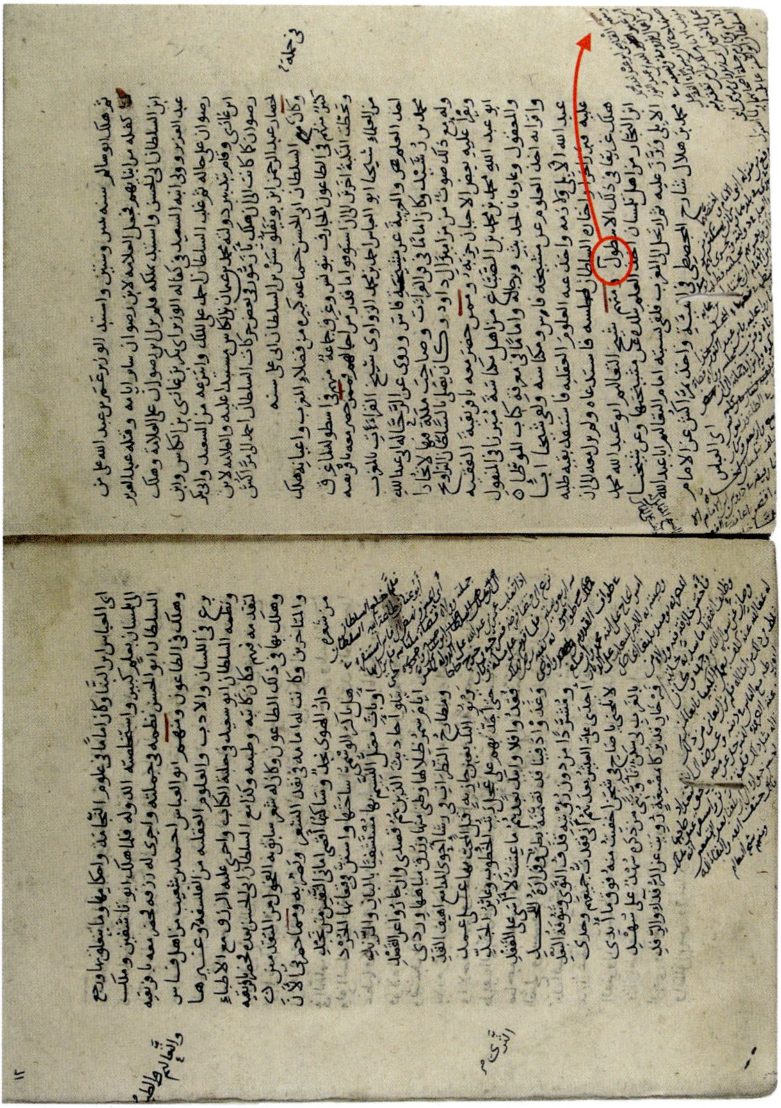

FIGURE 9.8 MS Ayasofya 3200, fols. 11^{b}–12^{a}
ISTANBUL, SÜLEYMANIYE KÜTÜPHANESI

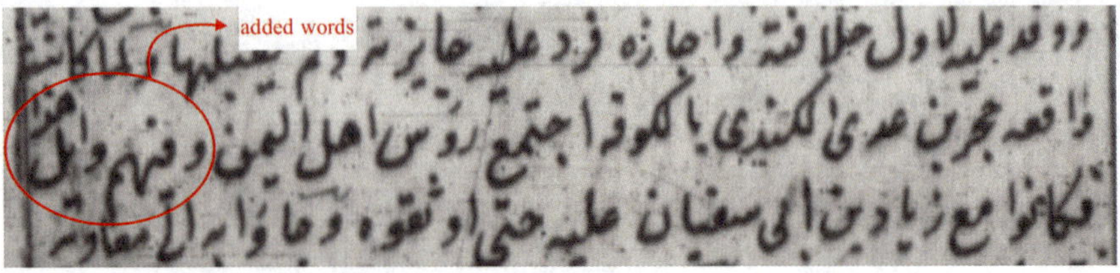

FIGURE 9.9 MS Taʾrīkh 109 mīm, fol. 1[b]
CAIRO, DĀR AL-KUTUB AL-MIṢRIYYA

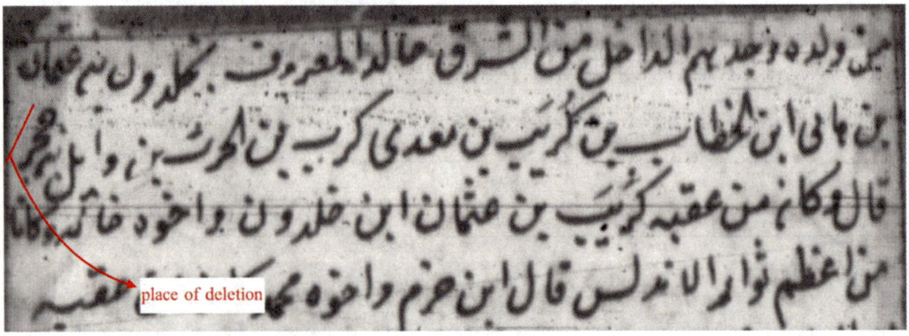

FIGURE 9.10 MS Taʾrīkh 109 mīm , fol. 2[a]
CAIRO, DĀR AL-KUTUB AL-MIṢRIYYA

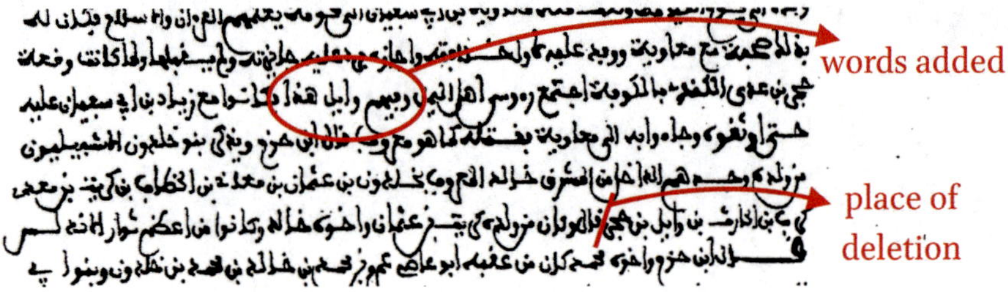

FIGURE 9.11 MS Ar. 1528, fol. 3[b]
PARIS, BNF

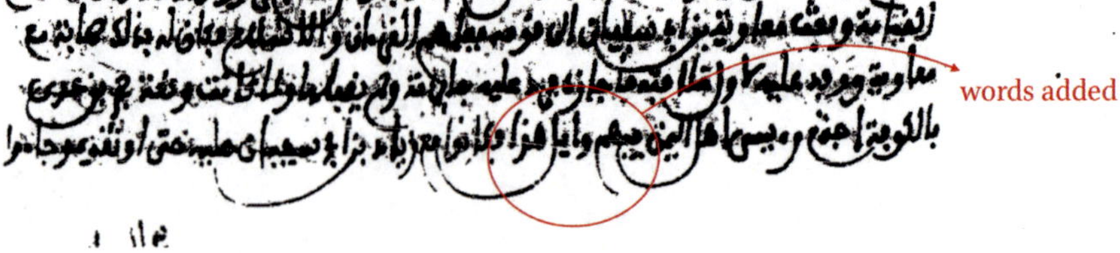

FIGURE 9.12 MS Ṭalʿat Taʾrīkh 2106, fol. 160[b]
CAIRO, DĀR AL-KUTUB AL-MIṢRIYYA

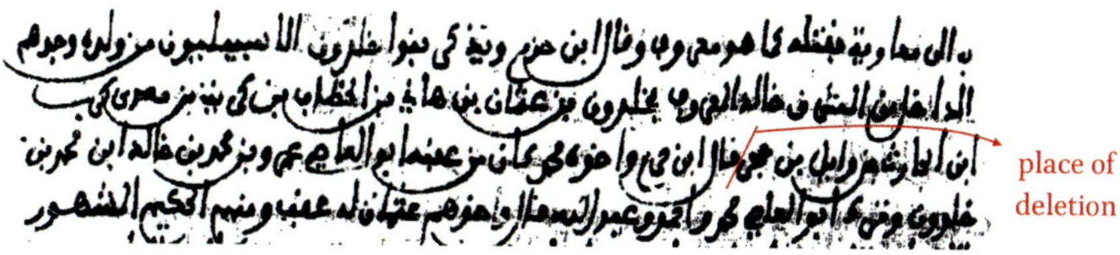

FIGURE 9.13 MS Ṭalʿat Taʾrīkh 2106, fol. 161a
CAIRO, DĀR AL-KUTUB AL-MIṢRIYYA

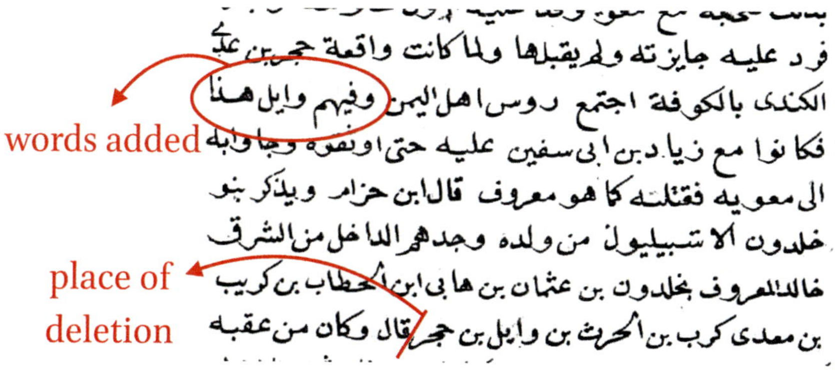

فرد عليه جايزته ولم يقبلها ولما كانت واقعة حجر بن عدي
الكندي بالكوفة اجتمع روس اهل اليمن وفيهم وايل هذا
فكانوا مع زياد بن ابي سفين عليه حتى اوثقوه وجاوا به
الى معويه فقتله كما هو معروف قال ابن حزام ويذكر بنو
خلدون الاشبيليون من ولده وجدهم الداخل من الشرق
خالد المعروف بخلدون بن عثمان بن هاني بن الخطاب بن كريب
بن معدى كرب بن الحرث بن وايل بن حجر قال وكان من عقبه

FIGURE 9.14 MS Esad Efendi 2268, fol. 2a
ISTANBUL, SÜLEYMANIYE KÜTÜPHANESI

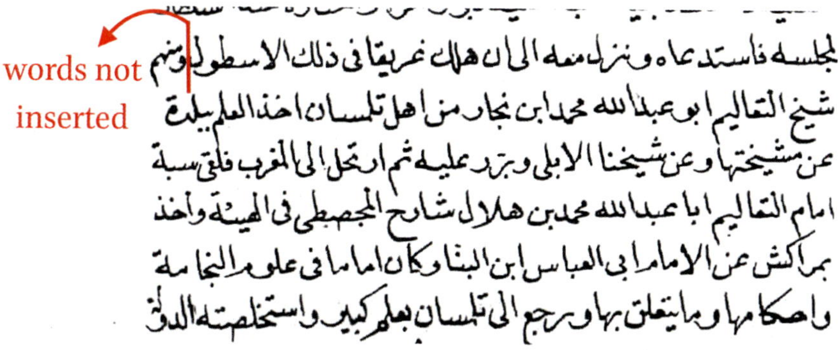

لمجلسه فاستدعاه ونزل منه الى ان هلك غريقا في ذلك الاسطول ومنهم
شيخ التعاليم ابو عبد الله محمد بن نجار من اهل تلمسان اخذ العلم ببلده
عن مشيختها وعن شيخنا الابلي وبرز عليه ثم ارتحل الى المغرب فلقي بسبتة
امام التعاليم ابا عبد الله محمد بن هلال شارح المجسطي في الهيئة واخذ
بمراكش عن الامام ابي العباس ابن البنا وكان اماما في علوم النجامة
واحكامها وما يتعلق بها ورجع الى تلمسان بعلم كبير واستخلصته الدولة

FIGURE 9.15 MS Esad Efendi 2268, fol. 13a
ISTANBUL, SÜLEYMANIYE KÜTÜPHANESI

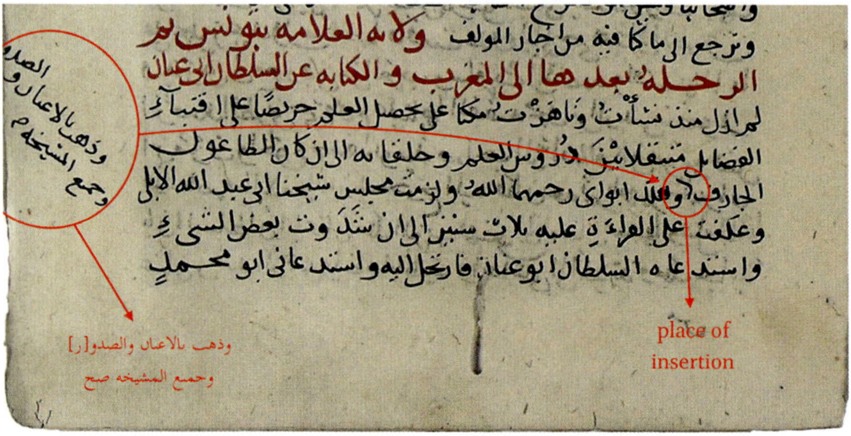

FIGURE 9.16 MS Ayasofya 3200, fol. 14[a]
ISTANBUL, SÜLEYMANIYE KÜTÜPHANESI

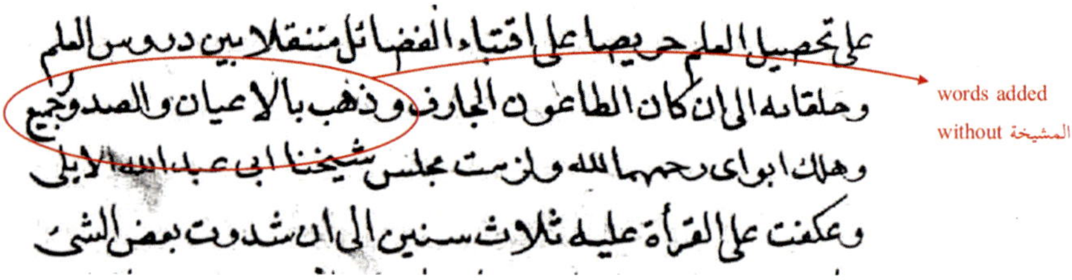

FIGURE 9.17 MS Esad Efendi 2268, fol. 15[b]
ISTANBUL, SÜLEYMANIYE KÜTÜPHANESI

CHAPTER 10

Les *safīna*s yéménites

Julien Dufour et Anne Regourd

1 Introduction

Comparé au format rectangulaire, le format oblong, ou "*safīna*", est, à l'instar du format carré, particulier dans la production de manuscrits en arabe. Il est ressenti comme localisé dans l'espace et le temps, voire abandonné, mais aussi lié à un type de livre et de support de l'écriture : l'exemple le plus emblématique de format oblong est en effet celui des premiers corans abbassides, sur parchemin[1]. Cependant, le format oblong a survécu au Maghreb et en Espagne, tout au moins jusqu'au XVe s., aux côtés de formats carrés et rectangulaires, pérennes, pour des manuscrits qui ne sont pas seulement des corans[2].

L'autre tradition de "*safīnas*" (*safīna*, pl. *safāyin*) désigne habituellement des anthologies poétiques persanes, empruntées à l'œuvre d'un seul ou plusieurs poètes. D'un format à l'italienne, elles s'ouvrent de la même manière qu'un calepin[3] (fig. 10.1) : lorsque le manuscrit est en position ouverte, le texte débute en haut du feuillet supérieur et se poursuit en haut du feuillet inférieur, si bien que le texte de deux feuillets à la fois peut être lu, ou du moins vu, en continu, de la même façon que le serait un projet panoptique d'enluminure sur deux feuillets. La ligne d'écriture peut être parallèle, perpendiculaire ou oblique par rapport au petit côté relié (dos de la reliure) et à la direction des décors marginaux[4]. En réalité, ce format oblong a abrité plus que des anthologies poétiques

1 Björkman, Ḳaṭʿ 742 : "Apart from these distinctions, it is worth noting that literary papyri have an almost square format whereas an oblong format, later on called *safīna*, was reserved for the Ḳurʾān".

2 Ainsi que l'a illustré une exposition récente du Louvre. Voir, Lintz et al., *Le Maroc médiéval*, formats oblongs : Coran, vers 1230, probablement à Marrakech (Istanbul, TSMK, inv. R. 21, fig. 3, p. 539) ; recueil de prières en hébreu copié à Fez en 1401 (Paris, BnF, ms. hébreu 657, fig. 1, p. 311) ; nombreux exemples de formats carrés. Sur la persistance de ce format oblong dans la partie occidentale du monde islamique et du format carré au Maghreb jusqu'au XIXe s., voir Gacek, *Vademecum* 34 ("Book formats"), qui cite Bosch et al., *Islamic bindings* 25.

3 Witkam, Nuskha 150, "noteblocks" ; Gacek, *Glossary* 69, "s.f.n., safīnah, (…) 2. note-pad" ; id., *Vademecum* 34.

4 On a pu dire que leur "utilisation rappelle celle du rouleau", Déroche et al., *Manuel* 60 ; Déroche et al., *Islamic Codicology* 53 ; Déroche et Sagaria Rossi, *I manoscritti* 67. On note des exemples de textes obliques ou horizontaux, à côté de textes horizontaux, par rapport au dos

dans les mondes persan, arabe et turc-ottoman, mais un lien s'est peu à peu constitué entre un type de texte et un format, au point que, par métonymie, des recueils poétiques ont été nommés "*safīnas*". Des travaux récents se penchent sur ce lien étroit pour le monde turc-ottoman[5]. Quant au format, il a été souligné que, parmi les différents types de recueils à disposition en persan, les *safīnas* étaient les seules à renvoyer à un format[6].

Au Yémen, la tradition des "*safīnas*-calepin" a perduré jusqu'au XXe s. et la désignation de recueils poétiques par le nom de *safīna* jusqu'à récemment[7]. Différents manuscrits examinés ici sont décrits par leur texte-même comme "*safīna*" et abritent une collection (*majmūʿ*) d'œuvres poétiques et de poètes différents[8]. Cette tradition n'a cependant pas été étudiée : au cours de cette étude, nous tâcherons de montrer que, bloc-note personnel, elle vient enrichir le giron des cas de manuscrits holographes.

2 Retour historique et définitions des recueils de type "*safīnas*-calepin"

La tradition des *safīnas* est attestée au Moyen-Orient par les sources scripturaires dès le Xe s[9]. Une *safīna* orientale du XVIe s. abritant une grammaire de Zamakhsharī, acquise par Leonardo Abel, qui a séjourné en Syrie de 1583 à 1586 et a continué à acquérir des manuscrits après son retour à Rome, est conservée à la Biblioteca Medicea Laurenziana de Florence[10].

Dans le monde persan, de nombreux exemples ont été relevés pour le XVe s., sans écarter le fait qu'il en existe toutefois de nettement antérieurs[11]. Pour

dans des anthologies poétiques dès le XVe s., voir par ex. le ms. BnF, ms. Suppl. persan 1798, Iran central vers 1450 ?, reproduit dans : Richard, *Splendeurs* 83 (n° 49) ; un intéressant exemple de la fin du XVIIe-XVIIIe s. a récemment été mis en vente, cf. Zisska & Lacher 4 (notice 14, pl. 2, fig. 14).

5 Gülgün Yazıcı, chercheuse invitée par la BnF, programme "Profession culture", a travaillé sur des *cönk*, entre autre des albums de poésies (*mecmu'atü'l-eşâr*) conservés dans les collections des manuscrits turcs en juillet et août 2013, m'a indiqué les *cönk*s comme recueils spécifiques de poésies populaires en dialectal. Par ailleurs, nos sincères remerciements vont à Sara Yontan pour sa relecture attentive des passages concernant les "*sefines*" ou "*cönks*".

6 Roxburgh, *Persian Album* 149 (chap. 4, "Reinventions of the Book", entre autres).

7 Cf. le recueil poétique al-ʿAmrī, *Safīna*.

8 BnF, ms. ar. 7084, fol. 17, les *safīnas* 5 et 6.

9 *Safīna*, dans le sens de collection de poésies notées et possédées par des individus, apparaît dans al-Thaʿālibī, *Tatimmat* 37-38, 54-55, 87. Cité par Wagner, *Like Joseph* 127.

10 Ms. Orientale 394, cf. Fani & Farina, *Le vie* 164 (n° 34, notice de S. Fani).

11 Richard, *Splendeurs* 55.

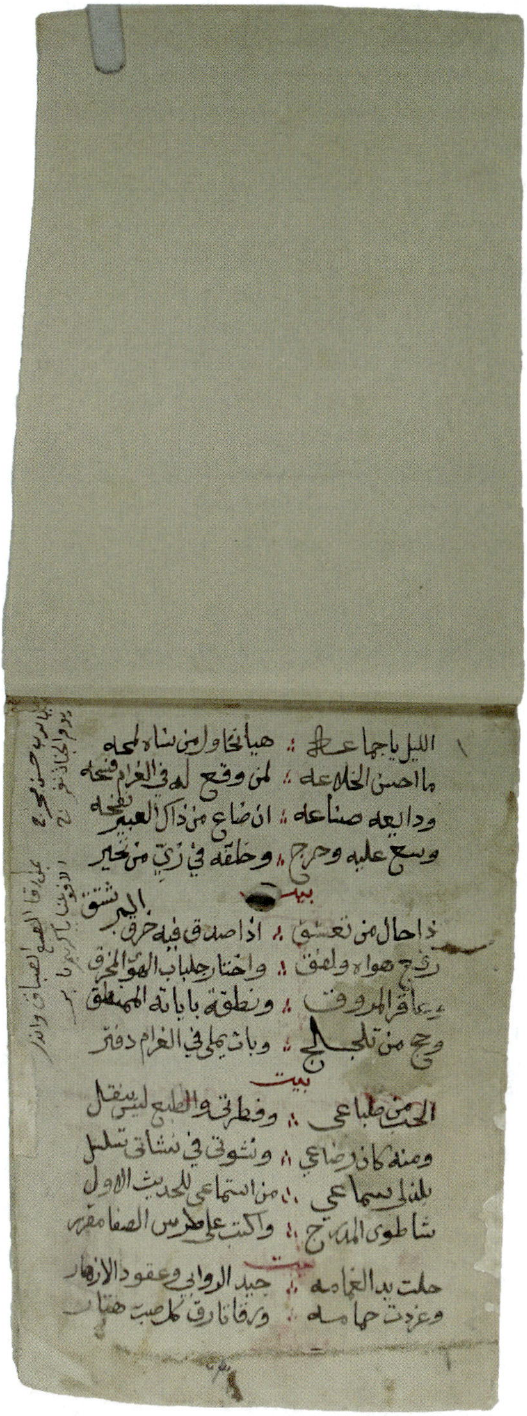

FIGURE 10.1
Ouverture en calepin. *Safīna* 2 (MS Adab 2336), *Dīwān d'al-Ahdal*, fol. 1-p. 23
SANAA, DĀR AL-MAKHṬŪṬĀT

preuve, cette copie de l'édition par al-Ṭūsī des *Éléments* d'Euclide, le *Taḥrīr Uṣūl Uqlīdis*, dont l'achèvement est situé vers 678-679/1280[12]. Mais le XVe s. est le moment où la production d'anthologies de cour voit s'élaborer une organisation de la page, l'usage de nouvelles techniques et le renfort d'enluminures, d'éléments textuels, telle la rubrication, et de tables des matières, afin de conjurer le "chaos" anthologique, produire un effet d'unité et finalement aider le lecteur à se diriger ou se repérer dans des manuscrits non foliotés; parmi cette efflorescence d'anthologies de diverses sortes figurent des "*safīna*s"[13]. Généralement décrites comme des anthologies de l'œuvre d'un ou plusieurs poètes, par différence avec les *dīvān*s et *kulliyyāt*s consacrés à un seul poète, ou avec les *majmūʿa*s et *jung*s, accueillant également de la prose[14], leur production et leur usage sont alors largement répandus[15]. Leur contenu est organisé, elles sont écrites sur du beau papier et sont illustrées[16]. Le mot de "*safīna*" viendrait du persan[17]. Le monde persan nous a légué de précieuses miniatures représentant des personnages portant des *safīna*s en biais, prises dans la ceinture[18]. Leur nom de "bateau" découlerait de leur format mince – largeur et

12 Voir Sotheby's n° 22.

13 Nous suivons Roxburgh, *Persian Album* 149. Voir l'analyse d'un groupe de *safīna*, 155 *sq*., et les exemples, *infra*, n. 649.

14 Voir la définition donnée par Roxburgh, Aesthetics 119-42 (surtout 137, note 1), et, surtout, id., *Persian Album* 152.

15 Pour le XVe s., on citera à titre d'exemple, par ordre chronologique, les manuscrits suivants: BnF, ms. suppl. persan 1425, ca. 1480, Hérat, Afghanistan; Bibliotheca Bodmeriana (Cologny, Genève), ms. 522, 888/1483, Nāʿim al-dīn Kātib, calligraphe de Shiraz; BnF, ms. suppl. persan 1798, Iran central?, ca. 1450; Chester Beatty, Dublin, ms. pers. 127, 1449, Hérat ou Shiraz; Biblioteca Nazionale Centrale di Firenze, ms. Cl.III.10, 1440?, Piemontese, *Catalogo* n° 147, tous décrits comme anthologies poétiques. Richard, *Splendeurs* 83, 100; Blochet, *Catalogue* 147, 332; Chester Beatty, Dublin, ms. pers. 122, probablement 1431, Hérat, et ms. pers. 127, déjà cité, fol. reproduits dans: Roxburgh, *Persian Album* 156 (fig. 80 et 81-83).

16 Le "papier coulé" est fréquent. Ce papier, qui annonce le papier marbré, s'apparente au papier "coulé romantique" occidental: il s'agit de projeter la couleur directement sur le papier et de procéder à un séchage incliné de la feuille; c'est ainsi que la couleur coule. Voir en particulier Teece, *Vessels of Verse* chap. 8 et 9, où le papier de *safina*s persanes du XVe-début du XVIe s. est traité comme un des aspects visuels de ces manuscrits. La réflexion prend ensuite un tour plus théorique en articulant la "débauche" de techniques décoratives et l'élaboration dans la conception d'ensemble des feuillets en regard, qui distinguent ces œuvres, fondamentalement visuelles, d'autres manuscrits persans, avec le caractère non narratif des textes qu'elles contiennent.

17 Déroche et al., *Manuel* 60: "On note aussi l'existence, dans le monde iranien en particulier, de volumes oblongs, à l'italienne (en persan *safīna*), …"; Déroche et al., *Islamic Codicology* 53; et Déroche et Sagaria Rossi, *I Manoscritti* 67. *Safīna* en persan, de même qu'en arabe, signifie "bateau".

18 Nombreux exemples, parmi eux, le ms. suppl. persan 1113 (BnF), un petit personnage d'une des illustrations de "la madraseh de Ghazan à Tabriz" et une illustration du ms. suppl. per-

épaisseur – et, par voie de conséquence, de leur transportabilité, qui est finalement partie intégrante de leur définition[19]. En fait, c'est de leur contenu qu'il s'agirait, une "science" transportable, un *vade-mecum* pour une pensée circumambulatoire, un *compendium* de textes à méditer, instructifs, édifiants et distrayants, reflétant le goût de leur propriétaire[20]. Les pratiques autour des *safīnas* ne s'arrêtent cependant pas là mais montrent que le plaisir peut être partagé, tout au moins avec l'aimée, et le texte qu'elles contiennent, lu à haute voix[21].

La BnF conserve deux *safīnas* dont le texte est en langues persane et arabe, toutes deux datées du XVIIe s. (ar. 3423 et ar. 3430). Il s'agit d'anthologies poétiques en vers et en prose. Le papier de la seconde, un papier oriental, a quelques feuillets colorés en vert et rosé. Un papier coloré rosé, avec quelques particules brillantes rappelant l'or, est collé sur les ais de la première.

La production de *safīnas* en arabe se poursuit du XVIIe au XIXe s., indépendamment du Yémen. Les genres poétiques abordés sont divers, y compris au sein du même recueil : on trouve des *qaṣīdas*, des *muwashshaḥāt*, des pièces courtes comme des *takhmīss* et des *mawāls*, ainsi que de la prose (anecdotes).

Les dimensions pour l'ensemble des aires et périodes décrites varient, aucun modèle ne semble s'imposer sur quelque 18 manuscrits observés[22]. Elles vont de 160 à 340 mm pour le grand côté et de 80 à 160 mm pour le petit côté, avec

san 1425 (BnF). Sur le lien lexicographique entre le terme "*safīna*", le sens de "bateau" (un générique ou un type de bateau) et son transport à la ceinture, cf. Roxburgh, *Persian Album* 152, 339 (note 7).

19 Roxburgh, Jong 11-14 : "The jong, or *majmuʿa*, contained an array of texts that were often densely copied over many folios to produce thick, comprehensive volumes. The safina, by contrast, was not only smaller in size but also had fewer folios : these features enhanced its portability ; it could be tucked under the belt".

20 Cf. Roxburgh *Persian Album* 152 ; plus loin, 158-159, analyse de deux recueils de cour réalisés par Shaykh Maḥmūd en 1460 pour Pīr Būdāq, gouverneur à Shiraz, dans une intention délicate, car il reflète les goûts de son destinataire. Un équivalent actuel pourrait être le lecteur de musique portable.

21 Voir par ex. Réunion des musées nationaux, *Louvre* n° d'inventaire OA7109 : 'le lecteur', Boukhara vers 1600-1630, "Partie centrale par Muhammad Charif Musavvir. Marges par Muhammad Murâd Samarqandi. Le lecteur tient une *safina*, un manuscrit au format 'langue de bœuf', réservé à la poésie. À l'origine, le prince n'était pas seul : lui faisait face, sur la page opposée, une jeune femme l'écoutant et lui tendant sa coupe d'or".

22 BnF, suppl. persan 1425 ; suppl. persan 1798 ; ar. 3423 ; ar. 3430 ; ar. 3424 ; ar. 3426 ; ar. 3428 ; ar. 3429 ; ar. 3454 ; ar. 3458 ; ar. 3459 ; ar. 3461 ; ar. 3585 ; ar. 7084 ; suppl. turc 1620. Les mss. de la Biblioteca Nazionale Centrale di Firenze, ms. Cl.III.106, Piemontese, *Catalogo* n° 157 et Cl.III.10, Piemontese, *Catalogo* n° 147 ; Biblioteca Medicea Laurenziana (Florence), ms. orientale 394.

une récurrence de 210-220 mm pour le grand côté de manuscrits des XVIIe et XVIIIe s. Mais il ne s'agit là que d'un premier travail d'observation, forcément limité.

Dans le monde turc-ottoman, ces recueils poétiques sont appelés "*sefine*" ou "*cönk*". En référence à leur format et à leur largeur exiguë, on dit aussi métaphoriquement "langue de bœuf". Le ms. suppl. turc 1620 de la BnF, daté de 1252/1836-1837, est un exemple de *cönk*, contenant de la littérature populaire turque. Il s'agit d'un don de Pertev Naili Boratav, spécialiste de littérature populaire turque. Sur le calepin, une note indique qu'il faisait partie de la collection de *cönk*s de Raif Yelkenci, un bouquiniste de renom ("Raif Yelkenci Cöngü 6"). D'après Gülgün Yazıcı, il s'agit d'un recueil de poésies, de genres très variés (*gazel, koşma, ilahi, düstur, semai*, etc.), et, comme c'est le cas de beaucoup de *cönk* de ce format, on y trouve aussi des notes, par exemple la comptabilité du matériel d'un chantier naval et des recettes de remèdes. Le petit côté mesure 85 mm pour 190 mm de hauteur[23]. La moyenne des dimensions de neuf manuscrits de format *safīna* de la Bibliothèque universitaire de Leiden (Universiteitsbibliotheek Leiden, UbL) est de 110 × 210 mm, cinq étant ottomans[24]. Les formats calepin antérieurs au XVIIe s. ayant été répertoriés ne semblent pas nombreux: ce pourrait être le cas du ms. UbL Or. 1088, ce que confirment les matériaux de la reliure (papier marbré et cuir, cf. n. 24). L'absence d'ais et donc la souplesse de ces manuscrits a été soulignée dans la foulée de remarques, applicables à la tradition persane, sur leur transportabilité et sur le caractère personnel de ces objets. L'usage de carnet des *safīna*s est renforcé par le fait que certains volumes aient été achetés "tout prêts", de la même manière qu'un article de papeterie[25].

---

23 Ce sont des dimensions que l'on trouve dans d'autres zones culturelles: le manuscrit suppl. persan 1798 (BnF), Iran central, ca. 1450, 190 × 82 mm. Mais il est possible que ce modèle très étroit ait eu la faveur des Ottomans et des Turcs. On trouvera une contribution récente à la question *sefina* et *mecmūʿa* dans: Aynur et al. (éd.), *Mecmūʿa*.

24 Scheper, *Technique* 260. Il s'agit des mss: Or. 1088, fin XVe/milieu XVIIe s., volume collectif de poètes turcs en turc, mais traces de persan et d'arabe (voir Schmidt, *Turcksche Boucken*), peut-être de la collection Warner; Or. 1090, note de propriété datée de 1591 et date la plus tardive collectée 1638-1639, abritant des modèles de lettres ou de parties de lettres en arabe, persan et turc, évoquant les recueils (*majmūʿ*) d'*inshāʾ*; Or. 1096, daté de 1658, contenant six poèmes mystiques en turc et un peu d'arabe; Or. 1097, non daté, anthologie de poésie, provenant de Turquie, en arabe; Or. 3071, non daté, carnet ("*notebook*"), principalement glossaire et notes géographiques, essentiellement en persan et latin, mais aussi un peu d'arabe et de turc, peut-être annotations de la main de Warner, selon Jan Schmidt. Nous remercions K. Scheper d'avoir eu l'obligeance de nous donner le détail de ces neuf manuscrits.

25 Pour l'ensemble, Scheper, *Technique* 313, 316 (note 39, ill. 173).

Deux autres *safīnas*, parmi les neuf exemplaires de la UbL juste mentionnés, revêtent un grand intérêt : les mss. Or. 14.637, daté de 1898, Macédoine, un carnet ("*notebook*") en turc, et Or. 14.638, non daté, provenant de Thrace occidentale, regroupant des poèmes et chansons en turc. L'un comme l'autre probablement propriété d'un derviche bektashi[26], ils montrent la circulation du modèle dans la zone d'influence ottomane.

Les *safīnas* en persan ou en arabe ont accueilli d'autres sujets que de la poésie, bien qu'exceptionnellement à notre connaissance. Outre la copie du *Taḥrīr Uṣūl Uqlīdis* d'al-Ṭūsī, la grammaire d'al-Zamakhsharī et le recueil (*majmūʿ*) d'*inshāʾ* déjà évoqués, on citera un *tafsīr* en persan daté des deux dernières décennies du XVIe-début XVIIe s. à la Biblioteca Nazionale Centrale di Firenze, Cl.III.106[27] ainsi qu'un recueil de fables, apologues, récits divers et anecdotes de 1165/1752, intitulé, dans l'*explicit*, "*safīna*" : le ms ar. 3585 (BnF).

La bibliographie sur le sujet des *safīnas* du Yémen est courte, si l'on veut parler d'une réflexion qui inclurait le format. Jaʿfar ʿAbduh Dafari (al-Ẓafārī) nous livre l'observation suivante, qui, selon Mark S. Wagner, ferait allusion au format : "A *safīnah* is generally a random collection of poetry owned by individuals who copy different poems either from books or *dīwāns* or as they hear them from singers and composers. They tend to have errors, no organization and a tendency to attribute poems to prominent *washshāḥīn*"[28].

Les recueils yéménites étudiés ici abritent de la poésie classique (*qaṣīdas*), appelée à Sanaa "*ḥakamī*", surtout par distinction avec le "*ḥumaynī*", un genre pratiqué – et probablement né – au Yémen, attesté depuis le XIIIe s[29]. M.S. Wagner indique, évoquant le célèbre salon de ʿAlī b. al-Ḥasan al-Khafanjī (m. vers 1766/1767), appelé "al-Safīna", à Sanaa, au XVIIIe s. : "At the same time, the word al-Safīnah also meant a scrapbook of poetry, primarily containing *ḥumaynī* verse", pointant peut-être une évolution dans leur contenu[30]. Le Yémen rassemble sous le terme de "*ḥumaynī*" la poésie qui s'écarte de la norme de la *qaṣīda* classique (classée, on l'a dit, dans la catégorie du "*ḥakamī*"), soit par sa forme (majoritairement strophique ou, lorsqu'elle n'est pas strophique, possédant deux rimes par vers), soit par sa langue, le plus souvent dépourvue des désinences flexionnelles dites *iʿrāb* de l'arabe classique et par conséquent qua-

26 Cf. Schmidt, *Catalogue* Or. 14.637, 484-9 ; Or. 14.638, 489-90.

27 Piemontese, *Catalogo* n° 157.

28 Dafari (al-Ẓafārī), *Ḥumaini Poetry* 25 (cité par Wagner, *Like Joseph* 127, n. 67). Nos remerciements chaleureux vont à Mark S. Wagner qui a bien voulu partager ses notes sur la thèse de J.A. Dafari.

29 Dufour, *Huit siècles* 30 et *sqq.*, 40, 41-42.

30 Wagner, *Like Joseph* 39.

lifiée de *malḥūn*, terme qui s'oppose à *muʿrab*. La langue "*malḥūn*" n'est pas forcément dialectale, mais il arrive qu'elle incorpore un nombre plus ou moins important de dialectalismes et qu'elle puisse alors être qualifiée de moyen arabe poétique. Le terme de "*ḥumaynī*" renvoie avant tout à des caractéristiques formelles (structure du poème en termes de strophes et de rimes, caractéristiques grammaticales et lexicales de la langue), sans préjuger d'un contenu pour ses poèmes : on verra figurer tour à tour, dans les *safīna*s examinées cidessous, des accents mystiques, du *ghazal*, du *madḥ*, etc.

Le terme de "*ḥumaynī*" semble propre au Yémen. Le sens large défini cidessus est celui que le mot a aujourd'hui, mais il est probable qu'à une époque ancienne, il ait eu un sens plus restreint, désignant une forme poétique particulière, sans doute le *mubayyat*. Le *ḥumaynī* yéménite s'est donné un visage qui lui est propre, mais l'usage de composer de la poésie strophique en langue "*malḥūn*" n'a rien de particulièrement yéménite et est abondamment attesté dans l'ensemble du monde arabophone à partir du XIIe siècle, en particulier – mais pas exclusivement – dans les milieux mystiques. Les formes d'origine andalouse du *muwashshaḥ* et du *zajal* sont sans doute celles qui ont connu la plus grande faveur dans la composition de la poésie dite "*malḥūn*".

Notons enfin qu'au Yémen le terme de "*ḥumaynī*" désigne une poésie qui s'inspire à des degrés divers d'une culture savante – y compris pour s'en démarquer. Il ne comprend pas normalement la poésie de tradition orale, tribale ou rurale[31].

C'est une poésie chantée et même dansée[32]. Son lien à l'oralité est attesté d'une autre manière : les élèves de Ḥātim b. Aḥmad al-Ahdal (m. 1013/1604), originaire de Moka en Tihāma, notaient dans leurs carnets ce qu'ils l'entendaient dire en transe[33]. Mais cet exemple est par définition difficile à généraliser : tiré d'un contexte mystique, il peut être le fait d'une personnalité, d'une part, et, d'autre part, le *ḥumaynī* a évolué vers d'autres thèmes après qu'il a gagné les hauts plateaux.

Dans les *safīna*s yéménites, le classique apparaît en principe d'abord, suivi du *ḥumaynī*. Il y a du *ḥumaynī* dans les *dīwān*s aussi, mais les *safīna*s, elles, ont recueilli un "*ḥumaynī* d'allure tribale, qui se caractérise par son ton, sa forme, ses mètres et des particularités de scansion – et bien que ses limites soient imprécises –, (un *ḥumaynī* qui) n'a pas eu l'honneur d'être rassemblé dans des *dīwān*s. Les auteurs mêmes en sont méconnus. Il a cependant envahi les *safī-*

31 Wagner, *Like Joseph* 11 *sq*.
32 Cf. le titre du livre de Dufour, *Huit siècles*, et Dufour, La *Safīna* 17, 25 et 26.
33 Dufour, *Huit siècles* 50.

nas. À quelle époque? Cela reste à déterminer"[34]. D'autres formes poétiques s'y ajoutent, parfois reliées à une aire géographique (peut-être un terroir). Et il arrive souvent que l'on y trouve des proverbes, devinettes, historiettes ou œuvres de prose.

Quatre noms, ceux de poètes majeurs pour avoir marqué une étape dans le développement de la poésie *ḥumaynī* postérieurement à l'époque rasūlide, reviendront fréquemment dans les *safīnas* étudiées: Muḥammad b. ʿAbdallāh b. Sharaf al-dīn (m. 1010/1601), petit-fils d'imam zaydite; ʿAlī l-ʿAnsī (m. 1139/1726), juge et haut fonctionnaire dans l'administration de l'imam al-Mutawakkil; et les Ānisī, père et fils, respectivement, ʿAbd al-Raḥmān al-Ānisī (m. 1250/1834) et Aḥmad b. ʿAbd al-Raḥmān al-Ānisī (m. 1241/1825), juges et hauts fonctionnaires.

3 *Safīna* 1. Ms. ar. 7084 (BnF)

Le ms. ar. 7084 fait partie du fonds légué par Georges Séraphin Colin à la BnF[35]. Sur la page de titre, après une *basmala* développée, une *ḥawla*, une *taṣliya* et "wa-baʿd": *"Hādhihi l-safīna majmūʿa min ʿiddat shuʿarāʾ mashriqī wa-ḥakamī wa-ḥumaynī wa-mukātabāt wa-naḥwa dhālika wa-bi-llāh al-tawfīq wa-huwa al-rafīq"*.

3.1 *Description du manuscrit*

1. Format oblong, ouverture "calepin" + cahiers, quinions?
2. Dimensions: 245 × 180 mm.
3. Papier: Abū Shubbāk, différents papiers de type A1, présent, au Yémen, dans des manuscrits de 1345/1926 à 1372/1956 et de type A2, relevé de 1324/1906 à 1386/1967, mais avec une présence forte jusqu'en 1940. Ce papier est aussi utilisé pour des formats rectangulaires[36].

---

34 Dufour, La *Safīna* 30.

35 Pour un historique de la collection Georges Séraphin Colin, voir Guesdon, Georges S. Colin.

36 Types A1 et A2, notre classification dans Regourd, *Manuscrits de la mer Rouge* (première moitié du xxe siècle) 92-8. Fourchette de datation, résultat d'une recherche récente à la Bibliothèque universitaire de Leyde, affinant les résultats d'une première enquête au Yémen, voir ibid. 112-6, et Regourd, *Papiers filigranés* 227-51 (chap. 8) et spéc. tableaux n° 1 (p. 234) et n° 16 (p. 236), Zabid, ms. m/ḥ 1, 170 × 240 mm, et 50/3, 240 × 185 mm. La recherche à Leyde a été rendue possible grâce à un financement "Brill Fellowship".

4. Texte parallèle au dos. Page de titre, titre présenté en triangle inversé, entouré d'un triple trait en feston à l'encre mauve et rouge. Dans l'ensemble du vol., rubrication et marques de section de vers à l'encre mauve.
5. Foliotation, paginations, nombre de lignes par page (désormais nb l/p) : 359 fol., commençant à la page de titre et s'achevant au dernier feuillet écrit, foliotation au crayon à mine, BnF 2014 ou 2015, placé au feuillet inférieur lorsque le ms. est ouvert. Pas de réclame.
6. Dates : ms. du XXe s.
   - page de titre, mention d'achat : "Ṣanʿāʾ Déc. 1929 // acheté 18 Riyāl = 18 × 12 = 216 frcs // environ 800 pages (400 folios)"[37].
   - fol. 133^{v}-135^{r} : poème de type *madaḥ* félicitant les Ottomans, i.e. Mustafa Kemal et le Sultan, pour leur victoire sur les Grecs, en 1340/1921-2.
   - fol. suivants, 135^{r}-138^{v} : controverse sur la consommation de *qāt*, datée, fol. 138^{v}, 1340/1921-1922.

   Auteurs identifiés :
   Qusṭanṭīn al-Naṣrānī ;
   ʿAbd al-Karīm b. Aḥmad b. Muṭahhar ;
   ʿAbdallāh b. Ibrāhīm b. Aḥmad b. al-imām ;
   Muḥammad b. ʿAbd al-Raḥmān b. Aḥmad Kawkabān.
7. Reliure : demi-reliure d'origine, dos plat de cuir brun. Plats de carton recouverts de toile grise. Feuillets collés sur les ais et feuillets de garde : papier Abū Shubbāk.

3.2 *Contenu et discussion*

Ce manuscrit du XXe s. porte une note d'achat à la date de 1929. La brièveté du séjour de G.S. Colin dans cette ville rend peu probable le fait qu'il ait été copié à sa demande, mais on observe qu'il ne contient pas de marques de transmission.

Le scribe anonyme introduit son recueil de la manière suivante : "Cette *safīna* rassemble [des textes] de nombreux poètes [de type] *mashriqī*, *ḥakamī* et *ḥumaynī*, des échanges poétiques épistolaires et autres choses du même genre". Le contenu et la structure du texte manuscrit ont déjà fait l'objet d'une publication détaillée[38]. L'ordre des genres, entre *ḥakamī* et *ḥumaynī*, n'est pas respecté. Le texte commence, sans préambule, par un poème introduit par : "*lil-Ṣafī Aḥmad b. Sunbul raḥimahu llāh taʿālā*". Les principes de l'accumulation ou la logique présidant à l'ordonnancement des poèmes échappent à la com-

37 Les doubles lignes obliques indiquent le passage à la ligne suivante.
38 Dufour, La *Safīna*.

préhension, par ex. entre les fol. 139 et 303v, ou même au sein de la série de poèmes des Ānisī, ʿAbd al-Raḥmān (m. 1250/1834) et son fils Aḥmad b. ʿAbd al-Raḥmān (m. 1241/1825) ; l'accumulation se fait plutôt par couches successives, à partir de sources diverses, sans plan d'ensemble prédéfini.

Aux fol. 304v-339v sont regroupées des poésies de *ḥumaynī* ancien, qui n'ont peut-être pas été copiées dans la continuité de ce qui précède, car l'écriture, quoique de la même main, est légèrement différente, comme si le scribe avait employé un calame plus large ou, en tout cas, plus souple ; l'encre violette, en outre, n'a pas exactement la même teinte qu'au feuillet précédent. Rien en revanche dans l'écriture ne la distingue de la section suivante[39].

Les auteurs de certains poèmes sont difficiles à identifier. Des poèmes sont anonymes, mais, il est vrai, la plupart se trouvent dans la section de poésie *ḥumaynī* ancienne (fol. 304 au verso du fol. 339).

Est indiqué pour un certain nombre de poèmes de la partie sur le *ḥumaynī* ancien le mode musical correspondant[40]. La poésie *ḥumaynī* est très majoritairement destinée au chant, même s'il n'est pas rare que le chant accueille également du *ḥakamī*.

4 *Safīna* 2. Ms. Adab 2336 (Sanaa, Dār al-Makhṭūṭāt), *Dīwān* d'al-Ahdal

Ce *dīwān* manuscrit de Ḥātim b. Aḥmad al-Ahdal (m. 1013/1604), poète soufi, né à Moka en Tihāma[41], est conservé à Sanaa (Yémen), dans le fonds de la Dār al-Makhṭūṭāt (désormais DaM) et porte la cote Adab 2336[42].

4.1 *Description du manuscrit*

D'après images numérisées.

1. Format oblong, ouverture "calepin", cahiers fixés sur le petit côté.
2. Dimensions : feuillets de taille variée, 260 × 185 mm, 240 × 180 mm.
3. Papier : non observé sur l'original.
4. Texte parallèle au dos de la reliure.

---

39 Ibid. 16.

40 Fait exceptionnel au Yémen, voir Dufour, La *Safīna* 18, qui note que c'est "le seul manuscrit yéménite qui indique pour un certain nombre de poèmes le mode musical correspondant". Voir Reynolds, Lost Virgins 69-105.

41 Voir Dufour, *Huit siècles* 50.

42 Al-Malīḥ & ʿĪsawī, *Fihris* 582, Adab 28 (dans le ms., 28 a été barré et 2336 a été rajouté sous un trait tracé sous "Adab 28") ; ʿĪsawī et al., *Fihris* ii, 1157-1158, cote Adab 2336.

5. Foliotation, pagination, nb l/p: 253 p., 113 fol.; pagination et foliotation au crayon à mine de plomb; foliotation postérieure à la pagination, qui a été raturée. Foliotation débutant au recto du deuxième fol. Nombre de lignes/page variable.
6. Dates: ms. du début du XXe s.
   En p. 191-fol. 83, colophon d'une moitié du manuscrit ("*wa-kāna l-farāgh min hadhā l-niṣf*"): 9 muḥarram 1323/16 mars 1905. Copiste: Ibrāhīm b. Ismāʿīl b. ʿAbbās, non identifié.
7. Reliure: apparemment récente, restaurée? Pas de feuillets dispersés.

4.2 *Contenu*

Il n'est traité ici que de la partie du manuscrit reproduite par les soins de la DaM[43]. Le manuscrit abrite au moins deux recueils de poésies différents: le *Dīwān* d'al-Ahdal et la *Safīnat Munāẓara bayn al-ʿinab wa-l-nakhl* de Zayd b. ʿAlī Kibsī[44]. C'est le premier recueil qui est analysé ici.

D'un point de vue littéraire, il est difficile de se reporter à un texte éponyme, car "Plusieurs *dīwān* manuscrits d'al-Ahdal sont conservés, qui semblent remonter à des recensions différentes."[45] La partie du manuscrit de la DaM en notre possession est un recueil de poésies de genres divers. Les attributions des poèmes sont rendues compliquées parce que les feuillets ont été intervertis. L'analyse du processus de compilation de la poésie doit tenir compte du fait que les feuillets, tels qu'on les trouve aujourd'hui assemblés sous une même reliure, accusent des lacunes. Le manuscrit est acéphale et la foliotation, raturée, commence au fol. 23. Les feuillets ont été ensuite paginés suivant

---

43 Tous nos remerciements vont au Directeur de la DaM pour avoir bien voulu autoriser la reproduction de ce manuscrit. Dans al-Malīḥ & ʿĪsawī, *Fihris* 582, le manuscrit est coté Adab 28 et est décrit ainsi: "Al-niṣf al-thānī, awwaluhu mabtūr wa-awwal al-mawjūd: (4 vers), ākhiruhu: (6 vers), nuskhat Ibrāhīm Ismāʿīl ʿAbbās, bi-khaṭṭ mutawassiṭ hadīth, fī 9 shahr muḥarram sana 1323 H. 191 ṣafḥa, mukhtalifa, 24 × 18 sm. Qāla fī nihāyatihi tamma bi-ʿawn Allāh taʿālā l-niṣf al-ākhir min dīwān al-Ahdal. // Al-shiʿr al-wārid bihi shiʿr ḥumaynī. // Mabtūr min awwalihi qadr 23 ṣafḥa idhā bada'a bi-l-ṣafḥa 24 bi-l-abyāt allatī dhakarnāhā fī awwalihi. // Bihi athar araḍa fī anḥā' mutafarriqa wa-qad kharibat fī awwalihi min al-ṣafḥa 24-59 wa-fī l-ṣafḥa 79, 84, bihi athar ruṭūba fī aṭrāfihi. // Yalīhi ṣafaḥāt mabtūra tabda' min raqm 192 bi-maqṭūʿāt shiʿriyya mukhtalifa ḥattā l-ṣafḥa 250. // Yalīhi Safīnat Munāẓara bayn al-ʿinab wa-l-nakhl li-l-shaykh Zayd b. ʿAlī l-Kibs (*sic*) wa-jawāb al-shaykh ʿAbdallāh b. ʿUmar al-Khalīl wa-lahumā muʿāriḍān Abī (*sic*) Bakr Muʿayyad wa-ʿalayhim al-jamīʿ ḥukm al-ʿālim Muḥammad b. Ismāʿīl al-Amīr". Repris par ʿĪsawī et al., *Fihris* ii, 1157-8, avec quelques corrections justifiées, tel al-Kibsī, mais l'introduction de deux erreurs, 191 ff. au lieu de 191 p. et ff, au lieu de page, 24-59, 79 et 84.

44 Nous n'avons pu identifier cet auteur. Il n'est pas mentionné dans: al-Ḥibshī, *Maṣādir*.

45 Dufour, *Huit siècles* 50.

leur nombre et leur ordre actuels. Mais l'analyse technique de la poésie, surtout de la rime, révèle des feuillets manquants. Néanmoins, certains sauts suscitent bien des interrogations sur le processus de compilation.

De manière générale, le recueil n'apparaît pas composé selon un plan. Les ruptures ne sont pas annoncées, par exemple par des rubriques. L'ensemble laisse une impression de pêle-mêle. D'un point de vue littéraire, l'ordre même d'apparition des genres poétiques à l'intérieur du recueil apparaît atypique, puisque la poésie classique (*ḥakamī*) vient habituellement avant le *ḥumaynī*.

Ponctuellement, on relève :

- a. p. 158 ; b. [p. 159][46]-fol. 69[47] : p. 158, poème *ḥumaynī*, sans rubrique introductive, sans doute de type *mubayyat* abababAB, interrompu brutalement au bas du feuillet. Il devrait en principe provenir du *dīwān* d'al-Ahdal, d'après les indications que ce manuscrit, aux feuillets désordonnés, donne, notamment la main, qui est celle du colophon.
  Feuillet inférieur, autre poème de style *ḥumaynī*, qui n'est pas pris à son début (de type *mubayyat* aaaA).
- a. [p. 164] ; b. p. 165-fol. 70 : suite et fin du poème précédent, suivi d'un nouveau poème, toujours dans le style *ḥumaynī*. Ils ne sont pas rubriqués en rouge contrairement à d'autres poèmes. Pour leur appartenance au *dīwān* d'al-Ahdal, mêmes remarques que précédemment.
- a. [p. 190] ; b. p. 191-fol. 83 : en b. p. 191-fol. 83, colophon daté de la seconde et dernière section du *dīwān* d'al-Ahdal, "al-niṣf al-akhīr min dīwān (…) al-Ahdal" [fig. 10.2].
- de : a. p. 192 ; b. p. 193-fol. 84, à : a. p. 196 ; b. p. 197-fol. 86, apparaissent des fragments de *ḥumaynī*, apparemment sans rapport avec le *dīwān* al-Ahdal. Le dernier poème est placé sur un feuillet distinct et tête-bêche par rapport au poème précédent ; les deux poèmes ne couvrent pas la totalité du feuillet [fig. 10.3].
- de : a. p. 198 ; b. p. 199-fol. 87, à : a. p. 232 ; b. p. 233-fol. 104, 2 premières l. : poèmes classiques (non-*ḥumaynī*), d'inspiration soufie. La p. 19 commence avec le début d'un poème qui est dans le *dīwān* publié d'al-Ahdal[48], suivi d'un court poème. Le poème du feuillet suivant fait aussi partie du *dīwān*

46 Les numéros de page sont notés entre crochets lorsqu'ils ne sont pas visibles (feuillets fragmentaires).

47 Lorsque le manuscrit est ouvert, le feuillet folioté apparaît, optiquement, comme feuillet inférieur, à l'exception du dernier feuillet du ms. portant un texte, le fol. 113. Les feuillets paginés sans numéro de feuillets (i. e. au recto) correspondent donc, optiquement, au feuillet supérieur.

48 Al-Ahdal, *Shāʿir* 123.

publié d'al-Ahdal[49]. Il s'agit donc visiblement d'une partie du *dīwān* classique d'al-Ahdal, qui débuterait abruptement ici.

– de : p. 233-fol. 104, l. 3*sq.*, à : a. p. 236 ; b. p. 237-fol. 106, poème *mubayyat* aaaA, rime en -ar, avec désinences d'*iʿrāb* – sans hiatus avec la partie classique de ce *dīwān*, rubriqué en rouge ; la mention "*bayt*" en rouge séparant les quatrains de ce poème n'apparaît pas dès le début du poème (voir a. p. 236 ; b. p. 237-fol. 106). Suit une *qaṣīda* classique, présente dans le *dīwān* publié d'al-Ahdal[50]. Les feuillets suivants contiennent eux aussi des *qaṣīda*s classiques, sans lacune, rubriquées en rouge. La section se finit au milieu d'une *qaṣīda* dont la fin n'apparaît nulle part ailleurs dans le recueil.
– a. p. 253-fol. 113 ; b. dépourvu d'écrit, texte rédigé d'une autre main, titre d'une œuvre totalement différente, insérée dans un jeu de triangles et d'horizontales, tracés d'un double trait, rouge et mauve, la *Safīnat Munāẓara bayn al-ʿinab wa-l-nakhl* de Zayd b. ʿAlī, suivie d'une réponse par le shaykh ʿAbdallāh b. ʿAmr al-Khalīl, puis d'une réponse faite aux deux premiers par Abū Bakr Muʾayyad, et enfin, d'un jugement du *ʿālim* Muḥammad b. Ismāʿīl al-Amīr.

4.3 *Discussion*

Recueil de poésie comprenant du *ḥakamī* et du *ḥumaynī*, avec colophon à la date de mars 1905.

Le manuscrit est acéphale. Il est probable que l'absence d'ordre dans l'apparition des deux parties de ce *dīwān* ne soit qu'apparente et résulte d'un accident, par exemple, au moment où la reliure actuelle a été réalisée. En effet, le début de la section de poésie *ḥumaynī* de même que la fin de la section de *ḥakamī* manquent, la section de *ḥumaynī* commence en cours de poème et le colophon qui clôture la section sur le *ḥumaynī* indique : "*tamma bi-ʿawn Allāh taʿālā l-niṣf al-akhīr min dīwān* (…) *al-Ahdal*". Le *ḥumaynī* constitue sans aucun doute la deuxième partie du *dīwān*, et, partant, l'on s'attend légitimement à une première partie consacrée au *ḥakamī*.

Dans l'ensemble, le manuscrit de la DaM n'en reste pas moins un rassemblement composite de poèmes parfois incomplets. L'absence de rubrique et les ruptures qui ne sont pas annoncées ne rendent pas l'identification des poèmes aisée. Il est possible qu'il abrite des versions inédites du *dīwān* d'al-Ahdal, issues de familles de manuscrits inconnus à ce jour ou bien puisées à une source orale.

49 Ibid. 131.
50 Ibid. 56 et suiv.

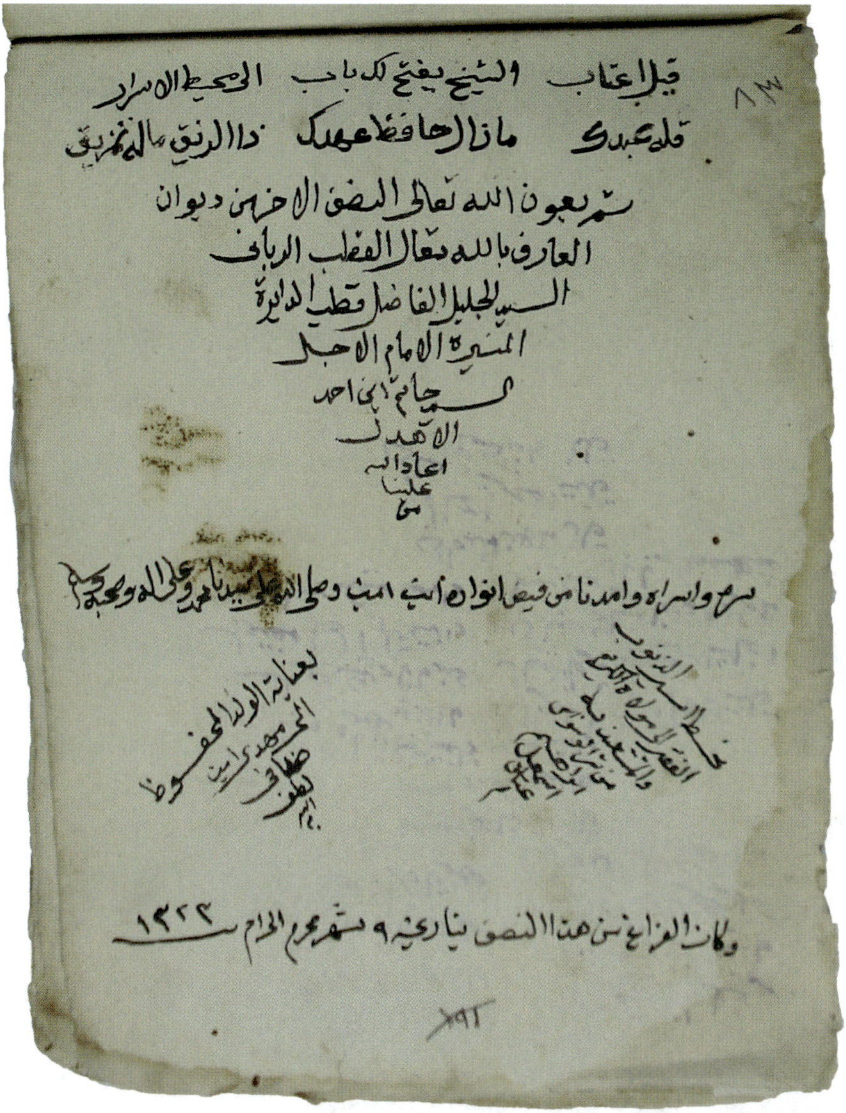

FIGURE 10.2 Colophon daté de la seconde et dernière section du *Dīwān* d'al-Ahdal, "*al-niṣf al-akhīr min dīwān* (…) *al-Ahdal*", Safīna 2 : MS Adab 2336, *Dīwān d'al-Ahdal*, p. 191-fol. 83.
SANAA, DĀR AL-MAKHṬŪṬĀT

FIGURE 10.3
Safīna 2, MS Adab 2336, *Dīwān* d'al-Ahdal, poèmes placés tête-bêche sur des feuillets distincts, p. 193-fol. 84 (fol. supérieur) et p. 191 (fol. inférieur).
SANAA, DĀR AL-MAKHṬŪṬĀT

5 *Safīna* 3. Le ms. Sharaf al-Dīn, collection privée

Ce manuscrit est conservé dans une bibliothèque privée de Sanaa, celle de Muḥammad Sharaf al-Dīn, dit Muḥammad Sharaf. Il a été consulté en 2004.

5.1 *Description du manuscrit*

N.B. : L'ensemble du manuscrit a été photographié. Nous ne disposons que des p. 5-9, puis 11-31. Elles sont toutes de la même main.

1. Format oblong, ouverture "calepin" + cahiers cousus ensemble sur le petit côté [fig. 10.4].
2. Dimensions : ca. 180 × 220 mm, un peu plus grand qu'un A5.
3. Papier : non observé sur l'original. Les feuillets sont prélevés dans un papier à la machine de couleur jaune sans marque, récent [fig. 10.5].
4. Le texte a été rédigé parallèlement au petit côté, celui où se trouve le dos de la reliure.
5. Foliotation, pagination, nb l/p. : nombre total de pages supérieur à 325 ; système de pagination entre parenthèses, en haut à droite, rappelant les livres typographiés ; autour de 20 l/p. Réclames.
6. Dates : ms. du deuxième quart du XXᵉ s. ?
   Auteurs identifiés : de la fin XIIᵉ-début XIIIᵉ s. au XIXᵉ s.
7. Reliure : récente, bloc de cahiers lié aux ais par une bande de tissu.

5.2 *Contenu*

Il s'agit d'un recueil de poésies *ḥumaynī* ; le *ḥakamī* est pratiquement absent.

Les p. 1-4 nous manquent. De la p. 5 jusqu'en haut de la p. 172, se trouve le *dīwān ḥumaynī* de Muḥammad b. Sharaf al-Dīn (m. 1010/1601)[51], *Mubayyatāt wa-muwashshaḥāt*, sans colophon. La fin du *dīwān* ou le début du texte suivant est marqué par deux traits horizontaux. Commence alors un recueil de poésies *ḥumaynī* diverses. Les auteurs sont surtout des poètes des XVIIIᵉ et XIXᵉ siècles, sanaanis ou de la région de Sanaa, de ces poètes dont l'œuvre circule surtout dans les recueils sans que, semble-t-il, il leur ait été consacré de *dīwāns* – la plupart d'entre eux se trouvent dans la *safīna* de Colin : ils sont donc plutôt connus. Chaque poète a sa section et l'agencement n'apparaît donc pas désordonné : les poèmes d'un auteur donné ne sont pas disséminés dans la *safīna* mais tous groupés ensemble ; ces groupes sont à leur tour rassemblés en quatre sections suivant la lettre initiale du nom du poète (en l'occurrence *mīm*, *nūn*, *hāʾ*, *yāʾ*), bien qu'à l'intérieur de chaque section l'ordre alphabétique ne soit pas strict.

51 Voir ci-dessus, 2., p. 324.

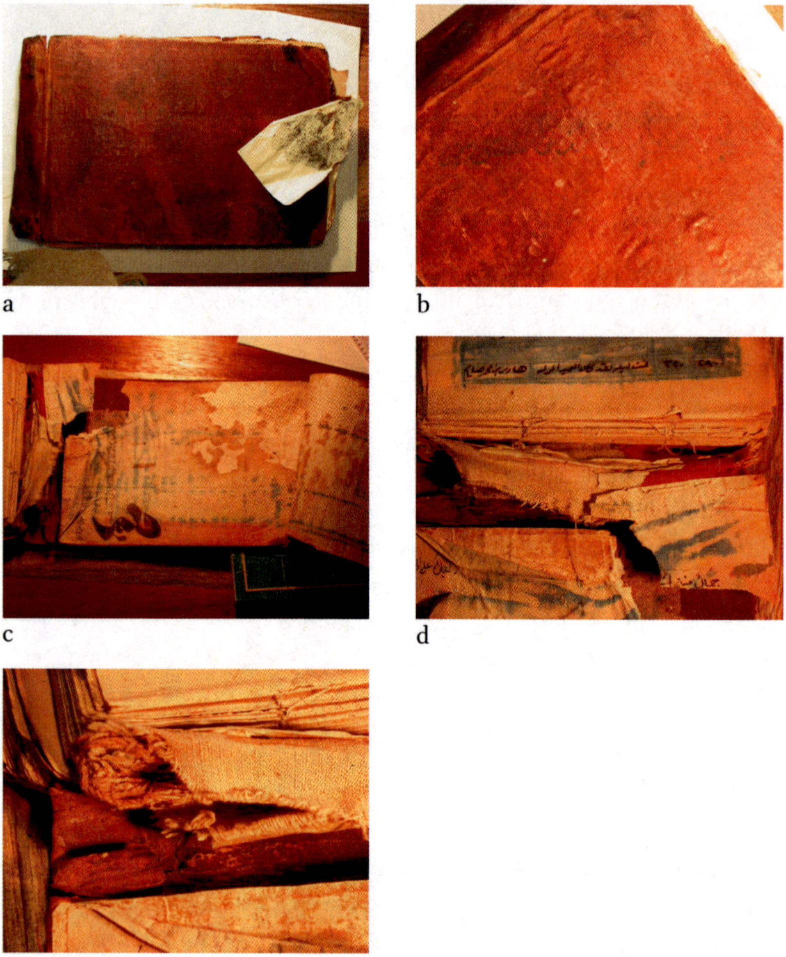

a b c d e

FIGURE 10.4 MS Sharaf al-dīn, collection privée, Sanaa. a. Reliure; b. Reliure, marque de propriété; c. Reliure, contreplat (partiel) et dos (vue interne), cahiers et couture; d. Cahiers et couture, gaze, contreplat (partiel); e. Tranchefile et dos (vue interne).

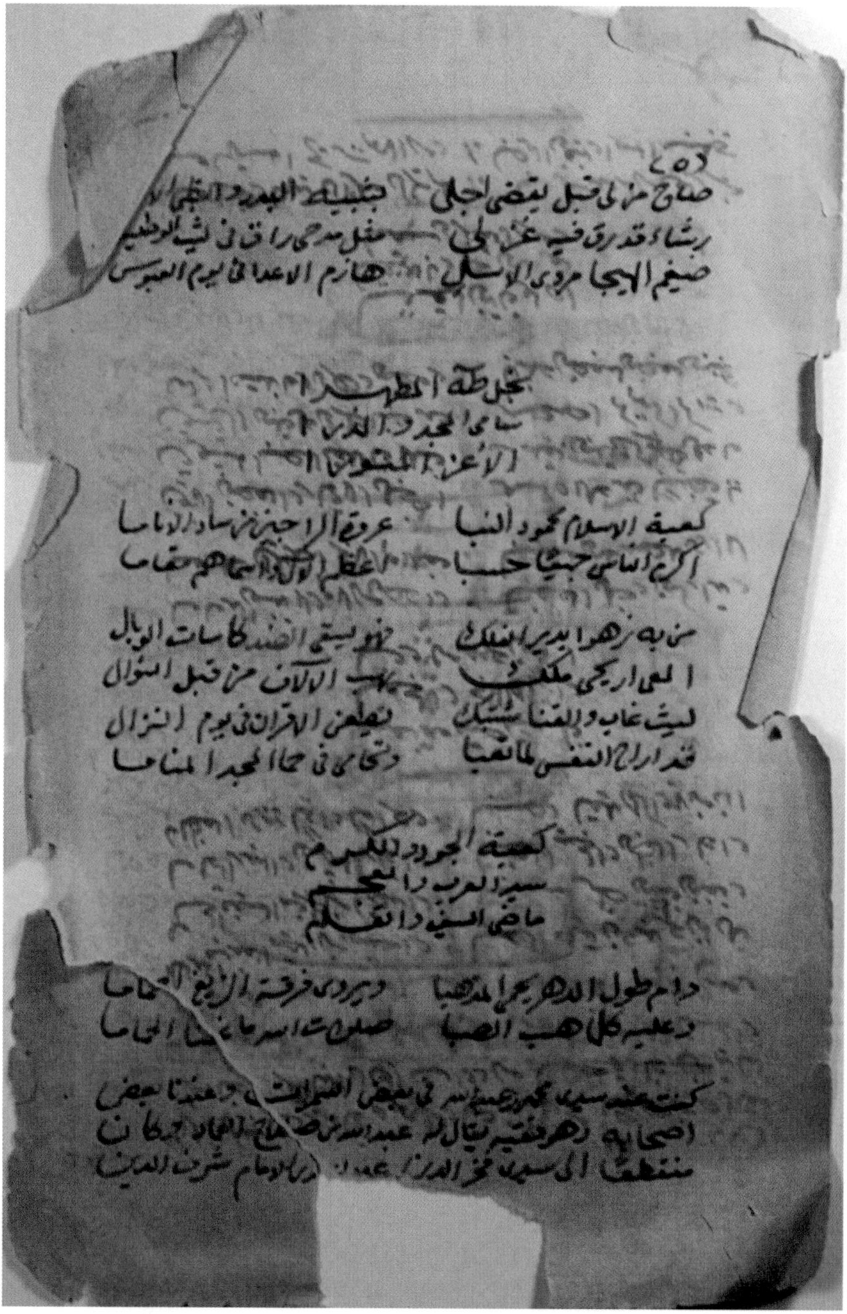

FIGURE 10.5 Papier. MS Sharaf al-dīn, collection privée, Sanaa.

Deux sections tranchent cependant :

a. P. 172-178 : poèmes de Mūsā b. Yaḥyā Bahrān (début XVIe s.) ;
b. P. 321-325 : des *muwashshaḥ*s de l'Égyptien Ibn Sanā' al-Mulk (fin XIIe-début XIIIe s.).

5.3 *Discussion*

Le manuscrit date du XXe s. (second quart ?). On note une *tatimma* sans date, suivie du nom, zaydite, du propriétaire, Hādī b. Muḥammad Ṣāliḥ. Il est fort possible qu'on ait affaire dans ce cas à une copie de manuscrit. Il contient diverses poésies *ḥumaynī*.

Les quatre manuscrits suivants appartiennent à la Fondation Zayd b. ʿAlī pour la Culture (Mu'assasat Zayd b. ʿAlī l-Thaqāfiyya, MZbAT), Sanaa. Numérisés dans le cadre du projet Yemeni Manuscripts Digitization Initiative (YMDI), ils sont accessibles sur le site de l'Université de Princeton (Princeton University Digital Library)[52].

6 *Safīna* 4. Ms. MZbAT ymdi_03_131 / Princeton 88435/cr56n2275

Ce manuscrit est catalogué sous le titre : *Safīna adabiyya taḥtawī fī awwalihā ʿalā Dīwān al-ʿAnsī*[53].

ʿAlī l-ʿAnsī (m. 1139/1726) était juge et haut fonctionnaire dans l'administration de l'imam al-Mutawakkil[54].

6.1 *Description du manuscrit*

D'après images numérisées.

1. Format oblong, ouverture "calepin".
2. Dimensions des feuillets (fiche électronique du site de Princeton) : 150 × 250 mm, avec variations : 150 × 200 ; 125 × 215 et 135 × 225 mm. Sur les 23 premiers fol. (p. 9-56), traces de rognure.
3. Papier : non observé sur l'original. En dehors des feuillets de garde, semble homogène.
4. Texte parallèle au dos de la reliure.

52 Pour plus d'informations sur l'YMDI, http://pudl.princeton.edu/collections/pudl0079, et http://ymdi.uoregon.edu/.

53 سفينة ادبية تحتوي في اولها على ديوان العنسي, texte intégralement en ligne, http://arks.princeton.edu/ark:/88435/cr56n2275.

54 Voir ci-dessus, *Safīna* 3.

5. Foliotation, paginations, nb l/p: 214 p., pagination au crayon à la mine de plomb. Nombre irrégulier de l/p.
6. Dates: jusqu'à la p. 56, fin XVIIIe s.?; début XXe s.
   - p. 31, poème, composé en éloge à l'imam al-Mutawakkil al-Qāsim (r. 1716-27) après qu'il a repoussé l'attaque des tribus contre Sanaa en 1138/1725-6.
   - p. 185-195,
     a. récit historique concernant l'imam al-Mahdī li-Dīn Allāh ʿAlī b. Muḥammad b. ʿAlī b. Yaḥyā b. Manṣūr b. Mufaḍḍal b. al-Ḥajjāj (m. 705/1305) et le rasūlide al-Malik al-Afḍal (m. 778/1377). Échange de poèmes et lettre de l'imam?
     b. P. 195, *tatimma* à la date du 18 dhū l-ḥijja 1318, soit le 8 avril 1901, écrite en lettre et en chiffre, de la main d'Ismāʿīl b. Ḥasan al-?

   Auteurs tardifs identifiés:
   - p. 9-54, al-ʿAnsī (m. 1139/1726); al-Ruqayḥī (m. 1749?);
   - p. 55 à fin: al-Samarjī (m. 1170/1757); ʿAbdallāh b. ʿAlī l-Wazīr (m. 1147/1734); Isḥāq b. Yūsuf al-Mutawakkil (m. 1173/1759?); Muḥammad b. ʿAbdallāh b. al-Imām Sharaf al-Dīn (m. 1010/1601); Yaḥyā b. Ibrāhīm Jaḥḥāf (m. 1118/1705).
7. Reliure: deux séries de dim., 170×285 mm, 170×270 mm (ais supérieur et inférieur?, fiche électronique du site de Princeton); plein cuir, rouge-brun; plats, décor à filets très fins: deux filets parallèles formant cadre rectangulaire, filet vertical central et filets obliques se croisant formant losanges; contreplat, cuir. Feuillets de garde.

6.2 *Contenu*

Le manuscrit abrite des poèmes, aussi bien que des extraits de texte en prose, historique ou "technique", ainsi que des notes de magie et de divination. Parmi les poèmes figurent deux *urjūza*s (p. 198-202; 204). D'après la fiche de Princeton, des variations dans la dimension des feuillets existent, que l'on ne peut localiser à partir d'une image. Cependant, les 24 premiers feuillets (p. 9-56) portent des traces de rognure. Le texte n'a pas été affecté; le dépouillement ne montre aucun texte disloqué, dont différentes parties apparaîtraient ici et là, et les deux seules interruptions repérées (p. 105 et 205) ne soulèvent la question de feuillets manquants que dans le cas de la p. 205.

À partir de la p. 56 apparaît une main qui réapparaît ensuite régulièrement, jusqu'à clore le texte manuscrit; les mains différentes de cette "main principale" sont, par comparaison, fugitives, et occupent parfois simplement des parties de feuillets laissées vierges (p. 106, 163, 165, 168, et, peut-être 171). Les pages précédant l'apparition de la "main principale", les p. 9 à 56, sont écrites de la même main, à l'exception des seules p. 54 et 55, "intercalaires". Elles se distinguent également par l'usage de rubrication et plus généralement d'encre rouge. La "main principale" coïncide donc avec la fin de l'utilisation d'encre rouge et signe également la fin du *dīwān* d'al-ʿAnsī (m. 1139/1726)[55].

6.3 *Discussion*

Ce recueil ne contient pas que de la poésie, mais des textes en prose, historiques ou traités, qui ne sont pas regroupés. On observe cependant des regroupements thématiques, par sujet, liant poésie et prose (p. 123-6) ou par type de poésie (p. 158-9, *maqṭaʿ*).

Le texte manuscrit débute par une phrase incomplète. Le *ḥumaynī* est quasiment absent (poèmes aux p. 55-6 et 205). Le principe de la composition d'ensemble, ainsi que l'organisation interne à la *safīna*, i.e. la succession d'une portion du *dīwān* d'un auteur à un autre, ne sont pas clairs, une impression que ne contribue pas à chasser l'absence de transition d'un texte – ou série de textes – à l'autre (hormis la rubrique annonçant une section de poésie d'al-ʿAnsī, p. 31) ou d'éléments d'identification du début du bloc suivant. Aucun principe d'organisation à l'intérieur des blocs ne se dégage à nos yeux.

La comparaison entre les cinq blocs communs à la *safīna* 4 et au ms. MZbAT ymdi_03_87 / Princeton 88435/rb68xd158, catalogué sous le titre : *al-Risāla al-ʿasjadiyya fī l-maʿānī l-muʾayyadiyya* [*safīna shiʿriyya*][56], qu'on nommera *safīna* 7, indique une alternance de ces blocs d'un manuscrit à l'autre :

	safīna 4, pages	Correspond à		*safīna* 7, pages
1.	9-13	→ ←	2.	287-289
2.	18-29	→ ←	4.	300-306
3.	31-55	→ ←	3.	290-298
4.	57-63	→ ←	5.	307-312
5.	108-122	→ ←	1.	274-287

55 Pour la description du contenu, voir Annexes, tableau 10.1, p. 358.

56 الرسالة العسجدية في المعاني المؤيدية, http://arks.princeton.edu/ark:/88435/rb68xd158. Elle ne fait pas partie de la collection de *safīna*s cataloguées dans cet article.

Pour le reste, les textes divergent.

On note la présence de devinettes (p. 18).

Le poème d'al-ʿAnsī, dont les quatre premiers vers furent improvisés "*fī l-majlis*" en salutation à l'imam al-Mutawakkil à l'occasion de la fête de rupture du jeûne, est un exemple de transmission de l'oral à l'écrit, du moins pour les quatre premiers vers (p. 33). Il est intéressant de trouver du *ḥakamī* attribué à al-ʿAnsī, dans la mesure où seule sa poésie *ḥumaynī* a été publiée à notre connaissance.

7 *Safīna* 5. Ms. MZbAT ymdi_03_142 / Princeton 88435/fj236338f

Ce manuscrit est catalogué sous le titre: *Safīna adabiyya wa-shiʿriyya taḥtawī ʿalā Muthallath Quṭrub wa-l-Rawḍ al-bāsim wa-l-Zājira li-l-umma ʿan isāʾat al-ẓann bi-l-aʾimma wa-ʿiddat qaṣāʾid wa-rasāʾil wa-mukātabāt wa-ashʿār*[57].

7.1 *Description du manuscrit*

D'après images numérisées.

1. Format oblong, ouverture "calepin".
2. Dimensions (site de Princeton): 155 × 255 mm, avec variations: 105 × 210; 105 × 230 mm.
3. Papier: non observé sur l'original. P. 5-6, 7-8/2 fol. de garde: croissant à profil humain dans un écu, certainement papier Abū Shubbāk (voir ici, *safīna* 1). Pavé écrit: p. 9-296, peut-être même papier; p. 296-312: différents papiers, voir 7., visiblement fol. ajoutés.
4. Texte en position variable par rapport au dos.
5. Foliotation, paginations, nb l/p: 312 p.; pagination à la mine de plomb; nb de l/p variable.
6. Dates: ms. fin XIXe-début XXe s. (p. 9-296).
   - p. 0: marque de propriété au nom de et de la main de Muḥammad b. Muḥammad b. Muḥammad al-Kibsī, à la date du début de ṣafar 1345, soit août 1926[58].
   - p. 12: date de composition, 25 jumādā l-ākhira 1037/2 mars 1628.
   - p. 138: texte datant de 1190/1776-7.
   - p. 232: texte datant de 959/1551-2.

57 سفينة ادبية وشعرية تحتوي على مثلث قطرب والروض الباسم والزاجرة للامة عن اساءة الظن بالائمة وعدة قصائد ورسائل ومكاتبات واشعار, http://arks.princeton.edu/ark:/88435/fj236338f.

58 Sur le manuscrit, année 345.

– p. 237 : réponse à la date de 1128/1716.
– p. 259 : mention au début du règne de Sélim II, 975-1567-8.
– p. 260 : bataille à la date de 1023/1614-5.

Auteurs identifiés : XIIIe, XVIIe et XVIIIe s.

Ibrāhīm Sāḥilī, Abū l-Qāsim Ismāʿīl b. ʿAbbād Ṣāḥib al-Ṭāliqānī, *al-Rawḍ al-bāsim fī l-dhabb ʿan sunnat Abī l-Qāsim* de Muḥammad b. Ibrāhīm b. al-Wazīr, *Zājir li-l-umma ʿan isāʾat al-ẓann bi-l-aʾimma* d'al-Mahdī li-Dīn Allāh (GAL, S II 563), Hādī b. Ibrāhīm b. al-Wazīr.

7. Reliure : dim. 175 × 360 mm (site de Princeton) ; ancienne, plein cuir, brun ; plats : décor géométrique conçu par rapport au format ; contreplats cuir. Cahiers ; p. 11-83 et 230-304, langues de papier récupéré (imprimé ou manuscrit) fixant ensemble deux feuillets volants (l'un au début, l'autre à la fin du bloc écrit ?[59]). P. 296-312 : rognés. Feuillets de garde. D'après l'état du bloc de texte, la reliure actuelle est postérieure.

7.2 *Contenu*

Le manuscrit s'ouvre sur des textes historiques en prose et se poursuit avec de la poésie. De particulière importance est le *dīwān* de Shams al-Dīn b. Aḥmad b. Aḥmad al-Ānisī (seconde moitié du XIXe s. ?), peut-être apparenté aux Ānisī père et fils (p. 41-165 ; p. 211-2 ; p. 199-191). S'y ajoutent quelques poèmes de ʿAlī l-ʿAnsī (p. 167-9 ; p. 202). Les poèmes sont tous en *ḥakamī*. Le *Muthallath Quṭrub* ne représente qu'une infime partie de l'ensemble. Dans la partie de texte débutant à la toute fin du manuscrit, se trouvent de nombreux textes en prose, essentiellement des épîtres à portée historique (*Risāla min al-Muṭahhar b. Sharaf al-Dīn ilā ahl Ṣanʿāʾ*, p. 216-24 ; *Zājira li-l-umma ʿan isāʾat al-ẓann bi-l-aʾimma min al-Mahdī li-Dīn Allāh*, p. 269-246 ; *al-Rawḍ al-bāsim ilā l-Sayyid Muḥammad b. Abī l-Qāsim min al-Sayyid Muṭahhar b. Muḥammad b. Muṭahhar*, p. 246-57) ; y figure aussi un texte de magie sous le nom d'al-Ghazālī (p. 266).

Du point de vue de la composition, on note ici aussi l'absence de préambule et des enchaînements abrupts entre poètes ou blocs de textes apparentés. L'architectonique de la reliure, les rognures, ainsi que le papier, indiquent certes le rajout des p. 296-312 et mettent en évidence un nombre important de feuillets volants à un moment donné, mais ne rendent pas totalement compte d'un désordre. Plusieurs mains sont à l'œuvre :

59 Cf. ms. ar. 3428 (BnF).

P. 9-16:	main A: *naskh* rond, *dāl* et *ṭāʾ* sous-ponctués, joli, ponctuation et vocalisation totales. Rédaction oblique
16-17:	main B: *ruqʿa* minimaliste assez régulière et élégante, très peu de ponctuation. Cette main prend le relais de A et le passe à C sans transition. Rédaction oblique
17-39:	main C: *naskh* élancé, grande maîtrise calligraphique, ponctuation abondante, vocalisation abondante, *dāl* non sous-ponctué. Texte droit et oblique
39:	main B': comme B mais moins régulier, plus penché vers l'arrière, très peu de ponctuation
41-165:	main D: *naskh* élancé mais moins souple que C, moins de différence plein/délié, ponctuation abondante, vocalisation irrégulière, mais présente, *dāl* et *ṭāʾ* sous-ponctués
166:	B'
167-170:	B": style indécis plutôt *ruqʿa*, peu de maîtrise de l'orientation du calame, ponctuation irrégulière mais pas rare, *tanwīn*, *dāl* et *ṭāʾ* sous-ponctués, pas très joli
170-180:	B'
180-188:	B"?
188-189:	*CHANGEMENT DE SENS DE LA SAFĪNA*
312-310:	E: espèce de *nastaʿlīq* / *naskh* assez horizontal, ponctuation irrégulière
309-305:	P. vierges
304-303:	Marques d'*ihmāl* (*rāʾ*, *sīn*, *dāl* sous-ponctués)
302-298:	F: *naskh* pas très adroit, peu de ponctuation, *dāl* et *ṭāʾ* sous-ponctués
297:	P. vierge
296:	début du (d'un) papier récurrent de la *safīna*
296-286:	B: élégant. Le corps du poème est écrit dans un style un peu différent de celui des notes marginales et interlinéaires, mais les deux sont sans doute du même scribe. C'est dans les notes qu'on reconnaît le mieux B comme p. 16-7
285-284:	Le corps du poème continue à être écrit par B, mais les notes sont de A
283-269:	A finit le poème seul
269-264:	B
264-261:	D
261-260:	espèce de *nastaʿlīq* qu'on ne trouve pas ailleurs, ponctuation irrégulière, *dāl* et *ṭāʾ* sous-ponctués
260-259:	B
259-237:	C, *dāl* sous-ponctué.

237-211 :	D
211-203 :	Sans doute toujours D, mais oscillation curieuse entre du *naskh* et quelque chose de plus ruqʿoïde
202 :	B
201-199 :	B'
199-191 :	B"' : style un peu plus ornemental que B, plus régulier que B', cherche des effets un peu comme B" dans l'étirement des traits horizontaux, mais y arrive élégamment contrairement à B", peu de ponctuation, quelques *dāl* sous-ponctués
191-189 :	B'.

Les mains A à D se retrouvent dans les deux 'parties' du volume, les mains E et F appartiennent au petit bloc rajouté. La main D est responsable de plus de la moitié des pages, suivie par la main A, avec 95 p[60].

7.3 *Discussion*

Le ms. est désigné par son propriétaire Muḥammad b. Muḥammad b. Muḥammad al-Kibsī comme une *safīna*.

Ici encore, le recueil admet, à côté de la poésie, des textes en prose montrant un goût prononcé pour les épîtres historiques. L'ensemble du recueil est en *ḥakamī*.

L'existence d'une deuxième main importante soulève d'intéressantes questions sur la façon dont ce recueil a été constitué et sur le lien entre son contenu, son commanditaire ou son propriétaire. L'accumulation de textes historiques donne tout de même un parfum d'ensemble à cette *safīna*, ainsi qu'une idée des centres d'intérêt de la personne à l'origine de la compilation.

8 *Safīna* 6. Ms. MZbAT ymdi_03_137 / Princeton 88435/p2676w837

Ce manuscrit est catalogué sous le titre : *Safīna shiʿriyya taḥtawī ʿalā dīwān al-Sayyid al-ʿallāma ʿAbdallāh b. ʿAlī l-Wazīr wa-qaṣāʾid li-ʿiddat shuʿarāʾ*[61].

8.1 *Description du manuscrit*

D'après images numérisées.

60 Pour la description détaillée du contenu, voir Annexes, tableau 10.2, p. 376.

61 سفينة شعرية تحتوي على ديوان السيد العلامة عبد الله بن علي الوزير وقصائد لعدة شعراء, http://arks.princeton.edu/ark:/88435/p2676w837.

1. Format oblong, ouverture “calepin”.
2. Dimensions (site de Princeton): feuillets 185 × 235 mm, avec variation: 145 × 210 mm.
3. Papier: non observé sur l’original. Possibles changements de papier aux fol. 81, puis 151, puis 261, puis 271.
4. Texte parallèle au dos.
5. Foliotation, pagination, nb l/p: 328 p.; pagination à l’encre rouge, p. 1-116 (la p. 1 correspond à la p. 81, la p. 116 à la p. 196), recouvrant l’ensemble du *dīwān* de ʿAbdallāh b. ʿAlī l-Wazīr et quelques œuvres de poètes divers; nb l/p: régulier, entre 22 et 24.
6. Dates: ms. 1348/1929.
   - p. o: marque indiquant que le texte est de la main du propriétaire, Muḥammad b. Muḥammad b. Muḥammad b. Ismāʿīl b. Muḥammad b. Yaḥyā b. Aḥmad al-Kibsī, à la date du 17 rabīʿ l-awwal 1348/23 août 1929.
   - p. 62: date de composition d’un *takhmīs*, 22 jumādā l-awwal 1346/ 17 nov. 1927, à Shahāra/Shihāra.
   - p. 140: mort d’un dénommé ʿUmar Shaykhān à La Mecque en 1113/1701-2.
   - p. 145: réponse faite à un Shaykh en 1118/1706-7.
   - p. 171: date cryptée dans le dernier hémistiche d’un vers, 1121/1709-10.

   Auteurs identifiés: du XIIIe au dernier quart du XVIIIe s.
7. Reliure: dim. 190 × 245 mm (site de Princeton); ancienne, plein cuir, brun; décor sur les plats avec filets, mandorle centrale et écoinçons.

8.2 *Contenu*

La note autographe de la p. o, par le propriétaire, compilateur et scribe, Muḥammad b. Muḥammad b. Muḥammad b. Ismāʿīl b. Muḥammad b. Yaḥyā b. Aḥmad al-Kibsī, désigne le manuscrit comme *safīna*. Parmi les poésies citées, deux vers de ʿAbdallāh b. ʿAlī l-Wazīr font l’éloge “d’une *safīna* qui contenait de la poésie”:

وقال في سفينة جامعة أشعار
سفينتك التي رقَّت وراقت – لديها القلب قد أضحى رهينة
وقد ضمّت بحورَ الشعرِ طُرًّا – ومِن عجبٍ بحورٌ في سفينة.

Ta *safīna* délicate et charmante a pris notre cœur en otage.
On y trouve tous les mètres (*buḥūr*) de la poésie:
quel prodige qu’un navire qui contient les océans!

p. 176

Les *dīwāns* de nombreux poètes se trouvent représentés dans la *safīna* 6. Le plus développé est celui de ʿAbdallāh b. ʿAlī l-Wazīr (m. 1147/1734), dont une première partie, p. 81-185, suit un ordre alphabétique ; l'autre partie, p. 197-217, est dédiée au *ḥumaynī*. Les p. 224-47 recueillent les poèmes et réponses de ceux que l'on pourrait nommer Banū Isḥāq. Leur font suite des parties conséquentes des *dīwāns* d'al-Sharīf al-Raḍī l-Mawsūʿī (m. 1016/1607-8), p. 251-73, d'al-Ṣafī l-Ḥillī (m. 750/1349), p. 274-87, d'al-ʿAnsī (m. 1139/1726), dans un jeu de réponses où l'un des Banū Isḥāq réapparaît (p. 290-8), d'Aḥmad al-Ruqayhī (m. 1749 ?), p. 300-6, et de Muḥammad Khalīl al-Samarjī (m. 1170/1757), p. 307-12. Des devinettes en vers se trouvent à la p. 300. On note une pièce en *sajʿ* (p. 186-9). Parmi les textes techniques, en prose, la section sur les calculs géomantiques pour localiser un objet caché, p. 69, revêt un intérêt particulier. Sont aussi consignées des anecdotes (p. 189-186).

Le texte commence sans préambule, il est précédé de feuillets réglés. Il est d'une main unique, celle de son propriétaire, Muḥammad b. Muḥammad Kibsī. Le texte manuscrit est distribué entre deux grandes sections, la première consacrée à la poésie classique (*ḥakamī*) et la seconde à la poésie *ḥumaynī*. Dans cette seconde section, même si des poèmes, dont les auteurs alternent, peuvent être regroupés par le système des réponses, on a encore ici des sauts d'un bloc à l'autre ou dans le temps sans transition, on a le sentiment d'une juxtaposition.

Le recueil a été exécuté avec soin, sur des feuillets réglés à la *misṭara*, avec un usage modéré d'encre rouge, des variations dans la couleur des encres noires, puis de l'encre mauve[62].

8.3 *Discussion*

Les deux vers de ʿAbdallāh b. ʿAlī l-Wazīr “à propos d'une *safīna* qui contenait de la poésie” (p. 176) confirment que le sens de “navire” pour *safīna* – ou l'association entre les deux notions – est bien présent dans les esprits. Ils laissent entendre aussi qu'une *safīna* peut être organisée autour d'un projet.

Dans une note autographe, al-Kibsī prend la peine de dire qu'il est à la fois le propriétaire de la *safīna*, son compilateur – ou l'auteur du recueil –, et celui qui a tenu le calame (p. 0). Cette indication fait entrevoir un lien personnel à l'objet. Al-Kibsī est par ailleurs propriétaire de la *safīna* 5, qui n'est pas de sa main.

62 Pour la description détaillée du contenu, voir Annexes, tableau 10.3, p. 396.

9 Discussion générale et conclusions

L'aire géographique de disponibilité des *safīna*s – tout du moins dont l'appartenance est attestée – pointe vers l'Asie, vers les pays du Shām, l'Iran, la Turquie et le Yémen. Dans différents domaines doctrinaux ou de la perception des sciences, le Yémen montre des affinités avec cet ensemble "culturel"[63]. Dater le phénomène au Yémen est difficile car un catalogue des *safīna*s yéménites (format et titres de poésies ou de recueils) qui soit pourvu d'une vision sur la durée et tienne compte des problèmes de conservation affectant les manuscrits privés reste à faire. Le salon, déjà évoqué, de ʿAlī b. al-Ḥasan al-Khafanjī (m. vers 1766-7), appelé "al-Safīna", qui se tenait à Sanaa atteste du lien entre *safīna* et poésie *ḥumaynī*, dès le XVIIIe s. Quant aux six exemples étudiés ici, ils se situent entre la fin du XIXe s. et le second quart du XXe s., assurant de la permanence de ces recueils. Ils semblent cependant être tombés peu à peu en désuétude, peut-être dès la seconde moitié du XXe s., si l'on en croit nos observations sur les hauts plateaux auprès des deux générations suivantes.

Cette étude est une première contribution à la question de la quiddité des *safīna*s yéménites, fondée sur un nombre encore limité d'exemples, mais suffisamment variés pour amorcer une réflexion. Ce sont bien des recueils (sing. *majmūʿ*) sous format oblong. Les textes qu'ils abritent sont en poésie aussi bien qu'en prose poétique ou prose, avec pour la prose des sujets variés (textes scientifiques, historiques, louanges, textes littéraires, …), l'ensemble présenté de manière chaotique. Plus qu'un "bateau" parce qu'il serait porté à la ceinture, les Yéménites ont vu dans la *safīna*, dans un trait d'humour typique des hauts plateaux, une allusion à l'Arche de Noé dont la mission était d'embarquer toutes les créatures[64].

Dans l'ensemble, cependant, la poésie émerge, corroborant le lien entre *safīna* et un genre d'écrit, le recueil de poésies, un lien que confirme l'usage qui, par métonymie, donne le titre de *safīna* à des recueils de poésies, indépendamment du format. C'est le cas ici de la *safīna* 2, qui abrite, aux côtés du *dīwān* d'al-Ahdal, la *Safīnat Munāẓara bayn al-ʿinab wa-l-nakhl* de Zayd b. ʿAlī l-Kibsī.

63 Voir par ex. les travaux du "Muʿtazilite Manuscripts Project Group" sur le *kalām* muʿtazilite.

64 Piamenta, *Dictionary* i, 224b-225a, atteste historiquement les sens suivants: "anthology of Yemeni folk literature [Ṣanʿāni songs] figuratively related to the Ark of Noah for its variegated selected items" (cite Al-Akwaʿ, *al-Amthāl* v(e) et n. 2), "or because it holds much of Yemeni folk legacy" (cite Ghānim, *Shiʿr* 8, et Rossi, Appunti 246), en même temps que les sens communs à l'arabe classique: "cf. oblong book, commonplace book" (cite Lane, *Dictionary* 1375c), "also a collection, a compilation" (cite Dozy, *Dictionnaire* i, 660a).

Quant au format oblong, on note que trois sur les six manuscrits décrits ici sont désignés par un locuteur (propriétaire, auteur de marque d'achat) comme *safīna*.

La présence de *ḥumaynī*, apparaissant *grosso modo* après la section de poésie classique (*ḥakamī*), sauf accident, et un cas, unique, de "*qaṣīda* en millefeuille", confère une spécificité textuelle aux recueils poétiques yéménites. Les exemples réunis ici confirment la valeur des *safīna*s comme source d'un *ḥumaynī* qui n'a pas sa place dans les *dīwān*s. Il est plutôt représentatif de ce qui circule sur les hauts plateaux entre la fin du XIXe s. et le deuxième quart du XXe s., à savoir la production des hauts plateaux eux-mêmes à partir du XVIIe s., mais aussi des poèmes de la première zone de développement du *ḥumaynī*, la Tihāma, avec le *dīwān* de Ḥātim b. Aḥmad al-Ahdal (m. 1013/1604, *safīna* 2). Il n'en reste pas moins que leur exploitation devra passer par un effort et des stratégies d'identification. Certains sujets, telles les merveilles d'Égypte, dont font partie les pyramides, partagés avec des *safīna*s ottomanes[65], ouvrent sur une recherche comparée des textes en prose, élargie à l'ensemble des recueils, et soulèvent la question de *topoi* littéraires communs. Si l'épaisseur des volumes yéménites rend difficile leur transport à la ceinture, l'existence de devinettes, d'anecdotes ou de *khabar*s rappelle le caractère tout à la fois éducatif et ludique attribué aux *safīna*s persanes, propres à agrémenter une pensée circumambulatoire. Avec devinettes et anecdotes, les poèmes courts (*maqāṭiʿ*), les *takhmīs*s et les *urjūza*s placent les *safīna*s yéménites dans la lignée du Suppl. persan 1798 du milieu du XVe s. et des recueils arabes du XVIIe au XIXe s. conservés à la BnF.

Certes recueils poétiques, mais dont la composition ou l'organisation générale ne semblent pas suivre un plan présent d'entrée de jeu : ils commencent sans préambule, on note des sauts d'auteurs et de périodes sans annonce, progression ou plan visibles ; des poèmes sont incomplets et même leur écriture interrompue. Les textes en prose ressemblent à des extraits. Aucun principe de compilation n'est décliné ou indiqué. L'unité textuelle, lorsqu'on la ressent, vient du choix des textes, comme dans le cas de la *safīna* 5, qui peut résulter d'un projet général, comme le laissent entendre les deux vers de ʿAbdallāh b. ʿAlī l-Wazīr (*safīna* 6, p. 176).

Chaque *safīna* offre un recueil unique. Il reçoit des auteurs multiples et la *safīna* 6, écrite de la main de son propriétaire, ne fait apparaître aucune œuvre de son cru. Feuillet après feuillet, c'est à une prise de notes personnelles que l'on pense, bien différente des notes de savant ou de recherche, sans doute

65 Voir Rieu, *Supplement* 725-6 (n° 1147), une *safīna* selon son titre, datée de 1052/1642, contenant un passage sur les Pyramides aux fols. 126-34 ; l'origine du ms. est incertaine : il ne fait pas partie de la collection Glaser.

davantage un choix de poésies et de textes en prose qui reflète le goût ou l'intérêt de son possesseur. Ce choix peut entraîner l'addition pure et simple d'une partie d'un autre manuscrit (les 55 premières pages de la *safīna* 4). C'est dans ces limites précises que la notion d'auteur (*authorship*) doit être pensée. Réalisées parfois avec soin, on y voit des traces de réglure, des rubrications et un jeu d'encre de couleur. C'est le caractère unique de chaque *safīna* qui en fait des holographes potentiels ; seule la *safīna* 6 correspond à la définition *stricto sensu* d'un manuscrit entièrement écrit par l'auteur (texte et main)[66], mais cela n'est pas suffisant pour remettre en question le lien générique aux holographes.

Les *safīna*s yéménites sont des codex. Parmi les exemples produits ici, on ne voit pas figurer de calepin acheté tout prêt à être utilisé[67]. La *safīna* 2 a reçu une reliure postérieure, tandis que la 5 a connu une étape de restauration.

Il est possible que la *safīna* 3 soit la copie d'une *safīna*. Le cadi Yaḥyā l-ʿAnsī a reçu en héritage la *safīna* de son grand-père[68]. Il n'est donc pas exclu que la copie de ces recueils soit commandée par des questions de transmissions familiales, qui pourraient aussi rendre compte de l'existence de mains différentes à l'œuvre, lorsqu'elles éclipsent la présence d'une main principale. Leur vente, comme tout manuscrit, à des personnes hors de la lignée est attestée par les cas de la *safīna* 1, du début du XXᵉ s., peut-être de la 5, en 1926, et de la *safīna* du cadi al-ʿAnsī, héritée de son grand-père, qu'il souhaitait vendre dans les années 1990.

Le *ḥumaynī* est lié à une culture savante et les connaissances de ceux qui le lisent et le pratiquent, on le voit ici, s'étendent à la poésie classique. La copie de textes écrits est un canal important, sans doute majeur, de la transmission des textes. Le poème d'al-ʿAnsī, dont les quatre premiers vers furent improvisés "*fī l-majlis*" en salutation à l'imam al-Mutawakkil (r. 1716-27) à l'occasion de la fête de rupture du jeûne, restitué dans la *safīna* 4 (p. 33), est non seulement un exemple d'improvisation, mais de transmission de l'oral à l'écrit, qui vient corroborer la description des *safīna*s donnée par Jaʿfar ʿAbduh Dafari (voir ici, 2., p. 324). Le *ḥumaynī* chanté est attesté à Sanaa dans ces réunions sociales où l'on mâche du *qāt* que l'on nomme *magyal*s, dont l'existence a été relevée dès

66 Nous suivons la définition d'holographe et d'autographe par Gacek, *Vademecum* 14-6 et ce volume, p. 55-6 ; v. aussi l'introduction de ce volume, particulièrement p. 3.

67 Les premiers manuscrits sur cahiers d'écolier relevés à Zabīd (Tihāma) remontent au début des années 1970.

68 Nos remerciements vont à Muḥammad ʿAbd al-Raḥīm Jāzim (CEFAS) pour nous avoir communiqué ces informations, ainsi que celles qui suivent sur la vente du manuscrit. Yaḥyā l-ʿAnsī est l'auteur d'ouvrages sur les calendriers agricoles au Yémen.

le XVIe s.[69] : ils ont dû être un haut lieu de “relevé” de textes, copiés ou entendus. Les *safīnas* recueillent et reflètent potentiellement une poésie, plus largement un *adab*, vivants, en train de naître. Beaucoup d'auteurs nous sont inconnus. Cette autre chaîne de transmission – orale/non écrite – en fait aussi une source importante pour l'étude de la poésie.

ʿAbdallāh al-Surayḥī abonde dans le sens d'une transmission orale et écrite des textes des recueils et ajoute qu'il n'y avait pas de maison d'oulémas, au Yémen, sans une ou plusieurs *safīnas*[70]. À partir de données encore bien minces, orales ou écrites, et en l'absence de relevés ethnographiques, on risquera que, recueils de lettrés pour des lettrés, elles ont tout à la fois une dimension personnelle et sociale. Identifiables immédiatement par leur format, elles posent socialement leur propriétaire ou leur compilateur. Voit-on en eux, dès que l'on reconnaît l'objet, un amateur de poésie, peut-être musicien? C'est plus difficile à tenir.

Entre texte et pratique, les *safīnas* sont, au Yémen, à la fois un texte et un objet, à la lisière de l'objet social et personnel. De manière significative, des manuscrits produits au Yémen qui sont parvenus en Éthiopie, de la circulation d'apprentis savants et de lettrés ou clercs dans les deux directions, il n'est jamais ressorti jusqu'ici, ni de format oblong, ni de recueil-*safīna*, parmi les manuscrits arabes, ni non plus de phénomène d'acculturation de ce type de recueil[71].

Bibliographie

Sources primaires

Al-Akwaʿ, I. b. ʿA., *al-Amthāl al-yamāniyya*, Le Caire.

Al-ʿAmrī, M. b. ʿA. (comp.) et Ḥ.ʿA. al-ʿAmrī (éd.), *Safīnat al-adab wa-l-tārīkh*, Beyrouth-Damas 2001.

Ibn al-Ḥusayn, A. *Majmūʿ rasāʾil al-Imām al-shahīd al-Mahdī Aḥmad b. al-Ḥusayn* (*ṣāhib Dhībīn*), ed. ʿA. al-K. A. Jadbān, Ṣaʿda 1424/2003.

Qushayrī, ʿA. al-K. b. H. et M. Ḥasan, *al-Rasāʾil al-qushayriyya*, Pakistan 1964.

Al-Thaʿālibī, *Tatimmat Yatīmat al-dahr*, Beyrouth 2000.

69 Dufour, J'ai ouï 14, 22; Lambert, *La Médecine* 39 et suiv. (chap. 11) sur les *magyal*s, 76 et suiv. sur le *ḥumaynī* en relation avec la musique.

70 Nos remerciements vont à ʿAbdallāh al-Surayḥī (Université d'Abu Dhabi et Bibliothèque nationale, Abu Dhabi).

71 Wetter, Manẓūma.

Sources secondaires

Al-Ahdal, Ḥ. b. A., *Shāʿir al-Mukhā Ḥātim al-Ahdal*, ed. ʿA. al-R. Ṭayyib Baʿkar, Sanaa 2005.

Aynur, H., et al. (éd.), *Mecmûa: Osmanlı Edebiyatının Kırkambarı*, Istanbul 2012.

Björkman, W., Ḳaṭʿ, dans *EI*² iv, 741-3.

Blochet, E., *Bibliothèque nationale. Catalogue des manuscrits persans*, Paris 1928.

Bosch, G.K., et al., *Islamic bindings and bookmaking. A catalogue of an exhibition*, Chicago 1981.

Canova, G., Sayf b. Dhī Yazan: history and saga, dans S. Dorpmueller (éd.), *Fictionalizing the past: Historical characters in Arabic popular epic. Proceedings of the workshop at the Netherlands-Flemish Institute in Cairo 28th–29th of November 2007 in honor of Remke Kruk*, Louvain-la-Neuve 2012, 107-23.

Chelhod, J., La Geste du roi Sayf, dans *Revue de l'histoire des religions* 171 (1967), 181-205.

Dafari (al-Ẓafārī), J.ʿA., *Ḥumaini poetry in South Arabia*, PhD diss., Londres, School of Oriental and African Studies, 1966.

Déroche, F., et al., *Islamic codicology. An introduction to the study of manuscripts in Arabic script*, Londres 2005.

Déroche, F., et al., *Manuel de codicologie. Introduction à l'étude des manuscrits en écriture arabe*, Paris 2001.

Déroche, F., et V. Sagaria Rossi, *I manoscritti in caratteri arabi*, Rome 2012.

Dufour, J., *Huit siècles de poésie chantée au Yémen. Langue, mètres et formes du* ḥumaynī, Strasbourg 2011.

Dufour, J., "J'ai ouï chanter les oiseaux": Musique, chant, danse et poésie humayni, dans *Quaderni di Studi Arabi* n.s. 7 (2012), 11-46.

Dufour, J., La *Safīna* de Colin: une source importante pour l'histoire de la poésie *ḥumaynī*, dans *Chroniques du manuscrit au Yémen* 15 (janv. 2013) (http://www.cmy.revues.org).

Fani, S., et M. Farina, *Le vie delle lettere. La Tipografia Medicea tra Roma et l'Oriente*, Florence 2012.

Gacek, A., *Arabic manuscripts. A vademecum for readers*, Leyde-Boston-Cologne 2009.

Gacek, A., *The Arabic manuscript tradition. A glossary of technical terms and bibliography*, Leyde-Boston-Cologne 2001.

Ghānim, M.ʿA., *Shiʿr al-ghināʾ al-ṣanʿānī*, Beyrouth 1973.

Guesdon, M.-G., Georges S. Colin au Yémen en 1929, dans *Chroniques du manuscrit au Yémen* 15 (janv. 2013) (http://www.cmy.revues.org).

Halm, H., al-Ḳus̲h̲ayrī, dans *EI*² v, 526-7.

Al-Ḥibshī, ʿA.M., *Maṣādir al-fikr al-islāmī fī l-Yaman*, Abu Dhabi 2004.

ʿĪsāwī, A.M., et al., *Fihris al-makhṭūṭāt al-yamaniyya li-Dār al-makhṭūṭāt wa-l-Maktaba al-gharbiyya bi-l-Jāmiʿ al-kabīr, Ṣanʿāʾ*, 2 vol., Qom-Téhéran 1425/1384/2005.

Lambert, J., *La Médecine de l'âme*, Nanterre 1997.

Lintz, Y., Cl. Déléry, et B. Tuil Leonetti, *Le Maroc médiéval. Un empire de l'Afrique à l'Espagne*, Paris 2014.

Al-Malīḥ, M.S., et A.M. ʿĪsāwī, *Fihris makhṭūṭāt al-Maktaba al-gharbiyya bi-l-Jāmiʿ al-kabīr bi-Ṣanʿāʾ*, Alexandrie s. d. [ca. 1398/1978].

Manqūsh, Th., *Sayf b. Dhī Yazan bayn al-ḥaqīqa wa-l-usṭūra*, Bagdad 2004.

Al-Maqāliḥ, ʿA. al-ʿA., *Shiʿr al-ʿāmmiyya fī l-Yaman*, Beyrouth 1986.

Paret, R., *Sirat Saif b. Di Yazan, ein arabischer Volksroman*, Hanovre 1924.

Piamenta, M., *Dictionary of post-classical Yemeni Arabic*, 2 vol., Leyde-New York-Copenhague-Cologne 1990.

Piemontese, A.M., *Catalogo dei manoscriti persiani conservati nelle biblioteche d'Italia*, Rome 1989.

Regourd, A., Manuscrits de la mer Rouge (première moitié du XXᵉ s.) : papiers Abū Šubbāk du Yémen et d'Éthiopie, dans A. Regourd (ed.), *The Trade in Papers Marked with Non-Latin Characters. Documents and History / Le commerce des papiers à marques à caractères non-latins. Documents et histoire*, Leyde 2018, 81-140.

Regourd, A., Papiers filigranés de manuscrits de Zabīd, premier tiers du XVIIIᵉ-milieu du XXᵉ siècle : papiers importés et 'locaux', dans D. Hollenberg, Ch. Rauch, et S. Schmidtke, *The Yemeni Manuscript Tradition*, Leyde-Boston 2015, 227-51.

Réunion des musées nationaux, *Musée du Louvre, Arts de l'Islam*, inventaire n° OA7109 : 'le lecteur', Boukhara, vers 1600-1630 (en ligne http://www.photo.rmn.fr/C.aspx?VP3=SearchResult&VBID=2CO5PCoXAKRYZ&SMLS=1&RW=1916&RH=863)

Reynolds, D., Lost virgins found : The Arabic songbook genre and an early North African exemplar, dans *Quaderni di Studi Arabi* n.s. 7 (2012), 69-105.

Richard, F., *Catalogue des manuscrits persans, Bibliothèque nationale de France, Département des manuscrits. Tome II : Supplément persan. Première partie, 1-524 ; Deuxième partie, 525-1000* (Series Catalogorum V/1-2), 2 vol., Rome 2013.

Richard, F., *Splendeurs persanes : manuscrits du XIIᵉ au XVIIᵉ siècle*, Paris 1997.

Rieu, Ch., *Supplement to the catalogue of the Arabic manuscripts in the British Museum*, Londres 1894.

Rossi, E., Appunti di dialettologia del Yemen, dans *Rivista degli Studi Orientali* XVII (1938), 230-65.

Roxburgh, D.J., Jong, dans *EIr* xv, fasc. 1, 11-4 (dernière mise à jour 17 avril 2012, http://www.iranicaonline.org/articles/jong).

Roxburgh, D.J., The Aesthetics of aggregation : Persian anthologies of the fifteenth century, dans O. Grabar et C. Robinson (éd.), *Islamic Art and Literature*, Princeton 2001, 119-42.

Roxburgh, D.J., *The Persian album, 1400-1600 : From dispersal to collection*, New Haven-Londres 2005.

Scheper, K., *The Technique of Islamic bookbinding. Methods, materials and regional varieties*, Leyde-Boston 2015.

Schmidt, J., *Catalogue of Turkish manuscripts in the Library of Leiden University and other collections in the Netherlands III. Comprising the acquisitions of Turkish manuscripts in Leiden University Library between 1970 and 2003*, Leyde 2006.
Sotheby's, *Arts of the Islamic world, London 7 October, 2009*.
Teece, D.-M., *Vessels of Verse, Ships of Song : Persian Anthologies of the Qara Quyunlu and Aq Quyunlu Period*, PhD New York University, 2013 (http://bobcat.library.nyu.edu/primo-explore/fulldisplay?docid=nyu_aleph003962106&context=L&vid=NYU&search_scope=all&tab=all&lang=en_US).
Vrolijk, A., J. Schmidt, et K. Scheper, *Turcksche boucken : de oosterse verzameling van Levinus Warner, Nederlands diplomaat in zeventiende-eeuws Istanbul/The Oriental collection of Levinus Warner, Dutch diplomat in seventeenth-century Istanbul*, Eindhoven 2012.
Wagner, M.S., *Like Joseph in beauty : Yemeni vernacular poetry and Arab-Jewish symbiosis*, Leyde 2009.
Wetter, A., Manẓūma, dans *Encyclopaedia Aethiopica* iii, 2007, 754-5.
Witkam, J.J., Nuskha, dans *EI*[2] viii, 149-53.
Al-Ziriklī, Kh. al-D., *al-Aʿlām. Qāmūs tarājim li-ashhar al-rijāl wa-l-nisāʾ min al-ʿArab wa-l-mustaʿribīn wa-l-mustashriqīn*, Beyrouth [5]2002.
Zisska & Lacher, *Catalogue de vente aux enchères* n° 64 Munich, 5-6 (nov. 2014).

Annexes : description du contenu des *Safīna*s 4 à 6

N.B. : les poèmes se faisant suite et appartenant au *dīwān* d'un poète, ainsi que les poèmes liés directement les uns aux autres (ex. réponses), ont été encadrés d'un trait noir épais, simple. *"Dīwān"* est pris dans un sens large, couvrant toute pièce poétique d'un même auteur.

Les textes juxtaposés liés par un thème sont, eux, signalés par un triple trait noir.

TABLE 10.1 Description du contenu de la *Safīna* 4

Remarque	***Incipit***	**Auteur**	**Page**
	Marque de bibliothèque. Autre marque (... الله وفى الله ؟)		1
Pages de garde vierges.			2-8
Partie supérieure, rubrication : le shaykh ʿAbd al-Raḥmān b. Muḥammad al-Dhahabī ayant demandé à ʿAlī b. Muḥammad al-ʿAnsī (m. 1726) de lui envoyer un exemplaire de son *dīwān*, celui-ci le fit en l'accompagnant de deux vers faisant allusion à Imru' al-Qays (m. ca. 550). Vers d'al-ʿAnsī, réponse du cheikh. P. 12 : virgules à l'encre rouge, marques de début et fin de vers et lettres rehaussées à l'encre rouge.	ذا وشي برد سا بري	علي بن محمد العنسي (m. 1139/1726)، عبد الرحمن بن محمد الذهبي	9
Réponse de ʿAlī l-ʿAnsī[72], introduite par, rubriqué : فأجَابه القاضي العلامه بقوله deux premiers vers en rouge.	أرخيم لحن موصلي	علي العنسي	13
Devinette en vers d'al-Ruqayḥī, sans doute, Aḥmad b. Ḥusayn al-Ruqayḥī, m. 1749, introduite par, rubriqué : من هنا اللغز / وللبديع احمد الرّقيحي مُلْغزاً فى أل وهو الـ... Marques à l'encre rouge de début, milieu et fin de vers. Lettres rehaussées à l'encre rouge.		الرقيحي (m. 1749 ?)	18

72 Comparer p. 9-13 avec *Safīna* 7, p. 287-9. Cité en *safīna* 7, 87 et 141.

TABLE 10.1 Description du contenu de la *Safīna* 4 (*suite*)

Remarque	***Incipit***	**Auteur**	**Page**
Réponse, introduite par, rubriqué: فاحابه حسين الحداد بقوله Début, milieu et fin de vers marqués à l'encre rouge. Lettre rehaussée à l'encre rouge.		حسين الحداد	18
Deux poèmes courts, introduits par, rubriqué: وله فى المكاتبه وله متغزّلاً et *maqāṭi*ʿ d'al-Ruqayḥī, introduits rubriqué: وله فى الحال والشّارب موريًا وله عفى الله عنه وله مقطوع P. 19, début, milieu et fin de vers marqués à l'encre rouge, lettres rehaussées à l'encre rouge.		الرقيحي	18-9
Introduit par, centré: وله متغزلاً	في الثغر در وفي الخدين توريدُ	الرقيحي	20
Poème détaché du précédent par un espace.	أدرها كؤسا من معتقة صرفا	?	20
Réponse au précédent poème? Poème détaché du précédent par un espace.	تبدّت فغاب البدر في الأفق واستخفا	?	23
Poème détaché du précédent par un espace. P. 26, début, milieu et fin de vers marqués à l'encre rouge.	ما للأسير بحبها إطلاقُ	?	25
Introduit par وله سقى الله حدثه ابلُ الرَّحمه مُتَغَزّلاً, rubrication dont lettres rehaussées à l'encre rouge dans la première moitié du vers, seconde moitié du vers à l'encre rouge. P. 27, début, milieu et fin de vers marqués par une virgule à l'encre rouge.	ما روى عن صبابة المشتاق	?	26

TABLE 10.1 Description du contenu de la *Safīna* 4 (*suite*)

Remarque	***Incipit***	**Auteur**	**Page**
Introduit par, rubriqué: وله من هذا الدّر النظيم والغزل الدى يترك الخلى سهم	هو الحب قد لاحت عليك مخايله	?	27
Poème détaché du précédent par un espace. P. 30, milieu et fin de vers marqués par une virgule à l'encre rouge, lettres rehaussées à l'encre rouge. *Tatimma* rubriquée, s. d.	طمع العاذل فينا ان نمارى[73]	?	29
Ouverture d'une section consacrée à al-ʿAnsī (m. 1726), rubriquée. Puis introduction au poème, un éloge à l'imam, sans doute al-Mutawakkil al-Qāsim (r. 1716-27), après qu'il eut repoussé l'attaque des tribus contre Sanaa en 1138/1725-6, rubriquée par surlignage de lettres à l'encre rouge. Début, milieu et fin des vers marqués par une virgule rouge. Lettres rehaussées à l'encre rouge.	سفت كمد الاسلام والبغي راغمُ	علي العنسي (m. 1139/1726)	31
Introduction au poème, rubriquée par lettres rehaussées à l'encre rouge, وله رحمه الله قالها صبحة عيد الفِطْر quatre premiers vers, improvisés "*fī l-majlis*" en salutation à l'imam al-Mutawakkil à l'occasion de la fête de rupture du jeûne, avec lettres rehaussées à l'encre rouge. Vers rubriqués. P. 33, marques à l'encre rouge en début, milieu et fin de vers. Lettres rehaussées à l'encre rouge.	ملك اغر ويوم عيد أزهرُ	العنسي	33
Premier vers détaché du poème. P. 36-7, marques rouges en début, milieu et fin de vers, lettres rehaussées à l'encre rouge. Rubriquées, mentions de Muḥammad b. ʿAbdallāh b. Ḥusayn b. al-Qāsim et de Zayd b. Muḥammad.	وما رضيت بالعبد منها كغيرها	?	35

73 Comparer p. 18-29 avec *Safīna* 7, 300-6.

TABLE 10.1 Description du contenu de la *Safīna* 4 (*suite*)

Remarque	***Incipit***	**Auteur**	**Page**
Introduit par, rubriqué: وللسد العلامه البليغ الحامل لوآ الادب والمجلى فى حلة البيان لكل من مارس الادب وداب محمد بن اسحق مكاتبا للقاضى العلامه على بن محمد العنسى رحمهما الله هده القصده التى عزت عن الاشباه Début, milieu et fin des deux premiers vers marqués par des virgules à l'encre rouge.	ذنبِ الجفا عند ذنب البين مغتفَرُ	العنسي	37
Réponse, introduite par, rubriqué: فاجابه سيدي محمد بن اسحق بقوله رحمه الله P. 42-3, milieu et fin des vers marqués par des virgules à l'encre rouge, lettres rehaussées à l'encre rouge.	يا صاحِ هذه شذا اهل الحمى عَطِرُ	محمد بن إسحق (m. 1167/1754)[74]	40
Au cadi al-ʿAnsī, introduit, rubriqué à l'encre noire et rouge: وللسد محمد المذكور للقاضى البليغ المذكور P. 43, milieu et fin des vers marqués par des virgules à l'encre rouge, lettres rehaussées à l'encre rouge.	اى صبر لم تفنه الأشواق	محمد بن إسحق	43
Poème détaché du précédent par un espace, mêmes mètre et rime que le précédent. Probablement réponse du cadi al-ʿAnsī.	هي شَمْسٌ له الثريا نِطَاقُ	العنسي ؟	45
Courte réponse de Muḥammad b. Isḥāq. P. 48, milieu et fin des vers marqués par des virgules à l'encre rouge, lettres rehaussées à l'encre rouge.	ايها السيد المكاتب عبداً	محمد بن إسحق	47

74 Cf. al-Ziriklī, *al-Aʿlām* vi, 30.

TABLE 10.1 Description du contenu de la *Safīna* 4 (*suite*)

Remarque	***Incipit***	**Auteur**	**Page**
Introduit par, rubriqué : من شعر السيد العلامة الحسين بن علي بن الإمام رحمه الله مكاتبا للقاضي العلامة علي بن محمد العنسي رحمه الله. Sans doute al-Ḥusayn b. ʿAlī b. al-Imām al-Mutawakkil, m. 1736. Dernier vers rubriqué. Milieu et fin des vers marqués par des virgules à l'encre rouge.	لقد زار... قد رقا	الحسين بن علي بن الإمام المتوكل (m. 1736 ?)	48
Réponse, introduite en gros caractères : فاجابه القاضى البليغ بهذه القصيده التى نظّم فيها اللئالى الفريده ولله درهما P. 50-1, milieu et fin des vers marqués par des virgules à l'encre rouge, lettres rehaussées à l'encre rouge.	عقيله ملك لو فرشت لها الطُّرقَا	العنسي	49
Introduction rubriquée : وكان السد حسن بن على هذا نادرة الدهر ومن حسنات الزمان التى اوجدها الكريم لاهل ذلك العصر جمع بين الهزل والجد مع علو الجَد وشرف الجد ومن شعره مادحا حاله ولله دره حيث جا باللّطافه وعدل عن الجداله	قمت في مركز الجمال بذاتك	حسين بن علي	51
Changement de main. Introduit par, rubriqué : وله بَلَّ الله ثراه بوامل رحمته Milieu et fin des vers marqués par des virgules à l'encre rouge.	سمعتُ فى روضِ الحمى بالبلا	حسين بن علي	54

TABLE 10.1 Description du contenu de la *Safīna* 4 (*suite*)

Remarque	*Incipit*	Auteur	Page
Introduit par, rubriqué: وله ايضا رحمه الله فى الحُميني البَديع متواسلاً الى الاله الكريم السميع. Tous les deux vers, "*bayt*", et *tatimma*, rubriqués. Milieu et fin de vers marqués par des virgules à l'encre rouge.	يا قديم الاحسان بلغوا... (؟)[75]	حسين بن علي	55
En milieu de p., passage à une autre main (dorénavant "main principale"). Parole de "*amīr al-mu'minīn*" ('Alī?). [À partir de la p. 56, les introductions ne sont plus rubriquées, mais centrées avec, parfois, des caractères plus grands. Les expressions qui reviennent sont: "وله رحمه الله", "غيره", mais peuvent être indiqués le nom de l'auteur ou le sujet du texte. Ne seront donc signalées ci-dessous que les entrées riches d'informations supplémentaires.]			56
Madaḥ dédié à al-Wazīr Aḥmad b. 'Alī l-Nihmī.	من ركب الشمس فى اغصان بلور	محمد بن خليل سمرجي (m. 1170/1757)	57
	بدت بصبح جبين لاح ابلجه	محمد بن خليل سمرجي	58
	وسلام معنبر العرق يرتاح	?	58
Introduit par, centré: محمد خليل سمرجي رحمه الله	سيف الجفون وسهم الناظر الغنج	محمد خليل سمرجي	59
Introduit par, centré: ولمحمد خلىل سمرجى يمدح صنعا واهلها	سقى جانبي صنعا دل سحابه	محمد خليل سمرجي	60
Introduit par, centré: وله ايضا مما قاله فى صنعا	خطرت من نحو نعمان تناجا	محمد خليل سمرجي	61

75 Comparer p. 31-55 avec *Safīna* 7, 290-8.

TABLE 10.1 Description du contenu de la *Safīna* 4 (*suite*)

Remarque	***Incipit***	**Auteur**	**Page**
Introduit par, centré : وله يمدح بير العزب	سقا البير براق الوميض المفلج	محمد خليل سمرجي	62
	زارت وصدر الليل فود شايب	محمد خليل سمرجي	62
Poème détaché du précédent. La moitié inférieure de la p. est vierge.	ولما تلاقينا وللشوق فى الحشا[76]	محمد خليل سمرجي	63
Introduit par, centré : للسد الحليل الاديب العلامه عد الله ن صلاح العادل كان من بلغا اهل صنعا المفلقن المجيدن فى جلتي النظم والنثر وله من النظم الوحيز المفرغ في قالب الا برىز والمعانى المسكره فى الاسالب الغربه النصره فمن نطمه على جهة الهحو والتنكيت ما كتبه الى السد اسمعيل فابع وذلك انه وعده بحايزة ابيات فبقى ... ايام لوصول الجا ىزه فلم ىشعر الا بوصول الموعود به وذلك قدحىن ذره واقزه قد استارضت ونحل حوفها وذهب اللب وىعا؟؟ العشريطيش من النسيم اذا دنا منه وىنفر من نغض الشياب وينبو عنه فلما تاملها وعرف محملها ومفصلها حعل هذه القصيده وارسلها اليه فضاق السيد اسمعل فابع لذلك درعا؟ واقبل نحوه يسعا مستدركا عثرته ومستقيلا من زلته واحزل له العطيه وهى هذه رحمه الله تعالى 1. Première partie (prose) 2. Poème	سلا هل الصب بعد النازحين سلا[77]	عبد الله بن صلاح العادل	64

76 Comparer p. 57-63 avec *Safīna* 7, 307-12. Malgré le changement de main, suite de la même série de textes que dans l'autre *safīna* ; si c'est le cas, celle-ci est plus probablement l'original (ou un ancêtre de l'original).

77 Voir *Safīna* 7, 7.

TABLE 10.1 Description du contenu de la *Safīna* 4 (*suite*)

Remarque	*Incipit*	Auteur	Page
Introduit par, centré : القاضى العلامه محمد ابن الحسن الحيمى Le tiers bas de la p. est laissé en blanc.	مغرالخيلا اين منه ملاذه	محمد بن الحسين الحيمي	65
Mubayyat	الصلاه تغشاك يا خير البريه	علي بن ابرهيم بن... الامير (cf. *safīna* 4, 97 ; *safīna* 7, 74, 244, 313-6)	66
Introduit par le nom de l'auteur du poème, centré.	لثمت ثغر عذولي حين سماك / فلذ حتى كاني لاثم فاك	جمال الدين[78] ابن نباتة	69
Introduit par le nom de l'auteur du poème, centré.	كيف الخلاص وقلبي بعض... اك	شمس الدين بن الصايغ	69
Introduit par le nom de l'auteur du poème, Muḥammad b. Yūsuf Talla'afrī (m. 696/1296), centré. Le poème connaît un autre *incipit*, "رُدّي الكؤوس...", ce qui implique sans doute en amont ردى lu fautivement ارى.	ارا الكوس التى فيها حمياك	التلعفري (m. 696/1296)[79]	70
Qaṣīda, introduite par, centré : وهذه القصيده للشهاب الرضى الموسوي يمدح الرسول صلى الله عله واله وسلم	هذا العقيق وتلك شم رمانه	شهاب الرضى الموسوي	70
Louange à 'Alī b. Abī Ṭālib, introduite, centré : وقال نغمده الله برحمته واسكنه فسح جنته يمدح امير المومنن وسد الوصىن على ابن ابى طالب كرم الله وجهه P. 75, partie inférieure du fol. laissée vierge.	غربت عنكم شموس التلاق	التلعفري	73

78 Le ms. donne : حمال الد ابن إلخ.
79 Voir *Safīna* 7, 10.

TABLE 10.1 Description du contenu de la *Safīna* 4 (*suite*)

Remarque	***Incipit***	**Auteur**	**Page**
Introduit par, centré : يمدح السيد بركات خان	خفرت لسيف الغنج ذمة مغفر	التلعفري	76
Introduit par, centré : وقال رحمه الله تعالى	اما ومواضي مقلتيها الفواصل	التلعفري	78
Introduit par, centré : وقال رحمه الله تعالى يمدحه	ميلوا بنا نحو الحزون ونكبوا	التلعفري	81
Introduit par, centré : وقال ايضا يمدحه	كتم الهوى فوشى النحول بسره	التلعفري	84
Introduit par, centré : وقال يمدحه ايضا	ضربوا القباب وطنبو بها القنا	التلعفري	88
Introduit par, centré : وقال رحمه الله يمدحه Partie inférieure p. 93 laissée vierge.	خطرت فما الغصن وهو ممنطق	التلعفري	90
Échange avec al-sharīf al-Mūsawī (al-Raḍī m. 1016 ?). Introduit par, centré : الحمد لله وحده Poème de Muhadhdhib al-Dīn introduit par : وهي avec extension du *yā*ʾ.	عذّبت طرفي بالسهر	مهذب الدين بن منير الطرابلسي	94
Poème introduit par وهي avec extension du *yā*ʾ.	بالحسن ثم الحسين... ال هاشم	علي بن ابرهيم الأمير (cf. *safīna* 4, 66 ; *safīna* 7, 74, 244, 313-6)	97
Texte formant un carré ; à l'intérieur, 4×3 lettres séparées en diagonale, en direction du centre, la lettre centrale est toujours un *sīn* : talisman ?			97
Introduit par, centré : لبعضهم	عادة الدهر بغيرته جنون	anonyme	98

TABLE 10.1 Description du contenu de la *Safīna* 4 (*suite*)

Remarque	*Incipit*	Auteur	Page
Introduit par, centré : للقاصى عبد القادر النويلى (؟) مكاتبا للسيد عبد الله بن على الوزير رحمهم الله تعالى	عد عن ذاك الحما والكثيب	عبد القادر النويلي ؟	98
Réponse, introduite par, centré : فاجاب سيدى العلامه السيد عبد الله الوزير رحمه الله بقوله واجاد	لا وقد تحت خدٍ مذهب	عبد الله بن علي الوزير (m. 1147/1734)	99
Introduit par le nom de l'auteur, centré.	لو رانا ليل بدرى لا اختفا / بدرك الباهى السنا فى حجبك	إسحق بن يوسف المتوكل (sans doute celui m. 1173/1759 ?)	100
Le tiers inférieur de la p. 101 est laissé vierge. Petite pièce en *saj*ʿ du même auteur sur *al-Rawḍa* ? Introduite par, centré : ومن قوله فى نعت الروضه عند ان حصل التفضيل لغيرها من المنتزهات فاطلق عنان القلم بقوله رحمه الله تعالى		إسحق بن يوسف المتوكل ؟	100-1
Introduit par une *ḥamdala*, suivie du titre ci-contre, soit "Récits et faits étonnants sur les pyramides d'Égypte", centré. La moitié inférieure de la p. 105 a été coupée avec un instrument tranchant. Le texte s'interrompt brutalement après la mention وقال غيره خلىلى, laissant un espace vierge. La partie prélevée n'est donc pas la cause de l'interruption du texte.	عجيبه فى ذكر الاهرامات	?	102-5
D'une autre main, d'un calame très fin, partie d'un vers, isolée. Le reste de la p. est vierge. Il s'agit du verso de la p. précédente, dont il ne reste qu'une moitié.		?	106
Page vierge.			107

TABLE 10.1 Description du contenu de la *Safīna* 4 (*suite*)

Remarque	*Incipit*	Auteur	Page
Retour à la main principale. Introduit par le nom de l'auteur, al-Ṣafī l-Ḥillī (m. 750/1349), dont le texte précise qu'il est "un poète du VIIe s.", centré من كلام الصفى الحلى من شعرآ القرن السابع فمن شعره فى الحماسه وعلو نفسه واجاد	لين ثلمت حدى صروف النواب	الصفي الحلي (m. 750/1349)	108
Poème introduit par, centré : وله رحمه الله تعالى Tiers inférieur de la p. 111 vierge.	سل الرماح العوالي عن معالينا	الصفي الحلي	110
Introduit par, centré : وقال رحمه الله تعالى يمتدح	ان لم ازر ربعكم سعياً على الحدق	الصفي الحلي	112
Introduit par, centré : وقال ايضا يمتدح الملك شمس الدن P. 115, partie inférieure prélevée, visiblement avant la copie du texte qui respecte ces nouveaux contours.	دت عقارب صدغه فى حده	الصفي الحلي	114
Introduit par, centré : وقال ايضا يمتدحه	انى لىطرىنى العذول فانثنى	الصفي الحلي	117
Introduit par, centré : وقال الصفي وهو بمصر الى الامام قاضي القضاة تاج الدين السبكي الحنفي	تركتنا لواحظ الاتراك	الصفي الحلي	119
Introduit par, centré : وله رحمه الله وقد سئم الاقامه والراحه واللهو واستاق اقاربه والحركه اليهم والتزم فى كل ىىت الجناس اللفظي فى شطريه فقال	لسيري فى الغلا والليل داجٍ	الصفي الحلي	120

TABLE 10.1 Description du contenu de la *Safīna* 4 (*suite*)

Remarque	*Incipit*	Auteur	Page
Introduit par, centré: وقال رحمه الله تعالى وقد كتب اليه الشيخ العالم المهذب محمود ن يحى النحوي الحلى من ماردن قصيده ادلها عبد العزز على انتُ ؟؟ ولمجدك التعظم والتعزز فاجابه بقوله	من لي بقربك والمزار عزُز	الصفي الحلي	121
Court poème fait de mots rares. Introduit par, centré: وقال رحمه الله تعالى وقد سمع احد الفضلا شعره فى ~~التحمس~~ فاستحسنه وقال لا عيب فه سوى قلة استعماله اللغه العربيه وغرب الكلام فكتب اليه	انما الخيربون والدردش[80]	الصفي الحلي	122
Extrait d'un traité d'astrologie. Le texte commence en haut de la p. 123, visiblement au milieu d'une phrase. Noms: Ibrāhīm b. Ismāʿīl b. Muḥammad et al-ṭabīb b. Qādir al-Shāfiʿī? Il enchaîne par une section (*bāb*) sur l'entrée de Saturne dans chacun des 12 signes du zodiaque et les conséquences sur l'année en cours en particulier au Yémen; elle s'achève au bas de la p. 124. Puis, suit la question des différentes manières de classer les signes du zodiaque selon leurs qualités. Enfin, la question du calcul du premier mois de l'année. Même main ("main carrée")? Copié en petits caractères, points diacritiques irréguliers.		?	123-6
Introduit par, centré: منصومه فى طالع الفجر	طلسم بطا ما فى المنارل بقتضي	?	126
Court texte, introduit par, centré: الحمد لله لبعضهم رحمهم الله Retour, semble-t-il, à la "main principale".	ان… منا الذى نحن فيه	anonyme	127

80 Comparer p. 108-22 avec *Safīna* 7, 274-87.

TABLE 10.1 Description du contenu de la *Safīna* 4 (*suite*)

Remarque	***Incipit***	**Auteur**	**Page**
Maqāṭiʿ de divers poètes arabes, dont Abū Nuwās. Introduits par une référence à l'auteur ou par le sujet, centré. P. 135 et 137, tiers inférieur de la p. laissé vierge.		divers poètes	127-37
Description de Damas par Ibn al-Wardī (m. 1348-9). Débute par le texte ci-contre.	قال ابن الوردي دمشق من اجل اقليم الشام	ابن الوردي (m. 1348-9)	138
Poème d'al-Shihāb al-Rūmī, sans doute Yāqūt, sur Damas. Introduit par: ولما وصلها الشهاب الرومي لم يطب له المقام بها و[تضـ]ـايق عليه الامر بها انشا يقول رحمه الله تعالى	فيا لله من زمنٍ عجيب	الشهاب الرومي ياقوت ؟ (m. 622/1225)	140
Maqāṭiʿ de divers poètes arabes. Introduits par غيره ou le nom de l'auteur, centrés. Citation d'al-Suyūṭī à l'année 820/1417-8. Le texte s'arrête au 2/3 de la p. 143 ; tiers restant, vierge.	*Maqāṭiʿ*		141-3
Retour à la main du traité d'astrologie ("main carrée") ? Introduit par, centré : الحمد لله وحده قال فى التتمه (؟) وحدىى ابو عبد الله محمد ىن حامد الحامدي (؟) قال عدى ىاى محمد الخازن... الصاحب ان عباد ينشد قصيدته فه الى اولها	هذا فوادك تهيا بين اهوآء	أبو عبد الله محمد بن حامد الحامدي ؟	144
Court poème, sans rubrique (*urjūza*). La moitié inférieure de la page est vierge. Sans doute main principale.	ملت بها فانتبهت رقودها	?	145
Autre main ? Un petit *khabar*, un *maqṭaʿ*, un poème d'al-Ṭughrā'ī, introduit par son nom, centré. Il s'agit probablement de Mu'ayyad al-Dīn Abū Ismā'īl al-Ḥasan b. 'Alī Ṭughrā'ī (m. vers 1121), alchimiste, poète et écrivain, le Ṭughrā'ī le plus célèbre et ce poème lui est attribué.	هب وهنا من الغوير نسيم		146

TABLE 10.1 Description du contenu de la *Safīna* 4 (*suite*)

Remarque	***Incipit***	**Auteur**	**Page**
Extrait d'un livre de médecine, introduit par une *ḥamdala*, suivi du texte ci-contre centré. Autre main ("main ronde").	هذا منقول من كتاب شرف اسرار الطب للعان تاليف محمد بن احمد بن علي الحموي رحمه الله	محمد بن احمد بن علي الحموي	147
Main inconnue? Récit historique sur al-Ḥajjāj (poète de Bagdad, m. ca. 941-1000), introduit par une *ḥamdala*. La page se finit par و من شعره يصف الأسد mais la page suivante (fol. différent) ne comporte pas la poésie annoncée.		?	150
La page commence au milieu d'un texte. *Akhbār* avec citations poétiques. Le texte des *akhbār*s s'achève dans la partie supérieure de la p. 157, dont plus des 3/4 est laissé vierge, à l'exception de quelques eulogies, peut-être d'une autre main. Retour à la main principale.		?	151-7
Au verso de la p. précédente, le texte commence sans transition par un vers de poésie isolé, suivi de غيره, centré, puis du premier *maqṭa*ʿ, puis de غيره, centré, puis du second *maqṭa*ʿ, enfin du poème de Zayd b. Muḥammad b. al-Ḥasan b. al-Qāsim b. Muḥammad, introduit par son nom, centré.	اتراه يكتم ما تحن طلوعه	Deux *maqṭa*ʿs anonymes, puis زيد بن محمد بن الحسن بن القاسم ابن محمد	158
Un *maqṭa*ʿ de chacun des deux poètes. Le second, Abū l-Ḥasan b. Manṣūr b. Ismāʿīl al-Tamīmī, est présenté comme un *faqīh* et poète égyptien, m. en 306/918-9.		أبو الصلت أمية بن عبد العزيز، وأبو الحسن بن منصور بن إسمعيل التميمي	159
Histoire, citation des *Ṭabaqāt* d'al-Subkī, au sujet de Niẓām al-Mulk (m. 1092), célèbre vizir des deux grands sultans seldjoukides, Alp Arslān (r. 1063-72) et Malik-Shāh (r. 1072-92). Introduit par le texte ci-contre, centré.	ابو الحسن بن علي بن اسحق العباسي الطوسي الوزير (...) الملقب بنظام الملك	السبكي	159

TABLE 10.1 Description du contenu de la *Safīna* 4 (*suite*)

Remarque	*Incipit*	Auteur	Page
Al-Qushayrī est décrit, dans l'introduction au poème, comme l'auteur d'*al-Risāla al-Ṭarīqa* (*sic*)[81], né en rabīʿ al-awwal 378 (= juin-juil. 988) et m. le dimanche 16 rabīʿ al-ākhir 465 (= 30 déc. 1072), d'après al-Subkī.	يا من تقاصر شكرى عن ايادیه[82]	الإمام القشيري النيسابوري	161
Un *maqṭaʿ*, introduit par, centré: ومن نطمه	لا تدع خدمه الاكابر واعلم	الإمام القشيري النيسابوري ؟	162
Même main que p. 146? Introduit par le nom de l'auteur, centré.	اهذه سير فى المجد ام سور	القاضي الفاضل عبد الرحيم	162
Partie supérieure de la p., deux vers de poésie isolés, main principale. Suivis d'un espace. Puis, *ṣifat sharāb al-tūt* (recette de la "boisson de mûres" tirée d'al-Ḥamawī), par la même main que le texte médical des p. 147 *sq*. ("main ronde").	صفة شرب التوت	الحموي (voir p. 147)	163
Trois vers de poésie, main principale, introduits par, aligné à droite, par une autre main: اىات فى سدق		?	164
Sur une page blanche, horizontalement: Coran VI, v. 79, suivi sans transition du v. 162; verticalement: 2 phrases, code d'écriture des lettres de l'alphabet? Est-ce par souci de remplir la page? Main inconnue.	Dont Coran		165
Autre main inconnue. Milieu et fin de vers marqués. Le texte s'arrête au premier tiers de la page. Sur la portion restante, quelques "graffiti", dans le sens vertical, essentiellement des séries de chiffres indiens.	لولا تحيه بعض الأَرسُم الدرس	العمري	166-7

81 Cette oeuvre n'est pas répertoriée par Brockelmann dans la *GAL*. L'imam Abū l-Qāsim al-Qushayrī est en fait né en rabīʿ al-awwal 376/986, cf. Halm, al-Ḳus̲h̲ayrī. Les dates indiquées par le texte ne laissent néanmoins aucun doute, il s'agit bien du célèbre soufi, dont on a ici l'attestation que l'œuvre était connue en pays zaydite, au début du XXe s.

82 Le poème est cité dans: Ḥasan, *al-Rasāʾil*. Voir la notice qui lui est consacrée.

TABLE 10.1 Description du contenu de la *Safīna* 4 (*suite*)

Remarque	***Incipit***	**Auteur**	**Page**
Main difficile à identifier, mais visiblement différente de celle de la p. suivante. Début du texte d'astronomie repris p. suivante, débutant par un titre de section (ci-contre). Suivi de 2 vers sur la connaissance des figures géomantiques, débutant par un titre de section (ci-contre). Puis sur la moitié inférieure de la p. laissée libre, jouxtant les 2 vers, *basmala*, *taṣliya* et proverbe ?, de la même main que p. 165, et lettres isolées témoignant d'un exercice d'écriture. Plus du tiers inférieur de la p. vierge.	باب في معرفة اشرف الكواكب السبعة باب في معرفة اشكال الرمل		168
Main inconnue jusqu'à présent ? Texte d'astronomie agricole, débutant par une *ḥamdala*, suivie par le titre de section repris de la p. précédente, différentes sections. P. 170, moitié inférieure vierge.	باب في معرفة اشرف الكواكب السبعة		169
Introduction d'un poème (*qaṣīda*). Plusieurs mains dont certaines malhabiles, qui suggèrent un exercice d'écriture. À l'encre verte, "*tajriba*".		?	171
Main ressemblant beaucoup à la "main principale", mais beaucoup plus régulière et plus anguleuse, qu'on nommera "main droite". Chronique tardive sur les Ayyoubides au Yémen (XVIIe s. ?), débutant par une *ḥamdala*, suivie du texte ci-contre.	تاريخ مختصر في ذكر أيام بني أيوب ودولتهم في اليمن الميمون وبني رسول وبني طاهر والأتراك	?	172-8
La "main droite" continue. Le texte est introduit par, en gros caractères : من كلام الشيخ أبو بكر الخوارزمي... رسالة كتبها إلى أهل طبرستان Il s'arrête à mi-page, p. 184. Dans la partie inférieure restée vierge, perpendiculaire au petit côté, *abjad* donnant la valeur de chaque lettre en nombre.	رسالة إلى أهل طبرستان	أبو بكر الخوارزمي (*adīb* persan, m. ca. 993)	178-84

TABLE 10.1 Description du contenu de la *Safīna* 4 (*suite*)

Remarque	***Incipit***	**Auteur**	**Page**
Récit historique concernant l'imam al-Mahdī li-Dīn Allāh ʿAlī b. Muḥammad b. ʿAlī b. Yaḥyā b. Manṣūr b. Mufaḍḍal b. al-Ḥajjāj (m. 705/1305) et le rasūlide al-Malik al-Afḍal (m. 778/1377). Échange de poèmes et lettre de l'imam ? P. 195, تم رقم ذلك, suivi, en lettre et en chiffre, de la date du 18 dhū l-ḥijja 1318, soit le 8 avril 1901. Mais il est difficile de savoir ce qui est daté. Quart inférieur de la p. vierge.			185
Toujours "main droite". Morceaux poétiques concernant les rois du Yémen préislamique, dont un poème de louange à Sayf b. Dhī Yazan[83], introduits par : لبعضهم رحمهم الله Le texte s'arrête au premier quart de la p. 197, le reste de la p. est vierge.		anonyme	196-7
Urjūza décrivant Sanaa. L'attribution de ce poème à Sharaf al-Dīn est inusitée. Introduit par, centré : منقول من مضومة محمد ن عد الله ن الامام شرف الدن رحمه الله يصف صنعا ومنتزها ىها فى هده الارجوره ولله دره فانترعت من دلك وصف حده لىكون مقابل ما اورد الـ... وعيره فى وصف الغوطه قال محمد بن عد الله الحمد لله	وقد توسمت حمىع ارضي	محمد بن عبد الله بن الإمام شرف الدين (m. 1010/1601)	198-202
Sans doute même main, mais calame beaucoup plus fin. Introduit par, centré : مما قاله القرونى[84] العلامه شرف الدين (؟)... الامام حفطه الله هذه القصىده الفرىده P. 203, *tatimma* ; le reste de la p. est vierge, à l'exception d'une *taṣliya*, écrite tête-bêche près du bord opposé au dos.	شمايل لا تنسا وان شغل الفكر	شرف الدين ؟	202-3

83 Cf. historique, Paret, *Sirat* ; Chelhod, Geste ; plus récent : Canova, Sayf ; en arabe, Manqūsh, *Sayf*.

84 Points diacritiques du *qāf* absents.

TABLE 10.1 Description du contenu de la *Safīna* 4 (*suite*)

Remarque	***Incipit***	**Auteur**	**Page**
Retour semble-t-il à la “main principale”. Vers d’Abū Nuwās, introduits par son nom, centré. *Urjūza* célèbre d’al-Aṣmaʿī (m. ca. 828/212-3), introduite par, centré : للاصمعي أرجوزة	كان ثيابه اطلعن من ازراره قمرا صوت صفير البلبل	ابو نواس (m. ca. 815/1201) الاصمعي (m. ca. 828/212-3)	204
Interruption de l’*urjūza* d’al-Aṣmaʿī (fol. manquants ?). Poème satirique burlesque en structure de “*qaṣīda* en mille-feuille”[85], avec alternance de distiques de *qaṣīda muʿrab* xAxA et de *bayt malḥūn* bbbA, le tout en *ṭawīl*. Le début du poème manque. Tiers inférieur de la p. vierge. Le papier de ce fol. est très abîmé.		?	205
Éclaircissement sur le sens à donner à certains mots employés par l’auteur, qui voulait parler de membres de la famille qāsimide[86]. Introduit par le texte ci-contre, centré. Seul le début du texte figure.	هذ[ا] سوال... كل المعاني الرامقة ما... الطباع و... في الاسماع للسيد يحيى بن ابراهيم جحاف والظاهر انه يقصد بمعناه بعض الخلفا من ال القاســـــــم	يحيى بن ابراهيم جحاف (m. 1118/1705)[87]	206
Pages de garde vierges.			207-13
Au stylo.	Tentative de table des matières du ms., vite interrompue.		214

85 Dufour, *Huit siècles* 129, 217 *sq*.
86 La dynastie des imams zaydites qāsimides a régné sur le Yémen de 1597 à 1962.
87 al-Ziriklī, *Al-Aʿlām* viii, 135.

TABLE 10.2 Description du contenu de la *Safīna* 5

Main	Remarque	*Incipit*	Auteur	P.
	Marque de propriété au nom de Muḥammad b. Muḥammad b. Muḥammad al-Kibsī, début de ṣafar 1345/août 1926.		محمد بن محمد بن محمد الكبسي	1
	Pages de garde vierges, plus courtes.			2-4
	Pages de garde vierges.			5-7
	Sur page de garde, tentative vite interrompue de table des matières du ms., au stylo, sans doute de la même main que dans la *safīna* ymdi_03_131.			8
A	Page endommagée qui devait être une des premières avant l'ajout des pages de garde. Bande de papier ajustant les deux parties du fol. séparées et restaurant le texte manquant, encre. Oblique/dos, *basmala*, texte à portée historique (épître ?) qui semble écrit par le fils de l'Imam al-Manṣūr bi-llāh al-Qāsim b. Muḥammad (m. 1029/1620).		Fils de l'Imam al-Manṣūr bi-Allāh al-Qāsim b. Muḥammad (m. 1029/1620)	9
–	Oblique/dos, nouvelle *basmala* et autre texte du même genre (autre épître ?). Date de composition, 25 jumādā al-ākhira 1037/2 mars 1628.		?	12
–	Oblique/dos, nouvelle *basmala* et autre texte du même genre, portant sur les conquêtes au Yémen (bas de page), suivi du nom de différentes villes (p. 15-16), Sanaa, Taez, Zabīd (autre épître ?)		?	15
A B	Changement de main, qui enchaîne, sans raison apparente.			16
B C	Changement de main, qui enchaîne, sans raison apparente. Formule religieuse conclusive en p. 18.			17

TABLE 10.2 Description du contenu de la *Safīna* 5 (*suite*)

Main	Remarque	*Incipit*	Auteur	P.
–	Parallèle, puis oblique/dos, introduit par, centré : وهذا الجواب من الامام (...) على الشريف مسعود بن إدريس بن حسن	جواب	الامام (...) على الشريف مسعود بن إدريس بن حسن	19-21
–	Parallèle, puis oblique/dos, introduit par, centré : وهذه ابيات للسد الجَلَيل العَالم النّبيل فخر الدن عبد الله بن المطهر بن محمد بن سليمن الحمزي تهنيه بقدوم الامام المنصور محمد بن علي السراجي عليه السلام إلى صنعاء وقد حط عليها عامر بن عبد الوهاب سته اشهر	قدِمتَ لنا واليُمن دونك والبشرُ	فخر الدين عبد الله ابن المطهر بن محمد ابن سليمن الحمزي	21
–	Oblique/dos, introduit par: وَهذه رِسَالة أَنْشَاءهَا الامام شرف الدين يحيى عليه السّلام نائبا عن الامام المنصور بالله محمد بن علي السّراجي عليه السلام إلى مَن وجّهَت اليه محرّضا على الجهَاد والغَاره الى صنعا حين احاطَتْ بها جنود عامر بن عبد الوهاب	رسَالة إلى مَن وجّهَت اليه محرّضا على الجهَاد والغَاره الى صنعا حين احاطَتْ بها جنود عامر بن عبد الوهاب	الامام شرف الدين يحيى	22-3
–	Oblique/dos, introduit par: وَللإِمَامِ شَرَف الدِّيْن عَادَتْ بَرَكَاتُهُ هَذِه الرِّسَالَة أَنْشَأَهَا فِي دَعْوتِه	الرِّسَالَة فِي دَعْوتِه	الامام شرف الدين يحيى	23-8
–	Oblique/dos, introduit par: وَهذه رِسَالةٌ للإِمَامِ شَرف الدّيْن عليه السلام أنشأها الى عَامِر ابن عبد الوهاب بن داود بن طَاهِر الطاهري فى سنه اربع عشر وتَسعمايه Date 914/1508-9.	رِسَالةٌ الى عَامِر ابن عبد الوهاب بن داود بن طَاهِر الطاهري فى سنه اربع عشر وتَسعمايه	الامام شرف الدين يحيى	28-39
B’	Notes marginales			39
B’ ?	Notes, sans doute de B’			40

TABLE 10.2 Description du contenu de la *Safīna* 5 (*suite*)

Main	Remarque	*Incipit*	Auteur	P.
D	يمدح أمير المؤمنين المهدي لدين الله (...) محمد بن أحمد	دهر أَغر ودولةٌ غَراءُ	شمس الدين بن احمد ابن احمد الآنسي (2e moitié du XIXe s.?)	41
–	Introduit par, centré : وقال يمدحه ايضا suivi d'une note à l'encre rouge d'une autre main.	سرا نحوكم ليلاً فصلَّى وسلمَا	شمس الدين بن احمد ابن احمد الآنسي	43
–	Après un espace, poème suivant. ٮهنيه ٮرواجه ٮاٮنه السّلطان احمد ٮن على الرصاص	أَلمت تهادَ (؟) او المعنفُ قد أَغفَا	شمس الدين بن احمد ابن احمد الآنسي	47
–	Introduit par, centré : وقال غفر الله له يمدحه ايض	ٮبدت بدورًا فى لىالي الذَّوايبِ	شمس الدين بن احمد ابن احمد الآنسي	49
–	Introduit par, centré : وقال يمدحه ايضا	ارحيق ٮابل ام سَماع بلابل	شمس الدين بن احمد ابن احمد الآنسي	52
–	Introduit par, centré : وله وقد اقترح عليه الامام هذا الوزن والقافيه واملا له بيتا على هذا P. 57 : partie d'une moitié de vers rubriquée.	ما رحت عن تلك الصِّباَ سايلا	شمس الدين بن احمد ابن احمد الآنسي	55
–	Introduit par, centré : وله ٮهٮٮه لطواٮف عسكر وصلت من الحبشَه	صنَعت لك الأَقدار ما لَا يصنَعُ	شمس الدين بن احمد ابن احمد الآنسي	58
–	Introduit par, centré : وقال ٮهنّيه ٮعود اٮنآيه من المشرق ٮعد الصُّلح	بدور التهاني مشرقات طوالعُ	شمس الدين بن احمد ابن احمد الآنسي	60
–	Introduit par, centré : وله ٮهٮيه ٮعد النَّحر	بطالِع السَّعد وافَا نحوك اللعيد	شمس الدين بن احمد ابن احمد الآنسي	62

TABLE 10.2 Description du contenu de la *Safīna* 5 (*suite*)

Main	Remarque	*Incipit*	Auteur	P.
–	Introduit par, centré: وقال ايضاً يحرضه على الجهاد	حكّم البيض فى رقابِ الأَعادي	شمس الدين بن احمد ابن احمد الآنسي	65
–	Introduit par, centré: وله في مفاخره الحيل والوانها حسبما اقترح عليه حماه الله Éloge des différents types de chevaux selon leur robe, avec des sections. Puis éloge des lances et javelots.	نفاخَرت صواهل الحيَادِ	شمس الدين بن احمد ابن احمد الآنسي	67
–	Introduit par, centré: وقال وقد اقترح المولى حفظه الله تعالى ان يخمس القصدة التى تحال الامام حى سدى احمد بن الحسن بن حمد الدن رحمه الله تعالى فقال	سارك الله من بالحسن انشا كا	شمس الدين بن احمد ابن احمد الآنسي	71
–	Introduit par, centré; وقال يمدح المحسن بن المهدى حفظ الله تعالى	وافتْ تَهادَا في ليالي الجعد	شمس الدين بن احمد ابن احمد الآنسي	74
–	Introduit par, centré: وقال يمدح الصَّادق بن المهدى على الله Corrections à l'encre rouge.	أَذابلٌ شيه أَم قَوامُ	شمس الدين بن احمد ابن احمد الآنسي	81
–	Introduit par, centré: وله يمدح سده يوسف بن المهدي حماه الله تعالى	أَكؤُسٌ بدرهَا عننَا كَا	شمس الدين بن احمد ابن احمد الآنسي	85
–	Introduit par, centré: وله يمدح سده المحسن بن المهدي	حطرت كخطَّارِ القَضيب السَّمهرى	شمس الدين بن احمد ابن احمد الآنسي	86
–	Introduit par, centré: وقال يمدح الصَّادق بن المهدي Mot dans la seconde moitié du 1er vers à l'encre rouge.	بدت في بهَا البدر بالبيه يحتالُ	شمس الدين بن احمد ابن احمد الآنسي	88

TABLE 10.2 Description du contenu de la *Safīna* 5 (*suite*)

Main	Remarque	*Incipit*	Auteur	P.
–	Introduit par, centré: وقال يمدح امير المومنين الهادي لدن الله وبهنه بعود اولاده من الحج	أَعلمتَ ما قال النَّسيمُ وقد سرَى	شمس الدين بن احمد ابن احمد الآنسي	90
–	Introduit par, centré: واقترح عليه الأمامُ ان يحرض علَى الجهاد وقرا له بيتاً يحذوه فقال غفر الله له	المجدُ فى شُهبِ الرِّمَاح الذُّبَّلِ	شمس الدين بن احمد ابن احمد الآنسي	93
–	Introduit par, centré: وقال يمدحه ويصف هدايا وصلت من الشام	جمعت بعلاك العرب والعجم	شمس الدين بن احمد ابن احمد الآنسي	95
–	Introduit par, centré: وقال ايضا يمدحه	بدَتْ كمحيا البدر في طالع السَّعدِ	شمس الدين بن احمد ابن احمد الآنسي	99
–	Introduit par, centré: وقال يَمْدَحُه	ضحك الصَّبَاحُ وازمعَ الدَّيجورُ	شمس الدين بن احمد ابن احمد الآنسي	101
–	Introduit par, centré: وقال يمدحه وبهنه بالانتقال فى الكنيه للخلافه من الهادى الى المهدى	أَبِالوحي امْ نُودتَ بالطُّور من سينَا / تكنيت بالمهدي وقد كنت هادينَا	شمس الدين بن احمد ابن احمد الآنسي	104
–	Introduit par, centré: وله يهنيه بانتصار سريته ووصول روس واسرى من المشرق وقرا له بيتاً يحذو حذوه وشرط عليه يضمنه فقال	نهج الخليفه واضح المنهاجِ	شمس الدين بن احمد ابن احمد الآنسي	107
–	Introduit par, centré: وقال يهنيه بعرسٍ من الاعراس واقترح عليه هذا	بدتْ كشمس الضُّحى فى جنح غريبِ	شمس الدين بن احمد ابن احمد الآنسي	108
–	Introduit par, centré: وله يمدحه ويهنه برجوع اولاده من الجهاد	سلسل أَحادث المسرَّى والهنَا	شمس الدين بن احمد ابن احمد الآنسي	111

TABLE 10.2 Description du contenu de la *Safīna* 5 (*suite*)

Main	Remarque	*Incipit*	Auteur	P.
–	Introduit par, centré: وقال يمدحه ويهنيه بزواج ابنته بالسيد الجليل عماد الدين يحيى بن علي بن المتوكل P. 115, mot commenté et commentaire à l'encre rouge.	عن مطلع الحسن بدر التّم قد سفرا	شمس الدين بن احمد ابن احمد الآنسي	114
–	Introduit par, centré: وقال ايضا يمدحُه ويهنيه ابتداً منه	حدثك عن ريًّا نفوحُ بريَّاهَا	شمس الدين بن احمد ابن احمد الآنسي	118
–	Introduit par, centré: وقال يمدحه ويهنيه بعد النحر	كرِّر حدث الوصلِ عن سعادِ	شمس الدين بن احمد ابن احمد الآنسي	121
–	Introduit par, centré: وقال غفر الله له وارسلها اليه الى السّلامه	أبحت لك السَّلامه في السَّلامه	شمس الدين بن احمد ابن احمد الآنسي	126
–	Introduit par, centré: وقال مهنيًا له ولاولاده بالاعراس وبعمارة حصن المواهب ايضًا	وافَت بحتَر في زي الدَّلالِ وفي	شمس الدين بن احمد ابن احمد الآنسي	127
–	Introduit par, centré: واقترح عليه المحسن بن المهدي ان يعارض القصده التى اولها يا نديمي بمهجتى افديك فقال يمدحه	أثناياكَ أَم بَناءيْ فيْك	شمس الدين بن احمد ابن احمد الآنسي	129
–	Introduit par, centré: وقال يهني المولى بوصول رسولٍ من سلطان العجم بهديةٍ له	نَعم هذهِ نَعْما وذا السَّفح نعمانُ	شمس الدين بن احمد ابن احمد الآنسي	131
–	Introduit par, centré: واقتدح (كذا) عليه المولى امداح الخيل ووصفها وقد امر بصمرها للطراد فقال غفر الله له	دعاهُ نديماهُ فقالَ دعاني	شمس الدين بن احمد ابن احمد الآنسي	136

TABLE 10.2 Description du contenu de la *Safīna* 5 (*suite*)

Main	Remarque	*Incipit*	Auteur	P.
–	Introduit par, centré: وقال في يوم العدير وبمدحه ايصا سنه 1190 Date: 1190/1776-7.	أيسليك عن ريَّا العزَّةَ سالفُ	شمس الدين بن احمد ابن احمد الآنسي	138
–	Introduit par, centré: وقال ايضا بمدحه حفظه الله تعالى	أَهاجك ومضُ البارق المتالق	شمس الدين بن احمد ابن احمد الآنسي	141
–	Introduit par, centré: وله عفر الله له وقد حصل بنه وبن جماعه من شعرا العراق والشام نفاحر فحكم بنه وبيهم ان يحعل كل واحد منهم قصده فى هذا المنوال الذى عليه هي وبذكر ما قد لقيه من رمانه وفراق احوانه واوطانه ومن فعل ذلك فى لىلة حكم له بالسبق فى مىدان البلاغه وعارصه عده من اوليك ومدح فى احرها الرسول صلى الله عليه واله وسلم	ألا حي ذاكَ الحيَّ من ساكي صنْعَا	شمس الدين بن احمد ابن احمد الآنسي	143
–	Introduit par, centré: وله عصى الله عنه بمدح امير المومنين المويد بالله ربّ العالمين رصوان الله عليه وبدكر العدير وما ورد فيه من فصائل امير المومنن عليهم	سلاَ إِن جرتما بالرّبِ طيًّا	شمس الدين بن احمد ابن احمد الآنسي	146
–	Introduit par, centré: وقال بمدح المهدى لدن الله وبهنّيه بهدبةٍ	افي اوج المواهبِ اصفهانُ	شمس الدين بن احمد ابن احمد الآنسي	148
–	Introduit par, centré: وقال بمدحه وبهيبهِ بعرسٍ حدث له	بمطلع شمس الشَّرق بتهج الغربُ	شمس الدين بن احمد ابن احمد الآنسي	151
–	Introduit par, centré: وقال بمدحه وبهبهِ باحذ (كذا) سراياه السَّيِد ا برهيم المحطوري في الشرف	ما بعدُ ا برهيمَ ا برهيمُ	شمس الدين بن احمد ابن احمد الآنسي	154

TABLE 10.2 Description du contenu de la *Safīna* 5 (*suite*)

Main	Remarque	*Incipit*	Auteur	P.
–	Introduit par, centré: وقال وقد اقترح عليه المولى حفظه الله ان يفعل قصيدة ويذكر فيها الصّلح الواقع بنه وبن على بن احمد ويحسنه ويذكر (؟) حسن حطابه له فقال غفر الله له و... (؟)	يحقن دمآءِ المسلمينَ لك الأجرُ	شمس الدين بن احمد ابن احمد الآنسي	156
–	Introduit par, centré: وقال موسيًا لامير المومنين حفظه الله ومحرضًا على الجهاد	تأمن (؟) بموسَى او بعيْسَى بن مريم	شمس الدين بن احمد ابن احمد الآنسي	158
–	Introduit par, centré: وقال يمدحه ويهنيه بنصر سراياه فى غزاةٍ غزاها على بعض الطّوايف	قضى القضَى بالذى تهواه والقدرُ	شمس الدين بن احمد ابن احمد الآنسي	162
–	Introduit par, centré: وله سامحه الله كتب بها الى الشيخ محمد بن الحسين المرهبي رحمه الله	أما خبر عن طيّهم طيب النَّشرِ	شمس الدين بن احمد ابن احمد الآنسي	163
–	Introduit par, centré: السلطان الملك الموىد الغسانى الى الامام محمد بن المطهر	روررك (؟) لا يعجل فما ات بعلها	السلطان الملك المؤيد الغساني (r. 696-721/1296-7-1321-2)	166
B'	Réponse, introduite par, centré, فاجاب الامام	باخر عن الدست الذى ات صدره	الأمام محمد بن المطهر	166
B"	Introduit par, centré, للقاضي العلامة البليغ المصقع جمال السلام على بن محمد العنسي يخاطب امير المومنين المتوكل على الله حفظه الله امين	دعوتَ قلبًا السعد وامتثل الدهر	علي بن محمد العنسي (m. 1139/1726)	167

TABLE 10.2 Description du contenu de la *Safīna* 5 (*suite*)

Main	Remarque	*Incipit*	Auteur	P.
–	Introduit par: وله طول الله عمره يخاطب المولى امير المومنين وحليفه الرسول الامين المتوكل على الله رب العالمين متع الله به الاسلام والمسلمين شافعا لتلك الدره الكريمه باحيها هذه فلست الاعلى المحار بيمه تعذر اليه حفظه الله عن الدحول الى مقامه السريف فالرحامه (؟) وعدم الصبر على ذلك وقرما (؟) فى موقف واحد للامام[88]	امام البريه جار الرحام	علي بن محمد العنسي	168
–	Introduit par, centré: وله يخاطب الزرير العظم الاستاد الجليل الكريم والقاصى العلامه الد... الفهامه سرف الاسلام ابا على الحسن بن لعب (؟) الحمى حفظه الله ورحمه	سدى لا فارق السعد حىّ	علي بن محمد العنسي	169
B'	*Khabar* et poème visiblement tirés d'*al-Jalīs al-ṣāliḥ al-kāfī wa-l-anīs al-nāṣiḥ al-shāfī* d'al-Muʿāfā b. Zakariyyā', séance 43[89]. D'autres versions du même poème circulent ailleurs sous d'autres noms, mais le manuscrit suit ici mot à mot le *Jalīs*.	يا ضمر اخبرني ولست بفاعلٍ	أحمر بن الحارث بن عبد مناة	170
–	Autre *khabar* et poèmes.	يخطى الي الموت من بين ما ارى	أنيس بن خالد	171
–	Texte du poème annoncé à la page précédente.	ابسُّ فديه النفس متنا فعدنه (؟)		172
–	Introduit par, centré: القول	حليلى هبا طال...	?	172

88 La mention "*ṭawwal Allāh ʿumrahu*" laisse entendre que le poète était encore vivant à l'époque où a été rédigée la rubrique.

89 GAL S I, 312.

TABLE 10.2 Description du contenu de la *Safīna* 5 (*suite*)

Main	**Remarque**	***Incipit***	**Auteur**	**P.**
–	Poème à l'encre rouge et noire.	مثلث قطرب	قطرب (m. 206/821)	173-6
–	Introduit par, centré: لاوتد (؟) الرحال حوار الافاق ابهم الساحلي السهر بالطوىحى المغرى (؟) وفانه ب 29 من (؟) فصده ىمدح امىر ملوك اليمن	خطرت كماد القا المقاطر	ابرهيم الساحلي الشهير بالطويحي المغربي ؟	177
–	Introduit par, centré: للسهاب محمود ىمدح ان...	ىصحدىا (؟) ىالحش كالروص ىهحه	الشهاب محمود	178
–	Introduit par, centré: للعاملى من الرىحانه	ىا ندىمى ىمهحتى افدىك	العملي	178
–	Introduit par, centré: للقاصى الفاضل عبد الرحم (؟)	اهده سر فى المحد ام سور	القاضي الفاضل عبد الرحيم ؟	179
B"	Introduit par للصاحب ابن عباد في مدح امير المومنين (...) علي بن ابي طالب commence au centre. La fiche électronique de Princeton précise: Abū l-Qāsim Ismāʿīl b. ʿAbbād *Ṣāḥib al-Ṭāliqānī*.	لاح لعسك الطلل	الصاحب بن عباد	180-4
–	Introduit par, centré: للقاضى العلامه محمد احمد السلفى مادحا لسلطان اليمن مولانا الحسن ان القاسم رصوان الله عليهما	كفا المحد فخرا ان عدا لك من سلا	القاضي محمد بن أحمد السلفي	185-8
Changement de sens du volume, qu'il faut lire à rebours, à partir de la dernière page				

TABLE 10.2 Description du contenu de la *Safīna* 5 (*suite*)

Main	Remarque	*Incipit*	Auteur	P.
E	Version versifiée du *Muthallath* de Quṭrub. Les mêmes mots à la rime, dans les trois premières colonnes, écrits à l'encre rouge. Poème attribué à Ibrāhīm al-Azharī, sur ce site, http://cb.rayaheen.net/showthread.php?tid=1799&page=1#p6493, http://www.al-mostafa.info/data/arabic/depot/gap.php?file=m010204.pdf, tandis que le site de Princeton indique : Muthallathāt Quṭrub by Muḥammad b. al-Mustanīr Quṭrub (GAL, S II 916).			312-1
–	Introduit par, centré : من كلام المقري في التعريب والترهيب وبعد احسن واحاد رحمه ورصى عنا وعنه Dans le ¼ de page demeuré vierge : بسم الموعظه العظيمه rien ne suit.		المقري	310
	Page vierge.			309
	Pages vierges, 2 fol. raccourcis (intentionnellement).			308-5
F	Introduction rubriquée.	سال الربع عن ضبآ المصلى	التلمساني	304
–	Introduit par : للبحر الفايض عمر بن الفارض rubriqué.	ا رق بدا من جانب الغور لامع	ابن الفارض (m. 632/1235)	304
–	Introduit par, centré : وله ايضا Tatimma.	نسخت بحبي اىة العشق من قبلى	ابن الفارض	304

TABLE 10.2 Description du contenu de la *Safīna* 5 (*suite*)

Main	Remarque	*Incipit*	Auteur	P.
–	Introduit par, rubriqué: [مـ]ـسائح الى الفارض	[شربنا علـ]ـى ذكر الحبيب مُدامةً / سكرنا بها من قبل ان يخلق الكرم	ابن الفارض	303
–	Introduit par, rubriqué: للحاجرى رحمه الله تعالى	هب لى حناية من زلة به القدم	الحاجري	303
–	Introduit par, rubriqué: للشيخ البكري رحمه الله	خلَقَت لوعتى بنار الخدودى	الشيخ البكري ؟	303
–	Introduit par, aligné à droite: للصفى الحلى في باب رد العجز على الصدر *Tatimma.*	يا بدنى للفراق ذب كمدًا / دب كمدا للفراق يا بدنى	صفى الحلى	302
–	Fol. à l'envers. Introduit par, aligné à droite:]هذه الفريده البلغه ~~والدى الدره~~ والدره الثمينه الدبعه لاخى العلامه ادب رمانه المدع الـ... اللبع الـ... الاسلام اسمعل محمد كبسى (؟) مكاتبا اى سد شمس سمر الحموى (؟) با ساعد (؟) Fol. rogné.	سلام على تلك الربا طيب النشر / يفوح على الارجا ويسموا على البدر	اسمعل محمد كبسى (؟)	301-2
–	Introduit par, aligné à droite: هدى الحواب الدي تررى البلغا فصاحةً فلو راه الطاهر لطاطأ راسه... لما طاب له بعدها اختراعاته... ولصارت هباءً اساها والدى العلامه الحجه عر الاسلام محمد بن اسمعل الكسى... حوابا علا احى العلامه... *Tatimma* dans la marge.	تسم ثغر البرق عن شنب الدر / والقض (؟) معتل الصبا نايم الزهر[90]		300

90 L'incipit évoque un poème d'Ibn al-Nabīh al-Miṣrī (époque ayyoubide): تبسم ثغر الزهر عن شنب القطر / ودب عذار الظل في وجنة الزهر.

TABLE 10.2 Description du contenu de la *Safīna* 5 (*suite*)

Main	Remarque	*Incipit*	Auteur	P.
–	Introduit par, aligné à droite: وهدى الحواب للحقير القاصر قابل به الدرر المكنونه[91] سامحه الله تعالى Trace de *tatimma* dans la marge.	سرت في دياجي ظلمة اللَّيل والشعر / عزال تحاكي طلعه الشمس والبدر		299
–	Deux poèmes. Le second, introduit par, aligné à droite: وهدى الحواب الفائق والانشا البليع الرائق للولد العلامه... الاسلام وباشيه سى الانام... محمد ن اسمعل ن احمد... رحمه الله (؟)	[تبسـ؟]ـمت الارحا فى واضح الثغر / ومال قصيب الىان بشرًا على بشر		298
–	Page vierge.			297
B	Parallèle/dos. Note, oblique/dos.	سرىا فى الهوى... معيا /... فكم ىوما معيىا	لسدى الحسين (؟) ان على	296
– P. 284-5, notes de A De p. 283, A	Perpendiculaire/dos, 6 à 10 vers/p. Introduit par, rubriqué à l'encre noire et rouge: هده القصده الفرىده للسىد العلامه الهادى ىن ابرهم ىن على ىن المرىصى الورىر رحمه الله إلخ Nombreux commentaires en marge, dont des noms; ils sont arrangés, évoquent des formes. P. 283, changement de main.	اليك اله العالمىن توسلى / بأحمد المحار اكرم مرسلٍ [كذا]	الهادي بن ابرهيم ابن علي بن المرتضى الوزير	295-71

91 أبو زكريا يحي بن موسى بن عيسى بن يحي المغيلي المازوني a écrit un الدرر المكنونة.

TABLE 10.2 Description du contenu de la *Safīna* 5 (*suite*)

Main	Remarque	*Incipit*	Auteur	P.
– P. 269-64, B	Parallèle/dos, suivi d'une *tatimma*, تمت القصيدة الفريده المفيده في ايمة التوحيد وشيعتهم اهل العقيده وسيرتهم الحميده الرشيده المشيده نفعنا الله بفضلهم واعاد علينا من بركاتهم وشركنا في صالح دعائهم امين اللهم امين وصلى الله على سيدنا محمد وعلى اله الطيبين الطاهرين. P. 269, dans les 2/3 inférieurs de la p., obliquement, *fāʾida*.	قصيدة في ايمة التوحيد		270-69
–	Oblique/dos. Titre, centré. P. 267, réponse d'al-Mutawakkil, introduite par, centré: وهدا حواب المتوكل عليه	كتاب من صاحب عمان الى الامام المتوكل		268-7
–	Oblique dans un sens et dans l'autre/dos, deux textes. Le second est introduit par: وكلام الغزالى فى حطه كتابه شفا العلال Suivis de noms, un carré magique et des versets curatifs, encre noire et rouge.	كتاب شفا العلال[92]	الغزالي، ابو حميد ؟ (m. 505/1111)	266
–	Oblique/dos, prose, louange à Dieu.			265-4
D	Parallèle/dos, introduit par, centré: من شعر السيد الحليل سرف الدن الحسين بن عد القادر رحمه الله تعالى قال يمدح النبي صلى الله عليه واله وسلّم	سقا رياضَ مغانٍ ضمّها إضم / صوتُ الحيَا وعلّيها دَامت الدِّيم	Sharaf al-dīn b. Ḥusayn b. ʿAbd al-Qādir	264-3
–	Parallèle/dos. Réponse sans autre précision, introduite par, centré: جواب عن ابياتٍ	اهلاً بهَا فهي انفاسُ ذكيّاتُ / نَدِيةٌ مَا لهَا نِدٌ نديّاتُ		263-2

92 La GAL S I 754, sous le n° 536, atteste l'existence d'un كتاب شفاء الغلال, une œuvre de *fiqh*.

TABLE 10.2 Description du contenu de la *Safīna* 5 (*suite*)

Main	Remarque	*Incipit*	Auteur	P.
Main inconnue	Parallèle/dos. Introduit par, centré: في نظم سدى سرف الدن الحسين ن علي ن المتوكل	أه كم اطوي على الضيم حناحي / واداجي فى العلى قالٍ ولاحي	Sharaf al-Dīn b. Ḥusayn b. ʿAlī b. al-Mutawakkil	261-60
B	Perpendiculaire/dos, poème précédé par la date de l'assassinat du sultan ʿUthmān, 1023/1614-5: ناريح فى السلطان عىمن لما قىله الحند [كذا] Suit un distique en *wāfir*: وصى عىمان سلطان البرايا / باسياف العساكر والحىود ووافته المىه فى السرايا / مورحه كعىمان السهىد *waṣā ʿUthmānu sulṭānu l-barāyā / bi-asyāfi l-ʿasākiri wa-l-junūdī wa-wāfathu l-maniyyatu fī l-sarāyā / muʾarri/akhatan* (*ou muʾarrikhuhū*) *ka-ʿUthmāna l-shahīdī* "Othman le prince des contrées est tombé sous les épées des soldats // Le trépas est venu le trouver parmi les bataillons, lui donnant une date en tant que Othman le martyr" Puis vient un autre distique sur le même personnage (**وفىه**), mais en *ramal*: قد وصى عثمان ظلما حىن خانه الحىودُ واللىالى ارحته ان عىمان سهىد *qad waṣā ʿUthmānu ẓulman / ḥīna khānathu l-junūdū wa-l-layālī ʾarrakhathū inna ʿUthmāna shahīdū* "Othman est injustement tombé lorsque les soldats l'ont trahi // Les nuits l'ont daté, Othman est un martyr" Puis viennent quelques vers introduits par فى الخم (peut-être non pas في الختم mais في الخيم?):	Poème		260

TABLE 10.2 Description du contenu de la *Safīna* 5 (*suite*)

Main	Remarque	*Incipit*	Auteur	P.
	ومرفوعه بالجر فى حال نصبها / مسكنه لا يسام الناس انسها *wa-marfūʿatin bi-l-jarri fī ḥāli naṣbihā / musakkinatin lā yasʾamu l-nāsu ʾunsahā* يعيس الورا فى طلها *yaʿīshu l-warā fī ẓillihā.*			
–	Perpendiculaire/dos, poème précédé par la date de 975/1567-8, à laquelle le Sultan Salīm aurait entamé son règne (Selim II, r. 1566-74). Introduit par, centré : باريح ولايه السلطان سلم سنه 975 Autre date, 1023/1614-5, alignée verticalement sur la première, renvoyant probablement à la fin du règne de Selim II.	باريح ولايه السلطان سلم تولا ملك الملك وابن ملكه / بعر واقبال وفخر واحسانى ce qui doit équivaloir à : تولّى مُليك المُلك وابن مليكهِ / بعزٍّ وإقبالٍ وفخرٍ وإحسانِ Puis on a : وله فى جماعه تخاصموا واصطلحوا مورخا 975 بصالح الاصحاب من بعد عداوات وصير / والحمد لله الى تاريخهم والصلح خير qu'il faut sans doute lire : يصالحُ الأصحاب من بعد عداوات وضير... Puis : وله مورخا رواحه بعض اصحابه 975 (il s'agit de la date d'un mariage عرسكم). Puis :		259

TABLE 10.2 Description du contenu de la *Safīna* 5 (*suite*)

Main	Remarque	*Incipit*	Auteur	P.
		وله نارح ولانه مراد السلطان لما اراد الله سع عباده / ولا مراد الملك حىر ىلاده i.e. لمّا اراد الله بيع عباده / ولّى مراد الملْك خير بلاده		
C	Alterne texte parallèle et oblique (2 directions)/dos, épître, vocalisée, signes d'*ihmāl* sur lettres variées, p. 252, marques de section à l'encre rouge, p. 248, phrase à l'encre rouge[93].	الزَّاجَرَة للأُمَّه عن اسَآءة الظَّن بالأَئِمة	الامام المهدى لدىن الله احمد ىن الحسن ىن احمد ىن القاسم ابن رسُوْل الله (m. 656/1258)	259-46
–	Même alternance/dos, prose, *al-Rawḍ al-bāsim ilā l-Sayyid Muḥammad b. Abī l-Qāsim min al-Sayyid Muṭahhar b. Muḥammad b. Muṭahhar*[94]. Introduit par, rubriqué, centré: يَلِيْهَا الرَّوْض البَاسِم إلخ	الرَّوْض البَاسِم الى السَّيد محمد ابن ابي القَاسِم مِن السَّيّد مُطهر ابن محّمد ابن مُطهر عَلَيْه السَّلام	مُطهر ابن محّمد ابن مُطهر	246-5

93 *Zājira lil-umma ʿan isāʾat al-ẓann bi-l-aʾimma min al-Mahdī li-Dīn Allāh*, GAL, S II 563. En ligne, *Majmūʿ rasāʾil al-Imām al-shahīd al-Mahdī Aḥmad b. al-Ḥusayn* (*ṣāḥib Dhībīn*), taʾlīf al-Imām Aḥmad b. al-Ḥusayn b. Aḥmad b. al-Qāsim b. al-Ḥasan b. ʿAlī b. Abī Ṭālib [612-56 H], Rawāʾiʿ turāth al-Zaydiyya, http://www.azzaidiah.com/kotob_mojamaah/aqeedh/magmou_rasayel_almahdi.html [dernière consultation 3/10/2019].

94 GAL S II, 561, *al-Rawḍ al-nasīm*, 1128/1716.

TABLE 10.2 Description du contenu de la *Safīna* 5 (*suite*)

Main	Remarque	*Incipit*	Auteur	P.
	Parallèles/dos, poèmes, introduits par *shiʿran*. Puis 2 vers d'un poème introduit par, centré : شعراً لمحون لىلى d'une autre main, peu soignée sans vocalisation, *dāl* sous-ponctué. Poème de Qays, le Fou de Laylā.	اىا شىه لىلى لا براعى فاىى / لك من بىن الوحوش صدىق[95]		244
	Parallèle et oblique/dos, texte en prose, vocalisé, contenant des poèmes, dont, p. 242, l'un de l'Imam al-Manṣūr, vocalisé. P. 243, sections de vers à l'encre rouge ; p. 242, introductions rubriquées, centrées, sections de vers marquées d'une virgule à l'encre rouge. Réponse et p. 237, sa *tatimma* avec date *yawm al-jumʿa* 9 shawwāl 1128/26 sept. 1716.			243-37
C	Main D. Parallèle et oblique/dos, prose.	المرسوم الوارد من السلطان سليمن ىن سليم خان الى المطهر ىن سرف الدىن فى خروج مصطفى ىاشا الى اليمن الميمون	السلطان سليمن ىن سليم خان	237-3
	Parallèle et oblique/dos, réponse d'al-Muṭahhar b. Sharaf al-Dīn/Muṣṭafā Bāshā, année 959/1551-2.	حواب المطهر سرف الدىن الى الابواب العاليه على ىد مصطفى ىاشا ىكدار ىكى رىد سانقا ودلك فى سىه 959		232-27
	Parallèle et oblique/dos, titre, centré.	صوره مكاىب قاضى الى قاضي		227-6

95 Il manque un mot dans le deuxième hémistiche, ce qui fausse le mètre. Le texte correct est :,

أيا شبْهَ ليلى لا تُراعي فإنني. لكَ اليومَ مِنْ بين الوحوشِ صديقُ.

TABLE 10.2 Description du contenu de la *Safīna* 5 (*suite*)

Main	Remarque	*Incipit*	Auteur	P.
	Parallèle et oblique/dos, titre en forme de triangle inversé.	صوره كاب تعوىد من حىدر باشا الى امير المومىن الموىد بالله ربّ العالمين فى الصُّلح واىشا القاصى فى الـ... عىد الله ىن الصدىق المحرفى رحمه الله تعالى	حيدر باشا	226-4
	Muḥammad b. ʿAbdallāh al-Ḥūthī, *Mirāth*, introduit par, centré : في مراث السىد العلّامه ىور الدىن محمد ىن عىد الله الحوثى الى الامير صفر الى محروس صعده	كتاب المراث	نور الدين محمد بن عبد الله الحوثي	224-1
	Oblique/dos. Introduit par, centré : ىىلوه كتاب للفقيه عىد الله ىن عىد الصمد المحرفى عن حىدر باسا الى الفقىه صلاح ىن ىحى الكاىب معاهداً له رحمه الله تعالى	كتاب للفقيه عبد الله بن عبد الصمد المحرفي عن حيدر باشا الى الفقيه صلاح بن يحيى الكاتب معاهذاً له	للفقيه عبد الله بن عبد الصمد المحرّفي	221-17
	Oblique/dos. Réponse, introduite par, centré : يتلوهُ جَوَابُ محمَّد وَلِيْ على القَاضي عَبْدُ الله المحرّفي	جَوَابُ	محمَّد وَلِيْ	217-6
	Oblique/dos, épître d'al-Muṭahhar b. Sharaf al-Dīn *ilā ahl Ṣanʿāʾ* introduite par, centré, en forme de triangle inversé : وهذه رسالَةٌ من المطَهَّر بن شرف الدِّين عَلَيلمْ إلى أَهلِ صَنعَا وبِلاَدهَا يحثُّهم عَلَى الجِهُاد في سبيل الله Même main. Suivent le titre de l'épître, 2 vers, d'une autre main, saisissant l'occasion d'un peu d'espace vierge, introduits par لمحبوب ليلى لما وصل مكه و... دات يوم حالس فادا داع دعا الىلى	رسالَةٌ إلى أَهلِ صَنعَا	المطَهَّر بن شرف الدِّين	216-2

TABLE 10.2 Description du contenu de la *Safīna* 5 (*suite*)

Main	Remarque	*Incipit*	Auteur	P.
	Parallèle/dos. Introduit par, centré: شمس الدين أحمد بن محمَّد الانسى عند دعوة الامام المتوكل علَى اللهِ عادت بركاته *Tatimma*	دعوة الامام المتوكل علَى اللهِ	شمس الدين أحمد بن محمَّد الانسي	212-1
C	Main D? Parallèle/dos, épître, introduite par, centré: هذه الرسالة التى انشأها الرصَّاص على لسانِ الحسن بن وهَّاس فوصع الحسن علهما حطه واضافها الى نفسه وهذه نسختها حرفاً حرفاً من عبد الله امير المؤمنين الحسن بن وهاس بن ابي هاشم بن رسول الله Même main. 1/3 de la p. laissé vierge, avec 3 vers de poésie d'un côté, 1 vers de l'autre, d'une autre main.	الرسالة على لسانِ الحسن بن وهَّاس	الرصَّاص	211-03
	Main B. Perpendiculaire/dos, poème introduit par: للقاصى العلامه على بن محمد العسى لما اعصمه ىته مطهر بن يحى فاحرح مه اعن الحلفه... له	بالبت اقسم او باهل البت سادت البشر	علي بن محمد العسي	202
	Main B'. Perpendiculaire/dos, *takhmīs* introduit par, centré: الاساب للكائد والحمىس لسدى محمد بن يحى (؟) المتوكل فى مدح اماما وسدنا المتوكل على الله حفظه الله	مدح الامام المتوكل على الله	محمد بن يحيى ؟ المتوكل	201-199
	Main B''. Perpendiculaire/dos, introduit par, centré, en forme de triangle inversé: ولله احمد احمد الاسى فى مدح الر... احمد بن عالب ابامه ولا... المكه المسرفه.	مدح	احمد احمد الاسي	199-4

TABLE 10.2 Description du contenu de la *Safīna* 5 (*suite*)

Main	Remarque	*Incipit*	Auteur	P.
	Parrallèle/dos, introduit par, centré : وللسىد المدكور ممدحا امىر المومىن المويد بالله رحمه الله يوم العدر	فى عىرى لك عن وحدى عىارات / وفى النابات عن وصفى اسارات i.e. في عَبرتي لك عن وَجدي عباراتُ / وفي النايات عن وصفي اشارات	احمد احمد الاسي	194-1
	Main B'. Perpendiculaire/dos, introduit par, centré : وللسىد الحلىل الحسن ىن عىد القادر ىن الناصر فى مدح النبى صلى الله علىه واله وسلم حده لمروس	مدح النبي	الحسن بن عبد القادر بن الناصر	191-89

TABLE 10.3 Description du contenu de la *Safīna* 6

Remarque	*Incipit*	Auteur	Page
Note autographe. Le propriétaire demande de bonnes choses à Dieu pour les croyants et les croyantes. Date : 17 rabīʿ al-awwal 13[48]/23 août 1929. Au stylo rouge, dans un coin, "raqam 68". Ce fol., plus court, a été collé sur le contreplat, masquant un texte ; une bande de papier a servi à ajuster.	هذه السفينة النفيسة بقلم مالكها الحقير الفقير الى مولاه الغني الكبير محمد بن محمد بن محمد بن اسمعيل ابن محمد بن يحيي بن احمد الكبسي عفى الله عنهم وجميع المؤمنين والمؤمنات وبـــــ 17 ربيع الاول سـنـه 48 ه ه ه		0

TABLE 10.3 Description du contenu de la *Safīna* 6 (*suite*)

Remarque	***Incipit***	**Auteur**	**Page**
Pages vierges. Réglures.			1-6
Introduit par وللسيد الجليل العلامه عبد الله بن صلاح العادل إلخ	سلا هل الصب بعد النازحين سلا / ام هل بغير هواهم عنهما اشتعلا[96]	عبد الله بن صلاح العادل (صنعاء)	7
Introduit par, aligné à droite: قال القاضي العلامه محمد بن الحسن الحسمى (؟ الحسمى ؟) رحمه الله	مغرا بحلا ا ن منه ملا د ه	محمد بن حسن الحشيمي ؟	8
Introduit par, aligné à droite: حمال الدن ابن ساته	لثمت ثغر عذولى حىن سمّاك	جمال الدين	9
Introduit par, aligné à droite: سمس الدن ابن الصايغ	كيف الخلاص وقلبي بعد اسراك	شمس الدين ابن الصايغ ؟	9
Introduit par (× 2), centré: التلعفرى	ارى الكووس اللتي فيها حميّاك	التلعفري (m. 696/1296-7)[97]	10
Introduit par, centré: لسدى العلامه الكرم بن الكرم بن بدر بن محمد بن الحسن بن القاسم بن محمد علىهم السلام	اتراه يكتم ما تحن ظلوعه	الكريم بن الكريم ابن بدر بن محمد بن الحسن بن القاسم ابن محمد	10
Introduit par, aligné à droite: لسدى اسحق بن يوسف المتوكل رحمه الله تعالى	لو رأنا الليل بدرى لا ختفا	اسحق بن يوسف المتوكل (m. 1173/1759)	10

96 Voir v, p. 339.
97 Voir v, p. 339.

TABLE 10.3 Description du contenu de la *Safīna* 6 (*suite*)

Remarque	*Incipit*	Auteur	Page
Introduit par, aligné à droite : قال سدى محمد بن عبد الله بن الامام شرف الدن رحمه الله نصف صنعا ومسرهاتها فى هده الارحوره إلخ Plus du ¼ p. laissé vierge.	وقد توسمت حمع ارض	محمد بن عبد الله بن الامام شرف الدين	15-1
Pages vierges.			16-23
Nombreux commentaires et usage d'encre rouge. Vers d'un trait plus épais. P. 62 : date de composition du *takhmīs* : 22 jumādā l-awwal 1346/17 nov. 1927, à Shahāra.	تخميس لمقصورة ابن دريد مرثي للحسن بن علي بن أبي طالب. ويبدو أن التخميس تم نظمه في شهارة سنة 1346 هـ		24
مقطع Introduit par, aligné à droite : قال ابن عنين		ابن عنين	63
مقطع Introduit par عىره		ابن عنين ؟	63
قصيدة Introduit par, aligné à droite : وقد ابدع اى الصابع فى وصف دمشق		ابن عنين ؟	63
Dans la marge, sur plus d'1/3 de la p. Introduit par : قال ابن الوردى	دمشق من اجل اقلم الشام مكانا واحسنه الخ	ابن الوردي	63
مقاطع À la fin du poème, début du texte d'Ibn al-Wardī (cf. p. 63) : دمشق من اجل اقلم الشام مكانا واحسنه[98]	عن دمشق	ابن الوردي	64

98 GAL G II, 140 ; S II, 174, n° 5a-5c.

TABLE 10.3 Description du contenu de la *Safīna* 6 (*suite*)

Remarque	***Incipit***	**Auteur**	**Page**
تمام ما قاله ابن الوردي عن دمشق وبدايته ص 63 في الهامش Le reste de la p. est vierge.	عن دمشق	ابن الوردي	65
Pages blanches.			66-8
Section sur l'extraction de quelque chose de caché par la géomancie (*al-raml*) en utilisant un carré quadrillé (*bi-l-tarbīʿ*). *Fāʾida*, avec recette médicinale.	باب في استخراج الخبيه من الرمل إلخ فائدة	?	69
Partie supérieure et inférieure de la p., vers introduits par: للحاجرى Au centre de la p., calendrier circulaire avec, du centre du cercle vers l'extérieur, les quatre saisons, les douze mois (calendrier solaire), les signes du zodiaque correspondants, et les 28 "étoiles", mansions lunaires (7 par saison). Sans doute un calendrier agricole. Utilisation d'encre noire et rouge.	بدر الدجا في فلك خديك قد انجمْ ذوّبتني بصدودك مثل ذوب الشمعْ	الحاجري	70
Quelques *ḥadīths* et anecdotes anciennes, introduits, horizontalement/au dos, par: الحمد لله سحانه مقول من العقد للفقيه شهاب الدن ابو عمرُ احمد ن محمد ن عد ربه رحمه الله فى المحاسه puis obliquement, فائده puis horizontalement لما احتضر قيس ن عاصم قال لبنيه يا نى إلخ puis obliquement, فائده			71

TABLE 10.3 Description du contenu de la *Safīna* 6 (*suite*)

Remarque	***Incipit***	**Auteur**	**Page**
Deux poèmes anonymes. Introduits par: منظومه فى طالع الفجر et ابيات فى بندق	Poèmes		72
Tableau de 12 colonnes sur 21 l. qui produit des versets du Coran si l'on lit une lettre sur sept.			73
Titre centré dans la p.	العقد الثمين في بيان الحق المبين لمولانا شيخ الاسلام وزينه الآل العلما العاملين الاعلام البدر المنير محمد بن اسمعيل الامير[99] نفع الله بعلومه المسلمين واعلى درجته من اعلا عليين	محمد بن اسمعيل الامير (cf. *safīna* 4, 66, 97; *safīna* 7, 244, 313-6)	74
Poème répondant à des doutes sur son ascendance, introduit par la *basmala* et une note en marge du poème.	بدرك يا رب الخلائق ابتدى	محمد بن اسماعيل الامير (cf. *safīna* 4, 66, 97; *safīna* 7, 244, 313-6)	74
Réponse des cadis d'al-ʿAns (en prose), introduite par: وبعد ذلك نذكر ما وجدناه من اجوبه العلما على اللّؤما من بنى العنسى جواب سيدى العلامه وجيه الدين عبد القادر بن محمد بن الحسين وسيدى العلامة النحرير وجيه الاسلام عبد القادر بن احمد بن عبد القادر رحمهم الله على الكتاب الواصل اليهما من القضاه بنى العنس الساكنين فى جبل برط لفظه changements de section rubriqués.		قضاة العنس	78

99 Muḥammad b. Ismāʿīl al-Amīr al-Ṣanʿānī, GAL S I, 612, 695.

TABLE 10.3 Description du contenu de la *Safīna* 6 (*suite*)

Remarque	***Incipit***	**Auteur**	**Page**
Introduit par, aligné à droite: قال السد العلامه الادب البليغ فخر الدن عد الله ن على الورير عليهم السلام محاطبا... على طريق الاقتنان الى سدى العلامه صبا الاسلام زىد ن محمد بن الحسن بن أمير المؤمنين القاسم P. 1 d'une pagination à l'encre rouge, dans un système différent de chiffres, commence ici; elle se clôt à la p. 116, soit p. 196 de la *safīna* actuelle.	طمعى قليل فى بدور الارض يا بدر السما فما اطيل عتابى	عبد الله بن علي الوزير (m. 1147/1734)	81
Introduit par, centré: وقال يمدح الحسين بن علي بن المتوكل	اذهلنى حالك يا معجب	عبد الله بن علي الوزير	81
Introduit par, centré: وقال ايضا الى السيد العلّامه المعير (؟ السعيد ؟) بن الحسن الحره (؟) رحمهما الله	ليس شقيقى من ابوه ابي	عبد الله بن علي الوزير	82
Rubriqué	حرف التا		84
	افدى الذى فصحت فى الحيد ناطقه	عبد الله بن علي الوزير	84
Introduit par, aligné à droite: وقال مكاتبا لسدى الحسين بن علي بن المتوكل رحمهم الله	قسما بالمصون من قسماتك	عبد الله بن علي الوزير	84
Introduit par, aligné à droite: وقال ايضا عند قدوم رمضان نقول عليه نعص اصحابه... هذا السوال	ما يقول الا كرمون انجبا	عبد الله بن علي الوزير	85
Introduit par, aligné à droite: وقال رحمه الله فى ثقيل	ثقيل تميد الارض منه اذا مشى	عبد الله بن علي الوزير	86
Introduit par, aligné à droite: وقال مرثيا الامير البليع سدى العلامه الادب شرف الاسلام الحسن ن عد القادر ن الناصر بن عد الرب رحمهم الله واىانا والمومىن والمومىات	اشقيق بدر الروض بعدك حده	عبد الله بن علي الوزير	87

TABLE 10.3 Description du contenu de la *Safīna* 6 (*suite*)

Remarque	***Incipit***	**Auteur**	**Page**
Rubriqué.	حرف الجيم		87
Introduit par, centré: وقال ومراحعا للشيخ عد الرحمن ن محمد الذهبي الدمشقى[100] نزيل مكه المشرفه القادم الى صنعا	وافى كشكل البدر فى جنح الدجى	عبد الله بن علي الوزير	87
Rubriqué.	حرف الحا		88
Introduit par, aligné à droite: دارت بن السد محمد ن حسن الكوكبانى رحمه الله وبن الشيخ مصطفى ن فتح الله مكاتبه فى روى الحا فقال على منوالها	راى فرقه من تحت طرته صبحا	عبد الله بن علي الوزير	89
Introduit par, aligné à droite: وقال مكاتبا لسدى حسن بن عد القادر بن الناصر	لا تنكروا وصف القد والملاح	عبد الله بن علي الوزير	90
Introduit par, aligné à droite: وقال ايضا رحمه الله Partie d'un vers à l'encre rouge.	افدى الذى قلبي على ما به	عبد الله بن علي الوزير	90
Rubriqué.	حرف الدّال		91
	أمَا آن أنْ تنسا عهودا ومعهدا		92
Introduit par, centré: وقال مطالعا حصره سدى الحق بن امير المومنين المهدى أحمد بن الحسن بن القسم عليهم السلام	ارى خطرات همك يا فؤادى	عبد الله بن علي الوزير	93
Introduit par, aligné à droite: وقال مهنيا لسيدى الحسن ن اسحق في عد الاضحى	ما العيد الا نحرهم العميد	عبد الله بن علي الوزير	95

100 Actif fin XVIIe-début XVIIIe s., voir *Safīna* 4, 9-13, et *Safīna* 7, 287-279. Cité dans *Safīna* 7, 141.

TABLE 10.3 Description du contenu de la *Safīna* 6 (*suite*)

Remarque	***Incipit***	**Auteur**	**Page**
Introduit par, aligné à droite: وقال مكاتبا للقاضى عبد القادر النزيلى والفقيه زيد بن صالح الشامى ومعاتبا	الا يا عمرو عنى قل	عبد الله بن علي الوزير	96
Introduit par, centré: وقال من قصيده رحمه الله	لولا اذكار شادن وشادى	عبد الله بن علي الوزير	97
Introduit par, centré: وقال رحمه الله	مرسل ومعى عليك في الحد	عبد الله بن علي الوزير	98
Introduit par: وقال معاتبا لصديق له	حيرانى عن اهل نجد ونجدى	عبد الله بن علي الوزير	100
Introduit par, aligné à droite: وقال رحمه الله مادحا لسيدى زيد بن المتوكل ومهنئًا له باعراس	ادرها كووسا بالهنا يا اخَى سعد	عبد الله بن علي الوزير	101
Introduit par, aligné à droite: وقال مكاتبا لبعض اصحابه وكان قد اسدى اليه معروفا	يا من سبانى بعين كم تلاحظنى	عبد الله بن علي الوزير	102
Introduit par, aligné à droite: وقال مجيبا على السيد العلّامه محمد بن الحسين بن يحيى الحمري رحمه الله تعالى	جار على ضعفى النوى واعتدى	عبد الله بن علي الوزير	103
Introduit par, aligné à droite: وقال فى حصان للسيد قاسم بن لقمان رحمه الله	لله من اشقر كميت	عبد الله بن علي الوزير	104
Rubriqué.	حرف الرا		104
Introduit par, centré: قال من قصيده	زفها بكرا على الشرط عقارا	عبد الله بن علي الوزير	104
Introduit par: وقال ايضا مكاتبا للسيد البليغ احمد بن احمد الآنسى رحمه الله تعالى	عذار رطيب فوق ريحانه خضرا	عبد الله بن علي الوزير	105

TABLE 10.3 Description du contenu de la *Safīna* 6 (*suite*)

Remarque	***Incipit***	**Auteur**	**Page**
Introduit par, aligné à droite : وقال ايضا وقد انتحله بعض شعرا اليمن ودوّنه	اضحى يوارى نفسه	عبد الله بن علي الوزير	106
Introduit par, aligné à droite : وقال من قصيده	اخدّك ذا سلع وهذى محاجره	عبد الله بن علي الوزير	106
Introduit par : وقال من قصيده	لمن هذه الزهر التى تحدرُ	عبد الله بن علي الوزير	108
Introduit par : وقال À partir de cette p., mots exécutés d'un trait plus épais.	كيف حالى يا سنبل بن سرور (؟)	عبد الله بن علي الوزير	110
Introduit par, aligné à droite : وقال مجيبا على الحكم شعبان سليم عن ايات	حذار امن معاشره العذارا	عبد الله بن علي الوزير	111
Introduit par, aligné à droite : وقال مطالعا حضره السيد محمد قاسم لقمان رحمه الله تعالى	من دون حطار قدك الخطر	عبد الله بن علي الوزير	113
Introduit par, aligné à droite : وقال مكاتبا لسدى الحسن بن عبد القادر ن الناصر ن عبد الرب رحمهم الله	يا روض ساطى (؟) البان لست بناظري	عبد الله بن علي الوزير	114
Introduit par, aligné à droite : وقال مجيبا على السد محمد بن قاسم لقمان رحمهما الله	بك فليتم الافتخارُ	عبد الله بن علي الوزير	116
Introduit par, centré : وقال معاتبا لصديق له	والذي يعلم سري علنا	عبد الله بن علي الوزير	117
Introduit par : وقال مرثيا للسد احمد مهدى بن يحى ن احمد السد الحمدى الكوكبانى رحمه الله P. 118, des blancs laissés par le copiste doivent correspondre à des passages illisibles dans l'original.	بيّن (؟) الصبح لذي (؟) عينين يَا / ايها اللاهي بصبح وسمر	عبد الله بن علي الوزير	117

TABLE 10.3 Description du contenu de la *Safīna* 6 (*suite*)

Remarque	*Incipit*	Auteur	Page
Introduit par, aligné à droite: وقال في السد حسن بن صلاح ن عز الدن وقد سعى به الى حصره الخلافه فسار إلخ	قل لنا يا ابن صلاح ما على	عبد الله بن علي الوزير	119
Introduit par: وقال مطالعا حضرة الشيخ زن العابدن ن سعد المنوفى (؟ المتولى ؟) إلى حضرة الخلافه	اه ما احلى التصابي وامر	عبد الله بن علي الوزير	119
Rubriqué.	حرف الزاي		121
Introduit par, aligné à droite: وقال مكاتبا لسدى العلّامه زند ن محمد ن الحسن ن الإمام رحمهم الله	نعم زمان السرور وافا	عبد الله بن علي الوزير	121
Introduit par: وقال ايضا	يا ابن صدر الكمال انت بحرا	عبد الله بن علي الوزير	121
Rubriqué.	حرف السين		122
Introduit par, aligné à droite: وقال إلى السيد على ن يحى العارضه	انا فى ربيع مقامها العبّاس	عبد الله بن علي الوزير	122
Introduit par, aligné à droite: وقال مهنيا لسدى العلامه محمد بن عبد الله ن الحسين ن أمير المؤمنين باعراس رحمهم الله	أيا من له حظّ من العلم وافرِ	عبد الله بن علي الوزير	123
Introduit par: وقال مكاتبا بعض اصحابه	اسبا بنفسك يا مولاي منتبها	عبد الله بن علي الوزير	123
Introduit par, centré: وقال ايضا رحمه الله	وحده الحق فى المقام النفيس	عبد الله بن علي الوزير	123
Introduit par, aligné à droite: وله الى سدى زند ن محمد ن الحسن رحمهم الله	ملأ الكاسات صرفا وحتسا	عبد الله بن علي الوزير	124
Rubriqué.	حرف الشين		126

TABLE 10.3 Description du contenu de la *Safīna* 6 (*suite*)

Remarque	***Incipit***	**Auteur**	**Page**
Introduit par, aligné à droite : وقال على \السان/ بعض اصحابه الى عامل فى الحفاش	اما فى هذه الدنيا هِلَالُ	عبد الله بن علي الوزير	126
Rubriqué.	حرف الضاد		128
Introduit par, aligné à droite : وقال مشيرا الى الموثرات عند الاصولىن	ما سبب الهجر بلا علة	عبد الله بن علي الوزير	128
Rubriqué.	حرف الطا المهمله		128
Introduit par, aligné à droite : قال على لسان نعض اصحابه	وحقك يا ابن الا كرمين ارومة	عبد الله بن علي الوزير	128
Introduit par : وكتب إلى سدى يحى ن على ن المتوكل	ارى قلبى مثل المثقف اذ يسطو	عبد الله بن علي الوزير	129
Rubriqué.	حرف العين المهمله		129
Introduit par, aligné à droite : وقال مكاتبا للسيد يحى ن إ برهم جحاف	مطالع الوصل قد بانت طوالعها	عبد الله بن علي الوزير	129
Introduit par, centré : وقال من قصدة	رعا زهرات القلب ثم اضاعه	عبد الله بن علي الوزير	130
Introduit par, centré : وقال من قصيده رحمه الله	سلا عندما بان الحبيب مودعا	عبد الله بن علي الوزير	131
Changement de calame ? Introduit par, aligné à droite : وقال مجيبا على سدى العلامه محمد ن اسحق ن أمىر المؤمنين رحمهم الله	داعي التصابي لفوادي قد دعا	عبد الله بن علي الوزير	131
Rubriqué.	حرف الفا		132
Introduit par, centré : وقال من قصيده	لك الله هذا مورد الوصل قد صفا	عبد الله بن علي الوزير	132

TABLE 10.3 Description du contenu de la *Safīna* 6 (*suite*)

Remarque	*Incipit*	Auteur	Page
Introduit par, aligné à droite: وقال مجيبا على سدى العلامه محمد بن زيد بن محمد بن الحسن بن أمير المؤمنين رحمهم الله	اسبكت قرطا او سبكت القرقفا	عبد الله بن علي الوزير	133
Introduit par, aligné à droite: وقال لما وصل سليمان باشا ناب جده الى حصره الخلفه بالمواهب بنفاس من الخيل والا… صحبة احمد اغا إلخ	شرّ فتمونا يا بني يافث	عبد الله بن علي الوزير	134
Rubriqué.	حرف القاف		135
Introduit par, aligné à droite: وقال لما وقف على كتاب مثال النعل النبوى للعلامه الفاسى مصوّرا بالذهب الاحمر فى نسحة عليها قلم العنانه	اى عيونى نزهى الاحداق فى / شبه نعل المصطفى فوه حديقه	عبد الله بن علي الوزير	135
Introduit par, aligné à droite: وقال من قصيده	لحظ الزهور اطال فى تحديقه	عبد الله بن علي الوزير	136
Introduit par: وقال ايضا	كم ذا جفونك بالدموع ترقرق	عبد الله بن علي الوزير	136
Introduit par, aligné à droite: وله من قصده الى سدى الحسن بن احمد بن الحسن بن أمير المؤمنين رحمهم الله	اثرها تسامى الشمس اوجا واشراقا	عبد الله بن علي الوزير	137
Introduit par, aligné à droite: وقال مجيبا على الحكيم شعبان سليم !	محيّاك ام بدر لشعبان مشرق	عبد الله بن علي الوزير	138
Introduit par: وقال معربا لسدى الحسن بن الحسن في ولده القسم بن يحى لما استشهد فى حفاش رحمهم الله	عز مولانا الحسين الملك فى / علم الاسلام ميمون الطريقه	عبد الله بن علي الوزير	139

TABLE 10.3 Description du contenu de la *Safīna* 6 (*suite*)

Remarque	*Incipit*	Auteur	Page
Introduit par, aligné à droite : وقال مرثيا للسيد الفاضل عمر شيخان المتوفى بمكه المشرفه سنه ثلاث عشره وماىه والف (1113) ووجهت إلى ولده محمد بن عمر سحابه (؟) رحمهم الله حميعا Date : 1113/1701-2.	مصاب له دمع المحاجر لا برقا	عبد الله بن علي الوزير	140
Rubriqué.	حرف الكاف		141
Introduit par : قال مجيبا على الشيخ عبد الرحمن بن محمد الذهبي[101] نزيل مكه المشرفه	امليك انت قل لى أم ملك	عبد الله بن علي الوزير	141
Introduit par, aligné à droite : وقال مجيبا على السيخ المذكور في هذه المتقدمة	لا وحمرا قد (؟) عتقت فى شفاتك	عبد الله بن علي الوزير	142
Rubriqué.	حرف اللام		143
Introduit par, aligné à droite : وقال مكاتبا سيدى الحسن ن على ن المتوكل الى الروضه رحمهم الله	الى مَ عن الرشا اسل	عبد الله بن علي الوزير	143
Introduit par, aligné à droite : وقال مجيبا على الشيخ مصطفى ن فتح الله الحموى القادم صنعا سنة 1118 Date : 1118/1706-7.	قد انصفتنى بالوصال / والبدر ينصف للكمال	عبد الله بن علي الوزير	145
Introduit par, aligné à droite : وقال مادحا لسيدى قاسم بن الحسين بن أمير المؤمنين لما نفده المهدي محمد بن أحمد إلى جهة القبلة (؟) وكان قد ظهر من حاشد وبكيل الخروج عن الطاعة	مل عن القول اذا لم تفعل / ليس غايات المُنا بالامل	عبد الله بن علي الوزير	146

101 Actif fin XVIIe-début XVIIIe s., voir *Safīna* 4, 9-13, et *Safīna* 7, 287-279. Cité dans cette *Safīna*, 87.

TABLE 10.3 Description du contenu de la *Safīna* 6 (*suite*)

Remarque	***Incipit***	**Auteur**	**Page**
Introduit par, aligné à droite: وقال ايضا على منوال قصيده القاصى العلامه الأدب على ن محمد العنسى[102] التى حعلها الى السد محمد ن قاسم لقمان رحمهم الله حميعا	منيتى ان ادخل الجنه يا / منيتى اما بفضل او عمل	عبد الله بن علي الوزير	148
Introduit par, aligné à droite: وقال ايضا مرثيا سدى اسحق ن أمىر المؤمنن رحمهم الله	مصاب على مرّ الجديدين لا يبلا	عبد الله بن علي الوزير	150
Rubriqué.	حرف النون		151
Introduit par, aligné à droite: وقال مهنيا لامىر المومنين المهدى محمد ن احمد ن الحسن بالشفا رحمهم الله	قميص الشفا ما حاطه قد انسانِ	عبد الله بن علي الوزير	152
Introduit par, aligné à droite: وقال ايضا وقد اقترح عليه بعضهم ذلك ولها مقتض حاص	اثرها عجاجا تلبس الجوّ اردانا	عبد الله بن علي الوزير	154
Introduit par, aligné à droite: وقال مرثيا للقاضى العلامه على ن احمد السماوى رحمهم الله بعالى وايانا	ارى دمع عينى من كل شان	عبد الله بن علي الوزير	155
Introduit par: وقال رثى سدى يحى ن الحسن ن القسم رضوان الله عليهم وعليا	اجلْ هدمت من شامخ المجد اركانُ	عبد الله بن علي الوزير	156
Introduit par, aligné à droite: وقال مرثيا لسدى الحسن بن الحسن ن القاسم رحمهم الله بعالى وايانا	ابدا كل من عليها فاني	عبد الله بن علي الوزير	157

102 M. 1139/1726.

TABLE 10.3 Description du contenu de la *Safīna* 6 (*suite*)

Remarque	***Incipit***	**Auteur**	**Page**
Introduit par, aligné à droite: وقال رحمه الله مرثيا للفقيه احمد بن عبد المؤمن النزيلى رحمه الله تعالى	ان امرا بالجلال فى كفن	عبد الله بن علي الوزير	158
Introduit par, aligné à droite: وقال مكاتبا للسيد محمد لقمان بعد عزمه من صنعا رحمهم الله وايّانا	يا بلبل البان طارحنى وكن خلَفا	عبد الله بن علي الوزير	159
Introduit par, aligné à droite: وقال مكاتبا لسدى محمد بن عبد القادر بن عبد الرب رحمهم الله وايانا	سلا هل سلا قلبي عن الرشا الغانى	عبد الله بن علي الوزير	160
Rubriqué.	حرف الميم		162
Introduit par, aligné à droite: وقال مادحا للنبي المكرّم والرسول المعظم محمد صلى الله عليه واله وسلّم على منوال قصيده سدى الحسن بن عبد القادر ايام اعتقاله فى قصر صنعا ورحمهم الله وايانا والمومنين والمومنات وغفر لنا ولهم جميع السيّات P. 163, espace laissé en blanc et vers écrit d’un trait épais à l’encre rouge.	يا اهل طيبه لى من وصلكم ذِمَمٌ	عبد الله بن علي الوزير	162
Introduit par, aligné à droite: وقال مادحا للامام المتوكل على الله القاسم بن الحسن لما استولى على بلاد القبلة إلخ	حنث الواشون فيما اقسموا	عبد الله بن علي الوزير	164
Introduit par, aligné à droite: وقال وقد نفذ إلى صنعا بنفوذ سدى قاسم بن حسن إلى بلاد الحجه إلخ	قساما اكده لام القسم	عبد الله بن علي الوزير	166
Introduit par, aligné à droite: وقال مرثيا للقاضى على بن يحى البرطى والقاضى حسين بن محمد المغربى رحمهم الله جميعا وايانا	مصاب له من حق الصيد احلام [كذا]	عبد الله بن علي الوزير	169

TABLE 10.3 Description du contenu de la *Safīna* 6 (*suite*)

Remarque	***Incipit***	**Auteur**	**Page**
Introduit par, aligné à droite: وقال مهنيا للسيد اسمعيل بن حسن الحره La somme des lettres du premier (et dernier) hémistiche donne la date de 1121H, soit 1709-10. Le calcul est détaillé et le résultat, 1121, est indiqué par une accolade, à l'encre rouge[103].	السعد لا يحتاج تنجيما	عبد الله بن علي الوزير	171
Rubriqué.	حرف الها		171
Introduit par, aligné à droite: وقال وقد ألف السد شرف الدن القاسم مؤلفا في حداول النحوم وسماه النجم الثاقب وطلب منه تقريطه	ردوا جدول العين الذى طاب سقياها	عبد الله بن علي الوزير	171
Introduit par, aligné à droite: وقال مكاتبا للسد محمد بن قاسم لقمان وجعله على هذا الاسلوب العجب رحمهم الله Le poème s'organise autour de l'*incipit*, dont chaque mot sert de point de départ à une manière alternative de compléter ce qui reste du vers. Chacun de ces vers 'latéraux' s'élève obliquement à gauche à partir du mot de l'*incipit* qui sert de point de départ, au-dessus et au-dessous de l'arête centrale formée par l'*incipit*, produisant ainsi un effet graphique[104]. Virgules et points à l'encre rouge pour marquer le milieu et la fin des vers.	كيف يخلو عن حكمة وصواب / زمن انت بيننا لقمانه	عبد الله بن علي الوزير	173
Introduit par, aligné à droite: وقال الى السد محمد بن قاسم لقمان اعتذارا من ترك التردد الى مقامه	يا ابن لقمان يا كريم السجايا	عبد الله بن علي الوزير	174
Rubriqué.	حرف اليا		174

103 Ce n'est pas exceptionnel d'avoir une date exprimée ainsi, à la fin de poésies, dans différentes régions du Yémen, entre le XVIIIe s. et aujourd'hui.

104 Même exercice dans le ms. ar. 3426 (BnF), fol. 65[v].

TABLE 10.3 Description du contenu de la *Safīna* 6 (*suite*)

Remarque	*Incipit*	Auteur	Page
Introduit par, aligné à droite : وقال مكاتبا للقاضى على ن محمد العنسى[105] والتزم التوريه فى الأغلب منها وسماها بعض الأدبا اهرامات مصر لاحكامها رحمهم الله وايانا	انادم من تلك العيون جواريا	عبد الله بن علي الوزير	174
مقاطع À l'encre rouge, aligné à droite, introduit, par : سلوا ذلك ما له من المقاطع قال أى (؟) السد البلع العلامه عد الله ن على الوزر		عد الله ن على الوزر	175
	اقنع بما قسم الرحمن واسال فكم	عبد الله بن علي الوزير	175
مقاطع Commencent dans la marge de gauche de la p. 175, perpendiculairement au texte central. Introduit par : وما قال من مقاطعه Les pièces suivantes ont une introduction ; p. 181, introduction à un *madaḥ* rubriquée. Certaines sont dans la marge.		عبد الله بن علي الوزير	175-81
Introduit par, aligné à droite : وقال معاتبا للسد الهمام العلامه الأمجد محد ن قاسم لقمان رحمهم الله وايانا	الا الى الشمس اعنى (؟) البدر مطلبي	عبد الله بن علي الوزير	182
Introduit par, aligné à droite : وقال جوابا على سيدى عيسى ن محمد عد القادر صاحب كوكبان	هزّت من القدر شيقا ماسا	عبد الله بن علي الوزير	183

105 M. 1139/1726.

TABLE 10.3 Description du contenu de la *Safīna* 6 (*suite*)

Remarque	***Incipit***	**Auteur**	**Page**
Introduit par, aligné à droite: وقال رحمه الله في تعداد ضيافات Les ¾ de la p. 185 sont vierges.	قسماً برز ابن الوزير ومعبل	عبد الله بن علي الوزير	184-5
Maqāma/Épître ? en *saj*ʿ peu aisée à suivre, évoquant de nombreuses anecdotes historiques plus ou moins célèbres. Introduit par une *basmala* et une *ḥamdala*, aligné à droite. Mots de section à l'encre rouge, et, p. 189, sections des vers marquées par des virgules et des points à l'encre rouge.			186-9
Introduit par, aligné à droite: للصفى الحلى سعرل لمحبوب له اسمه حسن	اذاب التبر فى كاس اللجين	الصفي الحلي (m. 750/1349)	189
Introduit par, aligné à droite: لسدى الحسين (؟) على ن المتوكل رحمه الله	ما زال ذكرك فى الظلام سميرى	الحسين بن علي بن المتوكل	192
Introduit par, aligné à droite: قال عمره	تعطف للاحبه كل حين	الحسين بن علي بن المتوكل	192
Introduit par, aligné à droite: للمحب الطبرى (؟) رواه الامىر العاصمى	يا جاعلا سنن النبي شعاره ودثاره	المحب الطيري ؟	193
Introduit par, aligné à droite: لسدى محسن 1\/ بن المنوكل رحمه الله البت الاول والثانى ولسدى حسن 2\/ ن على رحمه الله الثالث والرابع ولسدى يوسف 3\/ المتوكل \رحمه الله/ الخامس وللقاضى على 4\/ ن صالح ان ابي الرجال رحمه الله السادس والسابع	علام يهيج القلب وهو المتيم	Différents poètes	193

TABLE 10.3 Description du contenu de la *Safīna* 6 (*suite*)

Remarque	*Incipit*	Auteur	Page
Introduit par, aligné à droite : للسد محمد ىن احمد الحلال اشدت فى مقام فه سدى العلامه عىد القادر ىن احمد رحمهما الله عىد عزم المىصور بالله للحماد	فى دمه الله محروسا مدا الابد	محمد بن أحمد الجلال ؟	194
Introduit par, aligné à droite : فاحارها سدى العلامه وحىه الدىن عىد القادر ىن احمد بهذه الاىىات	فاعزم بجيش من النصر المبين ومن…	وجيه الدين عبد القادر بن أحمد	194
Introduit par, aligné à droite : للسيد عبد المعطى قىل انه كان بمجلس الامام المتوكل على اسمعىل ىن القسم علىهما السلام فدحل إلخ	سطى علينا امير المومنين سطا	عبد المعطي	194
Introduit par, aligné à droite : قال الفقيه العلّامه المفاضل صفى الدىن احمد ىن محمد قاطن رحمه الله مخطبا على تعلم العلم وىشره ىعد موت العلما والاساره الى من ىقوم ىذلك وفىه اساله الى مشاىخه وىرسه لهم رحمهم الله وايانا وحمىع المومىىن La pagination à l'encre rouge s'achève ici, dans cette numérotation à la p. 116. P. 196, ¼ inférieur laissé vierge.	يا طالب العلم صف القلب عن شوس	الفقيه صفي الدين أحمد بن محمد قاطن (m. 1198/1784)	195
Introduit par, aligné à droite : قال السىد العلامه الادىب التحرير (؟) ىخر الاسلام الفهامه الارىب عبد الله ىن علي الوزىر AAB CCC *mu'rab* llcllclclccl llcllclclccl ll llcllclclccl llcllclclccl llcllclclccl Sections des vers marquées à l'encre rouge par des virgules et une forme en escargot (*ḥaylazūnī*).	انصف قلبي الحبيب اذ وصلا	عبد الله بن علي الوزير (m. 1147/1734)	197

TABLE 10.3 Description du contenu de la *Safīna* 6 (*suite*)

Remarque	***Incipit***	**Auteur**	**Page**
Introduit par, centré: وقال ايضا ab ab ab AB *malḥūn* llcllclcl llclcll llcllclcl llclcll llcllclcl llclcll llcllclcl llclcll Nouvelles sections de 4 vers marquées par "*bayt*" à l'encre rouge, centré. Dans cette partie du *dīwān* réservée au *ḥumaynī*, le copiste s'efforce de consacrer une page à chaque poème, ce qui le conduit, au besoin, à achever verticalement dans la marge. Cet effort, surtout perceptible au début, s'essouffle ensuite progressivement à partir de la p. 208.	عليش يا بابلي النظر / يا حالي الشمايل	عبد الله بن علي الوزير	197
Introduit par: وقال رحمه الله ab ab ab AB ccc AB lclllcllcll lclllcl lclllcllcll lclllcl lclllcllcll lclllcl lclllcllcll lclllcl lclllcl lclllcl lclllcl lclllcllcll lclllcl Sections des vers marquées à l'encre rouge par des virgules et une forme en escargot. Nouvelles sections de 6 vers marquées par "*bayt*" à l'encre rouge, centré.	القلوب من ذى الذوايب ذوايب	عبد الله بن علي الوزير	198

TABLE 10.3 Description du contenu de la *Safīna* 6 (*suite*)

Remarque	***Incipit***	**Auteur**	**Page**
Introduit par, aligné à droite : وله رحمه الله تعالى وارسلها الى السد احمد المهدى الى قربه القابل aa aa aa AA llcllclllcllcl llcllcl llcllclllcllcl llcllcl llcllclllcllcl llcllcl llcllclllcllcl llcllcl Nouvelles sections de 4 vers marquées par "*bayt*" à l'encre rouge, centré, et *tatimma* à l'encre rouge dans la marge.	لولاك يا غصن لم اطرب لسجع الحمام	عبد الله بن علي الوزير	199
Introduit par, aligné à droite : وله رحمه الله تعالى وارسلها الى السدى زىد ىن محمد ىن الحسن llclllcl llclllclcll llclllcl llclllclcll llclllcl llclllclcll llclllcl llclllclcll llclllcl llclllcl llclllcl llclllcl llclllclcll Avant-dernier vers à l'encre rouge. Nouvelles sections de 6 vers marquées par "*bayt*" à l'encre rouge, centré ; avant-dernier vers à l'encre rouge. Dans la marge, vers à l'encre rouge, dont les parties sont réunies par un motif en nuage à l'encre rouge et sections des autres vers marquées par des virgules et escargots à l'encre rouge. *Tatimma* à l'encre rouge.	استغفر الله العظيم	عبد الله بن علي الوزير	200

TABLE 10.3 Description du contenu de la *Safīna* 6 (*suite*)

Remarque	***Incipit***	**Auteur**	**Page**
Introduit par, aligné à droite: وله رحمه الله الى شعبان سليم ab ab ab AB llclllcllcl llclllcll llclllcllcl llclllcll llclllcllcl llclllcll llclllcllcl llclllcll Nouvelles sections de 4 vers marquées par "*bayt*" à l'encre rouge, centré. Dans la marge, *tatimma* à l'encre rouge.	البارحه طبي الصريم الاغن	عبد الله بن علي الوزير	201
Introduit par, aligné à droite: وله رحمه الله مجيبا على السد احمد المنهدى رحمه الله ab ab ab AB ccc AB AB llcllclcll llcllclcll llcllclcll llcllclcll llcllclcll llcllclcll llcllclcll llcllclcll llcllclcll llcllclcll llcllclcll llcllclcll llcllclcll llcllclcll llcllclcll Nouvelles sections de vers marquées par "*bayt*" à l'encre rouge, centré. Dans la marge, vers à l'encre rouge et *tatimma* à l'encre rouge.	فتاك لحظيك يا محجب (؟)	عبد الله بن علي الوزير	202
Introduit par, aligné à droite: وقال رحمه الله تعالى ab ab ab AB llclllcll llclllcl llclllcll llclllcl llclllcll llclllcl llclllcll llclllcl Nouvelles sections de 6 vers marquées par "*bayt*" à l'encre rouge, centré, et *tatimma* à l'encre rouge.	ما هو السبب يا ريم رامه	عبد الله بن علي الوزير	203

TABLE 10.3 Description du contenu de la *Safīna* 6 (*suite*)

Remarque	*Incipit*	Auteur	Page
Introduit par, aligné à droite: وله رحمه الله تعالى ولها سرح طويل لـ... حشه التطويل ab ab ab AB lcllcllclllcl lcllcllcll lcllcllclllcl lcllcllcll lcllcllclllcl lcllcllcll lcllcllclllcl lcllcllcll Échos très nets du poème – sans doute postérieur – *Layt° shiʿrī limvh khilliy al-yawm iʿtadhar*. Nouvelles sections de 4 vers marquées par "*bayt*" à l'encre rouge, centré, et *tatimma* à l'encre rouge.	يا حمام اسعدينا بتبليغ السلام	عبد الله بن علي الوزير	204
ab ab ab AB CCC AB AB llclllclcl llclllclll llclllclcl llclllclll llclllclcl llclllclll llclllclcl llclllclll llclllclcl llclllclcl llclllclcl llclllclcl llclllclll llclllclcl llclllclll À l'encre rouge, "*tawshīḥ*" et "*bayt*". Dans la marge, vers et *tatimma* à l'encre rouge.	لى خل من بين الظبا شرد	عبد الله بن علي الوزير	205
Introduit par, aligné à droite: وقال رحمه الله ab ab ab AB CCC AB lcllclclll lcllcl lcllclclll lcllcl lcllclclll lcllcl lcllclclll lcllcl lcllclclll lcllclclll lcllclclll lcllclclll lcllcl À l'encre rouge, "*tawshīḥ*" et "*bayt*". Dans la marge, vers et *tatimma* à l'encre rouge.	الله المستعان يا خلّى	عبد الله بن علي الوزير	206

TABLE 10.3 Description du contenu de la *Safīna* 6 (*suite*)

Remarque	***Incipit***	**Auteur**	**Page**
Introduit par, aligné à droite: وقال عفى الله عنه ab ab ab AB llclll llclllclcl llclll llclllclcl llclll llclllclcl llclll llclllclcl À l'encre rouge, "*bayt*" et *tatimma*. Virtuosité calligraphique (*tafannun*) sur "*al-ḥajj*".	صلّى الاله يا اخوان	عبد الله بن علي الوزير	207
Introduit par, aligné à droite: وقال عفى الله عنه aaaA llclllclcll llclllclcll llclllclcll llclllclcll À l'encre rouge, "*bayt*" et *tatimma*.	لى خل مثل البدر طال مغيبه	عبد الله بن علي الوزير	208
Introduit par, aligné à droite: وقال عفى الله عنه ab ab ab AB ccc AB llclllclcll llclll llclllclcll llclll llclllclcll llclll llclllclcll llclll lclcll lclcll lclcll lclcll lclcll lclcll llclllclcll llclll À l'encre rouge, "*tawshīḥ*" et "*bayt*".	ما تاج كسرى او قصور قيصر	عبد الله بن علي الوزير	208

TABLE 10.3 Description du contenu de la *Safīna* 6 (*suite*)

Remarque	*Incipit*	Auteur	Page
ab ab ab AB cd cd cd AB llclllclcll llclll llclllclcll llclll llclllclcll llclll llclllclcll llclll lclcll lclcll lclcll lclcll lclcll lclcll llclllclcll llclll À l'encre rouge, "*tawshīḥ*" et "*bayt*".	قد نال عذولك كلّما [ما] تمنّى	عبد الله بن علي الوزير	210
Introduit par, centré : وقال عفى الله عنه ab ab ab AB ccc AB llclllcll llcllclll llclllcll llclllcll llclllcll llcllclll llclllcll llclllcll llcllclll llcllclll llcllclll llclllcll llclllcll À l'encre rouge, "*tawshīḥ*", "*bayt*" et *tatimma*.	اما وتغريد البلابل	عبد الله بن علي الوزير	211
Introduit par, centré : وقال عفى الله عنه ab ab ab AB lcllcllcll lcllcllcll lcllcllcll lcllcllcll lcllcllcll lcllcllcll lcllcllcll lcllcllcll À l'encre rouge, "*bayt*" et *tatimma*.	كم وكم لى ادارى شجونى	عبد الله بن علي الوزير	212

TABLE 10.3 Description du contenu de la *Safīna* 6 (*suite*)

Remarque	***Incipit***	**Auteur**	**Page**
Introduit par: وقال رحمه الله ab ab ab AB llcllclll llcllcllcl llcllclll llcllcllcl llcllclll llcllcllcl llcllclll llcllcllcl À l'encre rouge, "*bayt*" et *tatimma*.	صادت فوادی غزال الدور	عبد الله بن علي الوزير	213
Introduit par, centré: وفال رحمه الله ab ab ab AB lllcl llcllcll lllcl llcllcll lllcl llcllcll lllcl llcllcll Échos très nets de *Maʿshūq al-jamāl* de Sharaf al-Dīn (m. 1010/1601) À l'encre rouge, "*bayt*" et *tatimma*.	يا اهل الخيام / ردوا لطرفى منامه	عبد الله بن علي الوزير	213
Introduit par, aligné à droite: وفال رحمه الله ab ab ab AB llclllclcll llcll llclllclcll llcll llclllclcll llcll llclllclcll llcll À l'encre rouge, "*bayt*" et *tatimma*.	من منصفى من درى الجمانى	عبد الله بن علي الوزير	214
Introduit par, aligné à droite: وفال رحمه الله على لسان صديق له مات محبوبه ab ab ab AB llcllclll llcllcllcl llcllclll llcllcllcl llcllclll llcllcllcl llcllclll llcllcllcl À l'encre rouge, "*bayt*" et *tatimma*.	قالوا حبيبك فلان قد مات	عبد الله بن علي الوزير	214

TABLE 10.3 Description du contenu de la *Safīna* 6 (*suite*)

Remarque	***Incipit***	**Auteur**	**Page**
Introduit par, centré: وفال رحمه aaaA clllcllclllcll clllcllclllcll clllcllclllcll clllcllclllcll À l'encre rouge, "*bayt*". Le poème se termine au tiers supérieur de la p. 216, dont le reste est laissé blanc	اسالك بالنبي يا حبيب القلب ما لك	عبد الله بن علي الوزير	215
Introduit par, aligné à droite: وفال رحمه الله بعالى محاطبا لولده صلاح الدن ن عبد الله على الورىر رحمهم الله حمىعا ab ab ab AB llclllclcll llclllclcl llclllclcll llclllclcl llclllclcll llclllclcl llclllclcll llclllclcl À l'encre rouge, sections marquées par "*bayt*". Le poème s'arrête aux 2/3 de la p. 219, par une strophe incomplète et sans *tatimma*. Le 1/3 restant est laissé vierge.	اغنم شبابك يا صلاح تغنم	عبد الله بن علي الوزير	217
Introduit par, rubriqué: لبعصهم aaaA llclllclcll llclllclcll llclllclcll llclllclcll À l'encre rouge, "*bayt*" et *tatimma*.	متى متى بالوصل والتدانى	؟	220

TABLE 10.3 Description du contenu de la *Safīna* 6 (*suite*)

Remarque	*Incipit*	Auteur	Page
Introduit par, aligné à droite: وللقاضى العلامه الادب على ن العنسى رحمه الله واتى بها على لغه تهامه Mentionne la Tihāma, sa langue. ab ab llcllclll llcllclll llcllclll llcllclll À l'encre rouge, "*bayt*" et *tatimma*.	شابوك انا وامرفق بكره	علي بن محمد العنسي (m. 1139/1726)	221
Introduit par, rubriqué, aligné à droite: وللقاصى على ن محمد العسى الى السد محمد ن قاسم لقمان رحمهما الله Fin des vers marqué par un cercle à l'encre rouge et *tatimma* à l'encre rouge.	اوثقوا (؟) القلب وقالوا لي تسل	علي بن محمد العنسي	222
Introduit par, aligné à droite: وقال القاصى العلامه حمال الاسلام على ن محمد العنسى رحمه الله ما لفطه اطلعت فى بعض الكتب على نعل سىد المرسلىن صلى الله علىه واله وسلم ممثلة باحسن مثال وكان يخطر فى بالى نظم قصده فى مدح سىد المرسلىن صلى الله علىه واله وسلم إلخ À l'encre rouge, *tatimma*.	ما زلت النعل فى قول ولا عمل	علي بن محمد العنسي	223
Introduit par, aligné à droite: قال سىدى العلامه عر الاسلام محمد ن اسحق ن المهدى احمد ن الحسن ن القسم علىهم السلام *Tatimma* à l'encre rouge.	ايا بارق الجزعا (؟) هال الجزع ممطورُ	محمد بن إسحق بن المهدي أحمد بن الحسن بن القسم (m. 1167/1754)	224
Introduit par: وقال رحمه الله تعالى قصب قصب à l'encre rouge. Milieu de vers marqué par un escargot à l'encre rouge.	يا بروحى الذى (؟) تجلى لطرفى	محمد بن إسحق بن المهدي أحمد بن الحسن بن القسم	224

TABLE 10.3 Description du contenu de la *Safīna* 6 (*suite*)

Remarque	*Incipit*	Auteur	Page
Introduit par: وقال رحمه الله قصب قصب à l'encre rouge. *Tatimma* à l'encre rouge.	افاطم هل يمضى الزمان الذى مرا	محمد بن إسحق بن المهدي أحمد بن الحسن بن القسم	225
Introduit par, aligné à droite: وله رضى الله عنه مجيبا على والده عليهما السلام قصب قصب à l'encre rouge. Milieu de vers marqué par un cercle à l'encre rouge. *Tatimma* à l'encre rouge.	لا ومثواك بقلبي وهوى	محمد بن إسحق بن المهدي أحمد بن الحسن بن القسم	226
Introduit par, aligné à droite: وله رحمه الله قصب قصب à l'encre rouge. Milieu de vers marqué par une virgule et fin de vers par un cercle à l'encre rouge. *Tatimma* à l'encre rouge.	جودى بوصلك او بوعدك	محمد بن إسحق بن المهدي أحمد بن الحسن بن القسم	227
Introduit par, aligné à droite: وقال رحمه الله قصب قصب à l'encre rouge. Milieu de vers marqué par une virgule et fin de vers par un escargot à l'encre rouge.	أأَسْما انت الشمس لا انت يا أسما	محمد بن إسحق بن المهدي أحمد بن الحسن بن القسم	227
Introduit par, aligné à droite: وقال رحمه الله قصب قصب à l'encre rouge. *Tatimma* à l'encre rouge.	مرّت وقد جرت ذيول المرح	محمد بن إسحق بن المهدي أحمد بن الحسن بن القسم	228
Introduit par, centré: وقال رحمه الله قصب قصب à l'encre rouge. *Tatimma* à l'encre rouge.	وحمامة بالقرب منى نوحها	محمد بن إسحق بن المهدي أحمد بن الحسن بن القسم	228
Introduit par, aligné à droite: وقال رحمه الله تعالى وهو في السجن dernière l. de la p. 228, reprise p. 229, l. 1. *Tatimma* à l'encre rouge.	سرى طيفها ليلا الى السجن مشفقا	محمد بن إسحق بن المهدي أحمد بن الحسن بن القسم	228

TABLE 10.3 Description du contenu de la *Safīna* 6 (*suite*)

Remarque	***Incipit***	**Auteur**	**Page**
Introduit par, aligné à droite, à l'encre rouge: وقال وهو مما نظمه ايضا وهو واحوبه فى السحن رحمهم الله جمعا *Tatimma* à l'encre rouge.	لا تجزعوا ان طال حبسكم فما فى الحبس عاريا بنى اسحاق	محمد بن إسحق بن المهدي أحمد بن الحسن بن القسم	229
Introduit par, aligné à droite, à l'encre rouge: وقال مضمنا فى مليح قلع الطبب ثنيته وهو بديع قص *Tatimma* à l'encre rouge. Une première *tatimma*, erronnée, a été discrètement raturée.	لا كان هذا الطبيب من رجل	محمد بن إسحق بن المهدي أحمد بن الحسن بن القسم	229
Introduit par, aligné à droite, à l'encre rouge: وقال مضمنا قص	مهلا ورفقا يا مطوق ان لى / قلبا يطير متى صدحت ويخفق	محمد بن إسحق بن المهدي أحمد بن الحسن بن القسم	229
Introduit par, aligné à droite, à l'encre rouge, à l'exception de قص: وقال فى اللف والنشر المرتب قص وهو لسدى اسحق قاله فى محروس…	سقى الله هذا الروض اذ فيه كلما	محمد بن إسحق بن المهدي أحمد بن الحسن بن القسم	229
Introduit par, aligné à droite, à l'encre rouge, à l'exception du dernier mot: وقال سدى العلامه عر الاسلام رحمه الله تعالى قص	رمانى فاتن من مقلتيه	محمد بن إسحق بن المهدي أحمد بن الحسن بن القسم	229
مقاطع tous introduit, avec usage d'encre rouge.		محمد بن إسحق بن المهدي أحمد بن الحسن بن القسم	230-1
Introduit par, aligné à droite, dernier mot à l'encre rouge: وقال ايضا رحمه الله مجبا على القاضى احمد بن محمد الحيمى رحمه الله قص.	طوت نحوى الغلاه قطاه نفسى	محمد بن إسحق بن المهدي أحمد بن الحسن بن القسم	231
Copie d'une lettre. P. 232, usage d'encre rouge		?	232-3

TABLE 10.3 Description du contenu de la *Safīna* 6 (*suite*)

Remarque	*Incipit*	Auteur	Page
Introduit par, aligné à droite: ولسدى العلامه الادب الحسن اسحق الى سدى العلامه يوسف بن المتوكل على الله إسمعل رحمهم الله جمعا	دعوتك لما عيل يا سيدى صبرى	الحسن بن إسحق	234
Introduit par, aligné à droite: وله الى أخيه العلامه محمد بن اسحق رحمهما الله	تَلَطَّف فى تحيله الرسول	الحسن بن إسحق	235
Introduit par, dans la marge, aligné à droite, à l'encre rouge: فاجابه أخوه العلامه عز الاسلام محمد بن اسحق رضى الله عنهما P. 237, poème en marge introduit par "*qāla*" et *tatimma* à l'encre rouge.	تحمل عن احبتنا الرسول	محمد بن إسحق (m. 1167/1754)	236-7
Introduit par, aligné à droite: ولأخيهما فخر الإسلام عبد الله بن اسحق مجيبا على الحسن رضى الله عنهم Le poème commence en haut de la page. Cinq vers sont donnés puis le texte s'interrompt, le reste de la page est laissé vierge. Le poème suivant commence en haut de la p. 239.	دع العيس تذرع عرض الفلا	عبد الله بن إسحق	238
Introduit par, aligné à droite: ولسدى الحسن بن اسحق رحمه تعالى Dans la marge, poème introduit par, aligné à droite: وله رحمه الله *Tatimma* à l'encre rouge.	عرفْت قصدَك يا من / اهدى الى سوا كا	الحسن بن إسحق	239
Introduit par, aligné à droite: سمات الاسحار فى مراثى الحمار لسدى العلامه فخر الاسلام عبد الله بن احمد بن إسحق رحمهم الله	سحائب مدمعى قاضت سجالا	عبد الله بن أحمد بن إسحق	240

TABLE 10.3 Description du contenu de la *Safīna* 6 (*suite*)

Remarque	***Incipit***	**Auteur**	**Page**
Introduit par, centré: وله رحمه الله في الحمار ايضا	يوم موت الحمار يوم الحمار	عبد الله بن أحمد بن إسحق	240
Introduit par, centré: وله رحمه الله فى عرض المرثى اعشم	كأن حمارى من دجا الليل قطعة	عبد الله بن أحمد بن إسحق	241
Introduit par, aligné à droite: وسدى العلامه احمد بن يوسف بن الحسن الحسن حفطه مرثيا لذلك النجيب (؟)	جاد صوب الغمام اعظم عير (؟)	أحمد بن يوسف بن الحسين بن الحسن حفظه ؟	241
Introduit par, aligné à droite: وله ايضا فى عوض المرثى	وعير حباه الليل لونا وسيره (؟)	عبد الله بن أحمد بن إسحق ؟	242
Introduit par, aligné à droite: وله وقد عتب (؟) عله الفحرى حفطه مما جبا له	مصاب العير جشمنى النزالا (؟)	عبد الله بن أحمد بن إسحق ؟	242
Introduit par, aligné à droite: جواب الفحرى رحمه الله	أأعلا من على حسبا فطالا	أحمد بن يوسف بن الحسين بن الحسن حفظه ؟	242
Introduit par, centré: وللفحرى رحمه الله	ما شان مولانا الحسن	أحمد بن يوسف بن الحسين بن الحسن حفظه ؟	243
Introduit par: الجواب	عتب على اعلى سنَنَ	عبد الله بن أحمد بن إسحق ؟	243
Introduit par, aligné à droite: ثم فرضها الفحرى حفطه	عبرت بى نسمة من ادبك	أحمد بن يوسف بن الحسين بن الحسن حفظه ؟	244
Texte à l'encre rouge. Muḥammad b. Ismāʿīl al-Amīr, cf. *safīna* 4, 66, 97; *safīna* 7, 74, 313-6	يتلو ذلك ما وجدته من المراثى فى سيدى العلامه البدر المنير محمد بن اسمعيل الامير رضوان الله عليه		244

TABLE 10.3 Description du contenu de la *Safīna* 6 (*suite*)

Remarque	*Incipit*	Auteur	Page
Introduit par, aligné à droite : وقال سدى العلامه فخر الاسلام عد الله ن احمد ن اسحق رحمه الله ىعالى مرثيا للمذكور	هو الخطب لا خطب سواه يماثله	عبد الله بن أحمد بن إسحق	244
Introduit par : وقال سدى العلامه ىحى ن حسن ن اسحق فى الدر ايضا رحمهم الله حمىعا aligné à droite. Lettres ou mots d'un trait épais.	من الخطب ما يستاصل الصبر ناجمه	يحيى بن حسن بن إسحق	245
Introduit par, aligné à droite : وقال سدى العلامه وحىه الدن عد الرحمن ن على ن اسحق مرثيا للبدر ايضا رحمهم الله حمىعا Lettres ou mots d'un trait épais.	قضا العلم والارشاد بعد محمدِ	وجيه الدين عبد الرحمن بن علي بن إسحق	247
Introduit par, aligné à droite : تاريخ وفاة البدر المنير ايضا للسد العلاّمه محمد ن هاشم الشامى رحمهم الله Lettres ou mots d'un trait épais. Un quart de la page, partie inférieure, laissé vierge.	عز الاماجد من اهل المفاخر فى / طود من المجد لا اعنى به رجلا	محمد بن هاشم الشامي	250
Introduit par, aligné à droite : وقال الشريف الرصى الموسوى ىمدح رسول الله صلى الله عليه واله وسلم	هذا العقيق وتلك شم رعانه	الشريف الرضي الموسوي (m. 1016/ 1607-8)	251
Introduit par, aligné à droite : وقال رحمه الله ىعالى ىمدح أمىر المومنين على ن أبى طالب صلوات الله عليه	غربت عنكم شموس التلاق	الشريف الرضي الموسوي	254
Introduit par, aligné à droite : وقال رحمه الله ىعالى ىمدح السيد بركات خان ويهنيه ىعدومه من عىد الشاه صفى 50	خفرت بسيف الغنج ذمّة مغفر	الشريف الرضي الموسوي	256

TABLE 10.3 Description du contenu de la *Safīna* 6 (*suite*)

Remarque	*Incipit*	Auteur	Page
Introduit par, aligné à droite: وقال رحمه الله تعالى	اما ومواض مقلتيها العواصل	الشريف الرضي الموسوي	259
Introduit par, aligné à droite: وقال رحمه الله تعالى يمدحه	ميلوا بنا نحو الحجون (؟) ونكّبوا	الشريف الرضي الموسوي	262
Introduit par, aligné à droite: وقال ايضا يمدحه	كتم الهوى فوشى النحول بسره	الشريف الرضي الموسوي	265
Introduit par: وقال رحمه يمدحه Ici et ailleurs, de petits blancs de la taille d'un mot ou deux apparaissent dans le corps des poèmes, peut-être certains mots sont-ils illisibles dans l'original ?	ضربوا القباب وطنبوها بالقنا	الشريف الرضي الموسوي	267
Introduit par, aligné à droite: وقال رحمه الله تعالى يمدحه ويهنيه بختان ولده	خطرت فمال الغصن وهو ممنطق	الشريف الرضي الموسوي	270
Introduit par, aligné à droite: قال الصفى الحلى من شعرا القرن السابع فى الحماسه وعلو نفسه واجاب Lettres d'un trait épais.	لئن ثلمت حسدى من صروف النوائب	الصفي الحلي (m. 750/1349)	274
Introduit par: وله رحمه الله تعالى	سل الرماح العوالى عن معالينا	الصفي الحلي	276
Introduit par, aligné à droite: وله رحمه الله تعالى	ان لم ازر ربعكم سعيا على الحدق	الصفي الحلي	278
Introduit par وقال ايضا يمتدح الملك شمس الدين	دبت عقارب صدعه فى خده	الصفي الحلي	280

TABLE 10.3 Description du contenu de la *Safīna* 6 (*suite*)

Remarque	*Incipit*	Auteur	Page
Introduit par, centré: وقال ايضا يمتدحه	انى لينظرنى العدول فانثنى	الصفي الحلي	283
Introduit par, aligné à droite: وقال ايضا وهو بمصر الى الامام قاضى القضاه تاج الدين السبكى الحنفى	تركتنا لواحظ الاتراك	الصفي الحلي	285
Introduit par, aligné à droite: وله رحمه الله تعالى وسئم الاقامه والراحه واللهو واشتاق اقاربه والحركه اليهم والتزم فى كل ست الحاس اللعطى فى سطره فقال	لسيرى فى الغلا والليل داجٍ	الصفي الحلي	286
Introduit par, centré: وقال رحمه الله تعالى وقد كتب اليه الشيخ العالم المهنّب محمود بن يحى النحوى كل من ياردين قصده اولها عد العزيز على ات ويحدك فى العطم والعرير فاجابه بقوله	من لى بقربك والمقام عزيز	الصفي الحلي	287
Introduit par, aligné à droite: وقال رحمه الله تعالى وقد سمع احد الفضلا شعره فاستحسنه وقال لا عيب فيه سوا قل استعماله اللغه الغريبه وغريب الكلام فكتب اليه	انما الحيزبون (؟) والدر دبيس[106]	الصفي الحلي	287
Dans la marge, obliquement, du shaykh ʿAbd al-Raḥmān b. Muḥammad al-Dhahabī à ʿAlī b. Muḥammad al-ʿAnsī (m. 1139/1726) pour le remercier de lui avoir envoyé un exemplaire de son *dīwān*. *Rajaz*.	ذا وشى برد سابرى / ام سحر طرف بابلى	الشيخ عبد الرحمن بن محمد الذهبي	287

106 Comparer p. 274-87 avec *Safīna* 4, 108-22.

TABLE 10.3 Description du contenu de la *Safīna* 6 (*suite*)

Remarque	*Incipit*	Auteur	Page
Réponse introduite par: فاحابه القاضى العلامه حمال الدن بقوله aligné sur une colonne de vers, à l'encre mauve, de même que le premiers vers. P. 290, *tatimma* à l'encre violette.	ارحم لحن موصلى / تنظيم شعر الموصلى[107]	علي العنسي (m. 1139/1726)	289
Introduit par, aligné à droite, à l'encre mauve: وللقاضى العلامه حمال الدن ابصا على ن محمد العنسى الدى سبق إلخ	شفت كمد الاسلام والبقى (؟) راغم	علي العنسي	290
Introduit par: وله رحمه الله صحنه عند الاقطار عند سلامه للامام الموكل \رحمه الله/ ارحل منها فى المحلس اربعه ابات واخره المولى... ساما وهى قوله aligné sur une colonne de vers, à l'encre mauve. La moitié inférieure de la page est laissée vierge.	ملك اغر ويوم عيد ازهرُ	علي العنسي	291
Page vierge.			292
Pas de rubrique, poème pris en cours. *Tatimma* à l'encre mauve.	وما رضيت بالبعد منها كغيرها	?	293
Introduit par, centré, encre mauve, puis noire: وقال ابصا مكاتبا لسدى العلامه عز الاسلام الادب الكامل (؟) لوا الادب والمـ... فى حلبه السان لكل من حارس الادب ودأب محمد ن اسحق بن المهدى ن احمد ن الحسن بن القاسم علهم السلام وكان القاضى العلامه جمال الدن رحمه الله مقيما بوصاب بعد ارتحاله من صنعا	ذنب الجفا عند ذنب البين يغتفر	علي العنسي	293
Introduit par, aligné à droite, à l'encre mauve: فاجاب سدى العلامه الدر عر الاسلام محمد ن اسحق رحمه الله قوله	يا صاح هذا شذا اهل الحمى عطر	محمد بن إسحق (m. 1167/1754)	294

107 Comparer p. 287-279 avec *Safīna* 4, 9-13. Cité dans cette dernière *safīna* en p. 87 et 141.

TABLE 10.3 Description du contenu de la *Safīna* 6 (*suite*)

Remarque	***Incipit***	**Auteur**	**Page**
Introduit par, aligné à droite, à l'encre mauve: ولسدى العلامه عر الاسلام محمد ن اسحق رصى الله عنه ايصا الى القاضى العلامه على ن محمد العنسى رحمه الله Vers laissés blancs p. 296	أي صبر لم تفنه الأشواق	محمد بن إسحق	295
Introduit par, aligné à droite, encre mauve, puis noire: ومن شعر السد العلامه الحسن ن على ن المتوكل وكان هذا السد نادره الدهر ومن حسنات الزمان الى القاضى العلامه الادب اللبيب جمال الدن على ن محمد العنسى رحمه الله واىانا وجميع المومنين	لعدرار من... قدراقا	الحسين علي بن المتوكل	296
Introduit par, aligné à droite, encre mauve: فاجابه القاضى من البلع جمال الدن على ن محمد العنسى رحمهما الله بهذه القصيده التى نظم فيها اللالى الفريده	عقيلة ملك لو فرشت لها الطرقا	علي العنسي	297
Introduit par, aligné à droite, partie à l'encre noir clair: وقال سيدى العلامه الادب الحسن ن على ن المتوكل مادحًا خاله المهدى محمد ن المهدى لدين الله احمد ن الحسن ن القاسم	قمت فى مركز الجمال بذتك	يحيى بن علي بن المتوكل	297
Introduit par, aligné à droite, encre mauve: وقال ايضا رحمه الله	سمعت فى روض الحما بلابلا	يحيى بن علي بن المتوكل	298

TABLE 10.3 Description du contenu de la *Safīna* 6 (*suite*)

Remarque	*Incipit*	Auteur	Page
Introduit par, aligné à droite, encre mauve: وله فى الحمينى "*Bayt*" à l'encre mauve. aaaA lcllcllcllll lcllcllcllll lcllcllcllll lcllcllcllll[108]	يا قديم الاحسان يا جواد يا معطى	يحيى بن علي بن المتوكل	298
Introduit par, aligné à droite: للقاضى العلامه عبد القادر النزيلي مكاتبا للسيد \العلامه/ عبد الله بن على الورىر [ر]حمهما الله تعالى	عد عن ذكر الحما والكثب	عبد القادر النزيلي	299
Devinette en vers, réponse de Ḥusayn al-Ḥaddād, puis réplique à nouveau d'al-Ruqayḥī, introduits respectivement par, centré: فاجابه حسىن الحداد ىقول وله فى المكاتبه وله رحمه الله متغزّلا		أحمد الرقيحي	300
مقاطع tous introduits.		أحمد الرقيحي	300
Introduit par: وله متغزّلا	فى الثغر در وفى الخدين توريدُ	أحمد الرقيحي	300
Sans introduction (le copiste a laissé un blanc). P. 203, ¼ de la p., partie inférieure, vierge.	ادرها كووسا من معتقه صرفا	أحمد الرقيحي ؟	301
	ما للاسير بحبها اطلاق	أحمد الرقيحي ؟	304
Introduit par, aligné à droite: وله رحمه الله Lettres à trait épais.	ما روى عن صبابه المشتاق	أحمد الرقيحي ؟	304

108 Comparer p. 290-8 avec *Safīna* 4, 31-55.

TABLE 10.3 Description du contenu de la *Safīna* 6 (*suite*)

Remarque	*Incipit*	Auteur	Page
Introduit par, aligné à droite: وله رحمه الله	هو الحب قد لاحت عليك مخائله	أحمد الرقيحي ؟	305
Espace laissé entre le poème précédent et le suivant.	طمع العاذل فينا ان نمارى[109]	أحمد الرقيحي ؟	306
Introduit par, aligné à droite, d'une encre plus claire: هذه نبذه من شعر الأديب محمد حليل سمرجي رحمه الله فمن دلك ما انشاه بصنعا بمدح الورر صى الاسلام احمد ن على النهمى رحمه الله	من ركب الشمس فى اغصان (؟) بلّور	محمد جليل سمرجي	307
Introduit par, aligné à droite: وله رحمه الله	بدت بصبح جبين لاح ابلجه	محمد جليل سمرجي	308
Introduit par, aligné à droite: وله	سيف الجفون وسهم الناظر الغنج	محمد جليل سمرجي	309
Introduit par, aligné à droite: وله يمدح صنعا واهلها	سقا جانبي (؟) صنعا در سحابة	محمد جليل سمرجي	310
Introduit par, aligné à droite: وله مما قاله فى صنعا	خطرت من نحو نعمان تناجا	محمد جليل سمرجي	310
Introduit par, aligné à droite: وله يمدح بير العزب	سقا البير برّاق الوميض المفلّج	محمد جليل سمرجي	311
Introduit par: وله رحمه الله[110] suivi par: وله وقد التقا هو وا رهم المنوفى عند الكعبه فى الطواف alignés à droite.	زارت وصدر الليل فود شائب	محمد جليل سمرجي	312

109 Comparer p. 300-6 avec *Safīna* 4, 18-29.
110 Comparer p. 307-12 avec *Safīna* 4, 57-63.

TABLE 10.3 Description du contenu de la *Safīna* 6 (*suite*)

Remarque	***Incipit***	**Auteur**	**Page**
Introduit par, aligné à droite: قال السد الراهد العلامه العابد سدى حمال الاسلام وبلبل الابا الكرام العلما الاعلام الدر المنير على ن ابرهم ن محمد الامر رصى الله عهم وعا حمع المومىن والمومنات *Malḥūn* aaaA lclllclllcll lclllclllcll lclllclllcll lclllclllcll Moitié de la page laissée vierge.	الصلاه تغشاك يا خير البريه	علي بن إ برهيم بن محمد الأمير (cf. *safīna* 4, 66, 97; *safīna* 7, 74, 244)	313-6
Pages vierges.			317-28

List of Quoted Manuscripts

Afyon Karahisar

MS 702 (Gedik Ahmet Pasha Kütüphane; al-Awḥadī, *Mukhtār al-Dhakhāʾir wa-l-tuḥaf*)

Alexandria

MS 2125 dāl Tārīkh (Bibliotheca Alexandrina; al-Maqrīzī, *Untitled notebook*)

Ann Arbor

MS Isl. 605 (University of Michigan, Special Collections Library; al-Maqrīzī, *al-Mawāʿiẓ wa-l-iʿtibār*)

Baltimore

MS 591 (Walters Art Museum; al-Shīrāzī, supergloss on Sirāj al-Dīn al- Urmawī's *Maṭāliʿ al-anwār*)

Beirut

MS 1004 (American University of Beirut; Ibn Mufliḥ, *al-Tadhkira al-akmaliyya al-mufliḥiyya*)

Berlin

MS Or. oct. 3806 (Staatsbibliothek; al-Ṣafadī, *Ṣarf al-ʿayn ʿan ṣarf al-ʿayn fī waṣf al-ʿayn*)

MS Spr. 252 (Staatsbibliothek; Ibn Ayyūb al-Anṣarī, *al-Tadhkira al-ayyūbiyya*)

MS Spr. 1962 (Staatsbibliothek; Anonymous, *Majmūʿa*)

MS We. 71 (Staatsbibliothek, al-Harawī, *al-Gharībayn*)

MS We. 86 (Staatsbibliothek; al-Nuwayrī, *Nihāyat al-arab*)

MS We. 134 (Staatsbibliothek, fols. 1^r–31^v: al-Asdī l-Dimashqī, *Taʾrīkh bināʾ Dimashq wa-maʿrifat man banāhā wa-ṭaraf min akhbārihā*)

MS We. 408 (Staatsbibliothek; Ibn Mufliḥ Akmal al-Dīn, *Untitled notebook*)

Cairo

Microfilm no. 551 (and 554?) (Dār al-Kutub al-Miṣriyya; microfilm of MSS Ayasofya 3511–27, Süleymaniye Kütüphanesi, Istanbul; al-Nuwayrī, *Nihāyat al-arab*)

MS ʿIlm ʿarabī 125 (Dār al-Kutub al-Miṣriyya, fols. 41–89; al-Burīnī, *Sharḥ Qaṣīdat al-Bustī*)

MS ʿIlm ʿarabī 125 (Dār al-Kutub al-Miṣriyya, fols. 89–98; Ibn al-Jawzī, *Akhbār ahl al-rusūkh fī l-fiqh al-ḥadīth al-mansūkh*)

 | DOI:10.1163/9789004413177_012

MS Ṭalʿat Taʾrīkh 2106 (Dār al-Kutub al-Miṣriyya; Ibn Khaldūn, *al-Taʿrīf*)
MS Taʾrīkh 109 mīm (Dār al-Kutub al-Miṣriyya; Ibn Khaldūn, *al-Taʿrīf*)
MS Taʾrīkh 185 (Dār al-Kutub al-Miṣriyya; Ibn Khaldūn, *al-Taʿrīf*)
MS Taʾrīkh 5343 (Dār al-Kutub al-Miṣriyya; Ibn Khaldūn, *al-Taʿrīf*)
MS Taʾrīkh Abāẓa 6729 (Maktabat al-Azhar; Ibn Khaldūn, *al-Taʿrīf*)
MS Majmūʿa Taymūr 79 (Dār al-Kutub al-Miṣriyya; Ibn Ṭūlūn, *al-Thaghr al-bassām fī dhikr man wulliya qaḍāʾ al-Shām*)
MS Zakiyya 64 (Dār al-Kutub al-Miṣriyya; Ibn Khaldūn, *al-Taʿrīf*)

Calcutta
MS I 774 (Library of the Asiatic Society; al-Maqrīzī, *Mukhtaṣar Kitāb Qiyām al-layl, Mukhtaṣar Kitāb Qiyām ramaḍān, Mukhtaṣar Kitāb al-Witr*)

Chinguetti
MS Taʾrīkh 1 shīn (Ibn Khaldūn, *al-Taʿrīf*)

Copenhagen
MS Arab. Add. 83 (Det Kongelige Bibliothek; al-Ḥarīrī, *al-Maqāmāt*)

Damascus
MS 4325 (Maktabat al-Asad; al-Baylūnī, *Untitled notebook*)
MS 4805 ʿāmm (Maktabat al-Asad; al-Maqrīzī, *Untitled notebook*)

Dublin
MS Arabic 3101 (Chester Beatty Library; Ibn Ṭūlūn, *al-Multaqaṭ min al-Tadhkira*)
MS Arabic 3456 (Chester Beatty Library; al-Zawāwī, commentary on *al-Durra al- alfiyya*)
MS Arabic 3945 (Chester Beatty Library; Ibn al-Jawzī, *al-Birr wa-l-ṣila*)
MS Arabic 4731 (Chester Beatty Library; al-Karmī, *Qalāʾid al-ʿiqyān*)

Dushanbe
MS 1790 (Kitobhona-i milli-i Todjikiston; al-Maqrīzī, *Mukhtaṣar Durrat al- aslāk*)

Florence
MS Cl.III.10 (Biblioteca Nazionale Centrale di Firenze; Anonymous, *Untitled safīna*)
MS Cl.III.106 (Biblioteca Nazionale Centrale di Firenze; Anonymous, *Untitled safīna*)
MS orientale 394 (Biblioteca Medicea Laurenziana; Anonymous, *Untitled safīna*)

Gotha

MS Ar. 114 (Forschungs-und Landesbibliothek, Anonymous, *Untitled notebook*)
MS Ar. 1652 (Forschungs-und Landesbibliothek; al-Maqrīzī, *Itti'āẓ al-ḥunafā'*)
MS Ar. 1771 (Forschungs-und Landesbibliothek; al-Maqrīzī, *Durar al-'uqūd al-farīda*)
MS Ar. 1778 (Forschungs-und Landesbibliothek; Anonymous, *Mukhtaṣar Ta'rīkh Dimashq*)

Istanbul

MS 575 (Murat Molla Kütüphanesi; al-Maqrīzī, *Mukhtaṣar al-Kāmil fī ḍu'afā' al-rijāl*)
MS 3067 (Nuruosmaniye Kütüphanesi; Ibn Khaldūn, *al-Ta'rīf*)
MS 781 (Rağıp Paşa Kütüphanesi; al-Urmawī, *Maṭāli' al-anwār*)
MS 792 (Rağıp Paşa Kütüphanesi; al-Shīrāzī, *Sharḥ al-Muḥaṣṣal*)
MS A2832 (TSMK; Ibn Duqmāq, *Naẓm al-jumān*)
MS A2911/A1–3, A8–10, A12–17 (TSMK; Badr al-Dīn Maḥmūd al-'Aynī, *'Iqd al-jumān*)
MS A2911/B6–7 (TSMK; Badr al-Dīn Maḥmūd al-'Aynī, *'Iqd al-jumān*)
MS A2922 (TSMK; Ibn Shākir al-Kutubī, *'Uyūn al-tawārīkh*)
MS A2924/13–14 (TSMK; Ibn Khaldūn, *al-Ta'rīf*)
MS A2952 (TSMK; Shihāb ad-Dīn Aḥmad al-'Aynī, *al-Ta'rīkh al-shihābī wa-l-qamar al-munīr fī awṣāf ahl al-'aṣr wa-l-zamān*)
MS A3042/4 (TSMK; Ibn Khaldūn, *al-Ta'rīf*)
MS Atıf Efendi 1936 (Süleymaniye Kütüphanesi; Ibn Khaldūn, *al-Muqaddima*)
MS Ayasofya 1970 (Süleymaniye Kütüphanesi; al-Ṣafadī, *A'yān al-'aṣr*)
MS Ayasofya 2662 (Süleymaniye Kütüphanesi; Qāḍī-zādah al-Rūmī, *Sharḥ al-mulakhkhaṣ fī l-hay'a*)
MS Ayasofya 2968 (Süleymaniye Kütüphanesi; al-Ṣafadī, *A'yān al-'aṣr*)
MS Ayasofya 3007 (Süleymaniye Kütüphanesi; al-Dhahabī, *Ta'rīkh al-Islām*)
MS Ayasofya 3139 (Süleymaniye Kütüphanesi; Ibn Ḥajar, *al-Tadhkira al-jadīda*)
MS Ayasofya 3200 (Süleymaniye Kütüphanesi; Ibn Khaldūn, *al-Ta'rīf*)
MS Ayasofya 3362 (Süleymaniye Kütüphanesi; al-Maqrīzī, *al-Khabar*)
MS Ayasofya 3416 (Süleymaniye Kütüphanesi; al-'Umarī, *Masālik al-abṣār*)
MS Ayasofya 3511–27 (Süleymaniye Kütüphanesi; al-Nuwayrī, *Nihāyat al-arab*)
MS Ayasofya 4110 (Süleymaniye Kütüphanesi; al-Damīrī, *Sharḥ Lāmiyyat al-'Ajam*)
MS Ayasofya 4732 (Süleymaniye Kütüphanesi; al-Ṣafadī, *Taṣḥīḥ al-taṣḥīf wa-taḥrīr al-taḥrīf*)
MS Carullah 1310 M (Süleymaniye Kütüphanesi; Naṣīr al-Dīn al-Ṭūsī, *Ḥall mushkilāt al-Ishārāt*, copied by Quṭb al-Dīn al-Rāzī l-Taḥtānī)

MS Carullah 1442 (Süleymaniye Kütüphanesi; Ṭāshkūbrī-zādah, *al-Liwāʾ al-marfūʿ fī ḥall mabāḥith al-mawḍūʿ*)
MS Damad Ibrahim Pasha 822 (Süleymaniye Kütüphanesi; Ibn Sīnā, *al-Shifāʾ*)
MS EH1369 (TSMK; al-Nuwayrī, *Nihāyat al-arab*)
MS EH1405 (TSMK; al-Maqrīzī, *al-Khiṭaṭ*)
MS EH1472 (TSMK; al-Maqrīzī, *al-Mawāʿiẓ wa-l-iʿtibār*)
MS Esad Efendi 2268 (Süleymaniye Kütüphanesi; Ibn Khaldūn, *al-Taʿrīf*)
MS Esad Efendi 2317 (Süleymaniye Kütüphanesi; al-ʿAynī, Badr al-Dīn Maḥmūd, *ʿIqd al-Jumān*)
MS Esad Efendi 3733 (Süleymaniye Kütüphanesi; al-Dawānī, *Majmūʿa*)
MS Fatih 4197 (Süleymaniye Kütüphanesi; Ibn Iyās, *Badāʾiʿ al-zuhūr*)
MS Fatih 4338 (Süleymaniye Kütüphanesi; al-Maqrīzī, *al-Khabar*)
MS Fatih 4339 (Süleymaniye Kütüphanesi; al-Maqrīzī, *al-Khabar*)
MS Fatih 4341 (Süleymaniye Kütüphanesi; al-Maqrīzī, *al-Khabar*)
MS Fazıl Ahmed Pasha 242 (Köprülü Yazma Eser Kütüphanesi; Ibn Manda, *al-Tārīkh al-mustakhraj min kutub al-nās*)
MS Fazıl Ahmed Pasha 294 (Köprülü Yazma Eser Kütüphanesi; Abū Dāwūd, *al-Sunan* and *al-Marāsīl*)
MS Fazıl Ahmed Pasha 362 (Köprülü Yazma Eser Kütüphanesi; al-Bukhārī, *al-Jāmiʿ al-ṣaḥīḥ al-mukhtaṣar al-musnad min umūr rasūl Allāh wa-sunanihi wa-ayyāmihi*)
MS Fazıl Ahmed Pasha 831 (Köprülü Yazma Eser Kütüphanesi; al-Tustarī, *Kāshif al-asrār ʿan maʿālī Ṭawāliʿ al-anwār*)
MS Fazıl Ahmed Pasha 867 (Köprülü Yazma Eser Kütüphanesi; al-Shīrāzī, *Durrat al-tāj li-ghurrat al-Dībāj*)
MS Fazıl Ahmed Pasha 1618 (Köprülü Yazma Eser Kütüphanesi; *Collection of various texts*)
MS Feyzullah 1413 (Milli Kütüphanesi; Ibn Fahd, *Tajrīd al-Wāfī bi-l-wafayāt*)
MS Murat Molla 575 (Süleymaniye Kütüphanesi; al-Maqrīzī, *Mukhtaṣar al-Kāmil*)
MS Reisülküttab 862 (Süleymaniye Kütüphanesi; al-Mawṣilī, *Ghāyat al-wasāʾil ilā maʿrifat al-awāʾil*)
MS Şehit Ali Paşa 1847 (Süleymaniye Kütüphanesi; al-Maqrīzī, *al-Sulūk*)
MS Süleymaniye 830 (Süleymaniye Kütüphanesi; Shihāb al-Dīn Aḥmad al-ʿAynī, *Taʾrīkh al-badr fi awṣāf ahl al-ʿaṣr*)
MS Veliyyeddin 2390 (Beyazıt Devlet Kütüphanesi; Badr al-Dīn Maḥmūd al-ʿAynī, *ʿIqd al-Jumān*)
MS Veliyyeddin 2392 (Beyazıt Devlet Kütüphanesi; Badr al-Dīn Maḥmūd al-ʿAynī, *ʿIqd al-Jumān*)
MS Yeni Cami 763 (Süleymaniye Kütüphanesi; al-Ṭūsī, *Ḥall mushkilāt al-Ishārāt*)

MS Yeni Cami 887 (Süleymaniye Kütüphanesi; al-Maqrīzī, *al-Sulūk*)
MS Yeni Cami 888 (Süleymaniye Kütüphanesi; Ibn Khaldūn, *al-Muqaddima*)

Leiden
MS Or. 2a–2l (Universiteitsbibliotheek; al-Nuwayrī, *Nihāyat al-arab*)
MS Or. 19b (Universiteitsbibliotheek; al-Nuwayrī, *Nihāyat al-arab*)
MS Or. 95 (Universiteitsbibliotheek; al-Ṭūsī, *Ḥall mushkilāt al-Ishārāt*)
MS Or. 560 (Universiteitsbibliotheek; al-Maqrīzī, *Collection of opuscules*)
MS Or. 1088 (Universiteitsbibliotheek; Anonymous, *Untitled safīna*)
MS Or. 1366a (Universiteitsbibliotheek; al-Maqrīzī, *al-Muqaffā*)
MS Or. 1366c (Universiteitsbibliotheek; al-Maqrīzī, *al-Muqaffā*)
MS Or. 3075 (Universiteitsbibliotheek; al-Maqrīzī, *al-Muqaffā*)
MS Or. 14533 (Universiteitsbibliotheek; al-Maqrīzī, *al-Muqaffā*)
MS Or. 14637 (Universiteitsbibliotheek; Anonymous, *Untitled safīna*)
MS Or. 14638 (Universiteitsbibliotheek; Anonymous, *Untitled safīna*)

Leipzig
Vollers MS 0520 (Universitätsbibliothek; Nuqrakār, *Sharḥ al-qaṣīda wa-l-jawhara al-farīda al-mansūba ilā l-shaykh Abī l-Fatḥ al-Bustī*)
Vollers MS 0593 (Universitätsbibliothek; al-Ābī, *al-Qasḍ al-musirr fī kalām nathr al-durr*)
Vollers MS 0620 (Universitätsbibliothek; Shihāb al-Dīn Aḥmad al-Ḥijāzī, *Tadhkira*)

Liège
MS 2232 (Université, Bibliothèque d'Architecture, Lettres, Philosophie, Histoire et Arts; al-Maqrīzī, *Notebook*)
MS 2241 (Université, Bibliothèque d'Architecture, Lettres, Philosophie, Histoire et Arts; Anonymous, *Alf layla wa-layla*)

London
Papyrus 114, section 8, (British Library; "The Bankes Homer", *Iliad*, Scroll XXIV)
MS Or. 2916–9 (British Library; Anonymous, *Alf layla wa-layla*)
MS Or. 7969 (British Library; Naṣīr al-Dīn al-Ṭūsī, *Sharḥ al-Ishārāt*)

San Lorenzo de El Escorial
MS Árabe 687 (al-Dawānī, *Ijāza*)

Marocco
Private library, MS Jād (Ibn Khaldūn, *al-Taʿrīf*)

Montreal

MS RBD A22 (McGill University Library; *Qur'ān*)

Munich

MS Ar. 437 (Bayerische Staatsbibliothek; Ibn Duqmāq, *Naẓm al-jumān fī ṭabaqāt aṣḥāb imāminā l-Nuʿmān*)
MS Ar. 623–36 (Bayerische Staatsbibliothek; Anonymous, *Alf layla wa-layla*)

Oxford

MS Pococke 26 (Bodleian Library; Akmal al-Dīn b. Mufliḥ, *Untitled notebook*)
P. Oxy. 74.4970 (The Egypt Exploration Society, University of Oxford, Oxford University Sackler Library; Anonymous, Beginning of a medical handbook or speech)

Paris

MS Ar. 1528 (BnF; Ibn Khaldūn, *al-Taʿrīf*)
MS Ar. 1544 (BnF; Shihāb al-Dīn Aḥmad al-ʿAynī, *Ta'rīkh al-badr fī awṣāf ahl al-ʿaṣr*)
MS Ar. 1573–9 (BnF; al-Nuwayrī, *Nihāyat al-arab*)
MS Ar. 2144 (BnF; al-Maqrīzī, *al-Muqaffā*)
MS Ar. 3423 (BnF; Anonymous, *Untitled safīna*)
MS Ar. 3424 (BnF; Anonymous, *Untitled safīna*)
MS Ar. 3426 (BnF; Anonymous, *Untitled safīna*)
MS Ar. 3428 (BnF; Anonymous, *Untitled safīna*)
MS Ar. 3429 (BnF; Anonymous, *Untitled safīna*)
MS Ar. 3430 (BnF; Anonymous, *Untitled safīna*)
MS Ar. 3454 (BnF; Anonymous, *Untitled safīna*)
MS Ar. 3458 (BnF; Anonymous, *Untitled safīna*)
MS Ar. 3459 (BnF; Anonymous, *Untitled safīna*)
MS Ar. 3461 (BnF; Anonymous, *Untitled safīna*)
MS Ar. 3585 (BnF; Anonymous, *Untitled safīna*)
MS Ar. 3598–601 (BnF; Anonymous, *Alf layla wa-layla*)
MS Ar. 3602–5 (BnF; Anonymous, *Alf layla wa-layla*)
MS Ar. 3606–8 (BnF; Anonymous, *Alf layla wa-layla*)
MS Ar. 5046 (BnF; al-Ghazzī, *Untitled diary and poetry*)
MS Ar. 7084 (BnF; Anonymous, *Untitled safīna*)
MS Suppl. persan 1425 (BnF; Anonymous, *Untitled safīna*)
MS Suppl. persan 1798 (BnF; Anonymous, *Untitled safīna*)
MS Suppl. turc 1620 (BnF; Anonymous, *Untitled safīna*)
P. Rein. 2.82, inv. Sorb. 2070 (Sorbonne Université—Institut de Papyrologie; Dioscorus of Aphrodito, Petition enkômion addressed to Rômanos)

Princeton

MS Garrett 12G (Princeton University Library; al-Ḥusayn b. Muḥammad al-Ḥusaynī, *Idrāk al-sūl fī musābaqat al-khuyūl*)

MS Garrett 196B (Princeton University Library; Ibn Ṭūlūn, *Untitled notebook*)

MS Garrett 3520Y (Princeton University Library; Zayn al-Dīn ʿAbd al- Raḥīm al-ʿIrāqī, *Naẓm al-durar al-saniyya fī l-siyar al-zakiyya*)

MS Garrett 3570Y (Princeton University Library; al-Ṣafadī, *al-Tadhkira*)

Qom

MS 4 (Marʿashī Kitābkhānah; Ḥasan b. al-Muṭahhar, *Nahj al-mustarshidīn*)

MS 12388 (Marʿashī Kitābkhānah; al-Dawānī, *Untitled majmūʿa*)

Rabat

MS D1345 (al-Maktaba al-Malakiyya; Ibn Khaldūn, *al-Taʿrīf*)

Saint-Petersburg

MS B-1114 (Institute of Oriental Manuscripts; Anonymous, *Alf layla wa-layla*)

Ṣanʿāʾ

MS Adab 2336 (Dār al-Makhṭūṭāt; Anonymous, *Untitled safīna*)

MS Sharaf al-Dīn (private collection; Anonymous, *Untitled safīna*)

MS ymdi_03_131 (MZbAT; Anonymous, *Untitled safīna*)

MS ymdi_03_142 (MZbAT; Anonymous, *Untitled safīna*)

MS ymdi_03_137 (MZbAT; Anonymous, *Untitled safīna*)

Tehran

MS 1153 (Kitābkhāna-yi Millī-i Jumhūrī-i Islāmī-i Īrān; al-Ṭūsī, *Ḥall mushkilāt al-Ishārāt*)

MS 2301 (Library of the University of Tehran, Ḥasan b. al-Muṭahhar, *Marāṣid al-tadqīq wa-maqāṣid al-taḥqīq*)

Tunis

MS Ḥasan Ḥusnī ʿAbd al-Wahhāb (Dār al-Kutub al-Waṭaniyya; Ibn Khaldūn, *al-Taʿrīf*)

Unknown location

MS no. 42 sold at Christie's London, South Kensington (Private collection; Anonymous, *Alf layla wa-layla*)

Index of Names

Abbott, Nabia 14
ʿAbd al-Ḥamīd II (Ottoman sultan) 256
ʿAbdallāh b. Ibrāhīm b. Aḥmad b. al-Imām 332
ʿAbd al-Wahhāb, Ḥasan Ḥusnī 312
Abel, Leonardo 324
al-Ābī 262
Abū Fāris ʿAbd al-ʿAzīz (Marinid ruler) 301, 305
Adler, Jacob Georg Christian 11
Aḥad Aḥad 269, 270
al-Ahdal, Ḥātim b. Aḥmad 325, 330–8, 351–2
Aḥmad b. Manṣūr b. Muḥibb al-Dīn 270
Akkerman, Olly 1, 18
Alexander the Great 148n40
ʿAlī b. Abī Ṭālib 267, 365, 392n93
al-Amīr al-Ṣanʿānī, Muḥammad b. Ismāʿīl 334n43, 336, 400n99, 427
Ammirati, Serena 9
Āmulī, Ḥaydar 64
Andréas [de Caryste?] 39
al-Ānisī, ʿAbd al-Raḥmān 331, 333, 346
al-Ānisī, Aḥmad b. ʿAbd al-Raḥmān 331, 333, 346
al-Ānisī, Shams al-Dīn b. Aḥmad b. Aḥmad 346
al-Anṣārī, ʿAlī b. al-shaykh Ibrāhīm 97–8, 100, 106–10, 115–7
al-ʿAnsī, ʿAlī b. Muḥammad 342–6, 350, 353, 358, 360–1, 430
al-ʿAnsī, Yaḥyā 353
Apollonios 39, 43n18, 44
Arberry, Arthur J. 8, 11
Asan Buğā (al-Ṣafadī's slave) 69
al-Awḥadī 142–3, 149n43, 195–8, 230
al-ʿAynī 28, 277–98

Banū Isḥāq 350
Barqūq, al-Ẓāhir (Mamluk sultan) 152n58, 281, 283–4, 292, 294, 301, 305, 309, 311–2
Baybars, al-Ẓāhir (Mamluk sultan) 307
al-Bayḍāwī 74
al-Baylūnī, Muḥammad Fatḥ Allāh 264
Behzadi, Lale 2
Beit-Arié, Malachi 10
Ben Azzouna, Nourane 12
al-Biqāʿī x
Boiarov, Andrei 194–5
Bongianino, Umberto 13
Boratav, Pertev Naili 328
al-Bukhārī 27, 232–5, 252–3, 256–8
al-Bustī, Abū l-Fatḥ 262

Capasso, Mario 9
Cavallo, Guglielmo 9
Chartier, Roger 8n33, 14, 136
Chiron 39
Cicéron 40
Colin, Georges Séraphin 331–2, 339
Cratévas 39–40

al-Dabbūsī, Ẓahīr al-Dīn 64
Dafari (al-Ẓafārī), Jaʿfar ʿAbduh 329, 353
al-Damīrī x
David (Prophet) 296
al-Dawānī, Jalāl al-Dīn 74–5
Defrémery, Charles 139
Delsaux, Olivier 6, 7n22, 10
Déroche, François 12–3, 180–1, 183
al-Dhahabī x, 263
Dioscore d'Aphrodité 42–3, 45–8
Dioscoride 39–40
Dozy, Reinhart 7–8, 138–40

El-Leithy, Tamar 264
Euclide 326

Faraj b. Barqūq (Mamluk sultan) 286
al-Fāsī 13
Fatḥ Allāh b. Nafīs 283, 289, 291, 296–8
Fischel, Walter 307
Fraser, Marcus 12

Gacek, Adam 3–4, 14, 26, 62
Galien 39
Galland, Antoine 95–6
al-Ghazālī 141n17, 346
al-Ghazzī 261, 264–5
Gurrado, Maria 24

Hādī b. Muḥammad Ṣāliḥ 342

al-Ḥajjār, Abū l-ʿAbbās Aḥmad b. Abī Ṭālib 256
al-Ḥalabī l-Tādifī, Badr al-Dīn Abū ʿAbdallāh Muḥammad 59
Hämeen-Anttila, Jaakko 2
Ḥaram bt. ʿAbdallāh 270
al-Harawī 262, 291
Héraclide 39
al-Ḥijāzī, Shihāb al-Dīn Aḥmad 264
al-Ḥillī, Muḥammad b. Ḥasan b. Yūsuf b. ʿAlī b. al-Muṭahhar 73
Hirschler, Konrad 1
Houdas, Octave 13

Ibn ʿAbbād, Abū l-Qāsim Ismāʿīl Ṣāḥib al-Ṭāliqānī 346, 385
Ibn ʿAbd al-Hādī, Yūsuf 1
Ibn Abī l-Faḍāʾil, Mufaḍḍal 235
Ibn al-ʿAfīf al-Tilimsānī 153, 262
Ibn ʿAsākir 262n10, 264
Ibn Ayyūb al-Anṣarī 261, 264
Ibn al-Bawwāb 12
Ibn al-Dafrāwī, Shāhīn 314
Ibn Duqmāq x, 199, 263
Ibn Faḍl Allāh al-ʿUmarī, Shihāb al-Dīn 146, 231
Ibn Faḍl Allāh al-ʿUmarī, Badr al-Dīn 152n58
Ibn Fahd x, 145n33
Ibn al-Fakhkhār, ʿAbdallāh b. Ḥasan 310–1
Ibn al-Farfūr, Sharaf al-Dīn 269
Ibn al-Farfūr, Walī l-Dīn 269
Ibn al-Furāt 230, 263
Ibn Ḥabīb al-Ḥalabī 140, 228, 235
Ibn Ḥajar x, 142, 145n29, 150, 151n52, 152–5, 234n5, 309n30
Ibn Isrāfīl 269
Ibn Iyās x
Ibn Jamāʿa 16, 263
Ibn al-Jawzī 56, 62, 262
Ibn Kathīr 235
Ibn Khaldūn x, 13, 16–17, 28, 81n15, 283–7, 300–14
Ibn Mufliḥ, ʿAbd al-Kāfī 269, 272
Ibn Mufliḥ, ʿAbd al-Munʿim 269, 272
Ibn Mufliḥ, Abū l-Suʿūd Muḥammad 270, 272
Ibn Mufliḥ, Akmal al-Dīn Muḥammad b. Ibrāhīm 28, 260–75
Ibn Mufliḥ, ʿAlāʾ al-Dīn ʿAlī 269, 272
Ibn Mufliḥ, Badr al-Dīn Ḥasan 269, 272
Ibn Mufliḥ, Burhān al-Dīn Ibrāhīm b. Akmal al-Dīn 266–7, 269, 272
Ibn Mufliḥ, Kamāl al-Dīn Muḥammad 269, 272
Ibn Mufliḥ, Karīm al-Dīn ʿAbd al-Raḥīm 270, 272
Ibn Mufliḥ, Maḥmūd 269, 272
Ibn Mufliḥ, Muḥammad b. Akmal al-Dīn Muḥammad 270, 272
Ibn Mufliḥ, Muḥyī l-Dīn ʿAbd al-Qādir 269, 272
Ibn Mufliḥ, Muwaffaq al-Dīn ʿAbd al-Raḥmān 269, 272
Ibn Mufliḥ, Najm al-Dīn ʿUmar 267, 269, 272
Ibn Mufliḥ, Niẓām al-Dīn ʿUmar 265, 269, 272
Ibn Mufliḥ, Quṭb al-Dīn Aḥmad 270, 272
Ibn Mufliḥ, Radī l-Dīn Aḥmad 269, 272
Ibn Mufliḥ, Rashīd al-Dīn ʿAbd al-Jabbār 269, 272
Ibn Mufliḥ, Ṣadr al-Dīn Abū Bakr 269, 272
Ibn Mufliḥ, Ṣalāḥ al-Dīn Ṣāliḥ 270, 272
Ibn Mufliḥ, Shams al-Dīn Muḥammad 267–9, 272
Ibn Mufliḥ, Sharaf al-Dīn Abū Muḥammad ʿAbdallāh 267, 269, 272
Ibn Mufliḥ, Shihāb al-Dīn Aḥmad 269, 272
Ibn Mufliḥ, Taqī l-Dīn 269, 272
Ibn Mufliḥ, Walī l-Dīn Yaḥyā 269, 272
Ibn Muqla 12, 64
Ibn Musdī l-Andalusī l-Gharnāṭī 13
Ibn Muṭahhar, ʿAbd al-Karīm b. Aḥmad 332
Ibn Qawwām al-Bālisī 268
Ibn al-Ṣāʾigh 144, 154n70
Ibn Shākir al-Kutubī x
Ibn al-Shaṭṭī 262
Ibn Sīnā 59, 64
Ibn Sunbul, Ṣafī l-Dīn Aḥmad 332
Ibn Tāwīt, Muḥammad 300–3, 305, 307, 310–3
Ibn Ṭawq 265
Ibn Ṭūlūn 261–7
Ibn Turkī l-Shāfiʿī l-Azharī, Aḥmad b. Yūsuf b. Ḥamd 313
Ibn al-Wazīr, Hādī b. Ibrāhīm 346

Ibn al-Wazīr, Muḥammad b. Ibrāhīm 346
Ibn al-Zabīdī, Sirāj al-Dīn Abū ʿAbdallāh al-Ḥusayn 256
Ibrāhīm b. Ismāʿīl b. ʿAbbās 334
ʿImādī Hāʾirī, Sayyid Muḥammad 64
al-ʿIrāqī, Zayn al-Dīn ʿAbd al-Raḥīm 56, 62
al-Iṣbahānī, Abū l-Faraj 15
Ismāʿīl (ʿAlawid ruler) 312
Ismāʿīl b. Ḥasan al-… 343

al-Jaghmīnī, Maḥmūd 60n7, 66
Jaḥḥāf, Yaḥyā b. Ibrāhīm 343
Jamāl al-Dīn, Amīna 245
Justinien (empereur byzantin) 79
Juvin, Carine 13

al-Kabsī, *see* al-Kibsī
Kamāl 267
Karatay, Fehmi Edhem 277, 311–2
al-Karmī 60
al-Kātibī l-Qazwīnī, Najm al-Dīn ʿAlī b. ʿUmar 66
Kemal, Mustafa 332
al-Khafanjī, ʿAlī b. al-Ḥasan 329, 351
al-Khalīl, ʿAbdallāh b. ʿAmr or ʿUmar 334n43, 336
al-Khazrajī 268
al-Kibsī, Muḥammad b. Muḥammad b. Muḥammad 345, 348–50, 376
al-Kibsī, Zayd b. ʿAlī 334, 336, 351
Knysh, Alexander 194

Lehmann, Paul 6
Little, Donald P. 278

Machaon 39
al-Mahdī li-Dīn Allāh, ʿAlī b. Muḥammad b. ʿAlī b. Yaḥyā b. Manṣūr b. Mufaḍḍal b. al-Ḥajjāj 343, 346, 374, 392n93
al-Malik al-Afḍal (Rasulid sultan) 343, 374
Manetti, Daniela 45
Mantias 39
al-Maqdisī, Abū Muḥammad ʿAbd al-Ghanī b. ʿAbd al-Wāḥid b. ʿAlī b. Surūr 256
al-Maqrīzī x, 3, 7, 14–5, 18, 20, 22–3, 27–8, 136–231, 235, 263, 277–8, 283, 296
Marwān b. al-Ḥakam (Umayyad caliph) 237
Massoud, Sami 278, 296
al-Masʿūdī 268
McGuckin de Slane, William 279
Moritz, Bernhard 8, 11
Muʾayyad, Abū Bakr 336
Muʾayyad-zāda ʿAbd al-Raḥmān Efendī 74
Muʿāwiya b. Abī Sufyān (Umayyad caliph) 237
Muḥammad b. ʿAbdallāh b. Sharaf al-dīn 331, 339, 343
Muḥammad b. ʿAbd al-Majīd b. Abī l-Faḍl b. ʿAbd al-Raḥmān b. Zayd, Abū ʿAbdallāh 256
Muḥammad b. ʿAbd al-Raḥmān b. Aḥmad Kawkabān 332
Muḥammad Bak b. Manjak 261
Muḥammad, al-Nāṣir (Mamlūk sultan) 152n57, 233
al-Munajjid, Ṣālāh al-Dīn 8, 11
Muṣʿab b. al-Zubayr 237 301
al-Mustanṣir, Abū l-ʿAbbās Aḥmad b. Muḥammad (Ḥafṣid ruler) 301
al-Mutawakkil (Yemen) 331, 342–3, 345, 353, 360, 362, 389, 390
al-Mutawakkil, Isḥāq b. Yūsuf 343
Muzerelle, Denis 6, 24

al-Nahrawānī, Quṭb al-Dīn 262
al-Najdī 265
al-Naṣrānī, Qusṭanṭīn 332
Nicandre 39
al-Nuʿaymī 262
al-Nuwayrī 27–8, 151n51, 154, 232–59

Olszowy-Schlanger, Judith 10
Overgaauw, Eef 6

Pamphile 39
Parca, Maryline 42
Petrucci, Armando 9, 41
Pline l'Ancien 40

Qāḍī-zādah al-Rūmī 60, 62
al-Qalqashandī 151n57, 152n57, 173, 179
al-Qasṭallānī 256
al-Qazwīnī 66, 262
al-Qudūrī 277
Quintilien 40

Radicciotti, Paolo 40
al-Rāmīnī, Shams al-Dīn Abū ʿAbdallāh Muḥammad b. Mufliḥ b. Mufarraj b. Muḥammad 268
al-Rāzī l-Taḥtānī, Quṭb al-Dīn 59
Reisman, David 263
Riḍawī, Muḥammad b. Raḍī l-Dīn 64
Romanov, Maxim 22
Rück, Peter 24
Rufus 39
al-Ruqayḥī, Aḥmad 343, 350, 358–9, 433

al-Ṣafadī, Abū Bakr Muḥammad b. Khalīl b. Aybak 69
al-Ṣafadī, Abū ʿAbdallāh Muḥammad b. Khalīl b. Aybak 69
al-Ṣafadī, Fāṭima b. Khalīl b. Aybak 69
al-Ṣafadī, Khalīl b. Aybak x, 4–6, 27, 57, 69–70, 73, 80n10, 154, 234–5, 263
al-Ṣafī l-Ḥillī 350, 368
Sāḥilī, Ibrāhīm 346
al-Sakhāwī x, 142, 145, 150n50, 151n52, 154, 293
al-Ṣāliḥī, Aḥmad b. Mubārak 270
al-Samarjī, Muḥammad Khalīl 343, 350
Savant, Sarah 23, 95n55
Sayyid, Aymān Fuʾād 20, 137–8, 143
Sedeyn, Marie-Jeanne 10, 81, 86–9, 91–5, 97–9, 110, 127, 137n3, 158n79
Selim II (Ottoman sultan) 60, 346, 391
Senov, Alexander 194
Serikoff, Nikolaï 14, 160
Sextius Niger 39
Sezgin, Fuat 256
al-Shāfiʿī 267–8
al-Shāfiʿī, Ibrāhīm b. Muḥammad b. Ibrāhīm 264
Shāhrazād, *see* Shéhérazade
Shāhriyār 95
al-Sharīf al-Raḍī l-Mawsūʿī 350
al-Sharīshī, Jamāl al-Dīn Abū Bakr Muḥammad al-Mālikī l-Naḥwī 57
Shaykhān, ʿUmar 349
Shéhérazade 95
al-Shīrāzī, Muḥammad b. Pīr Aḥmad al-Shahīr bi-Arghūn 60
al-Shīrāzī, Quṭb al-Dīn 59, 64, 72
al-Shuwaykī, Aḥmad 269
al-Sinjārī, ʿAlī b. Muḥammad 152
Spies, Otto 277
Stutzmann, Dominique 25
Sulaymān (Ottoman sultan) 261
Sulaymān Āghā 60
Sulaymān b. Qubād 261
al-Surayḥī, ʿAbdallāh 354
al-Surramarī, Jamāl al-Dīn Yūsuf 56, 62

Ṭalʿat, Aḥmad Bey 313
al-Ṭanṭāwī l-Qarmūṭ, ʿAbd al-Razzāq 278
al-Tanūkhī, Sitt al-Wuzarāʾ Umm Muḥammad Wazīra bt. ʿUmar 256
Ṭāshkūbrī-zādah 66
al-Thaqafī, al-Mukhtār b. Abī ʿUbayd 237
al-Ṭūsī, Naṣīr al-Dīn 59, 60n6, 64, 66, 73, 326, 329

ʿUbayd Allāh b. Ziyād b. Abīhi 237
ʿUbayd Allāh b. Ziyād b. Ẓabyān 237
al-ʿUbaydī, Jalāl al-Dīn Faḍl Allāh 66
al-Udfuwī 27, 233–5, 248
al-ʿUmarī, Shams al-Dīn Abū ʿAbdallāh Muḥammad 69
al-Urmawī, Sirāj al-Dīn 60, 74
ʿUṣfūr 152–4

Vajda, Georges 8, 11
van den Boogert, Nico 13
van Hemelryck, Tania 6, 7n22, 10
Virgile 40

Wagner, Mark S. 329
al-Wazīr, ʿAbdallāh b. ʿAlī 343, 346, 348–50, 352
Wilson, Nigel 9
Witkam, Jan Just 156–7

Xénocrate 39

al-Yamanī l-Tustarī, Badr al-Dīn 74
Yāqūt al-Mustaʿṣimī 12, 14, 153, 169n113
Yāqūt al-Rūmī 15
Yazıcı, Gülgün 324n5, 328
Yelkenci, Raif 328
al-Yūnīnī, Quṭb al-Dīn 252
al-Yūnīnī, Sharaf al-Dīn ʿAlī b. Muḥammad 252, 256–7
al-Yūnīnī, Taqī l-Dīn Abū ʿAbdallāh Muḥammad b. Aḥmad b. ʿAbdallāh 256

al-Zabīdī 164n98
Zakī Pāshā, Aḥmad 239
al-Zamakhsharī 324, 329
al-Zawāwī, Abū Zakariyyā' Yaḥyā 57
al-Ziftāwī, Muḥammad b. Aḥmad b. ʿAlī 152n59, 153–4
al-Ziriklī, Ḫayr al-Dīn 8, 264
Zotenberg, Herman 96

Index of Places

Akhmīm 233
Aleppo 69, 265, 269, 282–3, 285, 290
Aphrodité 42–3, 45, 47–8

Baalbek 261
Byzantium 9–10, 26n117, 40, 47, 79

Cairo 15, 142, 144, 148n40, 152–3, 233, 237, 256, 262–4, 267–8, 282, 286, 294, 296
  Barjawān 144
  Citadel 144
  Genizah 264
  Khānqāh of Baybars 307
  Manṣūrī hospital 233
  Nāṣiriyya (*madrasa*) 233
  al-Qāhira al-Muʿizziyya 237
  al-Takiyya al-Sulaymāniyya 261

Damascus 1, 57, 144, 260–1, 263–7, 269, 282–7, 289–91, 370
  Abū ʿUmar (*madrasa*) 270
  Bāb al-Farādīs (cemetery) 269
  Bāb al-Ṣaghīr (cemetery) 270
  Bāb Tūmā 261
  Buzūriyyīn (quarter) 270
  Dār al-Ḥadīth (*madrasa*) 270
  Ḍiyā'iyya (*madrasa*) 256
  al-Jawziyya (*madrasa*) 270
  al-Maydān (*madrasa*) 269
  al-Muʿaẓẓama (*madrasa*) 266
  Qanāt al-ʿAwnī (*madrasa*) 269
  al-Ṣāḥibiyya (*madrasa*) 270
  al-Ṣāliḥiyya (*madrasa*) 267, 269–70
  ʿUmariya (*madrasa*) 1
  Umayyad Mosque 270
  al-Yūnusiyya (*madrasa*) 270
  al-Zāwiyya al-ghazāliyya 270
al-Daqahliyya 233

Fayoum 43–4, 47
Fez 301, 302n10, 323n2
  Qarawiyyīn (mosque) 301, 302n10, 303, 305

Hermopolis (Hermopolite) 43–5, 47
Hibeh 43, 47

Karak 261, 282, 284–7

Macédoine 329
Marw al-Rūdh 237
Marw al-Shāhijān 237
Medina 57
Moka (Tihāma) 330, 333
al-Murtāḥiyya 233

Oxyrhynque 44–5, 47–9

al-Qāhira (Zawzan) 237
Qūṣ 233, 286

Rome 25, 40, 324

Sidon 261
Shahāra/Shihāra 349, 398
St. Catherine's monastery in Sinai 264

Tabriz 74, 296
Thèbes 43, 47
Thrace occidentale 329
Tripoli 233, 243n48, 282, 285–6

Yemen 28–29, 262, 323–435

Zabadān 261

Index of Technical Terms

Abbasid 12, 323
Abbreviations (abréviations) 25, 43, 45, 47–8, 59, 64, 90, 252, 256
Abridgments (*mukhtaṣar*, *mūjaz*) 56, 260, 262, 262n10, 281, 293
Abū Shubbāk (paper) 331–2, 345
Additions (*also* insertions, inserts; *ilḥāqāt*, *mulḥaqāt*) 4, 20–1, 42n18, 43–45, 56, 59, 60, 67, 69, 83, 118, 137, 138, 139n12, 140, 149, 165n103, 168, 230, 238, 252n66, 296, 301, 301n5, 303, 308nn20–22, 353
Allograph 159, 170–5, 178, 183, 191, 193
Alteration 20, 149, 238
Anthology (*also* anthologist; anthologie) 2, 27–8, 47, 239, 262, 323, 324n4, 326–7, 328n24, 351n64
Apograph 20
Archetype (*also* original, exemplar; *aṣl*, *umm*) 6–7, 45, 56–7, 60, 67, 72–3, 75, 141n17, 142, 148, 164, 237, 239, 240n18, 252, 257, 301, 303, 305, 308–10
aṣl, *see* Archetype
Attribution (*also* identification) 2, 7–8, 10, 14, 18, 23–8, 39, 41–2, 47, 56, 64, 67, 76, 78–81, 89–90, 92–4, 95n53, 100, 109–11, 136–43, 146n36, 149n43, 153, 157, 160–2, 166–8, 176, 183, 189, 194–8, 200–1, 239–44, 247–8, 260, 262, 264–6, 270, 279–80, 300, 305, 309–10, 329, 332–4, 336, 339, 343–4, 346, 349, 352, 373–4
Authorial gloss (*minhiyāt*), *see* gloss
Authorial manuscript (manuscrit auctorial) 1, 3, 6–7, 20–1, 22n96, 27, 137, 142, 146–7, 158–9, 200, 228, 231
Authorship 1–2, 8, 266, 353
Autograph (autographe) 1, 3–4, 6–10, 16, 18, 25–7, 38–42, 45–50, 55–6, 228, 241n28, 265, 349, 350, 396
Avant-texte 21–2

Baseline (ligne de base) 12, 84–6, 92–4, 97, 99–100, 107, 110, 120, 122–5, 130, 132–5, 166, 169, 171–6, 181, 183n172, 185, 188, 190–3, 196
bayāḍ, *see* fair/clean copy
Binding (reliure) 4, 10, 20, 28, 69, 154n69, 265, 323, 328, 332–4, 336, 339–40, 342–3, 346, 349, 353
Blank (espaces [laissés] vierges) 3, 4, 26, 56, 69, 83, 140, 150, 164–5, 170–1, 193, 238, 245, 343, 347, 358, 364–8, 370–1, 373–6, 386, 388, 394–5, 397–9, 413–4, 422, 426, 428, 431, 433, 435
Bookhand 13–4

Calligraphy (*also* calligrapher; calligraphie, calligraphe) 4, 11–4, 27–8, 38, 42, 59, 63, 70, 80, 90, 137, 144, 150–5, 160, 173, 177, 181–3, 193, 232, 235, 238, 347, 419
proportionate styles (*mansūb*) 153, 154n69, 155
Cancellation (*also* deletion; rature; *ḍarb*) 3, 20–1, 28, 44–5, 47–8, 56, 69, 143n25, 149, 292, 301, 303, 308nn20–1, 309, 334, 425
Certificate of audition (*also* auditing statement; *samāʿ*) 8, 57, 234, 255–7
Chancery (chancellerie) 4, 63, 69, 80, 138, 140, 144, 148, 149n43, 151–2, 154, 164, 166, 177, 181, 233, 236, 252n65, 263
Collation 3, 20, 23, 64, 66, 73, 149, 231–2, 234–5, 252, 256–7, 266
Collectible (*also* collection, collectology, collector) 1, 14–8, 57n5, 164n98
Côlométrie 44
Colophon 2–3, 9, 26, 56–7, 60, 62, 64, 67, 69–70, 72, 74, 80, 91, 100, 108n84, 140–1, 146–7, 155, 228–9, 240–5, 247–8, 250–1, 261, 264, 295, 334–7, 339
Commentary (*also* comment, commentator; commentaire; *sharḥ*) 4, 6, 26n117, 47, 56–7, 59, 60nn7–8, 64, 66, 74, 80n9, 244, 248, 256, 260, 262, 381, 388, 398
Commonplace book (*tadhkira*) 2, 4–5, 21, 28, 260, 263–8, 271, 351n64
cönk, *see safīna*
Consultation note (*also* reading statement) 3, 16–7, 18n85, 27, 56, 141–3, 146–8, 197, 229, 257

ihmāl 347, 392
ijāza, see license of transmission
ikhtilās, see curtailment
ilḥāqāt, see additions
Inclination (inclinaison) 24, 84, 92, 107, 120–1, 156n76, 160–1, 182–3, 188, 279
Interlinear space/addition (espace/ajout interlinéaire) 3, 20, 43–5, 56, 83–4, 89, 93, 164
Invocation (*also* supplication, honorifics) 26, 44, 69, 72, 141, 244
iʿrāb 329, 336

jung, see *safīna*

laqab, see honorifics
Layout (mise en page) 4, 26, 41, 47–8, 50, 97, 158, 165–6, 238–9, 244n49, 248, 279
Letterforms 12, 69
 mabsūṭa 130–3, 160n94, 171–3, 183–4, 186, 193
 majmūʿa 172, 174
 makhṭūfa 172n120, 174, 193, 196
 malfūfa 174
 maqlūba 86, 122–3
 mardūfa 174, 196
 marshūqa 107, 175, 193
 mashkūla 132–5, 160n94, 162, 172, 173n124, 179, 183, 186, 189n182, 192–3, 196
 mashqūqa 108, 132–5, 174
 mawqūfa 169, 172
 mudghama 108, 124, 131, 135, 171, 174, 177, 179
 muḥaqqaqa 175–6, 183–4, 190, 193
 mukhaffafa 107
 mukhtāla 124, 134–5, 173
 mukhtalasa 130–1, 179
 mulawwaza 108, 173, 179
 mursala 170
 musbala 86, 122–3, 134–5, 175n134
 muʿallaqa 124, 171, 178–9, 183–4, 193, 196
 muʿarrāt 174
 rājiʿa 135, 174–5, 180–1, 183–4, 193
 wajh al-hirr 108, 135, 174
 warrāqiyya 107, 175, 190
Library 9, 16, 21, 60, 152n57, 164n98, 239n17, 252, 256, 305
License of transmission (*ijāza*) 2, 8, 56, 67, 69–70, 74, 141n17, 155, 256n69, 261n3, 266, 309n30
Ligature 12, 69, 85, 87, 97, 107, 127, 129–31, 134–5, 156, 158, 168–73, 175–8, 179n161, 180–2, 185, 188, 191–4, 208–9

madḥ 330
maghribī 12–3, 28, 81n15, 309–10, 312–3
magyal 353–4
majmūʿ (*also majmūʿa*; miscellany) 28, 260, 265–6, 324, 326, 328n24, 329, 351
malḥūn 330, 415, 435
mansūb, see Calligraphy
maqāṭiʿ 352, 359, 370
Margin 3–5, 165–6, 323
Marginalia—marginal annotations 20, 26–8, 43–5, 56–7, 59, 66, 69, 138, 149n45, 168, 198, 229–30, 252, 256–7, 261, 262n10, 265, 270, 296–7, 300, 305, 307–8, 310, 347, 377
mashriqī 13, 28, 309nn27–8, 331–2
matn 56
mawāl 327
Middle/Mixed Arabic (moyen arabe) 109n86, 167, 330
Miscellany, *see majmūʿ*
Mistake, *see* error
misṭara 27, 84, 165, 350
mubayyaḍa, see fair/clean copy
mubayyat 330, 335–6, 339, 365
muḥarrir, see calligrapher
mulḥaqāt, see additions
muwashshaḥa 327, 330, 339, 342
muʿrab 330, 375

naskh (*also naskhī*) 13, 14, 60, 64, 70, 160, 236, 238–9, 279, 309–14
nastaʿlīq 14, 67, 75, 347
Notebook 2, 4, 15, 21, 27–8, 56, 136–8, 139n12, 141, 145–6, 148–9, 159, 162, 164, 167, 192, 228, 231, 260, 263–7, 270–1, 328n24, 329
Notes 1, 5, 7–9, 15–8, 21, 23, 27, 38, 39n3, 43, 45, 47, 56, 59, 62, 64, 66–7, 74, 80, 82, 91, 139n12, 142, 146, 151n57, 157, 167, 194, 197–8, 228–30, 234, 237, 252, 260, 262,

264, 266, 268, 270, 300, 305, 307–8, 310, 328, 332, 343, 347, 349–50, 352, 377–8, 388, 396, 400

Oblique (*also* obliquity) 12, 89, 91, 106–7, 118, 121, 130–3, 170, 172–4, 176, 179, 182, 193, 323, 347, 376–7, 388–9, 392–4, 399, 411, 430
Opisthographe 41, 43, 44, 48
Oral (*also* orality; oralité) 2, 96, 237, 266, 330, 336, 345, 353–4
Orthoepics 12
Orthography (orthographe) 20, 40–1, 45, 50, 158, 166–8, 192, 238
Ostraca 39
Ownership (mark, statement, note; propriété: marque, note) 3, 16–8, 27, 56, 60n6, 67, 76, 142, 197, 261–2, 266, 268, 328n24, 340, 345, 349, 350, 376

Paleographic album 8
Paleography (paléographie) 1, 6, 8–14, 23, 25, 29, 49, 63, 79, 90, 93–4, 98, 109, 141–2, 144, 195, 201, 258
Paper (papier; *see also* Reuse) 4, 69, 83–4, 88, 97, 99, 118–9, 137–8, 159, 162, 165, 198, 230, 244, 326–8, 331–3, 339, 341–2, 345–7, 349
Papyrus 25–6, 38–9, 41, 43–50, 83, 323n1
Paratext 8–9, 27–8, 91
Parchemin 39, 83, 323
Philology 1, 9, 18, 22–3, 29, 110, 138, 141–2, 236, 252
Plagiarism 142, 263
Poetry (poème, poésie) 28–9, 39–40, 42, 44–8 233–4, 237–8, 262, 264, 268, 323–4, 326–33, 335, 342, 344–6, 348–51, 350–4, 358–61, 364–6, 368–75, 378, 384–8, 390–1, 393, 395, 398, 400, 411, 413, 415, 418, 422, 426, 429, 431, 434
Pressure (pression) 88, 93, 99, 124, 185, 189, 193, 198
Prosody (*also* meter) 237–8

qaṣīda 262, 309, 327, 329, 336, 352, 365, 373, 375
qāt 332, 353
Quire (*also* quinion; cahier) 56, 89n111, 158, 164–5, 234–5, 331, 333, 339–40, 346
Quotation 59, 239
Qurʾān (Coran) 12, 64, 150–1, 167, 181n168, 234, 262, 323, 372, 400

Reading statement, *see* consultation note
Reed pen (calame) 82, 83n24, 88, 106, 118–9, 153, 189, 333, 347, 367, 374, 406
Résumé (*also* summary) 15, 44, 145–9, 159, 162, 164, 165n102, 167, 174, 185, 188, 192, 228–9, 231, 257, 260, 292
Reuse (réemploi) 138, 140, 149, 164–5, 192, 263, 346
Rhymed prose (*sajʿ*; prose rythmée) 43, 350, 367, 413
Rhythm (rythme) 89, 99, 108, 126, 173, 181, 185, 188
Rubrication 4, 244n49, 248, 326, 332, 344, 353, 358–9

safīna (*also jung, çönk*) 28–9, 323–54
sajʿ, *see* rhymed prose
samāʿ, *see* certificate of audition
saut du même au même 149
Scroll (rouleau) 39, 41–5, 47–8, 164, 323n4
Seal (sceau) 9, 11, 115
Signature 3, 26, 55–6, 60n6, 62, 66, 69, 72–5, 79n8, 80n9, 91–2, 244, 266, 309n30
Sketch 21, 141, 148–50, 159, 167, 174, 182–3, 185, 188, 193, 228
Stenography (sténographie) 39, 179

tabyīḍ, *see* fair/clean copy
Tachygraphe 39
tadhkira, *see* commonplace book
taḥrīr, *see* fair/clean copy
tajrīd 57
takhmīs 327, 349, 352, 395, 398
taʿlīq 15, 60n6, 62, 67, 75, 311
taʿlīqāt, *see* Autograph
Textual criticism 1, 18–22, 300–22
Textual variants 20, 21nn90–93, 41, 43–5, 48, 64, 252, 257
Title page (page de titre) 3, 16, 41, 139–40, 252–3, 260, 268, 294, 307, 310, 331–2
Tremor (tremblement) 88, 90, 191–2, 194

umm, *see* Archetype
urjūza 343, 352, 370, 374–5

Verticality (for letterforms) 12, 84, 86, 92, 169–70, 172–3

waqf 9, 16n80, 28, 261, 265, 267, 301, 302n10

zajal 330

Printed in the United States
By Bookmasters